HUMAN SERVICES
CONTEMPORARY ISSUES AND TRENDS

Edited by

HOWARD S. HARRIS

Bronx Community College

DAVID C. MALONEY

Fitchburg State College

ALLYN AND BACON

Boston   London   Toronto   Sydney   Tokyo   Singapore

Vice President and Publisher: Susan Badger
Managing Editor, Social Work: Judy Fifer
Executive Editor: Karen Hanson
Editorial Assistant: Jennifer Normandin
Marketing Manager: Joyce Nilsen
Editorial-Production Administrator: Donna Simons
Editorial-Production Service: Shepherd, Inc.
Composition Buyer: Linda Cox
Manufacturing Buyer: Megan Cochran
Cover Administrator: Suzanne Harbison

Library of Congress Cataloging-in-Publication Data

Human services : contemporary issues and trends / [editors] Howard S.
  Harris, David C. Maloney.
     p. cm.
    Includes bibliographical references and index.
    ISBN 0–205–14656–2
    1. Human services. 2. Human services personnel. I. Harris,
  Howard S., 1942– . II. Maloney, David C.
  HV40.H784 1995   95–19044
  361—dc20   CIP

Printed in the United States of America

10 9 8 7 6 5 4 3   00 99 98 97 96

Contents

PART FOUR
HUMAN SERVICES: CAREER CONCERNS FOR HUMAN SERVICES
PROFESSIONALS   181

PART FIVE
THE HUMAN SERVICES CLIENTS: FAMILY ISSUES AND SPECIAL
POPULATIONS   231

PART SIX
HUMAN SERVICES: POLITICS, PROMOTION, AND DELIVERY SYSTEMS   311

PART SEVEN
EMERGING ISSUES OF TECHNOLOGY AND GLOBAL TRENDS   365

FOREWORD

The human services education movement began in response to the demands of the Great Society of the 1960s for workers who might be prepared in a shorter time and for more comprehensive service to persons with bio-psycho-social problems than traditional professionals. Each of the established professions is based on a single theoretical concept of the nature and treatment of such problems, but experience teaches that human service problems of people almost always involve a complicated blend of biological, psychological, social, economic, and political factors. What was needed was not so much a team of highly specialized experts in each of these disciplines, but a generalist worker who could use the best of each discipline in a pragmatic relationship to help clients solve their problems and empower themselves to function more effectively.

The human services worker was not to be atheoretical or purely empirical, but rather a multi-disciplinary practitioner, drawing from a basic knowledge of all the major disciplines, to advocate for each client what seemed pragmatically best for the circumstances. The worker was not to be a specialist in any particular technology or theoretical orientation. If specialized skills in these areas were deemed necessary, the worker was to negotiate for them for the client.

The human services movement enjoyed remarkable success in its early years, and it has continued to evolve over the past 25 years. However, it has also encountered challenges resulting from retrenchment in human services funding and the expansion of educational programs in the traditional professions, particularly by their moving to practitioner-training programs at Baccalaureate and Master's degree levels that for-

merly would have been unacceptable to those professions. At the same time, there have been remarkable changes in society's values and perceptions about many aspects of human service problems and society's response to them, including the role and status of women, the role of minorities, the role of public agencies versus that of private non-profit or for-profit services, etc. And there have been new realities to address—the spread of AIDS, the aging of the population, and the ongoing widespread use and abuse of mind-altering substances, especially among younger persons.

More than one hundred years ago James Russell Lowell wrote in "Once to Every Man and Nation":

> *New occasions teach new duties,*
> *Time makes ancient good uncouth;*
> *They must upward still and onward,*
> *Who would keep abreast of truth.*

And so it is today for human service educators! Educators and students must remain vigilant about changes in the field and be flexible to meet the new challenges with informed strategies.

This book contains a set of supplemental readings to address some of the changes facing the human services in 1995 and their inherent challenges for human services educators and practitioners. In a dynamically changing world it is essential that there be such a book issued every few years to assess and better respond to society's new occasions and new values.

Harold L. McPheeters, MD

PREFACE

The Human Services movement is presently continuing in its third decade of development. From its earliest beginnings the redirected emphasis has been on training and educating two-year and four-year undergraduates as entry-level professionals serving a wide variety of client populations with diverse needs in a broad system of delivery settings. The generic competencies of the human services professional reflect the continuum of inherent needs arising from social problems in crime and delinquency, chemical abuse and addiction, poverty, education, job training and employment, aging, mental illness, physical and sexual abuse, homelessness, and marriage and the family. Underlying these people-processing and people-changing skills are the equally important values and attitudes which shape the socio-emotional orientation of the human services worker in carrying out their specific client-centered job responsibilities. To these ends the human services education movement over the past twenty-five years has evolved to a well-defined body of knowledge, a generally universal set of analytical and clinical intervention skills, recognized career issues and problems of the profession, and awareness and response to new and emerging social problems and issues.

The rationale for this book arises from the recognition of the diversity and uniqueness found in the faculties that are teaching and training human-service entry-level professionals. At no other time or place in the human services education movement does one find a comprehensive publication of professional articles from a representative group of human services educators that depicts the content of two-year and four-year curricula. This book of readings brings together a wide diversity of such human services educators as well as supervisors, administrators and providers which together represents the history and spirit of the movement. The academic intention of this project was to extend the basic content areas found in introductory human services texts and to allow beginning human services students the opportunity to access more extended and elaborate information, data, and opinions which together reflect, more effectively, what exists as primary trends and principal issues found in the contemporary field of human services in the 1990s. To these ends, it is felt the book is long overdue and will reference the widest and most varied ideas of past and present human services educators on the most salient and emergent topics and concerns.

In organizing and producing the book, the editors have attempted to preserve the integrity of core content areas and have intended to create a representative set of materials which may routinely be found in courses introducing the field of human services to two-year and four-year students.

The book was designed to serve as either a single, primary instructional reference source or to be used as a required supplemental reading, which course instructors could choose and select reading assignment extensions or could assign all articles, chapter by chapter. The organizational layout allows students to quickly and clearly know what each chapter will try to accomplish. This is achieved by abstracts and specific learning objectives that precede each Part. Each Part is also followed by a list of key terms, pivotal discussion questions, and suggestions for further readings.

The flow of content begins in Part One with an extended view of the conceptual framework of the field of human services with historic references and contemporary reflections. In the lead chapter, Paul Cimmino discusses the many aspects of understanding what is human services, followed by an interesting exchange with Harold McPheeters. In Chapter 2, Jean Macht, with Douglas Whyte, presents the historical background necessary for an understanding of the human services movement.

The fundamental concerns of the training and development of professional skills, standards, and values are extensively discussed in Part Two. In Chapter 3, Edwin Simon presents field work experience as the centerpiece of a Human Services education program. The practical skills, knowledge, and values necessary for a successful human services worker are discussed by Lorence Long and Maureen Doyle in Chapter 4. Then, in Chapter 5, Judith Leff, Virginia Mulkern, and Stephen Leff explain an approach to worker training within the context of the trend toward community-based human services.

In Part Three, beginning with Chapter 6, Sally Fullerton sees theories as important for both classroom success and human service practice. In Chapter 7, methods of helping services for individuals are discussed by Anita Runyan, and helping services for groups by Barbara Somerville in Chapter 8. The remainder of this part is devoted to human services and education. In Chapter 9, Arthur Parlin and Kenneth Grew provide a historical perspective that explains the vast array of human services now available in schools. Rob Lawson and Peggy Anderson present an example of an innovative collaboration between human services and schools in Chapter 10. This part concludes with a concrete example by Michael Seliger of an education and training program designed to help people enter into the mainstream of society.

Part Four deals with issues important to anyone interested in being a human services worker. In Chapter 11, Naydean Blair discusses questions of law and ethics. Miriam Clubok discusses surviving and growing in a human services career in Chapter 12. Nan Littleton addresses the personal qualities necessary for a successful career in Chapter 13, and Frederick Sweitzer completes this part by dealing with ways to avoid burnout in Chapter 14.

Part Five focuses on specific client populations with regard to issues in the family and society. In Chapter 15, Maria Munoz-Kantha discusses family violence and helping the battered woman, followed by a Special Focus Feature in which Judy Morse provides the view of an agency volunteer. James Edell deals with the problem of child abuse in Chapter 16, and David Silberstein provides the approach he developed to help troubled youth in the next Special Focus Feature. Kathleen Niccum, in Chapter 17, discusses the issues of human services for older adults. In addition, providing services for homeless people is discussed by Lorence Long in Chapter 18, people living with HIV and AIDS by Wm. Lynn McKinney in Chapter 19, and alcohol and drug abuse by Marcel Duclos and Marianne Gfroerer in Chapter 20.

Part Six concerns human services' broad concern in regard to politics, promotion, and programs. In Chapter 21, Harold McPheeters discusses the political process. In a Special Focus Feature, Audrey Cohen discusses empowerment within the context of her training program. David Liederman, Madelyn DeWoody, and Megan Sylvester describe the child welfare delivery system in Chapter 22. The importance of prevention is emphasized by Iris Heckman in Chapter 23, and Joseph Mehr discusses the shift in community-based rather than institutional settings in delivering help in Chapter 24, and in a Special Focus Feature Mary Di Giovanni describes a community-based training program.

These introductory readings conclude with Part Seven—a section on emerging issues and trends. In Chapter 25, Rod Underwood and Michael Lee deal with research and evaluation in human services. In Chapter 26, Donna Petrie discusses the challenges of cultural diversity. Dennis Cogan describes international education in Chapter 27, and finally, the development of human services in Australia is presented by Rod Underwood and Michael Lee. In a Special Focus Feature, Tom Wisby emphasizes the importance of computer usage in human services work.

The enthusiasm and cooperation of these contributors in crafting articles for the introductory student made this book possible. We acknowledge and appreciate their efforts.

We acknowledge and appreciate the many people who helped bring this book project to completion. The authors would like to thank the manuscript reviewers: Ruth E. Andes, Genessee Community College; Winfrey M. Ruffin, Jr., Shippensburg University; Larry Sheffield, La Sierra University; Harry E. Smith, Baltimore City Community College; Dennis B. Cogan, Georgia State University; and Cynthia C. Tower, Fitchburg State College.

We received initial encouragement from Kevin Stone, former area Representative for Allyn and Bacon, and Jerry Higgins, Regional Sales Manager. The confidence and judgment of Karen Hanson, our Editor, was a source of continuous strength for us. We are also grateful to Allyn and Bacon for the support shown by Laura Ellingson for coordinating the review process, to Judy Fifer, Managing Editor for Social Work, and Donna Simons, Production Administrator, who navigated the process. The day-to-day effort in preparing the manuscript for production is due to the extraordinary efficiency and indefatigability of Jennifer Normandin, Editorial Assistant. Once in production, for the final perfect manuscript, credit must be given to Kelly Bechen from Shepherd, Inc.

We also acknowledge the work of Ann Bonner for the draft Code of Ethics now under consideration for adoption by NOHSE. Ann worked on Ed Newkrug's draft and was assisted in this undertaking by Miriam Clubok, Pat Baasel and Mary Kay Kreider.

We are most appreciative to Frank Dituri for granting us permission to display the art he creates from the images of infrared photography for the cover of this book. The image is entitled "Reaching In," from his Proximity Collection.

Perhaps most gratifying to us has been the excitement and anticipation of the project among our colleagues in Human Services education throughout the country such as Franklin Rother, Jim Carroll, and Mary Jane Dobson.

We thank Regina Wigfall and Monica Auld of the Social Sciences department at Bronx Community College who assisted us in many ways after long work days. Also, we are indebted to Carol Harris who devoted a good deal of her leisure time using her communication and word processing skills assisting us in various phases of this project.

H.H.
D.M.

PART ONE

HUMAN SERVICES DEFINED AND CLARIFIED

Part One includes two chapters that will provide a foundation for your understanding of the field of human services. You will learn about the different meanings and contexts of the term "human services." You will also come to appreciate the evolution of contemporary human services as a way of responding to a wide array of social and personal problems. You will find that the terms and ideas introduced in these chapters will reappear throughout the book and be useful in your human services career.

In Chapter 1 Paul Cimmino discusses the basic concepts and definitions in the field of human services. It will soon become apparent to you that "human services" is a complex term and that the field is very broad and varied. Paul Cimmino presents a strong case for human services as a distinct profession and field of study within the helping professions and within social sciences. As you begin your study of the human services profession, you will understand that you are a part of a movement that sees itself as one way that a just society expresses its concern for the worth and well-being of each person. You will better understand your future role as a human service worker as it compares with and is different from other professional careers in social work, psychology, psychiatry, and mental-health counseling. Human services is an "eclectic" field, which means that it draws upon and uses aspects of other fields such as clinical psychology and social work. Many of your teachers, who are human services educators, have had their initial training and experience in these other fields.

After reading this first chapter, you will come to realize the many different tasks undertaken by human service workers and how these tasks change with different consumer, or client, populations. You will also be aware of a wide variety of human service work, which, regardless of how this work is applied or carried out, is always involved in solutions to human problems and social issues. With these ideas in hand you will better appreciate the scope and range of human services and how these services attempt to change both individuals and society itself. At the conclusion of the article, as a Special Focus Feature, is a letter by Harold McPheeters that comments on aspects of the chapter. This letter will be of interest to you as you prepare for a career as a professional helper.

As you grasp these basic concepts you will need to know how the human service movement evolved to its present state, and how these professional services emerged to present-day form. Chapter 2 will help to provide the foundations and historical references to the human services field and will, along with Chapter 1, provide the general backdrop to later chapters, each of which will contribute special and important elaboration of details and issues. Together the chapters provide a continuous and comprehensive presentation of the professional field of human services.

In any first exposure to an academic discipline, professional field of work, or general subject matter, the introductory student will have the beginning need for a sense of "intellectual grounding" or an awareness from where these ideas or bodies of knowledge came, and how the field developed to the now or present condition.

In Chapter 2 Jean Macht, assisted by Douglas Whyte, provides a network of historical references, both remote and recent, which when woven together and understood in their shared continuity, will help better explain the breadth and depth of what is current and contemporary in the field. From the preceding chapter, students gained a basic understanding of human services as a concept and how that concept is applied to the "helping" professions. The chapter traces the history of human services from early values of altruism in various religious traditions to the impact of recent social and political forces. From this chapter you have an understanding of how this field of professional work and training began, how it developed over time, and what its major influences were.

Then, with a broader awareness of the origin and history of the human service concept and the emergence of the human service worker, the introductory student will better grasp and appreciate the still-developing nature of the skills, responsibilities, and issues in the professional field of human services. Part Two will discuss and describe the human services worker with specific reference to what is involved in the development and application of necessary skills and qualities of such persons. In Chapters 3 and 5, you will see what is involved in the field work segment of undergraduate human services training. In Chapter 4, you will learn skills and values necessary for human services workers.

**LEARNING OBJECTIVES FOR PART ONE:
HUMAN SERVICES DEFINED AND CLARIFIED**

In reading and studying Chapters 1 and 2:

- You will know the meaning of human services.
- You will be familiar with who the consumers/clients are in human services.
- You will understand three general ideas of human services—intervention, professionalism, and education.
- You will be able to describe a human service worker.
- You will be aware of the various delivery models in human services and how these systems reach people in need of help.
- You will be able to describe what is involved in training programs for undergraduate human service education.
- You will be aware of the origins of the human services movement.
- You will be familiar with the sequence and chronology of federal legislation that directly and indirectly impact upon the field of human services.
- You will recognize the major individual contributors in the field of human services.
- You will understand the most important social issues that have influenced the field of human services over time.
- You will be able to describe the recent historical factors and circumstances that have collectively impacted the continued development and growth of human services as a profession.

CHAPTER 1

BASIC CONCEPTS AND DEFINITIONS
OF HUMAN SERVICES

PAUL F. CIMMINO

INTRODUCTION

This chapter is dedicated to the development of basic definitions that describe and identify human services. However, any attempt to define human services in one sentence, or to use one description, is impossible. According to Schmolling, Youkeles, and Burger, there is no generally accepted or "official" definition of human services (1993, p. 9). Human Services is a multidisciplinary profession and reflects complex human interactions and a comprehensive social system. To understand human services, it is important to develop ideas that construct an organized perspective of the field. In this chapter, three general questions about human services are incorporated into the text. First, *"What is it, and what isn't it?"* Second, *"Who is helped and why?"* Third, *"How is help delivered and by whom?"* These fundamental questions tend to exemplify the basic concepts and definitions in human services. This chapter proceeds to introduce important terms, definitions, subconcepts, and concentration areas in human services, which are expounded upon by a host of authors who contributed their expertise in the formulation of this book.

The professional field of human services can be reduced to three basic concepts: *intervention* (needs and services); *professionalism* (applied practice and credentialling); and *education* (academic training and research). Each basic concept comprises important aspects of the human service field and identifies primary areas of the profession as well. The supporting background that nourishes *intervention*, *professionalism*, and *education* in human services is the history of the human services movement (Fullerton, 1990). The formal development of human services in society is located in the legislative, training, and service history of the field. This chapter attempts to offer a collective understanding of these important areas related to the professional development of human services. In this chapter basic concepts and definitions converge to generate a comprehensive and theoretical notion of human services in forming an overview of the field. To further assist the reader in developing thoughts about the human services profession, and to avoid ambiguity in the field, a medley of contemporary definitions of human services is presented later in the chapter.

Finally, an important letter recently written by Dr. Harold McPheeters (1992), which addresses the basic question of what comprises human services, is presented to close the chapter. McPheeters's letter was in response to a manuscript written by me in 1991. The paper proposes an idealistic model that defines human services in terms of its purpose and professional responsibility in society. Later in the chapter, the central ideas are summarized, providing an orientation to the thoughtful feedback from Harold McPheeters.

In my view, his written response contains landmark perspectives in development of the emerging human services field. Thus, the ideas stemming from my paper and McPheeters's response invite a judicious overview of this chapter for the reader's developing knowledge of human services.

THE BASIC CONCEPT OF PURPOSE IN HUMAN SERVICES

Human services is a term that reflects the need for society to help its members live adequate and rewarding lives (Eriksen, 1977). The human services field encompasses a variety of functions and characteristics. Human service activity is the act of people helping other people meet their needs in an organized social context. Thus, the human services function is a process of directed change taking place as the result of interaction between human service workers, clients, and organizations. Ideally, the changes human service workers attempt to facilitate are intended to assist clients in achieving optimum human potential in life. In order to help a variety of people in this fashion, the human service worker trains as a generalist and must be familiar with various approaches in the helping process (Schmolling, Youkeles and Burger, 1993, p. 146).

The human service orientation to helping people recognizes that clients are an intricate part of their environment. Today, the need for human services in society is obvious. Human services has emerged in response to the increase of human problems in our modern world (Mehr, 1986). The complications of living in a fast pace and transforming society causes massive stress on human conditions. Often people are unable to meet their own basic needs due to harsh social conditions and oppression (Ryan, 1976). Socialization for many individuals is deprived or detrimental relative to basic life needs. The problems people experience can be rooted in family backgrounds, education, economics, disease, disability, self-concepts, or legal matters. The human service model acknowledges these conditions as primary factors in human dysfunction but does not necessarily predetermine a person's capacity based on past or present life circumstances. The human service ideology of helping people focuses on the immediate needs and presenting problems of the client. This approach does not prejudge clients and recognizes that any person in need of human services is a legitimate consumer of services. By the same token, human services practice attempts to relieve human suffering while at the same time promoting independence from the human service system.

The conceptual evolution of human services as a professional helping process stems from historical movements in the field. The history of the human services movement is addressed in a later chapter. However, it is useful to mention the significance of this history in the development of a functional human service concept. The predecessors of today's human service and social welfare systems were the social reforms in England, which were particularly established in the Elizabethan Poor Laws of 1601. Prior to this legislation, the church assumed responsibility to relieve the poor and served in the capacity of a public agency (Woodside and McClam, pp. 38–43). Legislation stemming from the Elizabethan Poor Laws, and the Law of Settlement added sixty years later, initiated the idea of compulsory taxation to raise funds to help the needy, and established eligibility requirements (Woodside and McClam, pp. 42–43). These early developments in English social reform and legislation more than 350 years ago are bridges to contemporary human services in the United States.

The impact of social and legislative changes during the 1950s, 1960s, and 1970s fostered the creation of human services as it exists today (Woodside and McClam, 1990, p. 41). Stimulated by a response to deinstitutionalization in the 1960s, coupled with influences of the civil rights movement, along with a series of related legislation, resulted in the creation of a new "human service worker." Examples of important legislation in the development of contemporary human services are the Manpower Development Training Act of 1962; the Mental Health Study Act of

1955; the Social Security Amendments of 1962; the Scheuer Subprofessional Career Act of 1966; and the Community Mental Health Centers Act in 1963. Such legislation promoted the human services movement of the sixties and seventies, whereby a process ensued creating opportunities for training programs and progressive development in human services education. Consequently, a blend of services among agencies, social policies, academic programs, professional practice development, and people working together for social change formulate the helping process called human services.

HUMAN SERVICES INTERVENTION

Human Services Intervention is defined as a broad field of human endeavor in which the professional acts as an agent to assist individuals, families, and communities to better cope with crisis, change and stress; to prevent and alleviate stress; and to function effectively in all areas of life and living. Human Services Practice is conducted in the broad spectrum of human services in a manner that is responsive to both current and future trends and needs for human resource development, and committed to humanitarian values (Montana State University-Billings: Catalog 1991–93, Sexton, R., 1987).

The preceding definition of human services intervention reflects the functional role of the field in society. The degree to which there exists public support for human service programs is determined by the state of the economy (Schmolling, Youkeles and Burger, 1993, p. 24). Since sufficient funding for human service programs is inconsistent, fulfilling the mission of effective intervention in helping clients often fluctuates. Thus, the delivery capability of human services to the public is unpredictable and frequently inadequate in providing resources to sufficiently help clients. In spite of this condition, human services intervention remains committed to the values and priorities of society (Eriksen, 1977, p. 10).

Human services intervention is the bridge between people and various subsystems in society (Eriksen, 1977, p. 10). The intervention philosophy of human services reflects humanitarian values. In her earlier textbook, Karin Eriksen identified the following philosophical principles as fundamental to the delivery of human services:

1. Human Services are the embodiment of our national commitment to building a just society based on respect for people's rights and needs.
2. Every individual in our society is entitled to services that will prevent his/her pain, maintain integrity, enable him/her with realities, stimulate personal growth, and promote a satisfying life.
3. Prevention of people's problems and discomforts is as important a part of human services as restitution and rehabilitation after the fact.
4. The integration of human services is crucial to their effectiveness.
5. Human Services are accountable to the consumers.
6. Human Services Tasks and Goals.

The paramount goal of human services is to enable people to live more satisfying, more autonomous, and more productive lives, through the utilization of society's knowledge, resources, and technological innovations. To that end, society's systems will be working for its people. Putting people before paper (Eriksen, 1977 pp. 10, 11, 12).

The three primary models in the helping professions are the medical model, public health (social welfare) model, and human services model. Of these recognized interventions, the human service model views people, services and the social environment as integrated entities. The medical model and public health models, on the other hand, have an individualistic orientation to causation relative to people problems. For instance, the medical model concentrates on the individual and views clients as needing help because they are sick and refers to them as patients. From the medical model emerges the discipline of psychiatry at the end of the eighteenth century, and is closely related to the development of the human services profession. The public health model contends that individuals have problems that are also linked to social conditions and views disease as multicausal (Woodside and McClam, p. 89). Hypothetically, both of these models are based on determinism, suggesting that disease and social problems are an individual's responsibility, not society's, and if controlled they would have less effect on the human condition. The human services model expects disease and social problems to always affect the lives of people and focuses on providing services to help individuals deal with problems stemming from these conditions. Similarly, by using these models to describe and approach the problem-solving process, the human service worker is able to expand resources and systems for service delivery and intervention.

THE GENERALIST ROLES OF THE HUMAN SERVICE WORKER

The basic roles human service professionals play in the helping process were initially developed by the Southern Regional Education Board (SREB) while attempting to determine functional comparisons to other established professionals. The project also defined four levels of competence that are discussed later in this chapter to correlate with role functions. The SREB identified thirteen roles that human services workers perform that were derived by evaluating the needs of clients, families, and communities (SREB, 1969). These identical roles include the following:

1. *Outreach worker*—reaches out to detect people with problems and can make appropriate referrals for needed services.
2. *Broker*—helps people get to existing services and provides follow-up to assure continued care.
3. *Advocate*—pleads and fights for services, policy, rules, regulations, and laws for client's behalf.
4. *Evaluator*—assesses client or community needs and problems, whether medical, psychiatric, social, or educational.
5. *Teacher-educator*—performs a range of instructional activities from simple coaching to teaching highly technical content directed to individuals and groups.
6. *Behavior changer*—carries out a range of activities planned primarily to change behavior, ranging from coaching and counseling to casework, psychotherapy and behavior therapy.
7. *Mobilizer*—helps to get new resources for clients or communities.

8. *Consultant*—works with other professions and agencies regarding their handling of problems, needs, and programs.
9. *Community planner*—works with community boards, committees, etc., to assure that community developments enhance self-actualization and minimize emotional stress on people.
10. *Caregiver*—provides services for persons who need ongoing support of some kind (i.e., financial assistance, day care, social support, twenty-four-hour care).
11. *Data manager*—performs all aspects of data handling, gathering, tabulating, analyzing, synthesizing, program evaluation, and planning.
12. *Administrator*—carries out activities that are primarily agency- or institution-oriented (budgeting, purchasing, personnel activities, etc.).
13. *Assistant to specialist*—acts as assistant to specialist (e.g., psychiatrist, psychologist, nurse), relieving them of burdensome tasks.

The framework of the helping process in human services is characterized by the role functions and structures listed above, and not restricted to frontline workers who provide direct services; administrators and supervisors also facilitate service delivery.

THE SOCIAL IDEOLOGY OF HUMAN SERVICES

Eriksen's principles represent a social ideology about human services that parallels the needs of an individual living in society. Social policy advocates who hold humanitarian perspectives contend the previously mentioned conditions are individual rights that should be afforded to all people. Many of these scholars argue that humanitarian standards of living are constitutional rights. However, the U.S. Constitution does not specify living standards for citizens. To a large extent, the human life standards developed by humanitarian scholars are actually postulations drawn from language in the U.S. Constitution, the Declaration of Independence, the Bill of Rights, and a variety of subsequent federal and state civil rights legislation. For instance, in the opening remarks (second paragraph) of the Declaration of Independence it is stated, "We hold these truths to be self-evident, that all men are created equal, that they are endowed by their Creator with certain inalienable rights, that among these are life, liberty and the pursuit of happiness." Similarly, in the U.S. Constitution, Amendment XV, Section 1, states, "The right of citizens of the United States to vote shall not be denied or abridged by the United States or by any State on account of race, color, or previous condition of servitude."

One can see how expanding the meaning of this language from both documents can imply the right to be afforded a certain quality of life in American society. The degree of social obligation that government has in the role of promoting social equity, or empowering people to become self-suffi-cient, is a broad discussion that remains controver-sial among social policy makers and scholars. To a large extent, the present model of social welfare and human services delivery systems is not functionally consistent with the idea of society taking responsi-bility for the problems of its members. However, the notion of society taking partial responsibility for its members' hardships parallels the professional ideologies promoted in this chapter (Schmolling, Youkeles, Burger, 1993, p. 18). To date, social pol-icy relative to human services remains guided by an ideology of individualism and community derived from traditional perspectives. Conservative Ameri-can values continue to place emphasis on hard work, perseverance, and self-reliance. Thus emer-ges the concept of Americans as rugged individuals who believe in pulling themselves up by their boot-straps, a concept that remains the proforma of our society. This attitude translates into a community model of social services that supports programs dealing only with immediate sit-uations (human problems), and generally opposes programs that go beyond meeting basic survival needs (Schmolling, Youkeles, Burger, 1993, p. 18, 19).

Proactive Human Services

The concept of human services supports the empowerment of people to become self-sufficient and capable of meeting their own needs without assistance from human services. Therefore, human services aims to provide clients the kind of direct support that facilitates eventual emancipation and prevents a state of dependency on the system. This kind of assistance is referred to as the proactive approach to human services. This form of inter-vention utilizes strategies that invest in the preven-tion of problems and stabilization of client systems into the future. Idealistically, planning beyond the problem to help the client become socially self-sufficient is the heart of the professional human service model. However, a crisis-oriented, pluralis-tic society that has recently come to recognize the concept of multicausality and the impact of psy-chosocial stress cannot be expected to change from traditional (reactive) perspectives on human prob-lems to a prevention model or proactive perspec-tive in any short period of time.

Human services intervention is based in theory on fundamental values about human life that are woven into American heritage and more specifi-cally identified in various civil rights legislation. Professional perspectives of service delivery to clients recognize a standard of living for all people that promotes self-reliance, social perseverance, and a sense of personal gratification in social life. Linked to these values or life conditions are social values containing certain essential human needs. Since the human service worker is an agent of soci-ety who advocates for the psychosocial advance-ment of the individual, it follows that the human services model closely associates with civil rights legislation aimed at helping deprived population groups. Consequently, the identification of essential human needs is important for definitions of human service intervention and the development of basic problem-solving processes.

THE HUMAN SERVICES IDEOLOGY OF THE INDIVIDUAL

The general notion that problem behaviors are often the result of an individual's failure to satisfy basic human needs is a fundamental principal underlying human services practices. The human service model places a portion of responsibility on society for creating conditions that reduce opportunities for people to be successful by perpetuating social problems. The human service worker recognizes this condition and seeks to assist clients to adequately function in the same system that impairs them. A client may be in need of shelter, medical attention, transportation, education, food, emotional support, or legal services. Therefore, as an agent of a larger system (macrosocial systems), the primary focus of the human service worker is the needs of the individual client (microsocial systems). In this sense, the human service worker becomes an *agent of change in the client system, placing the person first in the value system of the helping profession* (Cimmino, 1993).

The focus of human service intervention on *human needs* is the essential task in determining service delivery. There are numerous concepts in the literature that propose definitions of human needs. One concept, developed by Abraham Maslow (1968), is a self-actualization theory in which he proposes a hierarchy of human needs that is applicable to the human services model.

The hierarchy Maslow conceptualized consists of five levels. At the base are basic **physiological needs** such as food, shelter, oxygen, water, and general survival. These conditions are fundamental to life. When a person has homeostasis with these basic survival needs, they are able to focus on **safety needs**, which involve the need for a secure and predictable environment. This may mean living in decent housing in a safe neighborhood. Given that safety needs have been fulfilled, the need for **belongingness and love** emerges. This includes intimacy and acceptance from others. When these three lower-level needs are partly satisfied, **esteem needs** develop in the context of the person's social environment. This relates to recognition by others that a person is competent or respected. Most people desire the appreciation and positive reinforcement of others. At the top of the hierarchy exists the need for **self-actualization**, having to do with the fulfillment of a person's innate potential as a human being. Maslow perceived self-actualized people as possessing attributes that are consistent with highly competent and successful individuals.

Although Maslow is considered a primary figure in humanistic psychology, there has been subsequent research to test the validity of his concepts. Follow-up research studies have been mixed; some results demonstrate support (Neher, 1991), while others refute the hypotheses (Schmolling, Youkeles, and Burger, 1993). Nevertheless, most people do live in a network of social relationships in which they seek external gratification in attending to their needs.

Another perspective of human needs is defined by Hansell's motivation theory (Hansell, Wodarczk, and Handlon-Lathrop, 1970; Schmolling, Youkeles, and Burger, 1993). This theory contends that people must achieve seven basic attachments in order to meet their needs. If a person is unsuccessful in achieving each attachment, ultimately a state of crisis and stress will result. Listed below are the seven basic attachments, accompanied with signs of failure of each one:

1. Food, water, and oxygen, along with informational supplies. Signs of failure: boredom, apathy, and physical disorder.
2. Intimacy, sex, closeness, and opportunity to exchange deep feelings. Signs of failure: loneliness, isolation, and lack of sexual satisfaction.
3. Belonging to a social peer group. Signs of failure: not feeling part of anything.
4. A clear, definite self-identity. Signs of failure: feeling doubtful and indecisive.
5. A social role that carries with it a sense of being a competent member of society. Signs of failure: depression and a sense of failure.
6. The need to be linked to a cash economy via a job, a spouse with income, social security benefits, or other ways. Sign of failure: lack of purchasing power, possibly an inability to purchase essentials.
7. A comprehensive system of meaning with clear priorities in life. Signs of failure: sense of drifting through life, detachment, and alienation.

Both Maslow's and Hansell's ideas about human needs provide a practical purpose for human service intervention. Essentially, human service workers attempt to find ways to help the client satisfy his or her unmet needs. The definition of the client situation or *presenting problem* generally relates to the sign of failures indicated above. Similarly, the identification of problems such as poor housing, lack of food, fear of neighborhood, detrimental relationships, and low self-esteem suggests a physical, social, or psychological crisis that blocks the development of a person and the ability to function such as implied by Maslow's and Hansell's theories of self-actualization and motivation.

CRISIS INTERVENTION

When human services intervention is required as the result of a sudden disruption in the life of a client that is precipitated by a situational crisis or catastrophic event, *crisis intervention* is the consequence. Often, in these circumstances, even those people who do not expect to become consumers of the human services system suddenly find themselves clients. The practice of delivering crisis intervention services is supported by *crisis intervention theory*. Studies and research in crisis intervention theory and practice are primarily the domain of sociology, psychology, social psychology, social work, community psychiatry, and social welfare policy. The practice of crisis intervention in human services was developed by a variety of clinical practitioners in areas such as nursing, psychology, medicine, psychiatry, and clinical social work (Slaikeu, 1990). The application of crisis intervention methods is a recent development based on various human behavior theories, including those from Freud, Hartmann, Rado, Erickson, Lindemann, and Caplan (Agulera and Messick, 1978; Slaikeu, 1990). Slaikeu (1990, p. 6) cites the Coconut Grove fire on November 28, 1942, where 493 people perished when flames devoured the crowded nightclub. According to Slaikeu:

Lindemann and others from the Massachusetts General Hospital played an active role in helping survivors and those who had lost loved ones in the disaster. His clinical report (Lindemann, 1944) on the psychological symptoms of the survivors became the cornerstone for subsequent theorizing on the grief process, a series of stages through which a mourner progresses on the way toward accepting and resolving loss (Slaikeu, 1990, p. 6).

The evolution of community psychiatry and the suicide prevention movement of the 1960s marks an important historical development in crisis-intervention human services. An important figure in crisis theory and the associated approaches in service delivery was Gerald Caplin, a public health psychiatrist. Some of his contributions are also discussed by Slaikeu (1990, pp. 6–7).

Building on the start given by Lindemann, Gerald Caplan, associated with Harvard School of Public Health, first formulated the significance of life crisis in adult's psychopathology. Caplan's crisis theory was cast in the framework of Eriksen's developmental psychology. Caplan's interest was on how people negotiated the various transitions from one stage to another. He identified the importance of both personal and social resources in determining whether developmental crises (and situational or unexpected crises) would be worked out for better of for worse. Caplin's preventative psychiatry, with its focus on early intervention to promote positive growth and minimize the chance of psychological impairment, led to an emphasis on mental health consultation. Since many early crises could be identified and even predicted, it became important to train a wide range of community practitioners. The role of the mental health professional became one of assisting teachers, nurses, clergy, guidance counselors, and others in learning how to detect and deal with life crises in community settings (Slaikeu, 1990).

The formal emergence of community mental health in the United States became a way to implement recommendations from the U.S. Congress Joint Commission on Mental Illness and Health, 1961. With strong support from the Kennedy administration to provide mental health services in a community setting (not restricting them only to hospitals), crisis intervention programs and the outreach emergency services were established as an integral part of every comprehensive community mental health system and necessary for federal funding.

A person who is experiencing a crisis faces a problem that cannot be resolved by using the coping mechanisms that have worked for them in the past (Aguilera and Messick, p.1). According to Woodside:

> *An individual's equilibrium is disrupted by pressures or upsets, which result in stress so severe that he or she is unable to find relief using coping skills that worked before. The crisis is the individual's emotional response to the threatening or hazardous situation, not the situation itself. Crises can be divided into two types: developmental and situational. A developmental crisis is an individual's response to a situation that is reasonably predictable in the life cycle. Situational or accidental crises do not occur with any regularity. The sudden and unpredictable nature of this type of crisis makes any preparation or individual control impossible. Examples are fire or other natural disasters, fatal illness, relocation, unplanned pregnancy, and rape. The skills and strategies that helpers use to provide immediate help for a person in crisis constitute crisis intervention (Woodside and McClam, 1990).*

People in crisis require immediate help and are in desperate situations. The human service philosophy (idealistically) is consistent with established crisis-intervention theory, which places the client's needs as a priority in the value system of the helping profession. For the human service worker, the value of putting people first is an important professional orientation, not just something that happens as the result of a crisis. In a crisis situation, the human service worker must quickly establish a working relationship and positive rapport with clients. The knowledge and skills necessary are important in supporting the client's sense of hope and eventual return to self-reliance (Woodside and McClam, p. 223). In most cases, there is more than one worker helping the client. Generally clients are involved in a social network of supportive programs that involve different agencies and stem from an assortment of referrals. Collectively, the human service system coordinates efforts that are designed to return the client to a pre-crisis state of functioning. This objective is usually accomplished as the result of well-coordinated service delivery and effective problem-solving skills.

CLIENT SYSTEMS IN HUMAN SERVICES INTERVENTION

To continue discussions about the basic concept of human services intervention, it is important to understand the *total view* of the practice field. Much like social work, human services is directed toward the resolution of client problems that are part of a larger and dynamic social system. The nature of the service delivery system encompasses two distinct levels of interaction: providing direct services (face-to-face) and encompassing the acquisition of services from larger social systems. The *client system* is the immediate condition of the client's psychological and social life circumstances. Client systems comprise many components, such as family relationships, social and cultural attributes, economic status, age, gender, employment, physical and mental health, legal issues, education, living conditions, religion, and self-esteem. In short, the client system involves the immediate environment having the most significant influence on the client's life and behavior.

Micro- and Macrosocial Systems in Human Services Practice

The human service worker provides direct services to the client, and is working simultaneous to the client system. For example, a worker can be assigned to an individual client that involves couples, family members, other workers, and agencies in the client system. In this context, the human service worker is engaged in two distinct systems called micro- and macrosocial systems.

A great deal has been written about micro- and macrosocial systems in the process of delivering human services that elaborates on the topic. However, a brief review of the concept can help the reader understand the basis of human services intervention in the social environment.

Every client lives in both micro- and macrosocial systems. The human service worker is enmeshed in these two systems. Microsocial systems include individuals, small groups, families, and couples. Macrosocial systems involve large groups, organizations, communities, neighborhoods, and bureaucracy. Whittaker explains:

The goals in macro intervention include changes within organizations, communities and societies, while micro intervention aims at enhancing social functioning or alleviation of social problems for a particular individual, family, or small group. Macro intervention relies heavily on theories of "big system" change (formal organization theory, community theory) drawn from sociology, economics and political science. Micro intervention tends to be based on theories of individual change drawn from psychology, small group sociology, and human development. Finally, we can distinguish differences in the strategies of macro and micro interventions. Macro intervention uses social action strategies, lobbying, coordination of functions, and canvassing; micro intervention typically relies on more circumscribed strategies directed at individual change: direct counseling, individual advocacy actions, and crisis intervention (Whittaker, 1975, p. 44).

Human services intervention is closely associated with micro- and macrosystems in relationship to the notion of *social treatment*. From a human services practice perspective, social treatment includes all those remedial efforts directed at the resolution of a client's problems within the context of the social environment (Whittaker, 1975). Theoretically, the client and worker move through micro- and macrosystems in a dynamic process, each bound by their social roles. By the same token, their relationship formulates a unique set of mutual needs and values as a result of the common objectives they share in problem solving and service delivery. In this sense, theoretical distinctions between macro- and microsystems are consistent for both worker and client. However, their circumstances in the social system are different, in that one is in the "client system," while the worker functions in the "human service delivery system." Each operate and negotiate within the boundaries of micro- and macrosystems of society. For example, a client system may include family relationships, housing, legal issues, and behavioral problems, whereas the human service worker as a provider must meet the needs of both the client system and the human service system.

Acting in a formal capacity, the human service worker must adhere to employment conditions (job description), social policy, professional ethics, and administrative aspects of service delivery. Human service providers operate in a maze of agency dynamics and organizational structures. This level of activity in the human services is generally in the scope of *macropractice*. In this context, the worker also deals directly with the client. Human service workers are most often face-to-face with clients either interviewing, counseling, working with the family, or doing something else to help them. This kind of intervention is called *micropractice*. The client system and the workers' system together set up a situational framework for professional human services intervention at micro and macro levels. This dualistic nature of professional practice is fundamental to the working model in human services. Further, it underscores how comprehensive and complex human service work in contemporary society really is.

INTRODUCTION OF THE SOCIAL HEALTH GENERALIST CONCEPT

Today's human service worker must possess special knowledge of the human service delivery system as well as client systems, and understand the impact of various environmental influences on human behavior and communities. Annexed to this knowledge base is the need for the worker to have competent communication skills so as to be effective with a variety of clients, and operate comfortably in different agency roles. Such demands of the modern worker produce the notion of a *social health generalist* in contemporary welfare, mental health, and human service systems (Cimmino, 1993). Compared with the mental health generalist concept of the 1960s and 1970s (McPheeters and King, 1971), the **social health generalist** sharply reflects the need for the human service worker in modern society to be prepared for today's challenges, which stem from rapid social change and related programmatic influences on economic restructuring of human service delivery systems. To work effectively in any human service agency today it is necessary for the worker to possess a functionally broader knowledge base of community resources, case management strategies, behavior, social policy, political influences, and understanding of which human factors impact the delivery of human services. Joseph Mehr (1988), elucidates the social health generalist notion when he discusses current conceptions of human service systems, and bases his book on a *generic human services concept* (Mehr, 1988, p. 11). In contrast, the mental health generalists of the past were primarily trained to focus on microsocial systems by providing direct assistance in institutional or closed settings. The social health generalist's basic training and professional orientation must address a wider spectrum of client conditions and supporting human service systems that conceptually go beyond the immediate client and agency environment.

The generalist concept is historically rooted in mental health technology systems. However, modern life in the 1990s demands that the need for human services reach beyond the mental health field. Therefore, the profession must expand the generalist concept to reflect what human service workers actually do in modern society. This condition was illustrated earlier in the discussion of *generalist roles the human service worker* performs in the formal helping

process. The academic and practice training in recognized human services programs today are designed to prepare a different generalist worker than in the past. According to Schmolling:

Many educators feel that the term 'paraprofessional,' widely accepted in the past, no longer accurately reflects the knowledge, abilities, skills, and training of graduates in recognized undergraduate human service programs of today. They feel graduates of such programs should be considered professional human service workers. The work roles and functions of generalist human service workers vary greatly. Generalist workers represent the largest number of workers and usually have the most contact with those in need. In some instances, the duties of the generalist workers are similar to those of professionals (Schmolling, Youkeles, Burger, 1993).

The social health generalist human service worker is capable of adjusting to a variety of settings in the human services field. Similar to the mental health generalist, the primary focus remains helping "target persons," either directly or indirectly. These target groups can be individual clients, families, small groups, or a neighborhood or community (McPheeters, 1990). Target groups refer to identified persons (clients) in need of human service intervention. However, the advancement of the term *human services* to include a wider spectrum of social, health, and welfare systems is a significant distinction from past concepts of the mental health generalist. For example, a human service worker today in a mental health setting is required to understand other service-delivery systems and social dynamics outside the place they are employed. This includes a knowledge base that integrates client needs with external and internal forces that influence service delivery, such as insurance requirements, diagnosis, and legal, community, or administrative complications. In today's human service industry the frequency of worker contact with clients and their families, as well as interagency collaboration, is steadily increasing for a variety of reasons. The framework of practice today reflects the notion that all clients are consumers and have the right to access an empowering process by way of the human services system (Halley, Kopp and Austin, 1992). Thus, the professional role of the contemporary human service worker scales the wall of institutional framework by comprehending conditions outside agency boundaries, and must engender an enormous level of social awareness and professional skills. Consequently, the decision-making capacity of the generalist in today's human service field requires a working knowledge of micro- and macrosystems within the social treatment model (Whittaker, 1977).

McPheeters describes the generalist as possessing the following characteristics:

1. The generalist works with a limited number of clients or families (in consultation with other professionals) to provide "across the board" services as needed.
2. The generalist is able to work in a variety of agencies and organizations that provide mental health services.
3. The generalist is able to work cooperatively with any of the existing professions.
4. The generalist is familiar with a number of therapeutic services and techniques.
5. The generalist is a "beginning professional" who is expected to continue to learn and grow (McPheeters and King, 1971).

McPheeters's characteristics are generally applicable to the notion of the new social health generalist. However, several important modifications to his previous description of the generalist concept is proposed to effectively address contemporary frameworks of service delivery, and justify the neologism of the *social health generalist*.

In his article, Dr. McPheeters places emphasis on the differentiation between the generalist and the specialist. He asserts that it is not based simply on the basis of division of labor. Rather, the generalist is concerned with all of the problems surrounding the client or family, whereas the specialist is focused in a specialized skill or activity (McPheeters, 1990, p. 36). McPheeters's characteristics describing the generalist can generally

apply to the new social health generalist concept. However, there are some important adjustments necessary that offer theoretical criterion for consistency with the contemporary human service field. The first concern is that McPheeters's second characteristic, "agencies and organizations that provide mental health services," must expand to include a larger view of the human services system. Replacing the term "mental health services" with *human services*, or *human services and related subsystems* seems more appropriate and fitting to today's human service worker. Similarly, his fourth characteristic states "the generalist is familiar with a number of therapeutic services and techniques." The focus here reflects a limited perspective in comparison to the practice framework and related concepts of the modern human service worker. Recognition of the need for a broader knowledge base involving multidisciplinary services and other theoretical frameworks is essential for human services to effectively operate in modern society. A professional knowledge base to include social systems, personality theory, and social treatment intervention strategies can more accurately point to the scope of information that today's worker must possess. With these two modifications, the mental health generalist concept can continue to provide professional foundations for today's *social health generalist worker*.

HUMAN SERVICES: WHAT IT IS AND ISN'T

At this point in the reading it seems appropriate to address the basic question of *what human services is, and isn't*. It has been established that human services is a helping profession in its own process of continuing development. Although human services is a helping profession, it cannot be all things to all people. At times this ideology must be brought into a realistic perspective of the human conditions that comprise psychosocial life and society. At best, human services is a process of negotiating social systems to respond in the best interest of people in need.

Human service workers spend an enormous amount of time dealing with large social systems and related subsystems. Similarly, they often find it necessary to expend a lot of energy sorting out bureaucratic issues to achieve problem-solving goals (Eriksen, 1977, p. 159). In this light, the profession of human services helps people meet important needs in life. The Allied Services Act of 1974 defined human services: "Human Services are those which enable the consumers of services to achieve, support, or maintain the highest level of economic self-sufficiency and independence" (Azarnoff and Seliger, 1982). Therefore, human services is a helping profession that places an emphasis on client systems and needs for specific service delivery.

Human services are delivered by a variety of people who are trained in different disciplines that make up this helping profession. Human services is not the only profession that practices human service work. In other words, persons specifically trained in human services, or having graduated from human services degree programs, cannot claim to be the only helping professional qualified to do human service work. The human service field comprises a number of other disciplines and related services. For instance, disciplines that often provide human services are medicine, psychology, rehabilitation counseling, social work, education, nursing, occupational and recreational therapy, psychiatry, corrections, etc. In this context, human services, as a profession and discipline, represent one aspect of a multidisciplinary helping professions field. However, the academic training in human services is founded on a systematic body of knowledge based on curriculum built on specific values and skills and the human service system. Therefore, human services does represent an identifiable academic discipline, social science, or profession (Cimmino, 1993).

Is or Isn't Human Services a Profession?

The question of whether or not human services is a legitimate profession arises frequently. For purposes of definition, human services—by meeting the criteria that it is an important occupation in society, requires special knowledge (academic training), and with relationship to other allied professions—qualifies as a profession (Woodside and McClam, 1994). Another important characteristic of a profession is the recognition of ethical standards to regulate membership activities (Woodside and McClam, 1990). A formal code of ethics in human services was formally proposed by NOHSE and CSHSE at the 1994 national conference. The board and council are recommending ratification of this important proposal to the membership at large.

Human services is a multidimensional professional field that encompasses a variety of functional and conceptual components. The human services movement underscores its professional development and the growth of certain social policies in the evolution of society. Human services itself is a generic term that refers to a variety of helping professions. Human services is not an exclusive profession, yet it seeks recognition as an academic discipline and organized profession with distinguishing qualities. Human services is a young, developing profession, academic discipline, and social science. The crux of the service delivery philosophy among those professionals who are contributing to the development of human services education and practice is to place the needs of people first in the value system of the helping profession. Further discussion about professionalism and professional development is presented in the next few pages and in other readings in this book.

WHO IS HELPED AND WHY

Human services are afforded to people who are in need of assistance in order to sustain an acceptable standard of living and to survive in society. Most clients of human services are experiencing crisis and stress coupled with other problems that impair social functioning. In general, human services selects target population groups of people who need assistance (Schmolling, Youkeles,

Burger, 1993). Thus, human service clients are usually members of target population groups. Often, these groups are identified as "at risk" because of the nature of their problems. The poor, elderly, adolescent runaways, homeless people, mental patients, abused children, disabled persons, and AIDS patients are all examples of groups that have been targeted as "at risk." Given the enormous amount of social problems and deprivation in society, there exists a significantly large number of at-risk target population groups. To identify all of them here would be impossible. However, they typically are made up of the lower economic social class and are frequently representative of minority population groups.

Human services has traditionally been associated with population groups in low socioeconomic categories. People from these categories are prone to be in at-risk situations, such as unemployment and chemical abuse, and are generally considered to be the potential populations for human services intervention. However, there have been recent developments which recognize the usefulness of human services in *normal population settings*. For example, employers have become interested in employee assistance programs that include human service interventions, such as dealing with drug and alcohol abuse with employees. Treatment, counseling, and prevention programs are rapidly being implemented in industry today.

The Federal Comprehensive Alcohol Abuse and Alcohol Prevention, Treatment and Rehabilitation Act, passed in 1970, was important for human services because it created an innovative approach towards the problem of alcohol abuse (Woodside and McClam, 1990, p. 75). This legislation required federal agencies to have alcohol abuse and prevention programs available to employees. The program emerged to become the better-known Employee Assistance Programs (EAP). Many corporations and employers now have these programs, and many provide a broader base of services including child care, retraining, marital counseling, recreation and health programs, diet and wellness education, etc. It is important to

note that many people who unexpectedly experience a crisis are often those who typically would not be candidates for human services. Individuals and families from middle and upper middle class categories frequently find themselves in need of some type of human services as the result of a situational crisis. Ultimately, people from any social class are potential clients for human services.

Human services focuses on the individual's psychosocial needs and is concerned with the whole person. A client's problem is identified through a process of understanding human needs relative to environmental conditions. In human services, the individual person's needs is examined within from the framework of the *client system* (neighborhoods, family, socialization factors, culture, education, economic situation, etc.). All people in need of human services are candidates for services. The human services model and supporting philosophical ideologies are based on serving the client's immediate needs at the time they are presented. This approach to the client, of being readily accepted as a legitimate consumer of the human services system, is consistent with the attributes and development of the human services movement (Woodside and McClam, 1994, p. 60). Stimulated by the civil rights movement and related legislation (e.g., Mental Health Study Act of 1955; Community Mental Health Centers Act of 1963; Johnson's Great Society), the human service model generates a proactive philosophy towards helping people in need.

PROFESSIONALISM AND PROFESSIONAL DEVELOPMENT

Most human service educators are convinced that human services is a profession (Clubok, 1984), and graduates of recognized human service programs in colleges and universities should be considered professionals (Schmolling, Youkeles, Burger, 1993). Other educators view human services as an evolving profession (Feringer and Jacob, 1987; Schmolling, Youkeles, Burger, 1993). However, there appears to be consensus among human service scholars that the general criteria necessary for the establishment of a human service profession have been met (Schmolling, Youkeles, Burger, 1993). The criteria needed to be a profession includes, but is not limited to, a professional organization and membership, related professional activities (such as annual regional and national conferences), professional journal, approval for college human service program curricula, and an organization to administer the approval process and establish academic standards (such as the Council for Standards in Human Service Education). Additional evidence of human services developing into a profession is the growth of the graduate programs in human services. However, other professionals in the traditional human services professions feel that until human service programs are accredited by an organization sanctioned by the Council on Post Secondary Accreditation, human services cannot be fully recognized as a profession. The struggle between traditional human service professions and the professional development of the generalist human service worker continues, involving money, status, and responsibility (Schmolling, Youkeles, Burger, 1993, p. 283).

Professionals adhere to a specific code of ethics that governs their activities. Each human services profession has its own ethical orientation. For instance, the National Association of Social Workers (NASW), the American Psychological Association (APA), and the American Psychiatric Association (APA-medical doctors), each possess a code of ethical standards. Human services education is committed to the ethical treatment of clients and co-workers. Human service professionals are also sensitive to the ethical treatment of other workers from allied professions (Woodside and McClam, 1992, p. 19). Although a code of ethics developed by the earlier National Organization for Human Services (NOHS) was printed in 1979, it was never formally adopted. The National Organization for Human Service Education (NOHSE) Board of Directors is currently directing attention to the development of a human services professional code of ethics. The NOHSE proposal is under review and evaluation by NOHSE membership, Council for Standards in Human Service Education (CSHSE), and the professional community. Plans are to reach consensus about the content of the code and formally adopt the proposed standards in the near future.

There are over 800 undergraduate human service programs in the United States, which establishes it as a recognized field in education and academia. With the number of programs and the thousands of graduates these programs produce annually, it is logical for human services to be considered an academic discipline. Since human service work directly involves human behavior and social interaction, as well as program evaluation and the analysis of society itself, it can also be considered a social science and there appears to be no limit on the potential for research studies under the title of human services. On a similar note, in 1988, for the first time, the Department of Labor's "Occupational Outlook Handbook" listed human services as a separate category and not as a subcategory of counseling or social work. Similarly, in the most recent release by the U.S. Bureau of Labor Statistics, opportunities for the *human service worker* are projected to increase by 71.2 percent between 1990 and the year 2000. The human service field was ranked high under the heading of "the fastest growing occupations."

The National Organization for Human Services Education (NOHSE) has its roots in the earlier Faculty Development Conferences sponsored by SREB in the late sixties and early seventies (Woodside and McClam, 1990, p. 66). Subsequently, NOHSE was established in 1975 in St. Louis. The original purposes for NOHSE follow:

1. *To provide a medium for cooperation and communication among human service professionals and faculty.*
2. *To foster excellence in teaching, research, and curriculum planning in the teaching of the human services.*
3. *To serve individual faculty and professional members in their career development and position placement.*

4. *To maintain a registry of members available to serve as consultants and resource individuals qualified in planning, developing, administering, and evaluating education and training programs relating to middle-level human services workers.*
5. *To encourage, support, and assist the development of students and graduates of human service programs (Woodside and McClam, 1990, p. 66).*

Much of the direct involvement concerning specific approval of education training programs now falls under the domain of the Council for Standards in Human Services Education. NOHSE, however, remains committed to the development of professionalism in association with high-quality education programs which produce skilled generalist human service workers. Today, NOHSE comprises seven regional affiliates which consist of the following organizations:

Southern Organization for Human Service Education (SOHSE)
Southwest Organization for Human Service Education (SWOHSE)
Western Organization for Human Service Education (WOHSE)
Northwest Organization for Human Service Education (NWOHSE)
Midwest/North Central Organization for Human Service Education (MNCOHSE)
New England Organization for Human Service Education (NEOHSE)
Mid-Atlantic Consortium For Human Service (MACHS)

The NOHSE Board of Directors holds formal meetings on two occasions each calendar year, once at the annual national conference and again at the annual summer meeting. The board of directors consists of executive committee officers, regional representatives, and an elected student representative who is a member of a recognized human service student organization which usually is affiliated with a program from one of the regions. NOHSE board meetings entail several days of planned agenda business. Since the NOHSE board meets twice annually, and board members travel from all around the country, the

meeting time is considered very valuable and requires dealing with many issues and making important decisions during each meeting.

Coexisting with NOHSE is the Council for Standards for Human Service Education (CSHSE). The Council for Human Services Education was established in 1979 to give focus and direction to education and training in mental health and human services throughout the country (CSHSE National Directory, 1991). CSHSE is an organization which establishes standards for quality assurance in human services training programs and approves them through a formal evaluation process that includes on-site visits and reviews. Similar to NOHSE, the Council is comprised of eight Regional Directors. These two organizations represent the core of human service education and professional development, and are shepherds of the human services movement. Recently, at the 1991 national conference, and at the summer board meeting the same year, NOHSE and CSHSE met together in a joint effort to strenthen a collaborative relationship. Since, members have met during the subsequent national conferences and summer board meetings. The purpose was for both organizations to share their respective visions about human services, its future, and how to improve the field. The conferences have developed to represent both NOHSE and CSHSE on a mutual basis in terms of organizational benefit and membership interests. Because NOHSE and CSHSE are of primary importance to the development of the human services profession, it is important that they work closely together to share expertise, information systems, and coordinate their efforts and directions in the best interest of the profession and human services education.

Human services continues to grow professionally. With programs from colleges and universities continuing to seek approval, and increasing professional activity, a progressive pattern of professional development has been established over the past two decades. This growth is taking place on both regional and national levels. The National Organization for Human Service Education (including regional affiliates), and the Council for Standards in Human Service Education are primarily responsible for the professional development of human services today. The purpose of this effort is to provide assurance that human service graduates from four-year programs are prepared and competent for entry level professional practice.

HOW IS HELP DELIVERED AND BY WHOM

Discussed in later chapters are topics related to persons who need help, and relevant issues regarding service delivery. The general idea surrounding how help is delivered and by whom directly involves *systems* and *people*. Human services is responsible for improving the well-being of others and attending to the needs of clients on a first and foremost basis (Woodside and McClam, 1990, p. 172). Of course, this involves the people in the system who deliver services, referred to as *human service worker*. The generic use of the term *human service worker* includes traditional professions in the human services field such as nurses, social workers, counselors, psychologists, ministers, and a variety of other health care professionals. However, many workers from traditional human service related disciplines hold advanced degrees (master or doctorate credentials) and their respective disciplines define them more as specialists in the broader context of human services.

The generalist human service worker deals with the client directly providing immediate supportive services, and occasionally performs some of the traditional counseling functions (Woodside and McClam, 1994, p. 173). Woodside and McClam refer to four levels of performance distinction regarding a *typology* of human service workers taken from a publication by the Southern Regional Education Board, "Staff Roles for Mental Health Personnel: A History and Rationale" (1979). A summary of these categorizations shows a direct relationship to educational preparation, training, and competence (1994):

Level one is an entry level category that includes those workers who have a few weeks or months of instruction and some in-service training. These

individuals may have little on-the-job experience. The technical/apprentice level is the second level, which includes those who have one or two years of formal training or experience. Sometimes these workers have earned an Associates of Arts degree. Level three, the associate professional level, includes workers with formal training or experience, usually at the baccalaureate level. Workers with masters or doctorate degrees are Level four, the professional/specialist level (Woodside and McClam, 1994, p. 173).

These human service workers are agents of change in both the *client system* and the *human service system*. They deliver service directly to the client, and serve as a conduit between the client and the human service system of organizational structures and bureaucratic administrations. Human services are provided by a variety of agencies and workers. Human service agencies range from social welfare programs to correctional, psychiatric/mental health, rehabilitation, special education, juvenile diversion, family support, child care/residential, special group interest support and intervention, and many other programs that fall into the human service field.

Providers of human services come from a variety of backgrounds and training orientations. In human services, the helper is defined as one who assists others and includes workers with extensive training, as well as those who have minimal or moderate training (Woodside and McClam, 1990, p. 159). This broader definition regarding who is doing the helping includes a wide range of personnel, such as psychiatrists, psychologists, and social workers, as well as paraprofessionals and volunteers. In this sense, there are many different ways of describing the human service worker. Similarly, there are many different levels of human service practice that necessitate various degrees of training and academic preparation for workers. The human service worker represents many different agencies and programs. For example, the job description and role of a probation officer compared with a child protective services worker, or child care worker in a residential center, are substantially different and tend to focus on different aspects in the client system. Consequently, human service workers are subjected to specific features (requirements) of their formal role and designated function in the human service system. Although human service workers may share similar values proscribed in the philosophy and ideologies of the profession, they must continually negotiate those values in the scope of their formal role as service providers. This condition applies to all human services including the traditional professions.

Where human service workers are employed has a direct bearing on their role and mission in the service delivery system. With the expansion of the generalist term to *social health generalist concept*, the meaning of helper takes on the responsibility of knowing about the inter-relationship between systems and services. This is a different orientation than the generalist worker of the past in human services (Woodside and McClam, 1990). Expansion of the knowledge base for today's worker allows a larger spectrum of job opportunities for new graduates, as well as providing a richer pool of trained generalists that have the basic skills and competencies to adjust to a variety of human service settings. The broadening of the generalist concept was not motivated exclusively by the needs of the human service job market, but rather by a progressive social and legislative process which stimulated an elevation of social consciousness about human living conditions. The human service generalist is a product of a society that is increasingly being held more accountable for the well-being of its members.

Who Is the Human Service Worker?

The human service worker is a person who resembles a typical citizen in most American communities. Human service workers and students tend to come from both lower and middle class social stratification groups (Collins, Fischer and Cimmino, 1994). Similarly, they are usually people who can relate to others in an empathic way (Bernstein and Halaszyn, 1989; Collins, Fischer and Cimmino, 1994; Woodside and McClam, 1990). In a recent study of human ser-

vice student profiles, which examines the influence of psychodynamic factors upon career choice (Collins, Fischer and Cimmino, 1994), it was reaffirmed that people who are drawn to human services tend to be sensitive to human conditions because of previous psychosocial-related experiences. Further, the study indicates that human service students generally come from middle class socioeconomic backgrounds, are older (or nontraditional) students, and have interpersonal patterns that were associated with the students' career choice of human services (1994).

The findings of the study suggest that family backgrounds of those students who participated reflected a traditional nuclear family structure. However, more than 80 percent of the students reported not being raised by both biological parents, and of those parents, 66 percent remain married (34 percent divorced or separated). The incidence of parent divorce among the students who selected chemical addictions as their major concentration was 54 percent, and only four percent of students with a major concentration in early childhood studies reported being raised by their biological parents. The study indicates the presence of similar characteristics to the Enoch (1988) findings regarding undergraduate social work students choosing social work because they want to help people. Similarly, human service students were also motivated by the need to help others (ibid., 1994). The human service field seems to attract students that have experienced some difficult aspects of life and are seeking to address those issues. The study further supports the idea that individuals entering the helping professions have values and attitudes that have been shaped due to social variables and experiences that influence career decisions (Collins, Fischer and Cimmino, 1994).

HUMAN SERVICES EDUCATION

Human services are vital to the core definition of the human service profession. The curriculum in human service programs is designed to adhere to the contemporary issues facing the human service worker. The content of the education programs training students and teaching them how to function in their professional roles must be progressive and reflect social and human conditions in society (Woodside and McClam, 1990). Consistent with the social health generalist term introduced earlier, the training of today's human service worker is a comprehensive task. Training programs must carefully balance an important client-oriented focus with the human service delivery system and the worker's formal role within that system. This multiple focus is an essential characteristic in human service education.

The Council for Standards in Human Service Education (CSHSE) is the primary organization that establishes academic guidelines for the curriculum in consummating a degree or training certificate in human services. Taken from the CSHSE Monograph Series (1989), the Counsel describes itself in the following manner:

> The Council for Standards in Human Service Education was established in 1979 to give focus and direction and training in mental health and human services throughout the country. The Council exits to help human service educators and college administrators who are interested in achieving maximum educational effectiveness and to formally recognize and approve programs whose competence warrants public and professional confidence.

CSHSE initially established a list of standards in collaboration with the Southern Regional Education Board in the 1970s. The CSHSE Handbook (1985, p. 1) asserts, "The Program Approval Project began in 1976 when the Southern Regional Education Board (SREB) met with task forces, represented national interests, conducted surveys for purposes of creating a set of training standards, and developed an educational program assessment model." Ultimately, the knowledge base reflected by the CSHSE demonstrated the perspective of professionals working in the field. Subsequently, in its development, the nature of the human services curriculum demonstrates the dual emphasis of commitment: to the human service delivery system and the worker on one hand, and to

the client and the client's environment on the other (Woodside and McClam, 1990).

In 1979, the Southern Regional Education Board (SREB) provided the results of their Job Analysis Survey which examined "what a worker is expected to do" and "what workers do to actually carry out their jobs" (Petrie, 1990, p. 37; McPheeters, 1979). The purpose was to establish skill standards and a competency base for all human service education programs. The importance of this endeavor by CSHSE, besides defining competency standards, is associating professional distinctions between human service training/degree programs and other related programs such as psychology, social work, and counseling. The importance of establishing human services as an exclusive discipline and profession is of paramount value to those students and practitioners who hold specific degrees and credentials in human services.

The perspectives grown out of the human services movement that underscore individualism and other social reforms are changing the system of service delivery by requiring more trained generalist practitioners at the line level. This condition in contemporary human service and social service programs unequivocally supports the notion that workers trained in formal human service education programs are indeed an important commodity in the industry of the helping professions and the social welfare service delivery systems. To this extent, the human service workers' significance in society is not only to officially help people, but to advocate humanitarian principles and human rights. Thus, human services is an educational discipline and deserving of its own professional identity within the traditional field of helping professions.

In his study "Undergraduate Training for the Human Services: Many Routes to the Same Field," Nilsson asserts: "One consequence of the career orientation of today's generation of college students is that there is an increasing variety of undergraduate academic programs seeking to prepare students for practice in the human services. The long standing competition between social work and psychology programs to attract and train students interested in human service careers has been joined by undergraduate counseling programs, clinical or applied sociology programs, and additional programs offering interdisciplinary human service programs." Andrew Nilsson continues, "Various programs in interdisciplinary human services now trespass upon territory traditionally held by psychology and social work education. Are such degrees really equivalent?" (Nilsson, 1990, p. 19). This points out the intimate relationship between student career orientations, human service education, and the systematic process of human services becoming a new profession. Although the term "human services" is loosely used to describe other terms such as social welfare or social services, it is becoming increasingly apparent that human services is a new professional field (Mehr, 1988, p. 14, 15).

An important obligation in the education of human service workers is to pose the question of why a person made the choice to become a human service worker. What motivates students to enter the field? As discussed earlier, often individuals are attracted to the helping professions because of their own previous experiences in life (Collins, Fischer and Cimmino, 1994). Human services students must be aware of their subjective tendencies or feelings and not unwittingly project them onto clients. Many human service education programs offer opportunities for students to explore their personalities and their relationships within the context of social structures that relate to human services intervention. The training and development of human service skills and competencies to some degree are predicated on the students' personality and temperament. Over and above the training emphasis, the profession requires a special kind of individual who can objectively tolerate difficult human conditions and social problems that are an intricate part of human service work.

Important areas in the training of human service workers include the development of problem-solving skills. This means being able to evaluate client problems and identifying appropriate intervention strategies. Developing a variety of other skills is important for the human service trainee, such as in interpersonal communication, information management, working knowledge of human resources and interagency linkage, planning service delivery to serve individual client needs, and case management. These areas, which call for specific skills and knowledge, will be addressed in the following chapters. However, it is important to understand that within the general definition of human services, education represents one dimension. Undoubtedly, education cannot be underrated; it is the fuel that generates the human service product by training and supporting students and practitioners. Similarly, it gears the focus and knowledge base in the training programs to remain progressive and flexible with the changes in society and related human conditions.

A MELODY OF HUMAN SERVICE DEFINITIONS

The following definitions of human services were selected in an idiosyncratic fashion from various textbooks and published articles. There is no particular order or ranking to how they are presented. Further, in no way can they be considered inferior or superior, more accurate or less accurate, in comparison to each other or to those definitions discussed in this chapter. The purpose of this section is to assist the reader in understanding the basic human services concepts and definitions within the context of this entire article and the larger professional field.

> *What exactly is human services? Defining that term has proven to be perhaps the most difficult and most crucial task in writing this book. In its broadest sense, a human service is going on whenever one person is employed to be of service to another. Human services is the unifying and integrating profession of our society's many social welfare subsystems—health, education, mental health, welfare, family services, corrections, child care, vocational rehabilitation, housing, community service, and the law (Eriksen, 1977, p. 8).*

"What are human services anyway?" is one of the questions most frequently asked by students. We would like to be able to provide an "official" or generally accepted definition, but there is no such thing. Hasenfeld (1983) suggested that human services are organizations designed to "protect and enhance the personal well-being of others." This is a rather broad definition that includes almost any kind of helping service. Azarnoff and Seliger (1982) discuss the definition presented in the Allied Services Act of 1974: "Human services are those which enable the consumers of service to achieve, support, or maintain the highest level of economic self-sufficiency and independence" (p. 1). It is clear that experts do not agree on the range or type of helping activities that should be included in human services. We propose the following somewhat arbitrary definition. Human services are organized activities that help people in the areas of healthcare; mental health, including care for retarded persons; disability and physical handicap; social welfare; child care; criminal justice; housing; recreation; and education. Another term that might be included is income maintenance, a term that refers to programs like unemployment insurance and social security that provide income to people who are unemployed or retired. It should be noted that human services do not include the help given by family, friends, or other primary supports. The help is provided by some type of formal organization" (Schmolling, Youkeles and Burger, 1993, p. 6).

Human Services is a phrase that is often used to group activities that focus on helping people live better lives. In the broadest sense, the human services include formal systems such as government welfare programs, education, mental retardation services, mental health organizations, child care programs, the physical health care and correctional services of the legal justice system. The phrase also has more specific meaning. Some authors have described its most important feature as a new consciousness among workers and clients in the formal helping systems. Others have focused on human services as a concept that embodies an integrated delivery of services to consumers. Still others have defined it as a sociopolitical movement that has aspects of a subtle revolution. Individual human service workers may focus on one or more of these factors as the most important aspect of human services, depending on their training, experience, and personal goals. The theme that all share is the improvement of quality of living for the most needy members of our society (Mehr, 1989, p. 3).

Human Services is also defined by its professionalism. Our discussion of human services further clarifies it as an emerging profession with unique characteristics. We feel that there exists a clear definition of human services, which combines characteristics of human service workers, clients, and organizations. Scholars approach the definition of human services by describing the purposes, historical context, and organizational structure of human services. Human services is committed to giving individuals and groups enough assistance to allow them to help themselves. From the human service perspective, the client and society have complex problems that demand a broad approach; helping must focus on both the client and the environment. The human service professional assesses the multiple needs of clients and refers them to the appropriate services, recognizing that complex problems require complex solutions (Lyon and Duke, 1981; Mehr, 1986). Human services has emerged in response to the increase of human problems in our modern world (Mehr, 1986). Many scholars include in their definition of human services the purposes of the organizations that deliver the human services to clients. Hasenfeld and English further describe the human service system as a combination of several parts of the social welfare system and the related resources, policies, programs, and technical knowledge (1974). Human service activity is seen in terms of the interaction between the client and the human service system; human services begin when the client and the system start to work on the client's problems. A function of the human service worker is to help clients develop their ability to assess fundamental needs and focus on them early in the helping process. Human services is a relatively new helping occupation, which is now becoming professionalized (Woodside and McClam, 1994).

The term "human services" has become popular in recent years. In some ways a euphemism, it refers to such services as education, health, mental health housing, welfare, counseling services to the aging, care for the retarded, recreation, corrections, criminal justice, family services, child care, services for the physical handicapped, vocational rehabilitation, and the like (Social Work Encyclopedia).

The functional definition of human services is based on acceptable standards of living in a civilized society. The *profession of human services* comprises an immediate organized social response to the recognition of human conditions which are detrimental to the survival of a person or persons living in society. Similarly, when *professional human service workers* determine that sufficient evidence exists which justifies the need for human services, it becomes the primary task of those workers to assure the delivery of specific human services which are intended to alleviate immediate suffering and assist individuals and families in acquiring and retaining acceptable standards of social and physical life needs (Cimmino, 1993, p. 15).

An Etiology of Human Services Definitions

The question of exactly what is *human services* is actually a major issue in our society because it reflects and relates to the current epidemic of social problems. The answer is not only vital to the development of professional human services, but to how human life is sustained in our society as well. In spite of extensive work by human service educators, authors, administrators, and practitioners, the human services movement and profession remain obscure to the general public and the allied professional community. From the literature, it appears that human services needs to be more than an academic program, credential, or

job. Professional development in contemporary human services represents a renewal of focus on client systems and human needs by placing the person and family first in the value system of the profession and society. In essence, the growth of human services as a profession, academic discipline, and social science fosters potential to become a factor in changing social policy and political positions towards domestic human conditions to be more supportive of humanitarian programs designed to enhance the quality of life for all people.

The statement above is a testimonial to the perspective and ideology of human services developed in a paper which was published in CSHSE Monograph Series (Visions) entitled, *"Exactly What Is Human Services? The Evolution of a Profession: Academic Discipline and Social Science"* (Cimmino, 1993). My objectives were to identify the importance of the human services profession by suggesting three primary reasons for professional development which are referred to in the paper as *pillars* (see Figure 1.1). The paper was presented at the 1991

FIGURE 1.1   Human Services Perspective in Reasons for Development
Source: Paul F. Cimmino, Ph.D.

NOHSE Conference in Seattle, and again in Oregon at the 1992 NWOHSW Regional Conference, to stimulate discussion toward building a vision about this new profession among scholars, educators, and practitioners in the human services professional community. My hunch was that a definition of human services would emerge in developing the paper since the research design was phenomenological and focused on existing literature in human services. The three pillars and corresponding reasons for professional development, which are described in the next paragraph, attempt to organize the gist of implications surrounding professional development at micro- and macrosocial system levels.

Much of the current literature in the field, such as studies published by the NOHSE Journal, address professional identity and status, descriptions of the field, definitions of service delivery systems, intervention, and the human service worker's role in the helping process (Cimmino, 1993). This emphasis in recent journal articles and other human service publications reflects the youthful growing pains of the field as well as the struggle for professional identity in human services education.

In my view, human services must become better defined and recognized as a profession. There is a great opportunity for the human services movement in society and education to be a contributing force for positive social change. The notion of conceptual pillars representing the primary foundations in defining human services is supported by three important reasons that parallel principles for professional development and represent the heart of human services. These reasons become the three *pillars* supporting the professional development of the human services field. The presentation below is representative of a brief overview and summation of the manuscript (see Figure 1.2).

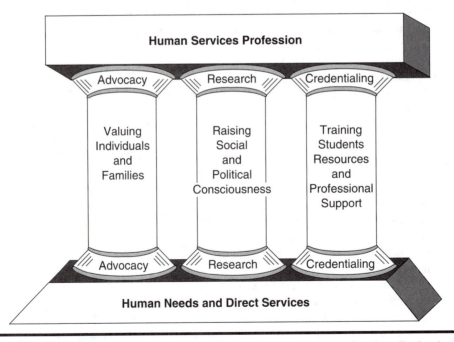

FIGURE 1.2   The Three Pillars Supporting the Development of the Human Services Profession
Source: Paul F. Cimmino, Ph.D.

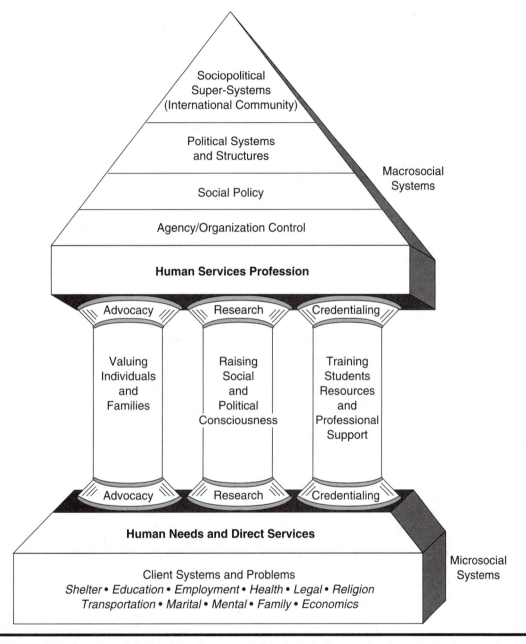

FIGURE 1.3   Functional Model of the Conceptual Principals in Human Services
Source: Paul F. Cimmino, Ph.D.

THREE REASONS FOR PROFESSIONAL DEVELOPMENT AND THE PILLARS

It is important to identify human services as a distinct profession that involves distinctive training of high quality workers for three primary reasons. These are operational reasons that serve simultaneously as functional roles in the development of the human services profession. They ultimately result in a *why, way, and how* phenomenon: (1) *why* the human services movement is so important to humanity relates to the *First Pillar*, "Putting people and families first in the value system of the helping profession and society;" (2) the *way* to accomplish human services professional objectives is through education, research, and social reform corresponds to the *Second Pillar*, "Expanding overall social and political consciousness;" (3) *how* to make human services more professionally recognized relates to the *Third Pillar*: "Training human service students is the basic resource for fueling change and professional development in the field" (Cimmino, 1993).

Ultimately, the helping process in human services operates in a larger social context that includes formal organizational structures, bureaucratic administrations, social policy, and a variety of interdeterminate and intermediate service delivery systems, as shown in Figure 1.3 on page 25 (Caputo, 1988, p. 73).

Dr. Harold McPheeters Responds

At the 1992 National Organization for Human Services Education Conference in Alexandria, Virginia, I had the distinct privilege of hearing Dr. Harold McPheeters give the keynote address. At the conclusion of his presentation, I spoke with him about human services and his discussion. During our conversation, I asked if he would be interested in reading my manuscript and comment on the ideas it developed. He agreed. Several weeks later, I received his four page written response. I was very impressed with his articulation and depth of reaction to the content of my study. Dr. McPheeters's response to "Exactly What Is Human Services," offers an expansion of insight to contemporary thinking about this relatively new field from its most noted professional figure and pioneer.

REFERENCES

Bernstein, G.S., and J.A. Halaszyn, (1989). *"Human Services"?. . . That Must Be So Rewarding.* Baltimore, MD: P.H. Brookes.

Caputo, R., (1988). *Management and Information Systems in Human Services.* New York, NY: Haworth Press, Inc.

Cimmino, P., (1993). "Exactly What Is Human Services? The Evolution of a Profession: Academic Discipline and Social Science." Bronx, NY: *Council for Standards in Human Service Education Monograph Series.*

Collins, R., J. Fischer, and P. Cimmino, (1994). "Human Services Student Patterns: A Study of the Influence of Selected Psychodynamic Factors Upon Career Choice." Bellingham WA: *Journal of the National Organization for Human Service Education* 14(1).

Erikson, Erik H., (1963). *Childhood and Society,* 2nd ed. New York: Norton.

Erikson, K., (1977). *Human Services Today.* Reston, VA: Reston Publishing Company.

Erdman, D.M., and R.J. Lundman, (1979). *Corporate and Governmental Deviance.* New York, NY: Harper and Row.

Frederick, H.S., and J.S. Jones, (1990). "Self-Understanding in Human Services Education: Goals and Methods." Kingston, RI: *Journal of the National Organization for Human Services Education* 9(1).

Fullerton, S., and D. Osher, (1990). "History of the Human Services Movement." Knoxville, TN: *Council for Standards in Human Service Education Monograph Series.*

Fullerton, S., (1990). "Development of Baccalaureate-Level Professional Education in Human Services." Knoxville, TN: *Council for Standards in Human Services Education Monograph Series.*

Fullerton, S., (1990). "A Historical Perspective of the Baccalaureate-Level Professional Education in Human Services." Kingston, RI: *Journal of the National Organization for Human Services Education* 9(1).

Kuhn, T.S., (1975). *The Structure of Scientific Revolutions*. Chicago, IL: University of Chicago Press.

Linzer, L., (1990). "Ethics and Human Services Practice." Kingston, RI: *Journal of the National Organization of Human Services Education* 9(1).

Macht, J., (1990). "A Historical Perspective." *History of the Human Services Movement, CSHSE Monograph Series* 9, 22.

McPheeters, H., (1990). "Development of the Human Services Generalist Concept." *History of the Human Services Movement, CSHSE Monograph Series* 31, 40.

Mehr, J., (1988). *Human Services, Concepts and Intervention Strategies*, 4th ed. Boston: Allyn and Bacon.

Nilsson, A.T., (1989). "Undergraduate Training for the Human Services: Many Routes to the Same Field." Kingston, RI: *Journal of the National Organization for Human Services Education* 9(1), 19–25.

Osher, D., (1990). "More than Needs and Services: Antecedent and Current Social Conditions That Influence the Human Services Movement." *History of the Human Services Movement, CSHSE Monograph Series*, 23–30.

Petrie, D.R., (1989). "Entry-Level Skills of Human Service Work." Kingston, RI: *Journal of the National Organization of Human Services Education* 9(1), 37–41.

Ryan, W., (1976). *Blaming the Victim*. New York: Vintage Books.

Schmolling, M. Youkeles, and W.R. Buger, (1989). *Human Services in Contemporary Society*. Pacific Grove, CA: Brookes/Cole.

Sherif, M., and C. Sherif, (1969). *Social Psychology*. New York: Harper and Row.

Simon, E., (1990). "The Challenge of the Future: Towards the 21st Century; The History of the Human Services Movement." Knoxville, TN: *Council for Standards in Human Service Education Monograph Series*, 101:115.

Slaikeu, K.A., (1990). *Crisis Intervention: A Handbook for Practice and Research*. Needham Heights, MA: Allyn and Bacon.

Whittaker, J.K., (1977). *Social Treatment: An Approach To Interpersonal Helping*. Chicago, IL: Aldine Publishing Company.

Woodside, M.R., and T. McClam, (1994). *An Introduction To Human Services*. Pacific Grove, CA: Brookes/Cole.

Woodside, M.R., and T. McClam, (1990). "Problem Solving in the Human Service Curriculum." Kingston, RI: *Journal of the National Organization of Human Services Education* 9(1).

Woodside, M.R., (1989). "Case Study Method: A Technique for Professional Development." Kingston, RI: *Journal of the National Organization of Human Services Education* 8(1).

LETTER TO PAUL CIMMINO
FROM HAROLD L. McPHEETERS

435 Forest Valley Rd., NE
Atlanta, GA 30342–2354
October 23, 1992

Paul F. Cimmino, Ph.D., ACSW
Montana State University—Billings
Department of Counseling and Human Services
1500 N. 30th St.
Billings, MT 59101

Dear Dr. Cimmino,

Now that we are back from our trip that included my talk at the NOHSE Meeting, I am nearly caught up with unpaid bills and unanswered letters. I have also read your "Exactly What is Human Services." I agree that there is a substantial need to provide a sharper conceptualization for Human Services, especially as it differs from Social Work, where there seems to be the greatest conflict with both sets of practitioners claiming the same turf. This has never been done well by either profession.

Most of the professions within the overall arena of Human Services rightfully claim a "humanitarian" base, but also most are also premised upon some theoretical foundation regarding the nature of Human Service problems and possible solutions. Thus much of medicine and the health care field assumes a biomedical causation and biomedical remedies, while psychology assumes a psychological/behavioral causation and set of interventions. Social work is theoretically based on the notion of social causation and interventions, and the early social workers functioned in that way. However, social work, especially case work, has drifted over into the psychological realm where many practitioners choose to practice what is much closer to psychological therapy than what most old-time social workers would have found appropriate. Perhaps this is because the scientific evidence for social causation and social interventions has been difficult to obtain and because the field has drifted to a strong "value oriented" base. Social work is based on a value system of beliefs far more than the other human service professions which tend to have more firm evidence for their work.

At times that value orientation causes social workers considerable internal conflict in practice. For example, they profess a belief in client self-determination, but in reality, they frequently find that the constraints of the fiscal/legal system in which they work does not allow the client to make his/her own decisions (e.g., the workers can't provide all the money the clients want or need; committed patients or prisoners cannot go home, even if they want to), and the workers find that they are actually the agents of social constraint. Another value of social work is its belief in democratic majority rule, but so many of their clients are in the minority. Then what?

My point is that there are inherent problems in making values (which often conflict with each other) the base upon which to build a profession, as social work has found. At the same time, there are severe limitations in building a profession on a single academic/knowledge base, because human service problems and their solutions require a broad bio-psycho-social perspective. Worst of all is a profession based on a narrow technology (e.g., psychoanalysis, surgery, behavioral therapy), because then every client's problems are seen in terms of the need for that specific technology.

The early work we did in this field was in the area of mental health technology—not broad human services. I have felt a bit uneasy as the academicians moved to the broader terminology of "human services" without making much change in their academic programs. However, I still feel that the basic concept of the "generalist" worker, as we defined it in mental health, and as you seem to do in your paper is the most appropriate orientation for the new field. In that formulation, the focus of concern of the worker is for the client and family and the totality of their problems/needs—not just one theoretical part of them. The worker is an advocate for that client, much as a family practitioner is the advocate for his client/family, doing what he can himself and making referrals to meet specialized needs, but even then keeping in touch and helping the specialist understand special needs, and following up after the specialist has done his "thing". The worker helps the client with all the bio-psychosocial aspects of his need, and needs a keen knowledge and appreciation of all of them. (In my judgement, many of the Human Services education programs have greatly devalued the biomedical aspects).

The worker must be quite analytical about the client's needs to assure that the client does not fall into prolonged dependency. This may be a difficult point for workers who focus too much on "humanitarian" needs; it can lead to fostering dependency if the distinction is not clearly understood. I believe "advocacy" is desirable, but at this level (the client level), I see it related to helping the client get what he needs in a system that would not ordinarily serve him.

These are all concepts that apply at the level of the individual human service worker engaged with individual clients and families. At higher academic and organizational levels I see Human Services working much more with the systems of services, creating new services, linking them more effectively and economically, etc. The advocacy here is more related to systems (economic, organizational, political, etc.). We need much more research in these areas. I get impatient with advanced human service educational programs that focus on preparing "therapists" for individual clients (Why not just switch those students to psychology or social work?), or that provide rather stereotyped education about organizational theory and management with little research to determine its relevance to human service systems. I believe that management concepts developed from manufacturing and business are in some ways actually antithetical to human services, but we need much more research to be sure.

I tend to be cautious about blaming the larger system of society for its short-comings in relation to the human services. In my judgement we in the human services have not done a good job of defining those problems and needs and especially what would be both effective and cost-effective interventions. American society is far too committed to a philosophy of competition and winning. The sorriest part of it is that the losers are seen as "deficient" or "bad" and thus to blame for and deserving of their own plights. We teach these competitive concepts in school, on TV, in books, in newspapers (right now we have both the World Series and the Presidential elections underway, and winning or losing on our national mind every hour). We need a gentler philosophy that says that everyone is important and must be brought to his/her level of greatest contribution and participation in our society—not just the winners, and that everyone has a stake in bringing about that state of our nation.

At the same time, we in the human services must be sure the we know what we are doing in our interventions and that they are cost effective. (A glaring example of such a current problem is the vast increases we have seen in recent years in institutional care for disturbed children/adolescents and alcoholics. They cannot be justified, and society is now saying so by establishing managed care organizations to control the "abuses". It is a discredit to the mental health establishment that it has allowed this to happen, but they "won" all those concessions to have those conditions "covered" by third party payment programs). We must not simply whine for more money and prestige for human services without assuring that we are making good use of our funds and talents. Human Services programs at advanced academic levels, with careful research, more refined program evaluation, and critical analysis (not just blind advocacy) could help us do better in those areas.

All this is a long way about to endorse your concept that human services puts the client/family at the center of concern and works to help in the totality of that person/family's bio-psychosocial realities—not just some theoretical portion of it. One problem you will experience at the highest conceptual level is that all the other human service professions will say that they do exactly the same thing. A careful analysis of what they *really* do will show that they focus on only a theoretical part of it, but then I'm not so sure that human service workers, as presently trained, are as well prepared in some of the broad bio-psychosocial aspects of the human need (the biomedical aspects and aspects having to do with anti-social behavior, corrections and criminology) as they really should be.

What kind of reaction did you receive to this paper? We surely need more attention to this kind of effort to more clearly define just what we are. There is great reluctance from legislators, third-party payers, etc. to accept any "new" professions that will simply raise the costs of human services to the public and the taxpayers. It behooves any new group to firmly establish its rationale for being and to sharpen the distinctions between it and other closely related professions in language and concepts that are practical and make sense to the larger society. Fuzzy abstractions will not cut the mustard.

I hope this helps.

Cordially yours,

Harold L. McPheeters

CHAPTER 2

HUMAN SERVICES
HISTORY AND RECENT INFLUENCES

JEAN MACHT
WITH DOUGLAS WHYTE

INTRODUCTION

Every movement has its antecedents and the human service movement is no exception. However, like most people in the helping professions, students and educators tend to be absorbed with the present, reacting to the burdens of clients, learning the skills that will relieve the pain of these needy folks, and warding off the burnout that accompanies the disparity between need and service availability. Consequently, seldom do we take that backward glance to learn how we arrived where we are today. Just what are those historical antecedents, attitudes and values pertaining to human life and quality of existence that shape and inform our practice?

An historical perspective is essential to any understanding of current conditions, to avoid the pitfalls of past mistakes, and to serve as a springboard for the evaluation of novel approaches. As has been proverbially observed, if we fail to learn from the mistakes of the past we are doomed to repeat them. Thus, the focus of this historical journey is the searching out of that lore, that heritage which most directly relates to the present mentality and disposition of the human services movement.

In accomplishing this, one is challenged by two concerns: how far back into remote history should the search extend and how much of the historical relevancy should be included? If one chooses the "short look," the perspective of the reader will be blunted. If one, however, elects the "long look," in both breadth and depth, the reader might become bored. Given the writer's penchant for history and digression, the temptation to take the "long look" is great, but temperance and moderation will prevail.

The Roots of Altruism

The practices, theories, and attitudes that originate and predispose care of the needy in our culture are influenced not only by historical occurrences but also by our unique national character. As a society we hold individual effort and independence in high regard, and yet we are also the most charitable nation in history. What country has so feverishly and extravagantly sought to rebuild its opponents after a war? What country has so actively and aggressively raised billions of dollars to relieve the plight of those distressed by hunger, disease, and ill fate? And yet what country has created a poverty culture in the midst of plenty and "conspicuous consumption"? Paradoxical? Certainly, but understandable in terms of an economic structure in direct contradiction to democratic ideals. This national character bears dramatically on our social welfare system with examples of service provision with the subsequent denigration of the recipient.

Many observers of social welfare institutions single out the Judeo-Christian tradition as providing the stimulus for benevolent actions. In fact, one might be led to think that Judeo-Christian religions invented humanitarianism, often equating Christianity with charity. History does not support this. No religion, philosophy, or movement has a corner on charity—or cruelty for that matter—but each in turn has influenced those of goodwill towards altruism and, in some instances, provided the justification for transgression by those who are less charitable.

From the beginning of recorded history and knowledge passed down by oral transmission, religion has been concerned not only with our vertical relationship to superior beings or a Superior Being, but also with the horizontal relationship of human beings with one another. The horizontal relationship addresses the ethics of religion, or what people ought to do, with the emphasis on the *doing*. Perhaps we can refer to these two aspects of any living religion as matters of faith or belief and matters of action or practice. The task of helping involves translating our belief statements into deeds appropriate to the circumstance.

We have limited information on how early peoples lived. However, experience with so-called "primitive" peoples whom anthropologists have met in the last one-hundred years suggests that a basic concern was probably for the success of the group or tribe, since human beings are designed to live interdependently within groups in order to survive. Anthropology informs us that even in antiquity, early peoples showed hospitality to strangers. Life-supporting sustenance was liberally shared for the common good and orphans were unknown because parenting was a shared task.

With the rise of major religions, doing unto others became formalized in sacred writings as well as in formal instruction and teaching by example. Buddhist teachings, four-hundred years before the birth of Christ, placed great emphasis on love and charity above all other forms of righteousness. Helping the needy was a condition for acquiring "good karma." Other Indian influences found in Hinduism instruct its followers to devote one's life to duty, family, caste, and community,

thus expounding the virtues of Dharma, or religious and moral law (Noss). Traveling east to China, the ethical principles of Confucianism are found in the law of reciprocity—simply the "Silver Rule," similar to the Golden Rule stated in reverse. Still farther east, in Japan, Shintoism absorbs the ethical doctrines of benevolence as outlined by the Buddha and Confucius (Noss). Jewish doctrine as embodied in the Talmud and the Old Testament teaches the duty of giving and, equally important, the right and obligation of those in need to receive. The testaments are replete with commands and admonitions to be charitable to the unfortunate—the sick, the old, the handicapped, and the poor. Following the traditions of the Hebrew prophets, emphasis on good deeds, love of one's enemies, mercy, and charity were a continual theme of Christ's preachings. Perhaps the most encompassing passage on Christ's ethical mission is phrased in Luke 4:18–21 (Noss).

> *The spirit of the Lord is upon me,*
> *For he has consecrated me to preach the good*
>   *news to the poor,*
> *He has sent me to announce to the prisoners*
>   *their release and to the blind the recovery of*
>   *their sight.*
> *To set the downtrodden at liberty,*
> *To proclaim the year of the Lord's favor.*

And finally, after the birth of Christianity, with the development of Islam as expressed by Muhammad, the Koran tells us that true piety is obtained by giving to the needy and all those who ask (Noss).

Beyond religious instruction, current research on prosocial behavior suggests that the roots of altruism may have a genetic link. Perhaps altruism is predisposed in the same manner as other abilities believed to be genetically linked, such as memory, logic, mathematics, and others. The impetus for much of the prosocial behavior research and its genetic link comes from Edward O. Wilson demonstrating prosocial behavior in animals (other than human), and Wilson extrapolated those results to human altruism. Such liberty has obviously provoked much controversy.

Despite the short supply of research in this area, one study of interest indicates that there is more cooperation between identical twins than fraternal, that relatives are more likely to help relatives than nonrelatives and that "helping in the face of danger is highly related to degree of blood relatedness" (Eisenberg). Of particular interest is the evidence that twins at an early age are keyed into behavior by each other, not just by their caretakers.

Eisenberg, in her work with Mussen (Eisenberg and Mussen), takes the position that "there is no doubt that humans have a biological potential for altruistic actions—otherwise they could not perform them." Less clear are individual differences in prosocial and altruistic behavior as genetically influenced. "The fact that humans have the biological potential for altruistic actions is not, however, sufficient evidence that individual differences . . . result from evolution or are genetically controlled" (Eisenberg and Mussen). Recent evidence, though, does show such individual variation as having some genetic link. The fact that during WWII many Germans, at great risk to themselves, tried to harbor and save Jews from the death camps, stands in testimony to individual variation.

Why some people come to the aid of others and some do not, certainly provokes continued and frustrating debate. Whether by nurture or by nature, and probably by both, the impulse to help the needy and the despairing is well established in our professional practices, our systems, and in the very fabric of everyday life.

ANTECEDENTS OF THE HUMAN SERVICES MOVEMENT

Despite the pronouncements of sacred writings regarding charity and the ethical and reciprocal arrangements of human beings, there has been a wide disparity between instruction and practice. This is obvious as we look at how societies have dealt with abnormal behavior (including what we now identify as mental illness). Further, each era has had its own view of disordered behavior, and the treatment afforded the disturbed has been a reflection of the prevailing views. Cyclically throughout history disturbance has been seen as a punishment for misdeeds, a curse resulting from possession by devils, a human weakness of character, or as ensuing from natural causes.

It is important for the reader to be advised that there will be a greater focus on mental illness in this chapter than might be expected. There is good reason for this in the unique history of the human services movement, as will become evident as you read further.

Early Peoples

Before recorded history, early peoples believed that events were controlled by a multitude of spirits. Indeed, spirits found their lodging in all matter, as well as in the elements. (This theological position of all things having spirits led to a respect for the earth and nature.) Certainly in some early groups, those exhibiting severe abnormality or inability to cope with life became ready scapegoats when there was an unproductive hunt, drought, flood, or any of a variety of natural disasters. To these early people, clearly those evidencing strange or inordinate behavior were possessed of evil spirits and therefore must be the cause of negative events.

Remains have been found by scientists bearing evidence of a procedure known as trephining. Since the person was possessed, logically the evil spirits must reside in the head. Consequently, it seemed appropriate to open a hole in the skull (usually accomplished with the use of a sharp stone or shell) to release the evil spirit. One cannot help but be reminded of the modern psychosurgical procedure known as lobotomy, where parts of the brain are surgically destroyed to control aberrant behavior.

The Golden Age of Greece

This period of history remains not only a time when politics, philosophy, and the natural sciences flourished, but a time when attitudes regarding problem behavior altered. Hippocrates, considered the father of modern medicine, rejected the concept of demonic possession and postulated that disturbed behavior was a function of natural illness and should be treated as such. This progressive view marks the beginnings of the medical model or disease concept. Whereas we can be concerned about this single-causation approach, those with problem behaviors were rescued from interventions based upon a premise of demonic possession. Unfortunately, the only people benefiting from this enlightened notion were the elite. The common person was still regarded as possessed and was treated accordingly. In fact, the democratic concepts birthed during this time only applied to upper class and privileged males. Slavery was still practiced, and the plight of the needy found no salutary response (Mehr).

Problem behavior has seldom been seen in its psychological and social sense. During this same time period, however, several hundred years before the birth of Christ, there was a precursor of the moral treatment movement and the therapeutic community model. It found its fruition at Epidaurus on the Peloponnesian Peninsula. The topography of the area affords a natural amphitheater as well as hot springs. Greek theatre was presented during the summer months (and still is today). Additionally, a sanitarium was constructed at Epidaurus for lodging and the guests were encouraged to bathe in the springs and attend the theatre productions. Unfortunately, this spa was again only provided for those of means from Athens as a retreat from the pressures of urban life and the complexities of a more sophisticated culture. Despite its restrictive clientele, Epidaurus was a glimmer of enlightenment.

The Medieval Period

Certainly, this period of history is remembered as one of the most bleak and inhumane of times. This era, from approximately the late fifth century A.D. until the Renaissance, beginning in the thirteenth century, is often referred to as the Dark Ages. Dark for several reasons; it was first of all so because there was little enlightenment. The Western world was under the domination of the Roman Catholic Church and the only literary efforts were produced by the early church fathers, often removed both literally and figuratively from their constituents. (The invention of movable type by Johannes Gutenberg did not occur until the middle of the fifteenth century. Thus all "literary" productions were laboriously copied by hand.) These works were written in Latin, which was not the spoken language of an illiterate people. Education and literacy were reserved for the priests and the upper class. Therefore, any hope for education and resultant progress was indeed limited.

Additionally, those who might challenge the authority of the Church intellectually or practically were labeled as heretics and subjected to extreme forms of punishment or death. Those persons exhibiting aberrancy were also accused of heresy and suffered similar plight. Those found to be heretical were often believed to be witches or warlocks possessed by the devil. Thus it seems we have a complete return to the thoughts of early peoples.

Searching out these troubled and rebellious souls was a major activity of the day and led to widespread witch hunts of proverbial fame. Despite the beginnings of enlightenment that came with the Renaissance, the hunts continued. Eventually, the Roman Catholic Church lost its corner on this activity to the leaders of the Protestant movement who were following fast with their own witch hunts.

The continuation of witch hunts travelled from Europe to the Colonies, reaching their height in Salem and nearby communities of the Massachusetts Bay Colony. By the close of the eighteenth century, thousands of people had been burned at the stake. It must be noted that most of the burning was selective to women (Long). Current information yields a picture of gross discrimination. Significant numbers of women labeled as witches were actually healing and soothing all manners of physical distress with herbal potions and natural healing ministrations. Obviously the medical profession, which was treating by bloodletting and leeching, was threatened. And so ends one of the most repressive and harsh periods of history.

The Renaissance

Significant to the history of helping is the shift of responsibility for the public's welfare from the domain of religion to the domain of government. The waning power of the Church, the Protestant Reformation, the decline of feudalism, rapid population growth and the subsequent rise of nationalism were all events and conditions that ushered in an era of enlightenment known as the Renaissance. Although not an entirely favorable period for the disturbed and wanting (not that any period of history has been), at least government programs were formalized.

The first such formalization occurred in 1536 under the reign of Henry VIII with a system of income maintenance and public welfare (Trattner). This was followed in 1601 by the establishment of the Elizabethan Poor Laws. These laws provided shelter and care for the poor only if and when the family defaulted in what has always been considered its responsibility as the primary caregiver (Trattner). The Poor Laws carried with them a system of classification whereby those that could work were relegated to "workhouses," those who could not work were sent to poorhouses or almshouses, and orphaned or abandoned children became wards of the state.

As with any public programming, the management of an ever-growing system became increasingly burdensome, resulting in a growing and impersonal bureaucracy leaving locals free to misuse and abuse their authority. This theme is played out over and over again as we shall see. However, at the same time there were glimmers of hope—including an asylum established in Valencia, Spain, noted for its humane and progressive treatment. Also, although seldom mentioned in historical chronicles, was the colony of Gheel in the Netherlands where townsfolk took into their homes disturbed people from all locales throughout the country (Trattner). A far less civilized solution for disturbed people was the founding of St. Mary's of Bethlehem in 1547. Bedlam, as it came to be known, rapidly became overcrowded, and uncaring caretakers chained their wards to walls in filthy, dungeon-like conditions.

Whereas the Renaissance ushered in an era of unparalleled expression in the arts of painting, sculpture, literature, architecture, and to a lesser extent music, the plight of the troubled, the disturbed, and the indigent, was eased little.

The First Revolution in Mental Health

The Rise and Fall of Moral Treatment and Other Early Monuments in the United States.   The rise and fall of moral treatment, often called the "First Revolution" in mental health, found its origin in 1792 when a French physician, Phillipe Pinel, unleashed the chains on some fifty "maniacs" at La Bicêtre Hospital in Paris (Hospital and Community Psychiatry). This act moved mental illness from the cauldrons of witches and the temptations of forbidden fruit to the rational perception of disorder as a pathological condition now relegated to the scientist and the humanitarian.

In England, William Tuke, an English Quaker, founded the York Retreat in 1796 (Hospital and Community Psychiatry). Influenced by Pinel and Tuke, the development of the mind, regularity of lifestyle, appropriate diet, exercise, diversion, and religious observance were the dominant practices in the establishment of retreats and asylums in the United States. The first such facility, the Friends' Asylum, was founded in 1817 in what is now Philadelphia, PA (Hospital and Community Psychiatry). Currently known as Friends' Hospital, it still serves the needs of the mentally disturbed. As positive as the initial efforts were, with the passage of time and expanded numbers entering the system, few could derive much benefit from the treatment offered (e.g., chronic disorders and permanent brain damage). The demise of moral treatment was brought about in barely thirty years (1820–1850) (Hospital and Community Psychiatry).

On the heels of the decline of moral treatment, and perhaps as a result of overcrowding pushing its overflow back onto the public, Dorothea Dix waged her own battle for the insane. Forced into retirement as a school teacher by poor health, Ms. Dix turned her efforts to teaching Sunday School. With her class, she visited numerous jails and almshouses and, finding the majority of those incarcerated were mentally ill, she took her fight for the mentally ill from Massachusetts to Washington and across the United States. Through her extraordinary efforts and personal commitment, hospitals for mental patients were established in nine states (and other cities around the world) by the end of Ms. Dix's life (Trattner).

Unfortunately, these facilities, like their earlier counterparts, became dumping grounds for the mentally ill and were soon overcrowded. The resulting deterioration led to widespread cries for reform. One of the more inspired suggestions for gentler treatment was to "farm-out" or "board-out" patients in the community. Massachusetts again was the forerunner in instigating change. Although the concept and subsequent implementation were considered successful, the project was short-lived and was never extended to other states on any large-scale basis. However, the movement toward community care served as a model concept for legislation nearly one-hundred years later (Hospital and Community Psychiatry).

The Industrial Revolution.   Revolution, according to Webster's, can be defined as "a sudden, radical, or complete change" (Trattner), and this is indeed what occurred during the latter half of the nineteenth and early twentieth centuries. Rapid industrialization brought about the dramatic movement of people from the nation's farmlands to our cities. What was in 1900 a 90 percent rural population became a 90 percent urban population.

These rural people flocked to the cities to find work. Immigrants came to find the American Dream (a nightmare for many).

I cannot help relating the story of Tillie (which was told to me by my daughter Rebecca, a volunteer at Willard State Hospital), a young immigrant of only 16, who in the early 1900s arrived in New York only to find that her appointed sponsor was not there to greet her. Wandering about the streets of New York, unable to speak English and explain her plight, her foreign tongue was interpreted by the local authorities as the babblings of the insane. She was incarcerated in New York City and later sent to Willard State Hospital in upper New York. Tillie died there at the age of 93 in 1980.

There were many Tillies. According to Bloom, at Worcester State Hospital (Massachusetts), the proportion of foreign born among all admissions climbed from 10 percent in 1844 to 47 percent in 1963. Further, nearly half of all first admissions at Worcester between 1893 and 1933 were foreign born and most were destitute. The connection of the cycle of poverty, alienation, and mental disorder is inescapable.

The effects of industrialization with its assembly line factories removed people not only from their roots but from the sources of satisfaction that come with creating a product from inception to completion. Emile Durkheim, a French theoretician, described this state of alienation as *anomie*. Little wonder that we witnessed increasing demand for new and different explanations for the origins of disorder.

In considering the impact of the industrial revolution, it is also important to remember that dependence on the factory meant that workers could easily be laid off and thus face unemployment (unemployment insurance didn't come about until the 1930s). This meant that individuals and families had to move around to maintain an income. Additionally, the industrial revolution looked upon the earth as simply a source of raw materials to be pillaged at will. Many of our environmental problems today developed from that manner of thinking.

The Settlement House and Charity Organization Societies Movements.

Throughout this narrative we have seen the needy and the disordered falling within the purview of the shaman, the priest, the physician, or a government authority. Each, in turn, attributing disturbance, or inability to function, to some internal causation, whether evil possession, a lack of faith, chemical imbalance, or just plain indolence. Seldom have those responsible for the plight of others looked to external conditions as possible causes. However, during this era of rapid industrialization, people like Jane Addams, Graham Taylor, and Lillian Ward not only recognized the role of societal conditions like poverty, homelessness, and lack of education, but they did something about it. With Hull House (1889), Chicago Commons, and Henry Street Settlement on New York's lower East Side, we saw not only the birth of social work but the beginning of social change agentry later to be formalized in laws and public policy (Trattner).

The settlement house movement was also a reaction to organized charity work. The Charity Organization Societies (COSs) were in the business of temporary relief and, as in an earlier period, charity workers sorted out the worthy from the unworthy poor, thus implying "individual and moral causes of destitution" (Trattner). Similarities existed between the two movements, however, in their use of volunteers, interest in people's spiritual as well as material conditions, and investigation before taking action.

There were other marked differences. The COS movement served the impoverished with immediate remediation. The settlement house movement was democracy in action, workers befriending and living among those they served. These settlement house leaders, like Jane Addams, were social reformers focusing on groups and the community. Their concern was with eliminating the sources of distress rather than merely alleviating distress. From these first

ventures, the growth in settlement houses increased from one hundred in 1900 to four hundred in operation by 1910 (Trattner).

Whether or not settlement house workers changed the world or merely improved a piece of it, the settlement house movement remains as one of the most significant model movements in the history of helping in terms of theory, commitment, and the spawning of reform.

The Second Revolution in Mental Health

Sigmund Freud.

At the same time as the birth of social work, and yet quite different in theory and remedy, is the work of Sigmund Freud. Freud's contribution must surely be regarded as among the more revolutionary in modern times and hence, his contribution is often referred to as the Second Revolution in Mental Health. Although the constructs of the id, ego, superego, and the promptings of the unconscious are impossible to directly observe, most of us sense an inherent accuracy in Freud's concepts. Freud's language has crept into our vocabulary with the ease of an old shoe. Its ready analysis "fits" and is difficult to resist, particularly with the scarcity of alternative explanations. Unfortunately, Freud asserted that deviant behavior is merely another form of physical illness, despite the absence of bacterial invasion and subsequent tissue damage. Consequently, deviancy should be "treated," thereby establishing the "one to one" as the treatment relationship of choice with the accompanying roles of doctor-patient motif. Despite this perpetuation of the medical model, with its concepts of diagnosis and treatment, Freud provides an alternative way of viewing disturbance and, with the behaviorists, turns our attention to childhood's early experiences as determining and offers a recourse that genetic, bacterial, or demonic determination disallow.

While we recognize the important learnings that came from the work of Freud, and Pinel before him, it is important to note that Pinel and Freud were part of the scientific revolution that began to grow during the Renaissance but flowered and bore fruit prolifically in the nineteenth and twentieth centuries. The development of the scientific method was an important advance for society. However, as with all change, there were negatives as well as positives. One of the negatives was a suspicion, often derision, for anything that could not be demonstrated by existing scientific methodology. Spirituality, concern for the connectivity of life among humans, animals, and plants and with however one defines the divine were one of those pieces looked at askance. There are still many helpers who cannot value the importance of such connectivity to the people they serve.

It is also important to recognize that "normality" and "abnormality" are always defined by the culture in which we live—as is the appropriate intervention to "correct" abnormality. The myths of a culture tend to both reflect and define those norms. For example, in the United States there is the myth that we should be able to "pull ourselves up by our own bootstraps." People who show more than a "normal" amount of dependence are considered abnormal or deviant in this society.

Compare that with the traditional Kung! society where all illness is believed to be inflicted by one of the gods. The entire community comes together for an all-night healing ceremony where one or more healers go into a trance. During that trance the healers go to the gods to plead for the lives of the people who are ill and will "pull" illness out of anyone in the group whom they mystically "see" as needing healing (Katz). This is an approach to intervention that involves the total community and the realm of the spirit in the helping process.

The Progressive Movement of the Early Twentieth Century

Looking back over the nineteenth century, the development of two very different modes of theorizing regarding human behavior can be traced. On the one hand the scientific approach (which hoped yet failed to find an organic cause to corre-

spond to each disorder) led to a plethora of medical interventions used widely today. Although sometimes providing relief for the immediate distress of symptoms, the medical or disease model has failed to cure. Indeed, it might be alleged that the model may thwart investigation into other possible and plausible explanations.

On the other hand, the increasing awareness of the impact of environmental conditions on the lives of individuals led to some very different conclusions about the causes of disorders. Freud's functional approach and the societal focus of early social work both identify environmental conditions as determiners of individual problems. According to Mehr, it was the functional or psychological approach that spawned the human service concept. No doubt, and Mehr suggests this in part, the growth of scientific investigation and the divergent growth of environmental interventions brought about the beginning fragmentation in the study of human problems into the subspecialties that exist today. With the fragmentation of study comes, inevitably, the fragmentation of care and the eventual fragmentation of those served by the system.

A variety of conditions, such as population shifts and technological advances, together with these new ways of looking at human behavior, brought about significant movement in addressing social ills. The progressives' strident outcry forced governmental response and thus increased the power of government both federally and locally. Following is a description of several of the issues and problems that achieved national attention and intervention.

Poverty.   During the early decades of the twentieth century, the United States became the wealthiest nation on earth (Schenk and Schenk). Increased technology brought with it not only riches but the means for the good life, or so it seemed. However, with the enormous influx of immigrants and the overcrowding of cities came an unequal distribution of our nation's resources. Poverty became rampant amid the luxury of the privileged. Although there appeared to be the monetary resources necessary to solve the problem of poverty, the mechanisms for redistribution were lacking. With the enactment of the Sixteenth Amendment (1913) to the Constitution, which provides for a federal income tax, a mechanism was created (Schenk and Schenk). Further, the amendment established government as the responsible agent. This, of course, paved the way for government to ultimately provide for a welfare system. Unfortunately, despite its new capacity to collect revenue, Washington was slow to develop programs to relieve poverty, a pattern that seems to have continued to the present.

Mental Hygiene.   As has often been stated, there is probably little original thought. The appearance of originality is the rearrangement of old ideas into a novel configuration. Therefore, with the community mental health movement of the sixties, we find the models of thought in previous times and movements. With the growing acceptance of environmental causation and as an alternative to the larger state complexes of an earlier invention, community-based hospitals, known as psychopathic hospitals (Bloom) were developed, along with the practice of aftercare. In fact, aftercare was deemed as critical to recovery as treatment in the hospital. Further, the concepts of early detection and intervention prompted Adolph Meyer in 1915 to propose that mental hygiene districts not only offer aftercare but prevent mental disorders (Bloom). Social workers were placed on the payrolls of mental hospitals to monitor the discharge and aftercare plans of patients, thus giving birth to psychiatric social work.

On the advocate side, following the publication of *A Mind That Found Itself*, the author, Clifford Beers, created in 1909 the National Committee for Mental Hygiene, which is known today as the National Association for Mental Health (Trattner). Beers and his colleagues, primarily former patients, spearheaded the movement to reform mental hospitals, and to spur efforts in discovering causes and means of prevention.

Mental Retardation.   Another area in which social workers played a critical role "was the movement for the identification, custodial care, special education, and social supervision of higher-grade defectives, the feebleminded, or retarded, as they are now called" (Trattner). The history of treatment of this population is particularly ugly, and even in the enlightened twentieth century attitudes toward characterological defects and interventions, such as death, sterilization, or segregation prevailed. Indeed, as many as fifteen states enacted sterilization laws (Trattner).

Social workers, through the National Committee on Provision for the Feebleminded, sought segregation during the reproductive years as an alternative. This measure involved the establishment of institutions to harbor the population that was always too large for the facilities available. Other remedies, modeled after the European parole and colony plans (placing out), were developed in America (Trattner). Since all of these measures failed to provide a safety net, attention was turned to organizing special classes for the mentally handicapped. This movement ultimately led to mandates to provide such educational benefits.

Child Welfare.   As a result of earlier efforts by social workers and concerned citizens, the White House, in 1909, held its first White House Conference on Children which has been held every ten years since that time (Trattner). The conference culminated in the establishment of the Children's Bureau within the Department of Labor to monitor child welfare, particularly in areas of health and labor abuses. Another outcome of the conference recommendations was the passage of the Maternity and Infancy Act of 1921 (Schenck and Schenck). Sadly, after eight years, the act's original appropriation was not renewed, falling to the pressure of the medical profession and an unsympathetic president (Trattner). However, these early movements permanently involved the federal government in the welfare of children.

Public Health. The intimate relationship between health and dependency is obvious. The financial and emotional burdens of illness, even on the affluent family, are overwhelming. Such recognition did not escape earlier crusaders in the field of public health. Sanitation science, medical technology, and social reform came together to set in motion a major attack on deadly diseases. Tuberculosis, the world's largest killer of the time, was the first plague to receive public health focus, and attacks on diphtheria and venereal diseases followed. The battle against these diseases demonstrated the effectiveness of modern administration and educational methods in preventing and treating disease. Once again, the state of New York took a leadership role, this time by means of a Public Health Law, to revamp health services (Trattner). The ensuing reforms brought public health out of the political arena and into the hands of experts. We continue to benefit from the public health movement mobilized by community organizers forcing governmental agencies into responsible action.

Civil Rights. The above discussion of issues and problems is not inclusive but does address those concerns that relate most closely to the human services field. Related and important to note in the civil rights arena, the Nineteenth Amendment guaranteed women's right to vote, as well as the founding in 1909 of the National Association for the Advancement of Colored People (NAACP) and the Urban League in 1910 (Schenk and Schenk).

The Crash and the 1930s. The Great Depression of 1929 became the "grim reaper" of private fortunes and plunged the poor into even greater depths of destitution. With millions out of work, the food lines formed and panhandling became a necessity for many, a way of life for some. The relationship between environmental and human problems could not have been made clearer (Schmolling, Youkeles, and Burger). Existing government agencies and private charities were vastly inadequate to meet the need.

With the defeat of Herbert Hoover in 1932, Franklin Delano Roosevelt brought in sweeping reforms known as the New Deal to create jobs and to provide direct assistance. Programs such as the Works Progress Administration (WPA) and the Civilian Conservation Corps (CCC) brought work and training to millions of the unemployed, while Aid to Dependent Children gave relief with direct cash transfers. Of course, the Social Security Act of 1935 was and has continued to be the most far-reaching legislative act to relieve economic disparity for those ravished by the stock market crash and to insure income and services for disabled and retired citizens. According to Russo, "the Social Security Act clearly indicated the direct involvement of the federal government in the welfare of its citizens."

Despite the dramatic events of the 1930s, including programs to address social inequities, the rise of unionism, and the heroic efforts to pull our country out of its worst depression, little happened to relieve the plight of the mentally disordered. Again our state systems were overcrowded and vile, as described in the *Snake Pit*. The mental hygiene movement of earlier decades had failed and the mentally ill were shunted off far from mind and sight. No other public health problem that affects more of our citizens and occupies more hospital beds has been so slow to receive attention.

It took the worst war in the history of the world, thousands of our GIs coming home with what was then called "battle fatigue," a fat economy and the scientific development of major tranquilizers (from Europe) to set in motion what has been called the Third Revolution in Mental Health.

THE HUMAN SERVICES MOVEMENT

The Third Revolution—The Beginnings

Most revolutions are sparked by single incidents—like Boston Harbor's tea-filled waters—reflecting seething discontent with unjust, cruel, and unusual treatment. However, the Third Revolution in Mental Health cannot be identified with a specific incident or thought. There was no sudden hostile act, no posted edict, no dramatic moment. It can be related to the giant Gulliver finally succumbing to the onslaught of countless Lilliputian arrows—more like acupuncture than lobotomy. The revolution could more accurately be labeled a movement that has proceeded with the speed of a tortoise. Nevertheless, there has been change, significant in scope and impact.

Like most postwar eras the nation was fat with prosperity and babies. These, however, were not the only boons. Not only were Veterans Administration (V.A.) psychiatric facilities jammed to overflowing, but state hospitals were admitting patients at an alarming rate into conditions that had deteriorated sharply during the war years. Attention, energy, and money turned to the assembly line, and the war effort took the focus from all other concerns, especially that of the human psyche. The state hospitals had not recovered from the setbacks of the depression of the thirties when they were once again preempted, this time by international conflict.

Conditions following the war were little different than the horror stories told by Dorothea Dix and Clifford Beers, and recounted in a new version by Mary Jane Ward of *Snake Pit* fame. These "hell holes" held nearly half of all the hospital beds in the United States. The history of mental health can hardly reflect a chronology of consistent progress. It is more a regression of national wits. These are the events that conspired to set the third revolution in motion.

Establishment of National Institute of Mental Health. Probably the single development that would ultimately become the basis of policy, monitoring, and glimpses of imagination was the enactment of the National Mental Health Act (Public Law 79–487), in July, 1946. It "created a Mental Hygiene Division within the United States Public Health Service, and a center for information and research that later became the National Institute of Mental Health (NIMH), [and] was designed mainly to develop preventive health measures" (Trattner).

Perhaps the greatest impact of this legislation is that it marks the first real involvement of the federal government in a nationwide movement to improve mental health. Aside from some federal support lent to the U.S. Public Health Service in areas that can be defined as mental health concerns (narcotics and V.A. psychiatric facilities), the federal government had disavowed any responsibility for the mental health of its citizenry. This retraction of support is particularly derelict when one considers the earlier involvement of the government in other health areas, such as tuberculosis, and the establishment of the National Cancer Institute, the National Heart Institute, the National Institute of Dental Research, and the National Microbiological Institute, all preceding NIMH. Not only had individuals dealt with mental disorder as a closet disease and built their Bedlams far from sight and mind, but the federal government seemed to also be afflicted with the same social blindness. All other public health problems have experienced far greater and more swift response than the most encompassing of all U.S. disabilities—mental illness.

Nonetheless, NIMH impacted significantly as an intellectual and financial source for innovation in the areas of training, research, and practice. It enabled states and private institutions to obtain federal funds for research, professional training, and community mental health programs (a forerunner of the current system). Unfortunately, NIMH had no authority to regulate or establish standards of practice pursuant to training. Also, most of the professionals receiving their training in public mental hospitals treated the more interesting cases and then left the institutional setting for more lucrative private practice. This condition clearly did not lead to more or better treatment. The great mass of the unserved and underserved remained so. However, despite its tardy start and mandated vicissitudes, the establishment of NIMH was a harbinger of things to come. There was now no turning back and mental health issues were to remain permanently and persistently in the public focus as a matter of public conscience and concern.

Movement Toward Community Care. Following the establishment of NIMH, changes were occurring rapidly in the field of mental health and societal conditions were also altering dramatically. With advanced technology, the cultural lag was widening and generational similarity was fast becoming a thing of the past. In 1952, Delay and Denken used *ataractic* drugs in Paris, thus initiating a biochemical treatment method that potentially reduced the number of patients in hospitals and afforded the possibility of community treatment (Adelson and Kalis). In fact, increasingly during this period, all human services (child welfare, corrections, aging, special education, etc.) were moving in the direction of community-based services, deinstitutionalization, rehabilitation and community support (McPheeters, personal communique).

In 1953, the publication of Maxwell Jones's *Therapeutic Community* brought a new social-treatment advance, the implementation of which had been made possible by the new drugs (Adelson and Kalis). In 1954, the U.S. Supreme Court desegregation decision (Brown v. Board of Education) signaled the beginning of an era of community and personal action and development that appeared to have the most profound implications for the civil rights movements of the 1960s (Adelson and Kalis).

Finally, the lag between need and care of the mentally disturbed affronted the public representatives who saw fit to examine the standard of the nation's psychological well-being. The time had come to examine approaches to mental health and the methods by which we dealt with the needs of our special citizens—the mentally retarded and those suffering from that most political of all illnesses, mental illness.

Feeling the weight of responsibility that comes from regarding a long-neglected issue, a Joint Resolution of the House and Senate (Public Law 84–182) brought into being a "nationwide analysis and reevaluation of the human and economic problems of mental illness" (Joint Commission on Mental Illness and Health). The Mental

Health Study Act of 1955, as it came to be called, stands as a landmark piece of legislation. For the first time the federal government financed through direct grants a comprehensive study of the way we were meeting the needs of citizens suffering from mental illness. The Joint Commission on Mental Health, made up of thirty-six member organizations, received this mandate pursuant to the provisions of the legislation, to conduct the study and to make appropriate recommendations.

The final report of the Joint Commission came out in twelve volumes in 1961. The final volume, *Action for Mental Health* (containing the committee's recommendations), was the major catalyst for one of the last pieces of legislation signed into law by John F. Kennedy. In February, 1963, nearly two years after the Commission's report, President Kennedy, in his message to Congress, said in part:

> *I propose a national mental health program to assist in the inauguration of a wholly new emphasis and approach to care for the mentally ill. This approach relies primarily upon the new knowledge and the new drugs acquired and developed in recent years which make it possible for most of the mentally ill to be successfully and quickly treated in their communities and returned to a useful place in society.*
>
> *These breakthroughs have rendered obsolete the traditional methods of treatment which imposed upon the mentally ill a social quarantine, a prolonged or permanent confinement in huge, unhappy mental hospitals where they are out of sight and forgotten. . . . We need a new type of health facility, one which will return mental health care to the mainstream . . . and at the same time upgrade mental health services (Mehr).*

By the fall of 1963, The Mental Retardation Facilities and Community Mental Health Center Construction Act (P.L. 88–164) was to deliver a minimum of five mental health services for their citizens through a series of local community centers (Hospital and Community Psychiatry). The mandated services included: short-term care, outpatient services, partial hospitalization, emergency services, and consultation and education. In 1965 the act was amended to provide grants for professional and technical staff, and subsequent amendments through 1973 extended the duration of the construction and staffing grants. A later amendment in July of 1975 extended and extensively revised the act. Special services for children, drug- and alcohol-dependent people, and the elderly, follow-up care and transitional living programs for discharged patients, and screening for referral of consumers to a state facility were added to the original five essential services.

Some of the principles embodied in the movement toward community care, according to Adelson, included a focus on prevention, on processes beyond the individual one-to-one relationship (e.g. groups, education, consultation, etc.), on new kinds of treatment facilities such as workshops and halfway houses, along with new treatment methods like family and group therapy. Further embodied in the movement was the concept of gatekeepers (police, teachers, hairdressers). Continuity of care, an increasing interdisciplinary focus, as well as increased research were further emphases of the model. Finally, of specific and special import was the understanding of social phenomena as it impacts on individual functioning.

Between October, 1965, and July, 1975, more than 1.3 million dollars were appropriated to community mental health centers, with staffing grants receiving the largest amounts. All fifty states have been recipients of these federal grants. However, since 1975, there has been a dramatic shift. Beginning with the Ford and Carter administrations, social welfare expenditures began a downward turn, but the significant cuts occurred during the Reagan administration with the move from categorical funding to block grants.

This sleight-of-hand maneuver by the federal government appeared at first glance to be a method of returning money to local authorities to determine the manner in which it should be spent. However, there was little correspondence in figures between prior government expenditures and the amounts designated in the block grants. It is clear that the Reagan administration wanted to get out of the welfare business and at the same time increase military spending by billions. Little changed during the Bush administration—except the country was plunged into greater debt—deeper economic recession, and higher unemployment. In general, statistics reflected that the United States was in decline and its citizenry was hurting.

Program increases failed to keep pace with current rates of inflation. Local government authorities as well as the private corporate sector have been called upon to pick up the slack. But local authorities appear to be as reluctant as their federal counterparts to generate through taxes the necessary funds to avoid deficit. The corporate sector, as yet, doesn't seem to be heavily invested in services unless there is some immediate investment return, e.g., productivity and better tax incentives.

Community Care: Problems and Promises. With the movement of care to the community and the dismantling of the large state hospital system, a policy known as "deinstitutionalization" was set in motion. This plan to return people to their communities, to reintegrate them into society, and to avoid the trauma of commitment is not only humane but seems theoretically sound. However, in practice, the plan has been a disaster. In 1960, the population of the nation's mental hospitals approached half a million; currently, it is a fraction of that number and still declining. Many of our largest state complexes have been closed.

Former patients who were released have been largely left adrift in urban settings, banished to inadequate and sometimes exploitative conditions without the support systems essential for rehabilitation. For many, deinstitutionalization has become a revolving door policy (a student paper once called it the "revolting door"—either as a slip or a deliberate comment) with frequently as many as one-half of all former patients returning to the hospital admission wards or, worse, joining the army of homeless and impoverished on the streets. What officials failed to foresee were the effects of, for some, decades of institutionalization, leaving most with an inability to control or self-regulate their lives and certainly needing much more than the community programs were equipped to deliver. The system had created a generation of "institutionalized" patients. With rapid diagnosis, short-term treatment, and quick release, similar treatment of the next generation can be avoided.

Despite the problems accompanying deinstitutionalization and the failure of government to fulfill the promise of enabling legislation (little more than half of the proposed community mental health centers were established), not all the failures can be attributed to policy and funding. The system itself has contributed to its difficulties. According to Nicholas Long, the developmental tradition of human services has been to respond to crisis situations rather than to engage in rational and long-range planning. He argues that the major deficiency is the lack of coordination of service elements rather than any perceived lack of relevance to the problems presented.

It's safe to agree with Long's first contention regarding coordination, but contrary to Long there has also been a lack of relevance. Practitioners have treated narrowly and from the confines of their disciplines, not from the expressed need of the consumer. Furthermore, many community mental health agencies have been poorly conceived or were established from existing mental health facilities operating out of general hospitals committed to the medical model and a treatment orientation rather than programming. Developed programs were factored out according to the medical model and became logical extensions of the systems from which their support derived. Support for this argument is reflected in the following quote by Perlmutter and Silverman:

> As the centers developed, mainly through medical institutions, they mirrored the traditional hospital organization. Thus the task of evolving new mental health services was embedded in a system whose participants were socialized into, and beneficiaries of, the old order. It is therefore not surprising that the legislation's innovative thrust was vitiated (Long).

The problem existing within agencies is not entirely the result of the "disease model" and the accompanying tendency to treat people from that perspective. It is also the result of failure to explore new avenues for helping people. It is the product of a persistent bias among professionals that they know what the consumer needs rather than a respect for the consumer's self-expertise. Perhaps this bias derives from the charity model—conceived in paternalism and nurtured in doing "for" rather than "with."

An additional problem confronting the community programs and concomitant with the existing myopia in agencies has been the continuing specialization, with a proliferation of agencies often offering a single service. Rather than increasing the quality of care in the broad spectrum of human services, these developments have fostered an insidious fragmentation in the system and the individual. The consumers served by diverse agencies and professionals are overwhelmed and frustrated by the variety of rules, regulations, practices, and policies they must follow to receive needed service. People already alienated by their problems are further isolated by bureaucratic functionaries who confuse, depersonalize, and verify the individuals' feelings that they live in an uncaring, unresponsive world. Aside from the personal toll, this state of affairs has resulted in tremendous gaps in the system. People are falling into these cracks; there are no bridges, no facilitators, no advocates to span the hurdles. Unfortunately, not only is the system fragmented, but it is often hostile, with agencies competing and fighting for funds and consumers. This division takes what should be a positive social reform and nullifies it, or worse, makes it damaging. The previous discussion has been a brief description of some of the major problems that beset the system of community care. As in the 1930s and other eras of national crisis, we have witnessed swift and decisive federal responses. Overhaul of the welfare system, a national health plan, reduction of the deficit, creation of jobs, and saving the environment are the promises of the Clinton administration. All of these ideals, along with an expanding population of the aging, of people with life threatening diseases (AIDS), or the impoverished and those living on the streets create the worst drain on the public coffers in history. Facing these needs will call for the sacrifices of all—perhaps even the most sacred of cows—social security.

The Emergence of the Human Service Worker

The term "human service worker" is being used here in preference to the term "paraprofessional." It refers to those people who serve on the front line of the helping process, spending the most time with and providing an extensive amount of service to the consumers. The term "paraprofessional," which literally means alongside the professional, has two serious drawbacks. First, it has become a term referring to people with little or no education or training. Secondly, it suggests that the paraprofessional is incapable of working independently of a professional.

Paraprofessionals have probably been around since the opening of the first mental hospitals. These paraprofessionals traditionally served as aides and attendants under the supervision of professionals, namely nurses and physicians. The system tended to create a dual categorization in which the aides or attendants functioned in a primarily custodial capacity as nonprofessionals, and the physicians provided supervision and care as professionals (with the nurses somewhere in the middle). However, there have been many instances when this group of caretakers contributed significantly to the treatment and rehabilitation of patients, clearly going beyond a custodial function. Dugger refers to this class of workers as the old paraprofessionals.

More recently, with the movement of care into the community and the reexamination of traditional models of treatment and a concern for the most efficacious deployment of personnel, several new classes or types of paraprofessionals or human service workers emerged. According to McPheeters (personal communique), the New Careers Program and the indigenous worker programs began in areas such as teacher aides, child care, and other areas before paraprofessionals found their way into mental health. In fact, McPheeters further contends "that mental health and health were among the last areas to respond, largely because those fields had become thoroughly professionalized and specialized" (1993). Impetus for the training of a new class of workers for our mental health population was provided by Dr. George Albee (1959) in a published monograph entitled "Mental Health Manpower Trends." This monograph, sponsored by the Joint Commission on Mental Health and Illness, documented the critical shortages of mental health professionals and projected even greater shortages if the pattern of long term educational programs for professional training persisted. Albee proposed, instead, the training of a new level of mental health worker in a much shorter period of time. This human resource and training recommendation was not acted upon until several years later as community programs expanded, drug and alcohol programs increased and the community retardation movement was introduced.

Despite the early lack of response to Albee's and others' recommendations, other social, conceptual and legislative events were occurring to promote what became the human service worker movement. The sixties were turbulent with civil rights causes raising clamorous voice. There was a new awareness of the relationship between social class and mental illness with the resulting disparity of services based on class distinction. The underclass population was simply not responsive to traditional methods of treatment—particularly "talk therapy." The professionals, drawn most usually from white, middle class ranks, lacked the skill or mentality to relate to those not sharing a common background. Aside from the inability of existing treatment modalities to deal with this population, there was a growing awareness that societal-cultural conditions were as equally productive of disorder as conditions or states within the individual. And furthermore, social conditions that were debilitating and discriminatory needed addressing. Social change became imperative and the human service workers, unlike most of their professional counterparts, were all for it.

Parallel to these events, at a conceptual level, an expanded definition of mental illness was evolving. In fact, the term "mental health" had been widely used for nearly two decades. Health in this context is referred to as a state of wholeness. Therefore, those suffering from disorder need to be brought to a state of wholeness or vigor, not merely marginal functioning or lives of silent desperation. With approaches stemming from the work of theoreticians like Fromm and Maslow, the condition of unhappy, unfulfilled lives came to be regarded as remedial and certainly undesirable. Problem-solving skills to help people better relate to peers, to say nothing of improving their ability to negotiate a complex society, were now within the realm of helping professionals.

Things were also happening in the legislative and social policy arena. The Antipoverty Program of the Kennedy Administration spawned the Economic Opportunity Act of 1964 (1965). The "indigenous" worker was an outgrowth of this legislation. The indigenous worker is someone who is a member of and shares similar life experiences with the target population to be served. Consequently, this person is better able to identify and deal with the consumer than the professional. This identification often provides special competence in mediating between the consumer and the agency. Employing this new class of workers not only affords relevancy to the underserved but by hiring individuals drawn from this population, the unemployment and subsequent poverty issues are also improved significantly (Levine et al.).

The Scheuer Subprofessional Career Act of 1966 administered by the Department of Labor to train and recruit entry-level workers for a range of human services provided implementation for a series of "New Careers." Numerous "New Careers" programs provided jobs for the poor and underprivileged. These workers were trained to help others in their community and by doing so became more fully aware of their own strengths.

Previously, we have described an indigenous worker as one who comes from the same social class and who shares the same value and attitude systems as the consumer population being served. Another category of human service workers are indigenous by virtue of specific difficulties that they have successfully overcome (Alley, Blanton, and Feldman). Recovering drug and alcohol abusers who become counselors to other abusers are examples of this type of indigenous worker. Unfortunately, as mentioned earlier, professional concerns regarding the competency of indigenous workers have resulted in considerable difficulty in integrating these workers into agency services, therefore losing their possible contributions.

Self-Help.   Another related spinoff of this type of approach that has been identified with this population has been the development of the "self-help" movement. Self-help provides a meaningful and viable alternative to services offered by agencies. Self-help groups have proliferated because, according to Riessman (Alley, Blanton, and Feldman), they are relevant, economical, nonprofessional, and apparently effective. Further, Riessman indicates that there are over a half million different self-help groups ranging from all varieties of abuse problems (e.g., alcohol, narcotics, food), to physical problems (heart disease, cancer), to support groups for families of individuals affected by the designated difficulty. A recent development has been self-help groups for people who are mentally ill.

Self-help groups are defined by Katz and Bender in the following manner:

> *Self-help groups are voluntary, small group structures for mutual aid and the accomplishment of a*

special purpose. They are usually formed by peers who have come together for mutual assistance in satisfying a common human need, overcoming a common handicap or life-disrupting problem, and bringing about a desired social and/or personal change. The initiators and members of such groups perceive that their needs are not, or cannot be, met by or through existing social institutions (Alley, Blanton, and Feldman).

The self-help movement cannot be underestimated in its impact as a meaningful alternative, particularly given the decline of other support systems like the family, the church, and the neighborhood. Professionals constantly refer consumers to such groups indicating their recognition of the efficacy of this kind of help. It might be added that given the difficulty of formal institutions to meet the needs of all people needing help, self-help groups are frequently the only assistance available.

Associate-Degree-Level Training Programs and the Role of SREB.[1]   During the mid-1960s, due to the rapid and fortuitous growth of community colleges in the United States, one vehicle was made available for collegiate career training in mental health. Community colleges were particularly appropriate to initiate this educational development. Locally based, nonresidential institutions could provide a ready supply of trained personnel for the emerging community mental health centers. Inasmuch as the students were drawn from the immediate area served by the colleges, continuity in staffing patterns could be established. Students were required to do placements at community agencies, which frequently led to employment following the completion of the associate of arts (or applied science) degree.

An additional asset of the community college is that they are considered by many to be the democratization of higher education. As such, these institutions afford inexpensive educational experiences to those students with marginal economic resources. With a dual mission of terminal career training and liberal arts transfer programs, the community colleges were uniquely suited to become the cutting-edge in mental health education.

Dr. Harold McPheeters, former director of the Commission on Mental Health and Human Services of the Southern Regional Education Board, located in Atlanta, Georgia, is considered by many to be the prime mover of human service education. The following excerpt from a letter written by Dr. McPheeters in June of 1993 clarifies and puts into perspective the role of the SREB:

> Our efforts with the community colleges began just before I joined the Board in 1965 when the NIMH awarded SREB a small grant to explore whether it might be possible and desirable to train mental health practitioners of some kind in those colleges which were being created at the rate of about one per week someplace in the U.S. Until about that time those colleges had never had training programs in health or human service areas, but a Kellogg Foundation grant had demonstrated that it was possible to prepare nurses at the Associate degree level instead of in traditional hospital-based diploma programs. SREB then received another Kellogg grant to expedite the development of those Nurse education programs in community colleges in the Southern region.
>
> Because of our contacts with the community colleges in that Kellogg program, NIMH sought us out to explore such possibilities in mental health. The first Associate degree program in mental health at Purdue University Extension in Fort Wayne had been funded, but was still in the planning stages. Their director attended our conference and received all of our working papers, final report, etc. That final report, *The Community College in Mental Health Training,* by Paul W. Penningroth,

---

[1]The SREB (Southern Regional Education Board) is an interstate compact organization of the fifteen Southern states, created by a resolution of the Southern Governor's Conference in 1948 to facilitate higher education through regional action. The Mental Health Manpower Division was added in 1954 to concentrate on mental health manpower and training. While the main support for SREB comes from the fifteen states, funding for special projects is provided through grants and contracts from Federal agencies or foundations.

found that it was both feasible and desirable to undertake such programs, but it was also suggested that some agency give overall direction to the effort to keep it from fragmenting. NIMH initially rejected that recommendation, but went ahead and funded six experimental programs across the nation.[2] NIMH turned down a grant request from us to provide overall leadership, but we re-submitted it the next year when we learned that seven additional colleges in our Southern region planned to undertake such programs on their own. Our request was funded the second time, and that was the project headed by Jim King.

Already it was apparent that the individual programs were headed in drastically different directions; some were training "little social workers," others "little psychologists"; others just aides for institutional programs for the mentally retarded, and others "little psychiatric nurses." The trend was to create some kind of "aide" to one or another of the established professionals. Thus one of our first efforts of that project was to host the sessions that defined the "mental health generalist" concept for the field. The publication, *Roles and Functions for Mental Health Workers,* was perhaps the most significant publication of all of our many publications in the field. Later we defined the curriculum goals in *Plans for Teaching Mental Health Workers* and many other publications related to developing jobs and introducing the new workers into the mental health agencies and evaluation of the entire movement. That first project was a five-year project, and in the last two years included faculty development conferences. NIMH asked us to invite faculty persons from the newly developing programs all over the nation, and that was when the project truly became national. Until then we invited persons from the out-of-region programs to participate (e.g., the faculty persons from the Philadelphia Community College), but we were not able to pay their costs unless we used them as working consultants (which we often did).

There were other paraprofessional efforts under way at that time—Margaret Rioch's program, the

New Careers programs in New York and Philadelphia, Audrey Cohen's program, and others. Most of them were difficult to coordinate, because they were so closely tied to specific agencies and the jobs of those agencies or to a specific philosophy (HLM).

From 1965 to the mid or late seventies, as many as 300–400 programs mushroomed across the United States. Most programs continued to be offered in the community colleges, but this educational initiative was also found in four-year colleges and some shorter training or certificate programs found their origins in agency settings. Most programs started as mental health technology or worker training programs, adopting the "generalist" approach as conceptualized by McPheeters (1973) and further identified by James King in the following manner.

1. The generalist works with a limited number of clients or families (in consultation with other professionals) to provide across-the-board human services as needed by the clients and their families.
2. The generalist is able to work in a variety of agencies and organizations that provide mental health services.
3. The generalist is able to work cooperatively with any one of the existing professions.
4. The generalist is familiar with a number of therapeutic services and techniques rather than specializing in one or two areas.
5. The generalist is a beginning professional who is expected to continue to learn and grow (SREB).

As reflected in the above description, these early pioneers felt that the work force shortage was not a quantitative problem but was a qualitative one. This new kind of worker needed to start with the needs of the consumer, since those needs are always broader than the coverage of existing professions.

[2]Daytona Beach Jr. College, FL; Metropolitan State College, Denver, CO; Sinclair Community College, Dayton, Ohio; Jefferson State Jr. College, Birmingham, AL; Community College of Philadelphia, PA; Greenfield Community College, MA.

The wisdom of the generalist approach takes on important meaning when it is considered that as the community programs grew, the traditional highly specialized professionals were unable by training or disposition to assume this role. All the social and practical needs of functioning in society had to be provided for the consumers, if they were going to make it outside of the institutional structure. No longer was the mental health worker to be the handmaiden of the existing professionals, but this worker had a new role, a developmental role, starting with the array of consumer needs predisposed by deinstitutionalization.

Methodology for training and educating the "generalist" focuses on knowledge, skills, and values. The knowledge base is acquired through a variety of general education, social science, and human service specific courses. Field placements, or practica, as well as skill training courses respond to the skills component of programs, and values and attitudes appropriate for working with needy people are incorporated across the curriculum and actualized in agency placements.

By the mid 1970s, retitling programs from mental health to human services became an increasing trend. In many cases, the Community Mental Health Centers, especially those established prior to the 1963 legislation, were professionally staffed and often located in general hospital settings. Administrators were reluctant to hire or even afford placements for associate level students. Parallel to the closing of this potential, human services was rapidly expanding its purview to include many needy and emerging populations. Services for the addicted, the aging, troubled youth, victims of every imaginable cruelty, physically and mentally handicapped children, and many others were being created to make a public and organizational response to conditions beyond the capability of families to manage. These often single-service agencies were eager to utilize the workers trained in the human service programs. Mental health programs changed their names to human services in response to an expanding definition of their training mission and the needs of the field as well as responding to political necessity in order for their graduates to obtain jobs. McPheeters and others have been concerned that many of these programs have taken on the broader human service title but have not really broadened their curricula to reflect the totality of human services.

The associate degree programs over the past decade have experienced little growth and while some programs have opened, many have had to close down. Providing sufficient institutional support has been a major problem as community college budgets have failed to keep pace with inflation. The job market is open to students, but the salaries or pay compare with wages paid to unskilled workers and many work "full-time" at "part-time" status without benefits. This continued failure to recognize the contribution of the human service worker jeopardizes all the populations served by a lack of workers or care from incompetent workers. Schools cannot attract students to an educational program that will fail to increase their earning potential over attaining only a high school diploma.

Interestingly, these conditions have spawned the growth of human service programs at four-year institutions. Students are increasingly furthering their education to gain credentials necessary to compete with professional workers. The four-year institutions have had their own battles to fight with schools of social work as well as their institutions, limiting the amount of hands-on experience for which the student can acquire credit. Several external degree programs (e.g., Thomas Edison in NJ) have offered a viable alternative with policies that offer credit for life experience and full transfer of all credits received in associate degree programs. A limited number of advanced degree programs in human services are also in place. While there is no solid data on this initiative, the impression is that these programs are experiencing growth.

Although a bit abbreviated, the previous discussion describes the growth and status of human service education today. From the original program at Fort Wayne nearly thirty years ago and the six programs two years later, the field has grown to a full fledged educational movement with hundreds of programs across the United States, Canada, and Australia. It has been called the Fifth Profession by Vernon James.[3]

The Development of Organizations.   Like any movement, the need to formalize its mission and content and to provide a forum for its constituents becomes not only desirable but necessary if the movement is to stabilize and grow. Several groups have been developed but only two have survived as national organizations. Once again we find the SREB involved in promoting both the National Organization for Human Service Education (NOHSE) and the Council for Standards in Human Service Education (CSHSE).

NOHSE was organized in 1975 at the St. Louis, MO, faculty development conference to promote communication and cooperation between professionals and program faculty, to advocate for human service faculty at the national level, and to continue to provide faculty development opportunities through annual meetings and conferences. In cooperation with CSHSE, NOHSE offers an annual conference for faculty, practitioners, and students. It also publishes regular newsletters and a journal.

A parallel development to NOHSE, encouraged by SREB, was the short-lived National Organization of Human Services (NOHS) for students and graduates of human service programs. This was an association of students and graduates of associate degree programs, numbering about four hundred at its height. NOHS conducted annual meetings and assisted in the development of a number of state and local chapters. Unfortunately, NOHS was dissolved in the mid-eighties. Currently, NOHSE welcomes graduates (practitioners who have graduated from human service programs) and students.

Following the initial support provided to NOHSE and NOHS, it became apparent that concerns regarding standardization of programs and licensure of workers was the logical progression to be addressed in the field. Most of the associate level programs developed locally, predicated on local needs. There were no overall standards to which to appeal. Amazingly, as documented by a national survey, the programs bore marked similarity, not by design, but most likely because the service needs emerging across the country had much in common. In any event, these commonalities needed to be formalized as a guide for program examination and for newly developing programs. Simultaneous to this concern was the failure of agencies to fully recognize A.A. graduates or to understand their deployment. Prospective employers needed to know what these workers were trained to do and to have verification of their competencies as well. Workers needed standardization to help foster a sense of identity. Commensurate to these concerns, NIMH again funded through SREB two projects to address these issues. One of these projects worked on the development of standards, guidelines, and an organization to provide voluntary program approval at the A.A. and B.A. levels.

Through this project, the Council for Standards in Human Service Education was incorporated in 1979 to give focus and direction to education and training in mental health and human services throughout the country. The CSHSE exists to help human service educators and college administrators to achieve maximum educational effectiveness, and to formally recognize and approve programs that warrant public and professional confidence. The approval process is designed to assist programs in self-study, evaluation, and continual improvement and to produce new, creative approaches to the preparation of human service practitioners at the

---

[3]Vernon James, former Chief of the former Paraprofessional Manpower Development Branch, Division of Manpower and Training Programs, NIMH. Dr. James is considered by many in the field as the paraprofessional of paraprofessionals. He came up through the ranks, starting as an entry-level paraprofessional.

undergraduate level. The CSHSE approval attests to a program's compliance with its standards.

The End of the Nineties and Beyond

Where do we go from here? What are the emerging issues and exigencies on the horizon that will demand attention and perhaps dictate public policy? Following is an attempt to identify some major problem areas.

Health Care. Clinton's health care plan will have a profound effect on reimbursement issues, delivery of service, and probably the current tax structure (or at least the manner in which the budget is allocated). Who will subsidize a significant change in our current system? Will the plan create a burdensome bureaucracy? Or will the changes be so minuscule that it will be difficult to note any real change? Why in all this has there been so little debate about the quality of care and the spiraling cost? The pressing needs of the growing AIDS victims, the startling numbers of "children having children," the homeless, and our aging are all populations that demand a profound change in health care coverage. Somehow, whatever ultimately occurs, there will be changes in our current health care systems whether by the government, insurance companies, employers, or providers.

Welfare. Increasingly, the American public seems to be questioning the wisdom of supporting or continuing our current welfare system. Some believe that our system (particularly Aid to Families with Dependent Children, hereafter AFDC) encourages illegitimacy, dependency, and fraud in the use of cash transfers and food stamps. Indeed, some feel that AFDC is largely responsible for the "crime wave" among youth—run amuck—by lack of supervision, poor or absent role models, and the absence of value transmission. Some folks possess a more benign attitude toward welfare regarding it as a necessary evil. Few view welfare as an appropriate response but just don't know what can be done about it. Any

intervention, such as curtailing support following the second illegitimacy, seems to many to punish the victim (in this case, the child) and indeed would not impact the problem anyway. The suggestion that orphanages be created and children removed from the mothers sends waves of panic and even rage through many.

How can we as thoughtful, caring helpers invent an alternative that is humane, does not reinforce dependency, and will afford dignity to our clients? When one looks at the enormity of the welfare bureaucracy, one has to wonder whom it really serves.

Managed Care. Managed care, with its emphasis on short-term treatment and measurable goals, will soon make our traditional approaches a dinosaur. Each year, the allowable length of stay in substance abuse programs becomes increasingly abbreviated. Interestingly, this direction may be a boon for the human services worker. The focus of human service education is on short-term interventions that emphasize raising levels of functioning with specific behavioral goals and utilizing a wide array of techniques. The days of long-term, one-on-one psychotherapy will be a luxury, not provided from the public coffers or the variety of third-party payers. Most professional therapists will become employees of managed care systems dictating the kind of treatment rendered and the term of that treatment. Potentially, and a bit frightening, is that the traditional understanding of doing what is in the client's best interest could shift to the best interests of the employer.

Needy Populations on the Increase

Needy population groups include, but are not limited to; the elderly, the mentally handicapped, and immigrants.

Elderly. With the graying of America, one can forecast one, and perhaps two, life stages beyond those identified by Erickson. Many people at age sixty-five can look forward to living thirty or forty more years, one-third of their total lives. As failing health and diminished functioning set in, we now have an old old population and those centennial fortunates will join the ranks of the ancient old. With each year of life, care needs increase exponentially and most families are unable to keep up with the demands of time, money, and emotional resources. The impact on social security systems is enormous and frightening. Older adults, within a few brief years, receive all that they have contributed to the system. Future generations are left to pay the balance and face the very real prospect of never receiving the same benefits.

Mentally Handicapped. Medical science has made it possible to extend the lives of the mentally handicapped appreciably. Many in this special population are among the aging with no family remaining to care for them or monitor their care. This possibility causes parents of the mentally handicapped to live in fear of what will happen to their child when they have gone—and for good reason. As one parent of a special child once remarked: "My child is a basement child. Every program she has ever been a part of was in the basement of a church, a school, or a community building." That mother was right.

Immigrants. Anyone that lives in Florida or other states that experience a rapid influx of aliens can readily attest to the increasing drain on their respective state budgets. Most such states are turning to the federal government, which mandates services without appropriations, to help defray the mounting costs. Are our immigration laws too lenient or too harsh? Are we protecting the jobs and safety of our citizenry? We are informed by history of our long heritage as a safe haven. With the political upheavals in the Caribbean and Central America, the failing economies in these areas, and the increasing hostility of our own citizens, action appears to be imperative.

The number of people dependent and in need of care is on the increase and the number of peo-

ple to shoulder this burden is on the decrease. This economic imbalance and its potential for national bankruptcy is not merely idle speculation.

There has been no attempt in this final portion of the chapter to cover the full range of problems and issues facing us, nor to prioritize. Rather, it is an attempt to provoke thought, to stimulate discussion, and to forewarn. There is much to be done!

SUMMARY

The forces that have shaped the human services movement in the United States are both varied and numerous. From the beginning of recorded history and from evidence acquired prior to written record, people have responded in some manner to those who exhibited aberrant behavior. Thus one sees, from early humanity down through the first great civilizations, into the medieval period, and on to our modern era, efforts ranging from the supernatural to the biological and humanitarian to explain and treat those in need.

From the Renaissance to the present day one can observe increasing involvement of governments as well as efforts in the private sector in caring for the distressed. Whether out of altruism or conflict (forced into action for political expediency), institutions, policy, and programs have come into being to house, to determine treatment methods, and to create systems for those in emotional, physical, mental, and economic need. The Elizabethan Poor Laws and the founding of institutions for the insane are examples of early government responses. The rise of moral treatment, the campaign by Dorothea Dix on behalf of the mentally ill, and the establishment of social work by Jane Addams and others in the Settlement house movement are all striking examples of the impact of individuals in the private sector to bring about change.

With the industrial revolutions, the revolutionary thinking of Sigmund Freud and the aforementioned pioneers, the groundwork was laid for the progressive movement of the early twentieth century. Legislation and policy addressed the problems of mental hygiene embodied in Roosevelt's New Deal, thus creating work programs and the granddaddy of all welfare programs, social security.

In recent history, following World War II, conditions were ripe to usher in the Third Revolution in Mental Health with the creation of NIMH and seventeen years later, Community Mental Health Centers Act. Additionally, Kennedy's antipoverty program spawned the Economic Opportunity Act as well as the Shever Subprofessional Career Act out of which grew the indigenous worker initiative and what has become known as the Human Service Worker Movement. The subsequent development of human service education has been a direct outgrowth of the need for training and education of these new workers to deliver a new kind of service to the ever-expanding needy populations. With the training and program development initiatives of SREB, the formation of organizations to bring cohesion to the field, and the establishment of over four hundred programs nationwide, the human service worker education movement has found a permanent place in higher education.

REFERENCES

Adelson, D. and B. Kalis, (1976). *Community Psychology and Mental Health Perspectives and Challenges*. Scranton, PA: Chandler Publishing.

Albee, G.W., (1959). *Mental Health Manpower Trends*. NY: Basic Books.

Alley, S., J. Blanton, and R.E. Feldman, (1979). *Paraprofessionals in Mental Health: Theory and Practice*. Springfield, IL: Human Services Press.

Bloom, B.L., (1977). *Community Mental Health: A General Introduction*. Pacific Grove, CA: Brooks/Cole.

Brennen, Earl C., (1974). "Paraprofessionalization and the B.A. Practitioner." *Perspectives on Social Welfare*. NY: MacMillan.

Brill, N., (1973). *Working With People: The Helping Process*. Lippincott.

Congress and the Nation, 1945–1964: A Review of Government and Politics in the Postwar Years, (1965). Washington, DC: Congressional Quarterly Service, p. 1224.

Dugger, J.G., (1975). *The New Professional: Introduction for the Human Services/Mental Health Worker*. Pacific Grove, CA: Brooks/Cole.

Eisenberg, N., (1992). *The Caring Child*. Cambridge, MA: The Harvard University Press.

Eisenberg, N. and Paul H. Mussen, (1989). *Roots of Prosocial Behavior in Children*. NY: Cambridge University Press.

Epstein, C., (1981). *An Introduction to the Human Services: Developing Knowledge, Skills, and Sensitivity*. Englewood Cliffs, NJ: Prentice-Hall.

Fisher, W., J. Mehr, and P. Truckenbrod, (1974). *Human Services: The Third Revolution in Mental Health*. Los Angeles, CA: Alfred.

Gartner, A., (1974). "The Effectiveness of Paraprofessionals in Service Delivery," *Human Services: The Third Revolution in Mental Health*. Los Angeles, CA: Alfred.

Harris, B., and J. Hiraoka, (1978). "The Human Services Worker: Definitions and Distractions." (Draft for discussion only.)

Hospital and Community Psychiatry, (1976, July). 27:7 507.

Hudson, B., (1973). "Changing Concepts in Utilizing Mental Health Workers." *Middle Level Mental Health Workers*. Atlanta, GA: Southern Regional Education Board.

James, V., (1979). "Paraprofessionals in Mental Health: A Framework for the Facts." *Paraprofessionals in Mental Health: Theory and Practice*. Springfield, IL: Human Services Press.

Jarvis, P.E., (1973, June). "Issues in the Development of Mental Health Worker Training Programs." *Middle Level Mental Health Workers*. Atlanta, GA: Southern Regional Education Board.

Joint Commission on Mental Illness and Health, (1961). *Action for Mental Health*. Basic Books.

Katz, R., (1982). *Boiling Energy: Community Among the Kalahari Kung!*. Cambridge, MA: Harvard University Press.

Levine, M., S. Tulkin, J. Intaglia, J. Perry, and E. Whitson, (1979). "The Paraprofessional: A Brief Social History." *Paraprofessionals in Mental Health: Theory and Practice*. Springfield, IL: Human Services Press.

Long, Nicholas, (1974). "A Model for Coordinating Human Services." *Administration in Mental Health*. Summer.

Macht, J. H., (1982, Spring). "What's in a Name? Or a Response." *Bulletin.* Council for Standards in Human Services Education.

McPheeters, H. L., and Jas. B. King, (1971). *Plans for Teaching Mental Health Workers.* Atlanta, GA: Southern Regional Education Board.

McPheeters, H. L., and D. Slavin, (1973, January). "The Human Service Worker: Issues in Implementing a Generalist Job Series." Atlanta, GA. Southern Regional Education Board.

McPheeters, H. L., (1993). Letter clarifying some aspects of the history of human services.

Mehr, Jos., (1988). *Human Services: Concepts and Intervention Strategies.* Boston: Allyn and Bacon.

Nash, K. B., Jr., N. Lifton, and S. E. Smith, (1978, June). *The Paraprofessional: Selected Readings.* Advocate Press (NIMH Grant M.H. 14082).

National Association of Human Services Technologies, "Goals of N.A.H.S.T." Monograph.

Noss, J. B., (1965). *Man's Religions,* 3rd ed. NY: MacMillan.

Rioch, M., (1966). "Changing Concepts in the Training of Therapists." *Journal of Counseling Psychology* 3.

Russo, J. R., (1980). *Serving & Surviving as a Human Service Worker.* Pacific Grove, CA: Brooks/Cole.

Schenk, Q. F., and E. L. Schenk, (1981). *Welfare, Society, and the Helping Professions.* NY: MacMillan.

Schmolling, S., M. Youkeles, and W. R. Burger, (1989). *Human Services in Contemporary America,* 4th ed. NY: The Free Press.

Simon, R., (1973, June). "The Paraprofessionals are Coming." *The Paraprofessionals Are Coming.* Atlanta: Southern Region Education Board.

SREB. (1973, June). *Middle Level Mental Health Workers.* Atlanta: Southern Region Education Board.

Trattner, W. U., (1974). *From Poor Law to Welfare State: A History of Social Welfare in America.* NY: The Free Press.

Vidover, R. M., (1973, June). "The Mental Health Technician: Maryland's Design for a New Health Career." Atlanta: Southern Region Education Board.

Ward, M. J., (1946). *The Snake Pit.* New York: Random House.

Wilson, Edward O., (1975). *Sociobiology: The New Synthesis.* Cambridge, MA: Harvard University Press.

Zax, M., and A. G. Specter, (1974). *An Introduction to Community Psychology.* NY: John Wiley & Sons.

KEY TERMS FOR PART ONE

In completing Chapters 1 and 2 in Part One you should now have a command of the following key terms, major concepts, and principal topical references.

Consumers
Generalist
Socialization
Crisis Intervention
National Organization for
   Human Services Education
   (NOHSE)
Community Mental Health
   Centers Act (1963)
Human Services
Intervention
Eclectic
Hierarchy of Needs

Employee Assistance
   Programs
Council on Standards in
   Human Services Education
   (CSHSE)
The "Great Society"
Southern Regional Education
   Board (SREB)
Allied Services Act (1974)
Lobotomy
Moral Treatment (The First
   Revolution)
Settlement House

Charity Organization Societies
   (COS)
Friendly Visitors
Psychoanalysis
Behaviorism
Social Security Act (1935)
National Institute of Mental
   Health (NIMH)
Therapeutic Community
New Careers Programs

PIVOTAL ISSUES FOR DISCUSSION OF PART ONE

1. What does the term "public social utilities" imply? How does this term reflect upon our society's responsibility to helping those in need? Do you think mental health services should be required on the Clinton administration's national health policies and programs?

2. What are the differences between human services and social work as professional disciplines?

3. How are people-processing agencies different from people-changing agencies? Give some examples of both.

4. What do you feel are the most important human needs that must be met in our society? How are these needs being met today? What might be the priorities in the future?

5. What role(s) have the church and religion played in the historical development of human services?

6. List five federal laws that have had the greatest impact on the human services movement. How have these legislations been related to the needs of the American people?

SUGGESTED READINGS FOR PART ONE

1. CSHSE Monograph, (1990). *History of the Human Services Movement.*

2. Bloom, B.L., (1984). *Community Mental Health: A General Introduction,* 2nd ed. Pacific Grove, CA: Brooks/Cole Pub. Co.

3. Trattner, W.I., (1986). *From Poor Law to Welfare State: History of Social Welfare in America,* 3rd ed. New York: The Free Press.

4. Kamerman, S.B. and A.J. Kahn, (1977). *Social Services: An Interventional Perspective.* Washington, DC: U.S. Govt. Printing Office.

5. Greenberg, Joanne, (1965). *The Monday Voices.* New York: Holt Rinehart and Winston.

6. Piven, Francis Fox and Richard A. Cloward, (1982). *The New Class War.* New York: Pantheon.

PART TWO

HUMAN SERVICES: PROFESSIONAL ROLES AND RESPONSIBILITIES

Part Two is concerned with the roles and responsibilities that characterize the work of a human services professional. Included here are three chapters that will enable you to appreciate the preparation necessary for a job as a professional helper. You will gain an understanding of the part played by the field practicum as well as the personal qualities, skills, knowledge, and values that you will need as a human services worker. Additionally, it will become clear to you that as the work settings change then the approaches to worker training must also change.

As a student planning to enter the human service profession you should know what to expect as an actual worker. Chapter 3, by Edwin Simon, is designed to fulfill that goal by featuring field practice as the centerpiece of a human services education program. You will learn about the field work experience as a part of your course of study and as an up-close look at what human service work is all about. You will understand the placement process, the need for supervision, good record-keeping, what goes into the evaluation process, and the role of the on-campus seminar. It will be apparent to you that a successful field work program depends upon the active involvement of the placement agency, meaningful integration with the academic curriculum and your willingness to cooperate in the supervision process. The evaluation and assessment procedures are designed to achieve standards of excellence. All of this is aimed at training you to be an effective worker.

Lorence Long and Maureen Doyle tell you in Chapter 4 about the values, different roles and responsibilities that characterize a human service worker. There are many personal qualities required to be an effective worker, some of these, such as being reliable, well-organized, focused, and attentive are necessary for success in a variety of fields. In addition, the human service worker must possess an array of special skills geared to the interpersonal helping process. In the chapter self-awareness and being able to help yourself is seen as a necessary condition for being able to help others. It will become apparent too, that your personal development is an ongoing process and, in part, results from what you learn in your helping work experiences. (This interplay of work and personal growth will be explored further in Part Four which deals with career concerns.)

Every work day becomes an opportunity for self-discovery and the continued improvement of priority skills such as communication and problem solving.

In the final chapter of this part, Judith Leff, Virginia Mulkern and Stephen Leff build on what you have learned in regard to the skills and qualities needed for human service work and acquaints you with the trend toward delivering services in community settings rather than large institutions. You will see how basic skills form the foundation for integrated work-based skills. The tendency is for more training to take place in the workplace. This is seen as part of a national effort to improve the school-to-work transition. Here in Chapter 5 providing services for people with disabilities is used as an example for presenting ideas that have applicability to a wide range of human services' consumer groups. The chapter provides a picture of the community setting in terms of an array of both provider agencies and worker roles. The human service worker will have to acquire specific skills and bodies of knowledge as part of the process of training accountability. The model presented here may gain national acceptance for training and credentialing entry-level human services workers.

This part has been concerned with very practical matters. However, as an introductory student you also should know the role of theory, methods and models of helping in the professional work of human services. This will be the next focus of the chapters in Part Three.

LEARNING OBJECTIVES FOR PART TWO:
HUMAN SERVICES: PROFESSIONAL ROLES AND RESPONSIBILITIES

In reading and studying Chapters 3, 4, and 5:

— You will gain an understanding of what is involved in undergraduate human services education.
— You will come to appreciate the importance and relevance of fieldwork, internships, and practicum experience.
— You will understand how students are educated, trained, and supervised in preparation for entry-level human services jobs.
— You will become familiar with generic human services training.
— You will be aware of the priority skills, knowledge and values necessary for successful job performance in human services.
— You will know how standards of excellence can be utilized in the process of credentialing human services workers.

CHAPTER 3

FIELD PRACTICUM
STANDARDS, CRITERIA, SUPERVISION, AND EVALUATION

EDWIN SIMON

INTRODUCTION

There is probably no aspect of human services education which has received more attention in recent years than what is often referred to as field work or field experience. Even the terminology used by educational institutions providing education for human services has become the subject of much discussion and, at times, even debate during the past forty years since the formalization of human services education. The idea that students preparing for careers in one of the helping professions should combine theory learned in the classroom with practice in an integrated learning experience is not new with human services education. Other helping professions and occupations developed education and training programs with such an approach beginning with the efforts of the Charity Organization Societies and the Settlement House movement as early as the 1890s and the early twentieth century.

For the purpose of this discussion the term "field practicum" will be used. Current terminology in use by the more than 500 human services education programs include the following: internship, externship, field work, field instruction, field practice and field practicum. More and more, field practicum has become the universally accepted term that describes the work experiences human services students engage in designed, directed, and supervised by the faculty of the college or university.

Field practicum is an integral part of the academic preparation of students pursuing a course of study in human services leading to either an associate or baccalaureate degree. In keeping with the general philosophy of human services education, that learning is preparation for doing, the field practicum component of the curriculum provides a supervised learning experience in professional practice. As a means of providing integration of theory and practice, the field practicum occurs (in almost all instances) concurrently with classroom instruction. Paralleling classroom curriculum, learning experiences in the field are designed to provide progression, continuity, integration, and testing by students.

In planning the field practicum program for human services students, faculty place particular emphasis on the needs of each and every student and the right to individualization. Students are assigned to work a specified number of hours (and days) under professional supervision in a variety of carefully selected and approved social, health, and human services community agencies which provide a variety of services to clients and other persons in need. The chief objective of the field practicum experience is to provide the student with an opportunity to engage actively in actual professional tasks which complement and reinforce classroom learning.

Field Practicum Standards. The content of the field practicum should be in consonant with the curriculum standards of the national educational program approval body, the Council for Standards in Human Services Education (CSHSE), as well as the curriculum policies and standards of the student's educational institution and its human services program.

The standards for field practicum as developed by CSHSE represent the current best thinking regarding preparation for entry into the field of practice. From an educational point of view, these standards demand and ensure precision and specificity in the definition of training and its critical elements. Ultimately, these standards relate to quality assurance, both in education and training and in the delivery of service by the graduates of human service educational programs even though the actual standards are necessarily general so as to allow for the diversity of programs across the country under the umbrella of human services education.

The several program approval standards specified by CSHSE related to field work reflect the importance placed on this learning component. The key elements of the standards applicable to field practicum include the following:

1. Students shall have actual work involvement with clients with opportunities to apply academically acquired knowledge and skills in the helping process.
2. There shall be gradual widening assumption of responsibilities when students are engaged in field work.
3. Students shall participate in regularly scheduled seminars on campus concurrent with the field work experience.
4. Students and field practicum agency supervisors and executives shall be provided with a written comprehensive manual for the field practicum prepared by the faculty of the human services program.
5. There shall be written contracts developed between the college and those agencies serving as approved field practicum sites for human services students.
6. There shall be a specifically designated minimum number of hours required for students to receive academic credit for the field practicum experience.

7. Faculty and cooperating agencies shall provide assurance of appropriate direct supervision of students on-site at field *practicum agencies.*
8. There shall be developed for each student an individualized written learning plan to form the basis for the student's field practicum assignments.
9. Students shall be provided with a formal evaluation by the field practicum agency supervisor to serve as a guide for student assessment and future learning needs.

FIELD PRACTICUM COMPONENTS AND RELATIONSHIPS

The field practicum experience has been described as a dual process engaged in by a set of "players" based upon a number of tri-partite relationships. The duality of the process includes both formal and informal processes, experiences, and requirements in which the various players or participants are engaged. The participants in the field include student (S), faculty (F), and agency supervisor (A). The interrelationships are between student and faculty, student and agency supervisor, and faculty and agency supervisor. The tri-partite functional relationships are at the same time usually both formal and informal processes. These are illustrated as follows:

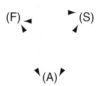

In addition to these relationships which are mostly formal, students as the key participants are often required to engage with other persons at school, including faculty and administrative personnel such as department chairpersons, deans, directors of field practicum, secretaries, etc. Students also relate in very meaningful ways with two other sets of participants: their peers or other students, and clients at the field practicum agency site. These are significant relationships for human services students. Although very little research has been done on the nature and impact of these relationships, their importance should not be overlooked or minimized.

Student Peer Relationships. The significance of student peer relationships, in particular, should not be underestimated. Whereas faculty and agency supervisors have controlling authority-laden relationships vis-a-vis students, the peer group (fellow students) serve a variety of important functions usually in a nonthreatening, nonauthoritative manner. These important functions include feedback, (unofficial) consultation, and most important support in the educational process.

Students often perceive themselves as powerless or (at best) disadvantaged in their relationships with faculty and agency supervisors who seem to have all of the power and authority on their side of the relationship. Evaluation, assessment of student learning and performance in the classroom and in field work, and the assignment of academic grades for the field practicum course are all in the hands of the players with the authority to make the required educational decisions and judgements. Therefore, it is no small wonder that students often experience much anxiety associated with the evaluation process—both the formal and the informal.

The student's relationship with peers is much less threatening. Fellow students are usually willing to play a supportive role for each other. In the formal setting of the field practicum seminar held on campus, students are usually very supportive of each other when they make presentations in class or when they discuss issues and problems they are experiencing in field work. Students often applaud other students when they make presentations. They also provide insight into problem areas or help to clarify issues. Students learn from each other in the formal setting of the classroom that they are not alone. They often share the same experiences as other students at the same stage in the learning process.

Students also learn that they are not alone through the peer process of interacting informally with each other outside of the classroom. For many students who at times express self-doubts about their ability to perform successfully in human services work settings, the peer relationships often provide the critical factors of much needed comfort, support, and insight. The informal student peer relationships are usually private and personal. Faculty and agency supervisors are not part of this process. Insofar as these informal relationships provide little or no threat from persons in authority, they can provide a safe place for students to express feelings, including anxiety and frustration about their field work experiences. For students preparing for careers in a helping human service profession, this fulfills a very important need.

Relationships with Clients. Student-client relationships are also significant for students. These relationships are central to the helping processes in human services. Learning by doing is the hallmark of human services education and in particular, the student-client relationship. Because it is so significant, some students are threatened by what they perceive to be their own powerlessness particularly with certain types of clients, including antisocial, difficult, uncooperative, incompetent, and/or disabled. Not being sure of themselves in such situations and relationships, students often project their own feelings onto clients. These feelings include frustration, incompetence, a desire for love and acceptance, and a need to control the situation.

Because students are a part of the student-client relationship they usually have difficulty in understanding and appreciating the relationship in an objective manner. Client feedback to students as students is usually not forthcoming because the client views the student primarily in the role and function as the worker—not as a student. In fact, in most instances, clients are not aware that their worker is a student. To the client he or she is a worker—a member of the agency staff. In those rare instances when feedback is forthcoming, it is hardly objective. Clients view and assess the situation and relationship through their own sets of eyes, with their own emotions, and their own unique subjectivity. Nevertheless, clients join the other major players that comprise the set of relationships for human services students in the field practicum. Students need to be responsive to all of the players—faculty, agency supervisors, peers (other students), and clients.

THE FIELD PRACTICUM PLACEMENT PROCESS

Most graduating human services students when asked what was the most significant part of their human services education usually respond with enthusiasm that the field practicum was the highlight of the educational experience. Field practicum is the place where it is all put together. It is where theory comes alive and is tested and challenged in practice. And because the primary goal of the supervised field work experience is to promote the development of the human services student into a competent human services professional, this goal is more likely to be reached when the field experience is a collaborative one involving the three main players—the school, the agency, and the student.

In creating an effective educational experience, attention must be paid to the process of student placement which determines where, when, who, and why students are assigned to agencies for the field practicum experience. Among the many questions posed that need to be answered are the following:

Which agency would be the most appropriate for each student?

What previous experiences and/or personal attributes should a student have as a prerequisite for placement in a particular agency?

Is the agency prepared to provide appropriate qualitative educationally oriented supervision for the human services student and by whom will the student be supervised?

Are the needs of the agency, the school, and the student compatible with regard to hours, days, assignments, skills, etc.?

These questions and other concerns indicate the complex nature of the human services field practicum student placement process. Therefore, educational institutions pay a great amount of attention to the process of student placement. Since placement is a faculty responsibility, most schools designate a particular person, usually a faculty member, to serve as the coordinator or director of field practicum placement. This person may be any one of the following: department chairperson, field practicum director, or internship coordinator. In some instances (depending upon the size of the human services program) it is a person who devotes full time to the field practicum program. In other instances it may be a part-time person or a full-time staff member who coordinates the field practicum in addition to other professional educational responsibilities.

Factors of Influence. Human services educational programs organize the field experience in very different ways depending upon several factors. Some of these considerations include:

The number of students in the program

The number of students to be enrolled in the field practicum

The number and nature of community agencies available and qualified for student placement

The number of faculty in the human services program

The specific curricular goals of field work in the human services educational program

General college/university policies regarding field experience for students

Student Involvement in the Placement Process. Human services students are also involved in the placement process in most educational settings. While the ultimate authority and responsibility for placement reside in the faculty, students have become active and important players in the process. In many schools students are given choices for placements or, in extremely rare instances, they may even be able to veto a placement if not to their liking or satisfaction.

Students are often encouraged to recommend agencies for placement which previously had not been approved by the faculty. Students, in some instances, are even encouraged and/or required to seek out their own placements rather than being assigned to an agency without student input. Based upon information received from other students preceding them in the field practicum, students often request specific agencies for placement. In any case, in more and more instances students have become involved as active players in the field practicum placement process. "After all," as one student put it, "whose education is it?"

However, even with student input as indicated, the faculty of the educational institution carries the leadership role and the primary responsibilities for making the essential connections among the school, student, and agency. The school sets the overall goals for the field practicum component and establishes the expected behavioral objectives for students entering the field of human services.

The school assumes these responsibilities by assuring that the following requirements are determined, inaugurated, and implemented:

1. Establish eligibility criteria for student enrollment in the field practicum including credits, academic standing, pre- and co-requisite courses, etc.
2. Schedule meetings, conferences, workshops, seminars, etc., to aid in the process of interpretation of field practicum requirements. Such meetings, etc., would be for faculty, agency personnel, and/or students.
3. Design and implement guidelines for the selection and continual use of agencies as field practicum sites for human services students.
4. Establish a school liaison representative who will relate to all parties involved in the educational endeavor.
5. Provide a comprehensive written field practicum manual which details all policies, procedures, requirements, and practices of the field practicum program as they relate to the various parties involved in the educational endeavor—faculty, field practicum director/coordinator, agency supervisor and/or executive, and student.
6. Develop procedures for on-going assessment of the field practicum program which will include faculty, agency supervisors, and students in the process.

GETTING STARTED

Most human services students want their field practicum experiences to be instructive, exciting, and gratifying. The process starts in most human services programs when the student expresses an interest in the field practicum course. The student may be required to complete and submit an application for the field practicum. This is done prior to or following attendance at a faculty conducted orientation session held either on a group or individual basis. In most instances, attendance at the field practicum orientation is mandatory. Once the faculty has informed the student regarding eligibility to enroll in the field practicum course, the process of agency selection and placement begins.

Students are often apprehensive about getting started beginning with being assigned to an agency either with or without student input. The amount and nature of student input allowed in the choice of a practicum agency placement varies across human services programs. In some programs, students are permitted (and even encouraged) to contact agencies and interview them on their own. In several instances students are actually required to interview agencies before placement. In programs at the other extreme, students are assigned to an agency and are given little or no choice. However, most human services programs allow students to state preferences and/or to become actively involved in the agency selection and placement process. Correspondingly, most agencies reserve the right to interview prospective students before accepting them for field practicum placement and reserve the right to reject students for placement.

There are a number of factors that are usually considered in the process of effecting agency field practicum placements for human service students, although some are more important than others. In as much as each student is different and brings to the experience a unique set of knowledge, skills, values, experiences, and personal needs and considerations, each field placement should be handled and made in its own special way. Individual factors to be considered include: transportation, scheduling, supervision, populations, problem areas, and agency value base.

Transportation.   Getting to and from the agency may be a problem for some students. Is public transportation available? Is it considered safe and does it have a convenient schedule for students? Is a driver's license required? Are students required to use their own car? Will the student have to transport clients? Does the agency provide insurance coverage for students? Will the agency reimburse students for transportation costs?

Scheduling.   Consideration should be given to student availability and the hours of agency operations. Is there compatibility of schedules? Is there any flexibility in case of illness, school assignments, examinations, personal commitments? Does the school have any specific schedule requirements that must be followed by students and agencies?

Supervision.   Although the college/university human services program will usually set minimum requirements and standards for the frequency and the amount of time to be allocated for student supervision by agency field practicum supervisors, some students may actually require more time and/or more frequent supervision. Considerations should also be given to the type of supervision provided by the agency. Is it individual, group, peer, or combination? Agencies vary widely with regard to what they will allow students to do as part of their field practicum assignment. There may be legal considerations. Some students will be allowed to have immediate one-to-one contact with clients, while others will delay such contact for several weeks (or even months). The variation in direct contact with clients by students can be explained by several factors. Among these are the nature of the agency services, the staff-client ratio, the complexity of the tasks performed by students, and the (possible) consequences of students making poor

judgements and/or acting in an unprofessional manner or with a lack of skillful dexterity. All of these may serve as justification(s) for providing close supervision of student field practicum experiences particularly during the beginning phase of the experience.

Populations and Problem Areas.   The ideal placement is one in which the student is exposed to and learns about many different populations in the community. These include ethnic, religious, racial, age, gender, and sexual orientation differences. The agency to which the student is assigned for field experience should capture the student's interest and provide a challenge to become actively involved in the helping process.

Although it is possible for students to learn something about human services in any field placement, students are most enthusiastic when they can immerse themselves rather quickly in an agency where they can easily relate to the primary client population (e.g., children, preschoolers, older adults, teenagers) in relation to those problems for which the agency provides services (e.g., chemical dependency, teen pregnancy, juvenile offenders, developmentally disabled, isolated senior citizens). It is important that, prior to placement, students reflect on what their areas of interest are and what age groups they prefer to work with.

Agency Value Base.   Another important consideration for human services students is the value base of the agency. Does the value base of the agency conflict with the student's own set of values? The conflict might be on religious or ethical grounds. For example, a student who believes that abortion is wrong (for whatever reason) may have a very difficult experience working in an agency where clients are routinely counseled and/or referred for abortions. Likewise, a student who is an orthodox Sabbath observer will probably have difficulty working in an agency which is open on the Sabbath and requires the student to participate in some or all programs on the Sabbath.

In many instances, a client's behavior and/or values may not be the same as the student's. As professionals, students learn to accept each client as a worthwhile person even though the client's behavior and beliefs are not condoned in every instance. Values are not fixed or permanent. Clients change, mature, and grow through experience. The same is true for students. It is a process that takes place over time and is influenced by many forces in the lives of clients and students. The agency experience is one of these forces.

In the process of obtaining a human services education, students become aware of their own basic value system and the values of the profession. Students become acutely aware (especially in the field practicum experience) of the impact of their own values on their interactions with others, particularly clients. Personal and professional growth occurs when students examine their own values and some of the stereotypes they hold.

However, students should not be forced to act against their basic principles and values. If a problem arises that causes conflict, the student should inform the agency field practicum supervisor as soon as possible. There are many possible solutions, including the transfer of the client to another worker at the agency. If necessary to resolve a difficult conflict situation, a three-way conference may be helpful. Such a conference would involve the student, the agency field supervisor, and a human services faculty representative, either the director/coordinator of the field practicum program or the instructor of the student's concurrent on-campus field practicum seminar. If the issues cannot be resolved through such consultations, the student may be reassigned to a different agency for the human services field practicum. However, it should be noted that such an action is very rarely taken.

FIELD PRACTICUM REQUIREMENTS

Having completed the process of agency placement, the student enrolled in the human services field practicum soon becomes engaged in an intensive learning experience. Although there are variations among the more than 500 associate and baccalaureate degree programs in human services, there are some required features common to most programs. These features include:

Supervision of students by professionals
Required hours of field work
Student logs and journal
Agency record keeping
Formal student evaluation
Concurrent on-campus field practicum seminar
Written assignments and reports
Agency visits by college faculty

While each field practicum placement is considered individually, it must meet several basic requirements in order to assure that the student receives an appropriate learning experience in an atmosphere of inquiry, trust, challenge, and growth.

Student Supervision. The agency that will serve as the field practicum site designates an experienced professional staff member to serve as field practicum agency supervisor. Ideally, this staff member is a skilled teacher as well as a skilled practitioner. The faculty member of the student's college/university responsible for administration of the field practicum is consulted and is ultimately responsible for approving the designated agency professional as the field supervisor of the human service student.

It is the responsibility of the agency supervisor to develop for each student an individualized "hands-on" assignment emphasizing service delivery appropriate for the particular student. Consideration is given to the student's maturity, previous experience in the field, academic status including year in school and courses taken, and career goals. Also considered are the school's requirements for specific experiences for all students and whether the placement is the student's initial or subsequent placement. Student assignments in the field practicum are open to continuous review and possible modification. Activities may be added and/or deleted to reflect student progress and learning needs as well as agency and school requirements.

Student involvement in the selection and modification of field work assignments takes place within the parameters of agency and school policies. The school faculty may be consulted in this process but the responsibility and authority to make or modify student assignments belong to the field practicum agency supervisor.

Differential Supervision. Effective supervision of staff as well as students has been an on-going problem and concern for most social and human services agencies. Supervision is the mechanism employed by agencies in assuring the fulfillment and maximization of agency standards, purpose, goals, and objectives. Supervision serves several functions—all important and deserving of some attention. Among the various functions of supervision are: (1) administrative, (2) educational, and (3) secondary leadership.

The administrative component involves a communication linkage, accountability of performance, task and work assignment and evaluation procedures. The agency field supervisor in human services is also responsible for the educational or teaching function. It is sometimes referred to as the "tutorial function." Students are learners who "learn by doing." Perhaps this function explains why the term often used to describe the agency field supervisor is "field instructor." The third function of supervision is called secondary leadership—a term used to describe what students do in carrying out some of the work responsibilities and performance tasks which ordinarily would be done by the supervisor if there was no student involved.

Supervisory Conferences. The student in the field is therefore subject to regular supervision. The student's work and progress will be monitored closely through the use of written reports, direct observations, and regularly scheduled supervisory conferences. The supervisor is responsible for ensuring that the conference is conducted free from interruptions. The day, time, location, and frequency are mutually agreed to by the student and the agency supervisor. Most human services programs require that students participate in a regularly scheduled conference of at least one hour in duration on a weekly basis. However, students will be at different stages which need to be accounted for in setting a schedule for student supervision. At the very beginning some students will need a high level of support requiring more frequent conferences and as they grow in their experiences, less time may be needed by some students.

Although the supervisor is primarily responsible for the conduct of the supervisory conference, the student may be asked to assume some responsibility as well. Some supervisors may request students to submit written work, journal entries, questions and concerns in advance of the conference. Students may also be encouraged (and sometimes required) to bring a written agenda to the supervisory conference in order to focus the conference content and maximize the use of available time for supervision.

Another area of concern for some students is the direct observation of their practice by the agency supervisor. This can be a threatening, anxiety-producing experience for some students. However, it is one way that the student's work can be monitored and evaluated ultimately for the purpose of providing appropriate feedback to the student concerning practice. This feedback is an essential part of the educational process in the human services field practicum.

Hours. Each field placement will be for a specified number of hours designated on a semester (or annual) basis as well as on a weekly basis. An example of an associate degree field practicum placement may be eight hours per week for fourteen weeks with a minimum requirement of 100 hours for the semester. A typical requirement for a baccalaureate placement which would occur in the student's last year might be fourteen hours (two days) per week for one full academic year (thirty weeks) with a minimum of 400 hours required for the year.

Students are informed of the specific requirements of their educational institution. The requirements are usually published in writing in the field practicum manual and/or college catalogue and are usually part of the written agreement form or contract that the student usually is required to sign prior to the start of field work.

Students are also expected to keep an accurate record of the hours they work in field work at the agency. The school and/or agency will provide the student with appropriate forms (time sheets) to be used for this purpose. The signatures of the student and the agency supervisor are required to attest to the accuracy and the completion of the required field work hours by the student.

Student Journals and Logs.   Human services students in field placement are required to keep a written record of their work and activities on the job. The student writes a daily log each day spent in the field. All of the logs combine to make up the student field practicum journal which provides a personal account of the student's field experiences, observations, evaluations, and interpretations. Students are expected to write not only facts and events (who, what, where, and how), but also to include an analysis of their personal reactions, thoughts, feelings and impressions. In addition, they are encouraged to include self-evaluation and introspective analysis of their own practice. It is also required that for each and every "significant" interaction reported, students will indicate how they made use of the agency supervisor and other personnel. This challenges the student to think and reflect on the helping process and how it affects outcomes, thus gaining experience in analytical thinking and writing which is an important hallmark of professional practice.

The student field practicum journal, viewed as one of the most important academic components of the student's human service education, will be submitted to the student's on-campus seminar instructor several times during each semester. Some human services programs require weekly submission. The minimum is usually three or four times per semester or once every three or four weeks. The content of the student journal provides the instructor with evidence of the student's activities and learning and ability to integrate the knowledge, skills, and values learned in the academic classroom and how these are being applied in the practice setting.

The seminar instructor monitors student activities in the field and carefully assesses student performance and personal and professional growth using the student journal as a major piece of evidence. The seminar instructor provides written feedback to each student after reviewing each and every journal entry thereby cultivating student competence and growth.

Agency Record Keeping.   In addition to the student journal which is submitted to the seminar instructor, the student may also be required to do other agency based recording. The agency supervisor will advise and instruct the student on what these requirements are, how they are to be done, timing, location of agency files, etc. In most instances, all entries made by students in official agency records must be cosigned by the student's supervisor who ultimately is responsible for all student assignments, performance, and productivity. Should there be any doubts or questions concerning these requirements, procedures, and policies, the student should consult, as soon as possible with the agency supervisor.

Agency Field Visits by Faculty.   Although the agency field supervisor is primarily responsible for what goes on in the agency and what experiences the student will engage in, the faculty of the human service program also plays an important role. Faculty of the human services program makes regular visits to field practicum agencies. These visits, made at various times, have several purposes which include the following:

1. Visits by the faculty member responsible for selecting and approving agencies to serve as field placement sites for human services students will usually be made prior to placement of any students. During the visit discussions will be held involving the faculty member (usually the director/coordinator of the field practicum program), the executive director of the agency, and the person(s) who are being recommended to serve as agency field practicum supervisor(s) of students placed at the agency.

2. Regular visits by the faculty member who serves as the instructor of the concurrent on-campus field practicum seminar will be made (at least) once during each semester. During the visit the faculty member will meet with the student's supervisor, the student, and other significant agency personnel for the purpose of assessing on an on-going basis the progress of the student in the field practicum.

3. Special visits to field practicum agencies may be made by the seminar instructor, the field practicum director/coordinator, and/or the human services program/department chairperson or coordinator. These visits will be made if and when special problems occur and may also be made upon request of the agency field supervisor and/or the student.

The On-Campus Seminar.   The concurrent on-campus field practicum seminar which usually meets for at least one hour on a weekly basis is designed for several purposes. Student problems encountered at the field practicum agency are frequently the basis for seminar discussions. Students learn much from their peers. They may be reassured to hear that others frequently experience the same difficulties, and they are encouraged to openly discuss their experiences in a critical fashion. Seeing the problem through the eyes of another student may help to clarify an issue and even suggest a much needed solution. At times, the seminar instructor may even encourage student ventilation of anger and frustration with "the system" so that they may continue to use their energies constructively.

When appropriate for the learning process, students discuss the contents of their journals in the on-campus field practicum seminar. The seminar instructor may, at times, extrapolate material from student journals in order to stimulate discussion in class on such issues as professional behavior, agency-client relationships, handling of difficult

situations, negotiating systems on behalf of clients, the use of supervision in the field practicum, and professional ethics. The issue of clients' rights and confidentiality often becomes an important topic for discussion in the seminar as students struggle with ethical, legal, and value issues in practice.

Seminar Assignments.   As part of the on-campus seminar the student will usually have to complete several assignments related to the student's field practicum experiences, the agency to which the student is assigned, and the community in which the agency functions. These assignments will usually be a combination of written and oral class presentations. The assignments and activities are designed to broaden the student's observational, research, and analytical skills.

Community Observation.   For example, a community observation report calls for the student to observe a specific community (usually the one in which the field practicum agency is located) and to analyze its strengths and weaknesses in terms of social, educational, cultural, governmental, and recreational resources. This assignment, which requires a written report also calls for an oral presentation in the seminar and a discussion conducted by the student. It helps the student identify and use important community resources and provides the ground work for the development of a community resource file by the student.

Agency Administration and Careers.   Another valuable learning assignment students may be required to complete for the field practicum seminar is usually assigned at the beginning of the student's field practicum experience. Through structured interviews of key agency personnel, the student collects pertinent information about the agency's history, goals and objectives, structure, services, funding sources, staffing patterns, and promotion procedures. This assignment helps the student to achieve an understanding and appreciation of the agency as a human service delivery system, and it allows students to explore career options, compare what human services workers in various jobs and agencies actually do, and increase their knowledge and understanding of human services fields of practice.

Students make oral presentations in the seminar describing their agencies, concluding with a discussion of career opportunities at the various agencies and their overall impressions. Students are also encouraged to collect brochures, pamphlets, printed forms, and other printed materials describing their agencies for distribution in class when making their agency presentations. Time is allotted in the seminar for questions and discussion by student peers and the seminar instructor.

Case Studies and Related Assignments.   Case studies and client analyses—school or agency based—are also used in the field practicum seminar, especially with advanced students in associate degree programs and in the upper-level baccalaureate field practicum. The purpose of the assignments dealing with case studies is two fold: (1) to increase the student's familiarity with and understanding of social, psychological and physical problems, thus increasing the student's awareness of what they can expect to encounter in various situations; and (2) to break down stereotypes often held by students about clients thereby increasing student ability to relate effectively with special and different client populations.

The use of case material in the seminar (especially the student's own cases) promotes the development of assessment skills and professional report writing. To supplement their learning and to aid in their understanding of the dynamics of case material and human behavior (including their own) students may also be required to read and report on specific articles from the professional literature on systems theory, problem solving theory and methodologies, and professional practice.

EVALUATION PROCESSES

Evaluation is a process that students (and faculty) in human services programs would sometimes

rather avoid if at all possible. But it cannot be avoided and, therefore, it needs to be addressed so that the processes and experience can be fruitful and productive for all concerned.

Many students fear the evaluation process because they perceive it as being personal and subjective. Some faculty would rather avoid the process because they have difficulty being subjective with students. The evaluation process can be made less threatening and more constructive to the extent that the subject (student) is evaluated on clearly stated objective criteria. The performance is evaluated, not the person. The evaluation process works best when a functional approach is used designed to enhance the educational process for students.

Accountability.   Increased demand for accountability in the human services field and in education generally has raised questions regarding the need for a clear and explicit connection between a human services program's educational objectives and the outcomes it produces. Many questions are raised by the process. Does the product (student) produce what it is supposed to? Are the objectives and learning components clearly and logically related to what goes on in the field practicum? Are there objective measures that can be employed to determine outcomes? What are these objective measures?

And just as student practitioners are held accountable for their performance with clients on the job, human service educational programs must be able to demonstrate the readiness of their associate and baccalaureate degree students upon graduation to perform competently as professional human service workers.

The process requires and begins with a set of clearly stated criteria that identify and explicate minimum practice and performance behaviors to be achieved by all students upon completion of the field practicum course. These criteria reflect the goals and objectives of the student's human services education program, the needs of the community human service delivery systems, and the standards and guidelines promulgated by the

Council for Standards in Human Service Education. In addition, the stated criteria for the field practicum are meaningful and useful to agency field supervisors as a teaching tool and to students as goal-directed guidelines for learning.

Purpose of Field Practicum Criteria. Field practicum criteria are necessary for assessment and evaluation of student practice performance. The specific (clearly stated) criteria link the overall objectives of the human services program with specific knowledge, skills, and attitudes required at various levels of professional practice and the various stages of the education process. The need to identify specific criteria forces schools to be clear about their educational goals and objectives and their relationships to human services education in general and to the specific human services programs and activities of the local community.

Criteria serve as important and necessary guides for faculty, students, and agency supervisors in assessing and evaluating student learning and the achievement of goals. Students can relate to the criteria and feel that the expectations are fair, reasonable, and achievable within the specific time frame of the field practicum assignment. Agency field supervisors are guided by the criteria in designating student assignments and assessing student performance in relation to expectations as specified in the goals and objectives and performance criteria for the field practicum. And the faculty of the human services program who develop the criteria and direct the process likewise engage in a process of assessment. When the field practicum learning process does not work, the specifics enable the faculty to locate the area(s) of concern and problems and effect the necessary modifications and/or effectively hold accountable one or more of the players in the tri-partite process.

Value for Students. Students often enter practice unprepared for a new (and sometimes different) approach to learning. To a great extent students are responsible for their own learning and much is expected of them as student interns. They often feel confused and lost in the process. Students need and look for guidelines. They need structure. They need to know what is expected of them. Specific, clearly stated field practicum criteria are valuable learning tools for students. The criteria are stated in writing in the field practicum manual, reviewed by the instructor of the on-campus field practicum seminar, and discussed in supervision conferences with their agency field supervisor. Students have the opportunity to question the criteria and gain clarification when necessary.

The functions that criteria serve for the field practicum are as follows:

Criteria enable students to view the goals and objectives for the field practicum as achievable over time, thus lessening anxiety and increasing motivation.

Criteria provide students with direction in the field practicum course.

Criteria allow students to engage in self evaluation comparing their own performance in relation to the criteria.

Criteria present objective measures for determining a grade for the field practicum course.

Criteria help students determine their readiness and/or suitability for the human services profession.

Criteria also help students clarify and develop specific career goals for themselves.

Value for Agency Field Supervisors. Field practicum criteria as determined by the faculty of the human services program are an essential and valuable source of support for all agency supervisors in that they help to facilitate the following:

Criteria enable the agency field supervisor to be in tune with the goals and objectives of the school's human services program and the behaviors that students are expected to achieve.

Criteria encourage supervisors to individualize students as learners.

Criteria guide and strengthen the teaching role of agency supervisors.

Criteria provide a base from which to formulate an assessment and conclusions about individual student performance in specific areas and in various settings.

Criteria heighten objectivity in evaluating student performance and increases the degree of accuracy in recommending (or assigning) a grade for the field practicum course.

Evaluation as an On-going Process. As an essential component of the process of education, evaluation should be on-going and continuous throughout the field practicum placement, whatever the period of time. Although formal written evaluations are done by the agency supervisor at the end of each semester (at a minimum), there should be no surprises at the end of the semester. The on-going evaluation process enables the student and the agency field work supervisor to see how well the student is applying knowledge, skills, and values to practice at various stages. They provide the opportunity for all parties concerned (especially the student) to take stock of the student's development as a human services worker. The written evaluation at the end of the semester serves as the basis for the required grade the student receives for the field practicum course.

In addition to the formal written evaluation which becomes part of the student's official record at the college, it is strongly recommended that midway in the semester the student and supervisor engage in a joint oral assessment of the student's field work and progress. Such assessment allows the supervisor and student to share common concerns, identify problems, chart progress, and make midcourse corrections before the end of the semester when the formal written evaluation is required. At this point, the school should be alerted to any serious problems in student performance.

Format and Procedures for Written Evaluation. The school is responsible for designating the format and procedures to be followed for the formal written evaluation. Most human services pro-

grams will make available to field practicum supervisors a printed evaluation form developed by the faculty. The form may be modified by the faculty from time to time having been "tested" in actual use. In almost all instances, field practicum agency supervisors are required to use the proscribed format, although supervisors will often add written comments should a situation warrant it. The focus of the evaluation form is always on the student's experience and performance.

Evaluation Criteria. The criteria to be evaluated in the formal procedure include content in the major areas of learning that describe expected performance by students at various stages in the educational process. The major areas of learning include: (1) student functioning within the service-delivery system, (2) within various environmental systems including the community, (3) within the client system, (4) as a learner (student), and (5) as a member of the profession.

In many educational programs these areas of learning are designated on the evaluation form with a check-off requirement with a range of responses from "superior—consistently exceeds requirements" to "inferior—consistently fails to meet minimum requirements." Space is also provided for narrative explanatory comments and examples that flesh out and explain the ratings. Students are, therefore, measured along a continuum on the basis of a series of clearly defined characteristics which include (but not necessarily limited to) the following:

Poise and self-control
Assertiveness
Personal appearance and demeanor as related to agency standards and requirements
Effectiveness in planning work responsibilities
Effective use of time
Ability to work within the purpose, structure, and constraints of the agency and its services
Ability to make suggestions for change in a responsible manner
Ability to identify and use community resources
Interviewing skills

Ability to recognize and interpret nonverbal behavior

Oral communication skills

Written communication skills

Ability to record with clarity, purpose, and promptness

Ability to assess situations in the client system and determine priorities

Ability to develop and maintain professional relationships with clients, staff, and community persons from various cultural, religious, ethnic, and racial backgrounds

Relationships with co-workers and staff of the agency

Effectiveness in providing services to clients as individuals, members of groups, and/or at the community level

Ability to effectively use supervision

Development of a professional self-awareness, including the need for continual professional learning, experiences, and growth

The above is not an exhaustive, definitive listing used in every human services program. However, it serves as a guide for students as they enter into and engage in the field practicum work experience and pause to consider the basis on which they will be assessed and evaluated, both informally and formally.

The Formal Process. The formal evaluation, completed and submitted to the school, is the responsibility of the agency field supervisor. However, it is based upon input from the student who is usually required to participate in an evaluation conference near the end of each semester or some other designated time frame. Evaluation should be discussed jointly after the student and supervisor have each reviewed the student's work during the semester. The supervisor then prepares the written evaluation based upon the discussion and shares it with the student who may, at this point, request some changes.

However, the student, even if there is some disagreement on the content, is required to sign the evaluation indicating that it has been read by the student and that the student has received a copy and has been given the opportunity to submit an addendum, if so desired. In case of disagreement, the student addendum is attached to the written evaluation prepared by the supervisor and is submitted along with it to the student's instructor for the field practicum course.

Three copies of the formal written evaluation and any addendum are prepared and signed. One copy is given to the student, one is kept by the supervisor for the agency files, and the third copy is submitted to the college field practicum instructor. The instructor, who is ultimately responsible for assigning a grade for the field practicum course will rely heavily, though not exclusively, on the formal written evaluation.

GRADING FOR THE FIELD PRACTICUM COURSE

Students are usually very interested in grades, how they are determined, by whom, criteria to be used, and other factors including the important question, "How do I get a good grade in the course?" To the extent that grading policies and procedures are spelled out in clearly stated specific terminology, much of the concern and anxiety of students about grades can be reduced or eliminated completely. What is required, therefore, is a clearly stated set of requirements and procedures that students can relate to.

Input for Assessment of Students. With rare exception, the ultimate responsibility for assignment of grades for the field practicum course resides with the faculty member who serves as the instructor for the student's concurrent on-campus field practicum seminar. The instructor will use the following data, information, and observations in assessing the student's work and achievement in the field practicum course which consists of two parts—field work and the on-campus seminar.

1. Information (formal and informal) provided by the agency field practicum supervisor
2. The formal written evaluation submitted at the end of the semester

3. Information from other agency personnel obtained at the time of the instructor's visit(s) to the agency
4. Direct observation of the student's work during visits made by the instructor to the agency
5. Student's logs and journal submitted during the semester
6. Information gleaned from individual conferences with the student and/or agency field practicum supervisor
7. Participation by the student in the on-campus seminar conducted by the faculty member
8. Written and oral assignments completed by the student for the on-campus seminar

Grades. Although there are some variations among human service programs as to the percentage or weight given to each of the above, the formal written evaluation submitted at the end of the semester by the agency supervisor carries the most significant weight—usually at least 50 percent—in determining the student's grade for the course.

There is also a variety of practices in the types of grades used in the field practicum course. The grades may be letter grades: A, B, C, D, or F—either with or without provision for pluses (+) or minuses (–). In other instances, colleges use a numerical grading system (0–100) and in a smaller number of programs other designations are used. These may include "pass-fail" or "satisfactory-unsatisfactory" or "credit-no credit."

Because instructors of the field practicum seminar have the responsibility of assigning grades for student efforts, they must rely primarily upon feedback from the agency field supervisor and possibly such evidence as they can collect from assignments. Emphasis is also placed on meeting deadlines. Faculty typically require that all assignments will be completed no later than the due date, that all logs and journals will be kept current and submitted when due, that students attend the seminar regularly and promptly, and that they show up for all scheduled appointments, conferences, and meetings required for the field practicum placement and evaluation processes.

If the student's grade is more dependent on agency work performance than on written assignments, then the student may earn a lower grade than the student believes is deserved if the student does inferior work in the field agency despite acceptable or even outstanding written work in the seminar.

Grading schemes are often somewhat subjective. One instructor may let the course grade be largely determined by the agency supervisor's recommendation and evaluation; another may weigh more heavily on written assignments and/or seminar presentations; a third may penalize a student for missing seminars; and a fourth may pass every student (when using a "pass-fail" system) as long as no problems occurred in the agency and all administrative requirements have been met by the student. The field practicum manual and course syllabus should state specifically the criteria used and how student grades will be determined.

Appeal Process. Most human services programs have an appeal process in place that students may use should they believe that the grade assigned is not a fair one and therefore does not accurately reflect the quality of their work performed in the field practicum course—including field work and the required on-campus seminar. The field practicum manual usually specifies what the appeal process consists of and what the student is required to do to take advantage of it. The steps of a typical appeal process might include the following:

1. Conference with the instructor of the on-campus field practicum seminar for the purpose of reviewing and gaining clarification as to how the student's grade was calculated.
2. If the student is not satisfied with the explanation, the next step would be a meeting with the director/coordinator of the field practicum program. The student will receive further clarification of the school's grading policies during this meeting and will also be given the opportunity to explain further why the student feels the grade is not fair.
3. The next step would be a meeting with the unit's administrative head—the program coordinator or department chairperson. Here, too, the student can receive further clarification, if necessary.

4. The student also has access, if still not satisfied, to meet with the academic dean of the college or university.

At steps 2, 3, and/or 4 a recommendation may be made to adjust the grade given to the student for the field practicum course. However, it should be noted that *only* the faculty member who is the course instructor has the authority to give or change a grade. All others in the appeal process may only recommend change. Nevertheless, a very strong recommendation based upon an intensive objective review of the student's performance in the field and in the seminar measured against the stated criteria may result in a change of grade for the student.

A FINAL WORD AND SUMMATION

There is no doubt that the field practicum is the central feature of education that prepares students for professional practice in the human services field. It is the mechanism that prepares students to integrate the three bases of professional practice: knowledge, skills, and values. Standards for the field experiences of students, as defined by the Council for Standards in Human Services Education, the national program approval body, represent the best available thinking regarding adequate preparation for entry into the human services field of practice.

The design, organization, and administration of human services internships is a shared responsibility involving the school, the field practicum agency and the student. The tri-partite relationship works best when all concerned parties recognize and carry out their special responsibilities.

The agency provides the student with individualized practice and observational learning opportunities that enhance student competency as a developing human services worker. The field practicum agency supervisor provides guidance and support through regularly scheduled supervisory conferences and an evaluation process that emphasizes the student's understanding of the implications of the field practicum experience.

The college/university human services program reinforces learning through the concurrent on-campus seminar designed to stimulate student thinking about theoretical concepts, practice skills, value considerations, and professional principles that are necessary for effective practice in the field.

Emphasis is placed on students developing self-awareness of their own talents, limitations, abilities, prejudices, and motivations for becoming human services workers. The field experience is also enhanced by its integration in the seminar through specific activities and assignments designed to facilitate this integration.

The collaborative model of the field practicum does not ignore the importance of student input. Students are involved at every point in the process including the selection of an agency to serve as the student's field practicum site, recommendations and requests for specific work assignments in field work, on-going assessment, and formal evaluation of student performance. All collaboration takes place within the parameters of the school and agency policies and a primary focus is on student education for practice.

REFERENCES

Acker, J., (1968). "Content for Methods Courses in Undergraduate Curricula for the Helping Services." In Teague, D. and D. Buck, eds. *Developing Programs in the Helping Services.* Boulder: WICHE, pp. 25–35.

Aldridge, M.J., (1983). *Developing and Rejuvenating Human Service Programs.* Council for Standards in Human Service Education, Monograph Series, Issue No. 3.

Aptekar, H.H., (1965). "Supervision and the Development of Professional Responsibility: An Application of Systemic Thought." *The Jewish Social Work Forum* 3:1, pp. 4–7.

Austin, M., J. Kopp, and P.L. Smith, (1986). *Delivering Human Services.* NY: Longman.

Becker, H.J., (1978). "Curricula of Associate Degree Mental Health/Human Services Training Programs." *Community Mental Health Journal* 14:2.

Brown, C., (1989). *Program Approval Manual.* Council for Standards in Human Service Education.

CSHSE, (1985). *Handbook,* 2nd ed. Council for Standards in Human Service Education.

CSHSE, (1986). *National Standards for Human Service Worker Education and Training Programs,* 3rd ed. Council for Standards in Human Service Education.

CSHSE, (1989). *Self-study guidelines.* Council for Standards in Human Service Education.

Dea, K.L., (1972). "The Collaborative Process in Undergraduate Field Instruction Programs." In Wenzel, K., ed. *Undergraduate Field Instruction Programs: Current Issues and Predictions.* NY: Council on Social Work Education.

DiGiovanni, M., (1989). "The Development of a Field Work Manual." In Tower, C., ed. *Field Work in Human Services Education.* Council for Standards in Human Service Education, Monograph Series, Issue No. 6.

Family Service Association of America. (1966). *Trends in Field Work Instruction.* NY: Family Service Association of America.

Fullerton, S., (1986). "Contracting with Field Placement Agencies." *The Link,* National Organization for Human Service Education 8:4.

Fullerton, S., ed. (1990). *History of the Human Services Movement.* Council for Standards in Human Service Education, Monograph Series, Issue No. 7.

Garrett, A., (1954). "Learning through Supervision." *Smith College Studies in Social Work 24.*

Hamilton, N. and J.F. Else, (1983). *Designing Field Education: Philosophy, Structure, and Process.* Springfield, IL: Charles C. Thomas.

Jacobs, E. and R. Feringer, (1985). *A Three Parameter Model for Planning, Monitoring, and Evaluating Human Services Field Experience.* Council for Standards in Human Service Education, Monograph Series, Issue No. 4.

James, V.R., (1981). *The Education and Training of Human Service Workers: An Analysis of a National System.* Unpublished doctoral dissertation, University of Massachusetts, Amherst, Mass.

King, M., (1986). "Field Work, a Collaborative Relationship." *The Link,* National Organization for Human Service Education 8:4.

King, M., (1988). "Collaborating for Quality: The Fitchburg Experience." *The Link,* National Organization for Human Service Education 10:3.

Kronick, R., ed. (1987). *Curriculum Development in Human Service Education.* Council for Standards in Human Service Education, Monograph Series, Issue No. 5.

Mandell, B. and B. Schram, (1985). *Human Services: Introduction and Interventions.* NY: John Wiley & Sons.

Mattson, M., (1968). "Learning through Field Experience." In Teague, D. and D. Buck, eds. *Developing Programs in the Helping Services.* Boulder: WICHE.

McKinney, L., (1988). "Field Instruction Ideas: University of Rhode Island." *The Link,* National Organization for Human Service Education 10:3.

Mehr, J., (1988). *Human Services: Conceptions and Intervention Strategies.* Boston: Allyn and Bacon.

Negron, C.V., (1989). "The Practical Aspects of Field Work Supervision." In Tower, C., ed. *Field Work in Human Service Education.* Council for Standards in Human Service Education, Mongraph Series, Issue No. 6.

Nesbitt, S., (1993). "The Field Experience: Identifying False Assumptions." *The Link,* National Organization for Human Service Education, 14:3.

Nilsson, A., (1989). "Undergraduate Training for the Human Services: Many Routes to the Same Field." *Human Service Education* 9:1, pp. 19–25.

Royce, D., S. Dhooper, and E.L. Rompf, (1993). *Field Instruction: A Guide for Social Work Students.* NY: Longman.

Russo, J., (1980). *Serving and Surviving as a Human Services Worker.* Pacific Grove, CA: Brookes-Cole.

Schmolling, P., M. Youkeles, and W. Burger, (1989). *Human Services in Contemporary America.* Monterey, CA: Brookes-Cole.

Shulman, L., (1983). *Teaching the Helping Skills: A Field Instruction Guide.* Itasca, IL: F.E. Peacock.

Simon, E., (1969). *Supervision as a Function of the Process of Administration of Social Agencies.* Unpublished paper presented in the doctoral seminar on practice, Wurzweiler School of Social Work, Yeshiva University, New York, NY.

Simon, E., (1989a). "Field Placement Evaluation: The Simultaneous Formal and Informal Processes." In Towe, C., ed. *Field Work in Human Service Education.* Council for Standards in Human Service Education, Monograph Series, Issue No. 6.

Simon, E., (1989b). "Field Practica Survey Results." In Tower, C., ed. *Field Work in Human Service*

Education. Council for Standards in Human Service Education, Monograph Series, Issue No. 6.

Simon, E., (1990). "The Challenge of the Future: Towards the 21st Century." In Fullerton, S., ed. *History of the Human Service Movement*. Council for Standards in Human Service Education, Monograph Series, Issue No. 7.

SREB. *A Guideline for Mental Health Programs at the Associate Degree Level*. Atlanta, GA: Southern Regional Education Board.

Tower, C., ed. (1989). *Field Work in Human Service Education*. Council for Standards in Human Service Education, Monograph Series, Issue No. 6.

Towle, C., (1962). "The Role of Supervision in the Union of Cause and Function." *Social Service Review* 36:4, pp. 396–407.

Urbanowski, M.L. and M.M. Dwyer, (1988). *Learning through Field Instruction: A Guide for Teachers and Students*. Milwaukee, WI: Family Service of America.

Uzak, S., (1988). "Field Instruction Ideas: University of New Mexico." *The Link*, National Organization for Human Service Education 10:3.

Wilson, S.J., (1981). *Field Instruction: Techniques for Supervisors*. NY: Free Press.

Woodside, M. and T. McClam, (1990). *Introduction to Human Services*. Pacific Grove, CA: Brookes-Cole.

CHAPTER 4

HUMAN SERVICES
NECESSARY SKILLS AND VALUES

LORENCE A. LONG
MAUREEN DOYLE

To be effective, human services workers need to possess a certain combination of personal qualities, knowledge, skills, and values.

Workers must be able to deal with people who are upset, angry, depressed, or confused, without being swept away by any of these feelings themselves. It is essential that workers be good listeners, yet be able to assert their own questions, statements, and judgments at an appropriate time.

Workers need to be well-organized in a way that allows them to deal with a complex workload, while being flexible enough to respond to interruptions. Workers must have a broad knowledge of human nature and social systems, yet be clear that each client is an individual, moving at his or her own pace toward self-discovery and the solution to his or her problem. It is desirable that workers display a deep interest in and commitment to their work, without neglecting their own development and their lives with their families and friends.

QUALITIES HUMAN SERVICES WORKERS SHARE WITH OTHER WORKERS

Many qualities needed by human services workers are the same as those generic characteristics required by architects, nurses, Wall Street brokers, carpenters, or any other workers. These include:

Being Responsible and Reliable. This cluster of characteristics involves being honest and taking responsibility for one's share of the work, as well as for the mistakes that one commits. It means carefully doing the work that has been assigned. It includes coming to work on time and staying until the designated worktime is over.

Addressing the Work in an Organized Way. Listening carefully to instructions, identifying sequences of tasks, allowing enough time for each part of the work, requesting assistance if time or resources are not adequate to get the job done, and asking for help if it is needed are all part of being organized. Workers are also expected to take the initiative when they know what to do, and to try to anticipate problems and work cooperatively to solve them. Sometimes the organized worker must drop everything to meet an emergency, and then reorganize to finish what had been begun earlier. Workers must be able to manage being interrupted without losing track of what they were working on before. The tasks that need to be done often exceed the time available to do them, so workers must prioritize, choosing what is most important to do first.

Listening Carefully, Paying Attention, Focusing Energy on the Task at Hand. Workplaces are full of and surrounded by distractions: competition between individuals and groups, personal concerns, conflicts, diversions and amusements, friendships, and other attention-getters. It requires discipline to focus on the work when these alternatives are close at hand.

Having a Constructive and Supportive Attitude.
The worker needs to be interested in learning, and should not be defensive about being criticized. Such a worker tends to assume that problems have solutions, even when the solutions are not obvious. She or he pitches in to do whatever is necessary. This worker treats other people—whether chief, clerk, or client—with respect, and understands that a key to success is to help clients, coworkers, and supervisors be successful.

Forming Positive Working Relationships with Others.
Workers are attentive to the human relations aspects of the job, willing to listen to colleagues' work-related problems, reaching out to coworkers and others to form links around common interests, and being attuned to others' culture and backgrounds.

The qualities we have listed would make any worker highly valued in virtually any setting, including human services organizations. Some readers may be surprised that we begin our discussion with these general qualities. Doesn't everyone know that these are required for success? In our experience, students and beginning workers are more likely to undermine their own success in the areas we have just outlined, rather than in those matters that are specific to human services.

SPECIAL SKILLS NEEDED BY HUMAN SERVICES WORKERS

Human services workers need the following skills:

How to Use One's Self to Help Others Move in a Positive Direction.
Sometimes a human services worker must interact powerfully with other people by setting limits, or confronting the other person, or engaging the person in an exciting activity. At other times, the worker might choose to be silent, let a client work out a problem on her or his own, or invite the client to join in a quiet activity. One must not only know how to do these things, but when to do each one in order to maximize the effectiveness of the intervention.

How to Communicate with Clients, Colleagues, and Others.
Workers are required to create a climate in which clients feel free to disclose whatever concerns them. Workers need to be able to hear what the client is saying without letting their own judgments get in the way. They must know how to use their imaginations in an empathetic way to understand how the situation looks from the client's point of view. It is important that they then find a way to let the clients know that they have been heard, using paraphrasing or some other technique for this purpose. "Being heard" includes recognizing and interpreting nonverbal, as well as verbal, forms of expression.

LISTENING TO THE WORDS, AND THEN SOME

Sarah's Cry for Help
Sarah came into the office holding her little girl firmly by the hand. "Can I talk to you?" she asked.

Fran said, "Sure. What's it about?"

"I don't know how to start," Sarah said.

"It's hard to talk about?" Fran asked gently.

Sarah was quiet for a moment. Then a tear ran down her cheek. Fran offered her ever-ready box of tissues. Sarah took one and blew her nose. Her eyes filled.

"Sad . . .," Fran said tentatively.

Sarah's daughter uttered a sound, but was immediately shushed by her mother, who gripped her hand even more tightly.

"She can sit over here in this chair," Fran said. The little girl, released, sat down, rubbing her hand.

Sarah said, "It's too much. I get to the point that when she makes a noise, I want to hurt her. I just can't control her."

"You want her to be quiet, and do what you want," Fran said.

"My mother had the same trouble with me," Sarah said. "I was a very bad girl when I was little."

"So you kind of see yourself in her, doing the same types of things," Fran said.

"Yes," Sarah said, and sighed. She sat back.

"It was really important to you to say that, I think," Fran said.

"Yes, it was. I don't want her to turn out like me. And she will, unless I can change her," Sarah said.

"You seem determined, but not sure how to make her life different from yours, and your life different from your mother's?" Fran made this last phrase a question, because she thought this is what Sarah meant, but she wasn't sure.

"Yes. I couldn't bear it if I ended up like my mother, angry and drunk every night with nobody to love me."

"You sound hopeless, lost, when you say that," Fran said.

"I feel hopeless," Sarah said. *"I guess I can't put it all on Susana, here."*

"She reminds you of the trouble you want to stay away from, but she isn't really the cause of the trouble."

After a pause, Sarah said, *"Right. I see that now. You saved me from doing something terrible."*

"I just listened to what you were saying, yourself," Fran said.

Workers must also communicate the rules and expectations of the agency or other providers clearly, so that clients understand what is required of them. Workers' own body language should correspond to their spoken language, to avoid confusing the client.

Workers are required to tell the agency clearly in both written (case record or log) and oral (case conference) form what the client needs and how the worker has responded. Case records follow a specific format, so that other workers can quickly find out the status of a client's situation, and in order to conform to the requirements of auditors from funding sources or regulatory bodies who are evaluating the agency's work.

Workers need to know how to use the telephone properly, communicating and receiving needed information accurately, completely, and clearly without breaking confidentiality and privacy rules regarding clients. Even acknowledging that someone is a client is a violation of the person's privacy, especially if such acknowledgement would tend to suggest that the person is HIV-positive or has some other stigmatized condition. As technology becomes more complex, new challenges arise. For example, computer monitor screens containing client data may be seen by unauthorized persons who visit a worker's office.

How to Operate Within the Agency's Framework to Solve Problems. Workers are required to observe situations and individuals as objectively as possible, being able to separate inference from observation.

SEPARATING INFERENCE FROM OBSERVATION

Emily's Silence

The family therapy team met to debrief after the session.

"Did you notice that Emily did not say one word during the whole session," Lloyd commented. *"She is so uninvolved in this family!"*

"I don't agree," Steve protested. *"I think that Lucy intimidates her. She talked last week, when Lucy was away."*

"I think she is getting ready to blast her father," Jeanine offered. *"Did you notice how she looked at him as though she could kill him? Next session there's going to be an explosion."*

"What are you all basing this on?" asked Jack. *"She was silent, and that's that. Since none of you asked her why she didn't say anything, you can make up any meaning you want. You just don't know."*

Everybody was silent for a moment after that.

Observations and assessments must be done with an agency's priorities in mind. When doing assessments, it is necessary for workers to distinguish between the more and less important elements of a situation. This might involve differentiating between a presenting symptom and its related underlying problem, or placing a style of behavior in the context of developmental levels or other critical issues.

FOCUSING ON THE IMPORTANT ISSUES

Walter

Desirée, a new worker at the day care center, called to a noisy three-year-old, "Walter, come here."

Walter responded gruffly, "Who you calling by my name?"

Desirée was about to reprimand him for his bad manners when her teacher said, "Isn't that good?! He's finally starting to speak in sentences!"

Desirée was shaken. She had assumed that her main goal was to make the children be well-behaved and polite. What the teacher said made her aware that she had been focused on an issue the teacher was not so concerned with.

Whatever activities are part of the agency's work—whether they be filling out forms, leading a group discussion, or advocating for a client—workers need to possess the skills involved. Workers also need to know emergency procedures, including how and when to contact emergency services personnel.

Workers need to be able to conceptualize a problem in terms of its relationship to the individual client's goals and to the goals of the program. Then they must break the problem down into objectives (what the worker, along with the client, will try to accomplish) and tasks (what needs to be done—and by whom—to achieve the objectives). Various parts of the problem may be selected for early action, either because they are the most emergent, or because they may be accomplished more easily. Skilled workers will be able to determine which parts should come first.

Workers also need to be able to make plans with clients (or sometimes for them, if the client is incapable) in a way that fits the client's abilities. Generally speaking, clients should participate in making plans for themselves to the extent of their capability, because this strengthens the clients' decision-making and problem-solving skills, as well as their self-esteem. Deciding things for clients should be a last resort. There is an old saying that applies here: "Whatever you do for me, I cannot do for myself."

Workers should be able to recognize the signs of progress that are appropriate and realistic for the client population they are working with.

SETTING REALISTIC GOALS FOR ONE'S WORK

Frank's Progress

Mary had been working with Frank, a developmentally disabled child, in an effort to reduce his self-injuring behavior. She was using positive reinforcement to increase the frequency of a replacement behavior. When she met with Cliff for supervision, Mary confessed to being discouraged.

"He is still doing it, no matter how hard I try," Mary sighed.

"How many times a day?" Cliff asked.

"He banged his head seventy-five times while I was on the unit," Mary said.

"And a week ago?" Cliff wondered.

"Let me look at my notebook. He averaged one hundred twenty-five times. Okay, so it's better. But he's still doing it."

Cliff said, "I believe that a forty percent improvement in a week is very good. You have to remember who you are dealing with. Frank has been institutionalized for nine years, and self-injuring behavior is one of his primary ways of stimulating himself. He's not going to stop it overnight. You are really doing very well."

"Oh," Mary said. "Well, I wish he would improve faster."

"Yes, I can understand that," said Cliff. "But you should expect that his improvement will slow down, and maybe reverse at times. You're doing better than you should have expected to, given his history."

DIFFERENCES BETWEEN INFORMAL AND PROFESSIONAL HELPING

Some people believe that all that is needed to be a professional helper is to have the desire to help. They base this assumption on their own personal experiences of helping a friend or family member, or babysitting for a neighbor's child.

Wanting to help is important. However, it can even get in the way of helping, if it is not disciplined by skill, knowledge, and values of respect and understanding. A standard exercise in our beginning human services courses at LaGuardia Community College is to ask students to list ways of helping that are not helpful. Every class comes up with a long list, often based on personal experiences. All of us have been offered unwelcome advice, been given incorrect information, had limits set for us that were unfair, been lectured to by someone who didn't understand, or been offered assistance when perfectly capable of doing something for ourselves.

One aspect of the professional helping relationship is the unequal status of the helper and the person in need. Usually the helper has more experience and skill, better knowledge of resources, and some emotional distance from the problem. Often the worker's emotional distance enables the person in need to see the problem more clearly, and to develop her or his own solution to the problem. It should be noted that different models of helping either emphasize or play down this difference in status (Corsini, 1989).

Family members and friends may have trouble maintaining that emotional distance, because they want to see a certain outcome. A professional helper—who is not vested in a particular outcome—should give the client information about various options, and explore with the client the benefits and difficulties associated with each one. The client must ultimately make an informed decision. If a helper persuades a client to choose a certain option, the client may blame the worker for a poor result. This may lead to a lack of trust between worker and client, and ultimately frustrate the helping process.

Another aspect of the professional helping relationship is that it usually lasts for a specific period of time. It is understood that the relationship will come to an end when the goals that have been set are accomplished, when the client's independence is more important than the remaining small gains that could be achieved by continuing, or when other factors intervene.

The professional helping relationship is clearly defined. Roles are specific, and responsibilities are clearly laid out. Often the helper's agency defines the ground rules for the helping activities and interactions, such as not giving clients money. Friendships and family relationships, on the other hand, are much more open-ended, shifting, and ambiguous, as they should be.

SPECIAL KNOWLEDGE NEEDED BY HUMAN SERVICES WORKERS

Agency-Related Knowledge. In addition to the many personal qualities outlined, effective human services workers need certain kinds of knowledge. Part of this knowledge must be about the agency that employs them. What are the agency's goals? When workers are clear about the goals, it is possible for them to make choices about competing claims on their time, and judgments about whether an activity that is being considered fits within the scope of the agency's focus.

It is helpful to know the agency's history. Which workers joined the agency first? What functions are the core functions and which ones were added later? What crises or scandals have "burned" the agency and led to defensive practices? All of these factors may explain otherwise puzzling attitudes and decisions.

Knowing the agency's philosophy about techniques and approaches is also helpful. Some approaches used elsewhere may be forbidden in a particular agency because of philosophical beliefs held by staff or board members. For example, some agencies are opposed to using behavior modification in working with clients, while others ground their approaches in behavior modification theories and practices. The agency's attitudes toward clients, government contracts, fundraising, interagency cooperation, and many other subjects will influence how workers are expected to proceed.

The worker must also be knowledgeable about the agency's accepted approaches and methods. If psychoanalysis, or reality therapy, or the Montessori method are used, the worker needs to read the literature being published about that particular approach.

Knowledge of the agency's organizational structure, roles, departments, and services is also essential for the worker to be effective. Knowing who to talk to about a particular problem, which department handles a certain matter, who supervises whom, whether the agency performs certain functions or refers them elsewhere, are important to a worker's success.

Familiarity with the agency's procedures is also expected of the worker. Whether procedures involve the agency's way of filling out a form, leading a group, writing up a psychosocial assessment, or taking a baseline on a child's behavior, the worker should thoroughly understand the reasons and regulations related to the procedure.

Knowledge about Clients and about the Field.
Workers are expected to be well-informed about general characteristics of the types of clients with whom they deal on a regular basis. If the clients have a particular developmental pattern or certain cultural characteristics, the worker would read about and discuss these matters with knowledgeable people. Workers would be expected to attend conferences and meetings about such subjects, and should regularly consult journals and other publications that present current information about their clients.

SHOULD HE RESPOND TO
A CULTURAL STYLE?

Chuck's Dilemma

Chuck was visiting Ron, who ran a cultural arts program in the downtown area. Chuck said, "Ron, I want to ask about how you relate to your Hispanic clients. I have been getting larger numbers of them uptown, and I am not sure what kinds of changes I should make in my style and the program's style."

"Well," Ron said, "one thing that I have had to get accustomed to is saying hello to people personally. They expect to pay their respects to 'el Don' when they come into the agency. I don't always feel comfortable about spending the time when I have some deadline, but I know they will feel hurt unless I ask them to sit down and talk about family for a little while, before they go on to their activity."

"I can see how that would be a problem for me," Chuck said. "I am not very available to clients. I expect staff members to do the face-to-face work. I don't mean that being distant is good, I just want to be as business-like as possible."

"I think some of your Hispanic clients will feel that there is something missing in your program, if they don't get to greet you," Ron said. "Most of them seem to want to be recognized by the head person."

"Okay, thanks," Chuck responded. "I can see I'm going to have to give this some thought."

In addition, the worker would attempt to keep abreast of new developments in the field. Human services concepts and approaches are always changing; what had been accepted as indisputable fact at one time can later be discounted. For example, until twenty years ago, it was widely thought that the short lives of developmentally disabled people were not affected by putting them in large institutions that, in many cases, provided very poor care. What we now know is that developmentally disabled people live just as long as other people; their short lives were the result of poor care. A worker needs to keep up with these trends, and must know where to find information about them.

Workers also need to know about the resources outside the agency that their clients must depend on. If new regulations are adopted by a referral agency, if public assistance grants are cut back, if a new program opens in the community, the worker should be aware and involved in helping clients deal with the new development. Workers make referrals to outside agencies. They need to know how these agencies function so that they can prepare clients for a successful referral. It is imperative that they identify and develop relationships with contact people at these organizations.

Dynamics of Working with Individuals and Groups.   Basic to nearly every human services activity is knowledge of the dynamics of relating to individuals: knowing about how relationships are formed, how they are worked through, and ended. Relationships are the primary tool of the human services worker. Human services workers also need to understand how groups function, so that they may make sense of what is happening in groups of people, including groups of colleagues as well as clients. A grasp of the concepts underlying these relationships is the basis for employing individual relationships and group dynamics to help clients move toward better lives.

VALUES FOR HUMAN SERVICES WORKERS

We have listed many professional and personal values in the preceding sections. Here are some that we believe deserve special emphasis:

Putting Clients' Needs First. Given that clients are the reason that human services agencies and roles exist at all, it is surprising how easily other elements—agency success, professional recognition, workload management, etc.—displace clients' needs as workers' first priority. This is especially distressing because clients are, once they enter the agency system, quite dependent on that system to meet their needs. Often the system is a mystery to the client; workers are the guides to what to expect, as well as how to negotiate the system. Workers may find it necessary to rearrange their schedules, stay after regular working hours, go into neighborhoods they would rather not enter, fill out multiple forms, etc., in order to meet the needs of clients. Workers are also empowered, within reason, to advocate within their own agencies on behalf of clients whose needs are not being met because of the system's inefficiencies. It should not need to be said that clients are not to be exploited in any way, sexually, emotionally, or financially. Workers sometimes make serious mistakes in this area because they come into human services expecting that someone will be grateful for their efforts. While this may sometimes actually occur, resentment at having to be dependent often keeps clients from expressing gratitude. Workers must find their per-

sonal gratifications in the work, in their comradeship with colleagues, or in some other area. They cannot be allowed to steal it from clients.

CLIENT EXPLOITATION

The Temptation of Martha
Gerda finally died, after long suffering. Her family was very grateful to Martha, who had managed the home care very efficiently and sensitively over seven years. Martha came to the house to pay her respects to the family. The subject turned to disposing of Gerda's possessions.

Gerda's older daughter was saying to Martha, "We are so grateful. You have always been there for us. Just let us know if there is anything we can do to show our appreciation."

As Martha thanked her perfunctorily, she turned and saw that a chair, which had been covered with a throw every time she had visited, was now revealed as the mate to her prized antique couch. She knew that it was worth several thousand dollars. And she suspected that the family did not know its value.

It should be understood that Martha, though a supervisor, was not well-paid. Unlike many human services workers, she was used to helping people who had more money than she did. Gerda's children were working people, comfortable but not wealthy.

"That's a very handsome chair," Martha said.

No Discrimination. Social agencies usually serve people who are discriminated against: older people, disabled people, poor people, people from stigmatized races or ethnic groups, people with a mental illness, etc. Often while serving one stigmatized group, agencies follow their community's other patterns of exclusion. For example, a senior citizens program operates on a club-like basis, excluding disabled people or representatives of a minority group. Because of the damaging effects of discrimination, human services workers must commit themselves to going beyond this minimal level of accommodation.

Bias is not just about groups—it also has to do with individuals. Workers may find one client appealing, and another disgusting. Each deserves to be treated fairly, however the worker feels about them.

Information-Sharing and Keeping. Human services workers often know the intimate details of their clients' lives. Clients trust that this information will be confidential, or they would never confide in workers at all. So workers must keep this information from others—family members, debt collectors, police officers, etc.—except when they are authorized to have it. Yet workers must share the information within the agency, so that the agency can respond appropriately when the primary worker is not available. Workers also offer the information to their supervisors, in order to learn how to be more helpful to clients, and to ensure that the work is being done properly. After all, the agency must monitor what the worker does. Another responsibility to share is when clients pose a threat to themselves or to others. This double responsibility—proper disclosure without unduly violating clients' privacy—is a cornerstone of a worker's integrity.

Being Truthful. Many people who enter human services as a profession are people who want to be liked. When someone at work asks them to give an opinion, they tend to sugarcoat it so the person will not be angry at them. This practice tends to obscure accurate understandings of what is going on in the work situation, and robs colleagues and supervisors of accurate feedback.

This does not mean that one should go around saying exactly what one thinks, no matter what. It does mean that workers need to look for the right time and place to say what they think. Critical opinions may be expressed in the form of a question, rather than a statement. It is desirable for workers to express themselves assertively, allowing for other people to have a differing point of view (Schulman, 1978, pp. 108–115). A goal for workers is to avoid assenting to an untruth, even if they do not feel they can tell the whole truth at that time.

SELF-AWARENESS AND SELF-MANAGEMENT

Responding to Criticism. Workers view criticism from colleagues and supervisors as an important aid in learning, and are expected to offer frank and open accounts of their work—including mistakes—to their supervisors and, when appropriate, to their peers. It is always tempting to try to explain, excuse, or apologize for errors. The useful response is to acknowledge mistakes, and to try to learn from them in a way that keeps the worker from repeating them very often.

Understanding One's Unique Ways of Acting, Responding, and Learning. Each worker has different ways of thinking about and getting involved in experiences with clients and other staff members. One worker will be sensitive to family dynamics, another one will be especially capable in confronting aggressive clients, and another will know all the regulations about public assistance by heart. Some workers will do best when they work in private, while others will thrive when collaborating in a team. An effective organization will use the different perspectives and responses of its workers in ways that allow each one to develop strengths and contribute them to the organization's life. Workers who want to grow will capitalize on their strengths and try to improve in their weak areas.

Managing One's Own Workload. Working always involves meeting deadlines. Often the deadlines are not coordinated; a new one falls at the same time as another. The presentation to the community group must be prepared and delivered at the same time as the monthly client statistics must be handed in. Workers must have a way to decide what is most important, and organize their time effectively. It is helpful if they know how to ask their colleagues for help in ways that do not lead to dependence but rather inspire, stimulate thinking, and spark renewed effort.

Knowing One's Limits.   The agency connection is what gives a worker legitimacy. As a worker for an agency, the worker is empowered to intervene in a deeply personal situation, access money and other resources, speak for and testify about clients in official proceedings, write records and reports that may determine the fate of individual clients or groups of clients, recommend that a child be removed from a family, plan programs that may involve large amounts of money and large numbers of people, and other powerful activities. Being rooted in the role that has been assigned to them is the worker's source of strength, authority, and authenticity.

Workers sometimes try to escape the limits of the calendar and the clock. There are so many interesting and worthwhile activities to become involved in that they overcommit their time and energy. Such overcommitment and its resulting stress leads to poor health, poor judgment, and erratic worker performance.

Workers are sometimes impatient to save the world, because the needs of people are so great and the obstacles to meeting them so formidable. They sometimes set unreasonably high goals for their clients, setting them up for failure because the workers want so much to succeed. Some inexperienced or emotionally needy workers think of themselves as "Lone Rangers" or knights on horseback, single-handedly rescuing clients from other insensitive workers. The truth is that one cannot carry out important and effective human services work alone. The cooperation of many others must be enlisted in order to meet any significant goal.

PRESCRIPTIONS FOR SELF-IMPROVEMENT

The preceding catalogue of skills, knowledge, values, and personal qualities may intimidate some readers. It is a formidable list. If you know human services workers, you may know that not all of them have all these characteristics, at least not all of the time.

How does one go about developing the characteristics? The need for them is not just a matter

of helping a worker improve; the clients need dedicated, expert, skillful, and sensitive assistance from workers. That may be the *first* prescription for positive personal development: not forgetting that it is all done for the benefit of clients. Some other rewarding aspects of human services work may include professional recognition, community leadership, close association with interesting and dynamic people, the opportunity to challenge the power structure, intellectual stimulation, an opening for new arrangements in society, personal power, and many other values that draw people into lives of service. But if these become more important than serving clients, the helping effort will probably lose its focus, and may even unwittingly harm clients.

The *second* prescription for positive personal development is to select our experiences carefully. None of us enter our roles fully formed. We grow into them, experience by experience. Often we learn more from our mistakes than from our successes. We all grow and change every moment. For that reason, it is important to select experiences that will help us grow positively. Work experiences early in the career of a human services worker will have an important formative impact, so it is critical that early experiences be carefully chosen. But even the most experienced workers are challenged to continually learn as the world changes around them.

The *third* prescription then is for the worker to form relationships with people who will challenge, stimulate, guide, and struggle in a positive way with the worker. The worker does not have to adopt the style or values of these people, although some may serve as role models. The joint process of learning with them is what is important. The beginning worker may, in turn, have an important influence on the others by asking seldom-heard questions, seeking explanations for customary ways of dealing with problems, or coming up with new ways of thinking about a topic. The process of dialogue and struggle, properly done, requires all participants to stretch and grow.

It is helpful if the worker can find these colleagues in the workplace; if not, they may be sought out in professional associations, civic groups, advocacy groups, or elsewhere. When a worker travels, it can be interesting to seek out human services workers who deal with similar problems in other locations, to see how they think differently about these problems.

A *fourth* prescription is to read the professional literature. There are many different ideas about how to serve the needs of clients. Reading professional journals and other works that deal with human need and ways to meet it can give workers new tools and new perspectives to address their daily tasks.

A human services worker is always in the process of becoming someone new. Thoughtful application of the prescriptions above will make the "new" someone a more effective, informed, and thoughtful worker.

REFERENCES

Brammer, L.M., (1988). *The Helping Relationship: Process and Skills,* 4th ed. Englewood Cliffs, NJ: Prentice-Hall.

Brill, N., (1990). *Working with People: The Helping Process,* 4th ed. New York: Longman.

Corey, M.S. and G. Corey, (1992). *Becoming a Helper,* 2nd ed. Pacific Grove, CA: Brooks/Cole.

Corsini, R.J. and D. Wedding, (1989). *Current Psychotherapies.* Itasca, IL: F.E. Peacock.

Egan, G., (1990). *The Skilled Helper: A Systematic Approach to Effective Helping,* 4th ed. Pacific Grove, CA: Brooks/Cole.

Kottler, J., (1991). *The Compleat Therapist.* San Francisco, CA: Jossey-Bass.

LaFramboise, T.D. and S.L. Foster, (1989). *Counseling Across Cultures,* 3rd ed. Honolulu, HI: University of Hawaii Press.

Napier, R.W. and M.K. Gershenfeld, (1993). *Groups: Theory and Experience.* Boston, MA: Houghton Mifflin Company.

Satir, V., (1989). *The New Peoplemaking.* Palo Alto, CA: Science and Behavior Books.

Schulman, Evelyn, (1978). *Interventions in Human Services.* St. Louis, MO: C.V. Mosby.

CHAPTER 5

PREPARING COMMUNITY SUPPORT WORKERS
A TRAINING MODEL BASED ON SKILL STANDARDS AND PERFORMANCE COMPETENCIES

JUDITH LEFF
VIRGINIA MULKERN
H. STEPHEN LEFF

THE CHANGING NATURE OF HUMAN SERVICES AND THE IMPLICATIONS OF THESE CHANGES FOR HUMAN SERVICE WORKERS

The service delivering systems for people with physical, emotional, and cognitive disabilities that affect their ability to live independently in the community are in the midst of profound changes. Increasingly, people with disabilities are living and receiving services in the community as opposed to large institutional settings. These services are being coordinated and provided by an array of staff with diverse backgrounds and levels of expertise. Bradley and Knoll (1990) have referred to these changes as a new paradigm in the delivery of human services.

The shift from an institutional to a community focus requires a new and different design of staffing patterns and staff training. Regardless of disability type, services are increasingly being delivered by *community support workers*. These individuals require training in new skills to implement the profound changes that are shaping the way we think about services for people with disabilities. This chapter describes and discusses underlying changes in the way services are being organized for people with disabilities, the need for specialized training for workers, and *a new educational model built on skill standards and performance-based education and training* for preparing new human service workers and retraining current ones.

Changing Delivery Systems

The philosophy underlying service systems for people with disabilities is in the midst of profound changes. Historically, people with disabilities were removed from the community and "placed" in large institutional settings that focused on medical and custodial care. In the mid-1960s, based in part on a recognition of appalling conditions in many of our nation's institutions, the focus began to shift to community-based treatment. This era of "deinstitutionalization" witnessed the movement of large numbers of people out of the institutions and into the community. Further, new admissions to institutions began to decline considerably. Community services were created to provide services to formerly institutionalized persons. However, in many cases, these programs have failed to replicate the scope of services formerly provided by institutions, and many individuals living in the community remain underserved.

Beginning in the mid-1980s a new paradigm, or model, emerged that is revolutionizing the way we think about designing services for people with disabilities. Fueled by dissatisfaction with existing models, demands from consumers and families, and an increasing recognition that people with disabilities—including those with severe disabilities—can live productive lives in the community if sufficient supports are available, this new paradigm acknowledges that people with disabilities are capable of making choices about their own lives, respects their right to do so, and focuses on individualized supports and empowerment. Bradley and Knoll (1990) identify four major attributes of this new paradigm, or delivery system.

The Importance of the Community.   The new paradigm rests on the fundamental belief that people with disabilities can, and should, live in communities as full participating members. The role of service providers is to identify and remove barriers to full community participation.

Emphasis on Human Relations.   People with disabilities have the same needs for social connectedness as any other persons living in communities. A fundamental task of service providers is to ensure that people make social connections and become fully integrated into the life of the community. These social relationships make it possible for people with disabilities to make use of natural supports in their communities.

Person-Centered Programming.   This view of services for people with disabilities argues against the notion of fitting people into available program "slots." Instead, functional supports must be designed to respond to the unique situation of each

individual in his or her community. People with disabilities should live in homes, not in programs, and they should work in jobs, not in workshops. Program planning must include the full array of family members, friends, service providers, advocates, and, most importantly, the consumer or person actually receiving the service.

Choice and Control.   The new paradigm rejects the notion that "the professionals know best." Instead, it recognizes the right of consumers to make choices about where and with whom they live, how they spend their time, and how they want their supports configured. The task for community support workers is to assist consumers in making informed choices and to ensure that meaningful choices are available.

This changing vision of how services should be delivered to people with disabilities has major implications for the types of workers required and the training these workers need. As Knoll and Recino note:

> . . . the basic values of personal choice and control, individual quality of life, valued roles, and full community participation for people with developmental disabilities does indeed require the fundamental transformation of words and practice inherent in the support paradigm. However, this promise will be lost if the field does not systematically re-educate itself and develop new workers who are both imbued in this new way of thinking and have the skills needed to undertake the far reaching changes that lie ahead (Knoll and Racino, 1992, p. 5).

DEFINITION OF THE COMMUNITY SUPPORT INDUSTRY

The community support industry that is emerging as a major force in the provision of services to individuals with severe disabilities is composed of those occupations and work settings that provide assistance to a variety of population groups to help them become integrated or reintegrated into their communities and to achieve their greatest levels of positive community participation and independent living.

Scope of the Industry

Client Groups. Individuals whose lives are affected by community support workers comprise a wide cross section of American citizens. Groups include adults with severe and persistent mental illness, children with serious emotional disturbances, adults and children with developmental disabilities, older citizens with physical or psychological infirmities who are living in the community, and adults and children with physical disabilities who live in the community.

Millions of people in this country live with disabling conditions that affect their ability to live independently.

— An estimated 6.6 million persons have *developmental disabilities* that limit their ability to perform major activities (Ashbaugh, 1992). Developmental disabilities include all physical, cognitive, and emotional disorders with an onset prior to age 22.

— It is estimated that between 1.7 million and 2.4 million adults have *severe and persistent mental illness* (Goldman, Gatozzi and Taube, 1981). Research suggests that the vast majority of these individuals can live productive lives in the community *if appropriate supports are provided.*

— Estimates of the number of *children with emotional disturbances* vary considerably. A recent study conducted by the Institute of Medicine estimates conservatively that approximately 12 percent of children under the age of 18 have emotional disturbances (IOM, 1989). Of these 7.5 million children, they estimate that half have a severe emotional disturbance that places them at risk for long-term disabilities and/or out-of-home placement. Because of the inadequacies of most local mental health systems, an alarmingly high number of children with serious emotional disturbances are taken out of their homes and placed in residential or foster care.

— A large number of Americans require *personal assistance* in daily living due to a number of physical impairments. The majority of these persons are elderly. The World Institute on Disability estimated that in 1985, 859,000 persons received personal assistance services through formal programs (WID, undated). This figure represents 11 percent of the estimated 7.7 million persons who are in need of such assistance.

Services Needed. The groups of individuals listed above clearly have some specialized needs

based on the type and severity of their disabilities. Community support workers need to be trained to deal with these differences. However, individuals with a wide range of disabilities also share substantial common needs that transcend the particular disability category. In the community, all of these persons must resolve problems related to housing, food, health care, income, education, employment, transportation, recreation, and developing social relationships. Specific services that community support workers provide for people with disabilities include:

— Assisting consumers to identify their options and make informed choices concerning where and how they will live;

— Training or mentoring in a range of life skills;

— Physical care and assistance;

— Psychological support;

— Vocational assistance;

— Counseling and guidance;

— Housing assistance;

— Legal assistance;

— Financial management assistance;

— Child care;

— Housekeeping;

— Transportation;

— Coordinating specialized services;

— Assisting consumers in developing social relationships;

— Assisting consumers to negotiate entitlement and other service bureaucracies;

— Assisting consumers to identify and mobilize natural supports in the community.

Occupations Providing Community Support Services. Currently, community support services are provided by a limited number and type of occupational groups. One of the major deficits in the way community services are currently configured is that the occupational groups providing these services tend to focus on one or a few specialized areas of need. Workers are not trained to provide the diversity of community support services required by people with disabilities who live in the community. The occupational groups that may provide some services to the population in need include:

— Trainer/mentor;

— Direct support staff;

- Vocational support staff;
- Residential support staff;
- Therapy aide;
- Services coordinator;
- Advocate;
- Teaching aide;
- Social service aide;
- Child care aide;
- Health care aide;
- Legal aide;
- Financial management aide;
- Case worker;
- Case manager;
- Personal assistant.

Work Sites. Several decades ago, people with disabilities received most services through large institutional facilities. Marked changes have occurred in the place of treatment, residential services, and employment services over the years for all disability groups. A few examples will illustrate the magnitude of this trend.

Treatment Settings. Historically in the mental health field, the major treatment site was the large state psychiatric institution. Over half a million individuals were residents of state psychiatric institutions in 1955. By 1986, this figure had declined to approximately 111,000—a decrease of 80 percent (NIMH, 1990a). Statistics on the growth of ambulatory mental health organizations demonstrate where the field has been moving over the past several decades. The number of ambulatory mental health organizations grew from 1,372 in 1970 to 2,221 in 1986. The number of additions to these settings nearly tripled during this same period, moving from 761,572 in 1969 to 2.2 million outpatients (NIMH, 1990b). Increasingly, the emphasis is on "wrap around" efforts designed to support children and adults with mental illness at home and schools.

Residential Settings. Four general trends are evident in the review of residential services for

people with mental retardation and related disabilities during the decade:

- Continued reduction in the use of large state institutions (down 37 percent or more than 100,000)
- Increased utilization of small facilities, i.e., those serving 15 or fewer individuals (up nearly 200 percent)
- Decreased overall rates of residential placement as a proportion of the total population (down 9 percent) with stabilization since 1982; and
- Particularly significant decreases in the rate of residential placement for children and youth, most dramatically in state institutions (down over 200 percent), but also in all types of residential placements (down 45 percent).

The growth in the Home and Community-based Waiver Program, the Medicaid-funded alternative to institutions, is an indication of the move to community-based supports. Between 1988 and 1992, the number of persons served under the Waiver more than doubled—48 states now utilize the waiver. More recently states have moved to supported living and family support services. These programs were recently given a boost from Medicaid under the Community Supported Living Arrangement (CSLA) program.

Employment Settings. As with other service areas, employment services are moving away from large segregated sheltered workshop settings and into the community via the supported employment initiative which began to take form during the mid-1980s. The Virginia Commonwealth University (OSERS, 1990) recently completed a national study of supported employment for people with all disabilities. Their data suggest a remarkable growth in the number of individuals receiving supported employment over a very short period. Between 1986 and 1989, the number of persons receiving these services grew from approximately 10,000 to nearly 52,000—*a 426 percent increase.* There is every reason to expect that this phenomenal rate of growth will continue, provided adequate staff is available.

Clearly, the trend in services for people with disabilities is away from large institutional programs that limit individual choice and maximize segregation and toward those models that are individualized, integrated into the community, and offer consumers choices in how they live their lives. Increasingly, *community support workers* are working in the full array of community agencies including:

- Individual homes and apartments:
- Community residences for adults and children with emotional or developmental disabilities;
- Community based agencies;
- Supported work environments;
- Sheltered workshops;
- Job sites;
- Schools;
- Nursing homes;
- Hospitals (including psychiatric hospitals);
- Day care centers for children, individuals with psychiatric or developmental disabilities, or the elderly;
- Shelters for the homeless;
- Community recreation sites.

These changes in work sites have profound implications for staff training. A decade ago, entry-level staff worked in settings that allowed for close on-site supervision. Today, this same entry-level staff is out in the community, working independently, with few opportunities for monitoring and supervision. They must have considerably more training. As Stein and Test have noted (1974, p. 669):

> —in vivo *community treatment is chaotic—surprise is the name of the game. The open community setting allows for an infinite variety of situations. In addition, each staff member spends most of his time working alone and must make on-the-spot decisions alone; an aggregate staff is not available for psychological or physical support or for diffusion of responsibility. Furthermore,* in vivo *treatment takes place on the patient's territory, resulting in reduced power of the staff. Finally, in addition to dealing with patients, staff members have to learn to relate to a variety of community agencies.*

Other Trends Affecting the Community Support Industry

Two major factors, in addition to the content and nature of community support work, are affecting the community support industry and have relevance to the education and training of community support workers. One factor is increased attention to what expert workers actually do in the industry workplace. This focus has been expressed, for example, in the development of "performance templates" for the human services (Albin, 1992), and "practice guidelines" in areas such as health and mental health (Eddy, 1992; Field and Lohr, 1992). The second factor is the interest in total quality management/continuous quality improvement.

The analysis of expert workers' practices has progressed the furthest in health care, where practice guidelines have been developed in an effort to control health care costs while maintaining quality (Eddy, 1992; Field and Lohr, 1992). However, there is a history of "job analysis" in the human services as well (Fine and Wiley, 1971). Total quality management is an approach to assuring product quality and customer satisfaction developed in Japan and based on the teaching of W. Edwards Demming, an American statistician (Albin, 1990).

Although the analysis of "best" practices and total quality management draws on the expertise of "shop floor" workers, both also stress collaboration between service consumers and service producers in defining and implementing services that are customer driven, effective, and efficient (Albin, 1990; Eddy, 1992; Field and Lohr, 1992; Taylor, 1992). Further, all efforts of these types are based on the idea that education and training must give workers the knowledge and skills to meet customer/consumer needs in an integrated manner that is both cost effective and consistent with consumer preferences. As one quotation, frequently cited in the continuous quality improvement literature, put it:

> Quality control begins with education and ends with education (Dr. Kaoru Ishikawa cited in Muther and Lytle, 1990).

Need for Specialized Training
for Community Support Workers

There is a consensus in the research and policy literature that there is a need for better training of community support workers. Several factors are noted in this regard.

Problems Related to Recruitment and Retention. The provider community is increasingly concerned about their ability to attract competent staff trained to meet the demands of community support work. O'Connor and Sitkei (1973), reporting data from a national survey of community mental retardation facilities, noted that over one-third (37 percent) of providers listed "difficulty of finding qualified staff" as one of the most serious challenges facing their organizations. More recently, Bruininks, Kudla, Wieck and Hauber (1980) surveyed over 2,000 community facilities serving people with mental retardation and noted that the most frequently reported problem faced by these facilities was the recruitment, retention, and development of staff. In this era of fewer financial resources, it is noteworthy that this concern was expressed more often than funding issues.

In addition to recruitment problems, staff retention is a crucial concern. Mitchell and Braddock (1991) recently completed a survey of over 1,600 institutional and community programs for people with developmental disabilities. This national study reported an annual turnover rate among direct care staff in community settings of 70.4 percent. This figure is 15 percent higher than that reported in the only previous national study of direct care staff, which was conducted in 1981 (Lakin and Bruininks, 1981). These data suggest that turnover has increased substantially during the past ten years. Ross's (1983) study of turnover among child care workers in residential care facilities reported a turnover rate of 30–50 percent each year, and 47 percent of that sample had been in their agency for twelve months or less. He also found that lack of career advancement opportunities was a key problem cited by 60 percent of subjects.

These extremely high turnover rates are costly in several ways. In the first place, it costs money to recruit staff and train large numbers of new staff. Secondly, there is the human cost involved when trusted staff members leave a direct care setting and clients are forced to establish relationships with new members. Several studies have documented that one of the major reasons parents favor institutional care over community alternatives is due to staff turnover in community residences (Meyer, 1980; Spreat et al, 1987; Heller et al, 1986).

Turnover is a complex phenomenon and multiple factors are undoubtedly involved in individuals' decisions to leave their jobs. However, the fact that staff members providing community services to people with disabilities are leaving their jobs so soon after starting suggests a poor fit between the attitudes and skills of these workers and their jobs. To the extent that adequate training makes new staff aware of the challenges of community support work and prepares them to deal effectively with these challenges, one would expect turnover rates to decrease. Job satisfaction also has been shown to increase, and turnover to decrease with the job enlargement possible given broadly-trained community support workers. Heretofore, jobs had been narrowed in part to accommodate the limited abilities of personnel available to fill them; this constraint can be loosened considerably, given the skills that better trained community support workers will carry. Further, knowledge and skills acquisition can lay the groundwork for a more articulated career ladder for community support workers, enabling them to move both vertically and horizontally within the field, as opposed to moving out of the field for career advancement.

Traditional Academic Disciplines Are Not Meeting the Needs of This Emerging Profession. The knowledge and skills required of community support workers are not the province of any academic or professional discipline. In fact, as Knoll and Racino (1992) note, many of the newer models for serving people with disabilities have not evolved as a result of formal policies within service systems, but from grass roots efforts to improve the lives of individuals. Many of the ideas are alien to professional training programs and in-service training provided by facility-based programs. As a result, there are few forums in which community support workers can obtain the requisite skills for doing their jobs.

Additionally, the few programs that are currently preparing people for community support work are geared toward post-graduate students. Clearly, there is a continuing need for professional staff with graduate level training. However, services research suggests that in many instances paraprofessionals are capable of providing community support services and are, in fact, a major component of the current workforce. In 1987, the number of employees providing direct care to persons with mental retardation in community-based residential settings alone (excluding those providing treatment and services in institutional settings and in day and other services) was estimated at 120,000 full time equivalent positions; 80,000 of these positions were held by persons without college degrees (Lakin, 1987). Similarly, research suggests that as much as 80 percent of direct care for persons with severe mental illness is provided by generalists and paraprofessionals (including individuals with bachelor's degrees) (DHHS, 1980).

There Is a Distinct Body of Knowledge to Be Imparted.   Despite the limited availability of formal curricula to train community support workers, there is an emerging body of knowledge that can be organized into an effective training protocol. The skills and qualities that are required include:

— Communication skills: workers need to cultivate excellent listening skills as well as ways of getting a message across in a way people can hear. It means being able to persuade, teach, express oneself, and defend oneself.
— Community organization skills: workers need to understand a community and know how to plan strategies to marshall community resources to meet the needs of its members.

— Advocacy skills: workers must do what it takes to change or create a situation that allows people with disabilities to obtain what they need. Community organization and advocacy are inexorably linked.
— Persistence: Workers will need determination to keep at the job because changes won't happen fast.
— Bridge building: This core skill area concerns making the connections to people and organizations that allow people with disabilities to develop real and meaningful roles for themselves. This is something that people with disabilities have traditionally had tremendous difficulty with because of the segregated nature of their lives. It takes connections to make connections.
— The ability and commitment to identify strengths in people and groups;
— Genuine respect for diverse perspectives and lifestyles;
— Skill and creativity in helping people become more aware and confident of their own abilities;
— Appreciation of when to step back and ability to help the individual or group assume decision making and action;
— Ability to analyze power relationships and help others to do so;
— Knowledge about how to gain access to information, not only about resources in the community, but also about government entitlement programs;
— Ability to reflect on and criticize ongoing processes, including one's own role in those processes;
— Autonomy: Human service workers increasingly will be on their own, with less direct supervision as they work to assist people to become independent, productive and included. Meeting the challenges of the job will require that people think on their feet and have good common sense.

The changing context of community services for people with disabilities requires a more highly skilled workforce. New work settings will require workers capable of performing diverse tasks with little on-site supervision. The development of skill standards is recognized by all stakeholders in the industry as an important next step in improving services to consumers, increasing the marketability of workers, and improving the efficiency and effectiveness of the industry. The existence of skill standards sets a high quality benchmark toward which educators can aim when preparing people for human services work. Beginning-level workers who have mastered the core body of knowledge and competencies contained in a broad-based set of skill standards for a whole industry will be ready to begin work in a range of entry occupations, with people requiring a variety of services, in various settings. They will also be prepared to learn the more specific skills required to work with different population groups. Their basic knowledge of the industry and core skills will help enhance the efficiency of service delivery and operations. This will increase their value to employers, which may lead to higher wages. Their knowledge of the industry structure will help them to foresee career opportunities which, in turn, should increase motivation for higher performance.

A NEW TRAINING MODEL FOR HUMAN SERVICE WORKERS

Preparing community support workers for the new *human services delivery system* will require a new *education and training model* that builds on the vision and reality of community-based services. We refer to this as an industry-based paradigm. *This paradigm has four components, linked by their emphasis on the industry workplace as both the source of education content and a primary locus of training.* The components of an industry-based approach to workforce education are: (a) collaborative planning among all stakeholders, (b) the "training occupation," (c) "integrated skill standards," and (d) combined school and work-based education (Education Development Center, 1992). In this section we will describe each of these components.

Collaborative Planning by Consumers and Other Stakeholders

Workforce education and training has important consequences for a number of stakeholders: employers, current workers, educators, students, and consumers of the products or services. All of these stakeholders must be involved from the

beginning in efforts to improve workforce education and training in order to: (a) ensure their needs are taken into account, (b) utilize their expertise, (c) legitimize their stake in the process and outcomes, and (d) gain "buy-in" from all parties to develop and implement the strategy. Each of these stakeholder groups has a unique and crucial role to play in developing innovative workforce education and training.

Employers.   Since the mid-1980s, employers have called for better educated workers (Carnevale, 1989). Much of the impetus for this has been realization that the United States is losing ground, in some industries, to foreign competitors. These competitors often produce higher quality goods with more efficient methods than do American producers (Dertouzos, Lester and Solow, 1989). In all industries, including those such as the human services industry that do not compete in the international marketplace, employers are recognizing the need to become more efficient—to cut costs and produce higher quality goods and services. A highly skilled workforce is considered the single most important requisite for greater productivity and higher quality production (National Center on Education and the Economy, 1990).

Even though employers are spending substantial amounts on worker training—about $30 billion per year (Government Accounting Office, 1991)—they still are dependent on the education system to meet their labor force needs. Workforce education must be targeted to these labor market needs. Employers know how their industries are developing and what the labor needs will be in the future. Their expertise is needed to help determine *what* subject matter should be learned and *how* the subject matter should be taught.

Current Workers.   Workers have an important stake in the improvement of workforce education and training because the acquisition of new skills and knowledge will allow them to advance their careers. Workers know better than anyone what tasks they perform in their jobs and what skills and knowledge are needed to perform these jobs. They also know the "craft" of their jobs—the subtle techniques that form the bridge between the skills and knowledge and successful performance. Therefore workers must play a central role in defining what people should learn for a given occupation, or group of occupations.

There are several techniques for analyzing the content of jobs, in which workers play an active role. These include intensive interviews with researchers, as well as focus groups and structured processes by which workers analyze the duties (major work responsibilities) and tasks (more specific pieces of work) they perform, and the knowledge and skills required to perform their work (Norton, 1985, V-TECS, Barley, 1993; Darrah, 1991–1992).

Current workers also should participate in the education of future workers. Work-based learning is most effective when trainees learn from experienced workers, such as in an apprenticeship program. In this kind of situation, students learn not only the skills but also the craft of a job.

Educators.   Educators (teachers and administrators) must be involved in efforts to improve the quality of both academic and work-related education. Experienced, skilled educators are knowledgeable about a variety of pedagogical techniques that facilitate learning. We will discuss some techniques that are particularly appropriate for our new education and training paradigm later in this chapter. By working closely with employers and workers, as well as through firsthand experience (such as internships in workplaces), they also can acquire the education content that people need to learn. This will allow them to blend the pedagogic techniques that are most appropriate for the education and training goals.

Students.   Students clearly are direct beneficiaries of collaboratively planned workforce educa-

tion programs. *All* students can benefit from greater knowledge of career options, and the education requirements for them. Ideally, general career awareness and exploration should be provided to all students before they enter high school. Students who have the biggest stake in a new workforce education paradigm are those at risk of dropping out of school, or those who will enter the labor force with little or no college education. These students must learn skills that are needed and valued in the workplace if they are to enter any occupation with career opportunities. Right now the education system is failing them (William T. Grant Foundation, 1988). Unlike other major industrialized countries, the United States has no system for preparing young people who are not going directly to college for meaningful work and careers.

We know that most of these young people become chronically unemployed or underemployed, drifting from one low-paid, dead-end job to another. They have a great stake in education and training programs that are industry-driven—that is, targeted to real workplace needs.

Industry-focused education and training is more likely to appeal to "at risk" or nonacademically-oriented students because it can incorporate real life applications more readily than can strictly academic approaches. It is important for these students to participate in collaborative planning to help educators and others better understand what subject matter and learning strategies would work best for them.

Consumers.   According to total quality management theory, all production should be consumer-driven. That is, the primary goal of producers should be to satisfy the consumer. It makes sense, therefore, for consumers to help design the programs to educate high quality future workers. The participation of consumers in the planning of education for future workers is particularly crucial in the human services industry. This is because human services consumers—recipients of services and their families—often are completely dependent on these services, usually have no alternative options, and have no control of the market. For these reasons, we emphasize the importance of consumer participation in the planning of education programs for human services workers. Having a say about the preparation of skilled, knowledgeable, compassionate service providers is one of the only sources of leverage (in addition to lobbying for social legislation and funding) that consumers have in the human services industry.

The Training Occupation

The second element of our training paradigm includes the concept of the "training occupation." Most workforce education programs developed in the United States have been targeted to narrowly defined occupations. Occupation-specific programs focus on a particular job, as traditionally defined by the industry or workplace. For example, in the human services, a narrowly defined occupation is a "vocational support staff person." A person who graduates from a training program designed for that occupation should be qualified to perform that particular job.

In contrast to a narrowly defined occupation, a "training occupation" is not an existing job, but a hypothetical composite of many related occupations that require a similar core of skills and knowledge. A training occupation in the human services could be a "community support worker," which combines the core of skills and knowledge required by a number of specific occupations, such as a vocational support staff person, trainer/mentor, residential support staff, services coordinator, advocate, social service aide, legal aide, and financial management aide.

Educating people for a training occupation has three very important advantages over preparing them for a narrowly defined occupation. First, broadly prepared workers will be more valuable to employers. They will be more flexible and capable of performing a variety of tasks in a range of work settings. Workers who have a broader base of knowledge and skills will have a more

complete understanding of the goals and work of the entire organization, so they will be able to respond to a broader range of situations. This means that employers will not need to invest as much in on-the-job training of entering workers.

Second, workers educated for training occupations will be more prepared to take advantage of both horizontal and vertical career moves. Because they can work in a range of work settings, in a number of different jobs, they will have a better chance for career advancement. Also, because they will be more flexible, they will be less likely to be laid off than other workers if employers decide to downsize.

The third advantage is that a training occupation more nearly reflects the reality of work performance than do traditional narrow occupations. Workers are being required to assume more work tasks, including management tasks previously performed by supervisors. Organizations striving for greater efficiency are eliminating some job categories and consolidating work tasks for remaining employees. Increasingly, teamwork—which requires individual members to understand the work of every team member—is replacing individual, compartmentalized work. The use of new technologies, such as computers, also is enabling individuals to perform a broader range of tasks.

In addition, work organizations are being required to produce a greater variety of products, to meet a broader range of consumer demands. This is true of organizations that create tangible products and those that provide services. In manufacturing, mass production in which an individual worker performs a single repetitive task, is being replaced by "flexible manufacturing," in which a worker (using computer operated machines that can be easily reprogrammed to produce different products) performs a variety of tasks to produce various products (Piore and Sabel, 1984). The manufacturing process, and the work tasks, can be changed at will to produce goods that are specifically designed to meet individual customers' requirements.

In the service sector, new concepts of how best to provide services to many consumer groups are changing the organization of service delivery in the direction of increased flexibility. The mass production of human service delivery, in which people with a variety of needs are kept in large institutions and provided a standard mix of services, is being replaced with a variety of community care options. The community-based services can combine modules of care into individualized service plans to meet consumers' varied needs. A person working in such a system needs a broad range of skills to provide the range and various combinations of services.

For these three reasons—greater value to employers, greater opportunities for career advancement, and better fit with the work requirements of changing work organizations and production methods—the training occupation is a more appropriate target for skill standards and for worker education than are traditional narrowly defined occupations.

Integrated Skill Standards

The development of standards of all kinds has increased dramatically worldwide since the mid-1980s. A standard is a set of criteria used to measure size, amount, quality, or other attributes of something relative to a benchmark (a desirable example). As trade, collaborative production, and international competition grow, standards are needed to ensure comparability of size, form, and other physical properties, as well as product quality, production efficiency, and health and environmental impacts.[1]

In response to evidence that American students are not learning as much as their counterparts in other countries, national education standards are being developed in the United States in almost every academic subject area (*Education Week*, June 16, 1993).[2] They have existed in most other industrialized countries for many years.

As one part of a growing effort to prepare higher skilled workers for the labor force, efforts are increasing in the United States to create skill standards for workers in many industries and occupations.[3] We first will describe skill standards and examine their uses. Then we will explain why the use of "integrated skill standards" fits best with our education and training approach.

What Are Skill Standards?   Skill standards are criteria for what people must know and be able to do to qualify for work in particular occupations or occupational clusters. Standards provide clear, measurable benchmarks for both the content (skills and knowledge) and the quality (level of performance) required. Their purpose is to ensure that people entering or continuing in an occupational area are qualified to perform it.

[1]Extensive efforts are under way to standardize standards from different countries into international codes. The International Standards Organization (ISO), a worldwide federation of national standards bodies, is developing uniform voluntary standards in such areas as communication (terminology, symbols); quality of raw materials and manufactured projects; storage, packaging and shipping; dimensions of machine parts; safety procedures; environmental protection; and training programs (International Standards Organization, 1984). These uniform standards are essential for growing international trade and technical collaboration.

[2]The European Center for development of Vocational Training (CEDEFOP) has been working since 1985 to cross-reference skill standards and certification among its member nations (CEDEFOP, Comparability of Vocational Training Qualifications: Guide, 1991). This is part of the preparation for unification of Europe into one economy and labor market. The aim is to facilitate the movement of workers freely across Europe and to help employers identify qualified workers in any country.

[3]In 1989, the National Council of Teachers of Mathematics developed the first national standards for what math should be learned at different grade levels in American schools, and for teaching methods. The National Research Council of the National Academy of Sciences is developing standards for science content, teaching, and assessment in the sciences. Similar efforts are under way in the fields of geography, history, social studies, economics, English, foreign languages, civics, the arts, and physical education.

Standards typically include criteria for academic knowledge and skills, such as reading, writing, physical sciences, social sciences, or mathematics. They also include specific technical skills required for jobs—such as drafting for engineers and architects, or laboratory skills for laboratory technicians and scientists. Increasingly, skill standards also include criteria for basic work readiness—such as the ability to organize and manage work, communicate with others, solve problems, make decisions, or work as a team member. These skills are not specific to any job category but are considered necessary for all workers.

Skill standards also include criteria for the level of mastery required for particular occupational groups. For example, the level of achievement required for a medical assistant in a physician's office is lower than that for a registered nurse, although many required skills and knowledge areas are the same. Other such criteria may be, for example, ability to work without supervision, or ability to perform a procedure within a prescribed length of time.

There are examples of skill standards in the United States, but widespread use is only now being considered. A number of skill standards are designed to meet increasing government regulations for environmental protection, consumer health, and worker safety. Some labor unions use skill standards, particularly in industries such as construction, in which the apprenticeship system is used for training. Mastery of precise performance standards is required to progress from apprentice to journeyman status. Some large companies are developing their own skill standards to evaluate prospective employees and to define skills and knowledge required for retraining or promoting current workers.

Skill standards are used by some schools, particularly technical schools and community colleges, as criteria for graduation from occupational training programs. A number of professional organizations also have set standards that members must meet in order to practice. Federal and state government regulations set performance standards for a number of occupations. For example, the Hospital Care Financing Administration developed the Clinical Laboratory Improvement Act, which stipulates education standards for various types of clinical laboratory workers.

In 1990, the U.S. Department of Labor organized the Secretary's Commission on Achieving the Necessary Skills (SCANS) in order to identify the basic "workplace know-how' needed by all workers, regardless of the industry and occupation they enter. After extensive research in a number of industries, they identified five *competencies* and a three-part *foundation* of skills and personal qualities that are needed by all workers (U.S. Department of Labor, 1991). The five competencies are:

— **Resources**: ability to identify, organize, plan, and allocate time, money, material, and facilities, and human resources;
— **Interpersonal**: ability to work with others in teams, teach others new skills, serve clients and customers, exercise leadership, negotiate, and work with a diversity of people;
— **Information**: ability to acquire, evaluate, organize, maintain, interpret, communicate information, and use computers to process information;
— **Systems:** ability to understand, monitor, correct, improve, and design complex social, organizational, and technological inter-relationships;
— **Technology**: ability to select, apply, maintain, and troubleshoot tools and equipment.

The three foundation skills are:

— **Basic Skills**: reading, writing, arithmetic/mathematics, listening, speaking;
— **Thinking Skills**: creative thinking, decision making, problem solving, seeing things in the mind's eye, knowing how to learn, reasoning;
— **Personal Qualities**: responsibility, self-esteem, sociability, self-management, integrity/honesty.

These SCANS skills are being incorporated into the comprehensive skill standards now being developed for a variety of industries and occupations.

Because the requirements for job performance in most occupations change frequently, due to both technological and organizational changes, skill standards must continually be updated. This requires periodic reexamination of jobs to determine how tasks and skill needs are evolving. The most obvious example is the automation of production. Increased use of computer controlled machines has revolutionized the work performed by machine operators in virtually every occupation, and required workers to abandon some manual skills and increase their understanding and ability to operate computer-driven systems.

Integrated Skill Standards.   Skill standards traditionally have been task-specific, designed to measure performance of discreet pieces of work. For example, a person training to become a vocational support staffperson might be asked to "demonstrate how you would teach someone to use the local employment office to find suitable job openings." The student must demonstrate mastery of a series of these individual tasks to be certified to enter that occupation. However, even if the student performs all of these tasks at the prescribed competency level to meet the standard, there is no means of assessing the student's ability to perform multiple, often simultaneous or overlapping tasks, as they occur in real life. There also is no means to measure how a student would respond to unanticipated problems that often require a person to make decisions and plan complex responses.

The "integrated skill standard" is in the form of a simulated, complex, work-based situation, often presenting problems to solve, and designed to measure performance of a number of interrelated tasks (Aring, 1991). In dealing with this situation (by means of both written answers and performance), the student will demonstrate mastery of a number of skills and a range of knowledge. For example, the student preparing to be a vocational support staffperson might be given the following situation:

> *John, who has a history of emotional disturbance and substance abuse, has just been discharged from Central State Hospital, and will be living in the Sara Francis House (a community-based residence). John wants to work, but has a poor work history and hasn't worked in eight years. You are meeting with John in a local McDonald's to help him plan how to do this. What would you do?*

This type of "integrated skill standard" requires the student to respond to a multifaceted situation, sometimes with unanticipated complications. To master the situation, she/he must demonstrate a variety of basic academic skills and knowledge, specialized human service skills and knowledge, generic work-related skills such as problem solving and decision making, and interpersonal skills such as communication and working in a team.

To meet the full criteria for a training occupation (such as a community support worker in the human services), a person would need to demonstrate mastery of a series of integrated skill standards. No one standard could capture all of the tasks, skills, and knowledge required to perform the total job. Also assessment criteria for level of performance (competency) would be attached to each task. To test a person's readiness to enter a training occupation, a larger number of integrated skill standards, requiring a greater number of tasks to be performed, would be required.

Unlike a list of discreet unrelated tasks, integrated standards link together tasks *in context*, as in a real work situation. Therefore, we think that use of these standards best prepares a person for the workforce.

Combined School and Work-Based Education

We have said that our industry-based education and training paradigm emphasizes the industry workplace as both a source of education content and a primary locus of training. We have explained how the participation of employers and workers in the planning process provides the industry-based content of education and training programs. The use of the training occupation and integrated skill standards further ensures that education is geared to the real life context of the industry workplace. We now discuss why industry must be a primary locus for education and training.

We know from our own experience that one of the best ways to learn something is to work alongside a role model or mentor and to practice what we learn in a real life context. This is how most of us learn the skills we use in our everyday lives. It seems logical, then, that the best way to learn many work skills is to study what an experienced worker does and to practice them in the workplace. This is the premise behind the apprenticeship training model.

This learning approach, however logical it may seem, is not the accepted one in the United States. There are two barriers that have blocked its use. One is the belief that academic learning is totally separate from vocational learning, and the other is the perception that learning takes place only in schools.

Academic vs. Vocational Learning

In our current education system, preparation for work is not a specific goal of schools. Education is focused primarily on the development of abstract thinking, toward the goal of creating a liberally educated citizen. Education standards, as they now are defined in the United States, state what people must know to graduate from an *academic* course of study, receive a degree, or qualify for entrance into the next level of academic education. An example is the Scholastic Aptitude Test. This type of education standard cannot be used to measure occupational preparedness. For example, a person might score a 720 on the Math SAT, but have no idea of the mix of skills required to work as an accountant or an engineer.

Only "vocational education" programs, or specific certificate programs, offer education and training for work. Vocational education is stigmatized in the United States as low level learning, requiring "lower order" skills (i.e., manual rather

than cognitive skills). The majority of students who receive high school, associate, or baccalaureate degrees are not specifically prepared to enter any occupation. Only at the graduate school level is workforce preparation a major focus (and then only in nonliberal arts areas, such as business, education, law, social work, etc.). Only at that level of education is vocational education considered respectable.

In reality, most learning and most work combine both abstract thinking and applied activity. For example, anyone who writes as part of their work must know how to put ideas together and express them in words. However, today they also must know how to type on a keyboard. A physician must know how to diagnose illness, as well as to use a stethoscope and fill out a report form. An automobile mechanic must know how to diagnose problems (often with the use of a computer), as well as to fix them. Separating out academic learning from applied learning is artificial.

There is much discussion now about the need to include "career preparation" among the goals of the country's general education system, and to set equally demanding achievement standards for vocational learning as for academic learning (Commission on the Skills of the American Workforce, 1990). If this occurs, the barrier between academic and vocational education will begin to break down.

The Locus of Learning
(Where Learning Takes Place)

The common assumption in our country is that learning takes place in schools and that work takes place in workplaces. Of course we know that learning is work for the student, and that workers learn some things on the job. But we do not generally think of the workplace as a place where students can learn.

In reality, the workplace is becoming increasingly a place where learning is a recognized activity. Growing numbers of companies are offering courses—ranging from computer operations to English as a Second Language—to employees. As employers recognize the need for continuous skill improvement and lifelong learning, they are offering more in-house education and training, as well as forming partnerships with education institutions to develop courses for employees. Virtually no American employers have yet conceived of their organizations as learning sources for young people who are not yet in the labor force, or workers who are not their employees.

This gap between the schools where young people learn, and the workplace where people work is beginning to break down. Companies are sending representatives to schools to talk about the work they do, and are offering company tours to classes. Schools are creating more internships and cooperative work experiences, in which students can spend time in workplaces exploring different occupations and work settings.

Educators are designing more curricula in which workplace applications are *infused* into academic subjects at all grade levels. For example, students learning math may learn how an architect uses geometry, or a medical technician uses algebra to measure results of physiological tests.

As the artificial barrier between academic and vocational learning breaks down, and as realization grows that learning occurs in many places besides the school room, opportunities will open for industry-based learning.

In the next section, we look at an example of such a learning system.

A National Example of an Industry-Based Education and Training Paradigm

The United States is virtually the only advanced industrialized country that has not developed a comprehensive system to prepare young people for the workforce or to retrain experienced workers. Therefore, we must look to other countries to understand how such a system works.

Extensive workforce preparation systems exist in a number of European countries, as well as in Australia and New Zealand. All of these systems contain some or all of the four components we have identified for our education and training paradigm (U.S. General Accounting Office, 1990). However, Germany offers the best example of all of these components functioning together, because it has the most highly developed workforce preparation system.

Over two thirds of German young people are prepared for the work force through an extensive apprenticeship strategy, derived from the guild apprentice training system of the Middle Ages (Munch, 1991). Apprenticeships are offered in 380 training occupations, representing over 20,000 occupations in the workforce. Apprenticeships are provided by most large employers and many smaller employers throughout the country, and apprentices are paid a stipend by the employers.

Students enter apprenticeships after completing secondary school, at age 15 or 16. They spend about three years in training, typically three to four days a week being trained in a work setting by a "master worker" and one to two days studying related subjects in a classroom. Students must meet nationally determined skill standards by passing rigorous final examinations consisting of oral, written, and performance-based tests. These are administered by the joint apprentice training committee comprised of educators, employers, and trade union representatives. People who pass receive "certificates of mastery," which qualify them for jobs in their occupational field anywhere in Germany. Employers throughout the country are assured that people who pass the exams and meet the skill standards are well prepared to enter the occupation cluster for which they were trained.

National level committees of employers, labor unions, and government develop apprenticeship curricula, skill standards, certification criteria, and examinations for individuals completing training programs. The standards stipulate the training plan, length of training, the knowledge and skills to be learned, and the examination requirements. It takes about three years to develop a set of new skill standards for an occupational cluster. Standards are revised about every seven to ten years (sometimes as frequently as every two years, if the occupation is changing rapidly) (Glover, 1993, pp. 38–39).

SUMMARY

Since the 1960s, a number of changes in both the locus of human services delivery and the increasing advocacy role of consumers and family members have placed new demands on human service providers. Foremost among these changes has been the shift of service delivery from large centralized institutions to smaller, decentralized community-based sites, the increasing demands of consumers and family members for personalized services that address individuals' unique needs, and increased inclusion of persons with disabilities into mainstream society. These shifts have generated the development of "community support systems," designed to meet consumers' basic living needs and to promote access to a range of services to enhance people's abilities to live in and participate in the community.

Traditional training programs have not taught human service workers, especially those workers without college degrees, the range of knowledge and skills needed to provide services to a variety of client groups, in varying settings within a community support system. There is a consensus in the field that current preparation of many human services workers is grossly inadequate. This poor preparation, and the resulting lack of fit between attitudes and competencies of these workers and the demands of their jobs, is one major cause of extremely high turnover rates in the industry.

The development of skill standards is recognized by all stakeholders in the industry as an important next step in improving services to consumers, increasing the marketability of workers, and improving the effectiveness and efficiency of the industry. The federal Departments of Education and Labor are currently providing support to coalitions of employers, educators, and labor unions to develop national skill standards for a number of industries (22 industries as of 1995). These coalitions are analyzing entry and mid-level occupations, requiring less than a baccalaureate degree, to create standards for what workers must know and be able to do. The standards will be used as output criteria for the development of career education programs in secondary and postsecondary schools and workplaces throughout the country. These projects will be assisted and coordinated by a National Skill Standards Board, composed of representatives from all of the relevant constituencies.

Human Services Research Institute, in collaboration with the Education Development Center, Inc., has been awarded a grant from the federal Department of Education to develop national skill standards for entry and mid-level positions in the human services industry. In order to do this, the project will:

— Identify the current and anticipated knowledge and skill requirements for people in entry and mid-level "community support worker" occupations in the entire range of industry work settings;

— Develop, based on these findings, standards for skills whose achievement will demonstrate mastery of the required bodies of knowledge and competencies;

— Develop mechanisms to have these standards validated by relevant stakeholders, including representatives from labor, the provider community, educators, human service workers, consumers, and family members;

— Propose these standards as benchmarks for the creation of high quality courses of study, curricula, and teacher development programs in secondary and postsecondary education;

— Define a process of updating these skill standards as new developments in the industry require the learning of new information, skills, and applications;

— Disseminate the information produced by this project to educators, employers, labor unions, consumer and family organizations, and other relevant parties.

In the upcoming years, as a human services student, you will be hearing and reading more and more about skills standards, accountability of treatment, and evaluating and credentialling worker competencies. We hope this article gives you a comprehensive awareness of current changes and issues in preparing human service workers.

REFERENCES

Albin, J. M., (1992). *Quality Improvement in Employment and Other Human Services*. Baltimore: Paul H. Brookes.

Aring, Monika, (1991). *Productive Chicago: Final Report*. Education Development Center.

Ashbaugh, J. W., (1992). "Estimates and Projection of the Number of Adults with Developmental Disabilities in the State of New Mexico and Their Demands for Services through the Year 2000." Human Services Research Institute, Cambridge, MA.

Barley, Stephen R., (1993). *What Do Technicians Do?* Ithaca, NY: Cornell University.

Barley, Stephen R. and Beth A. Bechky. (1993). *In the Backrooms of Science: The Work of Technicians in Science Labs*. Ithaca, NY: Cornell University.

Bradley, V. J. and J. A. Knoll, (1990). *Shifting Paradigms in Services for People with Developmental Disabilities*. Cambridge, MA: Human Services Research Institute.

Bruininks, R., M. Kudla, C. Wieck, and F. Hauber, (1980). Management Problems in Community Residential Facilities. *Mental Retardation* 18, 125–130.

Carnevale, Anthony P., Leila J. Gainer, and Ann S. Meltzer, (1989). *Workplace Basics: The Skills Employers Want*. San Francisco: Jossey-Bass Management Series.

CEDEFOP, (1991). *Comparability of Vocational Training Qualifications: Guide*. Berlin: CEDEFOP.

Commission on the Skills of the American Workforce, (1990). *America's Choice: High Skills or Low Wages!* Rochester, NY: National Center on Education and the Economy.

Darrah, Charles H., (1990). *An Ethnographic Approach to Workplace Skills*. San Jose, CA: San Jose State University.

Darrah, Charles H., (1991). *Workplace Skills in Context*. San Jose, CA: San Jose State University.

Department of Health and Human Services, Steering Committee on the Chronically Mentally Ill, (1980). *Toward a National Plan for the Chronically Mentally Ill*. Public Health Service, U.S. Department of Health and Human Services.

Dertouzos, Michael, Richard Lester, Robert Solow, and the MIT Commission on Industrial Productivity, (1989). *Made in America: Regaining the Productive Edge*. The MIT Press.

Eddy, D. M., (1992). *A Manual for Assessing Health Practices and Designing Practice Policies: The Explicit Approach*. Philadelphia: American College of Physicians.

Field, M. J. and K. N. Lohr, (1992). *Guidelines for Clinical Practice: From Development to Use*. Washington, DC: National Academy Press.

Fine, S. A. and W. W. Wiley, (1971). *An Introduction to Functional Job Analysis: A Scaling of Selected Tasks from the Social Welfare Field*. Washington, DC: The W. E. Upjohn Institute for Employment Research.

The Forgotten Half: Non-College Bound Youth in America, (1988). The William T. Grant Commission on Work, Family and Citizenship. Washington, DC.

General Accounting Office, (August, 1991). *Transition from School to Work: Linking Education and Worksite Training*. Washington, DC.

Glover, Robert, (January, 1993). *Developing a System of Skill Standards and Certification for the Texas Work Force*. Austin: Department of Commerce.

Goldman, H. H., A. A. Gattozzi, and A. C. Taube, (1981). "Defining and Counting the Chronically Mentally Ill." *Hospital and Community Psychiatry* 32(1), 21–27.

Gordon, Patricia, (1992). "A New Program for Direct Care Practice." *Brandeis Review*. Waltham, MA: Brandeis University. Fall, pp. 32–35.

Heller, T., M. A. Bond, and D. Braddock, (1986). "Family Reactions to Institutional Closure." *American Journal of Mental Retardation* 92, 336–343.

Institute of Medicine, Division of Mental Health and Behavioral Medicine, (1989). *Research on Children and Adolescents with Mental, Behavioral and Developmental Disorders: Mobilizing a National Initiative*. Washington, DC: National Academy Press.

International Standards Organization, (1984). *International Organization for Standardization*. ISBN 9–267–10086–6.

Knoll, J. A. and J. A. Racino, (1993). "Field in Search of a Home: An Exploration of the Need for Support Personnel to Develop a Distinct Identity." To appear in Bradley, V. J., J. Ashbaugh, and B. Blaney, eds. *From Vision to Reality: Transforming Service Systems to Systems of Support for Persons with Developmental Disabilities*. Baltimore: Paul Brookes Publishing Co.

Lakin, K. C., (1987). *A Rationale and Projected Need for University Affiliated Facility Involvement in the Training of Paraprofessionals for Direct-Care Roles for Persons with Developmental Disabilities*. Paper presented for the American Association of University Affiliated Programs for presentation to the Consortium for Citizens with Disabilities to support a recommendation for a Direct-Care Training Initiative in the 1987 DD Act.

Lakin, C. and Bruininks, (1981). Occupational Stability of Direct Care Staff of Residential Facilities for Mentally Retarded People. Minneapolis: Univ. of Minnesota Dept. of Psych. Studies.

Leff, Judith and Monika Aring, (1992). *Creating Skill Standards for Entry into the Bioscience Industry: Beginning and Mid-Level Laboratory Practitioners*. Newton, MA: Education Development Center.

Meyer, R.J., (1980). "Attitudes of Parents of Institutionalized Mentally Retarded Individuals Toward Deinstitutionalization." *American Journal of Mental Deficiency* 85, 184–187.

Mitchell, D. and Braddock, D., (1991). *Compensation and Turnover of Direct Care Staff in Developmental Disabilities Residential Facilities: A Summary of Results*. University Affiliated Program in Developmental Disabilities, University of Illinois at Chicago.

Munch, Jacob, (1991). *Vocational Training in the Federal Republic of Germany*. Luxembourg: CEDEFOP.

Muthler, D.L. and L.N. Lytle, (1990). "Quality Education Requirements." In Ernst and Young Quality Improvement Consulting Group, eds. *Total Quality: An Executive's Guide for the 1990s*. Homewood: Business One Irwin.

National Institute of Mental Health, (1990a). *State and County Mental Hospitals, United States and Each State, 1986*. Sunshine, J.H., M.J. Witkin, J.E. Atay, A.S. Fell, and R.W. Manderscheid. DHHS Pub. No. (ADM) 90–1706. Washington, DC: Supt. of Docs., U.S. Govt. Print. Off.

National Institute of Mental Health, Mental Health, United States, (1990). Manderscheid, R.W. and M.A. Sonnenschein, eds. DHHS Pub. No. (ADM) 90–1708. Washington, DC: Supt. of Docs., U.S. Govt. Print Off.

National Research Council, (November, 1992). *National Science Education Standards: A Sampler*. National Research Council. Washington, DC.

Norton, R.E., (1985). *DACUM Handbook*. National Center for Research in Vocational Education. Columbus, OH: Ohio State University.

O'Connor, G., and E. Sitkei, (1973). *The Study of a New Frontier in Community Services: Residential Facilities for Developmentally Disabled Persons*. Eugene, OR: University of Oregon, Rehabilitation Research and Training Center in Mental Retardation.

Office of Special Education and Rehabilitation Services, (1990). OSERS News in Print. Vol III, No. 3, 7–13.

Piore, Michael J., and Charles F. Sabel, (1984). *The Second Industrial Divide: Possibilities for Prosperity*. New York: Basic Books.

Ross, A.L., (1983). "Mitigating Turnover of Child Care Staff in Group Care Facilities." *Child Welfare*, Vol. LXII, No. 1, 63–67.

Spreat, S., J.L. Telles, J.W. Conroy, C. Feinstein, and J.J. Colombatto, (1987). "Attitudes Toward Deinstitutionalization: National Survey of Families of Institutionalized Persons with Mental Retardation." *Mental Retardation* 25, 267–274.

Stein, L.I., and M.A. Test, (1974). "Retraining Hospital Staff for Work in a Community Program in Wisconsin." *Hospital and Community Psychiatry*, vol. 25, pp. 669–672.

Stevens, R.L., (1990). *Challenges in Developing Quality Services Supporting Citizens With Developmental Disabilities Living in Community Environments: A New Approach to Professional Staff Training*. Copenhagen, Denmark.

Stevens, R.L., (1990). *Professional Pedagogical Assistance for Mentally Retarded in Community-Based Sheltered Care in Denmark*. Copenhagen, Denmark.

Stevens, R.L., *The Advanced Training of Social Pedagogues*. Copenhagen, Denmark.

Taylor, D., (1992). The Joint Commission Quality Assessment and Improvement Model. In Mattson, M., ed. *Manual of Psychiatric Quality Assurance*. Washington, DC: American Psychiatric Association, 69–78.

Thurow, Lester, (1992). *Head to Head: The Coming Economic Battle Among Japan, Europe, and America*. New York: William Morrow and Company.

U. S. Department of Labor, (June, 1991). Secretary's Commission on Achieving Necessary Skills (SCANS). *What Work Requires of Schools: A SCANS Report for America 2000*. Washington, DC.

U. S. General Accounting Office (GAO), (May, 1990). *Training Strategies: Preparing Noncollege Youth for Employment in the U.S. and Foreign Countries*. GAO\HRD 90-88. Washington, DC: U.S. Government Printing Office.

Viadero, Debra and Peter West, (June 16, 1993). "Standards Deviation: Benchmark-Setting is Marked by Diversity." *Education Week* Vol XII, Number 38.

Vocational Technical Education Consortium of States (V-TECS), (1991). *Commission on Occupational Education Institutions*. Decatur, GA: Southern Association of Colleges and Schools.

KEY TERMS FOR PART TWO

In completing Chapters 3, 4, and 5 in Part Two you should have an understanding of the following key terms, major concepts, and principle topical references:

Fieldwork	Student Logs and Journals	Community Support Worker
Internship	Supervisory Conferences	Performance-Based Training
Externship	Fieldwork Seminar	Deinstitutionalization
Council for Standards in Human Services Education (CSHSE)	Field Practicum Evaluation	Person-Centered Programming
	Case Record	Performance Templates
	Case Conference	Total Quality Management
Field Practicum Standards	Informed Decision	Education/Training Templates
Field Placement	Developmental Disabilities	Consumers
Field Supervision	Worker Self-Awareness	Integrated Skills Standards

PIVOTAL ISSUES FOR DISCUSSION OF PART TWO

1. When should human services students begin their exposure to field experiences? Should volunteer work be given college credit toward completing the baccalaureate degree? Why? Should past job (or perhaps life) experience be given credit? Why?

2. Why should students be required to carry professional liability insurance in field work placements?

3. Under what circumstances should field work students be denied placement in an agency and/or terminated from such a placement? How should fellow students be involved in the review and decision process?

4. Why is credentialling (i.e., licensure, certification, registration, etc.) a critical issue for future human services workers?

5. Make a list of the ten most important skills human service workers need to have; the ten most important bodies of knowledge; the ten most important values. Can these be measured or tested for in human services students? How? When? Where? By whom?

SUGGESTED READINGS FOR PART TWO

1. CSHSE. (1989, Sept.). *Field Work in Human Services Education.* Monograph Issue #6.

2. *Roles and Functions for Mental Health Workers.* (1969). SRED, Atlanta.

3. Maloney, D.C., (1982). *Field Work Manual.* Fitchburg State College Press, Fitchburg, MA.

4. Russo, J.R., (1980). *Serving and Surviving as a Human Services Worker.* Montenez, GA: Brooks/Cole Publications.

5. Schulman, E.D., (1991). *Intervention in Human Services: A Guide to Skills and Knowledge,* 4th ed. New York: MacMillan Press.

PART THREE

HUMAN SERVICES: THEORIES, METHODS, AND MODELS OF DELIVERING HELP

Part Three includes 5 chapters in which you will learn about the usefulness of theories (Chapter 6), and the different ways of helping individuals (Chapter 7) and groups (Chapter 8). You will also become acquainted with the history and current human services efforts in the schools.

You will recall that in Part Two you were exposed to a broad array of how skills and competencies are developed and expressed in the human service profession. As practitioners in the field exercise their roles and responsibilities, they do so from a variety of different theoretic frameworks and orientations. As you are trained in this field, you will realize the connection between how people are served in different intervention models and how these approaches are linked and grounded to broader, more conceptual views of how people develop and change.

In Chapter 6, Sally Fullerton presents a well-focused review of how theory is linked to practice, what general purposes theories provide, and how theory specifically is used and incorporated in human services intervention and education. In the upcoming chapters you will come to see how these latter points are expanded on and elaborated, and how theory and practice are continuously and consistently integrated within the professional field of human services.

After becoming acquainted with the importance of theory, you will read Chapters 7 and 8, which deal with practice. Here methods of direct helping for individuals and groups will be discussed. The work of the human service professional is based on a "generalist" model of generic skills. This chapter presents the practical application of these generic skills to individuals and groups. It will give you an opportunity, as a beginning student, to see how the human service professional applies his or her skills in working with these client situations. It will also show students how these skills are derived from, and reflect upon, a broad base of theoretical concepts and principles.

Individual human service work can vary extensively and can be directed to a wide variety of different clients. In Chapter 7, Anita Runyan discusses helping services for individuals. The chapter identifies both common and critical elements of effective individual human services, as well as showing numerous examples of student-centered experiences in field work that characterize the range and scope of human services work and its inherent diversity. These elements include "helper motivation," knowledge, and specific skills which, when acquired, have applicability in a variety of settings.

To expand the focus on how skills are applied in human services, Barbara Somerville, in Chapter 8, carefully outlines how human service workers are typically involved with clients as groups and what the introductory student should be aware of in studying group dynamics and group functioning. From this chapter you will know how groups are organized and how professionals in the field work with groups. You will also learn about the characteristics of groups, their stages of development, and the role of leadership.

Together these three chapters show how theories and methods work together and are applied with the two major categories of client intervention work, individual human services and work involving groups. As this material and information is digested and integrated, students like yourself will then better understand and appreciate the specific examples of how human services functions in a specific and common community-based setting, namely the local school system. This will be the focus of Chapters 9 and 10, which describe the functional application of human services to the community or local school district. In this situation, students can see how a wide variety of direct and non-direct services are delivered in a setting familiar to everyone.

In Chapter 9, Andrew Parlin and Kenneth Grew introduce the student to a broader and more historical description of how schools have progressively expanded their respective role in helping people. They provide an extensive reference to federally-sponsored programs that collectively help to improve school-based services to those physically, mentally, culturally, or educationally deprived or handicapped.

With this rich, descriptive backdrop you will more fully appreciate the contemporary efforts of collaboration between community schools and higher education described by Rob Lawson and Peggy Anderson in Chapter 10. This chapter discusses innovative and creative programs, projects, and models, as well as implications for future impacts on schools, families, students, agencies, and communities. You will be convinced that for our schools to accomplish their educational mission, it will be necessary for the human services effort to reach beyond the pupil to the family and community.

A Special Focus Feature by Michael Seliger is included here that describes a training model of helping by an educational program, the Bronx Educational Opportunity Center. The presentation includes a description of the work at the center and two case studies of individuals who were helped.

After completing Part Three you will be ready to explore some of the career considerations in the human services profession. Part Four will deal with legal and ethical issues, professional growth, personal qualities, and burnout.

LEARNING OBJECTIVES FOR PART THREE: THEORIES, METHODS, AND MODELS OF DELIVERING HELP

— You will understand the role and relationships of theory in the development of practices and techniques of helping others.

- You will know how agencies and schools work together in developing economic, efficient, and effective service programs.
- You will see how individual client services operate and what these services require from human service workers delivering those services.
- You will be familiar with how groups are employed in human services and what skills human services workers need in order to utilize group approaches.
- You will become aware of the evolution of human services in the history of education.
- You will be exposed to several examples of relevant models of human service delivery systems and how these models integrate students, clients, and services.
- You will see how groups of people of different ages can be successful in the delivery of human services.
- You will understand how schools are becoming critically important centers for community support services.

CHAPTER 6

THEORIES AS TOOLS AND RESOURCES FOR HELPING

SALLY FULLERTON

In human services, as in other helping professions, theory and practice are sometimes seen as two different realms. Some students, for example, view theory as required learning in the classroom and believe that when they leave school and get out into the "real world," they will put theory behind them and develop practice skills that are relevant to their clientele.

Similarly, some community service agency personnel claim not to have a theory base for their individual practice or for the service delivery system of the agency itself. In fact, practitioners have been criticized for operating too much from an impressionistic ad hoc basis rather than from an approach built on solid theory and research (Turner, 1986; Editors interview, W. B. Utting; 1984).

People who separate theory from practice generally see theory as unimportant, unrelated to practice, or even counterproductive. For example, some practitioners believe that basing their practice on a theoretical model would force them to treat all their clients the same without regard to individual, cultural, or situational differences. In reality, however, all human services work is based on a set of assumptions about human behavior and dysfunction, whether or not those assumptions have been articulated or organized into a coherent theory.

The purpose of this chapter is to examine the value of having a clearly articulated, coherent, and tested theoretical foundation for individual practice, for human service delivery systems, and for human service education.

WHAT IS THEORY?

A *theory* is a coherent statement of assumptions regarding a set of phenomena that provides a basis for explanation and prediction of those phenomena. According to Turner (1986) theory includes concepts, facts, principles, and hypotheses. *Concepts*, he says, are agreed-upon terms developed by a discipline to describe the phenomena with which it is dealing. *Facts* are aspects or relationships of the phenomena that have been empirically verified. *Principles* are general statements based on a set of concepts and facts. *Hypotheses* are hunches or predictions regarding the phenomena that are capable of being empirically tested. As hypotheses are tested, new facts emerge, which in turn provide additional support for the general theory or require some modifications of it.

To illustrate, these components of theory can be viewed in terms of theories of human development and behavior that are fundamental to human services work. These theories are composed of assumptions about how behavior is influenced by such things as internal human mechanisms, learned behavioral responses, and influences of the broader social environment. Examples of *concepts* used in these theories include genetic predispositions, motivation, operant conditioning, role taking, and social support. The *facts* upon which a theory is based are the research findings that support the general assumptions of that theory. For example, there is considerable empirical evidence that social support can moderate the amount of stress experienced by individuals (Whittaker and Garbarino, 1983). Examples of general *principles* are such statements as "all behavior is learned" or "social support buffers stress" or "alcoholism is a disease."

Theories are continually tested and modified through the generation and testing of *hypotheses*, which are derived from the theory. Examples of testable hypotheses are that anorexic behavior is related to low self-esteem, or that dropping out of school is related to juvenile delinquency. The testing and development of theory is done on all levels ranging from broad-scale scientific research studies to individual practitioners. Well-designed empirical studies are essential for the formal testing of hypotheses, which then contribute to the continual development of theories. Testing on an individual level is important also. As a practitioner working from a well-articulated theoretical foundation, you will test the theory daily as you observe how useful it is in helping you understand causes of problems and predict outcomes. This cumulative clinical wisdom will certainly help you modify your own personal theoretical model for practice. It could also form the basis for empirical research that could add to the general knowledge base.

How Is Theory Useful in Practice?

Kurt Lewin is credited (Turner, 1986) with the idea that nothing is as practical as a good theory. Indeed there are many ways in which a solid understanding of theory contributes to a practitioner's effectiveness. Six of these ways will be explored here:

1. Theory provides a guide for the kind of information to gather in working with individuals, families, groups, organizations, or communities.
2. Theory provides a framework for organizing and interpreting the information one acquires.

3. Theory provides a basis for identifying problem-solving alternatives, designing interventions, and predicting outcomes.
4. Theory provides a basis for designing preventive, as well as remediative, strategies.
5. Theory provides a means for improving accountability, consistency, and communication among workers in a given setting.
6. Knowledge of theory can enhance the confidence of practitioners.

Theory as a Guide for Information Gathering. Suppose that you have just started a new job in an agency that works with adolescent alcohol abusers. You are about to interview your first client, a young woman named Jane. The agency does not have a structured intake questionnaire. What kind of information will you seek about Jane and her situation?

Your basic theoretical assumptions about causation of alcoholism and related problems will guide your interview. For example, if you assume that genetic predisposition is an important factor in alcoholism, you would probably want to learn about Jane's family history regarding alcohol. If you believe that drinking patterns of youth are strongly influenced by family modeling or peer pressure, you would want a picture of the kinds of situations in which Jane uses alcohol, the other people present in these situations, and the kinds of pressure to drink that she feels in these situations. If your theoretical perspective includes the assumption that the normative structure of the social environment is an important determinant of individual behavior, you might want to gather information outside of your interview with Jane in order to learn more about the standards established by Jane's school and community regarding alcohol use. Whatever your theoretical approach, you will want to gather information to test your hunches (hypotheses) about what might be contributing to Jane's problems.

Workers without a clear understanding of their own theoretical assumptions risk collecting information they will not use; for example, asking certain questions simply because they believe it is customary to ask such questions; or they will omit questions that would result in crucial information for understanding and problem solving. Seeking information that is not useful could result in a waste of time for you and Jane, as well as a possible invasion of her privacy. Neglecting to seek certain types of information could seriously hamper your effectiveness in problem solving. The information-gathering stage of the helping process, therefore, is much more focused and purposeful if the interview questions are directly related to a coherent theory or group of theories.

Theory as a Framework for Interpretation. Suppose you have now had a very productive interview with Jane in which you have obtained a great deal of information about her and her situation. What do you do with all that information?

Since the concepts, facts, and assumptions of theories are organized into a coherent statement, an *organizational framework* is already available into which you can fit the specific information regarding this individual. As you fit the information about Jane into the framework of the theoretical model you are using regarding causation and consequences of alcohol abuse, research findings related to this theory will help you recognize patterns and guide your interpretation and understanding of Jane's situation. For example, theories of alcoholism have identified a progression of behaviors from experimental use to dependency. If you find that Jane's drinking pattern includes frequent episodes of solitary and secretive drinking, you would probably judge her problem to be much more serious than if she limits herself to party drinking only, since secretive drinking is typically further along in this established progression (Milam and Ketcham, 1983).

In basing interpretations on comparisons with research findings and theoretical assumptions, it is important to remember, of course, that the particular individual with whom you are working may not fit the pattern for a variety of reasons related to age, gender, race, culture, or individual uniqueness. Although researchers in recent years are paying more attention to selecting subjects representative of the diversity in our population, many research studies still do not have adequate sample selection. A good example of this is the recent revelation in the field of health that a number of long-accepted principles, based primarily on studies of male subjects, do not apply to women.

Even with theories and research findings which are drawn from studies of widely diverse populations, there may still be wide variations of responses among individuals within the studies. For example, research findings show that anorexia is more common among young women who have low self-esteem than among men, older women, or young women with high self-esteem. However, some subjects in these anorexia research studies who are men, older women, or women with high self-esteem may have anorexia—they just are not as likely to as the young women with low self-esteem.

It is also important to remember that the emphasis in human service work is on assessing and trying to understand the client's situation *with* the client rather than on making independent professional diagnoses of the client. Such collaboration serves as a constant reminder to keep the uniqueness of the client's situation in mind as one utilizes principles and research from theory.

Theory as a Basis for Selecting Interventions and Predicting Outcomes. The problem-solving model espoused by Woodside and McClam (1990 a,b) is the primary method of treatment in human services, and involves the steps of (1) problem identification, (2) goal setting, (3) development and assessment of alternatives, (4) decision making, and (5) evaluation. In terms of this problem-solving model, we have just discussed that operating from a theory base is important in acquiring and interpreting the information one needs in identifying and understanding a problem. Step 2, goal setting, is largely a *value* issue, where judgments are made regarding desirable outcomes; however, some theories imply desirable end states well. In steps 3, 4, and 5, theory provides a basis for predicting outcomes, i.e., for developing hypotheses about what would work in resolving the problem and for evaluating the accuracy of those predictions.

For example, suppose that your theoretical framework is based on sociological theories that individual behavior is strongly influenced by the norms and expectations of people in one's social environment, and in support of this theory, research shows that peer pressure is a powerful contributor to adolescent substance abuse. From this theoretical perspective you could predict that either reducing peer pressure or strengthening ability to resist peer pressure would reduce substance abuse in a group of adolescents. One or both of these could be used as *intervention strategies*. Although this theory and research suggest that substance abuse is a problem, whether your *goal* was responsible use or complete abstinence is also partly a value judgment. With clearly specified goals, intervention strategies, and predicted outcomes, you could systematically evaluate the effectiveness of your interventions. Without the use of theoretical principles and research as a foundation for generating alternatives and selecting an intervention, a worker is much more likely to rely on guesswork, or trial and error.

Theory as a Basis for Preventive Interventions.
During the last two decades, a great deal of interest has developed in learning how to prevent problems rather than waiting until they become serious before intervening. In the early days of efforts to prevent problems, however, it was difficult for workers to determine who should be the clientele and how people could be "helped" when they did not yet have "the problem." Well-researched theories of causation were the solution to this dilemma. By using the theories to identify the multiple factors that contribute to the development of a certain type of problem, like adolescent substance abuse for example, one could identify possible targets for change and youth who were most "at-risk." Prevention is discussed in much greater detail in another chapter in this book.

Theory as a Basis for Improving Accountability, Consistency, and Communication.   Consistency and communication among workers in a human service agency are facilitated if the workers share a common theoretical perspective. Teamwork is easier if workers share assumptions about causality, have common goals, and use similar intervention strategies. Using concepts with agreed-upon meanings adds precision to communication and reduces the need for lengthy explanations in staff meetings and report writing. For example, in an agency that uses a behavioral model, common understanding of such terms as base rates and reinforcement schedules would facilitate communication among the workers.

Accountability can also improve in an agency where workers operate within a clearly defined theoretical model, because program evaluation can be designed on the basis of the theoretical model and predicted outcomes of the agency's service delivery system. For example, in an agency that serves developmentally disabled adults within a behavioristic theoretical model, specific client behavioral outcomes could be delineated and data could be collected to see how well these outcomes were being achieved through the services delivered by the agency. Not only could individual workers in the agency be held accountable for accomplishing the specified goals of the agency, but the organization itself could be evaluated in terms of the effectiveness of its service delivery system.

Theory as an Enhancer of Practitioner Confidence.   There is support for the idea that practitioners who feel confident in what they are doing are more effective in helping clients (Frank, 1961). A helper who has a clear idea of what to explore in assessing a client's situation, can recognize patterns, is familiar with the research on problem causation, is about to make predictions based on the theory, and knows what has worked in similar situations can certainly proceed more confidently than one who has to rely on impressions of the moment. This confidence can be transmitted to the clients as well, making them more receptive to the intervention process.

A Theoretical Framework for Human Services

The theories we use in human services vary along many dimensions. They range in scope from comprehensive explanations of human behavior to theories regarding very specific behaviors. They range in perspective from biological to psychological to sociological explanations of the human condition. They vary considerably in the degree to which they have been empirically tested, and they vary in terms of their applicability across age, gender, race, or cultures.

A review of human services literature shows that no one particular theory predominates. Most articles in the *Human Service Education* journal do not articulate a theory base for the research presented. Introductory human services textbooks refer to a number of different theories regarding the human condition. The national standards for human service worker education, developed by the Council for Standards in Human Service Education (1983), are much more specific in delineating required skills than theories. This greater emphasis on skills is consistent with a proposed set of attributes of human services (Fisher, Mehr, and Truckenbrod, 1974; Mehr, 1986). One of these attributes states: "The focus for training human service workers is on learning skills rather than knowledge, but knowledge is not ignored" (Mehr, 1986, p. 14).

General areas of theoretical knowledge mentioned in the national standards include theories regarding human development; human systems— individual, group, family, organization, community, and society—and their major interactions; and major models of causation of problems and of healthy functioning (Council for Standards in Human Service Education, 1983).

Thus it appears that as the human services profession emerges, it is being built on a *pluralis-*

tic theory base. In doing so, it avoids the overdependence on a single theory that hampered the social work profession for many years, as discussed by Kendall (1986). She points out that as social work has moved from a dependence on psychoanalytic theory to a pluralistic conceptual base, it has become much more flexible in terms of ability to serve diverse populations and to engage in social change as well as individual change. There is indication that the counseling profession also, although never reliant on a single theory, is moving to embrace more broad systems theories as well as individualistic counseling theories (MacDonald, 1989).

Having a broad smorgasbord of theories from which to choose, however, can be very confusing to individual workers, particularly when the theories are offered as competing explanations. Students often feel they must choose one explanation and reject others—e.g., disease theory of alcoholism *versus* social learning theory; sociological explanations of delinquency *versus* psychological ones; nature *versus* nurture in human development. Since no one theoretical perspective adequately addresses the complexities of human nature, this kind of choosing necessarily limits one's perspective. On the other hand, becoming "eclectic," where one can draw on any one of a large number of theories at a given time, has pitfalls also. Although certainly more flexible, it is still hard for the worker to know which theory to use in a particular situation.

An alternative is to develop a *broad conceptual framework* for practice, which integrates a number of theoretical perspectives rather than treating them as competing explanations. A key concept in such integration is *multi-factored causality*, the assumption that any behavior is influenced by many different factors. A number of integrating frameworks have been described in the literature of various helping professions. One that will be described briefly here is called the *ecological perspective*.

Ecological Perspective.   An ecological perspective is not a theory per se; it is a broad framework or paradigm that can encompass a wide range of theories and integrate them with some underlying principles. Although there are a number of variations in the conceptualization and labels for an ecological perspective, all are grounded on these two basic assumptions:

1. Organisms are *interdependent* with their environment.
2. The interaction patterns of organisms and their environments are *dynamic*, resulting from *developmental and adaptive processes.*

Interdependence is a very important concept. It goes far beyond the idea that the environment affects individual behavior; even beyond the idea that individuals also affect the environment. Interdependence implies patterns of connectedness that we are only on the threshold of understanding.

Traditionally, Western scientific research has focused on isolating variables, on identifying single cause-effect relationships, while attempting to control for the effects of extraneous variables. The ecological paradigm suggests that we should be looking for interaction patterns among sets of variables rather than trying to identify single cause-effect relationships.

Systems theory is a good example of an examination of interaction patterns within groupings of people or other living beings, such as families, organizations, or communities. Commonality of purpose, communication patterns, and distribution of power are all aspects of interactions within systems. Although not synonymous with an ecological perspective, systems theory can be an important component of an ecological perspective.

Although an ecological assessment is much more complex than searching for one or two "causes" of a particular behavior, it also gives a much clearer understanding of the behavior. For example, what causes some children of divorce to have later adjustment problems? The simplistic answer is that it is the divorce—the breakup of the family as they knew it—that caused the problems. But a more penetrating examination shows that the relationship of the parents before and after the divorce, the reduced income level of the household in which the children live, combined with the necessity in some cases for a move to a new location and a change of school, and many other factors, all play a role in the ultimate adjustment. Further, these factors have a multiplicative rather than additive effect; in other words, the presence of one factor such as poor parental relationship interacts with the presence of another factor such as reduced income level, increasing the power of each.

One example of a significant interdependence that human service workers sometimes overlook is that an important part of the environment for the client is the worker and the setting in which the help is offered. Workers get so busy exploring other aspects of the client's world that they sometimes forget about how much the client is affected by the worker himself or herself and the service agency.

The second principle, that the interaction patterns are dynamic, is also important to remember in an ecological analysis. People are in a continual process of adapting to their environment and, with the rapid change in society today, that is not an easy task. If a family member leaves, the interaction patterns in the entire family have to be revised. If a community enacts a new law, everyone must adapt.

Some of the changes to which people must adapt are somewhat predictable. Human development theorists have identified a number of stages and developmental tasks that people encounter as they go through life. Group dynamics and organizational theorists have also identified typical stages these systems go through as they mature.

It is easy to see how a wide range of theories can be incorporated into an ecological perspective and used to help understand the interdependence of people and their social and physical environments. Sociological theories regarding social systems, stratification, role, labeling, deviance, and others; psychological theories regarding motivation, needs, learning, personality, human development, and others; biological theories regarding genetic makeup, hormonal imbalances, etc., all combine to help us understand the complex nature of the human condition.

Theory in Human Service Education

Gilchrist and others (1979) offer a model of education that can be useful in helping students learn how to use theory effectively. Effective education, according to the model, includes three necessary components: (1) information dissemination, (2) personalization, and (3) skill training for use of the information. Too often in colleges and universities, dissemination of information is the main focus and the other two areas are neglected.

In human service education, classes that offer students an opportunity to become familiar with a wide range of theories and supporting research are a good beginning. No doubt these are available to every human services student in some form, through general liberal arts courses as well as some specific human services courses. Several introductory human services textbooks (e.g., Schmolling, Youkeles and Burger, 1989; Mehr, 1986; Mandall and Schram, 1983) have chapters devoted to review of various theories underlying helping services.

In most human service education programs, there are probably also at least some opportunities for students to personalize what they have learned about theories and to develop their own personal conceptual framework for practice. A popular course offered at the University of Oregon is an example of this kind of opportunity. After a review of a full range of counseling and

social work theories, each student was required to write a major term paper describing his or her own conceptual framework for practice. Students drew from various established theories in defining the basic assumptions they made about human development and behavior. Related to these assumptions, they then described the general kind of goals toward which they would work (a values question), the kinds of methods they would use that would be consistent with their basic assumptions, and the kinds of populations and problems for which their approach would (and would not) be appropriate. Even though they recognized that their perspectives would change with experience, the assignment provided opportunity for them to explore various theories in relationship to their own personal beliefs and values.

Another opportunity, not only for personalizing the theoretical information but also for learning how to use it, is through supervised field study. Human service education standards require a substantial amount of supervised field study, so presumably these opportunities are available in all human service programs. In many programs, field placements are accompanied by theory-practice integration seminars in which students are encouraged to use various theoretical perspectives in resolving problems encountered in their placements. Sometimes these seminars also require students to find ways of applying specific theoretical principles in their agency work. Through these activities the students not only gain a deeper understanding of the theories and their applicability, but also gain the skills for using theory.

In summary, theories are powerful tools and resources for helping. Students who are familiar with a range of theories, who from this knowledge develop their own conceptual framework for practice, who are aware of the ways in which theory can be used and have the necessary skills, can greatly enhance their effectiveness as human service workers.

REFERENCES

Council for Standards in Human Service Education, (1983). *National standards for human service worker education and training programs.*

Editors interview, W.B. Utting, (1984). *New England Journal of Human Services* 4(1), 6–13.

Frank, J., (1961). *Persuasion and Healing.* Baltimore: Johns Hopkins Press.

Gilchrist, L., S. Schinke, and B. Blythe, (1979). "Primary Prevention Services for Children and Youth." *Children and Youth Services Review* 1(4), 379–391.

Mandall, B. and B. Schram, (1983). *Human Services: An Introduction.* NY: John Wiley & Sons.

Mehr, J., (1986). *Human Services: Concepts and Intervention Strategies.* 3rd ed. Newton, MA: Allyn and Bacon, Inc.

Milam, J. and K. Ketcham, (1983). *Under the Influence.* NY: Bantam Books.

Schmolling, P., M. Youkeles, and W. Burger, (1989). *Human Services in Contemporary America*, 2nd ed. Pacific Grove, CA: Brooks/Cole Publishing Co.

Shulman, L., (1991). *Interactional Social Work Practice: Toward an Empirical Theory.* Itasca, IL: Peacock Publishers.

Turner, Francis, (1986). *Social Work Treatment: Interlocking Theoretical Approaches.* NY: Free Press.

Whittaker, J. and J. Garbarino, (1983). *Social Support Networks: Informal Helping in the Human Services.* NY: Aldine Publishing Co.

Woodside, M. and T. McClam, (1990a). "Problem Solving in the Human Service Curriculum." *Human Service Education*, 10(1), 9–13.

Woodside, M. and T. McClam, (1990b). *An Introduction to Human Services.* Pacific Grove, CA: Brooks/Cole Publishing Co.

CHAPTER 7

HELPING SERVICES FOR INDIVIDUALS
PERSPECTIVES AND SKILLS

ANITA RUNYAN

INTRODUCTION

There are a multitude of helping services available for people who seek assistance outside their circle of family and friends. These range from services to provide information about such things as care for the elderly in the community to in-depth psychotherapy for individuals who may be suffering acute distress in dealing with the circumstances of their lives. What makes these services truly helpful, and what gets in the way of people receiving the help they need? Why are some human service workers sought out by people asking for help and why are others avoided if at all possible? What allows some people to get the help they need and move on in their lives while others seem to get "bogged down" in the service delivery system, remaining perpetual clients and often unhappy critics of the services they continue to receive?

The answers to these questions are complex, as complex as understanding the nature of humans. The sciences, the arts, and the humanities all bring knowledge to this understanding, and yet it is not complete. There is still a mystery involved. "As helping professionals we must seek to learn all that is knowable while always being mindful of the incompleteness of the task. Science and mystery are not incompatible principles. They yield both knowledge and reverence" (Berger, Federico, and McBreen, 1991, p. viii).

This chapter focuses on some of the important principles for providing effective services for individuals. It also looks at how these principles can be applied in many different contexts, while emphasizing the particular skills needed in the various roles. This information is presented from a framework that includes an ecological perspective on working with individuals and a perspective of reverence for the spirit within each individual.

Helper Motivation is the first section following the introduction. Human service workers are attracted to the field for many different reasons, but they usually have a strong commitment to helping others and, perhaps, some positive past experiences in receiving or providing services. In order to be effective, workers need to go beyond this to examine their motivations and their beliefs about the helping process. For example, the emphasis in human services is on **empowering** individuals to reach the goals they have set for themselves. Even if the worker is providing a specific service, such as assisting an individual to receive medical attention, it needs to be done within the parameters of the larger objective of empowerment. If a workers's satisfaction comes more from what he/she is able to do for the client and how grateful the client may be, the worker might question whether his/her motivation is compatible with the field of human services.

The next section is concerned with a number of elements critical to effective delivery of services. One such element is the ability to establish a good relationship. Helpers may have many insights that could be useful, but if clients do not trust the helpers and are unwilling to engage with them, there will be little progress. How does one establish a relationship characterized by mutual trust and respect? Another essential element is the understanding of basic principles of human behavior and the ability to use this understanding in practice with individuals. Helpers usually have had foundation courses and life experiences that contribute to this understanding, but what are some of the issues that stand out as one begins practice?

A third element is skill development. Helpers must develop the ability to assist clients in assessing their needs and discovering potential solutions, and then to assist them in implementing their solutions. Since individuals do not operate in isolation, but rather in their own unique environment, the influences of their family and other social systems must also be considered. What are some general skills needed by the helper working with individuals in many different settings?

The last section of this chapter discusses a variety of services that agencies offer and examines the skills that are the most pertinent in the delivery of these services. The author brings to this discussion her own experiences in practice, as well as observations and examples from her twenty years of experience with students completing field work in a variety of settings.

PERSPECTIVES FOR WORKING WITH INDIVIDUALS

People come to the human service worker for assistance with a variety of issues. Sometimes they are reluctant to come because they are not sure how they will be received, or they are not sure that they will actually get the help which they seek. Sometimes they do not tell their whole story, feeling that some of their concerns are irrelevant or fearing that the worker will find some of their concerns, or even themselves, unacceptable.

Other people may come demanding that they be given every service available. They have many problems in their lives with which they are unable to cope, and they would like the worker to "fix" things for them or for their families. They may be upset with services they have received in the past and impatient with whatever processes have been devised to deliver the current services. They may be embarrassed at their inability to cope on their own. They may fear that they will not get the help they seek.

How can the worker deal successfully with a wide range of individuals and with a multitude of available helping services? What personal qualities, knowledge, and skills will enhance the worker's ability to assist individuals in receiving the services they need?

Helper Motivation

Providing services is often a difficult job. There are so many people needing assistance, and so few resources to provide this assistance, that the worker can easily feel frustrated and become "burned out." There are certainly less difficult and higher paying jobs! So, to become a service provider one must first have a strong commitment to doing this kind of work. It is also important to examine this commitment to determine whether it is based on realistic concerns and beliefs that will carry one through the difficult aspects of the work.

Most people get a great deal of satisfaction from individual interactions in which they have been able to help someone. The person who has been helped is often quite grateful and responds in a warm and affirming manner. It gives us a good feeling to know that we are appreciated and our ability recognized. However, the human service profession has been built on the ideal of empowering individuals rather than on the worker simply providing answers or resources. The people who are helped to find the solution to their problems may be less in awe of the worker's ability, but they may feel very good about themselves and their own abilities as problem-solvers.

They may not even need the worker the next time! Although appreciation is nice, our satisfaction must also come from witnessing the individual's personal empowerment.

As human service providers, there may be many times when what we need to do is not appreciated at all. How will we respond then? Suppose that your job is to tell a teenager that he must go to an institution rather than returning home, when that is what he wishes to do. What if you receive hostility rather than gratitude? Will you be able to provide your own appreciation for having handled a difficult interaction in a caring manner?

Sometimes people who have been helped by a program in their past decide that they want to work with individuals who have similar problems. Perhaps they were delinquent in their youth, had an alcohol/drug problem, or were involved in the criminal justice system. They may be committed to providing the same kind of assistance that was helpful to them. This can be a very powerful kind of commitment, and often clients relate well to someone they perceive as having been through the same experiences they are having. There is a danger in this type of commitment, however. Sometimes helpers assume that their client's experiences are just the same as theirs and that the same interactions or solutions will be helpful. This often may not be the case since each individual is unique, and helpers may become disillusioned when their solutions are neither useful nor appreciated.

What, then, is important to consider when looking at your own motivation for becoming a helper? Some typical motives involve the need to make an impact in the world, the need to care for others, the need to return a favor (to emulate a role model), the need to be needed, the need for self-help, the need to provide answers, and the need for prestige and status (Corey and Corey, 1989). It is useful to recognize that our needs *are* involved in our choice of profession and that these do not necessarily have a negative impact on our clients. We may well be able to meet the needs of our clients at the same time that we meet our own needs. What is critical is that we recog-

nize our needs and ensure that they are not satisfied at the expense of our clients. For example, a survivor of sexual abuse decided that she wanted to work with sex offenders in a mental health agency. She thought that she had worked through her own issues about being victimized and that her experiences would be useful in the treatment of offenders. However, she found that she was becoming extremely emotional as she dealt with her clients and was unable to focus objectively on their concerns. After consultation with her supervisor, she elected to take another assignment and sought further counseling for her own issues.

Motivation may also be influenced at a philosophical or spiritual level. H.H. Dalai Lama (1991) talks about respect for all sentient beings, that it is nature's way for there to be harmony and a sense of responsibility. He says that a complicated philosophy is not needed; what is essential is "good heart," which involves love and compassion. He believes that everyone has this potential; that it depends on whether or not we care to value compassion. This "good heart" may be the essence of what is needed to provide services in a manner that respects and empowers the individual and which may, in turn, activate that individual's "good heart."

Essential Elements for Helping

Workers who wish to empower clients who come for assistance will be aware that they must view clients in the total context of their lives. A client may be asking for assistance in finding employment, but simply matching his stated skills with a job description may not help him to achieve the job stability and satisfaction he is seeking. Perhaps he has health problems such as allergies, or his particular cultural/religious beliefs put limitations on what he wishes to do, or he needs particular hours due to family responsibilities, or he has had difficulty in previous employment due to relationship problems with co-workers, or he lives some distance away, or he has any number of other factors that may influence his success.

Viewing clients in the context of their environment is taking an ecological perspective. From this perspective an individual is seen as being influenced by many interacting forces. These may include biological, psychological, social, economic, political, and physical factors. This view contrasts with more person-oriented perspectives where the problem is seen as being within the individual, and where the solution is seen as coming primarily from the expertise of the helper. An ecological approach to assisting clients is considered important in the human service professions, an approach leading to empowerment (Pardek, 1988).

In the preceding example, the worker, who takes an ecological perspective in helping the client to find employment, would want to engage him in looking at all of the relevant issues and at all of his alternatives for training and employment. If he needed medical attention for his allergies or counseling assistance regarding his difficulty with co-workers, the worker might refer him to the appropriate resources. If he later needed to engage in another job search, he would hopefully be much better prepared to successfully find satisfactory employment.

Providing services to individuals from an ecological perspective necessitates that workers have a broad range of knowledge and skills. They must be able to assess the range and levels of needs presented and to respond with appropriate services and/or referrals. A pregnant teen may need support in dealing with her family, but she may also need medical attention, nutritional counseling, planning for finishing her education, financial support, and parent training. Human service workers must be generalist practitioners in order to utilize a wide range of systems and resources. As generalists, workers have to understand enough to help people make choices, and then monitor the quality of services they receive from the service providers they choose (Berger et al., 1991).

Relationship.   Another critical element in delivering services is the ability to establish a relationship with the client that will provide the atmosphere where development and positive change can occur. It does not matter how much knowledge and technical skill a worker may have if she is unable to work cooperatively with the client toward the achievement of the client's goals.

"There now exists a wide variety of research evidence, from several different types of two-person interactions, to indicate that the quality of the helper-client relationship can serve as a powerful positive influence on communication, openness, persuasibility and, ultimately, positive change in the client" (Knefer and Goldstein, 1991, p. 22). The human service worker must come to the profession with some basic ability to establish positive relationships with others. Most people acquire this ability within their family and social groups simply as a part of their own personal interactions and development. The worker is then able to examine the important aspects of this basic ability and to build on those in ways that will be most helpful with clients.

Alfred Benjamin (1981) feels that part of creating a good relationship is having a genuine liking for people. He refers to this genuine regard as a "gift from heaven" (p. 43). He goes on to say that those who have not received this "gift" are neither better nor worse than other people, but they lack a trait that is indispensable in the helping professions. This seems a bit like the "good heart" discussed by the Dalai Lama (1991). Certainly the most effective workers will communicate their genuine caring, creating an atmosphere where trust and cooperative effort can develop.

Some would disagree that a worker must "like" the client in order to create a positive relationship. Gerald Egan (1990) prefers to see the issue as one of respecting rather than liking. He says that workers must show clients that they are basically "for" them, that workers want to be available to them and work with them in a genuine and open manner (p. 66). Some early research (Truax and Carkhuff, 1969) on essential elements for helping showed that empathy, warmth, and genuineness were critical to effectiveness in the process of giving help. Clients need to feel that they are heard and understood in a caring and genuine human interaction in order to move forward in difficult circumstances.

Russo (1985) in his book, *Serving and Surviving*, discusses a process for examining your feelings about difficult clients to determine if you dislike them because of the way they behave, or if you disapprove of your clients' behavior but still accept and respect them as human beings. He suggests keeping a journal with a factual description of the day's events, describing the actors, the circumstances and the outcomes; then asking yourself how you felt about what happened. At the end of the week or month use the journal for self-examination by asking yourself questions such as "What kinds of clients attract me?" "Which clients repel me?" and "What do I like most and least about my job?" (p. 51).

Although human service workers may not be in the position of establishing in-depth relationships with clients such as would occur in ongoing counseling or psychotherapy, a good relationship is still of primary importance for client assistance. Even if the relationship consists of only one contact, as in providing information about available medical resources, the quality of that interaction may mean the difference in whether the client actually follows through to receive the needed service.

We all have a need to be respected, to have our ideas heard and understood, to be accepted as who we are, and to be regarded with warmth and caring. Workers who are able to communicate this positive regard to clients may elicit this same regard in response. They will probably also feel good about themselves. According to Benjamin (1981), people who feel genuine warmth and liking toward others will also like themselves. They will not have a particularly strong need to have others like them, but this often happens because warmth seems to elicit warmth. It is this essence of humanity that is at the core of the strongest relationships and that we may hope to share in some small way with our clients.

Knowledge. Although a good relationship is a necessary element in providing services, it is not enough to establish such a relationship. Workers need to have some broad understanding of human behavior on which to base their choice of interventions with clients. According to Berger et al (1991), the four principal sources of behavior are biological, psychological, social-structural, and cultural (including spiritual). This is a broad base of knowledge, indeed, although you are probably familiar with some of the concepts in these areas from classes you may have already taken in sociology, biology, psychology, anthropology, economics, or political science.

The depth and breadth of your knowledge base will depend on the level of education you plan to achieve prior to providing services. The worker who plans to practice at the associate of arts level will have much less opportunity to develop an extensive knowledge base than the worker who completes a master's degree prior to practicing. What is important to your practice is that you are aware of the complexity of human behavior and aware that this complexity comes from the interaction of the various sources of behavior. This awareness will increase the likelihood that you will know when to seek assistance or to make referrals when faced with situations beyond your level of expertise.

In their book on human behavior, Berger et al (1991) discuss what they see as the four principal sources of behavior and the need for the practitioner to be able to select, integrate, and apply information from these diverse sources. Some important points from this discussion follow.

It is clear that part of human behavior is **biologically** determined. There is a great deal of discussion in current literature about the relative influence of genetics on behavior, and some sociobiologists contend that all social behavior can be explained genetically. However, there is evidence that the biological potential of individuals is influenced by culture and by psychological and social-structural variables. The **psychological** source of behavior results from people's perception, cognition, and emotional development. The personality structures that are developed from these processes mediate between individual needs and the environment. It is particularly important to understand the stages of development that occur from infancy to old age since different psychosocial tasks are postulated for each stage (Erickson, 1976). Like biological functioning, psychological growth and development are responsive to the cultural and socio-structural context in which they occur.

Social structures such as schools, the family, churches, and the political system organize social interaction so that it's possible for people to behave with some predictability. However, it is important to note that once such structures exist, they control behavior and seek to maintain themselves. When looking at behavior and the social environment, one must consider the impact of social-structural arrangements on biological and psychological development. **Culture** involves the values, knowledge, and material technology that people learn to accept as appropriate and preferred. It shapes our way of explaining the world and sets the limits of allowable behavior. It is similar to socio-structural bases of behavior in that it is usually not directly observable, although the effects of its influence are pervasive.

The authors summarize:

Each human being has a unique biological endowment that creates his or her behavior potentials. The degree to which this potential is realized, however, is heavily influenced by our culture, our psychological development, and our social-structural environment.

For example, a woman who is born with the potential for high intellectual achievement but who lives in a culture that does not value intelligence in women is unlikely to have many opportunities to develop her intellectual capacities to their fullest potential. If, for instance, her family values intellectual achievement and has sufficient economic resources, it may help her to take advantage of the educational resources society provides. If on the other hand, the family's values

concur with the culture's devaluation of education for women, or if the family lacks the economic resources needed to finance an education, the woman will most likely have few opportunities to develop her biological intellectual potential. Indeed, in such a situation she may even begin to think of herself as unintelligent or deviant if others treat her as such (Berger, et al., 1991, p. 31).

In addition to the broad area of knowledge just discussed, specific information about special populations may be critical to providing services successfully to individuals. For example, when working with a "differently abled" person with a physical or mental impairment, it is important to know about the social and legal steps taken trying to provide equal opportunity. Or, when working with substance abusers, it is important to know the physical effects of various substances and the treatments that have been found most effective. No one can be current on information regarding all populations, but it is important to seek out this knowledge as one begins work with an unfamiliar population.

Finally, it is important to note here that there are no absolutes when dealing with human knowledge. There are various theories of how personality develops, of what causes behavior, and of what interventions may be useful in practice. Scientists attempt to test these and to modify them as new information is revealed. However, this process is often faulty due to limited observations, incorrect methodology, or even faked data (Schmolling, Jr., Youkeles, and Burger, 1989).

A few years ago physics as a science was considered the ideal against which all other sciences should be judged. There was the belief that knowledge in physics could achieve absolute and final certainty. There has now been a paradigm shift, and even in this "hard" science, it is recognized that all concepts, theories, and findings are limited and approximate (Capra and Steindl-Rast, 1991). The new paradigm parallels the ecological or holistic perspective discussed earlier. Taking this perspective does not mean that we abandon our efforts to make interventions based on accumulated wisdom; rather, it involves the effort of understanding the dynamics of the whole and the acceptance of the element of "mystery" in the limits of this understanding.

Skill Development.   Students preparing to work with clients often discover that they have already developed many of the skills needed through previous interactions with friends and families and the informal helping performed throughout their lives. Others will discover that even though they have a sound knowledge base, it's quite a different matter to use this knowledge in the helping process. One of the challenging things about providing services is that each individual is unique, and this applies to both the worker and the client. This challenge is also what keeps the process of working with people endlessly intriguing as we seek to understand ourselves and others and to interact in ways that will bring about the most positive outcome for clients. To be effective, workers will need to continue to develop and refine their skills throughout their professional careers.

Students, who have already developed substantial skills through previous life experiences, often find it very beneficial to take practice courses that help them label their skills and organize their conceptual understanding of the helping process. In this way they are better able to build on skills that they bring and add new skills to their repertoire. For those students who come with fewer already developed skills, it is comforting to know that the needed skills can be learned through training. No one is born with helping skills intact; these are developed through awareness, understanding, and practice.

There are various models for skill development. One that many workers find useful is a model dealing with progressive stages of helping (Egan, 1990; Patterson and Eisenberg, 1982). **Stage I** involves responding to the client as the client is engaged in initial disclosure and self-exploration. **Stage II** involves integrative under-

standing on the part of the helper and a more in-depth exploration on the part of the client. In **Stage III** it is the job of the helper to facilitate action by the client, and it is the job of the client to test alternatives and to take action. The nature of the client and the help the client is seeking will determine the amount of time spent in any one stage. The adolescent who wants to deal with relationship problems at school may need longer in each stage than the individual who comes in to learn about housing resources in the community.

During the stage of **initial disclosure**, the worker is using skills that provide conditions that will build a trusting and working relationship. Some of these conditions were described in the section on relationship. Carl Rogers (1965) first presented these as **empathy, congruence or genuineness**, and **unconditional positive regard**. These involve understanding another's experience as if it were your own; being as you seem to be without a front or facade, consistent over time, and dependable in the relationship; and caring about your client without any conditions attached, being "for" and valuing the client out of respect for the client's basic humanity. Egan (1982) added the condition of **concreteness**, which is needed in the first stage as well as throughout the helping process. This involves using clear and specific language in dealing with the client's issues.

There are a number of specific skills involved in creating the conditions described above. Skills of **observation** must be refined in order to understand the behavior the client presents. **Matching** some of this behavior, both verbal and nonverbal, may help the worker understand the emotional state of the client; and this understanding may also be communicated, even without the client's conscious awareness of the matching process. For example, the client may use broad gestures and talk very fast in explaining concerns. If the worker notes this and uses the same type of gestures and fast pace in verbal responses, the client may feel a beginning comfort that the worker understands.

Restating or **paraphrasing** the client's statements helps both the worker and the client know if the worker is understanding correctly what the client is intending to communicate. The skill of **concreteness** is the ability to sort out ambiguous statements by clients and help them accurately portray their concerns. It is also the worker's ability to use clear and direct language without jargon when speaking to the client.

According to Egan (1990) the skills of practicing genuineness, positive regard, and respect are less straightforward because they involve the complexity of worker attitudes and behaviors imbedded in the communication process. However, in his training manual he suggests that workers can ask the following kinds of questions of themselves and of others: "Am I being my natural self? Am I being spontaneous (while being tactful), or is there something rigid and planned about my behavior? Do I avoid defensiveness, even if the client challenges me? Am I 'for' the client in a nonsentimental, caring way? Am I dealing with the client as a unique individual and not just as a 'case'? Do I avoid making judgments, and find ways of reinforcing the client for what he does well?" (Egan, 1975, pp. 58, 59).

In the second stage of **in-depth exploration**, workers use skills to build on the relationship developed in the first stage and to assist clients to a deeper understanding of the concerns presented. Workers continue to practice empathy through communicating what they understand from clients, but now they also communicate what they feel clients might be implying as well—**advanced empathy**. This is an invitation for clients to understand their concerns at a deeper level. Workers are also ready to use **self-disclosure** if they feel this will assist clients' understanding, but they only disclose in a way that keeps the focus on the client. Workers use **constructive confrontation** to provide clients with an external view of their behavior based on the workers' observations and to invite them in a caring way to explore the discrepancies that are apparent. Workers may also

use **immediacy** by talking about what is happening in the interaction between worker and client, as a way of helping the client explore his/her style and to look at alternative frames of reference.

In the third stage of **commitment to action**, workers use skills to help clients accomplish any goals that have emerged during the previous stages. These might involve making a decision, solving a problem, or securing needed resources. In this stage workers use all the skills of the previous two stages but also provide **directionality** to help clients look at alternatives and develop action programs. This skill involves teaching clients problem-solving methodologies and assists them in applying these to the concrete problems being addressed. Workers also provide **behavioral support** as clients work through their action programs. Workers use skills in all stages as they encourage, support, reinforce, and confront clients.

Patterson and Eisenberg (1982) talk about the importance of recognizing that these stages of the helping process are not necessarily linear. It is true that unless people clarify their concerns, it is not possible to establish goals, and unless goals have been established, it is not possible to effectively evaluate a possible course of action. However, it is not necessary that a person clarify *all* concerns before beginning to think about goals. Someone who has a family to support may want to find immediate financial resources and only then look more closely at career planning. In the same way, if a worker has moved to Stage II or III with a client who is trying to deal with an abusive spouse, a return to Stage I may be needed if the client loses her job and is temporarily unable to cope with the added disruption in her life.

There are other skills imbedded in this model of progressive stages of helping. Perhaps most important is the ability of **self-assessment**. We have to be aware of our own values, concerns, and behaviors in order to assist clients in assessing theirs without our biases interfering. We have to have some knowledge and skill in **problem-solving** and **decision-making** processes in order to be able to teach this to clients. We may also need to engage in **information giving** if there are issues about which our clients must be educated. We have to be able to apply our theoretical knowledge to our **assessment of client processes** in order to understand our clients' needs and help them understand the implications of their behavior. We have to develop **report writing** skills in order to make case notes and reports. We have to know about community resources and develop skill in **resource referral** if we are to help clients carry out action plans. We have to use **case management** skills in order to plan with clients, to maintain appropriate records, and to interact with other involved agencies. Finally, we need to be aware of issues of prevention and be able to assist clients with **prevention strategies** in order to help them achieve the objective of empowerment valued by the human service profession.

This may seem a formidable listing of skills to the beginning worker, but as you review these, you may be able to pinpoint those skills about which you already feel confident, as well as those you will need to develop. These are skills that all human service workers need to some extent, regardless of the setting in which they choose to work, but different settings will require sophistication in the use of some skills while requiring limited expertise in others. Job role will also influence the degree to which particular skills must be mastered. Since human service workers are trained as generalists, your ability to assess the appropriateness of your level of education and skill to deal with particular problems with which you are presented will be critical to your success as a service provider.

SKILL EMPHASIS IN VARIOUS CONTEXTS

The previous section dealt with the process of helping individuals and with some of the important general skills needed to assist them in achieving their goals. These skills will allow you to work in a variety of settings with different clients.

However, as you begin to work with a new population, it will be important to gather additional information about the particular needs of that group and about the skills that will be the most useful. The following vignettes are descriptions of positions held by field students in nine-month placements and some of the skills they most needed to refine in order to provide competent services. These are actual agency positions held by student workers with the names changed to protect privacy.

Prevention Services

Paula wanted to work with children of middle-school age and decided to take a position working with "at-risk" children at Lincoln Middle School. This is a school with a large population of children from low-income families, and the principal was interested in providing some special attention and advocacy for children who might be in danger of developing behavior problems.

Paula's primary concern in the beginning was to interact with the children in a way that would establish mutual trust and respect (Stage I skills) so that the children would confide in her about their problems. Paula came to the position with a very friendly, outgoing personality and a positive approach to life. She genuinely liked the energy of the children and enjoyed interacting with them, and the children liked her in return. Her position involved supervising various activities as well as supervising a "time-out" room where children were sent to study when they were having difficulty in the classroom. Her interactions with the children led to their coming to her on an individual basis to talk about personal difficulties.

In order to be the most helpful, Paula found that she needed to work on her listening skills. She soon learned that offering advice when presented with problems was of limited value to the students. They had heard a lot of advice before, and although they asked for her opinion, Paula noticed that they didn't really follow through on her advice. What they really wanted was to know that she fully understood what was happening to them and their feelings about this. When she began to use more paraphrasing and also helped them to be concrete about what was of concern to them, students began responding by trusting her with critical disclosures such as abusive situations at home or concerns about sexual activity.

As her relationship with these children deepened, she was able to help them develop some different perspectives on their problems and to confront them with some of their behaviors that were problematic (Stage II skills). In her work with one of the children, she was able to facilitate a discussion with the parent about a suspected pregnancy, and she provided support to both the child and the parent as they followed through with actions they had decided on to deal with the problem (Stage III skills).

As she worked with the children, Paula found that she had to look again at her own values. Her background was quite different than that of a number of the children, and she wanted to be careful not to impose her values on them as she was trying to be helpful. She also learned that she had to be very careful in her assessment of her ability to work with the presented problems. When faced with a potentially suicidal child, she knew that she needed to consult immediately with the school counselor since she did not have the training to deal with this issue.

She found that she needed to be very clear on the steps in the problem-solving process, clear enough that she could actually teach problem solving to the children so that they could use this process when faced with other difficult issues. She also found that she needed to learn a lot more about resources in the community so that she would know what might be available for her clients as they were involved in problem solving. Since referrals were generally made through the counselor's office, she did not need to carry out the important steps in the referral process. However, she did find her communication skills

critical in her interactions with the counselor, the principal, and the teachers who were involved with the children with whom she was working. These communications were mostly verbal, but she also wrote several reports on her work and on specific issues with which she dealt.

Paula was very successful in her position in the school, so much so that the principal decided to expand the position the following year. She was well-matched with the needs of the school, but she was also open to assessing her own skills and focused on expanding those skills that were most pertinent to her position.

Information and Referral

Jim was interested in helping people get the resources which they need, and he chose to work at the Washington Clinic. This is a community clinic that provides crisis intervention for people in psychological distress, both for drug-related problems and for problems of mental illness. The Washington Clinic also provides low-cost medical services and is the information and referral resource for the county in which it resides. Jim's position was to update the resource directory for the county and to provide referrals for clients, both in person for those who came into the clinic, and over the telephone.

Jim knew that he did not have counseling skills, but he felt that he knew quite a bit about resources and could make appropriate referrals. When he received feedback from his supervisor that he had been sending people to resources that were not meeting their needs, he realized that he needed to examine the skills he was using. One of the things he discovered was that he was suggesting possible resources without clearly understanding the needs of his clients. When a client presented a problem, Jim quickly provided some alternatives to try without really listening and helping the client to explore the issue. While it would have been inappropriate for Jim to facilitate the in-depth exploration needed for counseling on personal issues, he did need to ask open-ended questions and to paraphrase what he heard in order to be clear about the problem. He also needed to be aware of relationship building, no matter how brief the encounter, so that clients would communicate their concerns openly and ask whatever questions they might have about the best use of the resource.

As Jim developed more of these skills, he found that his interactions with clients flowed much more smoothly and resulted in more satisfaction for clients. He also discovered that his knowledge of some of the resources was not as thorough as he needed for this position, and he spent a lot of time learning the breadth and quality of services offered by some of the more complex agencies. He learned who the best people were to contact for quick responses, and he even visited a number of agencies so that he would have a better personal understanding of the agency when he described its services to clients.

Jim also developed his writing skills. As he updated the resource manual, he found that he needed to describe services in as clear and succinct a manner as possible. Other people using the manual needed to quickly grasp the objectives of a particular agency and the depth of services offered. They did not have time to read through any extraneous material while clients were waiting for their services. He also developed his organization and management skills. He needed to keep track of all the updated information coming in from agencies, to solicit information from new agencies, to develop a system for follow-up, and to organize all of this information in a manner useful for others. In addition to his other duties, Jim took on the responsibility for a newsletter sent to all of the agencies to update them on new or changing services available in the county. He found this a challenge, both to his writing skills and to his skills for managing information.

After some difficulties in beginning his work at the Washington Clinic, Jim began to appreciate the importance of his work for both the individuals to whom he provided referrals and to the county system. He became very knowledgeable about the multitude of resources available in the county, and he also became aware of some of the gaps in the service delivery system. If he were to have continued work in that agency, he would have been in a position to advocate for the development of new services to better fill community need.

Victim's Assistance

Mary chose to work with the county's Victim Services Program, which operates out of the district attorney's office. Her assignment was to be a Juvenile Victim Advocate. Services for victims of adults had been provided for a number of years, but the position of working with juvenile victims was a relatively new one. Her responsibilities included initiating contact with victims and victims' families, assessing needs, providing crisis intervention if necessary, referring to mental health providers and other community resources, accompanying victims and their families to court hearings, and dealing with restitution issues as appropriate.

Since this was a new program with the Juvenile Department, Mary needed to assess the procedures that had already been established to serve victims and to set up additional procedures as appropriate. Fortunately, she already had some excellent organization and management skills; still, she found it difficult to adapt some of the procedures used in the adult court system to that of the juvenile system. Her basic communication and relationship skills were invaluable to her in negotiating with probation counselors, judges, attorneys, and administrators in establishing a workable process to use in her role as victims' advocate. The fact that the Juvenile Department was anxious to make the new system work was also a real advantage in the negotiations that were needed.

In her direct work with the victims, Mary found it necessary to focus her efforts on assessment, crisis intervention, and referral. In assessing victims' needs, particularly victims of personal violence, it was important for Mary to evaluate their strengths and resources as well as the strengths and resources of their families and communities. Other factors such as medical and psychiatric concerns, ethnic and religious factors, social history, behavioral deficits or excesses, and motivation were also important (Austin, Kopp, and Smith, 1986).

Mary's Stage I skills were of substantial importance in the assessment process. She had a warm personal style that helped put people at ease and facilitated their sharing with her. However, she needed to hone her observation skills and to use the skill of concreteness as she helped clients with initial disclosure. In the beginning, Mary would end the interview with knowledge of a lot of the client's general feelings and concerns but without enough concrete information to make a good assessment of what would be the most helpful process or resource in meeting the client's needs. After discussing this with her supervisor, she made a list of what she needed to know from the client and was able to use this to be sure that she assisted the client in covering all of the important issues.

Some of Mary's clients, particularly victims of such crimes as sexual assault, required crisis intervention from her. According to Janosik (1984) assessment and planning are primary activities maintained throughout crisis work. The worker and the client need to agree on the goals of their work together and to define the shared responsibilities of the relationship. Cognitive, affective, and behavioral distortion by the client are characteristic of crisis, and being clear and concrete can help alleviate confusion and distress. Providing information about legal rights and supporting the client in participating in the court process can help to reduce feelings of helplessness. Mary continued to develop her skills in being direct and concrete throughout her work in this position.

Although important in all counseling relationships, the attitude of the helper in crisis work can be crucial in instilling hope that the problem can be solved. Counseling should be supportive in nature, aimed at reducing anxiety and reestablishing the victim's sense of worth and value. Mary's well-developed skills in demonstrating empathy and positive regard were very useful here. She was also able to help clients in gaining assistance from their informal family and community support networks.

She found that her excellent management skills were valuable in implementing the process of providing referrals for clients when other resources were needed. She was very thorough in discussing the purpose of the referral and in her assistance with the specifics of contacting the resource. She also used good follow-up procedures to see if the resource had been useful or if further support was needed for her clients to receive the service.

Case Management

Teens. Betty was interested in working with teenagers and chose a position in Community Services working with teen parents. Her position involved initiating contact with pregnant teens to provide information about available services and then to provide on-going support, education, counseling, and referral to other resources as needed. Many of these teens live with their families and some are involved with various school programs, so Betty's position included coordinating with these support systems as well. In addition to her case management duties, Betty also assisted in teaching a Life Skills Class and in developing various educational materials for information packets to be distributed to teen parent families.

Betty had three children of her own and had taken various parenting classes, so she felt confident about her knowledge in the area of parenting concerns. She also enjoyed interacting with people, which she did in a very warm and caring manner. She had an infectious sense of humor that facilitated her relationship with others and was particularly appealing to the teens with whom she worked. Many of the teens were in very difficult family situations, both in terms of relationships and economics, and it was important that they accept Betty as someone in whom they could trust and confide about these difficult areas of their lives.

Part of Betty's job was also to help the teens look at behaviors that were causing them difficulty, as well as behaviors needed to ensure that their babies would be raised in a safe and healthy environment. This meant that Betty needed some very well-developed relationship-building skills and skills to facilitate in-depth exploration (Stages I and II). Stage III skills were also emphasized since the teens needed to plan, make decisions, and carry out specific actions about health issues and about raising their children.

In addition, Betty needed to learn community resources well, so that she would have this information available as she worked with the teens to help them get information in such areas as nutrition, financial assistance, parent education, emancipation from families, child care, etc. She needed to be skilled in providing "follow-up" to be sure services were actually received and appropriately utilized. Since she was working with a number of clients, Betty also had to refine her management skills so that she did not forget appointments or dates on which follow-up needed to occur. Another area of importance was coordination with all the different agencies with whom she interacted for her clients. She often needed to check with schools, clinics, family members, and sometimes juvenile authorities.

Before she started this position, Betty already had a number of the relationship and personal management skills. One of the areas on which she spent energy was team-building skills within her own agency. The issues with which Betty and her co-workers were confronted were often very emotional, and sometimes traumatic, as when the life of a mother or baby was actually threatened. It was important that workers felt supported by each other and that they were able to ask for help if they were put in a difficult or dangerous situation. Another area that Betty wanted to develop was her ability to use community resources. At the end of her placement, her ability in resource referral was one of the areas in which she felt she had progressed the most.

The Elderly.   Carl had grandparents of whom he was very fond, and he particularly wanted to work in some capacity with an older population. He was gratified when he was accepted for a position with Senior Services as a case manager. A part of his position involved visiting with seniors who still lived in their own homes but who needed some outside assistance to do so. Another part of his job was to visit with seniors who could no longer care for themselves and were living in foster care or in some larger care facility such as a nursing home. He made scheduled visits every six months but would visit more frequently to assist with specific problems that were brought to his attention.

Carl communicated his interest and caring to his clients, and he was a good listener. His clients enjoyed talking to him and would often go on at length about issues with their children or about political concerns that they might have. Although Carl felt good about his relationship with his clients, he had some concern that it took him so long to find out about needs they might have and about the other information required to complete the forms for renewal of their services. After discussion with his supervisor, he realized that he needed to develop his skills in Stage II. He needed to listen for the implications of what his clients were saying about needs, and check this out with the clients. Sometimes he even had to interrupt his clients and refocus the conversation specifically on what needed to be discussed. He learned to do this by paraphrasing what the client had just said so the client knew he had understood, and then he would become very concrete about the issues to be addressed. Sometimes he also found confrontation important when clients were avoiding some important concern about their needs. The confrontation was in a very gentle and caring manner, and he found that his relationship with these clients deepened.

Carl found these Stage II skills also important as he moved on with clients to help them take needed action (Stage III). For example, a client might not be receiving good services from a housekeeper, and Carl would assist in the process of dismissing the current person and hiring someone else. Or there might be a problem in the interaction or services provided by a care giver, and Carl would assist in dealing with these issues. Carl also focused on learning specific information critical to the well-being of the elderly population, such as issues about kinds and amounts of medications that might interact dangerously in an older person and issues regarding mental functioning that might put the client in danger (Hashimi, 1991).

Since Carl was working for a governmental agency, he also had to do a great deal of paperwork in order to establish the eligibility of his clients for services. He learned to complete a number of the forms on the computer, which helped him to speed up the paperwork process; but he also focused on his writing skills so that he could complete his notes on his home visits in a brief manner while still including all the important information clearly. By the end of his placement, his supervisor felt very confident in reviewing his files and finding all of the critical information on which particular decisions had been based. She was also impressed at his continuing concern for his clients and his ability to establish an effective relationship with the limited contact allowed by the work load in that agency.

Client Supervision

Shelly decided to work with a sex-offender program in the County Youth Development Program. She had previous volunteer experience working with adolescents in a shelter care program and knew that she could relate well to adolescents. She also had taken classes on stages of child development and on sexual abuse, so she felt that

she had a good knowledge base for this position. Her job was to supervise juvenile sex-offenders to ensure that they did not commit additional offenses and to ensure that they were following the treatment plans that had been developed.

When she received new clients, she first helped them set goals for themselves that included any directives from the court. She then met regularly with them to offer support, problem-solving assistance, and referrals to other resources as appropriate. She also checked with their schools, families, and counselors to determine progress. The county uses lie detector tests, and she arranged for these as appropriate. If juveniles reoffended, her responsibility included taking them back to court and arranging for placements in other settings if they had to be removed from the community. Beyond her responsibilities with the individuals, she also assisted in presenting information in the sex-education program and in providing group counseling.

Shelly was a mature student who had a teenager of her own, and she felt quite comfortable in confronting her clients with inappropriate behaviors and in giving them information she felt they needed (Stage II). She also genuinely liked the juveniles and had a great deal of empathy with them. She had read the background information from their files and knew that most of them had multiproblem families and that many had been abused themselves.

Although her empathy and liking for the clients helped her to establish a beginning relationship with them, she felt that this was not enough. She found that the skills she needed to develop further involved responding to her clients in ways that would lead them to more exploration of their own feelings and behaviors. This included open-ended questions, paraphrasing, and reflecting back the feelings she observed in the clients (Stage I). She really already had these skills, but she didn't always remember to use them when she felt so strongly about what they needed to do. It seemed clearer and easier to simply give them advice, but this was of limited benefit to any real behavior change or feeling of empowerment on their part.

Another area of growth for Shelly was her own emotional involvement with clients. She became aware this was a problem when she had to recommend that one of her clients be institutionalized. She had discussed his situation with her supervisor and had explored all available alternatives, and she and her supervisor agreed that this was the correct decision. However, she could hardly bring herself to follow through; in fact, she became ill for several days after the decision was made. At this point, Shelly sought assistance for herself, assessed some of her own needs, and was then able to take a more objective stance with other clients.

Shelly had a unique opportunity to develop her report writing skills in this position since she was required to prepare the reports to the court when her clients went before the juvenile judge. Since there were legal conditions to be considered and her reports would be used by attorneys, she received careful training and supervision in developing this skill. She also had an excellent opportunity to use her team-building skills as she worked in cooperation with a number of community agencies to maximize her clients' potential for a successful completion of their probation. One of the areas she thought she would like to pursue, if she continued work in this agency, was the development of better resources for treatment/living facilities when her clients were unable to remain in their homes.

Shelter Care

Laura had held several volunteer positions in human service agencies, but she had never worked with adolescents. She decided that she would like to work with a boys' group home in a position where she could use her athletic skills in a therapeutic recreation position. Her job at the Mason Group Home was really broader than therapeutic recreation since she also provided supervision for daily living activities several days a week.

When she first arrived at Mason, she was anxious to be seen as a friend to the boys rather than an authority. She knew that she was closer to the boys' ages than some of the rest of the staff and felt this might provide her with an opportunity to gain the boys' confidence so that they would allow her to assist them in problem-solving efforts. Although Laura was somewhat shy and reserved in her approach to others, she was genuinely interested in the boys and was able to communicate this. There were always other staff present on her shift, and she had an opportunity to relate informally with the boys when they were doing chores or during free periods. After the first month she felt that she was beginning to establish a good relationship with a couple of the boys and was quite critical of some of the staff for some of the disciplinary measures they enforced.

The second month she was there, she was allowed to take a group of the boys out on a bowling excursion. Ordinarily another staff person would have accompanied the group, but one of the staff was ill and a volunteer went along instead. At first the group seemed to be having a good time and the evening progressed well. Then a couple of the boys got in an argument and began yelling and pushing each other. When she asked them to stop they paid no attention, and then others in the group joined in the argument. It ended by the management asking them to leave. She managed to get them all back to Mason, but both she and the group were angry and upset with what had happened. The next day when she approached one of the boys with whom she had been spending informal time, he told her that he did not want to talk about the issue they had previously been discussing. She felt that she had lost his respect due to the bowling incident.

After talking about the incident with her supervisor, Laura decided that she needed to take a more active role in dealing with behavioral problems in the home. Although it was nice to be seen as a friend by the boys, it was also necessary that she be seen as a staff member who could help them maintain control when that was necessary, and help them follow the established rules. She needed to learn to confront their inappropriate behaviors while still communicating caring for them as individuals. This was not easy for her to do, and she worked on the Stage II skills, particularly those of constructive confrontation and immediacy, throughout the rest of her time at Mason. Later in her placement, she did feel that she had learned to be a member of the staff team while continuing to relate well with the boys. The boys respected her staff position and several of them had also sought her out when they wanted to discuss family problems. She was even able to facilitate an important reconciliation between one of the boys and his mother.

SUMMARY

There are a number of important considerations when providing services for individuals. The first concern for potential helpers is to examine their motivations for helping and to see whether these are compatible with the goal of the profession to empower individuals in the helping process. It is also critical to develop an awareness of personal attributes and skills already acquired that will be useful in service delivery. The helping process requires the use of oneself

in a personal relationship with clients in order to be successful.

A broad knowledge base is also essential to the successful professional service provider. One must have an understanding of the complexity of human behavior and be able to look at individuals in the context of their environments. The amount of knowledge one can acquire is, of course, limited by the amount of education one undertakes. An individual can be successful in delivering some types of services without any professional degree; however, the key is the ability to assess the appropriateness of one's knowledge and skill for the service needed. The ability to assess the needs of clients and to make referrals to other, more appropriate, providers is an indispensable skill for the worker.

Service providers work in many different roles in a wide variety of agencies. In order to be effective, they must develop a range of skills. Within this range, there is a core of skills that the provider needs to utilize in the various stages of interaction with clients in almost any role or agency setting. As one moves into different positions working with varying populations, these "generalist" skills can continue to be used as the basis for service delivery, and more specialized knowledge and skill for work with a particular population can be acquired.

REFERENCES

Austin, M.J., J. Kopp, and P.L. Smith, (1986). *Delivering Human Services: A Self-Instructional Approach.* New York: Longman.

Benjamin, A., (1981). *The Helping Interview,* 3rd ed. Boston: Houghton Mifflin.

Berger, R.L., R.C. Federico, and J.T. McBreen, (1991). *Human Behavior: A Perspective for the Helping Professions,* 3rd ed. New York: Longman.

Capra, F., and D. Steindl-Rast, (1991). *Belonging to the Universe: Explorations on the Frontiers of Science and Spirituality.* San Francisco: Harper.

Corey, M., and G. Corey, (1989). *Becoming a Helper.* Pacific Grove, CA: Brooks/Cole.

Dalai Lama, H.H. (Speaker) and B. Moyers (Interviewer), (1991). *Spirit and Nature* (Video recording, conference, and interviews). New York: Mystic Fire Video.

Egan, G., (1975). *Exercises in Helping Skills: A Training Manual to Accompany the Skilled Helper.* Monterey, CA: Brooks/Cole.

Egan, G., (1982). *The Skilled Helper: A Model for Systematic Helping and Interpersonal Relating,* 2nd ed. Monterey, CA: Brooks/Cole.

Egan, G., (1990). *The Skilled Helper: A Systematic Approach to Effective Helping.* Pacific Grove, CA: Brooks/Cole.

Erikson, E., (1976). *Adulthood.* New York: W.W. Norton.

Hashimi, J., (1991). "Counseling Older Adults." In Kim, P.K.H., ed. *Serving the Elderly: Skills for Practice* (pp. 33–49). New York: Aldine De Gruyter.

Janosik, E.H., (1984). *Crisis Counseling: A Contemporary Approach.* Monterey, CA: Wadsworth.

Kanfer, F.H. and A.P. Goldstein, eds. (1991). *Helping People Change: A Textbook of Methods,* 4th ed. New York: Pergamon.

Pardek, J., (1988). "An Ecological Approach to Social Work Practice." *Journal of Sociology and Social Welfare* 15 (2), 133–145.

Patterson, L.E., and S. Eisenberg, (1982). *The Counseling Process,* 3rd ed. Boston: Houghton Mifflin.

Rogers, C.R., (1965). "The Interpersonal Relationship: The Core of Guidance." In Mosier et al., eds. *Guidance: An Examination.* New York: Harcourt, Brace and World.

Russo, J.R., (1985). *Serving and Surviving as a Human-Service Worker.* IL: Waveland.

Schmolling, P., Jr., M. Youkeles, and W.R. Burger, (1989). *Human Services in Contemporary America* 2nd ed. Pacific Grove, CA: Brooks/ Cole.

Truax, C. and R. Carkhuff, (1969). *Toward Effective Counseling and Psychotherapy.* Chicago: Aldine.

CHAPTER 8

HELPING SERVICES FOR GROUPS

BARBARA SOMERVILLE

Stephen is a human service worker in a large residential facility for seriously ill children and adolescents. The agency provides medical care, education, recreation, and counseling for its clients who, on average, remain there for several years. Stephen became aware that the teenagers really had no place to discuss typical topics of interest like dating, feelings about themselves, and their goals for the future. With his supervisor's permission, Stephen decided to organize what he called a "Rap Group" for eight teenage boys between the ages of fourteen and seventeen. He believed that by only having boys and keeping the age range narrow, the members would more easily be able to speak to and understand each other.

Stephen thought a lot about the goals of the group. What did he want the members to get from participating? He decided that two of the most important goals would be to help the boys achieve a sense of belonging and to help them develop friendships that would extend beyond the time of the actual group meeting. Other goals included learning to relate socially (listening, taking turns, being polite) and having the opportunity to discuss issues of concern to them. Stephen knew that many different goals could be achieved within the same group. He chose one of the smaller recreation rooms as the location and decided to offer refreshments. The group would meet in the evening for an hour once a week for twelve weeks. Stephen approached several of the boys individually, explaining his ideas about the group. Some were not interested but seven enthusiastically agreed to come. Stephen decided to run the group with seven and not add any members later as he felt it would destroy the cohesion that he hoped the group would develop.

On the following Wednesday evening at 8:00, the seven new group members arrived at the recreation room feeling a little nervous and unsure. Stephen was there to greet them. During the first meeting the members introduced themselves, had cake and soda, and talked about what would happen in future meetings. Some of the boys asked if they could meet at 7:30 instead of 8:00, and the group voted on this. They also voted on whether to have refreshments every week. Stephen thought it was important that the members make decisions together, rather than the leader deciding everything. After the boys left that first evening, Stephen was pleased. They had all shown up and all but one participated actively. (He would have to remember to try to involve that one boy in the next meeting.) They were talking and laughing on the way out so they must have felt comfortable with each other. It was a good beginning.

Stephen continued to meet with his group every week. Gradually, feelings of closeness developed among the boys as they shared their questions and concerns. They were able to resolve the few conflicts that occurred during the third meeting and at that point they decided to extend the time together from an hour to an hour and a half. Stephen worked hard with the group; his role changed as their needs changed. They talked about everything from girls to school to music. Some of the boys talked about the illnesses that brought them to live there. Sometimes the conversation was

139

light and sometimes it was very personal. Stephen was proud of them as he watched them listen to each other and offer suggestions and support. He was glad to see real friendships begin to develop among some of the boys. He knew they were making progress and that soon it would be time to end the group.

Stephen began the tenth meeting with the reminder that they had all agreed to meet for twelve weeks and that, in two weeks, the group would be over. The boys seemed amazed that the time had passed so quickly. They also seemed a bit quiet that evening and Stephen assumed they were reacting to the ending of the group. The following week they talked about how much they enjoyed coming to meetings and that they would miss them. They decided to plan a party for their last time together. Stephen knew that it was important to encourage them to share their feelings about ending and to evaluate the progress they made. The last meeting of the group went well. They had their party and talked about the group being over. Someone suggested that they continue for another twelve weeks. Stephen had already considered this but decided against it. The boys achieved a sense of friendship and belonging (two of the initial goals) that enabled them to discuss issues outside the group. They didn't need the group as much as they did in the beginning. Also, Stephen thought it was time to start a new twelve-week group, with other teens, so that they too could benefit from the process.

UNDERSTANDING GROUPS

From our birth until the time we die, most of us live our lives participating in groups. Our families, peer groups, church groups, and classes help us learn the norms of the society, enable us to acquire our values and beliefs, and help us to develop our identities. Groups afford us the opportunity to try out new roles; they are the place where we can get feedback so we can know how we appear to others. They give us a sense of security that comes from belonging. Members of a group provide encouragement, support, and sometimes concrete help for each other. They offer new perspectives. Considering the influence group participation has on the individual, it is not surprising that the human service workers would find merit in helping clients within the context of the small group.

Before we examine the place of groups in human services, it would be helpful to understand exactly what we mean by a "group." If you are in an elevator with six other people, are you part of a group? Is your family a group? What about your human service class? Let's begin by looking at some definitions of "group."

> *"Two or more people who, for longer than a few moments, interact with and influence one another and perceive one another as 'us'" (Myers, 1990).*

> *"Two or more people who share a feeling of unity and who are bound together in relatively stable patterns of social interaction" (Vander Zanden, 1990).*

In looking at these definitions, we can begin to see that groups have a certain set of characteristics that define them. If we examine these characteristics, we will begin to understand the nature of groups.

Two or More People.   While a group must have at least two people, there is less agreement about the maximum number of people that can be considered a group. Generally, we believe that a group must be large enough for it to achieve its goals (more about goals later) and small enough for the members to interact comfortably with each other.

Interaction.   Members of a group must interact with each other in some meaningful way. Several people standing together in a moving elevator usually don't interact significantly and so we don't view this as a group. Obviously, speaking and listening form the basis of interaction. Examples of interacting within a group might include cooperating in completing a project, working together to learn something new, solving problems, and resolving conflicts. When a group of adolescents meets regularly after school to play basketball they are interacting, as are a group of emotionally disturbed children who come together once a week to cook and bake.

Continuity. Members must interact over a period of time in order for them to truly be a group. If six students work together to rescue a cat from a tree on campus, would we consider them a group? Probably not, since their interaction took place for only a brief period of time. But those same students could be a group if they worked together during the semester on a term project, thereby interacting in an ongoing way over time. How long is enough time? Long enough for members to interact meaningfully, to influence each other, and to develop a feeling of "groupness" (this is explained in the next column). In some cases, as in therapeutic encounter groups, this can happen in the space of a single, intensive weekend. In other instances, like a group of resistant predelinquent adolescents who attend only occasionally and are poorly motivated, it could take months. It is not really the length of time that is important but rather what occurs during the time they are together.

Influence. Members of a group generally influence each other. This is especially true when members have been together for a long time or they share a strong sense of group identification. This influence can be seen in many areas: the group may affect the ways members feel, their attitudes, values, and goals, what they believe, and how they act and look. We have only to consider the adolescent peer group for many examples of group influence on the individual. Sometimes the influence may be subtle, and it may affect some members more than others, but it is still usually present.

Common Purpose. Group members usually have similar purposes or goals in coming together. Note that goals need not be identical,

they must just be similar enough so that the goals of each member can be met within the context of the group. Consider the lunch group at the senior citizens' center. While it is obvious that the members are all there to have lunch, one might be coming because the meal is free, another might attend for the chance to interact with others, still another might come just to have something to do during the afternoon. Their goals are not the same, but they are certainly compatible.

Feeling of "Groupness." Members generally share a feeling of "belonging" to the group. This feeling is difficult to define but can generally be described as a sense of unity, group spirit, or being inside rather than outside the group's boundaries. It usually develops gradually over time as members continue to interact with and influence each other on a regular basis. They come to identify with each other, to see themselves as having characteristics, experiences, or goals in common. This sense of identification promotes the feeling of "us." Often a group culture may develop that enhances the members' sense of being part of the group. Examples may include dress (like the jackets worn by a certain gang), rituals (like ending each group meeting with a song), norms (celebrating members' birthdays in a special way), even language (such as nicknames members may have for each other). These are certainly not always present but when they do occur, they tend to strengthen members' feelings of "groupness."

So in trying to decide whether your human service class is really a group, ask yourself these questions: Is the class small enough so that everyone can comfortably interact with everyone else? Do the students and professor actually interact with each other? Does the class meet over a significant period of time? Do the students and professor influence each other in any meaningful way? Do they have compatible goals that are being met in class? And finally, is there a feeling of unity or "us" in the class? If you can answer these questions in the affirmative, then you may consider your class a true group.

THE USE OF GROUPS IN HUMAN SERVICES

There is a great deal of variety in the way groups are used in human services. Most human services agencies run groups and some will conduct several different kinds, according to the needs of their clients. Zastrow (1993), Heffernen, et al. (1992), and others have described several different types of groups that may be found in human service settings. They vary in their purpose, activity, benefits to members, and skills required to lead them.

Recreation groups provide members with the opportunity for enjoyment and entertainment through sports, games, or crafts. They are found at Ys, community centers, hospitals, nursing homes, and other settings. Sometimes they arise spontaneously and may, in fact, be leaderless. In other cases they have leaders employed by the agency. One of their main goals is to provide members with the opportunity for social interaction. A number of people playing bingo in a nursing home would be an example of this type of group.

Skill-building recreation groups are often found in the same settings as simple recreation groups and have the same goals of providing diversion and the opportunity for interaction. However, they have an additional purpose: to teach or improve member skill in some activity such as sports, crafts, or cooking. Usually, the leader has some expertise in the activity being conducted. As members become proficient, self-esteem is often increased. An example would be an after-school basketball group at the local community center.

Educational groups provide members with the opportunity to acquire knowledge or more complex skills. They are different from classes in that they encourage more interaction among members and, in fact, this is one of their goals. They may be led by human service workers who have both the skill required to conduct groups and sufficient expertise in the area being taught. Examples would be assertiveness training groups, natural childbirth classes, and in-service training seminars.

Problem-solving groups may also be called task-oriented or decision-making groups. The goal of the group could be to solve a particular problem (like the lack of after-school care in a community) or make a decision that will affect many people (whether kindergarten in the public school should be extended to a full day). Although members may personally benefit in some way by participating in the group, their purpose in coming together, and their roles within the group, are related to the group's particular goals. Leadership in problem-solving groups may emerge from among the members or may be provided externally by the agency sponsoring the group. Examples would include consumer groups, community action groups, and task forces.

Socialization groups may be led by human service workers and are found in a variety of settings such as schools, prisons, psychiatric hospitals, and community centers. Their goals include helping clients to develop social skills, acceptable behavior, enhanced self-confidence, increased motivation, and more positive attitudes. They may be based on discussion or, especially with adolescents, may revolve first around an activity and then discussion. Socialization groups are very effective in working with delinquent and predelinquent youth.

Self-help groups are composed of people with similar problems or needs who come together to help themselves and each other. Leadership is usually selected from among the members, although sometimes human service workers may act as advisors. Depending on the group, the orientation might be recreational (like Parents Without Partners), therapeutic (like Alcoholics Anonymous), or problem-solving (for example, a group of parents of developmentally disabled children). Self-help groups are often found in churches, community centers, and hospitals.

Psychotherapy groups are usually led by trained professionals, often having advanced degrees. Used either alone or together with individual therapy, their goal is to help clients explore and resolve emotional problems. Family therapy and couples groups are special types of group therapy. Therapy groups are usually run in hospitals, mental health clinics, other social agencies, and by therapists in private practice.

STAGES OF GROUP DEVELOPMENT

Groups, like the people that comprise them, are not static entities. They are constantly evolving and changing as they move toward the achievement of their goals. If you were to look in on the first meeting of a couples group, for example, you might see eight or ten people appearing a bit awkward and uncomfortable. Perhaps a few would be sitting silently, others might be laughing nervously, not sure of what to say or do. Suppose that, several weeks later, you had the opportunity to observe the group again. Chances are you would find members very busy discussing issues of importance to them, asking each other questions, giving feedback, making suggestions. The uneasiness that you initially noticed would be gone and in its place you would find friendship and concern. Finally, some time later, you might find yourself looking in on the group once again, this time at one of its last meetings, and you may see that it has continued to change. Now members may be expressing regret, anxiety, or maybe even resentment that the group is about to end. Perhaps they're planning a party for the last session or exchanging phone numbers to ensure continued contact. Could these be the same people you observed months before who seemed to have nothing to say to each other? Can groups really change that much? Indeed they can, and do. We refer to these changes as the process of group development. Several small-group theorists have proposed models of group development in which they describe the stages that groups pass through from the time they are formed until they end. One of the most valuable models was proposed by Margaret Hartford (1971), who outlines ten stages, or phases, in the development of a group.

Pregroup Phases.   This is the first stage in the development of a group and, as such, it is one of the most important. There are three pregroup phases:

> *Pregroup private phase*: In this phase, a worker realizes that there is the need for a group and he or she decides to start one. The worker may or

may not discuss these intentions with others. He or she thinks about the group and makes all of the necessary decisions involved in the beginning (such as goals, number of members, length of meetings, location, and so on). At this point, the group exists primarily in the mind of the worker.

> *Pregroup public phase*: It is here that the worker's decision to form a group becomes known. Depending on the type of group, he or she may speak with each potential member individually to discuss joining (as in a psychotherapy group) or may send or post notices (as in a tenants' meeting). Potential members may be asked about their preferences regarding time, length of meeting, or meeting place.

> *Pregroup convening phase*: This is the point at which the members come together for the first time. They engage in introductions and small talk, try to find mutual interests, and attempt to present themselves favorably. Members may be anxious and may not be sure that they want to belong. The worker's main task at this stage is to help them develop trust and a beginning commitment to the group. This can be done in many ways, such as restating the goals of the group, asking members to discuss their expectations, pointing out areas of commonality. Sometimes structured group exercises are helpful. At this stage, the worker would also make known such things as number of weeks the group will meet, length of meetings, and whether refreshments will be served.

Group Formation Phase.   During this phase, group norms and group identity begin to develop. Members start to find their roles within the group; they become committed and begin to influence each other. They begin to see that they have common goals and they start working to attain them. They begin to see the group as an entity apart from other groups. This stage is very important because without it, the collection of people will never become a true group. The worker should help members clarify their goals and expectations, reinforce appropriate roles, encourage them to share and identify, and stress the positive aspects of belonging.

Integration, Disintegration, or Reintegration. This phase occurs in many but not all groups. This is a period when members are no longer on their best behavior. They may become disenchanted with each other and with the group, and they may show resistance, anger, hostility, or withdrawal. Power struggles may develop, and decisions already made may suddenly be reversed. The group may spend a great deal of time focusing on interpersonal issues in trying to resolve its conflicts. The worker's role during this phase would include encouraging discussion and resolution of conflicts and helping members see that this stage is a natural one in the development of groups. Sometimes, it may be necessary to change group purposes, roles, or tasks. For example, a worker has put together a group of concerned family members of patients in a chronic-disease hospital. The group decides to organize a trip for some of the patients with the hospital's permission. Each member has a task to perform (such as obtaining funds, arranging the bus, getting the food). At first, everyone is very enthusiastic, but as the group begins to move toward this stage, some members think the trip is too difficult to arrange. There is arguing about whether members are accomplishing their assigned tasks. One woman, who had often acted as a leader, becomes very bossy and the other members object. The worker must intervene here to help the group members solve their problems and regain their enthusiasm. In general, if the worker and members successfully resolve the issues that arise at this stage, the group will move forward into the next. However, if attempts at resolution fail, the group may not be able to continue.

Group Functioning and Maintenance Phase. This phase of group development is very appropriately titled—whether it involves adolescents discussing personal problems, community residents planning a new day-care program, or nurses organizing a holiday party on a pediatric ward. This is the stage in which most of the work of the group takes place. As the group becomes focused on achieving its goals, members become increasingly committed to the process and to each other. Defenses are lowered, genuine affection and trust are felt. Group identity is strong. Generally by this stage a group culture has formed and there are observable norms of behavior. For example, members may sit in the same place week after week; they may have group jokes that outsiders wouldn't find funny; they may always start or end the meetings in the same way. This is usually a period of strong cohesion within the group. If a new member entered now, he or she would certainly feel like an outsider. During this phase, the worker should praise the work of the group and encourage members' efforts. Depending on the style of leadership (discussed later), the worker may or may not actually participate, but should be ready to intervene if conflicts develop.

Termination Phase. This is an important point in a member's participation in a group; we will examine it again when we discuss worker skills later on. It is important to realize that at some point the group will either end or, if it continues, members will eventually leave the group. Endings generally are emotional times for people, and throughout the process of termination the worker must be alert to the reactions of members and be prepared to help them deal with their feelings. Like the beginning of the group, the ending has three phases.

> *Pretermination phase:* This refers to the period immediately before the ending of the group or before a member leaves. In a short-term group, the members have known from the beginning that the group will end but should be reminded in advance. The worker should help the members enumerate and evaluate the group's accomplishments and failures. He or she should encourage members to discuss their feelings and, if necessary, help them work through the difficulties they have in breaking ties. It should be remembered that the worker, too, may have feelings about terminating.
> *Termination:* This refers to the last session of the group or the last session for a particular member.

It may be a regular meeting or it may be a party or special activity that was planned in the pretermination phase. These might help to formalize the ending and make separation easier. At the last meeting some members may make plans to stay in touch in the future, especially if the group was a close one.

Posttermination phase: This stage in group development occurs only in some groups. Members may reconvene after the summer in a group that ended in June; some groups meet at regular or occasional intervals (like once or twice a year) much like a reunion, to keep in touch. Some groups that accomplish the task they were created to perform go on to become informal friendship groups. However, most groups in fact usually do end although some members may stay in touch.

In considering the development of any group, it is important to remember that although all groups may pass through stages as they grow and change, there is a great deal of variation in the timing and sometimes in the order in which the stages occur. At times a group might regress to a former stage, as when, for example, an unexpected change in leadership may cause a group to move from the Group Functioning and Maintenance Phase back to the conflict in the Disintegration Phase. Some groups may skip certain stages completely.

The leader has a great deal of responsibility in helping the group grow and develop. The definition of the leader's role and the tasks performed will change as the group moves from stage to stage. It is important, then, for the leader to be aware of which stage the group is in at any given time and the ways in which to help the group successfully negotiate that stage.

Some Factors to Consider in Forming a New Group

Suppose that you are a beginning human service worker employed in a nursing home. Although the facility is clean and the residents are well cared for, you've noticed that many of them seem bored and lonely. You've also seen that, except for meal times, few residents actually interact with each other. Your supervisor confirms your perceptions and asks how you might change the situation. You decide, then, to form a group. You realize that there are some important choices to be made in setting up your group and that these decisions will affect the experiences of both the members and the leader for the duration of the group's life. Let's examine these variables.

Group Goals. Before you begin to put together a group, you must understand your goals. Why do you want to run a group? What do you hope the group will accomplish? How might the individual members benefit from participating? In a nursing home, some examples of goals would include providing social interaction, learning a skill, increasing self-image, strengthening memory, and promoting independence of functioning. It is especially important to understand your goals because, as we will see, many of the decisions you will make in setting up your group will depend on how you define your goals.

Group Type. Once you are clear about the goals, you must decide on the type of group that would best help you and the clients achieve those goals. A bingo group, for example, would certainly help to relieve boredom and stimulate mental activity, but perhaps a discussion group might be a better choice. A discussion group would provide more interaction among members and might promote friendships that would continue to exist beyond the group. The point here is that there are many different types of groups that could be run in any particular setting; it is up to you to consider each type and choose the one that would best help meet the goals.

Group Size. How many clients should you include in your group? There are many factors to consider in making this decision. Among the most important are your goals and the type of group you've decided to run. A bingo or exercise group could obviously be larger than a discussion group. Another factor to consider in determining group size is the setting in which your group will take place; if you are limited to a small space, you must have a small group. It is also worthwhile to examine member characteristics here. Those with short attention spans or behavioral problems, for example, might do better in a smaller group where they would benefit from greater attention from the leader and other members. In general, you must be sure that your group is large enough for members to have a true group experience and yet not so large that some don't have an opportunity to participate.

Member Characteristics.   Factors such as age and gender may or may not be important to take into account in establishing a group. Once again, you must first look at your goals and then at the type of group you are creating. Age and gender are probably not important in most nursing home groups but they could certainly be significant factors in a group for adolescents in a community center. What about other member characteristics? Depending on the type of group and the nature of the client population, you may want to consider a potential member's level of motivation, attention span, personality, ways of dealing with frustration and anger, strengths and weaknesses, and life situation. In selecting members for your group, it's important to think about not only whether a particular client might benefit from the group experience but also the effect that person might have on other members and on the group process. A confused and aggressive nursing home resident might benefit from the social contact provided by a discussion group, but how would the other members' experiences in the group be affected by including this person? These factors must be carefully considered.

Group Setting.   To some extent, the location of the group will be determined by the type of group you're running. A cooking group tends to work best in a kitchen; a sport group may require a gym or other open space. In groups that focus on discussion as their main activity, the comfort and pri-

vacy of members should be the most important consideration in choosing a location. Factors such as size of room, seating, and lighting could promote or hinder interaction. Consider, for example, the difference between holding a therapy group in a classroom-type setting (large space, hard chairs, fluorescent lights, cold floor) versus the same group meeting in a room more like a living room with comfortable sofas, table lamps, and carpeting. While we acknowledge the impact of setting on group process, in reality many human service workers have little choice about where to run their groups. Agency space is often quite limited and sometimes we gratefully take whatever room we can get.

Closed- or Open-Ended Group.   A closed-ended group is a group in which membership remains stable for the life of the group. That is, certain members join the group when it is formed, they generally remain in the group throughout its duration, and no new members are added. An example of a closed-ended group would be a college seminar that usually begins and ends with the same students. In an open-ended group, new members are added as other members leave. While the number may remain constant, the actual membership changes over time. Alcoholics Anonymous groups are open-ended. There are advantages to both types. Open-ended groups are sometimes more dynamic, constantly changing as members come and go. They also eventually allow participation by a greater number of people. Closed-ended groups may become more cohesive as members come to feel comfortable with each other. Whether a closed- or open-ended group will work best depends on the goals of the group, the needs of the client population, and in some cases, the policy of the agency.

Number and Length of Sessions.   A long-term group is one that continues for months or even years. Long-term groups are often open-ended. A short-term group is one that will meet only for a specified length of time or number of sessions. A college seminar is short-term, usually meeting for one semester. Some group workers believe in the advantages of running short-term groups. Members often work harder on changing behavior or accomplishing tasks if they know they only have a limited amount of time to achieve what they've set out to do. In some cases, though, it would make more sense to organize a long-term group. Returning to our nursing home example, an activity or discussion group would best be long-term with continued social contact and mental stimulation to best meet the needs of the residents. The length of each session must also be determined, with the nature of the group and the needs of its members being considered. A therapeutic group of young addicts in recovery could last for hours, whereas a reality orientation group of confused clients might last only thirty minutes. The session must be long enough so that all members can participate and the group is able to make progress toward its goals. In some cases, time must allow a specific task to be accomplished or project completed. However, if a group session is too long, members may become bored and restless.

Selection of Program. Within the context of group goals and type, the leader must make some decisions about programming in the group. Programming refers to what the group will actually do when it meets; it is through programming that the goals of the group are reached. If a crafts group is being planned, thought must be given to the kinds of crafts projects that will be undertaken. If it's a cooking group, what kinds of food will be prepared and how will tasks be organized? What topics would be appropriate for a discussion group? Program, if appropriately chosen and carried out, will facilitate reaching group goals. It is very important to the success of the group that it be carefully planned in advance.

It is clear from our discussion thus far that there are many options, possibilities, and variables that must be considered during the group formation process. It is important that a group leader consider each of these in order to facilitate maximum effectiveness of the group.

Group Leadership

According to Zastrow (1993), leadership exists within a group whenever one person exerts influence over another and thereby helps the group achieve its goals. Most members, at times, engage in leadership behavior; however, in most groups the human service worker is generally the acknowledged leader. The ways in which the worker defines his or her role and performance in carrying out leadership tasks are crucial to the success of the group.

More than fifty years ago, Kurt Lewin and his colleagues (R. Lippitt and R.K. White), pioneers in the field of social psychology, identified three distinct styles of group leadership and described the ways in which they affect group performance. These are presented by Vander Zanden (1990) and are still considered current and valid today.

In the authoritarian style, the leader determines the policies of the group. He or she assigns tasks, gives detailed directions, and frequently praises or criticizes members according to their performance. While he or she is active within the leadership role, the leader rarely participates in the ongoing activities of the group. This type of leadership often produces a great deal of frustration among group members and feelings of hostility toward the leader. The group may be very productive as long as the leader is there, but members don't work nearly as hard when he or she is absent.

In the laissez-faire style of leadership, the leader remains passive and uninvolved; he or she may even be perceived by group members as withdrawn. The leader is willing to provide materials, help, and suggestions but generally does so only when these are requested. He or she tends not to evaluate member performance. In groups led according to this style, there may be high levels of aggression among members, and group morale and productivity are normally low.

Finally, according to the democratic style, the leader encourages the members to determine the group's goals and the means of achieving them. Alternatives are suggested, but it is the members who make the decision. This type of leader usually participates in the activities of the group and evaluates member performance fairly and objectively. In this type of group, cohesion is high. Members are happier, friendlier towards each other, and more group-oriented. They are motivated to work hard, even in the leader's absence.

The research by Lewis and others who study the small group clearly illustrates the impact of leadership behavior on group performance, goal attainment, and member satisfaction. Leadership style will vary, depending on the nature of the group, its stage of development, and the needs of the members. The personality of the leader will also affect the ways in which he or she carries out this role, much the same way that your professor's personality will affect the way classes are conducted. Be that as it may, what exactly does a group leader do? What skills are required to lead a group? How is the process of working with groups different from working with individuals? In a sense, there is a great deal of similarity between helping clients individually and in groups. In the first place, the values are the same. Human service workers believe in honesty, in the inherent worth of the person, in being nonjudgmental, in self-determination, and in confidentiality, regardless of whether the clients are being seen in a group or one at a time. The basic helping skills are also the same. Among them are observing, listening, questioning, assessing, clarifying, confronting, and giving feedback. (These are discussed in different contexts throughout the book.) These skills, and others, are necessary for the human service worker to have and use with individual clients and with groups.

Schmolling, Youkeles, and Burger (1993) have further identified seven skills that are involved more specifically in working with groups. These skills are: selecting group members, establishing goals, establishing group norms, intervening, promoting interaction, appraising and evaluating and, finally, terminating.

Let's examine the way these skills are used in practice.

Selecting Group Members.   In putting together a new group or replacing a member who has left an existing group, it is important for the worker to consider several factors, including personality, motivation, interests, and, perhaps, age and gender. The needs of the individual members, as well as the balance within the group, must be taken into account. The worker should approach potential members individually and explain the goals of the group and when and where it will meet. Participation is generally more successful if members know as much as possible about the group before it actually begins.

Establishing Goals.   As we've discussed, the group worker must be active in establishing goals for the group, sometimes with input from the members. A tenants' group, for example, may have as its goal to get the landlord to provide a night security guard. A community group of working parents might have as a goal the development of an after-school program for members' children. The worker must be careful to establish only goals that are feasible for the members to attain within the amount of time available.

Members have their own goals in joining a group. Some examples may be to resolve a personal conflict, to interact with others, or to do something useful. The single father who participates in the parents' group to build a playground may, in addition to wanting the playground, see the group as a way of meeting new people and having an evening out.

Establishing Group Norms.   The worker must be active in setting clear rules of behavior at the beginning of the group. This is important so that the group can work together to achieve its goals. Different norms would be significant in different groups. In a treatment group for substance abusers, maintaining confidentiality would be central to the functioning of the group.

The worker would explain to the members why it would be vital not to discuss the group with any nonmembers. In a group of community residents who come together to fund and build a playground, one important norm would be for members to carry out their tasks thoroughly and on time. If the members didn't do this, the playground would never get built.

Intervening.   A worker running a group must listen carefully and be ready to step in at any time. Sometimes, the leader might point out something he or she is observing (for example, that one member consistently arrives late, or one member often stands up for another). Sometimes the leader may make a suggestion, offer a different perspective, provide feedback, or help to settle a conflict. How much or how little the worker intervenes should depend primarily on the needs of the group and its members. But human service workers have their own styles of relating to others, which would affect the way they participate in the group process.

Promoting Interaction.   Positive interaction among members is generally necessary for the group to do the work it was intended to do. It also furthers the opportunity for mutual support and helps to develop group cohesiveness. Whether the group is baking a cake, planning a rent strike, or discussing the problems of childhood, it is important that members speak to each other and listen as well. How does the worker promote positive interaction among members? He or she may help members express themselves clearly; relate the concerns of one member to the concerns of another; encourage politeness, active listening, and taking turns. Also helping members to explore and resolve conflicts, if they exist, goes a long way toward promoting positive interaction.

Appraising and Evaluating.   The worker must continually examine what is occurring in the group. For example, he or she must evaluate how

well members relate to each other, the level of member satisfaction, the extent to which the group is moving toward attaining its goals, the presence of any conflicts or obstacles, and his or her own performance as group leader. Sometimes the leader may choose to involve the members in this evaluation. Depending on the outcome of the evaluation, he or she may decide to intervene in a specific way. If, for example, the leader determines that the group is not as organized as it should be, he or she may choose to help members assign tasks and responsibilities. Or, if he or she sees that the members are uneasy with each other, the leader may design a group exercise to increase familiarity. Evaluation, then, often implies action.

Termination.   A group may end for different reasons. If it is a short-term group meeting for a limited number of sessions, it will end at the last session. If the group was created to solve a particular problem, it will generally end when the problem is solved. Sometimes, as in the case of long-term groups, the actual group doesn't end but individual members may leave. This is, in a sense, a personal ending. As we discussed in the section on the stages of group development, the worker has some very specific tasks to achieve in the process of termination. He or she must, firstly, give the group notice, in advance, that the group will be ending. Even in a group that is scheduled to end, the members may not realize when the termination will occur. Secondly, as different people react to endings in different ways, the leader must allow members the opportunity to explore and express their feelings around the end of the group. Some may feel sad, anxious, or even angry. Thirdly, the worker may encourage the group to plan some sort of party or other celebration to make its ending. This is especially important in groups that have become particularly close. Finally, the worker might want to discuss with the members some plan for addressing issues or problems that may occur after the group is over. Termination is the last stage in the evolution of a group and, as such, it is important to handle it in a professional manner.

Skill in establishing and leading groups, like generic human service skills, are developed gradually over time. Knowledge gained in class, experience and supervision in the field, and on-the-job learning after graduation all contribute to the acquisition of these skills. One of the student's most important resources, though, is the ability to examine and critically evaluate his or her own feelings and behavior in working with groups.

REFERENCES

Hartford, M.E., (1971). *Groups in Social Work.* New York: Columbia University Press.

Heffernan, J., G. Shuttlesworth, and R. Ambrosino, (1992). *Social Work and Social Welfare, An Introduction*, 2nd ed. St. Paul: West.

Mehr, J., (1992). *Human Services*, 5th ed. Boston: Allyn and Bacon.

Meyrs, D.C., (1990). *Social Psychology*, 3rd ed. New York: McGraw-Hill.

Schmotting, P. Jr., M. Youkeles, and W.R. Burger, (1993). *Human Services in Contemporary America*, 3rd ed. Pacific Grove: Brooks/Cole.

Skidmore, R.A., M.G. Thackeray, and O.W. Farley, (1991). *Introduction to Social Work*, 5th ed. Englewood Cliffs: Prentice Hall.

Vander Zanden, J.W., (1990). *Sociology: The Core*, 2nd ed. New York: McGraw-Hill.

Zastrow, C., (1993). *Social Work with Groups*, 3rd ed. Chicago: Nelson-Hall.

CHAPTER 9

HUMAN SERVICES IN THE SCHOOLS
HISTORY AND FOCUS

ARTHUR W. PARLIN
KENNETH J. GREW

Education and the opportunity to acquire an education was, historically, an advantage controlled by the church. The religious leaders limited the possibility of education to those who supported the church and its goals. The occasion for an education increased during the Middle Ages with the invention of the printing press, and the dominance of the church as a ruling power declined. Two broad-based approaches to education grew out of the influence of the church. These theories, nationalism and developmentalism, while different in concept, had the same purpose. The intent of each doctrine was the preservation of a revolutionary government in the early eighteenth century.

The revolutions, one in America and the other in France, were viewed by monarchs as threats to their form of government. The various rulers sent their armies out to eliminate the revolutionary government espoused by these newly formed countries. The attacks promoted a strong patriotism among the French. The leaders of the Revolution recognized the value of maintaining the patriotic motivations present in the hearts and minds of the French people. The leaders also perceived the advantages and strengths inherent in a state-directed system of education whereby all people might be informed of the desirability of their form of government and be made aware of their rights, privileges, and liberties through this form of governance. The leaders clearly understood that in the education of children, their form of government would likely have an effective method for social control and a stronger guarantee of stability and permanence. This concept of using education to preserve and protect the nation from external attack and internal disintegration, developing national wealth and economic independence, and a national unity through common goals, ideals, and traditions espoused in a state-directed, national curriculum was the theory of nationalism.

The developmental theory of education, while having many of the same goals and objectives, seeks to reach them in a different manner. This theory viewed the *child* as the object of the educational process, not the country's continuance. These theorists believed education could change society for the better by changing the individuals who make up the society. They believed that the acquisition of rights and freedoms meant little to people unless accompanied by the advancement of their capabilities to profit from and use their liberties. They focused on the nature of the mind and how, psychologically, the mind worked with support for their theory evolving from the study of the development of children. More children were to be included in the educational system as the developmentalists increased their knowledge of the needs of children and how to address these needs in the educational system.

The motive for education in colonial America was religious. It emerged from the religious freedoms people sought in coming to

151

America. The pursuit of religious freedom grew into the struggle for independence, and ultimately resulted in the American Revolution, the Declaration of Independence, and the creation of public education as a way to prepare all citizens for their responsibilities.

There were two different opinions as to the relationship of education and government at the time of the founding of America. The Federalists, similar to the French, believed in the creation of a strong, highly centralized federal system for their instruction of the citizenry. The Jeffersonians espoused the view of the developmentalists. They believed that individuals, communities, and states should manage the business of education as much as possible. They believed that an educated, informed, and questioning citizenry would enable the country to persevere because people would satisfy their local needs instead of those imposed by a single federal system of national ideas and goals.

There was not a universal system of education existent at the time this debate was taking place in America, and there were many other weighty matters of state to be addressed. Therefore the leaders of the American Revolution acceded to the wishes of the Jeffersonians and reserved the responsibilities of education to the states through the provisions of the Tenth Amendment to the Constitution. It was clear from the public statements of many leaders of that time that the preparation of the individual for civic responsibilities was to be the aim of education in America. Thus, the American educational system selected the developmental approach for the education of its people in order to provide all people with the fullest realization of themselves, while preserving their freedom and their government.

There was little need for a student-support service in early America, since the economic life of the people did not demand high educational preparation for making a living. People were engaged in farming and agriculturally related trades for the most part. There was not a large population, and people lived in small groups that were somewhat distant from each other. Education was viewed as a largely private function or determina-tion of each family where attendance at school was optional and dependent on the needs of each family.

As American society grew and became more complex, the schools were driven to change to meet the needs of people. Economic success was linked to more and better education. The industrialization of America in the middle 1800s, created by the invention and introduction of machinery, caused specialization in the trades, increase in family wealth, growth in the population, an increase in immigration, and concentration of people in cities. The home was no longer self-sufficient. Along with these changes came increasingly insistent demands that all children be educated at public expense for a definite period of time each year and for a definite period of years. These demands led to the first compulsory attendance law in the country being enacted in Massachusetts in 1852. This was the birth of pupil services in the schools. The law required census taking and attendance monitoring by the school system. Larger and more affluent school districts hired clerks to conduct and tabulate the census and truant officers to monitor attendance. These people were paraprofessional or nonteaching people paid by the school system to carry out supportive services in the district.

Soon thereafter, the moral/religious roots of American education combined with the changing economic needs of society, where more employment opportunities were required for the growing adult population, resulting in the enactment of child labor laws. The child labor laws were enforced by the school attendance paraprofessionals. Children were required to secure guidance and approval, in the form of a written work permit, from these people if the children were going to be working. The children often disclosed family economic difficulties as the reason for their need to work. Again, the moral/religious foundations of the American education system, the concern for the development of the individual child, and the economic reality of limiting the number of working children led to additional social services in the form of food, clothing, and basic medical services for poor and indigent children. These services were viewed as reasonable and natural ways to accommodate the individual needs of children. As the specialization and number of the services grew, so did the use of support or paraprofessional staff to provide the services in an efficient and effective manner.

Student social and guidance services expanded further after World War I. The war identified the need of a system for the selection of men for specific jobs in the military. This was necessary to reduce the costs and time required to supply military units with trained soldiers. The emergency resulted in the use of skill testing of recruits. While lacking refinement, this preselection process worked. People recognized the wastefulness of personnel methods that ignored employees and potential employees so completely that no questions were ever raised as to whether people were doing the kind of work they were best fitted for or from which they secured the most enjoyment.

The success in the selection of draftees for military duties and the subsequent success of businesses in securing employees through skill testing led to the incorporation of group testing in the schools for purposes of educational training of the children in their areas of interest and ability. Psychological services developed concurrently, as did the concept of guidance services as a discrete pupil service staffed by specialized teaching staff and/or paraprofessionals. Over the course of time, guidance has evolved from a concept of group testing for vocational placement to a concept of career or lifestyle development and the sophisticated evaluation of scholastic ability and school achievement. Paralleling the growth in the status of guidance has been that of the early attendance and increased complexities of an urban society, and the application of science to everyday living. The launching of the first Soviet *Sputnik* satellite in 1957 created the spark needed to move the process forward.

Two federal programs also created opportunity for developing the field of pupil personnel services. They were the National Defense Education Act and the National Science Foundation Act, enacted in 1958. These laws contained incentive monies for states to stimulate and provide an improved education for individual students. Congress voted these laws into existence in an attempt to provide educational assistance to young people. The laws were modeled along the earlier military's Readjustment Act of 1944—the G.I. Bill of Rights—which had been so successful in helping individual servicemen adapt to the changed civilian life following World War II.

The National Defense Education Act was set up to improve the state statistical services and to encourage the coordination of services provided to all children. The National Science Foundation Act was structured to provide for the training of teachers in present day science and mathematics instructional procedures, to develop better teaching materials and instructional procedures, and to permit advanced training for advanced students.

The federal government continued its involvement in the process of expanding toward inclusion of 100 percent of the children in the school-attending population of elementary and secondary programs with added legislation. The legislation had direct and indirect influence on the growth of pupil personnel services, as well as a significant impact on the introduction of paraprofessionals into the regular school programs. The source of this movement was the National Science Foundation Act. School systems utilized some of the funding available from the program to institute science programs that included paid paraprofessionals. These aides were necessary because the role of the classroom teacher was expanded, and the teacher did not have the time to prepare equipment and materials for the science experiments, shop for the supplies, and do the record keeping associated with many of the experiments that related to the individual abilities of the child.

The use of paraprofessional assistants became more common when the federal government enacted Public Law 89–10, which is more commonly known as the Elementary and Secondary Education Act (ESEA) in 1965. This act required that compensatory education programs be extended to economically and educationally disadvantaged children in public and nonpublic schools. Under Title I of ESEA, funds could be and often were expended for almost any service that would reduce disadvantages. Other portions of ESEA provided for the supplying of instructional materials, including textbooks and library books, establishment of supplementary learning centers, and the furnishing of services not otherwise adequate or available to children in a particular school district. Enterprising school districts utilized the funds available through ESEA to hire specialized staff to teach reading and language arts, paraprofessionals to offer tutorial assistance outside of the regular classroom and complete much of the paperwork associated with the reports required by the programs, and administrators to coordinate the various functions and to seek additional federal funding.

As American society continued to grow in size and complexity, the trend to teacher specialization in the schools continued to grow. This growth was stimulated in part by the granting of collective bargaining rights to teachers. The collective bargaining process brought about an assessment and review of the duties and responsibilities of teachers. The assessments and reviews resulted in a division of labor into instructional and noninstructional duties. Noninstructional duties were delegated to administrative staff and/or paraprofessional staff. Examples of such delegations include lunchroom supervision, schoolyard monitoring, crosswalk guarding, and study hall monitoring.

The growth of the population and the increasing complexity of American society also created demands on the federal government. The demands were economic and political in nature. Economic demands came from employers who pressed for more literate employees trained in the sciences and able to make decisions. The political demands were being pursued by parents of children who were still not being integrated into the elementary and secondary schools.

The outcome of the efforts of the various groups was an increase in funding from the federal government to attempt to meet the expecta-

tions of the specific constituencies. Accompanying the money from the federal government was the requirement for even greater amounts of statistical data. The data was used to identify program successes, failures, and other possible specialized intervention. This process continued to generate additional administrative tasks to be completed and to identify new areas for specialized educational intervention. The more innovative educational interventions by the federal government often were categorical programs that were supported by corresponding legislation and regulations at the state levels.

One of the well-known examples of this approach for inclusion of previously excluded children in the educational process on the part of the federal government is Public Law 94–142. This law, more commonly known as the "special education bill," was enacted in 1972. The purpose of the bill was to extend public school programs to severely handicapped children and to expand the inclusionary age span for the delivery of educational services for these handicapped students from the traditional five to sixteen age chart to those in the three to twenty-two range.

This effort for inclusion traced its origin back to the Jeffersonian concept of developmentalism. Specifically, this group of people had the right to a free, public education but could not advance individual capabilities because access to that education was limited. Studies of the developmental ability of these children supported the inclusion of these children in the schools. And it was believed by many that the society could be changed for the better through the inclusion of this significant part of the society. Thus, Public Law 94–142 was enacted. The legislation stands as a fine example of the original intent of the founders of America in that there was a significant positive result for specific children, later for children in general, and finally for society as a whole, as will be discussed later.

The implementation of this special education bill followed the lines of earlier federal programs. Limited funds were disbursed to local school districts and the states with mandated expectations.

The funds could be used for a variety of materials, equipment, supplies, and staffing needs. The legislation contemplated specialization of personnel delivering services to the children. The legislation also considered a division of labor to include not only specialized teaching staff, but also paraprofessionals or special education aides. This division of labor and the formal introduction of a new specialized employment role in the schools was an effort to contain costs while providing services for a new group of students being educated within the schools.

The mandates of P.L. 94–142 resulted in the rapid proliferation of highly specific and specialized programs for handicapped children in the schools. Legal suits initiated by parents on behalf of the children also helped to generate changes in the educational process. Importantly, many of the alterations and modifications occasioned by the inclusion of the handicapped students occurred through the use of paraprofessionals. Educators expanded their study of children from the study of the child's mind and behavioral research to include studies of the physical development of children. Educators increased their knowledge of the needs of handicapped children. This increased practical knowledge, and the ongoing knowledge gained from behavioral research was combined with new research conducted on the physical and neurological development of children, and resulted in almost total inclusion of students with severe learning, and physical and/or neurological needs in school programs at the elementary- and secondary-school levels. The offering of these highly specialized programs became increasingly dependent on the services of a more technically proficient professional staff. Just as importantly, the success of these specialized programs came to rely on the contribution of a cadre of specialized paraprofessional staff.

The role of adults as helpers to classroom teachers has a rich history. Early studies report schools often invited parents and relatives of school children to volunteer their assistance in schools. The adults usually performed practical, everyday chores and duties that often took the teachers away from their instructional responsibilities. The tasks these volunteers performed were as mundane as helping children get their clothes on or off for school recess and as involved as checking to see that children were using correct procedures as directed by the classroom teacher. Over time, as society grew more complex and instruction covered more and more informational bases, more functions performed by classroom teachers were shifted to school volunteers. The volunteers, in turn, perceived their role as more than an aide to the teaching staff. They saw their services as paraprofessional and more indispensable to the success of the school.

While these changes occurred in the schools, there were material changes happening in the economic and social orders of the country that were to have a profound impact on the schools. The economy was being transformed into a global enterprise. International competition was created by the resurgence of the industrial foundations of Germany and Japan. Also, the emerging economies of newly industrialized countries such as Hong Kong, Singapore, Taiwan, South Korea, and Indonesia reduced the dominance of America in the world economy. This increase in economic competition created the need for students with increased competence in science, mathematics, and thinking skills. It also created the necessity for businesses to restructure their operational methods, and the requirement that the work force be retrained or cease doing business.

The significant redirections that occurred in the economy were matched by a shift in the attitudes and points of view in American society. The Civil Rights Act passed in 1964 spurred growing demands for equality in terms of racial, sexual, and educational opportunity. The number of single-parent families increased. It became necessary for both parents to work to support their desired life-style. Also, the schools started to become the local community center reserved for the education of children during the day, and the recreational and training center for adults during the afternoons and evenings. These momentous forces outside of the schools came together with events in the schools such as the surge in collective bargaining, the need for special education teachers, the requirement to integrate handicapped children, and the need to use paraprofessional staff to help educate and integrate the handicapped students to redefine the division of labor in the schools. This redirection of staffing patterns in the 1970s to include paraprofessionals was similar to the shift that occurred in the schools in prior years when specialization of the teacher staff occurred. The level of training for paraprofessionals evolved from an informed, experiential base to an informal, post-high-school training.

The movement to utilize paraprofessionals in the educational process was forced by several circumstances in the schools in the 1970s. First, there was a serious shortage of trained, certified special education teachers. A second reason for the shift to use of paraprofessionals was purely economic. A school district was not compelled to pay the high salary of a trained teacher now that regulations permitted use of paraprofessionals. Thirdly, the early programs for handicapped students were, for the most part, "pull-out" instructional programs.

The "pull-out" programs were essentially self-contained classrooms for the education of special education students. The regulations associated with P.L. 94–142 limited the number of students in these self-contained classes. The class size often was permitted to increase by some 50 percent when an instructional aide or teacher aide was present in the class. The special education teachers with teacher aides in their classroom had the aides perform noninstructional or quasi-instructional duties in the self-contained classroom so that the special education teacher could provide the instructional services needed to make the educational program of the student a more successful undertaking. The practice of utilizing the classroom aide to complete subprofessional tasks continued to grow. The special education teacher was required to produce a detailed individual educational plan for each special education student. The plans produced increased levels of academic, behavioral, and social achievement for the students. This success in turn required more detailed planning, greater demands on the teachers' time, and, over time, compelled the use of the instructional aide to complete the lower-level instructional tasks. These tasks included reading stories with the students, helping children complete worksheets, assisting students in test taking, and working with children on an ongoing basis as the children used technological innovations such as tape recorders, and later computers, to achieve mastery of educational materials.

The successful introduction of paraprofessionals into the educational process was noted by the teaching staff, researchers who analyzed the results being achieved, special education parents who wanted their children included in the regular classroom setting, and parents of regular education students who wished to have their children receive the benefits of an instructional aide in the regular classroom. Each of these groups of people was able to achieve its goal of expanding the use of paraprofessionals in the school setting. Teachers accomplished their goal of giving over mundane classroom tasks such as making copies of instructional sheets, taking lunch orders, collecting lunch and milk monies from students, supervising playgrounds, etc., to paid adult aides. The duties and responsibilities of these aides were judged to be more administrative in nature and, while important, not as important as the assignments of the instructional aides. Thus, a new category of paraprofessional, administrative aides, was introduced to school systems.

This striking growth of paraprofessional staffing continued in the 1980s. Special education parents, realizing the levels of success achieved by their children, sought to have their children more fully integrated into the everyday, regular classroom for the academic challenge and the social needs of their children. Initial responses of school systems to this request were often negative. Reasons for the negative responses included the increased costs associated with such moves, the reluctance of classroom teachers to accept special education students in their classrooms, reluctance of the special education teacher to have the special education students leave the successful setting of the self-contained classroom, and the difficulties associated with getting the more severely handicapped children around the school. Parents of special education students quickly turned to the federal bureaucracy and court systems to help them successfully force schools to expand the inclusionary model of developmental education first espoused by the Jeffersonians in early America to include special education and handicapped students. The intervention of the federal hierarchy and courts combined to literally knock down barriers and compel attitudes to change so the special education students could be included in the regular education programming.

The movement of special education students from the self-contained classroom to the regular classroom generated another division of labor within the ranks of the paraprofessional staff. The job of integration aide was added to the listing of instructional and administrative aide. The integration aide became the communication and instructional link for the teacher and the student, respectively. This aide implemented tasks contained in the individual educational plan of the student under the direction and guidance of the special education and regular education teacher. The position of integration aide is more often than not filled by a person who has a college education because of the duties associated with the position. The duties include easing the student into the academic and social order of the classroom, verifying that the student is meeting the goals designated in his or her individual education plan, collecting data to report the progress of the student to the teachers and parents, and helping maintain classroom discipline, as appropriate.

The success of the paraprofessional in the special education area did not escape the notice of parents of regular education students. The parents reasoned that if the special education and handicapped youngsters could benefit so greatly with the assistance of paraprofessionals, then their children would also have greater success with paraprofessionals in the regular classroom. This idea was supported by research that analyzed the results of programs that employed aides. The concept of using aides in all classrooms also gained momentum with the introduction of computer technology into the classroom. The technology spread like wildfire in the schools. The lack of skilled staff forced school systems to hire people to serve as computer aides. Thus, another category of paraprofessionals was added to the growing list of diversified support staff in the schools.

The staffing changes occurring in the elementary and secondary schools were noted by another group of educators, vocational educators. They, too, analyzed the results achieved through the use of aides and proceeded to successfully introduce the use of paraprofessionals in their programs. Students in the vocational schools have a greater potential for injury than those in regular secondary schools because of the high-powered equipment such as saws, presses, grinders, welding tools, etc., used in the vocational training programs. The use of aides in the various shop programs provided increased safety for the students and, over time, gave the teacher the same types of opportunities to use the aide as an instructional assistant as had occurred in the regular education programs.

The employment of paraprofessionals by school systems continued to be encouraged by the federal government through the rewriting of program guidelines. The guidelines were changed so that local school systems and state agencies could employ paraprofessionals. This process matured to a higher level in 1991 when the federal education bureaucracy shepherded a revamped vocational funding program through Congress. The new program, the Carl D. Perkins Vocational Education Act, was designed to improve the delivery of educational services to vocational students. Included in the guidelines was the opportunity to expand the paraprofessional field to include the technical preparation aide. The position was conceived as a means to bring adults trained in the emerging areas of technology into the vocational schools to prepare the students for the rapidly changing world of work. The blending of the professional and paraprofessional staff will enable the classroom teacher to provide the academic background and education needed by the students for employment in constantly changing areas; such areas include electronics, computers, drafting, auto repairs, hairdressing, heating, and ventilation and air conditioning, as well as the knowledge required for employment in emerging employment areas such as medical technology and biogenetics. This blending will permit the paraprofessional or technical preparation aide to provide, under the supervision of the teacher, practical skills for the student in the labs and workshops associated with the area of academic preparation.

As the nation grew in size, society became more complex and diverse and knowledge increased by immense proportions. A parallel change occurred in the field of educational administration to support the growing student population and to coordinate the diverse programming needed to serve the students. Additionally, as the population grew, the tasks of the teacher in the early one-room schoolhouse also increased. There were more students at different grade levels to educate, and the tasks of opening the school, such as tending fires to heat the building, cleaning of the building and the lavatories, repairing the building, etc., were recognized as noninstructional tasks that took away from the education of the child. The duties and responsibilities were parcelled out to new teachers by the principal teacher or head teacher as the school population increased. Thus, with the urbanization of the country and the call for required attendance in schools, the duties of the head teacher evolved into this new role of headmaster or principal and became more administrative in nature. The role also took on the responsibility of supervising the other teachers and developing curricular programs that educated the children for the times.

As the continued increases in student population and the explosion of knowledge caused a diversity in the curriculum, increased specialization of teachers, and a division of labor into instructional and noninstructional tasks, so that a discreet identification of administrative tasks occurred over time. The one-room schoolhouse began to separate into elementary and secondary levels of education. There were different curricular programs to be coordinated, more materials to be purchased, and distinct equipment was required for the schools. A person was hired to supervise these activities while the principals administered their buildings. The rapid mechanization of industry, the effects of compulsory education, the growth of knowledge, and the diversity of the specialized staff necessitated additional administrative staffing in larger districts and allowed the expansion of administrative staffing in richer school districts. The result was the hiring of assistants for the supervising administrator or superintendent.

The model for coordinating educational programs and services served until the 1950s. The advent of federal funding and increased accountability pressured the American system to continue to emphasize proven educational practices while developing educational services to assure the maximum development of each pupil. The administrative tasks were separated into instructional, or academic, and noninstructional, or pupil personnel services. This diversification of labor resulted in differentiated or specialized staff for these administrative areas. This model was further modified as the school systems expanded the school population to include special education and handicapped students and adult education in the 1970s. These specialty areas in administration were, in time, staffed by people trained and certified in the specialty.

The growth of a diversified employee group in the field of education has often seemed to be a topsy-turvy, accidental, political, or nondirected event. But, as shown in the broader view above, the growth and diversification of education in America has held true to its original concept of developmentalism. The schools have produced an educated, informed, and questioning citizenry that has enabled the country to persevere. The massive infusion of funding of the federal government and the subsequent intrusion by that government at the local levels through federal mandates, requirements, and guidelines since the 1950s have produced tension and stress in the local school system that have yet to be fully researched or appreciated. However, this involvement came about because of the need to include children who were being denied the opportunity for an equal educational opportunity by reason of their race, their sex, their physical difficulties, or their mental abilities. It is clear from a reading of the history of early America that change is more immediate today, the population exceeds the estimations of the Revolutionary leaders, the knowledge and information available today far exceeds that of colonial America, and the need to educate and re-educate people for the continual changes in the workplace were not foreseen by the founders of this country. Yet, the forward thinking people who developed our system of governance and education created a system that works.

We see today that new questions are surfacing every day about the role of the federal government in education. There is a movement to schools of choice where local systems and groups, again, seek to satisfy local needs for a strong education versus the needs imposed by a single system of national ideas and goals. While the business of education is no longer a private or purely local function, the success of the American approach to educating its people has resulted in success. As this chapter has tried to illustrate, the educational system grew, diversified, and became more complex as society grew, diversified, and became more complex. The schools diversified to provide instructional and support services for children. They also evolved from the early one-room schoolhouse to the large facilities of today where a differentiated staff of teachers, aides, and administrators educates and serves all children without regard to race, color, creed, handicap, or need.

As we look to the twenty-first century, we believe there will be a continued diversification in the staffing of schools. Recent research conducted by Pickett (1990) and Charter (1991), and the continued pressure to contain costs, lead us to speculate that staff growth and diversification will occur in the area of the paraprofessional staff. There will be increased training and certification required of staff members as they take on added responsibility for the continued inclusion of all children in the schools to ensure the maximum development of the individual child.

REFERENCES

Blalock, G., (1991). "Paraprofessionals: Critical Members in Our Special Education Programs." *Intervention in School and Clinic,* 26(4), 200–14.

Boomer, L.W., (1982). "The Paraprofessional: A Valued Resource for Special Education and Their Teachers." *Teaching Exceptional Children,* 14(5) 194–97.

Charter, P., (1991). "Who Will Teach Our Children?—Use of Bilingual Paraprofessionals in Special Education." Vista Unified School District, North San Diego County, CA.

Christinas, O.L., (1992). "Michigan Non-Mandated Aide Pilot Project." Michigan State Department of Education, Lansing, MI, Bureau of Information Management. p. 33.

Cabb, H. Jr., (1984). "Assessing the Role of the Paraprofessional." *Spectrum,* 2(1) 37–40.

Courson, F.H., and W.L. Heward, (1988). "Increasing Active Student Response Through the Effective Use of Paraprofessionals." *Pointer,* 33(1) 27–31.

Curlock, J.A., (1982). "Use of Cognitive Behavioral Interventions by Paraprofessionals in the Schools." *School Psychology Review,* 11(1) 64–66.

Eby, F., and C.F. Arrowood, (1934). *The Development of Modern Education.* New York: Prentice-Hall Inc.

The Encyclopedia of Education, L.C. Deighton, editor in chief, New York: The Macmillan Company and The Free Press.

Ford, J.R., (1982). "Connecticut Program Covers Classrooms of Absent Teachers, Provides Tutors." *Phi Delta Kappan,* 63(10) 702–03.

Hales, R.M., and L.B. Carlton, (1992). "Issues and Trends in Special Education." Federal Resource Center for Special Education, Lexington, KY.

Heck, A. O., (1929). *Administration of Pupil Personnel.* Boston: Ginn and Co.

International Encyclopedia of the Social Sciences, D.Z. Sills, editor, (1968). New York: The Macmillan Company and The Free Press.

Lindsey, J.D., (1983). "Paraprofessionals in Learning Disabilities." *Journal of Learning Disabilities,* 16(8) 467–72.

McKenzie, R.G., and C.S. Houk, (1986). "Use of Paraprofessionals in the Resource Room." *Exceptional Children,* 53(1) 41–45.

McKenzie, R.G., and C.S. Houk, (1986). "The Paraprofessional in Special Education." *Teaching Exceptional Children,* 18(4) 246–52.

Pickett, A.L., (1986). "Certified Partners: Four Good Reasons for Certification of Paraprofessionals." *American Educator: The Professional Journal of the American Federation of Teachers,* 10(3) 31–34.

Pickett, A.L., (1990). "Paraprofessionals in Education: Personnel Practices that Influence Their Performance, Training Needs, and Retention." Paper Presented at the Rural Education Symposium of the American Council on Rural Special Education and National Rural and Small Schools Consortium, Tucson, AZ.

Shear, B., (1966). "Administration of Pupil Personnel Services" in Edward Landy and Arthur M. Kroll, eds., *Guidance in American Education III: Needs and Influencing Forces.* Cambridge, MA: Harvard University Press. 238–57.

Stringham, G., (1982). "Noncertified Collective Bargaining: Education's Achilles Heal." NASSP Bulletin, 66(453) 100–07.

Trame, E.A., (1982). "Conform or Transform? Paraprofessionals in Physical Education." *Journal of Physical Education, Recreation and Dance,* 53(9) 62–63.

Vasa, S.F. et al., (1986). "Resource Guide for the Development of Policies and Practices in the Use of Paraprofessionals in Special Education," Project Assist; Research Guides for the Development of Policies and Practices, University of Nebraska, Lincoln, NE, Department of Special Education and Communication Disorder.

Wilds, E.H., and K.V. Lottich, (1964). *The Foundations of Modern Education,* 3rd ed. New York: Holt Rinehart and Winston.

CHAPTER 10

COMMUNITY-BASED SCHOOLS
COLLABORATION BETWEEN HUMAN SERVICES AND SCHOOLS AS RADICAL EDUCATIONAL REFORM

ROBERT LAWSON
PEGGY ANDERSON

It takes a whole village to raise a child.
—African proverb

Historically there have been many barriers that have impeded human service workers' accessibility to children in schools. The reasons are political, economic, and professional or, as it is more commonly called, "turf." It is time to create new paradigms to help society's most overlooked population: children and families in crisis.

According to Tyack (1992), "There is a long history in the United States of providing noneducational services to children in a school setting" (p. 19). Early programs attempted to provide health and social services in the school setting. The intent of these early efforts was to assist immigrant children in adjusting to their new culture. Locating these services in the school setting changed the focus from serving the family to serving the individual child.

Over the past forty years there have been increased cutbacks in social services and a move away from assisting the family as a whole. The last attempts at collaboration came during the Johnson Administration's War on Poverty. Collaboration was never truly achieved as new agencies were formed that completely by-passed schools. Most of these agency programs were eliminated during the Nixon Administration (Tyack, 1992). Programs were further threatened with the election of Ronald Reagan in 1980. His administration shifted the responsibility for human services to individual states, communities, and the private sector. In addition, the administration implemented cutbacks in major programs, as well as changes in eligibility. As a result of these decisions, important social service programs were affected (Woodside and McClam, 1990).

Edelman and Radin (1991) note that evaluation of programs over the past forty years has led to a contemporary model—colocation of human services in schools. According to Dolan (1992), colocation involves several agencies sharing space, either in a school or in close proximity to a school. Edelman and Radin (1991) further suggest that the results have been mixed, having more to do with the individuals involved than with the tangibility of the concept.

An increasing number of children and adolescents in today's society face an uncertain, often bleak, future. According to The National

Commission on Children Report, "Nearly 13 million children live in poverty, more than 2 million more than a decade ago" (Beyond Rhetoric, p. 24, 1991). Families are challenged by this escalation in poverty as well as an increase in crime, substance abuse, and single parent homes. Children who live in poverty also risk poor health and malnutrition. Neighborhoods are often dangerous, leaving families feeling isolated and frightened. Many of America's children live in violent homes, or often have no home at all. Heck (1987) notes that these children are "at-risk" of not achieving academic success without special care and attention (p. 4). Concurrently, an increasing number of these students are not being adequately served by the present configuration of social services. The National Commission on Children makes the following recommendation: "That all schools and communities reevaluate the services they currently offer and design creative, multidisciplinary initiatives to help children with serious and multiple needs reach their academic potential (Beyond Rhetoric, 1991, p. 210).

As is noted by these, as well as many other authorities on children and youth, it is imperative to work toward collaboration between schools and human services. This concept has many proponents but few models from which to learn. James Comer's School Development Model was implemented over twenty years ago (Dolan, 1992). Since that time, models have been designed throughout the country. While some have been more successful than others, all have been chosen based on the needs of the schools and communities they serve. Schorr (1988) notes that models—no matter what their circumstance—". . . provide a vision of what can be achieved." Further, the author suggests that consideration and study of these models can be a beginning of better understanding of the process of collaboration and interventions (p. 266).

COLLABORATION

All around the country, we've been forced to read the handwriting on the wall. Either we work together, or we don't continue to exist.

—Anne T. Pelletier

Mattessich and Monsey (1992) define collaboration as, "a mutually beneficial and well defined relationship entered into by two or more organizations to achieve common goals" (p. 7). According to Mark S. Homan (1993), in his book outlining community change, a collaborative process must include a series of steps in order to be successful. He lists those essential components as follows:

Steps to collaboration
1. Communication
2. Clear agreements
3. Decision making
4. Monitoring and evaluation
5. Recognition
6. Trust
7. Leadership

Melaville and Blank (1991) cite the importance of defining the difference between cooperation and collaboration. In cooperative arrangements, those agencies and institutions involved assist one another in meeting their individual goals but do not develop common goals. Cooperative agreements may include colocation of services, on-site referral to outside agencies, and possible in-service staff training. In addition, cooperative programs do not implement preventive or support services. In comparison, collaborative efforts must establish common goals. Collaborative strategy usually arises out of a need to change the delivery and configuration of services. These models offer a greater opportunity for change by agreeing to join together, utilizing resources, and jointly planning the programs. By effective delegation, the group can expect to achieve the goals set forth and avoid duplication and fragmentation of service.

CULTURES

In a culture that has been homogeneous for some time, there are a number of understood, unwritten rules by which people live. There is an ethos there, there is a mode, an understanding that "we don't do it that way."

—Joseph Campbell

Those involved in the collaborative process must be aware of the resources needed to achieve success. Obstacles to collaboration must be evaluated in order to reach the goals established by policy makers and effectively utilize resources.

Gardner (1992) suggests that teachers, as well as other school personnel and parents, must be part of the collaborative team. If they are excluded, opposition and lack of support can become issues. According to Kurtz (1988), parent participation is also beneficial to students' achievement. He feels that cultural differences can be an obstacle for parents and teachers. In further discussion the author warns that, "Teachers fear parents' scrutiny, and parents worry that any challenge to teachers may have a detrimental impact on their children's acceptance by their teachers" (p. 445). Professionals from different disciplines, as well as parents, inevitably view the child and family from different perspectives. According to Linda Kunesh of the North Central Regional Educational Laboratory, "If two people respect one another, they can make things work. That's why agencies interested in doing collaboration need to do some heavy-duty work on interpersonal relations and conflict resolution" (Melaville, Blank and Asayeah, 1993, p. 37).

Problems of "turf" protection constitute one of the most difficult barriers to successful collaboration. Professionals are trained to respond to challenges within their own system. Programs that have reported success in this area attempt to clarify the vision of each individual unit to make clear how these professionals fit into the model. It is important to stress each agency's contribution to the collaborative whole.

Jehl and Kirst (1992) and Golden (1991) assert that the issue of professional protection is due, in part, to the fact that the professionals involved in collaboration have diverse undergraduate and graduate training, use different professional language, operate in separate working cultures and have differing pay scales. Expanding on that subject, Edelman and Radin (1991) call for universities to begin teaching "across disciplines" to prepare future professionals to work in a collaborative setting. Further, the author notes the lack of interdisciplinary curriculum by stating

that, "University prestige is tied to specialization, to a specific discipline, not to integration" (p. 18).

Jehl and Kirst (1992), as well as Gardner (1992), report that co-equality is an important aspect of true collaboration. The three authors point out that no single agency can be allowed to have ownership of the process. There must be ". . . an atmosphere of mutual respect and collegiality for the efforts to be successful" (Jehl and Kirst, 1992, p. 7). This often necessitates staff training to achieve. This is an example of the importance of changing current ways of viewing problems—a paradigm shift.

Gardner (1992) warns that school-based services inevitably confront the issue of confidentiality. Requirements vary from agency to agency, which often makes the problem a difficult one to negotiate. One way to remove this barrier is the use of informed consent. This procedure uses parental consent forms designed for multiagency use. Grays Harbor Interagency Involvement Project (Akerlund and Carthung, 1990) has implemented the use of an interagency referral form for these purposes. In further discussion of this problem, Melaville and Blank (1991) suggest that, while arrangements are possible, they often require patience and, at times, legal consultation.

Co-eligibility, the ability of families to complete one form for establishing eligibility for several agencies, is an important goal of successful collaboration. Human service workers' values indicate that their client's comfort and integrity is of utmost importance. Co-eligibility removes the barriers to service delivery that may be difficult for families with multiple problems.

Co-location of services, another collaborative goal, removes a barrier common to families in need. Often, transportation is an obstacle that prevents clients from visiting agencies that are located far from one another. This is an added problem for families already burdened and highly stressed. Melaville and Blank (1991) suggest co-location as a way to bridge the gap between families and services. The authors describe this restructuring as, "The repositioning or co-location of staff from one organization to 'branch offices' located at other agencies' . . . . One-stop shopping centers" are another way to achieve more comprehensive service delivery. This arrangement provides several services at one location, thereby providing families with a single point of access (p. 9).

The American Association of College Teaching Educators calls for professional preparation programs that are responsive to the needs of America's children and youth. The educational needs of today's and tomorrow's youth are different from those traditionally served by the schools. It is imperative that programs meet the needs of students in today's society.

CHANGING PARADIGMS

Some men see things as they are and say, "Why?" I dream of things that never were and say, "Why not?"

—Robert F. Kennedy

Joel Barker (1990) defines a paradigm shift as: "a revolutionary new way of thinking about old problems." In further discussion, Barker suggests that this shift usually occurs when previous efforts fail to produce solutions to the problem (p. 27). By looking toward the changing paradigms of school/social service relationships, it is possible to envision the impact this shift will have on schools, children, family, and society.

A part of this shift is changing the usual negative approach to at-riskness to a more positive outlook. In addition, this change must include the stakeholders in society—youth, parents, teachers, business, and community workers. For example, in Snohomish County, Washington, there has been a community-wide program combining the efforts of several agencies involved with children and youth. The result has been an effective, integrated effort on behalf of the county's children.

An essential ingredient in the shifting of paradigms is the explanation and understanding of new terms. As a part of the human service and education collaborative model, it is important to define the terms as follows:

at-risk—those children, youth, and families who, because of multiple challenges, are likely to experience academic, economic, and lifeskills difficulties

co-eligibility—common criteria, procedures, and application forms for use by multiple agencies and institutions

co-location—a number of services sharing physical space

collaboration—a process of joining together education and human services with the intent to change the way in which services are currently delivered. A collaborative effort must share a common goal, as well as share decision making and evaluation duties.

cooperation—agreement made between schools and human service agencies to provide services to students and families. Information is shared but no common goals are developed in cooperative models.

family service worker—also known as a project coordinator, this is a professional who facilitates the collaborative process by assessing needs, coordinating services, assisting children and families in securing services, and establishing follow-up and assessment procedures

preservice—education at undergraduate and graduate levels that addresses the collaborative process and cross-training between disciplines

resiliency—resilient children possess the following attributes: social competency, problem-solving skills, a sense of his or her own identity, and a sense of purpose and future

school-linked services—a partnership formed by schools, health, and human service agencies to provide services to students

service learning—a process by which students learn by actively participating in community volunteer efforts. This process is integrated into students' academic curriculum and strives to help them develop a sense of civic responsibility and care of others.

A paradigm shift will significantly impact society as a whole. It will be especially important to the fields closely involved with collaboration—teachers, human service workers, business, government, and funding sources. It will most likely necessitate the implementation of a new profession—a facilitator trained in the collaborative process. Nissani and Garcia (1992) have assigned this professional the title of Family Service Worker. Currently, there is not a consistent educational requirement for this field. At this time, there are no existing programs that offer this type of comprehensive, structured curriculum. The authors state that, "Increasing professionalization of this role appears to be on the horizon" (p. 8).

Impact on Higher Education

The Renaissance Group (1992), formed by a small group of presidents and deans of education from colleges and universities across the country, met for the purpose of studying teacher reform and education. This group developed an action plan based on principles they viewed as important to teacher education. They assert that college and university programs have not kept pace with the changes in American society. In addition, due to the rapid changes taking place, the group recommends that community agencies work cooperatively with schools. Further, because the school has the most contact with youth, the group suggests that the school play a leadership role in joining these efforts. In order to achieve these goals, the Renaissance Group supports this type of education throughout the students' academic program, and calls for all disciplines of colleges and universities to share responsibility in the education of teachers.

One of the challenges of collaboration is the joining of professionals from different disciplines. Gardner (1991) calls for colleges and universities to participate in bridging the gap between professionals by designing curriculum that will teach collaborative skills to those in undergraduate and graduate programs. This type of training is known as preservice.

The University of Hartford has implemented a course entitled "Introduction to Education and Human Services." According to Dr. Fredrick Sweitzer, this course is designed as an interdisciplinary effort. It is co-taught by two faculty members, one from human services and one from education. A model of this course design is used to encourage further, more detailed student design. The University of Tennessee, Knoxville, has implemented a similar course design.

Tacoma (Washington) Community College's Human Services Program offers a class in Social Skills Training. James Carroll, Director of the Human Services Program, has created this course to teach the theory of social skills education and, in turn, teach the community college students how to take this knowledge into the community. The students are asked to observe "latch-key" programs, develop social skills education for the students and implement the training. After completion, the students evaluate the process.

At Western Washington University, Bellingham and Everett campuses, the Social Issues Institute was created four years ago by Dr. Lari Shannon and Rob Lawson. The idea was to create conjoint courses at the Everett campus, which is a self-supporting campus, that would appeal to abroad population. The Human Service Program is a part of the Woodring College of Education, although there had never been any collaboration with the teacher preparation programs. This, in part, was due to many of the cultural issues discussed earlier. Dr. Shannon taught in the teacher preparation area and Rob Lawson is an instructor in Human Services, but we are also administrators of the off-campus programs. By wearing both hats, it made it much easier for both to work through the many cultural barriers and, in essence, to start a new paradigm. We did not have any knowledge of this type of program being implemented at Western Washington University, or anywhere else for that matter. It was decided to design classes for four groups: students in education, students in human services, teachers, and human service workers. The philosophical or pedagogical base for the classes are as follows:

1. Study the problem or issue utilizing a holistic or systems view, especially recognizing the child in the family context

2. Provide assessment skills and tools
3. Study the impact of the problem on human development
4. Examine the impact on classroom and agencies
5. Study and develop collaboration between schools and human services
6. Increase knowledge and accessibility of community resources
7. Integration of current research in education and human services
8. Diversity training

After four years, the SII has offered courses that are considered to be prototypical themes—child abuse, poverty, youth gangs, and at-risk youth; but they also encompass other areas. These additional courses include Positive Discipline for the Whole Child, Utilizing the Meyers-Briggs and Learning Styles in Education and Human Services, Adult Sex Offenders, Burnout Prevention Strategies, and An Overview of Societal Issues: A Partnership of Human Services and Schools and Civic Responsibility and Service-Learning.

A future component of this new model or paradigm is to create a professional area for students who want to work as professionals in schools, but do not want to be teachers. Approximately 15% of the students interested in educational programs have previously had few options available to them other than obtaining graduate degrees in school counseling, social work, or becoming an educational aide. The plan is to create a certificate program that would educate students in school and human service cultures, the creation of collaborative relationships, advanced interpersonal skills (interviewing, groups & leadership), advocacy, program planning and assessment, child and family development, social policy, political systems, mediation, client assessment, community resources and self-care.

In Snohomish County, where the Everett Campus is located, collaboration is more than an idea, it is an everyday way of doing business. This is primarily due to the visionary leadership of many human service, educational, political, and business leaders, as well as funding agencies. In

May, 1993, under county leadership, a conference entitled "Kids' Futures" was held to address the needs of the county's children. Groups were formed to study children's challenges in the areas of schools, families, communities, and peer relationships. In addition, by direction of a county ordinance, the Children's Commission was formed to act as advocates for all children. This type of involvement in children's affairs has led to community involvement in the creation of a new paradigm and new positions in the schools. These professionals are known as Project Coordinators (Communities in Schools, 1993) and Family Service Workers (Nissani and Garcia, 1992). This is the key to the development of collaboration—there needs to be an emerging specialization within our universities for there to be an identity, which is also an ongoing problem in human services.

Impact on Teachers and Human Service Workers

These changes will impact the teaching and human service professions greatly. It is essential that these workers have the opportunity to learn through in-service and professional development.

The Washington State Communities in Schools Academy provides training for professionals working with collaborative efforts. Each professional designated to work as a project coordinator completes the training. The academy teaches issues of collaboration such as the process of change, strategic planning and goal setting, identification of needs and resources, management and leadership, mediation and conflict management, diversity training, and government issues. In addition, the training is offered for credit through Western Washington University's Social Issues Institute. The use of this academy training through professional development courses allows other workers—teachers, counselors, administrative personnel, human service workers—to enhance their knowledge of the collaborative process.

As previously mentioned, the Social Issues Institute offers courses in continuing education and professional development. The wide array of classes included in this institute serves the needs of educational and human service professionals. As well as quarter-long courses, many are taught in the evening and as weekend or week-long seminars, which allow professionals to attend these courses at convenient times.

The LINK project, a partnership between the Bellingham, Washington, community, the local school district, and Western Washington University, is intended to improve the academic skills of students, to empower youth to make a difference in their communities, and to integrate various ideas and traditions in the delivery of learning. The mission of the project is as follows:

> The LINK Project matches Western Washington University students with at-risk youth in the Bellingham School District in a variety of situations. Western volunteers work with English as a second language students, special education students, after school tutorial centers, and students in small group and one/one settings. The LINK Project is actively present in five schools, as well as maintaining a small presence in two elementary schools.
>
> The LINK Project staff is responsible for recruiting, training, and evaluating volunteers throughout the year. The LINK Project is also responsible for fiscal management, providing opportunities for reflection, and providing infrastructure for growth. The LINK Project has served as a catalyst and incubator to the creation and support or programs which serve the needs of Native American students, an eighth grade service learning project, and a mentoring program for students in the highly capable program who are at risk in a variety of ways.
>
> As a result of varied and extensive responsibilities the LINK Project staff has been unable to provide the level of support and services to its volunteers and to the K–12 at-risk population, which is needed for its continued success of the project. The LINK Project must enhance its management capabilities and expertise in order to provide a strong foundation for existing programs, and for the growth of new mentoring partnerships between Western Washington University and the Bellingham School District.

Professional Development of curriculum appears to be lacking in most colleges and universities. Only 5% of courses offered during summer quarter address the issues concerning both education and human services. The lack of this type of training is a missing piece in the process of collaboration between education and human services.

Implications for Students—Service Learning

In all of the articles and general public discourse on educational reform, curriculum reform tends to be the most controversial topic. There tends to be a great schism created within any community when there is discussion of revamping the 3 Rs. We will back away from this fight, for the moment. What we will focus on is an area that is familiar to all human service and education students: the concepts of experiential and service learning. What follows are excerpts from material written by Terry Pickeral (1993), a teacher in the Social Issues Institute and Director of Washington State Campus Compact:

> There are several converging missions: In the K–12 system there are persistent calls for basic skills + education of students for civic participation. The recent Governor's Commission on K–12 Reform identified four major educational goals; service-learning is a vehicle to accomplish several of them. Higher education is looking to the development and enhancement of "partnerships" to provide quality opportunities for students to learn. To quote from Washington's Higher Education Coordinating Board's 1992 Update of the Master Plan for Higher Education:
>
> "Washington has a strong tradition of voluntary partnerships among educational institutions and sectors. Hundreds of educational partnerships are in operation. Formed just last year, the Washington State Campus Compact focuses on service to the community. The Compact seeks to provide technical assistance and resources to member campuses, generate funding for competitive grant programs, facilitate networking and collaboration among campuses, involve faculty in linking curricula with service experience, and foster recognition of student service.

". . . Many postsecondary institutions already have integrated service-learning into their curricula through internships and cooperative education."

"Currently, the HECB supports service-learning by providing funding incentives for placing needy college students in work study positions with literacy providers and by funding institutionally created service projects."

"The State can benefit significantly from exploring the use of educational partnerships to: keep abreast of and help implement K–12 reform, improve teacher preparation and development programs, expand programs for at-risk youth and encourage expansion of public service learning."

Impact on the Family, Schools, Agencies, and Communities

James Comer, a pioneer in school reform, calls for communities to join together in charting the course for change. Comer states, "It's necessary to create an infrastructure for children, to bring people and places and organizations around them [together so] they will feel safe and secure and supported." The most important institution for children whose families are not able to provide the support they need is the school (Beyond Rhetoric, 1991, p. 210). Bonnie Benard's studies on resiliency (1993) call for families to be supported in "environments rich in protective factors of caring, high expectations, and opportunities for meaningful participation" (p. 4). Due to the fact that families have undergone a major societal change, it is even more important for schools and communities to take part in family care.

The concept of resiliency has become a driving force in the paradigm shift that is occurring in the work on collaboration in Snohomish County, Washington. A report on resiliency entitled, "Fostering Resiliency in Kids: Protective Factors in the Family, School and Community" by Bonnie Benard (1991) was summarized and embellished by Jim Teverbaugh, Coordinator for the Office of Children's Affairs, Snohomish County Human Services Department. The following is an outline of the main concepts from this work:

Individual personality attributes that contribute to resiliency

1. Social competency
2. Problem solving skills
3. Autonomy
4. Sense of purpose and future

Protective factors within a family

1. Caring and support
2. High expectations
3. Encourage child's participation

Protective factors within a school

1. Caring and support
2. High expectations
3. Youth participation and involvement

Protective factors within a community

1. Caring and support
2. High expectations
3. Opportunities for participation and involvement

Benard (1993) states that, "If we as adults and preventionists are truly concerned with preventing problems . . . then it is imperative that we make our central vision and mission the creation of supportive relationships with youth and their families" (p. 4). This will necessitate systemic change in all areas—families, communities, agencies and schools. The change must be fostered by shaping a climate open to participation by all stakeholders.

Models

According to Jehl and Kirst (1992), there must be encouragement for community involvement from parents, business leaders, and senior citizens. Promising models of community involvement in schools exist throughout the United States. These programs have a common mission—to make the school a center, not only of academic studies, but also of family support in addressing the challenges that take place outside the school walls.

According to Ascher (1990), there are several characteristics that successful collaborations share. The effort needs to be comprehensive, offering easy accessibility or directly providing services to clients. Secondly, these successful models often focus on prevention, moving beyond the usual cri-sis management. These collaborative efforts are also diligent in their move to eliminate professional barriers. In doing so, training is offered to build relationships between agency personnel. It is imperative to ask for teacher and parent input and to encourage communication between all parties. The employment of a facilitator is an important addition to the collaborative process. All participants must view the child as a component of the family, and the family as part of the community. Lastly, there must be a creative policy for accountability.

The School Development Model, a process begun over twenty years ago by James Comer, has operated on the belief that academic success is dependent on the school's ability to meet the social and mental health needs of children, as well as their families. Central to this model is the school management and governance team, which includes school personnel, parents, and members of the school community. In a team effort, these members work closely to enhance students' social and academic success. The program offers innovative services such as school-based mental health, parent education classes, and the sched-uling of school meetings at local housing pro-jects (Dolan, 1992). Schorr (1988) reports that the implementation of this program has shown an increase in academic test scores and a dra-matic increase in attendance in the two New Haven, Connecticut, schools where the program began.

Cities in Schools (1991) is another example of community-wide collaboration. This organiza-tion manages partnerships of schools, human ser-vice agencies, and business. In the State of Washington, work has begun to include state-level agencies and departments in collaborative models. In addition, an integral part of Cities in Schools is the recruitment of volunteers from local sources. In Snohomish County, Washington, Communities in Schools, in affiliation with Cities in Schools (1993), has joined with several corpo-rate partners to build a solid community-based plan. These corporations provide funding, pro-vide opportunities for students to observe busi-

ness operations, supply volunteers, and donate supplies for students.

New Beginnings, a partnership formed be-tween the San Diego, California, School System and local health and human service agencies, has been successful in designing a collaborative model. Initially, a needs assessment was com-pleted to determine the needs of the school popu-lation. With the data gathered, schools and human service agencies were able to coordinate efforts. For example, through an agreement between the school district and the Department of Social Services, students whose families receive public assistance are automatically eligible for free school lunch. This information is shared electronically, which eliminates further time and paperwork for families and agencies. In addition, work is being done to eliminate duplicity and ease regulations, therefore simplifying processes and providing ser-vices to families in a less fragmented, more effi-cient manner. In-service and cross-training between schools and agencies help to develop understanding and collegiality among personnel (Dolan, 1992; Jehl and Kirst, 1992).

North Middle School in Everett, Washington has developed an innovative model of collabora-tion. Through funding from the Community Health and Education Foundation and in partner-ship with Communities in Schools, Principal Chuck Lisk and his staff have designed a myriad of programs. A Family Support Center works to enrich the lives of students, staff, and families. The school has mental health and substance abuse counselors on site and provides support groups, as well as parenting classes in early evening hours, offering childcare and a meal to encourage family involvement. In addition, anger manage-ment classes, social skills training, and between twenty and thirty student clubs are offered on site. The use of positive reinforcement has been a large component in the development of this plan. In cooperation with local health agencies, institu-tions, and volunteer organizations, medical, den-tal and vision needs are attended to. Volunteers assist in screening, as well as transportation of students to appointments. Lastly, staff wellness is addressed as an important element in his holistic model. Exercise equipment, health screenings, and staff morale-boosting activities provide self-care opportunities for these teachers working with high-risk youth.

The emergence of a new career to facilitate these changes is of utmost importance to the success of collaboration. These professionals will act as advocates for policy change, as well as for students and their families. The family service worker, as described by Nissani and Garcia (1992), represents "the connection among education, children, families, and social services—the hub of community interest in child rearing" (p. 10). The University of Washington Center for the Study and Teaching of At-Risk Students (C-Stars), suggests that school-based interprofessional case management be utilized when working with "at-risk" populations. Lingo (1990) calls for the employment of a Behavior Disorders Service Manager—a full time case manager who has daily contact with students and is able to arrange services for them.

Lisbeth Schorr (1988) reports that researchers have concluded that academic success is most often achieved when the child is supported in a holistic manner. The author goes on to say that programs that are most successful in working with disadvantaged families offer a "broad spectrum of services" (p. 256). In her research regarding resiliency in youth, Bonnie Benard (1991) asserts that if a child does not have the basic needs of love, caring, and social support fulfilled in the home, it is of utmost importance for the school to provide this. She calls for partnerships through community collaboration—"between families and schools and between schools and communities" (p. 19).

CONCLUSION

Throughout this chapter we have discussed collaboration, the cultures of schools and human services, family, community and social change, and shifts in paradigms. As individual communities, neighborhoods, and school districts, we must create new ways of addressing the needs of children and families. The research is clear that there are successful models, but it is important to note that models should not be replicated. Models are made up of a myriad of unique variables that, if copied, may lead to terminal projectitis or failure. Just as a teacher or human service worker must be sensitive to the child and family context when designing a lesson or intervention, people involved in collaboration need to be aware of the fundamental rules and to follow them or purposely amend them for their unique process. Ascher (1990) suggests that the best programs are defined locally and are driven by the community's needs, history, and interests.

The collaboration of schools and human services is not the answer to all problems concerning children, but it can be a hopeful vision that includes all members of a community. Lisbeth Schorr (1988) states that we are all at-risk if one child is at-risk. We must unshackle from the myth that nothing works. We must remember that in education and human services, we are in the business of modeling, teaching, and giving hope.

And the Lord said to the Rabbi, "Come, I will show you Hell." They entered a room where a group of people sat around a huge pot of stew. Everyone was famished and desperate. Each held a spoon that reached the pot but had a handle so long that it could not be used to reach their mouths. The suffering was terrible.

"Come, now I will show you Heaven," the Lord said after a while. They entered another room, identical to the first—the pot of stew, the group of people, the same long spoons. But, there, everyone was happy and nourished. "I don't understand," said the Rabbi. "Why are they happy here when they were miserable in the other room, and everything was the same?" The Lord smiled. "Ah, but don't you see?" he asked. "Here they have learned to feed each other."
—Old Rabbinic Tale

REFERENCES

Akerlund, D., and H. Carthung, (1990). *Grays Harbor County Early Intervention Services.* Aberdeen, WA: Grays Harbor Pupil Services Cooperative.

Ascher, C., (1990). *Linking Schools with Human Service Agencies.* (Report No. EDO–UD–90–2). New York: ERIC Clearinghouse on Urban Education. (ERIC Document Reproduction Service No. ED 319 877).

Barker, J.A., (1990). *Discovering the Future: The Business of Paradigms* (Discussion guide). Burnsville, MN: Charthouse International Learning Corporation.

Benard, B., (1991). *Fostering Resiliency in Kids: Protective Factors in the Family, School and Community.* Portland, OR: Northwest Regional Educational Laboratory.

Benard, B., (1993). *Resiliency Requires Changing Hearts and Minds.* Portland, OR: Western Regional Center News.

Bruner, C., (1991). *Thinking Collaboratively: Ten Questions and Answers to Help Policy Makers Improve Children's Services.* Washington, DC: Education and Human Services Consortium.

Cities in Schools, Inc., (1991). *National and Local Overview.* Seattle.

Communities in Schools, (1993). (Information packet). Unpublished materials.

Council for Integrated Children's Programs, (1992). *What Kids Need.* Everett, WA: Snohomish County Department of Human Services.

Dolan, L.J., (1992). *Models for Research on Effective Schooling for Disadvantaged Students.* (Report No. CDS–R–30). Baltimore: Johns Hopkins University, Center for Research of Effective Schooling for Disadvantaged Students. (ERIC Document Reproduction Service No. ED 347 244).

Edelman, P.R. and B.A. Radin., (1991). *Serving Children and Families Effectively: How the Past Can Help Chart the Future.* Washington, DC: Education and Human Services Consortium.

Gardner, S., (1991). *A Commentary.* Washington, DC: Education and Human Services Consortium.

Gardner, S.L., (1992). "Key Issues in Developing School-Linked Integrated Services." *The Future of Children,* 2(1), 85–94.

Golden, O., (1991). *Collaboration as a Means, Not an End: Serving Disadvantaged Families and Children.* Boston: Harvard University, Kennedy School of Government.

Heck, D., (1987). *Challenges & Opportunities: The Transformation of Washington's School.* Seattle: Advance Washington.

Homan, M., (1993). *Promoting Community Change: Making It Happen in the Real World.* Pacific Grove, CA: Brooks/Cole.

Jehl, J. and M. Kirst, (1992). "Getting Ready to Provide School-Linked Services: What Schools Must Do." *The Future of Children,* 2(1), 95–106.

Kurtz, P.D., (1988). "Social Work Services to Parents: Essential to Pupils at Risk." *Urban Education,* 22 (4), 445–457.

Lingo, C. and N.A. Henry, (1990). *The Behavior Disorders Service Coordinator: A "Bottom-Up" Model to Providing Related Services.* Tucson, AZ: Rural Education Symposium of the American Council on Rural Special Education and the National Rural and Small Schools Consortium. (ERIC Document Reproduction Service No. ED 337 307).

Mattessich, P.W. and B.R. Monsey, (1992). *Collaboration: What Makes It Work.* St. Paul: A.H. Wilder Foundation.

Melaville, A.L. and M.J. Blank, (1991). *What It Takes: Structuring Interagency Partnerships to Connect Children and Families with Comprehensive Services.* Washington, DC: Education and Human Services Consortium.

Melaville, A.L., Blank, M.J., and Asagesh, G., (1993). *Together We Can: A Guide for Crafting a Profamily System of Education and Human Services.* Washington, DC: U.S. Department of Education and U.S. Department of Health and Human Services.

National Commission on Children, (1991). *Beyond Rhetoric: A New American Agenda for Children and Families: Final Report of the National Commission on Children.* Washington, DC.

Nissani, H. and W. Garcia, (1992). *Family Service Workers: Facilitators of the Integration of Education & Human Services.* Portland, OR:

Child, Family and Community Program, Northwest Regional Educational Laboratory.

Pickeral, T., (1993). *LINK and the Mentoring Resource Center.* Bellingham, WA: Western Washington University, LINK Project.

Pickeral, T., (1993). *Service-Learning: Various Notes.* Unpublished manuscripts. Western Washington University, Washington State Campus Compact, Bellingham, WA.

Renaissance Group, (1992). *Teachers for the New World: A Statement of Principles.* Cedar Falls, IA: University of Northern Iowa.

Russell, J.F., (1991). "The Relationships Between School Personnel Attitudes about At Risk Students, and At Riskiness of Student Population, and Effort Expanded for At Risk Students." Bloomington, IN: *Phi Delta Kappa.* (ERIC Document Reproduction Services No. Ed 344 876).

Schorr, L. and D. Schorr, (1989). *Within Our Reach: Breaking the Cycle of Disadvantage.* New York: Anchor.

Tyack, D., (1992). "Health and Social Services in Public Schools: Historical Perspectives." *The Future of Children*, 2 (1), 19–31.

Woodside, M. and T. McClam, (1990). *Introduction to Human Services.* Pacific Grove, CA: Brooks/Cole.

THE BRONX EDUCATIONAL OPPORTUNITY CENTER

A MODEL FOR HELPING THROUGH EDUCATION

MICHAEL SELIGER

The Bronx Educational Opportunity Center (EOC) is a unique part of New York's City and State University systems. It is one of ten centers (EOCs) located in impoverished communities in New York State. Each operates under State University of New York (SUNY) guidelines, with a mandate to serve educationally and economically disadvantaged adults. (Because it is located in New York City, the Bronx EOC is administered by a branch of the City University of New York (CUNY—Bronx Community College.) There is no charge for tuition or fees for the 1,200 or more people per year who attend classes at the Bronx EOC.

All of the EOC's students are "educationally and economically disadvantaged." With regard to education, this means that they were not adequately prepared by their previous schooling to take advantage of college or job-training opportunities, or to obtain more than a menial job requiring little skill and paying rather poorly. "Economically disadvantaged" means that the person's family income is not much above the national poverty level. (In New York City, the average welfare grant for a family of four is above the national poverty income guideline, but far below what the U.S. Department of Labor, Bureau of Labor Statistics indicates is needed for a family of four to be living above a poverty threshold.)

Students come to the Bronx EOC because they believe that learning there can lead them to a brighter future. They may be able to enter college (without spending valuable time there in non-credit remedial courses), gain a valuable occupational skill, or correct deficiencies in their language, reading, and math abilities.

The EOC is often seen by its students as their last chance to get ahead through education. Most have experienced failure in previous school situations. Most are not employed. Over 70 percent are women, the majority of whom are receiving Aid for Dependent Children, and are single heads of households with anywhere from one to eight children. Slightly over half are Latinos, mainly from Puerto Rico, the Dominican Republic, or Central America. Most of the rest are Black, but not from a single culture. Some grew up in housing projects in the Bronx, while others migrated from the South or from Caribbean islands like Jamaica. Some are immigrants from West Africa or Haiti. Some recent immigrants to the United States, from Cambodia and other Asian countries, and from Eastern Europe, also attend the EOC.

Each person who comes to the EOC comes with hopes, but also with needs that must be addressed if there is to be any chance of success. At the EOC, part of the challenge is to identify those needs quickly, and build the student's confidence in the EOC as a place where those needs can be addressed, as well as a place where the student can be treated with respect and given a realistic opportunity to progress towards her/his goals. Belief that each student's success is possible and expected is communicated by teachers, counselors, job developers, admissions advisers, tutors, administrators, clerical staff, and other support staff. The clean, modern facility, state-of-the-art equipment, and "learning climate" of the EOC itself also send the message to students that this is a place to learn, not to waste time; it is a serious place that can make students feel proud of being there, and offer security that their personal needs and motivations will be respected and addressed.

On the pages that follow, we will look at a few case examples of typical EOC experiences that can provide us with a multifaceted look at the complexities of addressing human service needs in an urban adult education setting. (The cases presented here are based on actual experiences of students and staff at the Bronx EOC, but actually are composites of those experiences. Names and situations are not intended to reflect the reality of any particular individual.)

Roberta Jackson learned about the Educational Opportunity Center when she attended Career Planning at the Southern Boulevard "BEGIN" Center. BEGIN is New York City's approach to the Federal Welfare Reform Act. Under federal law, recipients of Aid for Dependent Children should be provided opportunities to obtain employment or further education that can lead to employment, and given support-service benefits that make it possible and preferable to obtain and retain a job. The federal lawmakers recognized that a person on public assistance is not able to pursue education or training if he/she is responsible for caring for young children, and not likely to keep a job if the amount earned does not provide as adequately as public assistance for health care, housing, child care, and other services.

Thus, participants in BEGIN receive Training Related Expenses (TREs) for transportation, books, child care, tuition, uniforms, or tools, etc., during their training period, and receive transitional welfare benefits that cover the cost of health- and child-care during the first year that they are employed.

Roberta is 34 years old. She lives in an old tenement building in the Mott Haven section of the South Bronx. Roberta is the mother of three children, ages nine, seven, and four. The children live with Roberta's mother, who lives in a housing project about a mile from where Roberta lives. Roberta has been in and out of drug treatment programs and has spent time in the Bronx House of Detention. She is still legally responsible for her children, and wants to get a steady job with sufficient pay for her to move into a better apartment where she can have her children with her.

Roberta received a letter from the Southern Boulevard BEGIN program "inviting" her to come in for assessment and planning for entry into a job search or training activity. The letter explained transitional benefits and informed her that she was not required to come into the program at this time, because her youngest child is not of school age and there are insufficient child care services in the area. Without child care options, no parent of children under age six can be required to participate in BEGIN. Many, however, including Roberta, come in voluntarily, since this gives them a better chance of getting assistance with child care, and they know that they will be called later anyway.

BEGIN participants meet with a (welfare department) caseworker who quickly reviews their interests, prior schooling, and any experience they may have in the world of work. If the client is interested in looking for work, she is placed in a "job club," through which she is encouraged to prepare a resume, and make twenty contacts a week with prospective employers. If the client knows about a particular training program that she/he would like to enter, she/he may be referred to that program. Many people don't know what they want, however. These people are referred to Career Planning—two weeks of testing, exposure to various training and employment options, and other explorations of possibilities.

On one of the days that Roberta attended Career Planning, a Bronx EOC outreach specialist spoke to the group, describing the programs of instruction available at Bronx EOC. Roberta became interested in exploring the EOC's data entry training program. This program would provide computer keyboarding skills and experience in data entry, which would enable her to obtain work that typically pays between $6 and $7.50 per hour to start. The program did not require a high school diploma, but did offer participants the opportunity to prepare for the GED exam while gaining job-related skills. This combination appealed to her. The fact that the EOC also has a child care center for its students made the program even more attractive to her because good child care is often hard to find, and the opportunity to have her youngest child on-site while she attended classes was unusual and special.

Roberta came to the EOC, met with an admissions adviser who informed her of possible options, and scheduled a skills examination that measured reading and math levels on a standardized instrument. Roberta was nervous when she took the exam, and did not quite meet the entry requirements for either the EOC's GED class or data entry program. However, her scores were within a year of those required for entry into those programs. She was counseled by a case manager and a member of the EOC instruction team, and advised that she was eligible to participate in the EOC's learning lab (a computer-assisted learning environment where students master concepts at their own pace. A variety of methods of learning are used in the lab, including computer interactions, tutoring, small-group instruction, use of

workbooks, interactive video programs, etc.). Her advisers assured her that most people who spent twenty hours per week in the lab gained at least one grade in reading and math within ten weeks, after which she would be eligible for a future section of her preferred program.

Roberta participated in the learning lab for the next five months. During that time she spent twenty hours per week in the lab. She advanced two grade levels in reading, and three in math. She gained confidence and pride in herself, partly from her interactions with the instructional team in the learning lab, partly from occasional meetings with her counselor. While she attended the EOC, her youngest child attended the EOC's new child care center on the next block. They were able to have breakfast together at the child care center, and Roberta also came by as a volunteer and participated in the center's Parent Workshop series. These workshops introduced the concept of parents having a right and responsibility to know about the activities occurring in their children's schools.

By the time Roberta's daughter entered kindergarten the following year, Roberta had completed the data entry course and was employed. She also expressed interest in returning to the EOC or Bronx Community College to enroll in a child-care-worker training course. By the end of that year, Roberta was still employed as a data entry specialist, and had assumed an active role in her daughter's school-parent association.

Roberta achieved success by applying herself and realizing some of the potential that she always believed she had. To achieve that success she needed the assistance of a large number of individuals whose occupations all fit within the category of human service workers. These included:

■ *Caseworker* at the Southern Boulevard BEGIN Center. This City employee interviews at least fifteen people per day, using a format developed by a Research Specialist within the City's Department of Social

Services. The format, and the caseworker's listening and coaching skills, help the client to focus on options within the BEGIN program. As the result of this interview, Roberta was assigned to the Career Planning group. The caseworker also determined whether Roberta had any problems (like child care) that would rule out the possibility of her succeeding in her pursuit of employment or further education. (City caseworkers usually have college degrees and have passed a civil service entry screening and examination. Some individuals work in this capacity after partial completion of college.)

— *Supervisor* and *trainer* in the Career Planning unit. These two individuals manage groups of twenty to forty individuals, and work with new groups every few weeks. They must know, through research and review of information provided to them by central office staff, about a wide range of options that may be available to participants. They have the ability to interpret test results and counsel individuals on options that make sense, given the test outcome. They use their knowledge of training program options and career opportunities to bring information (and presenters) to the group. By providing options, they hope to keep the group members interested and motivated to find a career path that meets their needs and interests. (These positions are usually filled by experienced employees—normally with degrees and specialized training—of the Department of Social Services.)

— *Outreach worker* for the EOC has skills as a communicator to groups and individuals. Using verbal skills as a presenter to the Career Planning group, the worker should be able to demonstrate that the EOC offers meaningful opportunities for interested individuals. Knowledge of EOC programs and entrance requirements combined with this person's ease as a presenter should make the group comfortable and open to his/her message. The worker is able to respond to the group's questions because he/she has developed good listening skills, and has the information to put questions into a meaningful context. He/she also shares written materials about the EOC; the worker has prepared these, using writing skills and newly acquired competence in desktop publishing. (A particular outreach worker had recently completed a master's degree in guidance, and was fully bilingual. Some outreach workers are paraprofessionals who come from the

same background as the people that they are trying to recruit. Their own success enables them to speak as role models; their personal experience and success are useful in convincing others that success is attainable.)

— *Instructional team* at the EOC consists of classroom teachers, tutors, instructional lab managers, occupational skills specialists, and field mentors. Roberta took remedial classes in the instructional lab, and was guided by the lab manager and staff in finding her best modes of learning. (Roberta actually learned very comfortably sitting in front of a computer and interacting with the private screen. Sometimes she needed help from lab instructional personnel in understanding a concept or relating her knowledge to new situations presented on the computer.) When she moved into the data entry program, she participated in classroom instruction that involved some lecture-style presentations by instructors, but heavily emphasized practice and mastery of skills. Instructors in these classes spent time observing students' work at their computers, and providing feedback, encouragement, and clarification of appropriate techniques. They also conducted timed tests of speed and accuracy. Test results were the basis for prescribing next steps in the learning (or skill-sharpening) process. Before completing the course, Roberta was assigned to a work experience internship where she could apply her skills in a "real-world" situation, and return to the EOC knowing what skills still needed to be polished. Her field mentor was a staff person at the office where she was assigned for her work experience. The mentor was responsible for supervising Roberta, integrating her into the workplace, and providing feedback on her progress. (Most teachers, lab managers, and skills specialists have both academic and work-related training. Most possess degrees in the instructional area in which they work. Tutors are often individuals who are pursuing further education themselves, working part-time to earn their way through school while helping others attain mastery of learning skills.)

— *Counselors* and *case managers* help students like Roberta to identify problems that are affecting their ability to succeed in their (educational) pursuits. In addition to skills in listening and encouraging clients to express their concerns, counselors and case managers must have extensive knowledge of the resources available to assist their clients. Thus, when Roberta spoke with an admissions counselor at the EOC, she needed to be reassured that the EOC was the right place for her. The admissions counselor had to understand this need, and guide Roberta through discussions to enable her to focus on what she wanted and what obstacles threatened her ability to reach her goals. The admissions counselor initiated the process that led to Roberta's four-year old being enrolled in the EOC's child care center. Once enrolled in instructional programs at the EOC, Roberta was assigned to a case manager who worked with that particular program as part of a team committed to supporting student progress. This case adviser met with Roberta periodically to discuss progress and needs, and was always available in case special needs arose that required immediate assistance. The case manager also must respond to any indication that a student is in danger of not succeeding (e.g., attendance or grades are not satisfactory, or behavior is not fully appropriate). Roberta was dedicated enough not to require special attention for classroom difficulties, but did ask for assistance with housing and getting her family together under one roof. The case manager was able to initiate a process that would ultimately lead to Roberta being accepted into some new housing being built in the South Bronx by a nonprofit housing development organization. The case manager also served as an advocate and information manager with regard to inquiries from Roberta's public assistance case manager, who required periodic reports on her progress in order to sustain training-related expense benefits. The case manager also handled inquiries from family court and substance abuse agencies, on Roberta's behalf. (Many counselors and case managers hold advanced degrees and have specific training in counseling interactions. The EOC requires degrees and experience for these positions. There are some community-based organizations that value the ability to communicate and be understood by clients to the extent that some entry positions in this field can be assigned to paraprofessionals from the community.)

━ *Job placement specialists* are assigned to work closely with instructors and case managers at Bronx EOC. They are responsible for developing and maintaining contacts with prospective employers, and determining the skill and behavioral requirements that these employers want from prospective employees. They communicate these expectations to instructional and case management staff, to assure that students are pre-

pared with all needed competencies before they are referred to prospective jobs. The job placement specialist also communicates the employer's expectations directly to students, both in classroom groups and through individual meetings. Roberta learned that she would not be considered for employment until her keyboarding skills exceeded 300 strokes per minute. She also learned that employers expect steady attendance, punctuality, neat appearance, ability to follow directions, and ability to get along well with peers and supervisors in the workplace. (While job placement workers do not always possess college degrees, they must be articulate, well organized, and resourceful. Knowledge of the career fields in which they will be developing jobs is valuable. Understanding of the programs that produce the students to be placed is vital, since this is an occupation that requires building a reputation for wisely connecting employers to qualified applicants. Even one mismatch can be costly in terms of employer receptivity to future referrals.)

━ *Research and information team:* The service activity at the EOC is carefully documented. All human service workers must spend time producing and using written and computer-generated information. This information is compiled into a computerized Student Information System that tracks student programs, determines the type of interventions that were needed by the student in order to continue at the EOC, causes of dropouts, test scores at entrance and completion (and appropriate intermediate points). Staff involved in collecting and analyzing this data form the EOC's Research and Information Systems management team. While they are not human service workers in the strictest sense, the information that they collect and disseminate provides vital support for human service workers in instructional, support service, and placement roles.

Lydia Garcia came to New York from a small village in Honduras, near the Gulf of Fonseca. She has lived in the Bronx for three years. She lives with relatives in the East Tremont section of the Bronx. A fire in an unlicensed social club in the Bronx cost her two close friends last year. She might have been in the club at the time of the fire, too, if she hadn't been filling in for a friend as a cashier at a local Bodega that evening. Lydia is 23 years old, speaks limited English, and has difficulty comprehending written English. Most of the people she knows speak Spanish. Lydia would not need to learn much English if she just wanted to get along in her home community, but Lydia wants to become a nurse someday so she would like to improve her English, get a high-school-equivalency diploma, and go to college.

Lydia read about the EOC from an announcement that was posted at the church that she attends. Since it was a short bus ride (or a long walk) from her home, she went to inquire about its offerings. She was able to speak to a bilingual admissions counselor, who described the EOC's English as Second Language (ESL) program. She was scheduled to take a test of native language literacy, which demonstrated that she had a good grasp of Spanish from her studies in Honduras. Lydia was invited to attend the EOC's Spanish GED program, after which she would be able to enroll in ESL instruction. She agreed to participate, but found herself on a waiting list for several months before she actually joined the program.

While she enjoyed the classes and being among students at the EOC, Lydia's attendance was sporadic. She chose to work at the Bodega, or to babysit for her niece's child, instead of maintaining satisfactory attendance. Her counselor was alerted to the attendance problem, and invited Lydia to discuss her situation. She met with her counselor, who reminded her of the EOC's attendance policies, which allow no more than four absences per term. She already had four absences, plus several unexcused tardies.

Lydia's instructor and counselor met to discuss her situation. They agreed that Lydia had the potential to achieve the Spanish GED and move on to college, but they were concerned about her attendance and class performance. The instructor questioned her motivation for attending the course, and was ready to suggest that she be dropped from the course, but be permitted to re-enroll at the beginning of the next term. The counselor had learned from speaking with Lydia that Lydia was, indeed, highly motivated, but that she was facing a complex financial and personal crisis. She needed money to get through this difficult time, and felt that she had to put that ahead of her studies, even though she knew that education was crucial to improving her long-range situation.

The counselor convinced the instructor to give Lydia one more chance before suspending her for the term. The instructor agreed on the condition that Lydia spend additional time in the EOC's instructional lab receiving tutorial assistance to make up for time that she had lost. The counselor also arranged for Lydia to get top priority assistance from a job counselor, who was able to find a part-time job for Lydia. This job paid well enough for Lydia to rely on it, and not feel compelled to accept any opportunity to work regardless of its impact on her school situation. The part-time job's hours did not conflict with her school hours. Best of all, the job provided health benefits, which enabled her to be treated for minor ailments before they became major crises.

Seven months after she enrolled at the EOC, Lydia passed the Spanish GED exam. She continued at the EOC for four additional months to polish her English language comprehension and communication skills, and then enrolled in a bilingual college program.

After successfully completing the first year of her college program, Lydia came back to the EOC to thank her counselor for putting her on the right track. During the hour that she visited, Lydia's counselor introduced her to two students. The counselor felt that meeting Lydia would be valuable for these students, as each was struggling with situations similar to Lydia's. Being seen as a role model gave Lydia at least as much of a boost as it gave to the two students.

In Lydia's situation, a number of human service professionals were involved. These included instructors, tutors, job development specialists, and a counselor. The counselor's commitment to going the extra mile to support Lydia made a major difference in this case. The counselor's efforts included listening and counseling Lydia, advocating on her behalf, knowing resources that were available to help Lydia, and mobilizing those resources at the time they were needed.

Yet, all of this activity took place in a systemic context. This context, which is the operating procedures of the EOC, set the stage in which this positive intervention could take place. Among the elements of this context were the following:

- Rules and standards to which the student was expected to adhere.
- Procedures for instructional staff to alert the counselor promptly in situations where academic progress is at risk.
- A case-review process in which the counselor is expected to gather information about the student's situation in order to arrive at a decision on the most appropriate strategy for addressing the student's needs in the context of his/her situation.
- A collegial system in which the counselor is able to ask for, and receive, priority service for this student from the EOC's job development and placement team.

KEY TERMS FOR PART THREE

In completing Chapters 6, 7, 8, 9, and 10, you will have a command of the following key terms, major concepts, and principal topical references:

Theory	School Development Model	Empathy
Hypotheses	Group Leadership	Initial Disclosure
Principles	Group Cohesiveness	Unconditional Positive Regard
Pluralistic Theory Base	Intergenerational Service	Constructive Confrontation
Multi-Factored Causality	Models	Shelter Care
Ecological Perspective	Special Education Services	
Collaboration	Pupil Personnel Services	
School-Based Services	Exclusion and Inclusion	
At-Risk Children	Programs	
New Beginnings	Prevention and Promotion	

PIVOTAL ISSUES FOR DISCUSSION OF PART THREE

1. Make a list of short-range human services interventions; long-term interventions; direct service interventions; indirect interventions. How do these approaches differ with individual clients, as opposed to clients in groups?

2. Develop an outline for your own theory of personality development. Include three separate components: structure(s), dynamics, and how the theory would be applied to working with clients.

3. What is the Managed Health Care movement in mental health and human services? What are the major issues in this recent movement and how do they impact on the human services client, worker, and intervention services?

4. Give examples of how group approaches are used in human services. What are the advantages and disadvantages of groups?

SUGGESTED READINGS FOR PART THREE

1. Ivey, A.E., M.B. Ivey, and L. Simek-Downing, (1987). *Counseling and Psychotherapy: Integrating Skills, Theory and Practice,* 2nd ed. Englewood Cliffs, NJ: Prentice-Hall.

2. Sauber, S.R., (1983). *The Human Service Delivery System*, New York: Columbia University Press.

3. Leiter, M.P. and M. Webb, (1983). *Developing Human Service Networks.* New York: Irvington Press.

4. Hasenfeld, L. and R. English, (1977). *Human Service Organizations: A Book of Readings.* Ann Arbor, MI: University of Michigan Press.

5. Schram, B. and Betty Reid Mandell, (1983). *Human Services: Strategies of Intervention.* New York: John Wiley and Sons.

PART FOUR

HUMAN SERVICES: CAREER CONCERNS FOR HUMAN SERVICES PROFESSIONALS

Part Four deals with professional concerns of the human services worker and includes four chapters. Discussed here are law and ethics (Chapter 11), professional growth (Chapter 12), personal qualities (Chapter 13), and job burnout (Chapter 14).

As a professional helper you will be using your skills and knowledge to solve a wide variety of social and personal problems. Yet, you could be making serious blunders if you are unaware of the legal and ethical constraints placed on what you can do and how you can do it. In Chapter 11, Naydean Blair discusses the human service worker in relation to ethical and legal concerns. The thread running through the chapter is a recognition that the client should be treated as a person embodied and protected by rights. While there are ethical considerations such as confidentiality and informed consent, which will guide you whenever you work, the legal requirements may vary depending on where you are located, what agency you are employed by, and what kind of client you serve. In this chapter, Texas laws are used as an example, but there may be differences depending on the state in which you are working. The chapter is followed by a Special Focus Feature of the draft code of ethics currently under review by the membership of NOHSE.

Although you may be an "A" student, possess skills and knowledge, and be a very moral and ethical person, it will still be a challenge to have a successful human service career. Chapter 12, by Miriam Clubok, is devoted to giving you insight and encouragement in feeling satisfied and productive as a human service worker. The chapter discusses a variety of ways that will enhance your professional growth and insure your personal survival as you pursue your career in human services. The discussion emphasizes the concerns you should have for the client, self, and work setting. You will also find helpful the identification of eight tips, which, if followed, will enhance your personal and professional growth. The chapter is followed by a Special Focus Feature: The Human Services Worker, which is a joint publication of NOHSE and CSHSE. This piece will give you a succinct, generic job description of the human services worker.

In Chapter 13, Nan Littleton points out that success really depends on you. Your personal qualities, self-understanding, and ability to take care of yourself are critical criteria for career success and survival. The chapter discusses the role of personal characteristics and highlights the importance of positive thinking—that you must believe you can make a difference. There are also suggestions to follow that will lead to effective helping.

This part concludes with Chapter 14, by Frederick Sweitzer, which deals with understanding and avoiding job burnout. An awareness of both the intrapersonal and interpersonal sources of stress could assist you in avoiding this problem. Burnout may affect you directly in your career and also may impact you when, for example, one of your co-workers becomes burned out, and you have to assume additional work responsibilities.

As a human service professional, you should be prepared to work with clients with different kinds of problems. Part Five begins to acquaint you with specific aspects of different client populations.

LEARNING OBJECTIVES FOR PART FOUR:
CAREER CONCERNS FOR HUMAN SERVICES PROFESSIONALS

In reading and studying Chapters 11, 12, 13, and 14:

- You will become familiar with legal issues that impact the human service worker.
- You will understand the basic range of ethical behaviors that human service workers have to attend and adhere to in their work with consumers.
- You will know and appreciate what is involved in the development of a career in human services.
- You will understand which personal traits and characteristics are inherent to the human service worker and how these personality factors impact their professional effectiveness and career success.
- You will understand the problem of job burnout, how it develops, and how it may be dealt with best.

CHAPTER 11

LAW, ETHICS, AND THE HUMAN SERVICES WORKER

NAYDEAN BLAIR

INTRODUCTION

Human services has been struggling with its identity for many years. Although I've been working and teaching in the helping services, *I'm* confused. I cannot be sure that I truly understand all of the fundamental differences that set apart the various definitions. The students in my program in Houston are called mental health workers. A neighboring school with a similar curriculum calls its students human service workers, yet in another program nearby they are known as social work associates. To my knowledge these graduates compete for the same jobs and, when they get them, are expected to perform the same functions and have similar skills.

The confusion about what we call ourselves only adds to the dilemma when we consider law and ethics. Human service workers work in a variety of settings, with a variety of clients, patients, students, etc. Every state has a set of students' rights, clients' rights, patients' rights, and laws governing inpatient and outpatient services. There are privacy laws telling us what information can or cannot be placed in records or released. The list of rules and regulations is endless. As soon as you feel you have a comfortable grasp of the rules concerning nursing home care you get offered a wonderful position in child protection services. Time to start over.

Ethics are a different concern altogether. Are ethics and values the same? Who tells us what ethical standards we will work by? Most profes-sional organizations have established codes of conduct or ethical standards that provide guidelines for acceptable behavior on the job. Who knows if an ethical code is compromised? Who enforces these codes? I will attempt to address these and other issues concerning law and ethics in human services.

This personal experience article is not meant to provide you with a barrage of facts. It would be impossible to include all of the laws and ethical standards that apply to the variety of students and colleagues who may be reading this book. Instead, I will share with you some of the ethical and legal concerns that are frequently discussed within the topics. Many are issues brought up by interns in their weekly seminars.

EARLY DEVELOPMENTS

In order to have a formal set of professional ethics by which to work, we must first decide who we are, what our mission is, and with whom we will affiliate. As a group we became a separate entity when we gave ourselves a new name. By 1965 this country had reached a point where the demand for the trained generalist mental health worker was at the crisis point. The early 1960s with its War on Poverty brought with it the need for soldiers to fight this war. The Southern Regional Education Board (SREB) planted the early seeds for what is known today as the Human Services Training Movement. The SREB obtained a grant from the Experimental and Special Training Branch of the National Institute of Mental Health (NIMH) to work with community colleges, and provide institutions to develop the first training programs. These early training programs were predominantly called Mental Health; however, this terminology was changed to Human Service Worker to give the field the broader perspective it needed.

Many states do not have a method by which to credential a human service worker that does not have a minimum of a bachelor's degree. Recently, agencies like the National Association of Social Workers (NASW), and the National Association of Alcoholism and Drug Abuse Counselors (NAADAC), have developed appropriate exams to be used by states if they choose to test at a lower level.

The Council for Standards in Human Services Education (CSHSE) has been laboring since its inception to establish minimum standards of competency. CSHSE was created to develop a set of program training standards that would reflect the content of existing programs (Woodside, McClam, 1990). This was done on the assumption that the programs already in existence were based on community needs. Human service students who attend a program that is approved by CSHSE will have in their curriculum of studies, values, attitudes, and professional ethics training (standard 19, CSHSE Guidelines for Program Approval 1989). We have now answered the questions of what a human service worker is and how it is distinguished from other helping professionals.

Texas is one state that requires all counselors to be licensed. NASW and TCADA (the Texas equivalent to NAADAC have a licensing procedure for paraprofessionals. They have their own code of ethics and committees to enforce it. In the first year that licensure was required for substance abuse counselors, many ethical complaints were filed. These complaints were investigated and action taken.

WHAT ARE ETHICS?

Ethics by definition are "The study of the general nature of morals, and of the specific moral choices to be made by the individual in his relationship with others. The rules of standards governing conduct of the members of a profession" (American Heritage Dictionary). The same book goes on to tell us that "a moral is concerned with judging the goodness or badness of human action and character." My understanding, then, is that ethics and morals are very subjective.

Any topic that is subjective can have many variables. For this reason the codes of ethics for similar professions may be markedly different. For a good representative sample of the code of ethics for mental health professionals, I would like to recommend that you read the appendix of *Issues and Ethics in the Helping Professions*, 4th ed., 1993, by Corey, Corey, and Callanan, published by Brooks/Cole.

Tony Ellis in his article, "The Nature of Morality" (Barker and Baldwin, 1991), contrasts morality with a set of norms that we refer to as customs. He goes on to tell us that sometimes there is really not a good answer to why we do the things we do; it's just because everyone around us thinks it's normal for the times. Hopefully in human services, we have established customs that we feel are for the good of our clients. Of course, there are those who feel that we cannot police our colleagues, and so laws are passed.

CURRENT TRENDS THAT CAUSE CONCERN

One of the ways we help our clients is to model healthy behavior. Ethical problems must be faced openly and honestly. To do this we must take a close look at current trends that have caused so much distress in our industry.

One obvious problem that has facilitated many of the dilemmas we now face is agency survival. Social service providers are being held accountable now more than ever. Government funds are harder to acquire. Insurance companies want proof that a client will be healed. There is more competition for grants. Agencies that provide funding for training want to be assured that their clients will be able to get employment when they complete a program. In essence, the people who pay the bills want results.

In 1991 Texas began a study into the unethical practices of psychiatric hospitals within the state. Numerous complaints from consumers and concerned professionals prompted the action that led to the proposal of over one hundred suggestions for reforms to be made in this field alone. The study uncovered what is to be considered one of the largest scandals in Texas history.

Bounty Hunting

Bounty hunting is one of the oldest professions; however, one does not expect to find it in the mental health profession. Most states currently outlaw this in the medical fields, but the laws are vague or nonexistent in human services.

One of the most frequently used bounty-hunting techniques is to offer some kind of perk to professionals who refer to a particular hospital or clinic. These perks can be something as small as favors provided by the hospital such as fruit baskets, free literature, or elaborate lunches. These special treats can also be quite substantial. They may include vacations, free office space, or actual monetary kickbacks.

Many times bounty hunting can begin as a small unconscious act that seems to be an innocent give-and-take act. One example can be tied to recent trends. An institution may offer to provide free training programs or workshops to a company, business, etc., on topics such as drug testing, AIDS, or stress reduction. In return, this good relationship may prompt an employee assistance representative to refer employees to the facility. This institution may be offering the best available treatment; however, it may also simply have an excellent speaker's bureau. Who can be sure?

Advertising

Advertising and marketing is a multibillion dollar business. None of us are immune to the seduc-

tiveness of a good commercial or a nicely done billboard. A few years ago while driving down the freeway, I looked up to see a huge sign with a teenager, head in hands, looking very forlorn. The sign read, "is your child restless, easily bored, acting out, call us at . . . we provide a free evaluation and referral." Having two adolescents of my own and numerous friends hanging out at my house, I can safely describe most of them as restless and easily bored. What is "acting out"? I suppose it is something beyond what is normal. My fear is that it may be possible to exaggerate symptoms to come up with a diagnosis serious enough to have a child admitted to a residential facility for a twenty-eight day stay at perhaps $1,000 per day, the average covered by insurance.

Making services available to the public is part of the job of a good mental health worker. All advertising, of course, is not bad or unethical. We must, however, ask ourselves two questions: (1) Are we providing the least restrictive environment for care? (2) Who will benefit most from the service or treatment we recommend?

Accountability

Can we do what we say we can do? Can we provide a treatment that will improve the quality of living for our clients? Apparently not all of us can. One of the largest complaints is that many of our clients relapse into whatever it was that brought them to us to begin with. We simply do not keep honest or accurate statistics on our successes and failures. If we did, and were honest, we might discover that often our recovery rate is not good. Good, however, is a relative term. We all know we do not have cures, and that the clients must ultimately help themselves. The ethical concern here is that our clients, all of them, are vulnerable, as are their families. They must rely on us, the professionals, to learn from our mistakes in treatment plan development, follow through, and aftercare. We cannot wait for insurance companies or legislation to do this for us.

Many human service agencies rely heavily on public funding that requires a high degree of accountability. The records needed to substantiate progress, or rather success, are difficult to follow, time consuming to keep, and easily lend themselves to error. As a profession, human services has not traditionally done a good job initiating changes in this area.

Bissell and Royce (1987) have this to say about accountability and how to learn from our mistakes, "If we are to retain credibility and share useful information with one another about what works for patients and what does not, we must insist on quality data and well-defined goals." We must hold ourselves and each other accountable for, at the very least, providing the best care with the resources and knowledge we have available.

Sexual Impropriety

Most studies done on professional liability in the helping professions show that nearly 25 percent of the lawsuits are for some sort of sexual impropriety. Sexual contact is generally understood as physical touch of a clearly sexual nature (Markowitz, 1992). I am clearly astonished at how many of my colleagues have involved themselves in this type of blatant misconduct. At least 50 percent of the offenders are repeats. Most of the therapists involved believe that the behavior is harmful, or at the every least has no benefit for the client. Then for whose benefit is it?

One thing is very clear. Every ethical code in the helping professions that I have read forbids sexual misconduct with clients. The other fact is that an accusation does not really have to be substantiated for the therapist to appear guilty.

Example.   A few years ago, an intern that I was supervising was accused by a schizophrenic female client of touching her and propositioning her in inappropriate ways. The male intern emphatically denied the accusations, and insisted that the client was angry because he had not responded to her sexual interest in him. The student felt that it was my job as his supervisor to defend his innocence with the agency. Instead, I

called the on-site supervisor and removed the student from the placement with the agreement that the matter would be dropped. Did I believe the student was guilty? In fact, I did not. I did feel, however, that it would be better for the student in the long run to choose not to fight this battle. The student felt a sense of disloyalty from me, and it took awhile before his respect could be regained. The point is that these battles are lost even if innocence can be proven, which is difficult to do.

According to the American Psychological Association Insurance Trust, which is the major insurer for psychologists, sexual relationships between the client and therapist cost them more money in suits than any other type claim. For this reason a cap has been placed on how much can be recovered for such a suit.

Fraudulent Billing

Several years ago a family was referred to me whose son had just been released from a residential treatment center for substance abuse. The young man was in the facility for several months and the parents' portion of the bill was in excess of $57,000. Upon close examination the parents discovered that the statement contained charges for services that they were sure he did not receive. He was billed $100 each day for the services of the admitting physician, whom he saw about twice per week for ten minutes. He was billed for three hours of group therapy per day at $65 per hour. One therapy group had an average of twelve members; one was an education session with over forty residents. He was charged $45 per day for therapeutic recreation, which he discovered was for the use of the swimming pool and athletic facilities, since there was not a recreation specialist on-site. The list of charges goes on and on and averages $1,127 per day.

Currently there are states that do not levy criminal penalties for health care providers who fraudulently bill patients or insurance companies for services that are not necessary or not provided.

The suspicions that have brought us to this situation are not without cause. There have been many, many abuses. Consumers will be the ones to cause a radical change to occur. They will insist on better care and repeated lawsuits will force laws to be passed that will make us be accountable.

Cases to Review

It would be unlikely that any human service worker could get through a whole month of working in the field without being able to provide some example of a behavior observed that they felt was unethical, or perhaps breaking a basic law. Following are a few short stories that depict actual circumstances where beginning human service workers have had to stop and think twice before they realized they were being caught up in a questionable behavior.

Case A.   Lila, a woman in her mid-40s, had returned to school after raising three children. She was completing her final mental health practicum working on the adolescent substance ward of a private psychiatric hospital. The hospital staff was delighted with her skills and her ability to understand the turmoil many of these children have been through. After only a month at the hospital, Lila was co-facilitating a group of eight to ten adolescents. She was always well prepared and was offered a job with the company. A few weeks after she accepted a paid position, she was told there were going to be some staff cutbacks, and that she would have to double-up on group patients until further notice. The first afternoon was a nightmare. They had put the general psychiatric youth in with the substance abuse patients to bring the group number up to nineteen. Children were behaving inappropriately, and the group constantly needed several technicians available for control. After each session it took Lila two to three hours to properly document all of the charts about the client progress. She was told not to sign her name to the charts belonging to the psychiatric patients because that was not an area in which she was licensed to work.

This case illustrates some ethical and legal concerns. As a beginning worker we may be a little bit more cautious in expressing our concerns about such things as the unmanageable size of the group, or the fact that it could be very harmful to mix the general psychiatric clients with the CD clients. Little can be accomplished if we spend a large part of our time containing acting-out behavior. The issue of being asked to provide care in an area for which we are not trained or licensed is an issue on which we must take a stand.

Case B.   John, a newly licensed substance abuse counselor, was very excited when he got his first job with a halfway house that received state funds. After being on the job for only a few months, the facility was going to be examined for contract renewal. The staff was in a frenzy to insure that all records were up-to-date and files in order. John was asked to work overtime to audit files of patients, some of which had been discharged up to a year before his employment there. He was given an example and told how to properly document the records. He was told that this was usual, and that often the patient load was too heavy for a busy counselor to get all of the records done in a timely manner.

In essence, what John was being asked to do was falsify client records. Funding is an important issue; clients cannot receive care if funding is not continued. Facilities may lose their license if paperwork is not kept up properly. It is very true that keeping up with the piles of documents necessary is a cumbersome chore not enjoyed by many human service workers. Proper documentation requires a lot of time and most of us feel our time is better spent elsewhere. Cleaning up paper work problems left by our colleagues because of poor management cannot become our problem. This issue cannot be taken lightly, since we are often expected to do this unethical and illegal chore and we must know our position on the issue before entering an agency.

Case C.   Susan had always wanted to work with the elderly. Her first practicum was with a large established nursing care facility that had a wonderful reputation for providing excellent care. She was assigned to work with the lead social worker and found her guidance invaluable. Halfway through the semester an announcement was made that the facility would become a rehabilitation center. The residents that did not need rehab and were not covered under insurance would be assisted with relocation. The change was to be complete in thirty days. The process seemed to be going smoothly until Susan noticed that most of the residents were being strongly encouraged to move to one particular center that was not well known for its quality care, and was more expensive than the average. This concerned her. She consulted her supervisor who told her that she was doing what the management had told her to do, and that it was not her place to question.

Making referrals is one duty that will consume a lot of our time. Our clients are always in a vulnerable position when they need a referral, because they trust that we are giving them the best information we have available. They will most often go with whatever recommendation we make. It is our job and duty to make sure that we are informed about all of the most appropriate referral sources. If we knowingly refer for a motive other than wanting to provide the best care for a client, then there will be no question that we are acting unethically.

Case D.   Art was working at a day treatment center for mentally retarded young adults. He really enjoyed the physical activities, and it gave him great satisfaction when the young people seemed to be enjoying themselves. One afternoon when they were playing basketball, another worker became frustrated with the low level of one of the clients and very forcefully threw the ball, hitting the client in the face and causing a very bad bruise.

Art, disturbed by the incident, went to his supervisor to discuss his concern. The supervisor was supportive. Art, however, did not see a

change in his colleague's behavior and again approached his boss. This time the supervisor said that these people had accidents all the time, and that it would be better if he just did his job and went about his business.

With inexperience often comes self-doubt. Art was not sure what could be considered excessive force in this situation and, quite frankly, did not understand his client's right well enough to take a stand confidently on the issue. He did, however, have a real human feeling that this behavior was not right. This "feeling" that most of us have will most times be appropriate, and any action is better than none.

Lila, John, Susan, and Art all had similar but different ethical problems. All were new to the field, and all were questioning whether or not what they felt was wrong was truly wrong.

What do we teach human service students about working within a system? Woodside and McClam (1991) discuss being a good bureaucrat: learning to work within a system for the benefit of our clients. We take this a step further when we are being pragmatic. Let's face it, there is competition for most jobs out there. We cannot afford to challenge all of the details we may find that offend our value system. On the other hand it is important that we teach new workers in the field to know, at the very least, where their limits are and how to approach a situation to achieve the best results.

WHAT ABOUT THE LAW?

Human service workers have typically been afraid of issues dealing with the law. I believe this is for several reasons. First, we are intimidated by legal terms that tend to make us feel not so smart. Second, we think we will never need to know. Third, we often feel that we will always do a good job and that our clients will all think we're great. So why worry? These excuses will no longer be sufficient to even convince ourselves.

Over the past few years lawsuits have been rising at an incredible rate. One of the biggest reasons for this is that our clients are feeling a greater sense of empowerment. They are being heard and are no longer intimidated by physicians, therapists, or human service workers. We sometimes feel that because, as human service workers, we are not as liable as physicians. This is very untrue. Anyone can be sued.

Most laws are written in such a way that they are difficult to understand. The American Psychological Association publishes a series of books entitled *Law and Mental Health Professionals Series*. The books are each tailored by states and are divided into sections that are easy to read and understand. The books reference federal laws that may conflict, and provide additional resources if questions arise.

At a minimum, mental health professionals need to have an understanding of the laws in their state affecting how they conduct business.

Client Rights

Do clients have rights? We would like to believe that they do. Unfortunately, sometimes we will discover that this is only a myth. We have many prepared forms for our clients to sign. Some of these forms will cause them to give up their privacy rights. Some forms will release the agency from the responsibility of providing good service. All states have some basic rights published for mental health patients. It is the responsibility of every human service worker to know, understand, and be able to explain to consumers their rights in a language that they can understand. The working may need to be changed depending on the agency setting, but below is an example of a basic set of clients' rights.

Sample of basic rights for all mental health patients in the state of Texas

1. You have all the rights of a citizen of the state of Texas and the United States of America, including the rights of habeas corpus (to ask a judge if it is legal for you to be kept in a hospital), property rights, guardianship rights, religious freedom, the right to register and vote, the right to sue and be sued, the right to sign contracts, and all the rights relating to licenses, permits and privileges, and benefits under the law.

2. You have a right to be presumed mentally competent unless a court has ruled otherwise.

3. You have the right to a clean and humane environment in which you are protected from harm, have privacy with regard to personal needs, and are treated with respect and dignity.

4. You have the right to appropriate treatment in the most open place available that provides protection for you and the people around you.

5. You have the right to be free from mistreatment, abuse, neglect, and exploitation.

6. You have the right to be told in advance of any charges being made, the cost of services, sources of the program's reimbursement, and any limitations on length of services.

7. You have the right to fair compensation for labor performed for the hospital in accordance with the Fair Labor Standards Act.

8. Prior to admission, you have the right to be informed of all hospital rules and regulations concerning your conduct and course of treatment.

Communication

9. You have the right to talk and write to people outside the hospital. You have the right to have visitors in private, make private phone calls, send and receive sealed and uncensored mail.

Confidentiality

10. You have the right to review the information contained in your medical record. If your doctor says you shouldn't see your record, you have the right to have, at your expense, another doctor of your choice review that decision. The right extends to your parent or conservator if you are a minor (unless you have admitted yourself to services) and to your legal guardian if you have been declared by a court to be legally incompetent.

11. You have the right to have your records kept private and to be told about the conditions under which information about you can be disclosed without your permission.

12. You have the right to be informed of the current and future use of products, of special observation and audiovisual techniques, such as one-way vision mirrors, tape recorders, television, movies, or photographs.

Consent

13. You have the right to refuse to take part in research without affecting your regular care.

14. You have the right to refuse any of the following:
- surgical procedures
- electroconvulsive therapy
- unusual medication
- hazardous assessment procedures
- audiovisual equipment
- and all other procedures for which your permission is required by law

15. You have the right to withdraw your permission at any time in matters to which you have previously consented.

Care and treatment

16. You have the right to a treatment plan for your stay in the hospital that is just for you. You have the right to take part in developing that plan, as well as the treatment plan for your care after you leave the hospital.

17. You have the right to be told about the care, procedures, and treatment you will be given; the risks, side effects, and benefits of all medications and treatment you will receive, including those that are unusual or experimental, the other treatments that are available, and what may happen if you refuse the treatment.

18. You have the right not to be given medications you don't need or too much medication, including the right to refuse medication that is mood-altering or mind-altering, unless the right to refuse has been specifically taken away by court order.

19. You have the right not to be physically restrained unless your doctor orders it and writes it in your medical record. If you are restrained, you must be told the reason, how long you will be restrained, and what you have to do to be removed from restraint. The restraint has to be removed as soon as possible.

20. You have the right to meet with a staff responsible for your care and to be told of their professional discipline, job title, and responsibilities. In addition, you have the right to know about any proposed change in the appointment of staff, professional or otherwise, responsible for your care.

21. You have the right to request the opinion of another doctor at your own expense. You have the right to be granted a review of the treatment plan or specific procedure by another doctor who works for the hospital.

22. You have the right to be told why you are being transferred to any program within or outside the hospital.

At this point clients are told that if they have any questions or complaints concerning these rights, they can call the appropriate state office and are given the toll free number.

Please note that there are special rights for persons apprehended for emergency detention and special rights if they are voluntary patients. These rights include such things as how long they can be detained without a hearing, and the right to discharge themselves.

Many states use federal laws such as the Federal Confidentiality Regulations as a guide when developing standards for care. There may also be sets of rights established for special populations such as the elderly, and mentally or physically challenged clients. When you choose to work with a special needs population it is your duty to keep abreast of changing laws.

Confidentiality

To most of our clients, confidentiality means that we will keep what they tell us private. Many actually believe that we will tell no one. Little do most of them know that there are many people and many reasons information told in confidence may be shared. Our laws and code of ethics will dictate most of the guidelines. However, ultimately, our good judgment will provide us with the most prudent answer.

Human service professionals need to have a clear understanding of the privileged communication laws in their state. In Texas, for instance, the laws are different for civil and criminal cases. In criminal cases, the mental health worker-patient privilege is not recognized (Shuman, 1989). Every state has different definitions, exceptions, and waivers.

Under certain conditions there are common reasons for breaching the personal relationship we have with our clients. Most often, these are (1) the duty to warn and the duty to protect laws, and (2) in most states, child abuse. The duty to warn and protect laws has been passed in many states after the California Supreme Court ruled that a college psychologist did not take all of the needed precautions when a student confided that he was going to kill a woman, who was easily identifiable, after she returned from a trip. The woman, Tatiana Tarasoff, was eventually killed and a lawsuit was filed by her parents. Although the psychologist notified the campus police and wrote a formal letter of concern, he did not notify the woman or her family (Corey, Corey, and Callanan, 1993). If an intended victim's name is unknown, it's important to know how long a client can be restrained.

Protecting a client from himself or herself is another area human service workers wrestle with frequently. There is no doubt that a confidence must be broken to save a life. Our often volatile clients have so few healthy coping skills that suicide seems, at times, to be the best answer. Although most of us are not in the position to be able to detain clients when we are concerned, we must have at our fingertips the resources and referrals necessary to protect human life.

Child abuse is against the law in every state. Reporting procedures may vary, but as a general rule, all people involved in the helping services are obliged to report cases of child abuse, even if it breaks confidentiality.

When training our beginning mental health students, we always have them actually verbalize to their clients the exceptions to the confidentiality pact. We also encourage them, when they get to their practicum sites, to inform clients if information will be disclosed in staff meetings and what the information will be used for.

Confidentiality is an even tougher issue when we discuss group work. We may have a good feeling for our genuine desire to keep confidence, but it's almost impossible to control the actions of twelve other people. The best rule of thumb is to discuss the issue openly with the group up front. It may often be necessary to screen more closely and perhaps have forms signed if you feel particularly insecure about a group. Corey, Corey, and Callanan (1993) discuss in some detail ways to encourage confidentiality in groups and go on to relate exceptions to the confidentiality rules.

Domestic Issues

Every client population will have domestic issues to be resolved. Although it is best for us not to give legal advice, we must know some basic civil law to assist us in making wise referrals. For example, states vary in their opinion about who is a minor, who will pay child support, statute of limitation for reporting child abuse, and the list goes on.

Basic Department of Education Laws

The laws pertaining to education and schools in your state are valuable tools to possess. Who is entitled to an education, and under what provisions are special needs provided for? What are the assessment tools available through the school system that may save your clients time and money? Who is considered a student? This information is especially important for those parents who have children in their twenties in college. When can students be considered independent and qualify for financial aid on their own?

Truancy, guardianship, and residency laws will also come in handy, as many of our clients will have difficulty in this area. Laws pertaining to minors are often different and unexpected.

Insurance

Insurance rules and regulations can and will change constantly. Insurance laws will dictate many things to a human service worker. Some examples are how long and what kind of treatment can be provided. The trend recently is to allow hospitalization for emergencies only. Both medical and mental health procedures must almost be a life-or-death situation to be covered. Outpatient services are encouraged, and new treatment methods are being developed to accommodate these regulations.

Insurance may also dictate the kind of documentation that will be kept on a client. In 1979 Congress passed the Privacy Act (P.L. 96–440) protecting third parties from the abuse of a search warrant. Many states have laws overriding this public law.

A relatively new term in our profession is managed health care. What this really means is that someone other than a mental health professional may be telling us what is best for our clients. Employee assistance professionals have been learning the hard way that a marriage must occur between the insurance companies, the employers, and health care providers (Young, 1993). Managed health care will be very similar to what our clients understand as health maintenance organizations (HMO). As part of our public understanding and education skill, we may be called on to interpret what services are covered, which will most certainly affect our referrals.

ETHICS AND CULTURE

Lately human service professionals have come to realize how necessary it has become to have a basic understanding of cultural differences if we are going to provide quality, ethical care. Many cities have become so diversified that it is impossible to work effectively, in any profession, without at least a few tools for being culturally appropriate. Daisy Kabagarma in her book *Breaking the Ice, A Guide to Understanding People From Other Cultures* (1993), provides us with six keys to help prepare us to be culturally neutral.

1. Genuine interest. Genuine interest is cultivated by a realization that culture is a relative concept, and that our interests need not have the hidden agenda of wanting to affirm beliefs in our own culture.
2. A sense of curiosity and appreciation. An openness to appreciate behaviors that are different from our own.
3. Empathy—the ability to place ourselves in another person's place. To be able to feel the same kinds of feelings.
4. Nonjudgmental. Understanding before passing judgment.
5. Flexibility. Be open to changing our own behavior to fit the situation.

6. Childlike learning mode. Allow yourself to accept new meanings.

People are people, and the laws for working with all cultural groups are the same. The difference lies in remaining ethical, not imposing our own values, and protecting the rights of all without breaking the law.

Preparing to be Ethical

For most of us, our basic sense of right and wrong will guide us in the right direction. We'll remember what we've been taught by our parents, our teachers, our religion, and our community. We'll choose a few special people to use as models. We'll study the laws and codes of ethics of our professions. We'll make some mistakes, and learn many lessons. There are a few suggestions I can add to assist you in becoming and remaining an ethical human service worker:

1. Write your own personal code of ethics. Use one of the professional codes such as the APA or NASW as a guide and put it in your own language. Be flexible and willing to change as you mature.
2. Continually solicit feedback from colleagues. Get a second or third opinion if you feel in doubt about a behavior or belief.
3. Keep yourself healthy. You must be well to assist others in staying well. Understand your motivations and you'll be able to keep firm your boundaries.
4. Know your limitations and refer a client before you give incorrect, illegal, or unethical information.

SUMMARY

Human service work is a relatively new field of study and has yet to define itself clearly. Organizations such as the Council for Standards in Human Services Education and the National Organization of Human Services Education have brought the field a long way by publishing literature specific to the field. A basic brochure, *The Human Service Worker*, is available by writing to CSHSE, Mental Health Program, 5514 Clara Rd., Houston, Texas 77041.

REFERENCES

Barker, P.H., and S. Baldwin, (1991). *Ethical Issues in Mental Health.* London: Chapman and Hall.

Bissell, L., and J.E. Royce, (1987). *Ethics for Addiction Professionals.* Haxeldon Foundation.

Corey, G., (1991). *Theory and Practice of Counseling and Psychotherapy.* Pacific Grove, CA: Brooks/Cole.

Corey, G., M.S. Corey, and P. Callanan, (1993). *Issues and Ethics in the Helping Profession.* Pacific Grove, CA: Brooks/Cole.

Fullerton, S., and D. Osher, (1990). *History of the Human Services Movement.* Council for Standards in Human Service Education, Monograph Series.

Kabagarama, Daisy, (1993). *Breaking the Ice, A Guide to Understanding People from Other Cultures.* Boston: Allyn and Bacon.

Maeder, T., (Jan. 1989). "Wounded Healers." *The Atlantic Monthly.*

Markowitz, L., (Dec. 1992). "When Therapy Does Harm, Crossing the Line." *The Family Therapy Networker.*

McClam, T., and M. Woodside, (1990). *An Introduction to Human Services.* Pacific Grove, CA: Brooks/Cole.

Lum, D., (1992). *Social Work Practice and People of Color.* Pacific Grove, CA: Brooks/Cole.

Shuman, D.W., (1989). *Law and Mental Health Professionals,* Washington, DC: American Psychological Association.

Smith, M., (Sept 22, 1992). "Psychiatric Reforms Are Proposed." *Houston Chronicle,* Houston, TX.

Young, V., (Jan. 1993). "Managed Care." *The Advisor.* 4(6) 1–4.

ETHICAL STANDARDS OF HUMAN SERVICE PROFESSIONALS (PROPOSED)

NATIONAL ORGANIZATION FOR HUMAN SERVICE EDUCATION

PREAMBLE

Human services is a profession developing in response to and in anticipation of the direction of human needs and human problems in the late twentieth century. Characterized particularly by an appreciation of human beings in all of their diversity, human services offers assistance to its clients within the context of their community and environment. Human service professionals, regardless of whether they are students, faculty, or practitioners, promote and encourage the unique values and characteristics of human services. In so doing human service professionals uphold the integrity and ethics of the profession, partake in constructive criticism of the profession, promote client and community well-being, and enhance their own professional growth.

The ethical guidelines presented are a set of standards of conduct that the human service professional considers in ethical and professional decision making. It is hoped that these guidelines will be of assistance when the human service professional is challenged by difficult ethical dilemmas. Although ethical codes are not legal documents, they may be used to assist in the adjudication of issues related to ethical human service behavior.

Human service professionals function in many ways and carry out many roles. They enter into professional-client relationships with individuals, families, groups, and communities who are all referred to as "clients" in these standards. Among their roles are caregiver, case manager, broker, teacher/educator, behavior changer, consultant, outreach professional, mobilizer, advocate, community planner, community change organizer, evaluator, and administrator.[1] The following standards are written with these multi-faceted roles in mind.

THE HUMAN SERVICE PROFESSIONAL'S RESPONSIBILITY TO CLIENTS

> *STATEMENT 1* Human service professionals negotiate with clients the purpose, goals, and nature of the helping relationship prior to its onset, as well as inform clients of the limitations of the proposed relationship.
>
> *STATEMENT 2* Human service professionals respect the integrity and welfare of the client at all times. Each client is treated with respect, acceptance, and dignity.
>
> *STATEMENT 3* Human service professionals protect the client's right to privacy and confidentiality except when such confidentiality would cause harm to the client or others, when agency guidelines state otherwise, or under other stated conditions (e.g., local, state, or federal laws). Professionals inform clients of the limits of confidentiality prior to the onset of the helping relationship.

[1]Southern Regional Education Board, *Roles and Functions for Mental Health Workers: A Report of a Symposium*. Atlanta, GA: Community Mental Health Worker Project, 1967. Used with permission.

STATEMENT 4 If it is suspected that danger or harm may occur to the client or to others as a result of a client's behavior, the human service professional acts in an appropriate and professional manner to protect the safety of those individuals. This may involve seeking consultation, supervision, and/or breaking the confidentiality of the relationship.

STATEMENT 5 Human service professionals protect the integrity, safety, and security of client records. All written client information that is shared with other professionals, except in the course of professional supervision, must have the client's prior written consent.

STATEMENT 6 Human service professionals are aware that in their relationships with clients, power and status are unequal. Therefore they recognize that dual or multiple relationships may increase the risk of harm to, or exploitation of, clients, and may impair their professional judgment. However, in some communities and situations, it may not be feasible to avoid social or other nonprofessional contact with clients. Human service professionals support the trust implicit in the helping relationship by avoiding dual relationships that may impair professional judgment, increase the risk of harm to clients, or lead to exploitation.

STATEMENT 7 Sexual relationships with current clients are not considered to be in the best interest of the client and are prohibited. Sexual relationships with previous clients are considered dual relationships and are addressed in Statement 6 (above).

STATEMENT 8 The client's right to self-determination is protected by human service professionals. They recognize the client's right to receive or refuse services.

STATEMENT 9 Human service professionals recognize and build on client strengths.

THE HUMAN SERVICE PROFESSIONAL'S RESPONSIBILITY TO THE COMMUNITY AND SOCIETY

STATEMENT 10 Human service professionals are aware of local, state, and federal laws. They advocate for change in regulations and statutes when such legislation conflicts with ethical guidelines and/or client rights. Where laws are harmful to individuals, groups, or communities, human service professionals consider the conflict between the values of obeying the law and the values of serving people and may decide to initiate social action.

STATEMENT 11 Human service professionals keep informed about current social issues as they affect the client and the community. They share that information with clients, groups, and community as part of their work.

STATEMENT 12 Human service professionals understand the complex interaction between individuals, their families, the communities in which they live, and society.

STATEMENT 13 Human service professionals act as advocates in addressing unmet client and community needs. Human service professionals provide a mechanism for identifying unmet client needs, calling attention to these needs, and assisting in planning and mobilizing to advocate for those needs at the local community level.

STATEMENT 14 Human service professionals represent their qualifications to the public accurately.

STATEMENT 15 Human service professionals describe the effectiveness of programs, treatments, and/or techniques accurately.

STATEMENT 16 Human service professionals advocate for the rights of all members of society, particularly those who are members of minorities and groups at which discriminatory practices have historically been directed.

STATEMENT 17 Human service professionals provide services without discrimination or preference based on age, ethnicity, culture, race, disability, gender, religion, sexual orientation, or socioeconomic status.

STATEMENT 18 Human service professionals are knowledgeable about the cultures and communities within which they practice. They are aware of multiculturalism in society and its impact on the community as well as individuals within the community. They respect individuals and groups, their cultures and beliefs.

STATEMENT 19 Human service professionals are aware of their own cultural backgrounds, beliefs, and values, recognizing the potential for impact on their relationships with others.

STATEMENT 20   Human service professionals are aware of sociopolitical issues that differentially affect clients from diverse backgrounds.

STATEMENT 21   Human service professionals seek the training, experience, education and supervision necessary to ensure their effectiveness in working with culturally diverse client populations.

THE HUMAN SERVICE PROFESSIONAL'S RESPONSIBILITY TO COLLEAGUES

STATEMENT 22   Human service professionals avoid duplicating another professional's helping relationship with a client. They consult with other professionals who are assisting the client in a different type of relationship when it is in the best interest of the client to do so.

STATEMENT 23   When a human service professional has a conflict with a colleague, he or she first seeks out the colleague in an attempt to manage the problem. If necessary, the professional then seeks the assistance of supervisors, consultants or other professionals in efforts to manage the problem.

STATEMENT 24   Human service professionals respond appropriately to unethical behavior of colleagues. Usually this means initially talking directly with the colleague and, if no resolution is forthcoming, reporting the colleague's behavior to supervisory or administrative staff and/or to the professional organization(s) to which the colleague belongs.

STATEMENT 25   All consultations between human service professionals are kept confidential unless to do so would result in harm to clients or communities.

THE HUMAN SERVICE PROFESSIONAL'S RESPONSIBILITY TO THE PROFESSION

STATEMENT 26   Human service professionals know the limit and scope of their professional knowledge and offer services only within their knowledge and skill base.

STATEMENT 27   Human service professionals seek appropriate consultation and supervision to assist in decision-making when there are legal, ethical, or other dilemmas.

STATEMENT 28   Human service professionals act with integrity, honesty, genuineness, and objectivity.

STATEMENT 29   Human service professionals promote cooperation among related disciplines (e.g., psychology, counseling, social work, nursing, family and consumer sciences, medicine, education) to foster professional growth and interests within the various fields.

STATEMENT 30   Human service professionals promote the continuing development of their profession. They encourage membership in professional associations, support research endeavors, foster educational advancement, advocate for appropriate legislative actions, and participate in other related professional activities.

STATEMENT 31   Human service professionals continually seek out new and effective approaches to enhance their professional abilities.

THE HUMAN SERVICE PROFESSIONAL'S RESPONSIBILITY TO EMPLOYERS

STATEMENT 32   Human service professionals adhere to commitments made to their employer.

STATEMENT 33   Human service professionals participate in efforts to establish and maintain employment conditions that are conducive to high quality client services. They assist in evaluating the effectiveness of the agency through reliable and valid assessment measures.

STATEMENT 34   When a conflict arises between fulfilling the responsibility to the employer and the responsibility to the client, human service professionals advise both of the conflict and work conjointly with all involved to manage the conflict.

THE HUMAN SERVICE PROFESSIONAL'S RESPONSIBILITY TO SELF

STATEMENT 35   Human service professionals strive to personify those characteristics typically associated with the profession (e.g., accountability, respect for others, genuineness, empathy, pragmatism).

STATEMENT 36   Human service professionals foster self-awareness and personal growth in themselves. They recognize that when professionals are aware of their own values, attitudes, cultural background, and personal needs, the process of helping others is less likely to be negatively impacted by those factors.

STATEMENT 37   Human service professionals recognize a commitment to lifelong learning and continually upgrade knowledge and skills to serve the populations better.

CHAPTER 12

HUMAN SERVICES AS A CAREER
PERSONAL SURVIVAL
AND PROFESSIONAL GROWTH

MIRIAM CLUBOK

ACKNOWLEDGING MOTIVATION

"You're going to do what?" "You'll never get rich." "You'll be bogged down with paper work and bureaucracy." "Why not accounting, computer science? Why human services?" Who hasn't heard these questions and more after revealing that human services has been chosen as a career? Usually these questions are answered in a superficial manner; the answers seem easy. But with reflection, it soon becomes clear that persons really choose human services for more complex reasons. Success in human services requires that individuals identify their true motivation for this work, at least for themselves if not for friends and relatives.

Most persons, when asked, say they chose human services because they like people. They may cite times when others came to them for help and how they liked being a listener. Some may say that they have had problems they overcame; therefore they can help others do the same. Some point to individuals who have helped them, so they wish to become helpers in return. While all of these statements are true, they may also be viewed as explanations for entering the profession that do not address the deeper-level motivations that people may have. When asked to reflect more deeply, helping people will come in touch with a different set of needs and motivations. They will admit such things as liking to feel needed; liking to feel in control and powerful; lik-

ing to feel important; enjoying being viewed as knowledgeable; and liking to be liked. At first glance, admitting these feelings seems distasteful, even selfish. But human service workers are humans with human needs, wants, and desires. To deny these basic motivating forces is dishonest and possibly dangerous. It is neither bad nor selfish to have these feelings, but if one refuses to acknowledge them, the danger lies in the likelihood of the worker unconsciously using the client to meet the worker's needs. When we are in touch with, for example, our need to be liked and depended on, we may be more likely to recognize that doing too much for the client is really meeting our need, not the client's. In their discussion of how personal needs impact the helping relationship, Danish, D'Augelli, and Hauer (1980) emphasize that all students should analyze their needs for becoming helpers to identify what is personally rewarding and to recognize how their needs will influence the helping process.

IDENTIFYING WORRIES

Just as being in touch with personal needs and motivations is essential to success in human services, so is being in touch with the worries and fears every student has as the protection of school is about to end, and entry to the real world of work approaches. Although a myriad of fears and concerns could be identified, generally they fall into three categories: fears about the clients, fears about oneself, and fears about the work environment. Facing these fears directly and examining them can help the new worker deal more realistically with his or her responsibility and expectations.

Concerns for Client

One of the most frequently stated worries involves the student's fear that he or she will not be able to help or may even harm the client. The fact is, however, that we cannot help every client, and survival in the field demands our recognition of this. Some clients resist change, often preferring a painful status quo to taking a risk. For some, all available options are poor ones, easing some aspect of the problem but creating new concerns. It is important to remember that making no choice because all options are flawed is also a choice. Ultimately, choices for change and responsibility for outcome are the client's, not the worker's. The worker, however, must assume primary responsibility for the helping *process*. That is, the worker must have or seek out relevant knowledge about the client's situation; must utilize his or her skills to create and maintain a helping relationship; must engage the client in problem solving and identification of all available choices; and must operate in a professional manner, applying all of the basic attitudes and values that are inherent in ethical practice (respect for individual dignity, client self-determination, confidentiality, etc.).

Concern for Self

Another common worry is that one may become too emotionally involved with a client. The truth is, workers cannot avoid becoming emotionally involved with clients, to some extent. Most of those who enter the human service field are naturally empathetic and caring individuals. These qualities cannot always be turned off at 5:00 P.M., and to expect so creates an unrealistic and unachievable

goal. Instead, it is important to accept the fact that entering human services will place emotional demands on the worker, but to avoid becoming overwhelmed, some attitudinal and behavioral restructuring is needed. One of the most important attitudinal factors all workers need is a high degree of self-awareness. This is necessary in many aspects of human service work, but is certainly critical to avoid the emotional exhaustion that can result from getting too involved with clients. All workers should learn early in their careers to constantly evaluate their behaviors and feelings. To do so does not make one selfish or egocentric, as some may fear. Instead, it helps sharpen the focus on clients or problem situations by forcing the worker to consciously identify what works, what doesn't, and what behaviors or actions may be originating from the worker's own unmet needs. When a worker learns to constantly think about his or her own behavior and attitudes toward clients, internal alarms will sound when signs of being too involved begin (too frequent telephone calls, extended interviews, disproportionate amount of time worrying about the client, etc.). Honest self-reflection can help identify the reasons for the involvement, separate worker and client responsibility, and help the worker step back to evaluate what is happening in a more objective manner. After a worker's self-awareness has helped to identify danger signs, appropriate attitudinal and behavior changes must take place. Being realistic about one's own responsibility for the client, setting limits, utilizing supervisory and peer support, and involvement in satisfying personal relationships and activities outside the workplace are some of the major ways workers can distance themselves from over-involvement.

Most new workers are concerned that they do not have enough knowledge or skill to be effective. While for some, this concern may paralyze them into inaction, for most, it is a useful concern that motivates workers to stay self-aware about what new knowledge or skills are needed, to seek out that information, and to constantly try to improve practice. Frankly, it is the new worker (or more experienced worker, for that matter) who insists he or she knows the "right" way to do everything, and that his or her decisions are "best," who poses much more risk than the worker who admits there is more to learn and a variety of choices that can be made. The fact is, that human service workers operate in situations where complete knowledge of facts and outcomes is impossible to achieve, so as responsible professionals, workers must learn to accept their limits while constantly striving to improve their practice. All human service workers must make a personal commitment to acquiring new knowledge and improving skills throughout their professional careers.

Work Environment Concerns

A third category of concerns deals with the work environment. New workers worry about whether or not they will get along with their colleagues, and whether or not they can get along without the support and protection provided by the college environment. They worry about whether or not they can balance the demands of their personal and professional lives, and whether or not they can have an impact on problems in their work environment. While all of these concerns are valid, most new workers find that they can be dealt with if they utilize for themselves the same skills they have learned for working with clients. Use of relationship-building skills works with colleagues, as well as with clients. Application of problem-solving techniques helps in one's own life, as well as with clients. Understanding the organization and bureaucracy in which one works is critical to professional survival and the possibility of effecting change (Lauffer, 1984). Learning to anticipate difficulties and identifying early signs of personal and professional problems is also essential.

THE ETs

While survival and professional growth in human services careers require that workers consider their own motivating forces and confront common worries, it is also helpful to have some specific guiding principles that can increase one's chances for a successful, satisfying career. What follows is what this writer calls her Eight Tips, or "ETs," i.e., identification of behaviors and qualities that, if internalized and used routinely, will likely maximize personal and professional rewards.

Be Professional in Attitude and Work Habits. Much has been written about whether or not the human services is a profession (Clubok, 1987; Fullerton, 1990), but the resolution of that issue is not a prerequisite for the necessity for human service workers to behave in a professional manner. What is meant by "being professional"? Clearly, a long list of qualities could be presented, but basically one must begin by demonstrating personal traits such as being collegial and polite in relationships with clients and colleagues. Using tact to achieve one's ends, learning to be appropriately assertive but still cooperative, managing time effectively, and accepting realistic limits to workplace changes all contribute to "professionalism." Critical, but too often ignored qualities are dependability and punctuality. Many employers, when calling about references, identify these as their number-one concern. Agencies cannot function well (and indeed can suffer serious repercussions from such behaviors as missed deadlines or meetings), nor can workers meet their obligations to clients if they are in the habit of being late or missing appointments or deadlines. Finally, it is important for professionals to be clear about their role, but not to interpret it too narrowly. In other words, sometimes, when situations demand it, a "professional" worker will need to file, type letters, or do other tasks that may not be a specific part of one's job description. A professional attitude demands flexibility and a willingness to step in to meet needs when special circumstances arise.

Continue to Concentrate on Writing Skills. Proofread! Proofread! Proofread! No matter how much knowledge or skill one has, if written work contains misspellings, grammatical errors, or is poorly organized, the worker risks being identified as less competent than he or she may really be, and the agency risks being viewed as careless and nonprofessional. Furthermore, sloppy writing is often accompanied by sloppy documentation, and that could, conceivably, result in legal action against the worker and/or agency. It behooves all human service workers to take a close look at their writing skills and work to improve them. Career advancement is much less likely for individuals who, although able to relate well and think well, cannot translate their ideas to the printed page.

Do Not Compartmentalize Knowledge Areas. Those who think psychology is psychology, sociology is sociology, and interviewing skills are interviewing skills are making a serious mistake. All areas of knowledge relate to one another, and virtually all areas (theoretical and practical) have potential applications to practice situations. To breathe a sigh of relief once the good grade is achieved, thinking (for example): "now I'll never have to worry about identifying those psychological defense mechanisms or demonstrating understanding of role theory concepts," can jeopardize optimal practice. Successful workers must learn to translate knowledge, value concepts, and skills to practice situations. Given any case situation, one should habitually ask oneself: "On what knowledge areas must I draw? What values must be operationalized here? What skills must I use? In what areas must I be particularly self-aware?" Every class or workshop offers potential for application in practice settings. To set aside or compartmentalize that information is irresponsible. The more able one is to identify practical applications from class material, the higher success one will have in practice.

Be a Critical Thinker. Understanding problems, making decisions, and initiating change will create fewer new problems if one carefully analyzes facts, considers alternate reasons for behavior, and avoids making assumptions. Because it is natural for human service workers to want to be "helpers,"

there is a tendency to make assumptions and to jump to solutions or interventions before all of the relevant facts are known. In many cases, knowledge of even a few more details of a problem situation will lead to an entirely different definition of the problem, and thus to a different direction for intervention. This point underscores the importance of good data collection, making and testing hypotheses, and the necessity to identify alternate meanings for client behaviors. Application of critical thinking skills in one's professional life is equally important and can help avoid many difficulties in career decisions.

Use Self-Talk. This tip refers to the necessity of having self-awareness and utilizing self-questioning skills to understand one's needs, feelings, and behaviors. Successful human service workers should acquire the habit of automatically questioning themselves and their decisions. Such questions as what is the *purpose* of this interaction? What do I wish to achieve? What knowledge do I need? Am I maximizing the client's right to self-determination and confidentiality? Am I really conveying a nonjudgmental attitude? Have I considered all explanations for behaviors and options for change? The list is endless, but acquiring this habit will unquestionably improve one's effectiveness in all professional situations.

Learn from Experience. In all situations, even negative ones, there is something to be learned. The habit of identifying what one can learn should begin in the classroom and should never end. Begin to question what is happening in every situation. Why is it boring, demoralizing, or unproductive (as the case may be)? What could be changed, and how? How can I use what I've learned from this in the future? It is no accident that professionals refer to their work as "practice." Human service workers "practice" their profession, and that word implies that all situations are not perfect, but that we have the ability to identify what is working and what is not, and to utilize that information to improve in the future.

Take Responsibility for Learning.   As a student, one needs to learn to speak up if material or instructions are incomplete or unclear. Students must learn to take initiative in utilizing all of the resources available to them (instructors, field supervisors, library) to seek out additional relevant knowledge and skills. This responsibility does not end when one's degree is conferred. When no longer faced with the learning demands of college, the responsibility for continued learning and professional growth falls squarely on the new worker. All human service workers should identify early in their career with their primary professional organization, National Organization for Human Service Education, and take advantage of the opportunities it offers, including its publications and national and regional conferences. Workers should regularly read several journals relevant to their area of work to keep informed of new knowledge and skills. Participation in a variety of workshops and professional meetings is critical for effective practice, professional growth, and career development.

Take Care of Yourself.   If one were to master all of the previous ETs, one would soon become stagnant and exhausted without attention to this final, critical one. It is not by chance that the human service field is replete with major publications about stress and burnout (Burnard, 1991; Edelwich, 1980; Pines and Aronson, 1980; Wessells et al., 1989). As new workers begin their careers, their high levels of energy and unrealistic expectations may develop into frustration and chronic disappointment unless conscious attention is paid to prevention. Workers must learn to separate their professional and private lives and develop off-the-job satisfactions and relationships. Learning to accept responsibility for oneself, prioritizing responsibilities, identifying ways to vary one's work responsibilities, finding professional and personal supports, creating personal goals, and giving oneself tangible rewards are some of the ways human service workers can

achieve the personal satisfaction needed to survive in a demanding career.

CAREER ENTRY AND MOBILITY

Preparation for entering the field of human services requires attention to several factors. Certainly, one must prepare a good resume, and should rehearse for a variety of interview questions and situations. Finding employment often requires looking broadly at the field, and utilizing not only obvious sources (civil service opportunities, health and welfare directories, telephone books), but also less obvious sources such as private employers, personal contacts, and organizations that may offer opportunities for human service work but under less familiar job titles. It is also important that one be prepared to address the issue of what human service means, and particularly how it is similar to and different from social work (Clubok, 1984). New professions are misunderstood professions. The ability to concisely explain the nature and goals of one's training and the specific skills acquired can "sell" a worker to an employer likely to be unfamiliar with the human service degree.

Finding a position, however, is only the first challenge. Mobility within the field is another. To maximize one's opportunity to advance in the field, it is often necessary to further one's education, i.e., acquiring an advanced degree or specializing in specific knowledge and skill areas. In addition, the importance of "networking" in human services cannot be overemphasized. Many opportunities arise as a result of contacts and acquaintances made through professional workshops and conferences and community contacts. It is an unfortunate irony, however, that often advancement in the human service field places the worker in supervisory or management areas, removed from direct contact with the people and clients who inspired him or her to enter the field in the first place.

There is no question that there are many opportunities to enter and advance in the human service field. Success in doing so, however, is more likely if one acknowledges personal motivation for human service work, confronts fears, and learns and internalizes the ETs. While the ETs may be easy to memorize and may even seem somewhat obvious, in reality, if workers are honest in self-appraisal, they will admit difficulty applying them conscientiously and in many instances will find themselves making excuses for *not* applying them.

Those who choose human services as a career must expect to be faced with many frustrations, including misunderstanding of the human service profession itself, turf issues with traditional professions, insufficient financial rewards, unappreciative clients, and decreasing funding and community resources accompanied by increasing caseloads and workplace demands. So why not accounting or computer sciences? The answer lies in the immeasurable rewards available in human services that compensate for the limitations. Few other fields, if any, offer the variety, challenges, opportunity for creativity, and personal satisfaction that comes from knowing that one has made a positive impact on individuals or the community. Change, when it occurs, even small change, can be exhilarating. Of course there are potential hazards and frustrations, but enthusiastic, thinking individuals, armed with knowledge, self-awareness, and problem-solving skills can inoculate themselves against much of this. With discipline and determination, new workers can enter, survive, and grow in the field of human services, creating for themselves an exciting professional career and a satisfying personal life.

REFERENCES

Burnard, P., (1991). *Coping With Stress in The Health Professional: A Practical Guide.* New York: Chapman & Hall.

Clubok, M., (1984). "Four-Year Human Service Programs: How They Differ From Social Work." *Journal of the National Organization of Human Service Educators,* 6, 1–6.

Clubok, M., (1987). "Human Services: An 'Aspiring' Profession in Search of 'Professional' Identity," in R. Kronick, ed., *Curriculum Development in Human Service Education,* Council for Standards in Human Service Education Monograph Series, Issue No. 5, 1–7.

Danish, S., A. D'Augelli, and A. Hauer, (1980). *Helping Skills: A Basic Training Program.* New York: Human Sciences Press, Inc.

Edelwich, J., and A. Brodsky, (1980). *Burnout: Stages of Disillusionment in the Helping Professions.* New York: Human Sciences Press, Inc.

Fullerton, S., (1990). "A Historical Perspective of the Baccalaureate-Level Human Service Professional." *Human Service Education,* 10: 53–61.

Lauffer, A., (1984). *Understanding Your Social Agency,* 2nd ed. Beverly Hills, CA: Sage Publications.

Pines, A., and A. Aronson, (1980). *Burnout: From Tedium to Personal Growth.* Riverside, NJ: The Free Press.

Payne, R., and J. Firth-Cozens, eds., (1987). *Stress in Health Professionals.* Somerset, NJ: John Wiley & Sons.

Wessells, D.T., A. Kutschner, I. Feeland, F. Selder, D. Cherico, and E. Clark, eds., (1989). *Professional Burnout in Medicine and the Helping Professions.* New York: The Haworth Press.

THE HUMAN SERVICES WORKER
A GENERIC JOB DESCRIPTION

A JOINT PUBLICATION OF NOHSE AND CSHSE

HUMAN SERVICES

Making a Difference in People's Lives

The field of human services is a broadly defined one, uniquely approaching the objective of meeting human needs through an interdisciplinary knowledge base, focusing on prevention as well as remediation of problems and maintaining a commitment to improving the overall quality of life of service populations. The human services profession is one that promotes improved service delivery systems by addressing not only the quality of direct services, but by also seeking to improve accessibility, accountability, and coordination among professionals and agencies in service delivery.

Human Service Workers

Nature of the work—"Human services worker" is a generic term for people who hold professional and paraprofessional jobs in such diverse settings as group homes and halfway houses; correctional, mental retardation, and community mental health centers; family, child, and youth service agencies, and programs concerned with alcoholism, drug abuse, family violence, and aging. Depending on the employment setting and the kinds of clients served there, job titles and duties vary a great deal.

The primary purpose of the human service worker is to assist individuals and communities to function as effectively as possible in the major domains of living.

A strong desire to help others is an important consideration for a job as a human services worker. Individuals who show patience, understanding, and caring in their dealings with others are highly valued by employers. Other important personal traits include communication skills, a strong sense of responsibility, and the ability to manage time effectively.

Generic Human Service Worker Competencies

The following six statements describe the major generic knowledge, skills and attitudes that appear to be required in all human service work. The training and preparation of the individual worker within this framework will change as a function of the work setting, the specific client population served, and the level of organizational work.

1. *Understanding the nature of human systems: individual, group, organization, community and society, and their major interactions.* All workers will have preparation that helps them to understand human development, group dynamics, organizational structure, how communities are organized, how national policy is set, and how social systems interact in producing human problems.

2. *Understanding the conditions that promote or limit optimal functioning and classes of deviations from desired functioning in the major human systems.* Workers will have understanding of the major models of causation that are concerned with both the promotion of healthy functioning and with treatment-rehabilitation. This includes medically oriented, socially oriented, psychologically-behavioral oriented, and educationally oriented models.

3. *Skill in identifying and selecting interventions that promote growth and goal attainment.* The worker will be able to conduct a competent problem analysis and to select those strategies, services or interventions that are appropriate to helping clients attain a desired outcome. Interventions may include assistance, referral, advocacy, or direct counseling.

4. *Skill in planning, implementing and evaluating interventions.* The worker will be able to design a plan of action for an identified problem and implement the plan in a systematic way. This requires an understanding of problems analysis, decision-analysis, and design of work plans. This generic skill can be used with all social systems and adapted for use with individual clients or organizations. Skill in evaluating the interventions is essential.

5. *Consistent behavior in selecting interventions that are congruent with the values of one's self, clients, the employing organization, and the Human Service profession.* This cluster requires awareness of one's own value orientation, an understanding of organizational values as expressed in the mandate or goal statement of the organization, human service ethics, and an appreciation of the client's values, life-style and goals.

6. *Process skills that are required to plan and implement services.* This cluster is based on the assumption that the worker uses himself as the main tool for responding to service needs. The worker must be skillful in verbal and oral communication, interpersonal relationships, and other related personal skills, such as self-discipline and time management. It requires that the worker be interested in and motivated to conduct the role that he has agreed to fulfill and to apply himself to all aspects of the work that the role requires.

Where Human Service Workers Work

Working conditions vary. Human services workers in social service agencies generally spend part of the time in the office and the rest of the time in the field. Most work a 40-hour week. Some evening and weekend work may be necessary, but compensatory time off is usually granted.

Human services workers in community-based settings move around a great deal in the course of a work week. They may be inside one day and outdoors on a field visit the next. They, too, work a standard 40-hour week.

Human services workers in residential settings generally work in shifts. Because residents of group homes need supervision in the evening and at night, 7 days a week, evening and weekend hours are required.

Despite differences in what they are called and what they do, human services workers generally perform under the direction of professional staff. Those employed in mental health settings, for example, may be assigned to assist a treatment team made up of social workers, psychologists, and other human services professionals. The amount of responsibility these workers assume and the degree of supervision they receive vary a great deal. Some workers are on their own most of the time and have little direct supervision; others work under close direction.

Human services workers in community, residential care, or institutional settings provide direct services such as leading a group, organizing an activity, or offering individual counseling. They may handle some administrative support tasks, too. Specific job duties reflect organizational policy and staffing patterns, as well as the worker's educational preparation and experience.

Because so many human services jobs involve direct contact with people who are impaired and therefore vulnerable to exploitation, employers try to be selective in hiring. Applicants are screened for appropriate personal qualifications. Relevant academic preparation is generally required, and volunteer or work experience is preferred.

Job Outlook

Employment of human services workers is expected to grow much faster than the average for all occupations through the year 2000. Opportunities for qualified applicants are expected to be excellent, not only because of projected rapid growth in the occupation, but because of substantial replacement needs. Turnover among counselors in group homes is reported to be especially high.

Employment prospects should be favorable in facilities and programs that serve the elderly, mentally impaired, or developmentally disabled. Adult day care, a relatively new concept, is expected to expand significantly due to very rapid growth in the number of people of advanced age, together with growing awareness of the value of day programs for adults in need of care and supervision.

While projected growth in the elderly population is the dominant factor in the anticipated expansion of adult day care, public response to the needs of people who are handicapped or mentally ill underlies anticipated employment growth in group homes and residential care facilities. As more and more mentally retarded or developmentally disabled individuals reach the age of 21, and thereby lose their eligibility for programs and services offered by the public schools, the need for community-based alternatives can be expected to grow. Pressures to respond to the needs of the chronically mentally ill can also be expected to persist. For many years, as deinstitutionalization has proceeded, chronic mental patients have been left to their own devices. If the movement to help the homeless and chronically mentally ill gains momentum, more community-based programs and group residences will be established, and demand for human services workers will increase accordingly. State and local governments will remain a major employer of human services workers, and replacement needs alone will generate many job openings in the public sector.

Salary Range

According to limited data available, starting salaries for human services workers ranged from $12,000 to $18,000 a year in 1988. Experienced workers earned up to about $23,000 annually, depending on the amount of experience and the employer.

Employment

Human services workers held about 123,000 jobs in 1990. About one-fourth were employed by the State and local governments, primarily in hospitals and outpatient mental health centers, facilities for the mentally retarded and developmentally disabled, and public welfare agencies. Another fourth worked in agencies offering adult day care, group meals, crisis intervention, counseling, and other social services. Some supervised residents of group homes and halfway houses. Human services workers also held jobs in clinics, community mental health centers, and private psychiatric hospitals.

Examples of Occupational Titles of Human Service Workers

Case Worker	Family Support Worker
Youth Worker	Social Service Liaison
Residential Counselor	Behavioral Management Aide
Case Management Aide	Eligibility Counselor
Alcohol Counselor	Adult Day Care Worker
Drug Abuse Counselor	Life Skills Instructor
Client Advocate	Neighborhood Worker
Social Service Aide	Group Activities Aide
Social Service Technician	Therapeutic Assistant
Probation Officer	Case Monitor
Parole Officer	Child Advocate
Gerontology Aide	Juvenile Court Liaison
Home Health Aide	Group Home Worker
Child Abuse Worker	Crisis Intervention Counselor
Mental Health Aide	Community Organizer

Intake Interviewer

Community Outreach
Worker

Social Work
Assistant

Community Action
Worker

Psychological
Aide

Halfway House
Counselor

Assistant Case
Manager

Rehabilitation Case
Worker

Residential
Manager

NOHSE: A History of Commitment

The National Organization for Human Service Education (NOHSE) was founded in 1975 at the 5th Annual Faculty Development Conference of the Southern Regional Education Board. NOHSE grew out of the perceived need by professional care providers and legislators for improved methods of service delivery. NOHSE, with the early support of the National Institute of Mental Health and SREB, has striven to promote excellence in Human Service delivery in an increasingly complex world.

Through the professional efforts of NOHSE members, many programs of care have been developed to address unique social, behavioral, and educational issues in society. NOHSE's focus includes supporting and promoting improvements in direct service, public education, program development, planning and evaluation, administration, and public policy.

Members of NOHSE are drawn from diverse educational and professional backgrounds. Professional backgrounds and experience in corrections, mental health, child care, social services, human resource management, gerontology, developmental disabilities, addictions, recreation, and education reflect this diversity.

The applied philosophy of NOHSE addresses the diverse needs of the society by supporting educators and professionals in developing innovative models of service and education.

Purposes of NOHSE

1. To provide a medium for cooperation and communication among Human Service organizations and individual practitioners, faculty, and students.
2. To foster excellence in teaching, research, and curriculum development for improving the education of Human Service delivery personnel.
3. To encourage, support, and assist the development of local, state, and national organizations of Human Services.
4. To sponsor forums via conferences, institutes, and symposiums that foster creative approaches to meeting Human Service needs.

Council for Standards in Human Services Education

Founded in 1979 to improve the quality, consistency, and relevance of human service training programs, the Council for Standards in Human Service Education (CSHSE) is the only national organization providing standards and assistance to accomplish these goals. The Council achieves its purpose by:

1. Applying national standards for training programs at the associate and baccalaureate degree levels;
2. Reviewing and recognizing programs that meet established standards;
3. Sponsoring faculty development workshops in curriculum design, program policymaking, resource development, program evaluation, and other areas;
4. Offering vital technical and informational assistance to programs seeking to improve the quality and relevance of their training;
5. Publishing a quarterly Bulletin to keep programs informed of Council activities; training information and resources, issues and trends in human service education.

Through a membership of educational programs, the Council provides an organization and an opportunity for all constituencies of the undergraduate human service field to work together in developing and promoting sound programs of human service training as the essential foundation for effective and relevant service delivery.

CHAPTER 13

PERSONAL QUALITIES IN A SUCCESSFUL HUMAN SERVICES CAREER

NAN LITTLETON

INTRODUCTION

Who is an effective helper? What are the characteristics of an effective helper? There has been considerable research conducted in this area. Specific characteristics and conditions have been identified that we know are mandatory in order to be a capable helper. I will identify and discuss those characteristics and practices personally and heuristically viewed as the most critical to being an effective helper.

HISTORY

In the early sixties the helping professions were challenged by studies that suggested that a significant number of individuals who received counseling and therapy to deal with their problems were no better off than those who did not receive professional help. Subsequent studies showed that long-lasting effects of counseling and psychotherapy appeared in only about 20 percent of the cases. In further examination of such research findings, it was discovered that individuals who received professional counseling or psychotherapy either stayed the same (showed no improvement), got significantly better, or got significantly worse. From these studies it was discovered that these positive, neutral, or harmful effects could be determined by the level of functioning of the counselor, i.e., the counselor's effectiveness (Rogers et al., 1967; Truax and Carkhuff, 1967).

Carl Rogers is one of the early pioneers in the field of studying the conditions necessary to facilitate the growth of persons in counseling, therapy, classroom, and corporation settings. As a result of his and others' extensive research, conditions have been identified that are necessary to create the kind of trusting and supportive environment where a person can grow, flourish, and trust sufficiently to make the changes they so desperately want in their lives.

According to Rogers (1957) there are therapeutic conditions that are "necessary and sufficient" for promoting constructive change in others. Effective helpers have to develop an understanding and high level of skill in creating the type of safe environment that supports and facilitates their client's abilities to make significant life changes. Such conditions are genuineness, realness (helper's congruence), acceptance and caring (unconditional positive regard), and empathic understanding.

Before discussing each of these characteristics and conditions in more detail, the reader is reminded that it is a goal of most mental health/ human service undergraduate programs to translate these somewhat abstract concepts into teachable skills. Typically, introductory counseling courses teach the skills necessary to create this kind of therapeutic environment. Field placement courses give undergraduates an additional setting outside the classroom in which to practice the development of these skills.

CREATING THE ENVIRONMENT

As previously stated, numerous and continuing studies of what we call helping relationships identify essential ingredients that characterize effective helping (Rogers, 1957; Strupp, 1986). These characteristics include the helper's ability to demonstrate genuineness, realness, acceptance, warmth, respect, and empathy. Following is a brief description of these characteristics.

Genuineness is that quality that communicates to the client that the helpers are who they say they are. That is, the helpers' actions are consistent with the helpers' words. Their actions signify that they are who they say they are. The helpers' values are displayed in their day-to-day activities and behaviors. Realness is the helpers' willingness to display their humanness. It is being open and honest with the client. It is felt by the client when helpers do such things as appropriately self-disclose, acknowledge that they don't have all the answers when they don't know something, and be willing to laugh at themselves and their humanness. Acceptance refers to the helpers' ability to admit the validity of their client's position in a nonjudgmental and nonevaluative manner. Warmth is the helper's ability to express a sense of caring, appreciation, and positive regard for the client, both verbally and nonverbally. Respect for the individual includes the helper's belief in the client's inherent worth, significance, and right to be treated with dignity. Respect also includes the helper's belief in the individuals' capacity to be personally responsible for making their own decisions and following the direction they themselves set for their lives. Empathy refers to the helper's ability to understand the internal frame of reference of the client. It is the helper's responsibility to be committed to gaining an understanding of where clients are truly coming from and to really hear clients from their point of view. For effective helping, it is imperative that the helper see the client's reality from that client's perspective. Finally, empathy is the ability of helpers to verbally share with their clients an accurate picture of their world, their experiences, and their feelings. In research conducted by Truax and Carkhuff (1965), helpers who demonstrated high levels of empathy facilitated the process and outcomes of their clients. On the other hand, those helpers who displayed low levels of empathy and understanding had client outcomes that indicated no change or their condition worsened.

To summarize, these are the conditions that an effective helper must be able to create and communicate so that individuals can trust sufficiently to make critical changes in their lives. Therefore, in order to be effective helpers, we must develop the skills necessary to create such an environment.

THE ROLE OF PERSONAL CHARACTERISTICS

According to Woodside and McClam (1990) more and more research supports the notion of the importance of the personal characteristics of the helper in effective helping. While appropriate methods and techniques and the client's own role in the helping process are vitally important, the following paragraphs in this chapter will discuss the third critical component of the helping process. That is, the attitudes, beliefs, values, and behaviors that the counselor/therapist/teacher/ helper brings to the helping relationship. It is these components that define and influence the helper's role and responsibility during the helping process (Rogers, 1965).

Understanding Who I Am

One of the common characteristics found in studies of effective leadership, effective teachers, effective executives, and effective CEOs is that people who are effective, people who are really good at what they do, people who get results, all possess a keen understanding of who they are. That is, they understand themselves, and they understand that this self-understanding is an ongoing process. Successful individuals know that understanding who they are is a daily journey, that it is an everyday adventure into deeper self-discovery, and they are committed to this everyday exploration. This means they have resolved to do the daily work necessary for understanding who they are.

There cannot be enough emphasis placed on how important it is to understand who we are in order to be effective helpers. Many of the great philosophers have reflected on the critical nature of understanding the self. Among these great philosophers, Socrates said that, "the unexamined life is not worth living." Before I can create the kind of growth-producing environment described in the preceding paragraphs, I must know myself. In order to facilitate clients in discovering who they are, I must know who I am. Before I can deal with a client's problems, I have to be willing to deal with my own problems. This doesn't mean that I come into this helping relationship without problems. It does mean that I know what my problems are, and that I am committed to working them through. It also means that I have resolved not to let them interfere with the client's problem-solving process. It does mean that I don't burden the client with my problems. It does mean that I will stay focused on the client's problems rather than dealing with my own problems when I'm involved in a helping relationship. It does mean that, before I can help anyone else, I have to be able and willing to help myself.

Therefore, in order to be effective at anything, i.e., an effective parent, helper, therapist, counselor, leader, or supervisor, I have to know who I am . . . I have to understand myself. I have to know where I am coming from in my attitudes, beliefs, and behaviors. I have to know why I am who I am, and how I got where I am today. It's also important to have some clear understanding of where I want to be, where I want to go, and what my goals are for my future. Just like my clients, I will have goals and dreams, and I will need to have a plan to achieve those goals and dreams. I must have an understanding of how I am going to get there, the

steps I'm taking to achieve the goals for my life. If I can do this for myself, then maybe I can facilitate others doing that for themselves.

Self-Concept

Self-concept is my image of myself, my abilities, my worth as a human being. It is part of my identity as a person. In order to understand who I am, I must have an accurate concept of myself. There are many ways of developing a strong self-concept. Knowing our strengths and being aware of those areas in which we are not as strong is a beginning. As effective helpers we need to also be aware of areas where we don't have as much information and skill as we might need in order to be helping a particular person in a specific situation. We must also know our likes and our dislikes. We need to know what motivates us to do the things we do. This requires looking inside ourselves on a continual basis to understand our own value system and our own philosophy in order that we may enjoy a full appreciation of who we believe we are.

Not only must we be able to answer the question "who am I?" but we must also be able to articulate our purpose. Part of understanding our purpose is knowing why we have chosen to be a helper. Challenging oneself in a quest for self-understanding, as discussed in the preceding paragraphs, will greatly enhance the self-concept.

Beliefs about Others

Another part of our becoming effective helpers and understanding ourselves is defining for ourselves what we believe about others. Ideally, we have a particularly theoretical underpinning that we use in understanding the human being. We know what our beliefs are concerning human behavior, and these beliefs are based on our own life experiences, as well as knowledge of the theories of human behavior developed by experts in the field of personality theory. As we study these personality theories, typically there will be one theory that we will be drawn to and that will match some of our beliefs. We will then be able to use that theory as a foundation for the work we are doing with others in helping them grow and develop to become all they are capable of becoming.

Self-Care

In addition to understanding ourselves and who we are, our strengths and weaknesses, what motivates us, how we got where we are, where we want to go, why we want to be in the helping professions, and our beliefs about ourselves and others, we also have to be committed to staying healthy. We first must define what health is in our own life, and how this health is reflected in our own personal life. It is this author's opinion that health does not just mean physically healthy. Health is reflected in all areas and aspects of our lives, health in our social lives, emotional health, and health in our spiritual lives. It also refers to seeking and working to maintain healthy relationships. This includes relationships with neighbors, parents, children, brothers and sisters, co-workers, friends, and lovers. It also means being healthy in my relationships with the people I come in contact with every day; those who are so important to my getting through the day, such as cashiers, those who help me get what I need in terms of purchases, the waitresses and waiters, and attendants at the service station. It means that I strive to maintain the most healthy and functional relationships possible with everyone, and that I understand that my life is more than just my one-on-one relationships with those who are closest to me.

Such commitments to developing and maintaining healthy relationships show that helpers have some understanding that they are like tiny stones thrown into a big pond. The ripples that the pebbles make flow out and touch every other molecule of that pond. It demonstrates that the helpers have at least a beginning awareness, if not a complete awareness, of their interconnectedness with the rest of the world. It shows that they understand that we live in a global world and are connected to all others in this universe.

Owning Our Fears

Part of knowing who I am is being aware of my fears. Fear is one of the greatest blocks to human growth. When we fear, we stop. Fear can keep us and our clients locked into incredibly self-defeating behaviors. The good news is that being aware of that which I fear means that I can do something about it. It is only through this initial awareness that I can decide to move fear aside and get on with my life. In order to conquer my fears and facilitate clients moving through their fears, I must first recognize the fear, own it, and then mobilize the courage to move through it. It is important to remember that I cannot ask my clients to do anything that I myself am not willing to do. Therefore, I must be willing to deal with my fears if I am going to be encouraging clients to deal with their fears.

Acknowledging Differences

In addition to knowing who I am as a helper and as a human being, I must also know who my clients are and from where they came. This includes being aware of such things as cultural and life-style differences. As helpers it is our responsibility to understand and acknowledge that there really are cultural and lifestyle differences. It is the helper's responsibility to find out what those differences are in a direct and sensitive manner. One way to do this is to openly discuss cultural and lifestyle differences with our clients. We must be willing to ask our clients about cultural and life-style values, customs, beliefs, attitudes, and behaviors. We must also be willing to frequently ask our clients if what they are doing fits their cultural needs. This, then, becomes a joint exploration and identification of cultural and life-style values, needs, and behaviors with the clients we are working with. We have to acknowledge and be aware that differences do exist and take this information into consideration when we are helping to move our clients from where they are now to where they want to be.

Not only must we be aware of cultural and life-style considerations, but we also have to acknowledge that we don't have all the answers within ourselves for the problems that we are going to be facilitating people in solving. Therefore, we have to be willing to tap into other resources. We must learn networking skills. We also need to know the policies and procedures, and be willing to make appropriate referrals. We have to be willing to use whatever resources we can come up with individually, and in consultation with others, to facilitate the growth of our clients and ourselves. It is not just the growth of our clients we are concerned with; it is also our own growth and development. Remember, the more effective the helpers are at taking care of themselves . . . the more effective helpers they will be.

FINAL THOUGHTS

While this chapter has discussed many of the personal characteristics of effective helpers and reviewed the environmental essentials conducive to therapeutic change, there are three prerequisite conditions that must exist before anyone can be helped to grow and change. The first condition is that the helpers must believe that they can help these individuals. The second condition is that individuals have to believe that the helpers can help them. The third condition is that the helpers and the client must like each other. If any of these things is absent from the helping relationship, there is a very little chance of helping being effective.

Application Suggestions

1. Make a list of your personal and professional strengths and weaknesses.
2. Prepare your own personal philosophy of life. Include your beliefs, attitudes, and values about yourself and others.
3. Prepare a mission statement for your life. Describe and define your life's purpose.
4. Define what health means for you. Make a list of those things you do to create and maintain health in your life.
5. Evaluate yourself as a helper. What do you see as your strengths and your weaknesses? How might you insure your effectiveness as a helper?

REFERENCES

Carkhuff, R.R., (1983). *The Art of Helping.* Amherst, MA: Human Resource Development Press.

Rogers, C.R., (1951). *Client-Centered Therapy.* Boston: Houghton Mifflin.

Rogers, C.R., (1957). "The Necessary and Sufficient Conditions of Therapeutic Personality Change." *Journal of Consulting Psychology,* 21, 95–102.

Rogers, C., E. Gendlin, D. Keisler, and C. Truax, (1967). *The Therapeutic Relationship and Its Impact.* Westport, CT: Greenword Press.

Strupp, H.H., (1986). "Psychology: Research, Practice, and Public Policy (How to Avoid Dead Ends)." *American Psychologist,* 41(2), 120–130.

Truax, C.B., and R.R. Carkhuff, (1967). *Toward Effective Counseling and Psychotherapy.* Chicago: Aldine.

Woodside, M., and T. McClam, (1990). *An Introduction to Human Services.* Monterey, CA: Brooks/Cole.

CHAPTER 14

BURNOUT
AVOIDING THE TRAP

H. FREDERICK SWEITZER

INTRODUCTION

Picture three human service workers, all of whom work at a mid-sized human service agency. The first is an efficient, happy professional. She arrives most days full of energy and enthusiasm, getting in a little early to check her mail and phone messages, read logs, do some paperwork and compose herself before beginning to work with clients. She works quickly and efficiently, yet seems to have time to talk to co-workers who need her opinion, or to clients who need some extra attention. She is a tireless advocate for her clients in the community and at staff meetings, and it is a joy to watch her with them. She seems to have a feel for each one. Her paperwork is almost always in on time and she has authored or co-authored several proposals for new programs and approaches at the agency. She works extra hours a few days each week and sometimes takes work home on weekends, but she doesn't seem to mind and it doesn't appear to drain her energy.

The second worker often seems resentful and exhausted, but she is still trying hard to do a good job. She finds that she has to work weekends and evenings to stay caught up, and even this isn't working anymore. She sometimes forgets appointments or misses deadlines, but snaps at people who remind her about these things. She has not been out with family or friends in months, although she occasionally goes out for beers on Friday with some other workers. Lately her supervisor has been leaning on her to work more efficiently.

The third worker never arrives before her shift begins, and is often late. She takes a break each morning and afternoon, regardless of what is going on, and leaves precisely at the end of her shift, often arranging to leave a little early. She refuses to take work home or work on weekends under any circumstances. She interacts with clients as little as possible, is often short and impatient with them, and is heard to make cynical, disparaging comments about them in the halls and even in staff meetings. She is skeptical of any new ideas, rebuffs any attempts to involve her in change efforts, and makes fun of more enthusiastic workers. Her supervisor usually has to ask two or three times for reports or other paperwork, and when it does come in, it is not done well. She complains loudly about her pay, the clients, and "the system."

Of course the three portraits are stereotypes, but even if you've only been in the human services field for a little while you have surely met people who are similar to these three. Perhaps you were on the receiving end of teachers, counselors, or other human service workers who fit these types. What may surprise you is that these three descriptions could all be of the same person, at different points in her career. Worker number three, of course, is burned out and her clients and co-workers are paying the price along with her. Chances are, though, that most burned out workers didn't start out that way, nor did they get that way quickly or abruptly. Most new workers swear they'll never be "like that." But burnout sets in slowly, usually without your knowledge. Worker number two is showing signs of burnout, but may not understand the phenomenon or want to admit it. One of the major misconceptions that new workers have is that burnout only happens to "bad" workers— something they are not and will never be. Certainly you want to see yourself as more similar to the first worker than the third. Don't be convinced, though, that it can't happen to you. It can, and once you are deep in burnout it is very difficult to turn it around. This chapter is about burnout prevention. It will help you examine ways that you can prevent burnout before it happens and recognize it when it begins.

WHAT IS BURNOUT?

Burnout is the result of persistent, job-related stress. This phenomenon has been examined in a variety of professional contexts, and there are lots of definitions of burnout. Christine Maslach, who has written extensively on burnout in the helping professions, emphasizes that burnout is a progressive process. Its results include: physical and emotional exhaustion, rendering the worker depleted and drained; depersonalization of work and clients, so that the worker feels detached and even callous; and reduced personal accomplishment (Maslach, 1982). The exhaustion is not just physical, it is emotional, and even spiritual. The person feels irritable, and displays negative attitudes towards the clients. Productivity declines and the person often feels isolated and withdrawn. No two people are alike; we all manifest stress and the onset of burnout in sightly different ways. However, there are some common warning signs. Carey Cherniss, another author who has written on burnout in the helping professions, compiled this list (1980):

Resistance to going to work	A sense of failure
Anger and resentment	Guilt and blame

Discouragement	Fatigue
Clock-watching	Postponing client contacts
Not returning client phone calls	Stereotyping clients
Lack of concentration	Cynicism
Increasingly "going by the book"	Sleep disturbance
Frequent colds or flu	Frequent gastrointestinal disturbances

Everyone probably experiences at least some of these symptoms some of the time. However, if you see a rise in frequency in any of them, pay attention. It does not necessarily mean you are burning out, but it could be a warning. Also, just because you aren't experiencing any of the symptoms on the list doesn't mean you aren't under stress; you may have some ways of showing stress other than the ones listed here. Additional reading on stress and burnout may help you recognize some of the ways that you show stress. You also need to determine how much stress you can take before you begin to be negatively affected. Don't hold yourself to someone else's standards. You may know a colleague that seems to be able to take more than you, but that does not make him or her a better worker or a better person. Furthermore, if either of you pushes beyond your limits, then you will start to burn out, and you will be less effective very quickly.

Burnout in Human Services

Anyone can experience burnout, and there are lots of high stress occupations. People in the helping professions, however, seem especially vulnerable. The kinds of people who select human services as a career are typically concerned with people and their problems, attuned to human suffering, and anxious to make a difference. These very qualities make them vulnerable to working too many extra hours, or to putting their clients' needs ahead of their own (Cherniss, 1980b; Corey and Corey, 1993; Mandell and Schram, 1983). There are also many features of human service work that can cause stress. Clients are often not appreciative of your efforts, change often comes slowly and sometimes is not seen for years, many agencies are understaffed and underfunded, and neither the pay nor the prestige are equivalent to other professions.

What Causes Burnout?

Just from reading the previous paragraph you may be wondering about who is to blame for burnout. Is it caused by the behavior and attitudes of individual workers or the characteristics of the agency and the work they do? The answer is that both factors are involved. Certainly, some attitudes are necessary for human service work, such as patience, empathy, and tolerance for ambiguity (for an excellent discussion, see Mandell and Schram, 1983). If you don't have them, or cannot develop them, you will burn out in a hurry. It is also important to have realistic expectations for your work. Both Russo (1993) and Bernstein and Halaszyn (1989) have written excellent books describing what new workers can expect. There are also signs of burnout that you should not ignore, and many lists of "do's and don'ts" designed to prevent burnout; your agency may even have one. For example, some authors and agencies will tell you never to see clients outside of your regular hours or shift, and some agencies offer recreation programs as stress reducers. The trouble with these prescriptions is that they may be true in general, but not for you.

On the other hand, some of the conditions described above are not the fault of individuals; they are characteristics of some human service organizations. It is possible to think about any organization as being "healthy" or "unhealthy," although that is a discussion outside the scope of this chapter (see Moracco, 1981). However, even within accepted definitions of health, caseloads, clarity of expectations, the amount of feedback and support offered, the nature or the clients, and the quality of communication all vary from setting to setting.

Burnout Prevention

Burnout is a result of the interaction between the worker and the work setting. This interaction is highly personal and individual. No two people are going to react the same way to a work setting, and you will find that you respond differently to the different agencies where you work. Therefore, I recommend you take a view of burnout that is similarly personal; instead of thinking about burnout in general terms, think of it in terms of yourself. The most important thing you can do to prevent burnout is get to know yourself better than you do. As discussed earlier, you need to learn to recognize the ways in which you show stress. You also need to learn what stresses you. The answer to this question is both interpersonal and intrapersonal. Human service work involves many interpersonal relationships, and all of them have the potential for stress. As you think about the people you are going to work with, don't think in terms of good and bad clients, supervisors, co-workers and work situations. Instead, pay careful attention to the things that stress *you*. These are interpersonal sources of stress. However, the reason people react differently to the same situation is that they have different personalities. Surely you can think of someone you know or work with who gets upset over things that don't bother you, and vice versa. Your personality will leave you vulnerable to stress and burnout in ways that the worker at the desk next to you is not. These are intrapersonal sources of stress. You need to try to understand what it is about you that makes you vulnerable to being upset by certain events. By understanding these two factors, and the way they interact for you, you can take steps to prevent burnout from occurring, or to stop it quickly when you see it starting to happen.

There is a lot to know about burnout and this chapter is not going to cover it all. It is devoted to helping you develop self-awareness, specifically focusing on where and why you are vulnerable to burnout. If you understand more about why and how certain situations are stressful, the stress of those situations will lessen somewhat and you will have some clues about ways to combat burnout in our professional life.

INTRAPERSONAL STRESS

You enter the human service profession with a unique set of values, hopes, and motivations. Your life experience has given you certain strengths and also some areas that are sensitive or painful. Your strengths are an important asset in preventing burnout. Your sensitive and painful areas make you vulnerable to burnout in some unique ways. The more you know about that, the better you can prevent it. Specifically, it is important for you to be aware of the needs you bring to your work, of any unresolved or partially resolved issues you may have, and of some of the fears about yourself that underlie some of your responses and response patterns.

The Needs You Bring

At some point in your education someone has probably asked you to think or write about the reasons you are considering human services as a career. Understanding and reminding yourself of these motivating factors can be a source of strength. Yet every one of them leaves you vulnerable to burnout in some way as well. Corey and Corey (1993) discuss several possible reasons for entering human services, or needs that workers bring with them, including the need to make and impact; the need to care for others; the need to help others avoid or overcome problems they themselves have struggled with; the need to provide answers; and the need to be needed. They also point out that each one of these motivations can cause problems.

There is an important distinction between wanting and needing. All the reasons listed above are good ones for entering human services, providing you substitute "desire" for "need." For example, wanting to care for others is fine, but as Corey and Corey point out, it is not fine if you always place caring for others above caring for yourself. Sometimes what you need conflicts with

what the agency wants or needs. For example, you have worked a very full week and are very tired. Your supervisor explains that someone is out sick and asks if you would mind working over the weekend. If you choose to say yes to these requests from time to time, that is fine. However, if you find that you cannot say no, ever, then you may be someone who needs to put others' needs first in order to feel good about yourself. That can happen for a lot of reasons, but none of them offset the price you will pay if you don't learn to attend to your own needs as well as those of your clients. Eventually, you will be headed for burnout. Take some time to think about your own motivations for entering human services. If those desires turn into needs, in what specific ways will you be vulnerable to burning out?

Unresolved Issues

Each of us has struggled with different personal issues in our lives. You may have had a prolonged struggle with one of your parents during adolescence. You may have been a victim of abuse or assault. Perhaps you wrestled with substance abuse or an eating disorder. These struggles leave us all with issues that are unresolved, or partially resolved. For example, you may have overcome your eating disorder, but the memory of those days may still be very painful for you. These issues could be thought of as your "unfinished business." This unfinished business does not have to come from some traumatic event or a particular struggle such as those described above. Family patterns are another source (Corey and Corey, 1993; Sweitzer, 1990). For example, if you were always the "mediator" in your family—the one who stepped in, calmed people down, and helped them resolve their differences—you may have some very strong feelings about conflicts. It may be hard for you to see someone in conflict and *not* step in to help, even though in some cases it is best to let people work it out for themselves.

Transactional Analysis (or TA) is another useful perspective for uncovering your unfinished business. There are many books on TA, but one excellent one is *Born to Win*, by James and Jongeward (1971). According to Transactional Analysis, all of us have within us a number of ego states, which are cohesive systems of thoughts, feelings, and actions. All ego states are always present, but we act out of certain ones at certain times. They are often referred to as "tapes" because you can sometimes actually hear them in your thoughts. They are also called tapes because they are believed to be the result of messages you received and internalized (or "recorded") growing up. Many of those messages may be helpful to you. Those that are not helpful may comprise a piece of your unfinished business.

A full discussion of ego states can be found in the sources listed below, but a brief one will be undertaken here. The ego states can be divided into three groups: parent, child, and adult. When you are acting in a parental way toward yourself or others, you are likely to be in your parent ego state. The Nurturing Parent is the part of you that is sympathetic, warm, and supportive of yourself and others. The Critical Parent, on the other hand, lets you (or others) know what should and should not be done. When you act, think, and feel as you did when you were a child, or in a child-like way, you are acting out of your child ego state. The Natural Child is the part of you that is spontaneous and uncensored. The Adaptive Child is the part that obeys the rules, compromises, and tries to get along. Finally, the Adult ego state is the one that is rational and deals with objective reality. It separates fact from opinion and calmly assesses the costs and benefits of certain courses of action.

Although some of the ego states may sound more attractive to you than others, they all have the potential to help you or hurt you. Too much or too little of any of them can be a problem. For example, too much criticism can make you unsure of yourself, but too little can also cause anxiety; you never know when you are doing something right or wrong. Cooperation and compromise are necessary to get along in the world, but people with too active an Adaptive Child can have trouble

being appropriately assertive. Also, although ego states exist in all of us, they have different amounts of strength or energy, depending on the person. For example, I may find that my Critical Parent ego state is very active; I find myself thinking, feeling, and behaving out of that state often and vividly. You, on the other hand, may have a relatively quiet Critical Parent and a much more active and energetic Nurturing Parent. The situation you are in can also make a difference. You may find, for example, that your Adaptive Child is relatively quiet, except when you are around authority figures.

This is not the place for a full discussion of all the ego states, but you should be able to see their utility in uncovering your unfinished business. If you are overly critical with clients, or quick to take yourself to task for the smallest failure, if you have trouble setting limits with clients or co-workers, or if you often find yourself fighting the urge to do something really rebellious, like skipping work or shouting at your boss, you may be dealing with an imbalance in the ego states. You are encouraged to explore TA further (see Corey and Corey, 1993; Corsini and Wedding, 1989; Dusay, 1977; James and Jongeward, 1971).

Finally, your unfinished business can come from your membership in certain societal subgroups. Your vulnerable areas are not just the result of your personality or of your childhood and family experiences. They are also the result of your experience in society as a member of racial, ethnic, gender, and other subgroups. If you are a member of a group that has been discriminated against, you may have a hard time with clients who express prejudice, especially toward that group. If you are a member of a "majority" group, such as males, whites or heterosexuals, and you have thought about issues of discrimination, you may feel guilty, or very hesitant, around members of oppressed groups.

The point here is not that you must not have any unfinished business; all of us have some. However, you need to be as aware as you can of what that business is and how those "sore spots" may be touched in your work. Often past struggles are the reason people choose human service work. They want to help others deal with or avoid problems that they experienced and feel their experience will be an asset. Corey and Corey (1993) point out that your experience certainly can be an asset and can help you establish empathic connections with clients. However, they also point out that some workers can unconsciously want clients to confront or resolve issues that they themselves have not yet resolved. This is also called projection (Sweitzer and Jones, 1990). An example of this kind of projection occurs when a worker who struggles with expressing anger encourages his clients to express theirs at every opportunity.

Even if your unfinished business is not part of the reason you selected human services as a career, human service work will often stimulate those issues. Suppose you are working with a substance abuse population. As you work with a particular client, he begins to discuss his struggle with an overcritical father. Even though you have not had experience with being a substance abuser, you have had a similar struggle with your father or some other parent figure. You are likely to be touched by this client in some ways that seem mysterious at first. You may find yourself thinking about him when you are at home, or when you wake up in the morning. This kind of preoccupation can be very draining. Also, some clients have an uncanny sense for your sore spots, and will use them to manipulate you. If you have a strong need to be liked, for example, the client may withhold approval as a way to get you to relax a rule or go along with a rationalization.

Learning to recognize your unfinished business is an important part of burnout prevention. If you accept and face these issues, you are less likely to blame your clients or yourself, or to need your clients to act in certain ways. You may also want to use a support group, a self-help book, a therapist, or some other approach to personal growth in order to have a place to deal with these issues and to absorb the emotional fallout of having them stimulated at work.

Fears About Yourself

One of the most frustrating, stressful situations anyone can be in is one in which they find themselves doing something they don't want to do, or reacting in a way they don't want to react. Here are some examples:

— Your supervisor offers you some constructive criticism. As the conversation goes on, you find that you are getting angrier and angrier and are having a hard time listening. You keep coming up, mentally or verbally, with defenses for every criticism, and you imagine yourself telling the supervisor off.

— You are at a staff meeting in which an important policy is being discussed. You have something to say but can't seem to say it. Since others are very vocal, it is easy, although frustrating, for you to just sit there.

— You are struggling with your relationship with one of your clients. A co-worker who seems very skilled asks you how it's going with that client and, to your surprise, you hear yourself saying that things are fine.

— A client calls you at home and asks that you meet him right away. The matter does not seem like an emergency to you, but you leave your family at the dinner table and drive to meet your client.

These are not situations in which you find later, after much reflection, that you made a mistake. They are situations in which you know immediately afterwards, or even during the situation, that you are not responding the way you want to. In fact, almost as soon as it is over, you can think of several ways to handle the situation that would have been better. Think about situations like this that have happened to you. Jot a few of them down.

Thinking About Difficult Situations

One very useful method for understanding yourself and learning from your experiences is to keep a journal and try to write in it every day. Record the events, thoughts, and feelings from each day that seem significant to you. If you get in the habit of writing, the journal can be useful in several ways, one of which is to learn more about the kinds of situations we have been discussing. Gerald Weinstein developed a method of reflecting on events that will be helpful to you here (Weinstein, 1980; Weinstein et al., 1975). Take a moment at the end of the day to recall any events that stand out in your mind. Pick out one or two (they can be positive or negative). Divide a piece of paper into three columns. In the left hand column, record each action taken by you or others during the event. Record only those things that could be seen or heard, such as "she frowned," "he said thank you," or "they stomped out of the room." List them one at a time. Now read down the list and try to recall what you were thinking when the different actions occurred. When you recall something, enter it in the middle column, right across from the event. For example, you may have been thinking "What did I do now?" when the people left the room. Finally, read the list again and try to recall what you were feeling at the time each action and thought occurred. Record what you recall in the extreme right hand column. For example, you may have felt embarrassed, confused, or angry when they walked out. An example of this sort of analysis is included in Table 14.1. Take a look at it before proceeding.

You may find that these are isolated incidents, or that they occur with just one person. You may also find, however, that these responses are part of a pattern for you. You may find that, in general, you are defensive about criticism, unable to speak in meetings, unable to say no to clients, or to ask for help. Gerald Weinstein calls these tendencies dysfunctional patterns (Weinstein, 1981). Dysfunctional patterns are groups of thoughts, feelings, and actions that occur in response to a particular group or class of situations. See if you can identify any of these patterns in your work. Try using the format suggested by Weinstein (1981):

> *Whenever I'm in a situation where _____, I usually experience feelings of _____. The things I tell myself are _____, and what I typically do is _____. Afterwards I feel _____. What I wish I could do instead is _____.*

Here is an example to help you:

> *Whenever I am in a situation where I feel angry at a client, I usually experience feelings of anxiety and self-doubt. The things I tell myself are "Take it easy. It's not that bad. There's probably a good explanation, and besides, you don't want to upset him." What I typically do is smile, joke, or protest very weakly. Afterwards I feel like I let us both down. What I'd like to do is find a clear, respectful way to tell the client what is upsetting me.*

Your journal is an excellent source for discovering these patterns. Look for common themes in your actions, thoughts, and feelings. Also, look for common themes in the events that caused those thoughts and feelings. Consider the situation analyzed in Table 14.1. It may be an isolated incident, but it may also be true that the person who wrote it has a pattern of hesitancy with difficult clients, or of becoming confused about rules and procedures.

These patterns come from a variety of places. You may have had a difficult experience or set of experiences that "taught" you to react this way. They may come from your ego states, or from the role you played growing up in your family (Corey and Corey, 1993). According to Weinstein, however, at the heart of these patterns is a "crusher" statement, which is a statement about ourselves that we do not want to hear. The pattern protects us from the crusher. In the example above, the crusher might be "I'm a mean, vindictive person. I have no compassion and people should be afraid of me." The pattern protects you; you believe that if you *do* confront a client it will confirm that you *are* that mean and vindictive person. In the example of the worker who is reluctant to speak up in meetings, the crusher might be "I'm stupid. I don't belong here. If I answer wrong everyone will see." As painful as the pattern is, it protects the worker from the crusher, which is even worse. If you are struggling with a dysfunctional pattern, discovering the crusher is the key to change. Just telling yourself "I'm not going to do it anymore" won't help; you've probably told yourself that many times already.

TABLE 14.1   Situation Analysis Technique

ACTIONS	THOUGHTS	FEELINGS
I am sitting in the lounge with several residents. John walks in and sits down. There are several chairs available but he sits right in front of me.	This guy is always looking for trouble. What is he doing?	Nervous, uncomfortable
I say hello. He nods. I continue my conversation with the residents.		
John squirms around in his chair several times. Finally, I notice the outline of a pack of cigarettes in his pants pocket (a clear violation of house rules).	What is his problem? Damn. He has cigarettes and I'm supposed to take them away and take points. He has a terrible temper. He set this whole thing up.	Annoyed, angry, anxious
When I look up he is looking right at me.	I have to do something now. He knows that I saw them.	Embarrassed, more anxious
I say, "What've you got in your pocket there John?"		
John: "Where?"	Here we go.	
Me: "Right there"		
John: "Nothing! What are you talking about?"	He's not going to make this easy. I'm trying to be nice.	Nervous and angry
Me: "The cigarettes. You obviously wanted me to see them."		
John: "I did not! So what are you going to do about it anyway?"	If I punish him now he's going to do something worse.	Confused, uncertain
Me: "What do you think I should do?"	I'm stalling and he knows it.	Stupid
John: "I think you should leave me alone." His face is getting red.	I'm tired of this nonsense.	Angry, resentful
Me: "If you wanted that you shouldn't have come in here. You could have just gone outside and smoked, you know."	I can't believe I just suggested he break a rule. I just wouldn't have had to deal with him if I hadn't seen him.	Upset at myself
John: "Go take a flying leap (expletives deleted)!!" He jumps to his feet.	Uh oh! Are there any other staff around? I have to calm him down. The other kids are watching me.	Scared, self-conscious, alert

TABLE 14.1   *(continued)*

ACTIONS	THOUGHTS	FEELINGS
Me: "Look, if you just give me the cigarettes, I won't report this."	Maybe this will work.	Hopeful
John: "They're mine. No one takes my property!" He is clenching his fists.	He's not going to get physical over this. Is he?	Frightened
Me: "You're not allowed to have them here and you know it. I should take points away."		
John: "Do I get them back?"	I can't give them back.	Confused, desperate
Me "I don't know. I'll think about it."		
John: "All right, but only because I like you."		
Me: "Thanks."	Thank God. I wonder if I did the right thing though.	Relieved, embarrassed, angry

Irrational Beliefs

Albert Ellis offers another way to look at specific situations in which you are not responding the way you want to (Ellis and Grieger, 1977; Ellis and Harper, 1975). He believes that situations like the ones described are stressful because of what we believe they mean. Often we have irrational beliefs about how we are supposed to be. No one can live up to them and no one should, but we keep trying. When we fail, it is evidence that we are not the person we want to be. These beliefs often take the form of "shoulds" or "musts." Below are some beliefs to which human service workers are vulnerable, drawn from the work of Ellis, Corey and Corey (1993) and Bernstein and Halaszyn (1989):

> I must be successful with all my clients.
> I must be outstanding, clearly better than others I know or hear about.
> I must be respected and loved by my clients.
> Clients should listen to me and push themselves to change.
> I should always enjoy and grow from my work.

Hopefully, you can see how these beliefs, especially the first three, might be operating in the four exam-ples described earlier. Earlier we discussed the distinction between having goals for your clients (wanting) and needing them to behave in a certain way. Here, too, all these statements contain noble aspirations; it's fine to want them. But when you believe you must have them you are letting yourself in for stress, because none of them are achievable.

Your Fears and Burnout

These situations and patterns contribute to burnout in several ways. The situations are stressful, as is the knowledge that you didn't handle them the way you wanted to. If you are struggling with a pattern, not only are the situations stressful but the knowledge that you keep falling into the pattern, sometimes, despite vowing not to, adds to your stress. Finally, many of these situations and patterns will keep you from making the progress with clients or having the relationships with supervisors and co-workers that you want.

If either of these approaches to examining your fears about yourself is interesting to you, you can explore them further. All the sources listed in this section discuss ways to overcome crushers or replace irrational, stressful beliefs with more rational, encouraging ones. It takes focus and practice, but it will pay off for you in your work and your life.

INTERPERSONAL STRESS

There are three main groups of people you will interact with on the job: clients, co-workers, and supervisors. Each can be a source of great satisfaction and in some cases can give you lots of support. However, each can also be a cause of stress. Learning what behaviors in clients, co-workers, and supervisors are difficult for you is an important step in preventing burnout.

Clients

Although your experience with clients may be limited, even if you have spent a few hours volunteering at an agency you already know something about how you react to clients, and you can learn more by reflecting on your experience. Before going on with this chapter, try this exercise. Think of a client you enjoy(ed) working with. Don't worry about why you enjoyed it; just get a picture of that person in your mind. Now describe the person in as much detail as you can, including both physical and behavioral characteristics. Here is a partial list of things to consider:

> What does s/he look like? What is s/he wearing?
> Recall the tone of voice, the body language, the gestures this person uses.
> What kinds of emotions have you seen that person display? Under what circumstances?
> How does s/he react to you? To other clients?

Do this for as many clients as you can. Now try the same thing for clients you do not enjoy. Again, try to avoid analyzing yourself or them to discover why you don't enjoy them. You can also use your journal, and the three-column processing described earlier.

If you look back over the descriptions of people and incidents you kept, you may see some patterns emerging. You may begin to see elements that are common to several different incidents, thereby getting clues to what kinds of clients, behaviors, or

emotions are hard for you and which ones are easier. For example, you may notice that all of the clients you do not enjoy are loud or aggressive in some way. As you review several incidents in your journal, you may notice that in many of the stressful situations a client challenged your authority in some way. See how many of these common elements you can find.

Perhaps you have some ideas already about what client behaviors you find most stressful, or think you might find most stressful. The list below was compiled from the work of Cherniss (1980b), Corey and Corey (1993), and Russo (1993). Read it and see how you react to each client. If you are not sure, that's a good answer to give. In some cases you may be speculating; that is, you may never have actually experienced this behavior in clients but you have an idea how you would react. That's fine, too, but remember that you may respond differently when it actually occurs. Keeping a journal is a good way to check yourself.

> Clients who "play the game"; they go along with agency rules but they're not really making progress.
> Clients who lie to you.
> Clients who manipulate you to get something they want but cannot have.
> Clients who are never satisfied with what you have to give; they always seem to need more.
> Clients who are prone to angry outbursts at you.
> Clients who blame everyone but themselves for their problems.
> Clients who are always negative about everything.
> Clients who are sullen and give one-word answers or responses.
> Clients who ask again and again for suggestions and then reject every one.
> Clients who refuse to see their behavior as a problem.
> Clients who are very passive and won't do anything to help themselves.

In their book, *Issues and Ethics in the Helping Professions,* Corey, Corey, and Callanan (1993) stress the importance of values awareness in relationships with clients. A value difference with a client over a matter of importance with a worker can be very stressful. The worker must decide whether to expose the difference by telling the client about it, and further, whether to try and influence the client to change his or her values (they call this "imposing" values). Of course the first step is to be aware of what your values are, especially in areas that may be challenged by your clients or your work. Some of the key areas discussed in their book include sexuality, race, the right to die, religion, and homosexuality. They also discuss value differences that can arise from cultural differences between workers and clients. The book contains a very useful chapter on values and many self-tests covering a wide range of values issues.

Some of your reactions to the hypothetical clients listed above may be due to value conflicts. For example, suppose that honesty and straightforwardness are strong values to you. For you, to be dishonest is wrong. Of course, you are dishonest occasionally, but you know it is wrong when you do it. You may be dealing with a client who has different values. In her experience, being honest, especially with human service workers and other authorities, means being taken advantage of by a service delivery system she perceives as unfair. For example, in some states a woman on welfare will have her benefits reduced if she is married, even if her husband is not employed. One way to lessen the stress of client interactions is to try to understand the values underlying their behavior. That way it will seem less like a willful transgression, although you may still object to (or in some settings even punish) the behavior.

A final issue concerning client-related stress concerns the extent to which you may, consciously or unconsciously, be relying on clients to meet needs that should be met in other ways. For example, some workers need clients to make progress in order to feel successful. They will not say so directly and may even be unaware of it themselves, but the high level of stress they feel from any client failures indicates this pattern. There is an important, but subtle, distinction here. Of course you *want* your clients to make progress; you want that progress for *them*. However, when you *need* your

clients to succeed you set yourself up for stress. Not all clients can or want to succeed, yet they all need your attention and respect, and you will need to be able to find satisfaction in working with them even when they don't make the progress you hope for. Another need most people have is to feel that their work is respected. Often human service workers find that their work is misunderstood and not valued by peers, family members, or people in the community. This gap can lead workers to depend on clients to provide them with a sense of respect. Also, many human service workers have to set limits with clients, and for many people that is difficult to do. A client in a residential program may challenge a rule. A client in a community agency may press you to give more assistance, services, or time than s/he is entitled to. A worker in those situations needs someone to confirm or validate the necessity of the limit setting. The client is not usually going to do that; in fact, they may often be angry about the limits being set. Workers who need that validation from clients spend unnecessary time and energy trying to get clients to *agree* with the limit, when all they really have to do is be willing to abide by it.

Here is another exercise to try. List all the things you want from your work, such as intellectual stimulation, the knowledge that you are doing some good, continued professional growth, and so on. Now list the things that might happen on the job that will give you the things you listed as wants. How many of these involve clients? For each one that involves clients, make sure there are other people and situations that can serve to meet that need as well. Another useful exercise is to list all the things you hope your clients will accomplish. Make a long list, and don't worry about how achievable the goals are. Then go back over your list and eliminate unreasonable goals. You should then have a list of goals that are reasonable to hope for. Ask yourself, though, whether you need your clients to achieve any of them. If so, ask yourself why. Lots of goals are reasonable to hope and strive for; none are reasonable to demand or need.

It has probably already occurred to you that there can be a connection between interpersonal and intrapersonal sources of stress. As you have thought about your reactions to the clients discussed in this section, you may see ways in which your unfinished business, your ego states, or your dysfunctional patterns all affect your client interactions. In turn, you may find that in answering the questions posed in this section of the chapter you will get clues to some intrapersonal issues that are operating for you.

You may also, at this point, be wondering what you are supposed to do with all this awareness. After all, your clients are not going to change, at least not right away. So now that you have some ideas about what clients are difficult for you and why, what can you do about it? One strategy is to learn more about the clients, and about yourself. If you find out more about a particular client or client group, about the psychological and social factors that influence their behavior, their actions may not seem so mysterious and stressful. If you do not understand why you react in a certain way to a client or a prospective client, do some further self-exploration. You can also take deliberate steps to modify your emotional reactions to certain clients, as discussed in the section on intrapersonal stress. You can also let supervisors and co-workers know that you will need some extra emotional support in dealing with a certain individual or group. However, while you can and should pursue all these avenues, it may well be that there are certain individuals or client populations that you should not work with, at least right now.

Supervisors

Your relationship with your supervisor is one of the most important ones in your professional life. It can be a wonderful source of learning and support. It can also be a major contributor to burnout. Notice that I did not say that your supervisor can provide support or cause burnout. As in any relationship, what happens with your supervisor is a result of the attitudes and behavior of both parties. You do not have to like your supervisor for the relationship to be productive, although it helps. You do, however, have to make sure that you are getting what you need. The better you know yourself the better you will be able to communicate your needs to a supervisor. For example, it is important for you to consider how you react to criticism, praise, or to the knowledge that you have made a mistake.

While it is true that there are some supervisors who are not very good at their jobs, and you may have one of them someday, it is also possible to have a poor relationship with a perfectly competent supervisor. That is because no one approach to supervision works best for everyone. Here are two exercises to help you understand what is important to you in a supervisor. As you did with clients, take some time to recall supervisors you have had, in human services or other settings, with whom you had a good relationship. Describe that person in as much detail as you can. Don't worry yet about what it was that made the relationship a good one, just write the most complete description possible. Do the same exercise for any supervisors with whom you had a difficult or unproductive relationship. Now go back and look at your descriptions and see whether there are some characteristics that all the successful—or unsuccessful—supervisors had in common.

Next, consider some specific aspects of supervision, and several possible approaches to each one. You may have experienced many of these approaches in the supervisors you have worked with. Think about which ones seemed to work for you. If you have not had much experience, try to imagine how you would react to each of the approaches.

Data Collection.   Supervisors have different ways of finding out how you are doing. In a direct supervision approach, your supervisor works alongside you or observes you directly. Self report means that you meet with your supervisor and tell him or her what you have been doing. Using a peer review approach means that other workers in the agency observe your work and report to your supervisor about your progress.

Frequency of Contact.   Some supervisors will set aside an hour or more each week to meet privately with you, while others may schedule private meetings less frequently or not at all. One approach is to wait for you to initiate a meeting, or to wait until the supervisor senses a problem or has a concern. Some supervisors hold group meetings with several of their workers. Some don't schedule meetings at all, but will pull you aside for a conversation if they see something particularly noteworthy. Finally, some supervisors are open to meeting with you outside of scheduled time, and some are not.

Format. Supervisors will set up supervision time differently. Some supervisors follow a structured format and some are more flexible. Some supervisors, while not following a structured format, are always the one to set the agenda for the meeting; they come with issues they want to discuss. Others will discuss only those concerns and issues that you bring to the meeting. Still others will reserve time for both.

In some cases, there is a mismatch between a worker and a supervisor. For example, you may be very sensitive to criticism and be working with a supervisor who is especially blunt. If you have a supervisor who does not work alongside you, having him or her show up to observe you may make you nervous. On the other hand you may not like having your supervisor base his/her opinion of you on reports from other people. You may prefer an unstructured approach while your supervisor is very structured, or vice versa. Another important point to remember is that you may need different styles of supervision at different points in your career, or in a specific job. You may, for example, need a high level of structure in your first job, or in your first few months at a new job, and then less as time goes on. A mismatch can occur when a supervisor does not change his or her style to match your changing needs. Therefore, you may recall a supervisor who was terrific in a job you had a few years ago, but that same supervisor would not be as effective for you today.

Of course, you will be better off if you can adjust to a variety of styles. However, if you have such a mismatch, it can contribute to burnout in two ways. It can be a direct cause of burnout in that it is a stressful relationship, or it can be an indirect cause in that you are not getting the support and guidance you need to grow and to meet the emotional challenges of your work setting. If you are clear about what you need and why you are not getting it, you may be able to approach your supervisor and discuss the situation. If it is thought of and described as a mismatch and not as a failing on the part of you or your supervisor, you will increase the chances that you can both make some changes and work out a successful relationship.

Co-workers

Although your supervisor may be one of the most important professional relationships you have, your relationships with your co-workers are an important factor in burnout as well. There are many more of them than your supervisor, and you will probably spend more time with them. Often it is your co-workers who teach you the ropes of the agency, especially the unwritten rules that are such a powerful part of life in any organization. They can also be models and sources of support for you as you attempt to balance the many and sometimes conflicting demands placed on you by clients, supervisors, agency rules, and your own professional ideals and aspirations. When your relationships with co-workers are not good, it adds another source of stress to your work life and also denies you a potential source of support (Maslach, 1982).

Difficulties with co-workers are sometimes the result of a personality conflict; a certain amount of that is unavoidable. However, you may also find yourself frustrated with or resentful of the way some of your co-workers approach their jobs. I am not talking here about people who cut corners or avoid their responsibilities. You may see a co-worker who brings a lot of energy and commitment to the job, but applies it in a way that puzzles, or even troubles you. You may find yourself wondering what is wrong with that person. It may be that the person simply has a different approach than you. It is possible to have value differences with co-workers just as with clients. Some of your co-workers may have a different theoretical perspective than you do. Thinking of the differences as differences, as opposed to trying to decide who is "right," will help you live with, and even learn from, this diversity rather than be stressed by it.

Russo (1993) offers another productive way to look at these differences. He says that in adjusting to competing demands there are three general patterns of adjustment: identification with clients, with co-workers, and with the organization. He stresses that these are not personality types, but rather choices that can be and are made by many different kinds of people. Workers who identify with clients believe their primary responsibility is to effect change on their clients' behalf. They are often impatient with policies and procedures, with professional codes of conduct, and with "the system." Those who identify with co-workers see their primary allegiance to a professional code. These codes are issued by many different professional organizations, and are very useful guides to professional conduct. However, those who identify with these organizations follow these rules and codes rigidly, with little regard for the nuances of individual clients and organizational settings. Finally, those who identify with the organization adhere to the rules and codes of the organization itself, rarely even considering deviating from them.

In reading these descriptions, you may find yourself drawn to one or the other, although not everyone falls strictly into one of these categories. Most likely, some seem strange, overly rigid, or even wrong to you. Russo, however, stresses that people often move from one category to another over the course of their careers, and that there is a legitimate case to be made for each position.

Understanding these categories may help you be more accepting of co-workers whose priorities are different from your own.

CONCLUSION

Lots of talented people leave the human service field because of burnout. While there is nothing wrong with changing careers, it is always sad to see someone who has the potential for a long and successful career leave the field early and often bitter. You may find that human services is not for you; however, you should be able to avoid burning out. This chapter has tried to acquaint you with the role of self-awareness in burnout prevention. No two people have the same experiences in human services. That is because each person is unique, as is each agency and client group. If you understand the things about you and others that may lead you to burnout, you can take a more productive, proactive approach to stressful situations. You don't need to see yourself as weak or incompetent, or others as bad supervisors, co-workers, or clients. Instead, you can think of the situation as a mismatch, and think about ways to make changes in yourself and/or in the situation.

There are a lot of other things about burnout that you may be interested in knowing. The books and articles referenced at the end of this chapter contain interesting and important information on dealing with burnout once it begins, the characteristics of clients and organizations that may lead to burnout, and comprehensive stress management plans that will help prevent burnout from occurring.

REFERENCES

Bernstein, G.S., and J.A. Halaszyn, (1989). *Human Services? . . . That Must Be So Rewarding.* Baltimore: Paul H. Brookes Publishing Co.

Cherniss, C., (1980a). *Staff Burnout: Job Stress in the Human Services.* Beverly Hills, CA: Sage Publications.

Cherniss, C., (1980b). *Professional Burnout in Human Services Organizations.* New York: Praeger.

Corey, G., M.S. Corey, and P. Callanan, (1993). *Issues and Ethics in the Helping Professions,* 4th ed. Pacific Grove, CA: Brooks/Cole.

Corey, M.S., and G. Corey, (1993). *Becoming a Helper,* 2nd ed. Pacific Grove, CA: Brooks/Cole.

Corsini, R.J., (1989). *Current Psychotherapies,* 4th ed. Itasca, IL: Peacock.

Dusay, J., (1977). *Egograms: How I See You and You See Me.* New York: Harper and Row.

Ellis, A., and R. Grieger, (1977). *Handbook of Rational Emotive Therapy.* New York: Springer.

Ellis, A., and Harper, R.A. (1975). *A New Guide to Rational Living.* Englewood Cliffs, NJ: Prentice Hall.

James, M., and D. Jongeward, (1971). *Born to Win.* Reading, MA: Addison-Wesley.

Mandell, B.R., and B. Schram, (1983). *Human Services: An Introduction.* New York: John Wiley and Sons.

Maslach, C., (1982). *Burnout: The Cost of Caring.* Englewood Cliffs, NJ: Prentice Hall.

Moracco, J., (1981). *Burnout in Counselors and Organizations.* ERIC/CAPS.

Russo, J.R., (1993). *Serving and Surviving as a Human Service Worker,* 2nd ed. Prospect Heights, IL: Waveland Press.

Sweitzer, H.F., and J.S. Jones, (1990). "Self-Understanding in Human Service Education: Goals and Methods." *Human Service Education,* 10(1), 39–52.

Weinstein, G., (1980). "Asking The Right Questions." *Journal of Humanistic Education,* Vol. 4, p. 1–4. Spring.

Weinstein, G., (1981). "Self Science Education." In J. Fried, ed. *New Directions for Student Services: Education for Student Development.* San Francisco: Jossey Bass.

Weinstein, G., J. Hardin, and M. Weinstein, (1975). *Education of the Self: A Trainer's Manual.* Amherst, MA: Mandella.

KEY TERMS FOR PART FOUR

In completing Chapters 11, 12, 13, and 14 you will have a command of the following key terms, major concepts, and principal topical references.

National Association of Social Workers (NASW)	Billing Fraud	ETs
	Confidentiality	Career Mobility
National Association of Drug Abuse Counselors (NAADAC)	Informed Consent	Genuineness
	Rights of Refusal	Transactional Analysis (TA)
	Managed Healthcare	Intrapersonal Stress
"Bounty Hunting"	Privacy Act (1974)	Interpersonal Stress
Accountability	Health Maintenance	
Sexual Misconduct	Organization (HMO)	

PIVOTAL ISSUES FOR DISCUSSION OF PART FOUR

1. Make a list of what you believe to be your best personal qualities. How do these individually relate to your work as a human service worker? What are your major personal weaknesses? How do these traits act as barriers to your professional effectiveness?

2. How do helpers violate their client's rights? Why is sexual misconduct a major issue in the profession? What can be done to correct this problem?

3. How can human service workers protect themselves from legal professional liabilities?

4. Describe your career goals in human services. What requirements will you need to meet in order to achieve these objectives?

5. What are the signs of job burnout in human services? How can you plan to avoid or minimize this professional dilemma?

SUGGESTED READINGS FOR PART FOUR

1. Woody, R.H., and Associates, (1984). *The Law and the Practice of Human Services.* San Francisco, CA: Jossey-Bass.

2. Barton, W.E., and C.J. Sanborn, eds., (1978). *Law and the Mental Health Professions: Friction at the Interface.* New York: International University Press.

3. Corey, A., and G. Corey, (1989). *Becoming a Helper.* Pacific Grove, CA: Brooks/Cole Pub. Co.

4. Corey, G., M. Corey, and P. Callahan, (1993). *Issues and Ethics in the Helping Professions,* 4th ed. Pacific Grove, CA: Brooks/Cole Pub. Co.

5. American Psychological Association, (1987). *Casebook on Ethical Principles of Psychologists.* Washington, DC.

6. Herlihy, B., and L. Golden, (1990). *AACD Ethical Standards Casebook,* 4th ed. Alexandria, VA: American Association for Counseling and Development.

PART FIVE

THE HUMAN SERVICES CLIENTS: FAMILY ISSUES AND SPECIAL POPULATIONS

As a student and as a human services professional it is important that you understand the characteristics of different client populations as well as the human services responses to them. You may be on a job that requires dealing with different clients on a daily basis. Additionally you may have to change jobs and work with other client populations. In any case the more you know, the greater flexibility you will have. The first three chapters deal with client populations that relate to what can be termed family issues: domestic violence, child abuse, and the elderly.

In Chapter 15, Maria Munoz-Kantha discusses domestic violence in terms of the dimensions and explanations of the problem, as well as the human service response. You will be able to identify the battered woman and understand the pattern of violence and the impact on the family. Effective human service responses have to address all of the components of the family. The chapter concludes with a Special Focus Feature by Judy Morse which gives the point of view of a volunteer for a family shelter. Many agencies that you may work in are privately funded and depend upon the concern of citizen volunteers and benefactors that may serve on its board of directors, support the mission, and promote the agency goals in many ways such as getting out a newsletter.

In Chapter 16, James Edell discusses child abuse and neglect in terms of its extent, characteristics, and strategies for helping. You will understand the different ways children are maltreated and how to identify them. You will also learn about intervention approaches to treatment. Child maltreatment along with domestic violence both reflect family crisis and disorder. Frequently horrifying examples are exposed in the national media. On one level, society's response has to be with prevention programs. In the Special Focus Feature, the Rite of Passage, an innovative mentoring community is presented by David Silberstein as one way to overcome family deficiency.

In Chapter 17 by Kathleen Niccum you will read about providing help to the increasing population of older adults. You will learn to identify the physical, psychological, and social aspects of aging as well as understand the special needs and special issues of older adults. Many older adults are no longer in a family situation. Additionally, you will understand what human services are provided typically, and the different career opportunities in this rapidly expanding area of human services.

The next three chapters will present special and specific considerations for human service workers who deal with three currently significant client groups: the homeless individual, the person living with HIV/AIDS, and the clients dealing with alcohol and/or substance abuse and addiction.

In Chapter 18, Lorence Long discusses the variety of different reasons why individuals become homeless, the range of different types of homeless people, the special problems associated with being homeless, and the nature and scope of services typically available in dealing with this problem. This human service client population has increased tremendously in numbers and has challenged the human services delivery system in all areas of the United States. In studying this chapter you will have a command of basic and essential knowledge related to homelessness, and you will become more aware of its extensiveness and frequency.

Another critically fast-moving number of human service clients emerge from the HIV/AIDS epidemic. Lynn McKinney, in Chapter 19, presents to you a comprehensive and practical description of the problem of the HIV/AIDS infection and its far-reaching implications. From this chapter you will solidify your understandings of how this disease develops, how it is transmitted and spreads, what are the major effects of the infection, and how these client needs are addressed within the human services field. You will also appreciate the special nature of this tragic social problem and unique challenges it presents to the human service professional.

In concluding this part, Marcel Duclos and Marianne Gfroerer in Chapter 20 detail the special needs and demands of the alcohol and substance abuse client. In this chapter you will better comprehend the scope of the problem of alcohol and substance abuse and learn about the beginning issues of how to work with these human services clients. Education, prevention, and intervention programs are discussed, and the need for specialized training and credentialing is discussed and defended.

In all, Part Five will acquaint you with solid and relevant examples of present-day human services client groups and the special problems they challenge the human service worker with. In Part Six you will learn about the role of advocacy, our political process for human services, and an important trend in delivery systems.

LEARNING OBJECTIVES FOR PART FIVE

In reading and studying Chapters 15, 16, 17, 18, 19, and 20:

— You will be familiar with human services issues associated with domestic and family violence.

— You will know about the range and variety of human services programs and issues dealing with senior adults and the aging process.

— You will understand the current dynamics and causes of child sexual abuse and what responses and resources are typically available within human services.

— You will appreciate and comprehend the origins of homelessness, populations affected, and what is being done in human services to help these individuals and families.

— You will know the current scope and trends in the problem of the HIV and AIDS epidemic and what the major emerging support considerations are in human services.

— You will know about the needs of the substance abuse and dependency client and what training and services are provided by human services professionals.

CHAPTER 15

DOMESTIC VIOLENCE, BATTERED WOMEN, AND DIMENSIONS OF THE PROBLEM

MARIA MUNOZ-KANTHA

Throughout history, society has disregarded family violence and its implications on the family system regardless of the fact that earlier theorists made attempts to bring it to the attention of the public. Benjamin Wadsworth, an influential seventeenth century New England writer on marital ethics, wrote:

> *If therefore the Husband is bitter against his wife, beating her or striking her (as some vile wretches do) unkind carriage, ill language, hard words, morose peevish, surely behavior; nay if he is not kind, loving, tender in his words and carriage to her; he then shames his profession of Christianity, he breaks the Divine Law, dishonours God and himself too, the same is true of the Wife too. If she strikes her Husband (as some shameless, impudent wretches will) if she's unkind in her carriage, give ill language, is sullen, pouty, so cross that she'll scarce eat or speak sometimes; nay if she neglects to manifest real love kindness, in her words or carriage either; she's then a shame to her profession of Christianity . . . the indisputable Authority, the plain Command of the Great God, required Husbands and Wives, to have and manifest very great affection, love and kindness to one another (quoted in Morgan, 1966).*

This social issue is presenting a serious problem for society because violence against women and children has increased in the last twenty years. The physical abuse of women is increasingly recognized as a serious, widespread community problem that must be addressed by the medical, legal, law enforcement, academic, corporate, political, religious, and human services fields. Every year in the United States, three to four million women are beaten in their homes by their husbands, ex-husbands, boyfriends, lovers, or family members. These women often suffer severe emotional and physical injuries that can result in death.

The last two decades since the 1960s witnessed a new national awareness of violence faced by women and children. Prior to the 1970s the focus was on rape by strangers or acquaintances. Violence in the family system was viewed as an intrapsychic issue rather than a societal widespread problem. In the past fifteen years, much data on violence against women has been gathered with regard to prevalence and outcome in the area of advocacy, medical care, mental health, criminal justice, and academic communities (Browne, 1986 and Schechter, 1982). Major feminist movements, research, and policy initiatives now address aggression within the family system. Rape laws have been amended to protect victims of assault by marital partners. Nearly every state has infiltrated new legislation addressing domestic violence.

In 1972, the first refuge for battered women opened in Britain. Others soon opened throughout Britain (Sutton, 1978), and other parts of Europe, the United States, Canada, and Australia (Warrior, 1976), as activists travelled throughout countries sharing ideas and providing support for opening and expanding new refuges.

The battered women's movement has now extended throughout much of the world, providing shelter and support, and working for social change. Although several books have been published on the topic of wife assault and family violence, few researchers considered the impact of this behavior on the children who were exposed to this violence. Most of the early literature focused on the incidence of violence against women and society's inadequate response represented by community agencies, justice, health, and social service systems (e.g., Gelles and Straus, 1988). The impact of the violence on the child was not considered unless the child was physically abused as well.

Early studies on shelters for battered women began to identify the needs of children admitted to the shelters with their mothers for safety. At least 70 percent of all battered women seeking shelter have children who accompany them, and 17 percent of the women bring along three or more children (MacLeod, 1987). Shelter staff pointed out that the women were most vulnerable and that the children presented themselves with a number of emotional, cognitive, and behavioral problems that required immediate intervention. However, the times when the children needed their mothers the most as a nurturant provider, the mothers were unavailable, as a result of their own overwhelming needs related to their victimization.

Given the complex nature of this problematic public issue, how do human services workers deal with battered women and their children? Both societal and intrapsychic determinants of reactions to "battered women" may determine how human services workers respond and intervene in providing services.

The increased utilization of human services workers over the past two decades is enormously high. Today the single largest category of personnel providing direct services to children and families are paraprofessionals. The most recent trend has been the development of bachelor's degree programs in human services. Despite the degrees, we are finding gaps and problems with curriculum development. Students are confronted with their own reactions to societal problems and are requesting more training in identifying issues, dynamics, and interventions.

Extent of domestic violence problem

1. According to FBI statistics, wife beating results in more injuries that require medical treatment than rape, automobile accidents, and muggings combined in this country. Their statistics for 1984 indicated that 2,116 spouses were killed by their mates. Another study conducted in 1988 by Stark and Flitcraft revealed that spouse abuse occurs in 20 to 30 percent of all families.
2. Family violence calls comprise about 25 percent of all calls to most police departments.
3. Eighty-six percent of police injuries are reported to be caused by calls involving domestic violence (confrontations with the batterers).
4. Violence against women and children is pervasive and does not discriminate; it cuts across lines of income, color, class, and culture. There are many variations, ranging from the most subtle and indirect to the most blatant, including psychological, emotional, and verbal abuse. These variations include sexual harassment, rape, incest, prostitution, economic deprivation, genital mutilation, murder, and oppression. Testimonies from an international hearing on violence against women held on February 13, 1993, at the Church Center in New York emphasized the need for society to recognize violence against women as a human rights violation and not as a private family matter. They estimated that 1,000 women per year are killed by their husbands or partners. Women from all over the world testified and revealed their inner pain within a cultural context. Women within many different cultures are seen as property of the husbands. In fact, wife beating is expected when a woman "steps out of line," in spite of religious and cultural practices against violence.

Sources of the problem

1. **Alcohol**—Alcohol is involved in at least 60 percent of the cases. However, alcohol is not the cause, it is only the excuse or defense level of rationalization for violence (Fitch and Papantonio, 1983).
2. **Sex Role Stereotypes—Power Issues**—Men are taught and conditioned that to be masculine is powerful, to control is normal. It is common in many homes to stress the values and beliefs that designate the man as the authority figure and the woman as subservient. Of course, not all women in these relationships experience abuse, but a traditional marriage does tend to reinforce certain gender roles. Many women are also

taught early in their development that to be feminine is to be helpless, dependent, and vulnerable.

3. Cultural Values and Norms—Our cultural values, social norms, family expectations, and psychological processes work together to encourage men to be abusers and women to be abused. Historically, women have been oppressed and beaten with the acknowledgement of their families, friends, and community. Within my own clinical practice, I have treated battered women from various socioeconomic levels, cultures, religions, and races involved in cases in which family members interrupted acts of violence and continued to reenact the process by keeping it a secret for the sake of not shaming the family.

4. Cycle of Intergenerational Abuse—A wife or woman batterer has often learned from his father (identification with the aggressor) that a real man expresses his anger by using his fist, not by crying or verbalizing his frustrations. In this process, the male also learns to disrespect women and the woman learns to inherit her mother's passivity by watching her get exposed to years of abusive behaviors. For some couples there seems to be a pattern of violence that is repeated from generation to generation. Some families perceive violence as normal; it is internalized to the point that defenses like denial, aggression, suppression, anxiety, and identification with the aggressor play an important role. In some families the abuse is infiltrated among siblings as well as between parents and children, therefore creating blurred boundaries within the contextual family system.

5. Low Self-Esteem—A wife beater usually feels inferior and powerless in other areas of his life. It does not matter whether he has an excellent job or is unemployed, he feels unsuccessful, angry with the self, and worthless. This is when the batterer displaces and projects his own anger onto his wife or partner. A woman who endures this kind of abuse internalizes inferiority, hopelessness, worthlessness, and a temporary form of helplessness.

6. Economics—Many battered women are housewives with no money of their own, no work skills, and dependent children. However, it is important to note that there is a high number of professional women who stop working to take care of their children, later finding themselves in a trapped situation. Women in these situations usually tend to get depressed and lost in the shadow of the "super woman" issue. Often, this depression is correlated to the experience of living with extreme emotional and physical stress and deprivation for an extended period of time.

7. Specific Causes of Violence—In a domestic violence situation, anything can precipitate abuse: a bad day at work, a delayed dinner, unpaid bills, an affair, or accusations of infidelity. Often, there is little awareness or insight into the level of abuse to come at the time that the abuser starts to abuse. His vision is microscopic not macroscopic.

8. Societal Denial—The last two decades have been marked by a growing public awareness of wife assault or wife beating. The belief that all family life is safe and secure is shattered by the alarming frequencies of reported cases. Yet, this topic that was once considered a family secret or acceptable behavior seems to be interwoven with the very fabric of society's attitudes and values. Extensive data in this area remain shocking to society; yet, our statistics on violence continue to rise. Denial continues to be a major problem. An example would be the most recent famous and controversial case involving the great football player O.J. Simpson, America's All-American football hero, a mentor to many and a model for all. In spite of his long problems with domestic violence towards his ex-wife, O.J. continued and continues to be idealized, protected, supported, and rallied around; there seems to be more public sympathy for him than for his victimized ex-wife.

CHARACTERISTICS OF ABUSE

Abuse has several dimensions. It can be emotional, physical, or sexual. It can occur every day or once in a while. It can happen in public places, or in the privacy of someone's home. Abuse can leave a woman with bruises and bumps on her body, or leave inner emotional pain that no one else can see. Here are some common characteristics of abuse.

Physical Abuse

Does her partner:

— Hit, slap, shove, bite, cut, choke, kick, burn, or spit on her?
— Throw objects at her?
— Hold her hostage?
— Hurt or threaten her with a weapon such as a gun, knife, chain, hammer, belt, scissors, brick, or other heavy objects?
— Abandon her or lock her out of her house or car?
— Neglect her when she's ill or pregnant?

■ Endanger her and children by driving in a wild, reckless way?

■ Refuse to give her money for food and clothing?

Emotional Abuse

Does her partner say or do things that embarrass, humiliate, ridicule, or insult her? Does he say:

■ You are stupid, dirty, crazy.

■ You are a fat, lazy, ugly whore.

■ You can't do anything right.

■ You are not a good mother.

■ Nobody would ever want you.

■ You don't deserve anything.

■ Your mother is a whore.

Does he:

■ Refuse to give her attention as a way of punishing her?

■ Threaten to hurt her or the children?

■ Refuse to let her work, have friends, or go out?

■ Feel threatened by her assertive and competent friends?

■ Force her to sign over property or give him her personal belongings?

■ Take away gifts that he gave her when he becomes angry?

■ Brag about his love affairs?

■ Berate women?

■ Accuse her of having love affairs?

■ Manipulate her with lies, contradictions, promises, or false hopes?

■ Hide money from her and the children?

Sexual Abuse

Does her partner:

■ Force her to have sex when she does not want to?

■ Force her to perform sexual acts?

■ Criticize her sexual performance?

■ Refuse to have sex with her?

■ Force her to have sex when she is ill or when it puts her health in danger?

■ Force her to have sex with other people or force her to watch others having sex?

■ Tell her about his sexual relations with other people?

■ Have sex that she considers sadistic, or sex that is painful?

Destructive Acts

Does her partner:

■ Break furniture, flood rooms, ransack, or dump garbage in her home?

■ Throw food and pots out of the window?

■ Slash tires, break windows, steal, or tamper with parts of the car to break it down?

■ Kill pets to punish or scare her?

■ Destroy her clothes, jewelry, family pictures, or other personal possessions that he knows are important to her?

WHAT IS DOMESTIC VIOLENCE?

According to Evelyn White, abuse and battering are used interchangeably to describe a relationship with a partner who hurts a woman physically and/or emotionally. However, there are some differences in their meaning. This awareness can be helpful to the human service worker when providing assistance to a victim of domestic violence. She refers to **battering** as a means of punching, hitting, striking, or the actual physical act of one person beating another. **Abuse** may include physical assault, but it also covers a wide range of hurtful behavior. Threats, insulting talk, sexual coercion, and property destruction are all a part.

Domestic violence is a general term used to describe the battering or abusive acts within an intimate relationship. For example, a shelter worker, counselor, social worker, psychologist, or legal advocate who helps battered women and their children might say that she or he works in the field of domestic violence.

Physical abuse, emotional abuse, sexual abuse, and destructive acts are all dimensions of domestic violence. Some forms of abuse are considered serious offenses that can be prosecuted; others are simply behaviors that no one should tolerate. A woman's partner has no more right to hit, threaten, or hurt her than a stranger in the community or streets. A woman has a right over her body, mind, and soul; it is to be respected and should not be violated or demeaned.

Battered Woman

The term "battered woman" was first described by a women's movement in Britain. It was a powerful phrase. The everyday word "battered" had been successfully used to describe persistently abused children; much later the phrase was utilized by the movement to convey the traumatic experience of persistent and severe violence against women. Many believed that the problems associated with violence are primarily perceived as contextual, associated with the violent repression of men. Therefore, allowing women to escape this predicament and release themselves from violence and its consequences is vital (Dobash and Dobash, 1992).

How Does Battering Begin and Continue?

Battering can begin at any time during a relationship and continue throughout it. It can happen in a companion relationship, on a first date, on a wedding night, and after good and bad times. Statistics show that many men are under the influence of alcohol or drugs when they become violent or abusive. However, it is important to note that substances do not cause the abuse. In some families it is repeated from generation to generation and can start at any interval.

The Cycle of Battering

Dr. Lenore Walker describes the cyclical pattern of battering as a process that can only be ended when the batterer takes responsibility for his abusive behavior. Only he can change or learn how to control his behavior. Within the cycle of violence the **first stage** refers to the process by which a man is irritable, uncommunicative, and quick-tempered. He may claim to be upset about his job and have a short attention span. He breaks dishes, throws

objects, has shouting fits, but then quickly apologizes. It is during this period that the abused woman may report feeling as though she is walking on egg shells. She makes an attempt to pacify him in every which way in order to prevent him from having another explosive episode. When there are children involved, quite often they, too, learn quickly to pacify their father's violent behavior. An adolescent child in my private practice described her feelings:

> I had to help my mother because she was afraid, I felt I needed to protect her, it was so frightening, while I was in school it was difficult to concentrate because I always feared coming home to a **dead body**. I remember life at home as extremely violent, my father cut my older brother's arm with a machete while my brother protected my mother. Following this, he threw my older sister down the stairs and knocked out my other brother's tooth. It was a nightmare. Now I am a victim of abuse; I let my boyfriend beat me, at times I feel I deserve it.

The **second stage** is what Dr. Walker describes as an increase in the tension to physical or verbal explosion. It can be precipitated by a disagreement, traffic ticket, late meal, or misplaced keys. This can trigger the batterer into a violent rage that can result in his attacking the person he is closest to. During this stage an abused woman may be beaten for seemingly minor or nonexistent reasons. Another woman in my practice reported that her husband beat her following a dinner party they held for some business associates. He accused her of being provocative and too outspoken. He criticized her clothing and also accused her of wanting him to lose the business deal.

Dr. Walker refers to the **third stage** as the "honeymoon phase." The batterer becomes extremely loving, gentle, kind, and apologetic for his abusive behavior. The client described above stated two days later in her session: "He loves me, he is genuinely sorry. I think it was the alcohol and cocaine that did it, after all, he just bought me that beautiful house in Rye, NY. . . . He promised me that he would never hit me again. . . . After all now he feels successful and just like his father. . . . You know his father is just like him. . . . My mother-in-law puts up with it. I'm sure we'll be fine." The battered woman believes these promises because she doesn't want to be beaten again, nor does she want to lose what appears to be a caring and nurturing provider. In this stage her partner romances her, brings flowers, buys gifts, takes her out to dinner, and spends extra time with the children. She believes that her household has been magically transformed into the classic happy family. She enters a period of denial and repression, overlooking the previous dynamics. Another client reported "he lost his job because of his temper; upon his return home, he beat me so badly, that my children begged him to stop while they cleaned up the blood off my body. One more time we were forced to go on welfare. He became enraged at any little thing like the children making a little noise. I was forced to work nights in a cleaning company. One evening I returned home to find my eight-year-old boy tied up to the bed post, beaten and scared. I found my husband crying in the living room, begging for mercy. I felt sad for him, he apologized and said he would never do it again. I believed him; his sadness and tears manipulated me. For the next few weeks he was wonderful to me and the children. Another incident occurred when I came home early and found him in bed with my ten-year-old daughter. I was devastated it was my fault, you know things would be better if he found a job. We eventually dropped welfare and had two incomes. I believed him." In reality the honeymoon phase wanes. It presents the battered woman and her children with a dilemma; they fall gradually from power, prosperity, or influence.

Behavioral Characteristics of Domestic Violence

Batterer.   As stated earlier, batterers are found in all socioeconomic levels, all educational, racial, ethnic, and age groups. Vicki D. Boyd and R.S. Klingbeil (1984) have outlined clearly the psychological and behavioral characteristics:[1]

— Poor impulse control, limited tolerance for frustration, explosive temper, rage

— Stress disorders and some psychosomatic complaints

— Emotional dependency, subject to secret depressions known only to family

— Limited capacity for delayed gratification

— Insatiable ego needs and qualities of childlike narcissism

— Low self-esteem; perceived unachieved ideals and goals for self, disappointment in career, even if successful by others' standards

— Makes frequent promises to change and improve

— Perceives self as having poor social skills; describes relationship with mate as closest he has ever had; remains in constant contact with family

— Possessive, jealous, controlling, and hovering over mate

— Fearful of abandonment by family, and fear of being alone

— Violates others' personal boundaries, takes no responsibility for his actions, failures (marital, familial, or occupational), or violent acts

— Absence of guilt emotionally, even after cognitive awareness

— Intergenerational history of abuse

— Frequently uses children as pawns and exerts power and control through custody issues; may kidnap children or hold them hostage

Battered Mate.   The battered mate transcends all socioeconomical, educational, religious, ethnic, and age categories. Typically, they exhibit the following characteristics:

— Psychologically, verbally, and physically abused; frequently sexually abused

— Engage in excessive minimization and denial

— Long-suffering, martyr-like endurance of frustration; passive acceptance; internalizing anger and displacement

— Stress disorders and psychosomatic complaints are common

— Unsure of ego needs; have problems with determining differentiated self

— Economically and emotionally dependent; subject to depression, high risk for secrets, drugs/alcohol, and home accidents

— Unrealistic hope that change is imminent, belief in "promises"

— Gradual increase of social isolation, including loss of contact with family and friends

— Constant fear, which gradually becomes cumulative and oppressive with time

[1]Used by permission of Springer Publishing Company, Inc., New York 10012.

— Emotional acceptance of guilt for mate's behavior, believes that "mate can't help it"
— Intergenerational patterns of abuse in the family system
— Poor self-image, depression, low self-esteem and post traumatic disorder
— Feels powerless in child custody issues, lives in constant fear, and worries about children being kidnapped from shelter, school, and community

Battered Children.   Battered children are psychologically abused, and may be verbally and sexually abused. Children in battered homes are characterized by:

— A combination of limited tolerance for frustration, poor impulse control, martyr-like suffering, internalizing and externalizing anger
— Sadness, depression, stress disorders, and psychosomatic complaints; absences from school; predelinquent and delinquent behavior
— Poor definition of self; problems with trust and pseudomature behavior, often becomes the caretaker; role reversal
— Increased social and peer isolation or complete identification with peers; poor social skills
— Bargaining behavior with parents; attempts to prove self; compliant, but may run away; feelings of powerlessness
— Constant fear and terror for own life as well as parents' lives; confusion and insecurity
— Little or no understanding of the dynamics of violence; often assumes violence to be the norm
— Continuation of abuse patterns in adult life
— Poor problem-solving and conflict-resolution skills; may use violence as a problem-solving technique in school, with peers, and with family (appears in preschool years); demonstrates aggression or passivity
— Poor sexual image, uncertain about appropriate behavior, confused about role models, immature; identification with aggressor (violent parent)
— Heightened suicide attempts, murderous thoughts about parents, prone to negligence or carelessness
— Feeling used and powerless in all decisions

CHANGING ATTITUDES

The recognition of domestic violence as a deeply rooted problem in our society has come from several sources, most notably the women's issues movement and antirape organizers. Grassroots activists and human services professionals have borrowed counseling and organizing principles from the rape crisis movement to illustrate and address the similar plight of the battered woman. As public consciousness about sexism and its violent impact on all women's lives began to grow, shelters for battered women and their children opened, and social and legal reforms began to take place. Abused women took flight and organized supporters across the country.

Although it continues to face many cultural and economic challenges, the battered women's movement is here to stay. Abused women should be made aware that there is no need to feel shame about domestic violence. They should be educated about the physical-, emotional-, and sexual-abuse counseling programs that are working to change the attitudes of battered women, their children, and batterers.

Given the complex nature of this problem, theorists have developed interventions and techniques that have been helpful to the counseling professionals working with battered women and children. The optimal goal in dealing with domestic violence is to keep the abuse from ever happening again, to prevent the explosive elements in a potentially abusive family system.

STRATEGIES AND INTERVENTIONS

Battered women who leave their homes frequently stay at the house of a relative, friend, or neighbor for a few days or months. There they hope to get support, comfort, safety, and distance from the batterer. Others choose to contact a battered women's hot line, where they get help with immediate intervention and referrals. A woman usually makes the first contact with the shelter by calling a 24-hour hot line. She may have read about the shelter or gotten the number from a friend, doctor, church, social service agency, library, school, police officer, or through a public service announcement or newspaper. During the hot line call the staff member evaluates the needs of the woman and the ability of the shelter to provide services. Usually women who have significant chemical dependencies or severe mental health problems are referred to more appropriate services where there are professionals to help via an interdisciplinary approach. Those who have been abused and are in need of shelter discuss their current situations with staff members and review the current services available for shelter placement. If admission is indicated, a staff member will review the circumstances and make a decision whether to admit. If there is no room, then a referral is made to another shelter. Once a decision to admit has been made, the living arrangements, fees, and guidelines are reviewed. However, no woman is rejected because of income or status. The woman is then asked to participate and cooperate in shelter life. Once an agreement has been made, travel arrangements are made either by giving the victim specific public transportation directions to the shelter or by arranging pickup by the shelter staff. When the woman and her children arrive at the shelter, they are greeted and oriented by a member of the staff who assures them safety, makes an assessment, and reviews shelter rules and routines. The family then meets the other families. Within twenty-four hours, the client is assigned a counselor who will continue to obtain information for intake and necessary services. These goals may include a methodology to include legal services, finances, school arrangements, medicaid, emergency funds, and support counseling for all members. Some shelters refer to a case manager as the primary counselor and advocate for the family.

Services Available

— **Counseling**—Short-term therapy, crisis intervention, assessment of psychological needs of women and children.
— **Support Groups**—Group discussions revolve around each member's perceptions, peer support, and role modeling, especially in the area of problem solving and conflict resolution. Activity groups are provided for relaxation, as well as the enhancement of everyday living skills.
— **Family Sessions**—Family sessions are provided to help the client and children have a better understanding of family violence, current crisis, relocation, and conflict resolution.
— **Legal Services**—A legal advocate will be available to provide information on a woman's legal rights and options. Clients will also be informed about family court laws and acts.
— **Outreach Services**—Outreach services are also provided to the community whereby an assessment can be done in the area of need, advocacy, counseling, and referrals to appropriate facilities.
— **Empowerment**—Each woman will be oriented to the cycle of battering and intergenerational patterns of abuse, and their impact on the family system. They will become empowered to work through their issues in a therapeutic environment with the appropriate support staff, volunteers, and advocates.
— **Children's Program**—This program provides a fun, safe place for children to play and explore their feelings through the course of play and artwork. The counseling component provides the children with individual sessions to work through their feelings of aggression, anger, sadness, and trauma.
— **Community Education**—Domestic violence programs conduct presentations and seminars to community groups, professional associations, civic clubs, schools, training institutes, parent groups, and other institutions about family violence and related issues. They promote awareness of the scope of the problem, provide concrete information about available services, and offer information on recruiting volunteers and advocates for legislation and lobbying.

Leaving the Shelter

The average stay in a shelter for battered women is ninety days. When the family prepares to leave the shelter, an exit interview is conducted and follow-up contacts are made. Referrals to transitional housing, appropriate agencies, or to nonresidential service programs are made to provide support for the woman and children as they readjust to life outside of the protected environment. If the woman returns home to the abuser, she is advised to seek nonresidential counseling with her abuser. The goal of the shelter staff is to assist the woman in whatever choice she makes without judging that choice, regardless of personal opinion.

Counselor Intervention and Self-Awareness

Treatment of a battered woman and her children is extremely difficult for the family, counselor, and community. The thought of someone being abused presents conflict for all involved. It is important for counselors to be aware of their feelings while working with battered families. Dr. Kim Oates (1986) refers to the battered professional as one that can identify with the client in a nonproductive way. Sometimes they are not aware that their feelings of anger lead them to overidentify with the battered client. In situations like these, Oates advises that counselors seek their own counseling to work through these feelings prior to making an attempt to work with battered families.

Lastly, human services workers must be ready to make an assessment and work with the battered family in a productive fashion to promote a healthier and a more positive environment.

CONCLUSION

It is quite difficult to realize that although public awareness and understanding of domestic violence in our society has greatly advanced over the last decade, statistics on battered women and children continue to rise. In spite of the challenge, we recognize that it is our responsibility to raise and develop healthier families. We hope to guide our children and their families to safety, success, and challenging endeavors, without having to expose them to personal and familial violence. This pain is multilayered and can, in a sense, create a fragmented self, family, and society, which are not easily repaired.

The achievements of the battered women's movement are massive and inspiring. The goal of social change is macroscopic, with serious implications for the improvement of the institution of family, gender issues, and the psychological development of children. The achievement of such goals relies on the commitment of staff, community, public policy, legislation, advocates, educators, human services, volunteers, criminal justice system, and community-based programs. At the very least, their collaborative efforts have shown support for women throughout the world and have brought the issue to the public arena.

REFERENCES

Boyd, V., and Klingbeil, K.S., (1984). "Behavioral Characteristics of Domestic Violence." Revised in Seattle Washington. A. Roberts, ed. *Battered Women and Their Families.* New York: Springer.

Browne, A., (1986). "Assault and Homicide at Home: When Battered Women Kill." In M.J. Sakes and L. Saxe, eds. *Advances in Applied Social Psychology,* Vol. 3. Hillside, NJ: Lawrence Erlbaum.

Dobash, E.R., and P.R. Dobash, (1992). *Women, Violence and Social Change.* Routledge, London: Chapman and Hall Inc.

Fagan, J. and A. Browne, (1982). "Violence between spouses and intimates." In J.A. Reiss and J.A. Roth, eds. *Understanding and Controlling Violence.* Washington DC: National Academy Press.

Fitch, F.J., and A. Papantonio, (1983). "Men Who Batter: Some Pertinent Characteristics." *Journal of Nervous and Mental Disorders,*171(3), 190–192.

Gelles, R.J., and M.A. Strauss, (1988). *Intimate Violence.* New York: Simon and Schuster.

Jaffe, P., D. Wolfe, and S. Wilson, (1990). *Children of Battered Women.* Beverly Hills, CA: Sage Publications, Inc., The International Professional Publishers.

Jaffe, P., S. Wilson, and L. Zak, (1986). "Emotional and Physical Health Problems of Battered Women." *Canadian Journal of Psychiatry,* 31: 625–629.

Krugman, S., (1987). "Trauma in the Family: Perspectives on the Intergenerational Transmission of Violence," in B.A. Van der Kolk, ed., *Psychological Trauma.* (pp. 127–151). Washington, DC: American Psychiatric Press.

MacLeod, L., (1989). *Wife Battering and the Web of Hope: Progress, Dilemmas, and Vision of Prevention.* Ottawa: Health and Welfare Canada.

Morgan, E.S., (1966). *The Puritan Family.* Westport, CT: Greenwood Press, Publishers.

Oates, K., (1986). *Child Abuse, A Community Concern.* New York: Brunner/Mazel, Inc.

Schechter, S., (1982). *Women and Male Violence.* Boston, MA: South End Press.

Stark, E., and A. Flitcraft, (1988). "Violence Among Inmates: An Epidemiological Review," in *Handbook of Family Violence*. New York: Plenum.

Steinmetz, S. K., and M. A. Straus, (1974). *Violence in the Family*. New York: Harper and Row.

Sutton, J., (1978). "The Growth of the British Movement for Battered Women," *Victimology*, (3–4)2: 576–584.

Walker, L. E. A., (1984). *The Battered Woman Syndrome*. New York: Springer.

White, E., (1985). *Chain, Chain, Change*. Seal Press. Library of Congress.

Warrior, Betsy, (1976). *Working on Wife Abuse*, 1st ed., subsequent editions published annually, Cambridge, MA.

AN AGENCY VOLUNTEER

JUDITH S. MORSE

Social issues surrounding domestic violence had always been one of my concerns. I had time, and more importantly, I wanted to volunteer my services. A director could not have staged the following events more flawlessly. The director of the Northern Westchester Shelter for Victims of Domestic Violence asked me if I would be interested in serving as a member on their board of directors. I quickly learned that I, as a volunteer, could give as much or as little time as I wanted. So much needed to be done, that any amount of time given was considered generous. Board meetings were held one evening a month and committee meetings were called as needed. This did not seem to be an unreasonable amount of time to give. I floundered for the first two years, not knowing how I would enjoy spending my time. After all, volunteering is supposed to be fun. It took me two years to find my niche.

First I served on the personnel committee. We spent one night every other week discussing staff problems: Our goal was to revive an antiquated personnel policy. We attempted to balance favorable working conditions with shelter needs, and salary fairness with limited finances. Some board members attended every meeting, some came when they could. We had no experience in this area. For me, it was a long, frustrating, and tedious process—we did not accomplish our goal by June, and a new committee was formed the following September. Fortunately, a volunteer with personnel expertise joined our board, and became the much needed addition to this committee. The following year I became involved in fundraising. Friends of the shelter and I devoted the entire month of August to putting together a picnic scheduled for September. I equated this endeavor with planning a wedding. I ran through the gamut of emotions—aggravation, anxiety, enjoyment and self-gratification. The major stumbling blocks were arranging for the band, caterer, tee shirts, grounds, etc., for little or no cost. When I resumed teaching in September, I was exhausted. However, the memories of the camaraderie surrounding the event made the effort worthwhile.

Gradually, I gravitated toward the quarterly newspaper, the *Hotline*. The *Hotline* is the shelter's link with the community; it lets the public know of our existence and the services we provide. We distributed the paper by mail and also hand-delivered to community sites frequented by the public. First, I became an assistant, and then began to think that this could be for me. The development coordinator and office staff participated in this endeavor.

Together, we decided what articles were appropriate to print. Shelter news is always interesting and it is important to give proper credit to private companies, corporations, or individuals who give services, grants, or donations to our organization. Recognition of staff or board members' accomplishments are equally important. No one appreciates being forgotten. It is also necessary in every publication to inform the community at large what the world is doing to deter family violence: i.e., new or proposed legislation, politicians' positions, court case rulings, etc. Frequently it was difficult to report some of the events because I lacked accurate and current information.

Due to budgetary problems, our development coordinator and other staff members were laid off. At this time I accepted the job of editor, naively thinking that I would receive the articles from contributing members of the board and staff for the *Hotline*. I quickly learned that if I wanted the articles printed, I would need to write them. (Thank goodness for computers and spell-check!) Before I delivered the *Hotline* to the publisher, I formulated a mock-up of the paper, since having the publisher do this adds to the cost of the publication. Publishers don't seem to have respect for weekends. Many times my husband and I have had to proofread the paper on the weekend, because the printing was scheduled to begin early Monday morning.

Gathering articles for the *Hotline* is an ongoing process. Before the latest *Hotline* is off the press, I'm preparing for the next issue. When the *Hotline* is due to be published, my energy and thoughts are on nothing else. I can relate it to writing a major term paper for a college course. My husband and I eat a lot of take-out.

I no longer call myself the editor of the Hotline; I am Managing Editor and Production Consultant. I enjoy the challenge, work deadlines, and excitement of creating this paper. For me, volunteering as a member of the board of directors is more than attending monthly meetings and occasionally writing a check. I became involved because I like being involved. Volunteers are the backbone for the Northern Westchester Shelter for Victims of Domestic Violence and many other human services organizations.

CHAPTER 16

CHILD MALTREATMENT AND ABUSE
THE PROBLEM AND HUMAN SERVICES

JAMES EDELL

INTRODUCTION

Child abuse occurs every day. Following is an example that received national attention and became a contemporary symbol of child abuse.

> *Early Monday morning, November 2, 1987, six-year-old Lisa "Steinberg" (it was discovered later she was not legally adopted) was rushed to St. Vincents Hospital. EMS workers picked her up unconscious from the bathroom floor in the apartment of Joel Steinberg, an attorney, and his companion, Hedda Nussbaum, a former writer and editor of children's books. The girl was covered with bruises, brutally beaten by Steinberg several times the day and evening before, the last time fatally for "staring" at him. One of the bruises on her head was delivered with such force that her brain shifted position inside her skull (a condition known as subdural hematoma). Subsequent investigation and court hearings found that Steinberg had also frequently brutally battered Nussbaum, his companion; she and Lisa had come to the attention of police as well as medical and Special Services for Children authorities several times in the past. After three days in the hospital in a coma, and with her brain permanently damaged, life support equipment was removed (Fontana, 1991).*

Renewed concern over child abuse as a major social problem emerged in the 1960s. The main agents were Dr. C.H. Kempe, a pediatrician, and his associates who practiced medicine in Denver, Colorado (Corby, 1987). Their work with children led them to conclude that severe physical maltreatment was a problem more common than previously thought. Kempe published his findings in 1962 in a now classic article in the *Journal of the American Medical Association* in which the term "battered child syndrome" was first used (Kempe et al., 1962).

The article focused on children who were physically battered by their parents or caretakers, and argued for psychological factors as the dominant cause of abuse. Unrealistic parental expectations for children, he argued, frequently led to frustration and physical abuse. The abuse, in Kempe's view, was likely to continue and worsen unless some form of intervention took place. Above all, Kempe's concern was to protect the child, and his model of intervention was either to remove children from the parents or place them in the hospital, and then treat the parent (Kempe et al., 1962, p. 17–24).

Kempe and his associates widely influenced how disciplines such as medicine, psychology, social work, and human and social services understand, treat, and prevent child abuse. The emerging public concern from his efforts with child maltreatment brought two major benefits. First, it resulted in more funding allocated to research on child abuse, and over time, other theories and broader perspectives have developed (Fontana, 1991). Today, three decades of research and intervention have produced a basic knowledge—though it is still incomplete—concerning incidence, cause, treatment, and prevention. Second, the increased public attention to child abuse spurred widespread governmental involvement. By 1968, all fifty states had enacted some form of law that mandated reporting of suspected child abuse cases. In 1974, after ten years of debate and controversy, Congress signed the Child Abuse Prevention and Treatment Act (PL 93–247) into law. While individual states determine their own definitions of maltreatment, the federal legislation helped to create standards to identify and manage child abuse cases (McCurdy and Daro, 1993).

Despite the thirty years that elapsed since Kempe's article focused national attention on child maltreatment, the case of Lisa Steinberg shows that the problem is still present. As Dr. Fontana, Chairman of the Mayor's Task Force on Child Abuse and Neglect, and Medical Director of the New York Foundling Hospital, has said, "we rediscover child abuse whenever an abused child's death makes headlines. This, our reawakening, is Lisa's legacy" (1991, p. 6).

THE PROBLEM OF CHILD MALTREATMENT

What Is Child Abuse?

What child abuse is has been the subject of debate and disagreement since Kempe's article. An effective definition of child maltreatment, Mayhall and Norgard (1983) point out, should include (1) what is legally considered harmful to the child; (2) when and what must be reported; (3) when intervention occurs, how, and by whom; (4) what is "imminent danger" and when does it occur; and (5) when is the court system justified in intervening in the family, overriding the authority of the parents (possibly terminating their parental rights) to protect children. The debate turns on one central issue: the definition given to child abuse determines the establishment and enforcement of child abuse laws (for a description of how Child Protective Services use the law to determine whether child maltreatment has occurred, see the section Human and Social Service Response). It is not surprising, then, that

the original Child Abuse Prevention and Treatment Act signed into law in 1974 has undergone two major revisions, reflecting the complexity of the maltreatment problem. The current definition is:

> *Child abuse and neglect means the physical or mental injury, sexual abuse or exploitation, neglectful treatment, or maltreatment of a child under the age of eighteen, or the age specified by the child protection law of the State in question, by a person (including any employee of a residential facility or any staff person providing out-of-home care) who is responsible for the child's welfare under circumstances which indicate that the child's health or welfare is harmed or threatened, thereby as determined in accordance with regulations prescribed by the Secretary (Child Abuse Amendments of 1984, Section 102).*

What Is the Extent of the Child Abuse Problem?

The question of the extent of the child abuse problem is subject to wide debate. The debate centers on two issues. First, while the federal government helped to establish a set of standards to identify and manage child abuse cases through the Child Abuse Prevention and Treatment Act, it is still the individual states that determine definitions of maltreatment, procedures for investigation, services that are offered, and systems of data collection (McCurdy and Daro, 1993). Thus, part of the problem in estimating the number of child abuse cases nationwide is the lack of uniform procedures across the states for collecting data. For example, forty-two states have a central reporting registry. But half of those states maintain statistics on the calendar year while the other half use a fiscal year. Methods of counting child abuse cases present more of a problem. While some states count two or more reports of the same episode of maltreatment as one report, other states consider these as separate reports (McCurdy and Daro, 1993).

Despite these difficulties, the National Committee for the Prevention of Child Abuse (NCPCA) each year since 1986 has conducted a survey of federally appointed liaisons for child abuse and neglect in each of the fifty states. This survey obtains data on (1) the number of child abuse reports and the characteristics of those reports; (2) the number of child abuse fatalities; and (3) changes in funding and how that affects services offered to children (McCurdy and Daro, 1993).

The NCPCA estimates that in 1992, 2,936,000 children were reported to state Child Protective Service (CPS) agencies as alleged victims of abuse. That makes 45 children per 1000 reported for maltreatment in the U.S. (McCurdy and Daro, 1993); 45 percent of these were due to neglect, 27 percent to physical abuse, 17 percent to sexual abuse, 7 percent to emotional maltreatment, and 8 percent other.

The forty states that were able to provide data for 1992 (forty-nine states responded to the NCPCA query; nine could not provide data) recorded an average 7.8 percent increase in reports of child abuse between 1991 and 1992. Child abuse reports have grown at an average of 6 percent per year during the period 1985 to 1992 (Daro and Mitchell, 1987). While it is difficult to sort out the relative contribution of increased public awareness, changes in reporting systems and actual cases to the increased number of reports, most state liaisons contacted by NCPCA stated they believed the increase to be due to a real increase in maltreatment, resulting from increased economic stress and substance abuse.

The second and more serious problem in estimating the extent of the child abuse problem stems from the reliance upon "formal reports," that is, the number of reports of maltreatment made to child protective services discussed above. Such formal reports, critics charge, may seriously underestimate the incidence of maltreatment. Evidence for this position comes from studies and interviews with random samples of individuals which reveal higher rates of maltreatment than do formal reports (Straus et al., 1980).

One study done in 1980 estimated that between 3.1 and 4 million children are kicked or punched by their parents at some point during their childhood. These shocking findings were not substantiated in a follow-up study done ten years later. That study showed a decrease in the most serious forms of physical violence, but did substantiate previously reported levels of pushing and slapping. Moreover, interviews with random samples of individuals corroborate the findings in these surveys. The gap between cases "formally reported" and the actual incidence suggested by the foregoing reports was highlighted by the National Incidence study. This study showed that only 33 percent of the cases identified by professionals throughout the country were ever formally reported (Westat, 1981).

Neither the formal reports nor the interviews with random samples give a definitive statement about numbers. They do, however, provide a base to discuss the extent of the problem and the frequency of the types of maltreatment. As Daro points out, the figures "make a powerful case for public intervention" (1988, p. 15).

What Are the Consequences of Maltreatment?

Any consideration of the consequences of child maltreatment must focus on concern for human suffering, and its individual, social, and moral effects. First, child abuse causes physical trauma. In addition to bruises, serious injuries such as fractures, subdural hematomas (bleeding inside the skull), and so on, children who are abused may suffer from serious and recurrent medical problems, such as damage to the central nervous system, leaving the child with seizures, mental retardation, and sensory deficits. Not directly related to the episode of abuse are medical problems such as lack of immunizations, inadequate hygiene, poor nutrition, and anemia, among others (Martin, 1980).

Abused children are also at risk of various psychological problems, such as mental retardation, learning disorders, and language delays. Evidence for this risk comes from clinicians and from research that have documented maltreated children to have more developmental problems compared to control groups. Maltreated children are also at greater risk for depression, fearfulness, and mistrust towards adults, lack of age-appropriate relationships with peers, as well as poor self-image (Elmer, 1977).

Second, there is the issue of what happens to maltreated children as they grow into adulthood. The most obvious long-term effect of abuse is its influence on how abused children later parent their own children. The concept of generational transmission of abuse was posited first by Steele and Pollock (1971). While an abused child who later became an abusive parent is commonly referred to in the literature as a cause of maltreatment, research on it is not conclusive (see the section Who Are the Perpetrators of Maltreatment? for a discussion of this issue). Other long-term consequences of abuse include delinquency, criminal behavior, school dropouts, teenage parenthood, and increased risk of repeating violent assaults on others (Martin, 1980).

Third, given these consequences, it is not surprising that there are increased social costs associated with medical care, hospitalization and rehabilitative services, emergency placements and foster care, special education, counseling, etc. More difficult to assess, but no less real, are costs associated with adult criminals, criminal justice system and incarceration, and loss of earnings (Daro, 1988, p. 149–155).

Finally, there are quality-of-life issues. Abused children may be unhappy children and adults, face bouts of clinical depression, and experience difficulties in relationships, especially those of love or attachment (Martin, 1980).

FOUR TYPES OF MALTREATMENT

Kempe's original article focused on physical abuse. Further research has expanded Kempe's focus on this one dimension of maltreatment to elaborate a typology of four kinds of abuse: physical abuse, neglect, emotional maltreatment, and sexual abuse. Such research has organized maltreatment into groups that share more or less sim-

ilar kinds of characteristics and therefore similar underlying causes and types of intervention.

Legal definitions of child abuse and maltreatment vary from state to state. In the following section, New York definitions will be used as a guide.

Physical Abuse

Kempe's concept of the "battered child syndrome" informed both the research and public campaign against child abuse. Hence the popular image of the maltreated child is one who has been physically battered, and this form of maltreatment has wide public recognition as abuse.

A physically abused child is one less than eighteen years of age whose parents or legal caretakers inflict (or allow to be inflicted) a physical injury (other than an accident) that creates risk of death, disfigurement, or impairment of health or function of any body organ (New York State Family Court Act, Section 1012[e]).

Recent research has challenged lumping all physical abuse cases into one category, suggesting that physical abuse is too broad a term, one that encompasses variation not only in abusive behavior but also types of families that commit the abuse. Gil (1981) suggested dividing up physical abuse into levels of severity, since cases involving broken bones or permanent brain damage—as in the case of Lisa Steinberg—merit more concern and a different level of intervention than cases with minor physical bruises. Other studies have focused on grouping cases of physical abuse into clusters based on characteristics of families. Different studies identify and use different characteristics to categorize families. Boisvert (1972, p. 475–476), for example, collected data on characteristics of perpetrators, age of the child, and the nature of the injury. Kent et al. (1983), by contrast, developed subgroups based on the type of intervention most likely to be successful with certain families. For example, Kent's category "spare the rod" referred to families that need to learn modes of discipline other than corporal punishment.

About 27 percent of cases reported to child protective services in 1992 involved physical abuse. Severely abused children tend to be younger than those experiencing "minor" forms of abuse. More children who are physically abused are hospitalized compared to other forms of maltreatment. Physical abuse—more than any other form of maltreatment—causes the abuse-related deaths among children. In 1990, there were 1,060 confirmed fatalities resulting from child abuse and neglect in the United States; in 1991, there were 1,176; in 1992, with incomplete data, there were 869 confirmed fatalities, although the projected figure was 1,261 (McCurdy and Daro, 1993, p. 15). Between 1990 and 1992, 59 percent of these fatalities were due to physical abuse (McCurdy and Daro, 1993, p. 16).

How Is Physical Abuse Identified? Physical abuse leaves marks on the body that are observable; consequently, it tends to be easier to identify than other forms of maltreatment. Reports of physical abuse generally come from observations of children made by physicians, health care providers, teachers, day care center personnel, friends, or neighbors.

What Are the Warning Signs? The typical warning signs of physical abuse include bruises, burns, welts, scars, repeated accidental injuries, and broken bones. Besides medical evaluation, a key piece of information used to separate abuse from accidents is the parents' ability to explain the injury (see Table 16.1) (Weston, 1980, pp. 241–50).

Physical Neglect

If physical abuse is the most popular image of the abused child, cases of neglect are perhaps the form of maltreatment most removed from public awareness. Yet, it is the most widespread form of child maltreatment. In 1992, 45 percent of the total number of maltreatment cases reported were for

TABLE 16.1 Indicators of Physical Abuse

Physical Indicators
- Bruises and welts
- Burns
- Fractures
- Lacerations or abrasions
- Human bite marks
- Frequent injuries that are "accidental" or "unexplained"

Behavioral Indicators
- Wary of adult contact
- Apprehensive when other children cry
- Behavioral extremes: aggressiveness, withdrawal
- Frightened of parents
- Afraid to go home
- Seeks affection from any adult

Parent's Behavioral Indicators
- Seems unconcerned about child
- Misuses alcohol or drugs
- Disciplines child too harshly
- Has a history of abuse

Adapted from: Weston, James, "The Pathology of Child Abuse and Neglect." In *The Battered Child,* C.H. Kempe and R.E. Helfer, eds. Chicago: University of Chicago Press, 241–271.

neglect. Between 1990 and 1992, 37 percent of confirmed child abuse and neglect fatalities were due to neglect (McCurdy and Daro, 1993, p. 4).

A case of neglect refers to a child less than eighteen whose physical, mental, or emotional condition has been impaired (or is in danger of becoming impaired) because of a lack of a minimum degree of care. This breaks down into failure to (a) supply the child with adequate food, clothing, shelter, education, or medical care, even though they are financially able to do so, or are offered the means to do so; and (b) provide the child with proper supervision (e.g., by using drugs or alcohol, etc.). Neglect also refers to children abandoned by their parents (New York State Family Court Act, Section 1012[f]). NCPCA estimates that during 1991 and 1992 at least 4,696 children were reported abandoned by eighteen states (only twenty-three states collect data on abandonment; eighteen provided information for the survey). There are problems in estimating abandonment: the small number of states that collect data give an incomplete picture and the system of data collection in many states does not have a separate category for abandonment, so these cases are lumped under neglect (McCurdy and Daro, 1993, p. 12).

Research portrays neglect as a homogenous grouping: certain characteristics of families tend to be associated with neglect in the majority of cases. These characteristics include lack of adequate financial and material resources that limit the family's ability to care for children. For example, 51 percent of children reported for neglect lived in single-parent families; 43 percent of these caretakers were unemployed (AAPC, 1986). Other characteristics include poor housing and living conditions and large, multiproblem families (BPA, 1982). Above all, one factor consistently associated with neglect is lack of social support. Children who are neglected come from families that often are completely isolated from an informal network of social supports among family and friends. Research portrays one type of family consistently involved in neglect: a poor and socially isolated family, where the needs of the child are lost in the struggle for daily existence (Cantwell, 1980). It is not surprising that neglect, more than other forms of maltreatment, is likely to occur by itself and not in combination with other forms of maltreatment. Consequently, studies differentiate among neglect cases on the basis of behavior—educational neglect, medical neglect, abandonment, etc. (Miller, 1982). Neglect as a category of maltreatment contrasts with physical abuse, where researchers have separated out different types of families.

How Is Neglect Identified?   Like physical abuse but to a lesser degree, neglect results in observable signs that are noted by people who are in daily or frequent contact with the child, such as teachers, welfare caseworkers, day care personnel, physicians, or health care workers.

What Are the Warning Signs?   Suspicion of neglect does not turn on observation of a single episode of behavior; rather, it is a consistent lack of clean clothing or regular hygiene that results in skin or other medical conditions as well as consistent tardiness or absenteeism from school that are considered signs of potential neglect (see Table 16.2) (Miller, 1982).

The impact of neglect on children is severe. One study showed that neglected children received the lowest rating in self-esteem and confidence. Families that neglect children appear to be among the most resistant to intervention (Elmer, 1977).

Emotional Maltreatment

Emotional maltreatment is defined as the "impairment of emotional health" and "impairment of mental or emotional condition." These refer to a condition of substantially reduced psychological or intellectual functioning, and include behavior

---

TABLE 16.2   Indicators of Neglect

Physical Indicators
- Consistent hunger, poor hygiene
- Inappropriate dress
- Consistent lack of supervision
- Abandonment

Behavioral Indicators
- Begging or stealing food
- Poor school attendance
- Constant fatigue

Parent's Behavioral Indicators
- Misuses drugs or alcohol
- Disorganized home life
- Isolation from friends
- Chronic illness
- Exposes child to unsafe living conditions

Adapted from: Weston, James, "The Pathology of Child Abuse and Neglect." In *The Battered Child,* C.H. Kempe and R.E. Helfer, eds. Chicago: University of Chicago Press, 241–271.

related to failure to thrive, control of aggressive impulses, acting out, and misbehavior (New York State Family Court Act, Section 1012[h]).

Emotional maltreatment is pervasive. It tends to occur with other forms of maltreatment, unlike physical abuse or neglect, which tends to exist alone. The National Clinical Evaluation Study found that sixty percent of all abuse cases in 1983 were accompanied by emotional maltreatment. Yet, the practical problems in measuring emotional maltreatment, assessing its impact on children, and developing effective treatment make it the most ambiguous form of maltreatment. First, it is not as visible as physical abuse, or even neglect—constant criticism and shouting don't leave visible marks on children—and its consequences are more difficult to pinpoint. Second, not all states have statutes that mandate reports of maltreatment. These difficulties account for why, until recently, emotional maltreatment was omitted from policy and research. In fact, emotional maltreatment has been considered a "residual category," covering behaviors not in physical abuse, neglect, and sexual abuse categories (Daro, 1988, p. 35). These difficulties are reflected in the low reporting of emotional maltreatment: In 1992, only 7 percent of all child maltreatment reports were for emotional maltreatment (McCurdy and Daro, 1993).

In an effort to clarify these ambiguities, research has attempted to subdivide the emotional maltreatment category into small groups that make identification and treatment easier. Dean (1979) identified three types: (a) emotional neglect; (b) emotional assault (verbal attacks); and (c) emotional abuse (acts that prevent development of a positive self-image). Another study focused on differentiating the category in terms of behavior: rejection, coldness, inappropriate control, and extreme inconsistency (Garbarino, 1977). In addition to these efforts at categorization, the medical profession has identified "Munchausen syndrome" as a form of emotional maltreatment. This refers to a situation where parents believe the child is ill, or exhibit "paranoid' thinking about the child's health—and may even make frequent visits to different doctors—despite all medical evidence to the contrary (Woollcott et al., 1982).

Given these difficulties, it comes as no surprise that researchers so far have been unable to develop a profile of parents who emotionally maltreat children, as they have in neglect cases. Characteristics of families that emotionally maltreat children are also found among those who physically abuse children, such as lack of parenting skills and social isolation, making identification and treatment of cases much more difficult.

How Is Emotional Maltreatment Identified? Identification is made by someone who has specialized daily or frequent contact with the child or family, such as a school counselor or a therapist.

What Are the Warning Signs?   Common warning signs include speech disorders, lags in physical development, and failure to thrive. Parents who emotionally maltreat children blame or belittle the child, withhold love, or don't seem to care much about the child's problems (see Table 16.3) (Carroll, 1980).

TABLE 16.3   Indicators of Emotional
Maltreatment

Physical Indicators
- Speech disorders
- Lags in physical development
- Failure to thrive

Behavioral Indicators
- Habits, e.g., sucking, rocking
- Conduct disorders, e.g., antisocial, destructive
- Behavioral extremes

Parent's Behavioral Indicators
- Treats children in family unequally
- Blames or belittles child
- Cold or rejecting, withholding love

Adapted from: Weston, James, "The Pathology of Child Abuse and Neglect." In *The Battered Child,* C.H. Kempe and R.E. Helfer, eds. Chicago: University of Chicago Press, 241–271.

Sexual Abuse

The concern over sexual abuse as a major problem is reflected in the growing numbers of reports for this form of maltreatment. In 1992, 17 percent of all maltreatment reports involved sexual abuse (McCurdy and Daro, 1993, p. 4). If neglect cases tend to be associated with poverty, sexual abuse cuts across socioeconomic boundaries and is found in all communities and at all income and educational levels.

A sexually abused child is one less than eighteen years of age whose parents or legal caretakers commit (or allow to be committed) a sex offense against the child, or allow the child to engage in, or promote using a child in sexual performance (New York State Family Court Act, Section 1012[e]).

Children reported as sexually abused are generally female (75 percent of cases) and older compared to other forms of maltreated children. Interviews with random groups of adults suggest that sexual abuse may also occur when children are younger, and many victims may be boys. In 50 percent of the cases, a parent or step-parent is responsible for the abuse; the remaining cases involve other adults who are usually known to the family (Kempe, 1980).

How Is Sexual Abuse Identified?   Identification of sexual abuse is difficult since verbal reports and physical symptoms are not available in most cases. Identification, therefore, depends on observation of the behavior of victims of sex abuse, their family members, or even a self-report at a later age. Social workers and others must be trained to identify the physical and behavioral signs of abuse.

What Are the Warning Signs?   Children who are sexually abused often have difficulty walking or sitting, have pain in the genital area, or suffer from sexually transmitted disease. Moreover, such children often have poor peer relationships, withdraw from social contact, or demonstrate infantile behavior. Parents who abuse children often misuse

alcohol or other drugs, or lack social and emotional contacts (see Table 16.4) (Kempe, 1980).

Public awareness of sexual abuse has led to instruction in schools to prevent abuse. Such instruction has included lessons on both inappropriate touching, and the child's disclosure of such acts to someone they trust. How effective prevention efforts are that rely on children is unknown and poses an important research question.

Who Are the Perpetrators of Maltreatment?

Studies have identified various characteristics of families that contribute to a higher likelihood of maltreatment. These range from psychological disorders and limited income and material resources to stress caused by unemployment, among other situations. But who are the people who abuse children? Fontana has written that they "are not usually monsters or seriously deranged individuals, but rather parents deserving of help" (1991, p. 13). Research findings support this statement. Severely disturbed and psychotic individuals constitute no more than 10 percent of all cases of maltreatment (Kempe and Kempe, 1978).

TABLE 16.4   Indicators of Sexual Abuse

Physical Indicators
- Pain or itching in the genital area
- Venereal disease
- Bruises in genital area

Behavioral Indicators
- Unusual sexual behavior or knowledge
- Reports sexual abuse
- Withdrawal, fantasy, or infantile behavior

Parent's Behavioral Indicators
- Protective or jealous of child
- Encourages child to engage in prostitution
- Lacks social and emotional contacts

Adapted from: Weston, James, "The Pathology of Child Abuse and Neglect." In *The Battered Child,* C.H. Kempe and R.E. Helfer, eds. Chicago: University of Chicago Press, 241–271.

Rather, most parents who maltreat children suffer from various personal disorders or internal conflict. For example, Sever et al. (1982) studied sexually abusive families and noted that 71 percent abused alcohol. Moreover, Olson (1976), focusing on development of psychological profiles of parents who maltreat children, found a high percentage have rigid or authoritarian personalities, emotional immaturity, or drug or alcohol dependence. Divorce and remarriage also pose a risk factor for maltreatment. Research noted that children in step-parent families showed a higher incidence of sexual abuse and other forms of maltreatment (Russell, 1984).

Finally, as noted earlier, childhood abuse of the parent is one of the most widely cited causal factors of maltreatment. Hunter (1979) studied 255 mothers who gave birth to premature babies. Nine out of ten of the mothers who abused their babies had a history of abuse, lending support to the concept of generational transmission of abuse. However, 17 percent of the control group who did not abuse their babies also reported a history of past abuse. The data clearly show that while not all abused children grow up to become abusers themselves, an increased risk exists. Why some abused children become abusive parents and others do not is unknown.

Why Does Maltreatment Happen?

Three basic theories are used in research to explain child maltreatment: (1) psychodynamic, (2) learning, and (3) environmental. These broad theories try to elucidate the relationship between either a specific individual (perpetrator of maltreatment) or set of environmental conditions to the incidence of maltreatment.

Psychodynamic Theories. Psychodynamic theories emphasize the psychological problems of parents and consequently their levels of personal and social functioning in explaining why abuse occurs. The theory argues that individuals with personal problems or severe or moderate psycho-

logical disorders are less able to care for their children. It is not a deficit of skills: such parents do not have the personal capacity to care consistently for children. For example, parental depression can contribute to abuse. The intervention model following from a psychodynamic perspective is therapeutic services provided to individuals, families, or groups. The nature and duration of therapy would vary according to the type and severity of maltreatment (Steele, 1980).

Learning Theories. In contract to psychodynamic theories, which focus on psychological problems of parents, learning theories emphasize lack of skills and knowledge. According to this theory, abuse occurs because parents don't know how to care for their children. The theory argues that parents can be taught how to care for children through learning new information or skills. Such information is imparted in parenting education classes and support groups (Steele, 1980).

Environmental Theories. The theories covered so far have focused on the individual. The final theory moves from the individual focus to broader environmental conditions. Rather than psychological problems or lack of skill, this perspective looks at macrolevel factors such as poverty, racism, and sexism as causes of maltreatment. For example, poverty and a lack of material resources are associated with child neglect. Other researchers identify a correlation (if not causal relationship) between pornography and sexual violence/abuse towards women and children. Moreover, critics charge, poverty and the social conditions it produces—unemployment, underemployment, poor housing, lack of access to education, and health care—underlie the psychological problems and lack of knowledge that psychodynamic and learning theories attempt to address.

The intervention model suggested by this approach seeks policy changes to reduce poverty, improve housing, health insurance and access to health care, and increase vocational training and employment opportunities (Martin, 1980).

Ecological Model.   None of these perspectives is incorrect, but each one alone is insufficient to explain maltreatment. The causes of maltreatment probably lie in individuals and society. The use of ecological theories in social work, developed by Germain and Gitterman (1980), focuses not just on the individual or on society, but rather the interaction between these two domains, and the impact of those interactions on children. The challenge for research is to specify these interactions and refine existing typologies of maltreatment so that cases with similar patterns of causation can be grouped together to enhance prevention and treatment efforts.

SOCIAL SERVICE RESPONSE: MANDATED REPORTING AND CHILD PROTECTIVE SERVICES

In 1973, the New York State Legislature signed into law the Child Protective Services Act of 1973 (CPSA). Other states have similar laws; as with the definitions of abuse, New York will be used as a model to explain the general process. CPSA mandates certain persons and officials to report cases of suspected child abuse and maltreatment. It specifies what must be reported, and how a report is to be made, as well as the penalties for not reporting and the legal protection afforded to those who report.

Whenever child abuse or maltreatment is suspected, New York Social Service Law mandates that a report be made immediately by telephone. Oral reports are made to the State Central Register of Child Abuse and Maltreatment (SCR). Social Service Law also mandates that a written report be filed with the local child protective services (CPS) within forty-eight hours of the oral report. Generally, information given during the oral report includes the names and addresses of the child and parents or caretakers; the child's age, sex, and race; nature and extent of the injuries or maltreatment. Reports can be made even if information is missing. Written reports are admissible as evidence in judicial proceedings relating to child abuse. Moreover, any person or official or institution that acts in "good faith" in making the report has immunity from liability, both civil and criminal, that might result from the report. Conversely, a person who willfully fails to make a report is subject to penalty (a Class-A misdemeanor).

What Happens When a Report Is Made?

Once a report is made to the Central State Register, Social Service Law mandates that local child protective services investigate the report and provide or arrange, and monitor services for children and families.

Investigation

The goal of the investigation is to determine if "credible evidence" of abuse exists. Credible evidence is evidence that is worthy of belief. The investigation involves fact-finding through interviews and observation. The CPS caseworker will contact people able to give information relevant to the case. These include the reporter, children, parents or caretakers, school personnel, physicians and health professionals, service providers, relatives, and neighbors.

Determination and Assessment

The final step is determining whether the report is "indicated" or "unfounded." This determination must be made within ninety days of the oral report. After the facts are gathered, they are compared to statutory definitions of abuse and maltreatment, and a decision is made as to whether there is credible evidence of abuse. During this process, the stresses in the family are evaluated. This process normally includes an assessment of the child's behavior and level of developmental functioning; the parents' capacity to care for the child; past and current family functioning; potential harm to the child; environment; and supports to the family. Specific problems are also assessed, such as health problems, marital conflict, housing conditions, and substance abuse.

If the investigation determines that credible evidence does not exist, the report is considered "unfounded." If the investigation determines that credible evidence exists, the report is "indicated," and the family is offered appropriate services. When the report is indicated, a service plan is developed for the child/family that aims to ensure the child's well-being, and preserve and stabilize the family. Service plans usually contain a description of the problem, an assessment of individual problems and needs, as well as goals to be achieved. The services needed to attain the goals are specified along with their expected duration.

Service Provision and Monitoring

Services can be provided by the New York State Department of Social Services or from community-based agencies. The caseworker is responsible for arranging/coordinating and monitoring the services delivered.

In cases where the child's injuries are severe, there is a past history of abuse, and the parents refuse to cooperate, Child Protective Services turns to Family Court. The role of the court is to impose treatment or protective services on the parents. In some cases, a police officer, caseworker, or physician (in the capacity as member of a hospital) can take the child into protective custody. This occurs under specific conditions, i.e., when the child is in "imminent danger" and there is not enough time to apply for an order of temporary removal from Family Court. It carries responsibility to take specific actions such as bringing the child to an area designated by rules of the Family Court and making reasonable efforts to inform the parents of the child's placement.

Child Protective Services workers often use emergency foster care placements during investigation or following confirmation of a report to ensure the safety of the child. Foster care is defined as "full-time, substitute care of children outside their own homes . . . [that] occurs in fam-

ily homes, group homes and institutions" (Encyclopedia of Social Work, 1987). After abuse is substantiated, Green and Haggerty (1968) estimate that when children are returned to their homes, there is a 50 percent chance that abuse would continue, and a 10 percent chance death might occur. While it is preferable to maintain children with the family, workers weigh the social/emotional damage created by removal of children from the parents and their placement in foster care to the potential harm if children remain with parents. In general, the goals are to minimize the number of children placed in foster care and the length of their stay. As of May 1993, New York City foster care caseload was 48,560.

A large number of community-based agencies provide therapeutic and other services to families that maltreat children. Such services follow a psychosocial model built on the premise that effective intervention rests on combining provision of therapeutic services to individual clients with community or social interventions. The psychosocial model dominates service planning at community-based agencies, which takes place in multidisciplinary teams (formed of medical, legal, mental health, and social service specialists) that review reports and assess treatment needs.

Services are offered from a family perspective, that is treating the family as a unit as opposed to individuals, usually over six to nine months. Direct services to parents may include parenting education, hospital-based perinatal services, group therapy, home visitor services, and various support groups.

Services to maltreated children include therapeutic day care, outpatient psychiatric treatment, and various special services for adolescents. Also, crisis-intervention services exist that respond immediately to families in distress, such as 24-hour hotlines or crisis nurseries. Finally, caseworkers provide concrete services to families, which include resolving problems related to income, housing, medical care, public assistance, day care, vocational training, and employment opportunities.

TABLE 16.5   List of Mandated Reporters

Physicians	Peace Officers
Surgeons	School Officials
Medical Examiners	Residents
Coroners	Interns
Police Officers	Registered Nurses
Dentists	Hospital Personnel
Osteopaths	Christian Science Practitioners
Chiropractors	Day Care Center Workers
Podiatrists	Foster Care Workers
Social Service Workers	Mental Health Professionals
Law Enforcement Officials	Psychologists

Source: New York State Social Services Law, Section 413.

WHAT STUDENTS OF HUMAN AND SOCIAL SERVICES SHOULD KNOW ABOUT CHILD ABUSE AND MALTREATMENT

Students should be aware not only of the legal definitions of abuse and maltreatment, but also the physical and behavioral indicators of abuse.

Under New York Social Service Law (Section 413), certain persons and officials are required to report suspected cases of child maltreatment. These reports are made when (1) there is reasonable cause to suspect that a child is abused or maltreated; or (2) if the parent or legal caretaker states from personal knowledge, facts or conditions that would constitute abuse. See Table 16.5 for a list of mandated reporters.

Observation of indicators of abuse is often the only way caseworkers can identify suspected cases of abuse (see Tables 16.1–16.4 for the indicators of abuse). The presence of one of these signs, however, does not automatically signify abuse; there may be

legitimate explanations. If physical or behavioral signs of abuse occur frequently, however, in sufficient number or as part of a pattern, it is cause to suspect child abuse or maltreatment and make a report. The mandated reporter does not have to be certain that abuse exists before reporting; cases are reported when they are suspected, based on existence of signs and the reporter's experience and training.

CONCLUSION

Thirty years after Kempe's original paper, studies of child abuse have elaborated a set of theoretical frameworks, models, and empirical findings that contribute to understanding the basic parameter of the problem—its causes, incidence, treatment, and prevention. Though far from complete, such knowledge consistently points out one central fact: knowledge alone is insufficient; it needs to be put into action individually, socially, and politically to be effective.

REFERENCES

American Association for Protecting Children, (1984). *Highlights of Official Child Neglect and Abuse Reporting.* Denver: American Humane Society.

Berkeley Planning Associates, (1977). *Child Abuse and Neglect Treatment Programs: Final Report and Summary of Findings from the Evaluation of the Joint OCT/SRS National Demonstration Program in Child Abuse and Neglect.* Prepared for the National Center for Health Services

Research under Contracts No. 106–74–120 and No. 230–75–0076.

Boisvert, M., (1972). "The Battered Child Syndrome." *Social Casework,* 53 (October), pp. 475–480.

Cantwell, H.B., (1980). "Child Neglect." *The Battered Child.* C.H. Kempe and R.E. Helfer, eds., 183–197. Chicago: University of Chicago Press.

Carroll, C.A., (1980). "The Function of Protective Services in Child Abuse and Neglect," C.H. Kempe and R.E. Helfer, eds., in *The Battered Child*. 275–287. Chicago: University of Chicago Press.

Corby, B., (1987). *Working with Child Abuse*. England: Open University Press.

Daro, D., (1988). *Confronting Child Abuse: Research for Effective Program Design*. New York: The Free Press.

Daro, D., and L. Mitchell, (1987). *Deaths Due to Maltreatment Soar: The Results of the Eighth Semi-Annual Fifty State Survey*. Chicago: National Committee for Prevention of Child Abuse.

Dean, D., (1979). "Emotional Abuse of Children." *Children Today*, 8 (July-August), 18–27.

Elmer, E., (1977). "A Follow-Up of Traumatized Children." *Pediatrics*, 59 (February 1977), 273–279.

Fontana, V.J., (1991). *Save the Family, Save the Child*. New York: Dutton.

Garbarino, J., (1977). "The Human Ecology of Child Maltreatment: A Conceptual Model for Research." *Journal of Marriage and the Family*, 39 (November) 721–735.

Germain, C.D., and A. Gitterman, (1980). *The Life Model of Social Work Practice*. New York: Columbia University Press.

Gil, D., (1981). "The United States versus Child Abuse," in L. Pelton, ed., *Social Context of Child Abuse and Neglect*. New York: Human Services Press.

Hunter, R.S., and N. Kilstrom, (1979). "Breaking the Cycle in Abusive Families." *American Journal of Psychiatry*, 136, 1320–1322.

Kempe, C.H., (1980). "Incest and Other Forms of Sexual Abuse," C.H. Kempe and R.E. Helfer, eds., in *The Battered Child*. pp. 198–214. Chicago: University of Chicago Press.

Kempe, C.H., F.N. Silverman, B.F. Steele, W. Droegemueller, and H.K. Silver, (1962). "The Battered Child Syndrome." *Journal of the American Medical Association*, 181(17):17–24.

Kempe, R.S., and C.H. Kempe, (1978). *Child Abuse*. Cambridge, MA: Harvard University Press.

Kempe, R.S., C. Cutler, and J. Dean, (1980). "The Infant with Failure-to-Thrive," C.H. Kempe and R.E. Helfer, eds., in *The Battered Child*. pp. 163–182. Chicago: University of Chicago Press.

Kent, J., H. Weisberg, B. Lamar, and T. Marx, (1983). "Understanding the Etiology of Child Abuse: A Preliminary Typology of Cases." *Children and Youth Services Review*, 5(1): 7–29.

Mccurdy, M.A., and D. Daro, (1993). *Current Trends in Child Abuse Reporting and Fatalities: The Results of the 1992 Annual Fifty State Survey*. National Committee for Prevention of Child Abuse.

Martin, H.P., (1980). "The Consequences of Being Abused and Neglected: How the Child Fares." C.H. Kempe and R.E. Helfer, eds., in *The Battered Child*. pp. 347–366. Chicago: University of Chicago Press.

Mayhall, P.D., and K.E. Norgard, (1983). *Child Abuse and Neglect*. New York: John Wiley and Son.

Miller, K., (1982). "Child Abuse and Neglect." *Journal of Family Practice*, 14(3) (March): 571–595.

New York State Family Court Act, Sections 1012 (e, f, h).

Olson, R., (1976). "Index of Suspicion: Screening of Child Abusers." *American Journal of Nursing*, 76 (January), 108–110.

Russell, D., (1984). *Sexual Exploitation: Rape, Child Sexual Abuse, and Sexual Harassment*. Beverly Hills: Sage.

Sever, J., and C. Janzen, (1982). "Contradictions to Reconstitution of Sexually Abusive Families." *Child Welfare*, 61(5) (May), pp. 279–288.

Steele, B., (1980). "Psychodynamic Factors in Child Abuse." C.H. Kempe and R.E. Helfer, eds., in *The Battered Child*. pp. 49–85. Chicago: University of Chicago Press.

Steele, B., and C. Pollock, (1971). "The Battered Child's Parents." A.S. Skolnick and J.H. Skolnick, eds., in *Family in Transition*. Boston: Little Brown.

Straus, M.A., (1980). "Stress and Child Abuse." C.H. Kempe and R.E. Helfer, eds., in *The Battered Child*. pp. 86–103. Chicago: University of Chicago Press.

Straus, M., R. Gelles, and S. Steinmetz, (1980). *Behind Closed Doors: Violence in the American Family*. Garden City, NY: Anchor Press.

Westat and Development Associates, (1981). *National Study of the Incidence and Severity of Child Abuse and Neglect*. Prepared for the National Center on Child Abuse and Neglect under Contract No. 105-76-1137.

Weston, J.T., (1980). "The Pathology of Child Abuse and Neglect." C.H. Kempe and R.E. Helfer, eds., in *The Battered Child*. pp. 241–272. Chicago: University of Chicago Press.

Wolock, I., and B. Horowitz, (1979). "Child Maltreatment and Material Deprivation Among AFDC-Recipient Families." *Social Service Review*, 53 (June), pp. 175–194.

Woolcott, P., Jr., T. Aceto, Jr., C. Rutt, M. Bloom, and R. Glick, (1982). "Doctor Shopping with the Child as Proxy Patient: A Variant of Child Abuse." *The Journal of Pediatrics*, 101(2) (August), pp. 297–301.

RITE OF PASSAGE, INC.[1]
A MENTORING COMMUNITY

DAVID SILBERSTEIN

*They experience confusion about their sexual iden-
tity . . . their self-esteem is unsteady . . . they
repress their ambition and inquisitiveness . . . they
exhibit learning problems . . . they have trouble
respecting moral values and accepting responsibilities . . . they have little sense of duty or obligation toward others. The absence of limits also
makes it difficult for them to act with authority or
to respect the authority of others. Their insufficient
internal structure results in a certain laxity, a lack
of rigor, a general inability to organize their lives
effectively. All such behaviors are rooted in deep
revolt against patriarchal society. This revolt mirrors to the father the consequence of his absence.[2]*

As a result, many of these youth do not feel
welcome in society. Ethnologists who have studied the contemporary patterns of violence within
the male peer subculture and the organized youth
gangs in this country, point to the intense alienation and apathy these young people experience.
Almost invariably, these youth have had no father
in the home. More than 70 percent of black and
hispanic young men convicted of felonies involving violence (assault, rape, homicide) were children of teen mothers without partners. What has
made this group phenomena so difficult to transform is that the youth today have tended to organize themselves in their own firmly cemented
antisocial rites of passage. These "rites" serve as
a substitute for positive contact with the adult
male community. Not trusting the primary male

figure in their lives (their fathers) these boys project contempt and mistrust for all men.

Statistics show the overwhelming majority of
violent crimes in America are committed by males
(88.6 percent!) and that violent crimes by males
are on the increase (between 1985 and 1989 an
increase of 32 percent to 442,522 arrests nationwide) and that juveniles in custody have increased
30 percent in the last ten years! We all know the
connection between crime and drugs.

*Clearly, the research and statistical informa-
tion indicates that as more and more boys are
raised without their fathers or other significant
positive male role models (as is the case of most of
the youth in foster care) violent crime increases.*

Where are the fathers and other male family
role models for these boys? In agrarian and village
societies, where economic conditions supported
the intact family, sons and fathers spent much time
together. The sons knew about their fathers' work.
It was visible to them. Boys were taught work
skills by their fathers and took on roles modeled
after their father as well as other elders.

But today's conditions are radically different.
Today's missing fathers are casualties themselves
of drugs and alcohol, bigotry, chronic poverty, violent environments, and inadequate education in a
highly competitive marketplace. Even many of the
so-called "successful" men in America are absent
from the lives of their sons. Workaholism, divorce,

---

[1]Rite of Passage, Inc. is a not for profit New York State Corporation.
[2]Corneau, G., (1991). *Absent Fathers, Lost Sons.* Boston: Shambhala Publications, Inc.

economic demands, and emotionally absent fathers all contribute to the average time men spend with their children: nine minutes per day.

THE NEED FOR A SPECIAL MENTORING APPROACH

These adolescents have special needs that can only be fulfilled by caring men if they are to successfully manage the transition into manhood.

A community of men, caring men, conscious men, responsible men, have come together with these adolescent boys with absent fathers for the purpose of initiating them into manhood—mentoring the boys as the man themselves become more whole as a result of their "fathering"—or perhaps the term should be "uncle-ing."

In tribal society, fathers rarely initiated their sons alone. It was the men of the entire *community* that performed these rites. Today's "rites" are being administered by such a group of men who have voluntarily come together to form a healing community as men and boys share metaphor, experience and bonding.

While many independent living skills programs attended by foster care adolescents address themselves to important "rites of passage" such as a high school diploma, obtaining gainful, productive, and hopefully meaningful employment and the material rewards that accompany such success—*young men need to be able to experience an internal process of initiation that includes the development of a balanced, principled, value-centered life, a solid sense of identity, a feeling of worth and direction, as well as aspirations and goals which can be fulfilled.* This process must also take into consideration issues of living amongst a diversity of cultures (racial harmony), relations with other men (beyond competitiveness), relations with woman (beyond sexism and woman bashing), and relations with nature (environmental awareness).

The *cross-cultural community of men* in **"Rite of Passage"** *demonstrate* their willingness to include these boys in this vital internal initiation process. It is amongst this community that the boys are learning to be responsible, productive citizens who live with integrity and make positive contributions to themselves, their families, their communities, and the world.

PROGRAM GOALS AND OBJECTIVES

The overall goal of the program is to facilitate the successful and holistic transition from adolescence into adulthood for boys in foster care. A secondary goal is to develop an innovative program model which can be replicated within the child welfare/foster care system as well as community-based organizations. The program is expected to have a positive impact on the educational, vocational, social, emotional, cultural, and spiritual lives of the participants.

PROGRAM DESCRIPTION

Phase I: Mentor Training

The **Rite of Passage** program recruits, screens, trains, and forms communities of male mentors from various ethnic and racial backgrounds for the purpose of bringing men together in community and then reaching out to mentor boys within the context of the community mentoring model.

There is a three-month training period in which men meet weekly in facilitator-led meetings of 2.5 hours each, with the emphasis on community building. Here, men have an opportunity to get to know each other on a deeper level than the culture traditionally fosters. Beyond talking sports, business, politics, conquests, and opinions, men share their authentic experiences, feelings, fears, emotional woundedness, passion, joy, aspirations, and purpose. They share their experience in relationships with wives, lovers, children, fathers, mothers, men, and women. And they focus on the question, "What does it mean to be a man in today's society?"

It is in these initial twelve meetings that the seeds of community are sown by skilled group facilitation. Using effective and tested models in the development of men's groups, the **Rite of Passage** facilitator creates an invaluable network of support for the men. It is a safe haven—a place where men can be who they truly are without the constraints of male competitive behavior. The men share something else as well; they share a purpose, a common vision for boys, and a shared stake in the future. It is this commitment, this shared action, which also bonds the men.

During this three-month period some men may opt out of the program ("deselect" themselves) as they learn more about what is entailed in being in community: the rigorous honesty necessary to make it work, showing up on a regular basis, the willingness to go beyond individual opinion and positionality to accomplish group tasks, the time commitment, being accountable, being one amongst many, and being vulnerable in front of other men.

Men who choose to continue on after this initial period undergo a rigorous weekend Mentor Training Program, which grounds the participants in the distinctions of "community," "mentor," and "rite of passage." Using initiative games and team-building exercises such as a low-ropes course, men experience the accomplishment of community tasks that no man could possibly do alone. These facilitator-led "games" followed by debriefing sessions further bond the group. Using the inquiry method, the men are asked, "Who do you need to BE to be in community?" "Who do you need to BE to be a mentor?" "Who do you need to BE to create an opening for boys to see and create a future for themselves that they had no idea existed?"

The training also includes presentations and discussion on the following relevant topics: adolescent development; the foster care experience; understanding the implications of abuse and neglect; effective problem solving; goal setting; techniques for support; building relationships with young men; establishing healthy boundaries and substance abuse issues.

During the training, the men undergo a "rite of passage" (a high-ropes course). Rites of passage are discussed from a sociological and histor-ical perspective and the men are invited to create additional rites of passage to experience throughout the year. This prepares the men for their role in creating a meaningful and appropriate rite of passage for the boys at the end of a year.

Mentor trainees perform a community service project at the training site followed by a discussion on "giving service." This aspect of the Mentor Training grounds the men in the creation of and the participation in giving service.

Giving service in the form of a community service project with men and boys is an important element of the **Rite of Passage** program.

Giving service—a profoundly integral part of the success of 12-Step programs—teaches putting the ego aside for the greater good, stepping outside of one's own problems to share the gifts that are inherently within us, and demonstrates that the way to receive is by giving. Giving service is also consistent with the spirit of volunteerism in America. Fifty percent of Americans volunteer in some fashion at some point in their lives.

Completion of the Training.   After completing the training, mentors make a one year *written* commitment to: attend two monthly meetings with the boys; attend two monthly meetings of men only; be available for individual meetings with an adolescent at least one time per month (minimum 2 hours); be available at least five weekend days per year for a retreat or camping trip or other special events.

Mentors also agree to being coached in the community mentoring process by the facilitator and to be accountable to the group as a whole.

Sufficient time for discussion (as much as is necessary) is spent on making the COMMITMENT. Clarity is of utmost importance. All community members must know what is expected of them and what they can expect from each other.

The training underscores the need for men to keep their word. Staying true to the commitment, doing what we say even when we *don't feel like* or when the *going gets tough* (and it will), is "what separates the men from the boys."

Phase II: Enter the Boys

Traditional mentoring programs match young people one on one with adults based on vocational/career interests and focus on the educational and employment dimension. This program emphasizes a *community* of responsible men sharing experiences with the boys on a wide variety of male-related issues in large and smaller group formats as well as individual one-to-one encounters. The advantages of this format are manyfold. A partial listing of positive outcomes follows.

1. The boys will witness men of cultural diversity willing to be a community. Largely, these boys live in monoracial communities unaccustomed to interacting on an intimate basis with people from other racial and ethnic backgrounds. This community mentoring experience will broaden their racial repertoire and enhance their fluidity in the world of work as well as prepare them for good citizenship in a racially diverse society.

2. The boys will witness men of different ideas at times "agreeing to disagree" and they will learn that differences are to be respected amongst men and, in fact, that difference adds vitality to community. The boys will witness and participate in conflict resolution processes, which are by definition nonviolent.

3. The boys will encounter men's discussion regarding difficulties and successes in relationships with women. Hearing the experience of men will underscore that relationships that work take commitment and are based on more than sexual energies. Frank discussion on relationship with conscious men will tend to soften the firm belief in the "masculine mystique" of many hypermasculine boys with absent fathers.

4. Boys will witness that white men and black men with no experience in foster care also have absent father issues. The boys are not alone with these issues. Feeling that other people can relate to a problem which one thought was unique to oneself is the beginning of coming out of isolation, sharing one's problem and being able to receive support from others. This is the beginning of healing the "father wound."

5. The boys will experience a sense of acceptance amongst a *community* of men. They will know that a group of "strangers" cared enough about themselves, the boys and the community at large to give them this gift of mentorship. The boys will know that if this experience is possible once, it can be replicated in the "real world."

6. The boys will have an opportunity to learn about the work lives of numerous adult males, which will be invaluable for them in their vocational choices and searches.

7. The boys will learn about the educational attitudes, accomplishments, and goals of many men. Sharing these experiences and how they relate to the world of work will serve to enlighten the boys *first hand.*

8. The young men will take their clue from the older men whether the community is a safe place to be, a safe place for true expression where self-doubts can safely be explored without mockery. This might well be the first time that this level of honesty is available for a young man and it is his opportunity to learn more about himself and connect with other men and boys.

9. The boys will witness the response from a community of men and other boys regarding their behavior that may be self-destructive, anti-social or generally nonproductive. Within a safe, nonjudgmental, group-facilitated environment, a boy will have the support necessary to weigh such behavior in relation to the wisdom of the group. This presents a unique "window of opportunity" for a boy to get outside himself and objectively view his actions, patterns, and attitudes.

10. A boy may receive support for *positive* behavior that he might ordinarily consider "not manly." This kind of support reshapes a boy's definition of what it is to be a man, thereby letting go of stereotypically rigid definitions, which tend to lead to self-limiting behaviors at best and violent antisocial acting out at worst.

11. The adolescents will be part of an experience in community building as members of the group (men and boys) have direct input in establishing ground rules and in planning for group activities. The boys will learn the dynamics of consensus; namely, that the group's decision may override a particular individual's choice without the threat of violating an individual's basic rights or necessitating the individual's exclusion from the group.

12. The boys will witness and participate in working side by side with men in special volunteer community projects, entrepreneurial projects, outdoor challenges such as a ropes course or camping trips, computer learning, and the art of self defense (aikido). They will learn how men work and how men play. It is the objective of the program to provide both an effective format for boys to transition into responsible adulthood while allowing for the opportunity to experiment at what works best *and* to establish a nation-wide model for replication.

CHAPTER 17

HUMAN SERVICES FOR OLDER ADULTS

KATHLEEN J. NICCUM

The "graying of America" is quite visible, with 21 percent of its population fifty-five years of age or older (Redmond, 1986). Within that statistic, 13 percent are over sixty-five, with the fastest growth in the nonwhite population, especially Latinos and Asian Americans (Gelfand and Yee, 1991). By the year 2030, it is expected that one-fifth of the population in the United States will be over sixty-five. The U.S. Department of Commerce (cited in Katz and Karuza, 1992) reports that the United States has the fourth largest population of adults sixty years of age and older in the world. The increasing number of older persons is creating a new market for service programs such as travel agencies, adult education, human services, and most aspects of health care.

Older adults are more different than alike. Physically and psychologically they age at different rates, and what is true for one seventy-year-old may not be true for another. Many people know older adults who are "old" at sixty and others who are "young" at eighty. A person's health, outlook on life, and agility often affect how old or young one feels. This is because the aging process is a combination of genetic and environmental factors which include one's activity level, attitude, diet, stress, and lifestyle.

PHYSICAL ASPECTS OF AGING

The aging process begins at conception and continues throughout one's lifetime. Many of the changes associated with the normal aging process are very slow and gradual. For instance, one's vision changes with age. Decline in visual acuity begins in early adulthood but usually does not interfere with a person's functioning until much later in life. By the age of fifty or fifty-five years, most people wear glasses or use reading glasses to accommodate the changes in their vision. The effects of aging on visual changes include: reduced visual acuity, reduced accommodation (decreased flexibility of the lens), reduced capacity to adjust to changes in illumination (dark adaptation), shift in color vision, and increased susceptibility to some types of visual illusions (Huyck and Hoyer, 1982).

A hearing loss may begin in one's early twenties and progress slowly throughout life. Approximately 30 percent of the older population in the United States is affected by a hearing loss, which can frequently be alleviated by the use of hearing aids. A major auditory loss that can occur later in life is called presbycusis, which is due largely to deteriorative changes in the middle ear. It mainly affects the discrimination of pitch (especially higher tones) and the threshold for hearing high-frequency tones.

The other senses also show a slight decline with age, although many people do not notice the changes. In addition, older adults tend to have less physical strength and stamina than younger people. In general, though, people adapt to the physical and perceptual changes of aging with little awareness of its process.

Although older adults are now healthier and live longer than they did at the turn of the century, they still account for over one-third of all health care costs. They continue to have more chronic conditions with arthritis, hypertension, and heart conditions as some of the most common ones (U.S. Senate, 1991). Even though 80 percent of older people have at least one chronic condition, only 20 percent of people sixty-five and older have some degree of disability associated with it (Katz and Karuza, 1992).

Alzheimer's disease, a progressive, degenerative disease that attacks the brain and results in impaired memory, thinking, and behavior, affects only 10 percent of the population over 65 years of age. However, more than 50 percent of nursing home residents have this disease or a related disorder. Early symptoms of the disease include forgetfulness, shortened attention span, trouble with simple math, difficulty expressing thoughts, changing or unpredictable moods, and a decreasing desire to try new things or meet new people. As the disease progresses, the symptoms become more debilitating and include: severe loss of memory (including dressing skills and names of family members and friends), mood and personality changes (including outbursts of anger and suspicion), total loss of judgment and concentration, an inability to complete routine household tasks, and the inability to care for personal hygiene.

A number of illnesses and conditions, such as drug reactions, thyroid problems, and malnutrition, may manifest similar symptoms to those of Alzheimer's disease. Thus, it is very important that people have thorough evaluations (physical, neurological, and psychological) to eliminate potential causes which might have a cure. Alzheimer's disease occurs when there are changes in the nerve endings and brain cells which interfere with normal brain functions. There are various theories about why these changes occur, but there is no conclusive cause of Alzheimer's disease. Likewise, there is no cure for this debilitating illness, although some treatment methods may slow down the progression of the disease (About Alzheimer's Disease, 1985).

PSYCHOLOGICAL ASPECTS OF AGING

Old age is a developmental stage of life. Exactly when this occurs depends upon which develop-

mental theory is being used or what resource is being referenced. There is no one consistent age range that identifies middle age or older adulthood among the lifespan theories or by society or the government. For instance, the Age Discrimination in Employment Act (ADEA) uses forty as the time when age discrimination occurs, while the government frequently uses the age of sixty-five for full entitlement to its aging programs, such as Medicare and Social Security. Other organizations, such as the American Association of Retired Persons (AARP) accepts members as young as fifty while many senior discount programs start at age sixty or sixty-five.

Often, it is presumed that older adults become more rigid, set in their ways, stubborn, grouchy, and crotchety as they age. These are stereotypes and are not supported by research related to the aging process. Grouchy seventy-year-olds were probably grouchy 20-year-olds. However, there are a number of emotional events, such as the death of a loved one or a move to a nursing home, which may affect behavior. Thus, it is important when working with older adults to avoid age stereotypes and to focus on the individual and his/her current circumstances.

Aging also has an effect on various aspects of intelligence. For example, crystallized intelligence (knowledge acquired through experience) depends on sociocultural influences and encompasses the skills one learns in school and through acculturation, including verbal comprehension, numerical skills, and the ability to perceive relationships and formal reasoning. Crystallized intelligence continues to improve with age (Peterson, 1983).

Fluid intelligence, on the other hand, refers to one's general mental ability independent of acquired knowledge, experience, or learning. It depends more on genetic endowment and consists of the ability to perceive complex relationships, use short-term memory, create concepts, and use abstract reasoning. Fluid intelligence begins to decline slightly during the middle years and slowly continues to decline throughout the remainder of life (Peterson, 1983).

Older adults often seem to have more diffi-culty learning and remembering information than younger people. Hayslip, Jr. and Kennelly (1985) suggest that age differences in learning may be a product of the interaction between cognitive and noncognitive influences. Cognitive influences refer to basic learning processes, including mem-ory function as it relates to learning, intelligence, and problem-solving skills. Noncognitive factors which affect learning include: (a) health, (b) the ability to see and hear, (c) the ability to under-stand and build upon past experiences, (d) energy level, (e) the ability to overcome the fear and inhi-bition that could limit involvement in the learning process, and (f) the motivation to learn (Lowy and O'Connor, 1986; Peterson, 1983).

Depression and low morale may create mem-ory complaints and decrease learning performance. Depression, which is prevalent in the older popula-tion, is frequently associated with the fear and anx-iety of real or anticipated losses. Many of these losses are indirectly related to aging, such as loss of income with retirement, loss of health with chronic conditions, and loss of family and friends through death. Biological changes within the cen-tral nervous system and the increase of physical ill-nesses, as well as the side effects of medications, also may contribute to the higher incidence of depression. Symptoms of depression include: changes in appetite (eating more or less); changes in sleep patterns (sleeping excessively or disruptive sleep); changes in activity level (decreased or agi-tated, purposeless); loss of interest in hobbies or usual activities; low self-esteem; guilt; decrease in ability to think, understand, and concentrate; and thoughts of suicide. In addition, older adults have more psychosomatic complaints, more frustration with memory impairment, withdrawal behaviors, apathy, and increased alcoholism (Frengley, 1987).

Overall, healthy aging means making adjust-ments and adapting to change as needed. In the later years of life, some changes, especially those associated with illness, may occur with little or no warning. Gradual changes in physical ability are easier to adapt to than sudden changes. However, a positive attitude, flexibility, and philosophical beliefs help many people to accept change, even sudden ones, and to continue to look forward to the future.

ECONOMIC ASPECTS OF AGING

Although there has been a steep decline in poverty for both men and women following the Social Security Act amendments in the 1960s, older women are much more likely to have incomes below the poverty level than men. In 1987, the poverty rate for older white women was 12.5 per-cent; for older white men, it was 6.8 percent; for African-American women, it was 40.2 percent; and for African-American men, it was 24.6 per-cent. Thus, older men and women often have dif-ferent financial and social resources available to them, some of which are influenced by gender and race (Hess, 1990).

The life expectancy for women is estimated to be seven years longer than for men. Although a portion of this difference in mortality can be explained by hormonal and genetic factors, much of it is due to acquired risks and health habits. However, as women increase their stress levels and acquire unhealthy habits, the difference in mortal-ity rates is beginning to narrow (Hess, 1990).

According to the U.S. Bureau of the Census (cited in Hess, 1990), American men who are 65 and older are almost twice as likely to be married than women of the same age group, who are three and a half times more likely to be widowed. Thus, more older women live alone and are more likely to enter a nursing home if an illness makes it dif-ficult to maintain their own home. In contrast, older men who become disabled are more apt to be cared for at home by their spouse. Thus, even though women usually live longer than men, they do not necessarily have a better quality of life.

CULTURAL ASPECTS OF AGING

Cultural diversity is a growing part of American life. Human service workers need to know about cultural and racial differences (among and within races and cultures) to best meet the needs of older minorities. For instance, within the Native American population, the elderly are respected, seen as a source of strength, and receive social support from their families. However, this may be less true for some families who do not live on a reservation (Yee, 1990).

The African-American population has traditionally been viewed as taking care of its own family. Many African-American older adults live in intergenerational families or at least help with child care. Throughout the years, African-American women have been a significant source of strength and support for their families. Thus, older women may be more respected than older men in the African-American culture (Yee, 1990).

Overall, the Latino/Hispanic population has a strong extended-family orientation which can provide a sense of belonging and security to its members. For this population, family often includes biological family members, as well as close friends and the godparents of any children. Godparents traditionally have social support privileges in addition to family responsibilities in the Latino culture (Yee, 1990).

Although there is diversity within and among minority groups, these populations share more similar life experiences with each other than they do with the white population. Most, if not all, of the minority populations have had experiences with racism, with its prejudices and stereotypes. They have been forced to have inner strength to help them adapt in their life struggles. In turn, these strengths have helped them adjust to their own aging challenges (Yee, 1990).

NURSING HOMES

Approximately 5 percent of people over the age of sixty-five live in long-term care institutions, primarily in nursing homes. Over 70 percent of nursing home residents are women (predominantly white women) and the majority are over eighty years of age. Although most older adults prefer to live in their own homes, they move to nursing homes when they are no longer able to live alone, when family members are unable or unwilling to assist them, or when there are no community services available to help meet their needs.

Adjusting to life in a nursing home is difficult for many people and requires a number of dramatic adjustments. There are major losses to handle including a decrease in independence, a loss of privacy, a decrease in a personal sense of control, a loss of personal possessions, an inability to come and go at will, and a drain on financial resources. Frequently, the nursing home is viewed as the place to die and, in reality, the majority of the residents never return to their homes or communities. Many nursing homes do not provide adequate mental stimulation or opportunities for independence, personal empowerment, socialization, community involvement, or independence.

AGE DISCRIMINATION

It was during the 1960s that Robert Butler (the former director of the National Institute on Aging) coined the term "ageism" to mean a process of systematically stereotyping and discriminating against people because they are old (Butler, 1975). Age discrimination, which is often more subtle than other forms of discrimination because of the false stereotypes that equate age with ability, has been prevalent for generations. Typical myths and stereotypes include: (1) aging is a constant downhill decline, (2) older people are unproductive, (3) there is a marked decline in intelligence after middle age, (4) people get senile as they age, and (5) older people cannot learn new things.

Age discrimination has hampered the ability of many older people to obtain employment or to further their careers. To address ageism problems the Age Discrimination in Employment Act (ADEA) was passed in 1967 to promote employment based on ability rather than age. It has been amended since that time and presently prohibits discrimination on the basis of age in hiring; job retention; compensation; and other terms, conditions, and privileges of employment. It protects workers who are forty years of age and older, and it has eliminated mandatory retirement for all but a few careers which are still being studied for safety factors. Even though research has been refuting age stereotypes as early as the 1920s and 1930s, many ageist beliefs still remain today.

Older Workers

The labor force is getting older and employers are beginning to recognize that older workers are an untapped resource. Presently, approximately 30 percent of workers leave their careers while in their late fifties or early sixties. For those who are sixty-five and older, 46 percent were employed in 1950, compared to 16 percent in 1988 (The Older Worker, 1988). Although people are retiring younger, many retired people start new careers or look for part-time work that offers flexibility in days and hours of work. Older adults are now healthier, better educated, better informed, and more active than in the past, which makes them better candidates for continued employment—barring age discrimination.

As the work force gets older and the labor pool of young people shrinks, employers are being challenged to address the issue of employing and training older workers. A number of studies indicate that many managers foster some prejudices toward older workers. For example, a 1985 study by AARP concluded that overall, human resource managers perceived older workers positively and valued their experience, knowledge, work habits, and attitudes. However, the managers also harbored some negative perceptions which included the view that older workers were resistant to change, had physical limitations, did not learn new tasks quickly, and were not comfortable with new technology (AARP, 1987). Another survey of corporate managers found that managers said they valued both older and younger workers. However, they believed there were more difficulties in changing older workers, did not attribute positive motives to older workers

who desired retraining, favored the career development of younger workers, and viewed the older worker as less likely to be promoted (Peterson and Coberly, 1988).

Overall, the work performance of older workers does not support the above negative beliefs. In general, the attitudes and work behaviors of older employees are compatible with effective organizational functioning. Older workers have greater job satisfaction and greater loyalty to their organization, resulting in a lower turnover rate than that of younger employees. Furthermore, the rate of absenteeism for healthy older adults is less than their younger counterparts. The older population also has fewer injuries on the job, but if there is an injury, the recovery time is longer (Doering et al., 1983).

Older Clients

It is important for human service workers to understand the aging process and to avoid the trappings of ageism with its myths and stereotypes. It also is helpful to know that negative attitudes, low self-esteem, and depression may be barriers to learning, seeking social services, or participating in counseling or activity programs.

Human service workers will benefit from assessing the individual needs of the older adult/client with whom they work. It will be helpful to gain information about the person's background, past experiences, culture, strengths, limitations, interests, needs, and motivation level. This information can then be incorporated into the planning of training/retraining programs, educational or activity programs, and intervention and social service programs.

Developing rapport, trust, and respect is vital in building a relationship with an older person. Often, the human service worker will be younger than the client, thus making it important to establish one's credibility. It is critical to never "talk down" to an older client, even if the person suffers from Alzheimer's disease or another form of dementia.

When working with people who have hearing problems, be sure that the person has heard the entire question or instruction to avoid inappropriate responses. If the person asks to have information repeated, it may help to lower voice pitch. This will benefit those who cannot hear higher frequency pitch and who have difficulty distinguishing vowels and soft consonants such as *s, p, f, th, sh,* and *ph.* Also, it is helpful to face the hearing impaired person when talking, to talk slower, and to have the person's attention before beginning to speak.

PROGRAMMING TECHNIQUES

Research in Gerontology (the study of aging) has shown that healthy older people continue to learn as they age. However, they may benefit from the use of specific teaching techniques to enhance their learning. Many adults become more cautious with age which makes it appear that they need more time to do tasks and to answer questions (less likely to guess). Thus, they will need more time and encouragement to respond in learning situations.

Older adults also may benefit from teaching techniques which help them organize information to be remembered. Often, they are less likely to spontaneously organize new information as a way to aid remembering it. A helpful tool could be the use of advance organizers which involve organizing information into categories, sequences, or relationships. Examples of advance organizers which human service workers might use during an educational program include providing handouts on a given topic, a written outline of what will be covered during a training session, or verbally giving an overview of the program's agenda.

Older adults also need more time to recall information once it is learned. When planning programs for this population, it is helpful to use a slower pace, incorporate their previous knowledge and experience when possible, focus on one task at a time, avoid time limits, and give lots of positive feedback. In addition, repeating and rephrasing information during a learning session will enhance its retention. Mediators, which involve the association of a word to be learned with some other word, image, or story, is another example of how to increase learning performance. Also, short breaks may be beneficial if the learning activity lasts more than 30 minutes (Sterns and Doverspike, 1987; Peterson, 1983).

The use of concrete examples and maintaining a clear focus may be helpful in individual/group counseling, discussion groups, and educational programs with older adults. This type of approach may decrease anxiety, enhance the understanding of the client, and assist in staying on topic. Older adults may benefit from learning to set goals and time lines, use brainstorming techniques, and address specific problems. There may be a tendency for the client to ramble and talk about a number of problems, so the human service worker will need to help the client stay focused for the best results.

Older persons' past experiences may block, modify, or enhance their participation in various kinds of programs. For instance, they may be reluctant to participate in government entitlement programs or social service programs because of their pride and belief that seeking help is a sign of weakness. They may not seek counseling because of a previously learned belief that they should be able to deal with their own problems, or that "normal" people do not receive help. They may not participate in educational programs because they have the misperception that they are too old to learn. In learning situations, if they have been taught to do a task a certain way, it may take a great deal of time to unlearn the task and then to relearn to do it another way. Or, they may resist learning something that is contrary to what they had learned previously, thus making it difficult to integrate the new information (Harvey and Jahns, 1988).

Past experiences, however, also can make learning more meaningful. For example, sometimes it is easier to apply information to a new task if there is a way to relate to it. Likewise, past experience can provide a bridge for combining the old with the new, especially if the new knowledge now makes the old information more meaningful and useful (Sterns and Doverspike, 1987).

A desire to participate and learn is important for learning to take place at any age. Older adults may have an interest in learning but fear failing at the task, be anxious about participating, or believe that they are not able to learn new information. In mixed age groups, they may fear failing in the eyes of their peers or doing less well than younger participants. Human service workers will need to be aware of the potential reluctance of older clients to enroll in programs. To encourage participation, the human service worker may need to change the format of a program or help the clients work through the reasons they are hesitant to get involved.

Research has shown that age decrements in learning ability are affected by health, as defined by the presence of chronic disease such as coronary artery disease, arteriosclerosis, and hypertension. In addition to poor health, chronically ill people may be depressed, have low morale, and more fatigue than their healthy peers, which can impair their learning. Although knowledge can be empowering and can aid decision-making skills for most people, it is imperative for chronically ill people. Providing patient education can help people to understand the physical and psychological aspects of their illness and may help them to maintain independence and a sense of control over their lives. Human service workers will need to account for chronic conditions whenever they program activities, educational tasks, or other services for chronically ill older adults.

The physical setting where older adults receive services, educational programs, or come to participate in activities is important to consider when programming for this population. For a community-based group, the place should be on a bus line, have parking close to the building, and be handicap accessible. In any setting, the room should be free from noise distractions. The noise level could hinder the learning process, since some older adults may not hear well or their attention may be drawn toward the noise rather than attending to what is being said. In addition, increased lighting is needed to compensate for potential visual problems and glares. Also, because of poor circulation, many older adults prefer a warm room with temperatures often in the upper seventies.

Some equipment and teaching materials may need to be considered differently for older age groups. As people get older, certain colors such as dark green, blue, and violet become harder to see as the lens of the eyes become yellow. However, red, yellow, and orange stay more vivid and, thus, become the preferred colors to use on flipcharts and printed material. It also helps to use large print, write legibly, and have a contrast between the paper and ink. If using film projectors, be aware that it takes a longer time for older adults to adapt to light and darkness. Thus, it will help to wait a short time to start a film after the lights have been dimmed. After a film, lighting should be restored slowly, and there should be a short interval before people get up and move around.

When working with older adults who live in nursing homes, the human service worker should address the psycho-social needs of the residents and help them feel empowered in their restricted environment. Also, it is important to avoid both labeling residents as patients and focusing on their illnesses. Residents need to have mental, physical, and social stimulation regardless of their mental status. They need to have individualized care plans that reflect their individual needs (medical and emotional), and they need to be treated with respect. It is important, too, for residents to have a sense of personal control, to make choices, to have privacy, to have a support network, and to participate in their care as much as possible. Although some residents are not alert to time and place, they still should be treated as adults with dignity and respect. Overall, human service workers help older clients in a number of different ways. They may provide educational programs or training sessions geared toward the needs of older learners. They may assist with retirement issues, the adjustment to widowhood, or other issues related to the aging process. In addition, they may help older clients learn new skills, develop new hobbies, expand their interests, and learn how to empower and enrich their lives.

JOB OPPORTUNITIES

As the population ages, more social services will be needed to meet the needs of older adults. Human service agencies will need to target more efforts toward the rural and the minority elderly. These two populations may need more assistance than the general older population but may be more reluctant to ask for help. Human service workers may have to do more home visits and learn about the older client's culture to establish a supportive, therapeutic relationship. It also may be helpful to become fluent in a second language, such as Spanish, to decrease the language barrier when working with minority clients (such as Latinos) who may still be struggling to learn English. Many programs will be aimed at helping people maintain their independence which, in turn, may help to maintain or increase their self-image or self-esteem.

There is an increasing need for case management skills to plan and organize services and resources needed by many older adults to remain independent. This may involve coordinating and integrating a variety of services from different programs. For instance, a person may need low-cost housing; Meals-on-Wheels (a program that delivers hot meals to older adults in their homes or at a designated site); assistance with medication costs; transportation; and involvement in a social, therapeutic program to decrease loneliness, isolation, and depression.

Working with older adults can provide an enriching experience and an opportunity to learn from the wisdom and life experiences of the client. Human service workers who want to work with older adults can find employment in a variety of settings. For instance, they may want to work in a corporation and assist in providing training/retraining programs, wellness programs, or elder-care services. In a long-term care facility (retirement center or nursing home), a human service worker might work as an activity director, social services director, coordinator of volunteers, admission coordinator, or marketing coordinator. There also are employment opportunities in senior citizen centers, adult day-care programs, community multi-service centers, area agencies on aging, home-care programs, respite programs, and organizations which provide advocacy services. In addition, human service workers may be involved in programs that provide training and education; counseling and group work; crisis intervention; or helping older clients access community resources such as housing, transportation, and financial assistance.

Human service workers who have an interest in working with older adults may find employment opportunities by completing a two-year associate degree or a four-year baccalaureate degree. Some colleges also offer a Gerontology Certificate which requires a student to take a certain number of courses in Gerontology and complete a practicum in a setting with older adults. It will be beneficial for human service workers who work with older adults to understand the aging process (physical, psychological, and sociological aspects) and to know how to use specific techniques which enhance learning in later life. In addition, knowledge about cultural diversity, advocacy, and caregiver issues will be important.

The large number of baby boomers (those born between 1946–1964) have had a major effect on the trends of society through each of their developmental stages. As they get older, they will influence how older adults are viewed and what services will be available. Older adults are now healthier and wealthier, and are apt to stay in the mainstream of society. It is likely they will demand more community services, leisure services, receive more retirement education, have second and third careers, and require more health services. It is an exciting and challenging time to be working with older adults and there should be ample employment opportunities for human service workers in a variety of settings.

REFERENCES

About Alzheimer's Disease, (1985). South Deerfield, MA: Channing L. Bete Co.

American Association of Retired Persons, (1987). *Workers 45+: Today and Tomorrow.* Washington, DC: American Association of Retired Persons.

Butler, R.N., (1975). *Why Survive? Being Old in America.* New York: Harper and Row.

Doering, M., S. Rhodes, and M. Schuster, (1983). *The Aging Worker: Research and Recommendations.* Oklahoma City, OK: Sage.

Frengley, J.D., (1987). "Depression." *Generations* 12 (1):29–33.

Gelfand, D., and B.W.K. Yee, (1991). "Trends and Forces: Influence of Immigration, Migration, and Acculturation on the Fabric of Aging in America." *Generations* 15(4):7–10.

Harvey, R.L., and I.R. Jahns, (1988). "Using Advance Organizers to Facilitate Learning among Older Adults." *Educational Gerontology* 14, 89–93.

Hayslip, B. Jr., and K.J. Kennelly, (1985). "Cognitive and Noncognitive Factors Affecting Learning among Older Adults." In B. Lumsden, ed. *The Older Adult as Learner* (73–98). New York: Hemisphere.

Hess, B.B., (1990). "Gender & Aging: The Demographic Parameters." *Generations* 14(3): 12–15.

Huyck, M.H., and J.J. Hoyer, (1982). *Adult Development and Aging.* Madison, WI: Wm. C. Brown.

Katz, P.R., and J. Karuza, (1992). "Service Delivery in an Aging Population: Implications for the Future." *Generations* 16(4):49–54.

Lowy, L., and D. O'Connor, (1986). *Why Education in the Later Years?* New York: Macmillan.

Peterson, D.A., (1983). *Facilitating Education for Older Learners.* San Francisco: Jossey-Bass.

Peterson, D., and S. Coberly, (1988). "The Older Worker: Myths and Realities." In R. Morris and S. A. Bass, eds. *Retirement Reconsidered: Economic and Social Roles for Older People.* New York: Springer, pp. 116–128.

Redmond, R.X., (1986). "The Training Needs of Older Workers." *Vocational Education Journal* 61, 38–40.

Special Committee on Aging, United States Senate, (1991). *Developments in Aging: 1990 Volume 1* (Rept. 102–28, Vol. 1), Washington, DC: U.S. Government Printing Office.

(1988, December 22). "Labor Trends." CD Publications, Silver Springs, MO. J. Van Ryzin, ed. *The Older Worker.* p. 7.

Sterns, H.L., and D. Doverspike, (1987). "Training and Developing the Older Worker: Implications for Human Resource Management." In H. Dennis, ed. *Fourteen Steps in Managing an Aging Workforce.* New York: Lexington, pp. 97–109.

Yee, B.W.K., (1990). "Gender & Family Issues in Minority Groups." *Generations* 14(3):39–42.

CHAPTER 18

HUMAN SERVICES
FOR HOMELESS PEOPLE

LORENCE A. LONG

PROLOGUE

Before 1980, homeless people in the United States numbered a relatively few substance abusers and some unhospitalized people with a mental illness. Since that date, a number of factors, including the booming cost of real estate, a shrinking job market with declining real wages, and expanding substance abuse joined with other factors to multiply the numbers and types of homeless people. An industry has developed to meet their needs. This chapter is a description of the programs, workers, and clients who participate in that industry.

DESCRIPTION OF THE PROBLEM

A homeless person is one who has no right to a living space. Other people do have such rights, through ownership, payment of rent, or through an enforceable relationship with a person who has the right to be in a particular living space (see Jahiel, 1992, Chapter 1, for a discussion of official definitions).

Thus a person who pays rent to live in a farm shed is homeless because the shed is not a living space. Residency in the shed could not be enforced, even though the person paid rent. Following the same train of thought, a person who lives in a car or in a subway tunnel is homeless, because the space is not legally a dwelling.

For a different reason, a person who is staying in a friend's apartment is homeless or at the edge of homelessness, because he or she may be ousted from the living space at the whim of the friend. The most recent prior residence of homeless people has usually been someone else's living space where the homeless person was staying temporarily, and was then asked to leave.

Homelessness is a problem that almost never appears by itself. People become homeless because of another problem: family conflict, substance abuse, unemployment, low income, mental illness, physical illness, and so forth. Thus, there is no single pattern or cause of homelessness, and no standard approach or service that would be effective for all homeless people.

Once a person becomes homeless, she or he may have very different experiences than other homeless people. Some people live on the street, while others live in shelters or with friends. Each of these situations has its special challenges, and each influences the homeless person in certain ways.

If a person goes through many difficult experiences while being homeless, these may limit the person's ability to resume life in his or her own living space. Those homeless people who must make the most profound adjustment to their status would be those persons who live outdoors or in a nonliving space, such as in a subway tunnel. In order to survive in these settings, a person must adjust to the following conditions:

- the fear of abuse or attack.
- the need to be constantly alert, with little sleep.

- the difficulty of surviving extremes of weather.
- the lack of a balanced diet.
- strained relations with other people.

Making these adjustments over a period of time has the paradoxical effect of making being indoors unbearable to many such survivors.

Living in shelters often has its own drawbacks. These may include bullying by other residents (or groups of residents), actual physical or sexual abuse, and theft of belongings by residents or staff. Lack of privacy is very common in shelters, as is the regimentation—everyone must do everything at the same time and in the same way—that usually accompanies institutional living. Overcrowding may make all of the above factors worse. There may be no organized activities or services, and badly prepared food. The general lack of resources tends to create dependence on the staff for every small attention or service, sometimes accompanied by dictatorial or preferential treatment by staff members.

Staying with friends or relatives may also have its problems, especially if the living space is overcrowded. Tensions between those living together may reach a point where conflict breaks out and the homeless person must leave. This type of accommodation is frequently the first stop on a series of steps within homelessness. A common transition to homelessness begins with staying in one or more friends' apartments, and then moves on to shelters or the street as these temporary arrangements break down.

The task of surviving as a homeless person may keep the person from having any time, energy, or motivation to address the problem that led to homelessness in the first place.

SOME TYPES OF HOMELESS PERSONS

Here is a thumbnail sketch of a "typical" homeless person:

Luke lives in a cardboard box behind a maintenance shed at the local cemetery. He avoids contact with other people, but keeps up a busy conversation with himself. He gets enough to eat by sifting through the dumpsters at several local restaurants. He has severe skin problems from poor personal sanitation, body vermin, and exposure.

Here is another "typical" homeless person:

Francine is staying with her two children in the Salvation Army's family shelter. She fled her abusive husband in another city. She came here, hoping he wouldn't track her down. One of her children is very restless and active, unable to stay still for more than a moment. The other child has a severe case of asthma. Both have been out of school for a month and a half while Francine has been traveling from place to place (Molnar, 1988).

Consider a third "typical" homeless person:

Dorothy is living in the big city for the first time. She is staying in an abandoned warehouse with four other teenagers, also runaways or throwaways. She left her home in the Midwest to avoid the screaming fights she had with her aunt who has raised her since she was six months old. The fights were mostly over Dorothy's boyfriends and what time Dorothy should come home on a school night. Dorothy is supporting herself by providing (mostly) oral sex to men who drive down the Boulevard looking for young women to do what Dorothy does.

Perhaps less obvious types of homeless people would be:

- Juan, who works full-time, but doesn't make enough money to afford a room or apartment.
- Steve and Rose, a husband and wife whose family of five is staying doubled-up in his brother's apartment while he looks for another job.
- Joyce, a woman with three children who now lives in a shelter for single women because her children were taken away when her substance abuse got in the way of her parenting.
- Jack, a Vietnam-era veteran who begs on one of the main streets for quarters to support his habit of smoking rock cocaine.
- Tasha, a pregnant young woman who was ordered to leave her mother's house when her condition was discovered.

The list of situations could go on and on. Each is different in some important way from the others.

SERVICES FOR HOMELESS PEOPLE

The types of services that homeless people need are as varied as the types of situations they experience. Their most important needs are those common to every person:

Food	Housing	Clothing
Medical care	Income	Employment
Bath or shower facilities	A dependable routine	Belonging to other persons and a place
Safety	Privacy	

Note that "shelter" is not listed as a general human need. While shelter is useful as a temporary aid for persons who have no place at all, it is not adequate as a long-term arrangement. People need housing, which may be defined as a living space where a person or her/his family has a right to be. Such a place must be safe, secure, private, and adequate in terms of space, temperature, and accessibility.

Some homeless people may also need the following:

Education	Job training	Social services
Substance abuse treatment	Supervised housing	Psychiatric treatment
Rehabilitation services	Individual or family counseling	Case management services

To be effective, services must be delivered in a manner that the homeless person will accept. In providing services to Luke, for example, the service must take into account his extreme discomfort in relating to other people. He has made many adjustments to succeed at living outdoors. If he is to begin to live in a more customary way, he has to adopt a whole new set of behaviors.

What will work with Luke? Should he be approached boldly with requests for immediate change, or gently over a period of time? Which of the many services he needs—mental health, personal sanitation, nutrition, housing, etc.—should come first? Can these services be delivered where he is, or will he have to come indoors in order to receive them?

Some Types of Services for Homeless People

The range of services for homeless or near-homeless people is very broad. If homelessness is viewed as a process, rather than a state of being, some services are aimed at the early part of the process. These include:

Eviction Prevention Services. Many tenants become homeless because they do not know their rights. The landlord usually has a lawyer to facilitate the eviction process, but the tenant often does not have a legal representative. Private or public funds may be used to ensure that tenants' rights are safeguarded, and that unwarranted evictions do not occur.

Diversion Services. Interventions by this type of program involve the anticipation or interruption of the homelessness process by reaching out to offer resources or counseling to those likely to become homeless or who are at the point of homelessness. The resources might include providing money to pay a high rent, money to pay back rent, family crisis counseling, or conflict resolution services. (Note that many common supports and services fulfill the diversion function. Helping a person who is unemployed get a job, providing family counseling, providing financial support through public assistance, and overcoming discrimination in housing and employment all lessen the likelihood that people will become homeless.)

Special challenges for planners and workers in providing these services include how to identify those individuals or families most at risk so that action can be taken before they cross over the line into homelessness. Another obstacle to overcome is the difficulty that community leaders and funders have in conceptualizing and devoting resources to preventive, rather than remedial—the more common tendency—services (National Housing Institute, 1993).

Once a person does become homeless, other types of services may be available. In some communities, these may be the only types of services that exist. Services vary enormously from community to community. Some localities do their best to deny any support to homeless people on the theory that homeless people will then go elsewhere.

Some of the types of services for people who are homeless are:

Shelters.   Shelters may be buildings devoted to temporarily housing homeless people, or they may be hotels, motels, or other lodging places that are used for the same purpose. Shelters may have one-day stay limits or may allow guests to remain indefinitely as long as they obey the rules. Since shelters are often crowded and usually provide little or no privacy to their guests, many people cannot tolerate the closeness, noise, confusion, and conflict that result.

Some shelters are structured as transitional shelters, introducing the guest to programming that prepares the guest to live in permanent housing. The program may include orientation to tenant-landlord relations, rent-paying, minor maintenance of an apartment or room, connection with services and other resources in the neighborhood where the client will live, and so forth. The success of transitional shelters is closely related to the availability of decent, affordable, permanent housing when the client has completed the program.

Workers in shelters need to find ways to help guests move toward permanent housing even though staying in the shelter may provide more benefits for the guest. This must not be done through making life in the shelter miserable for them, but through helping them prepare to move on. Another type of challenge is to treat guests fairly—which does not always mean treating each one exactly the same. Some shelter staff members find themselves treating all guests punitively when one or two of them are guilty of breaking rules. This approach can create a residence where everyone is miserable. The alternative is to (a) get to know the guests as soon as they enter, (b) form relationships with them,

(c) observe them systematically during their stay, and (d) involve guests in governance issues so that they can help the staff make decisions about rule-breaking.

Food Programs.   Food programs may be involved in preparing and offering food directly to homeless people, or they may be networks of scavengers and suppliers who locate and distribute free or inexpensive food to the direct providers.

Food pantries are one type of direct service food program. They provide unprepared food to both homeless and housed poor people who prepare and consume the food off the premises of the food pantry. Soup kitchens, a second type, cook and serve meals to homeless people and others who appear at a specified time or day.

Food suppliers to homeless services may gather, store, and distribute government surplus foods, leftover prepared food from restaurants or caterers, and private donations of food from manufacturers and food producers. They supply soup kitchens, food pantries, and shelters. These programs address a problem of hunger that is wider than homelessness.

Some homeless people qualify for U.S. government food stamps. In some cases when they are living in shelters, they pool their purchases so that everyone living there may enjoy a better menu.

Challenges for those who work in this area include providing for the special dietary needs of people who may have been severely malnourished in the recent past. It is essential to offer the appropriate foods to some who may need special diets because of diabetes or other medical conditions. Another challenge is providing sound nutrition for pregnant women and for young children and infants.

Health Care.   Because of their exposure to severe weather conditions, poor nutrition, lack of personal sanitation, and risk of injury, many homeless people have serious medical problems.

Their lack of access to regular medical care over a period of time may mean that conditions that would ordinarily be easily treated have advanced to a critical state. In addition, standard health care services for poor people impose conditions— repeated visits, long waits, fragmented care, impersonal or condescending service—that present insuperable barriers to participation by homeless people.

All of these conditions have led to the development of special medical services for homeless people. These services typically make themselves available in shelters, soup kitchens and day programs where homeless people gather. They offer more personal attention and are attuned to the typical problems and attitudes of their patients. The services offer direct medical care and screen for more serious problems that may require referral to a hospital or substance abuse program. In many cases, the medical service tries to establish Medicaid eligibility for a patient, partly to garner reimbursement for the services it provides, and also to give the homeless person access to other medical facilities.

Among the challenges for human services workers in this area are:

— Making a successful referral to a standard medical service, given the bureaucratic barriers that keep many people from getting the medical help they need.

— Achieving a helpful balance between exasperation at the behavior that has led to the homeless person's overlapping emotional, medical and social problems, and a too-sympathetic provision of service without raising expectations for changes in self-destructive behavior.

— Avoiding being manipulated to provide medicines that may be sold on the street to get money for drink or drugs.

Substance Abuse Programs.   Abuse of alcohol or some illegal drug may lead a person to become homeless as she or he becomes increasingly unable to focus on paying rent or working steadily. Substance abuse may also develop into a problem after a person has become homeless (Wright,

1989, p. 99). The homeless person may try to deal with depression, low self-esteem, symptoms of mental illness, physical pain, or other problems through the use of drugs or alcohol. Substance abuse then makes it difficult for the person to be willing to face the emotional challenge of getting his or her life together. It is easier to continue with the lifestyle that is buffered by the substance abuse.

Many shelters and other homeless programs deal with substance abuse by simply barring all persons who have obviously taken too much of some mind- or mood-altering substance. The person may be required to stay out for a stated period of time. This protects the shelter from the fighting, damage, and demoralization that often accompany on-premises substance abuse. In a few cases, it may bring the excluded person to realize that substance abuse must be stopped. More often, substance abuse continues until the person suffers an accident or health emergency. Then the person is taken to a hospital for treatment, and there is an opportunity to raise the question of substance abuse treatment when the patient has recovered from the injury or ailment that brought him or her into the hospital.

It is impossible to provide substance abuse treatment while a person is "living rough," as the English call living outdoors. The street dweller must be housed, either in a hospital (perhaps for detoxification) or in a low-expectation shelter while her or his nutrition, personal sanitation, and level of fear are brought near normal. These changes alone may produce positive personality and behavior changes. Once the person is stabilized, expectations can be raised. Group and individual counseling sessions, assessment of mental and physical health needs, detoxification, and other processes may begin. The person may be moved to another shelter or to a place within the same shelter where abstinence is expected. This is a high-status program which is clean, pleasant, and may offer various perks in terms of flexible routines, small stipends, better food, etc. Alcoholics Anonymous-type groups will probably be an important aspect of the program. Referrals may be made to residential drug or alcohol treatment programs. As the person makes further progress, referrals to permanent housing may be made, and work begun on helping the person define and realize other personal goals.

The most difficult challenge for workers in this area is the high relapse rate of their clients. Workers must learn not to take such failures personally, and to hope that the next time the client abstains, he or she will be able to maintain abstinence for a longer period of time.

Mental Health Services. Many commentators on the problem of homelessness have blamed psychiatric hospitals for contributing to the problem of homelessness by discharging long-time patients who should have been kept in the hospital (Torrey, 1988). It would be more accurate to say that psychiatric wards and hospitals contribute to the severity of homelessness by refusing to admit people with mental illnesses until they reach a critical state of danger to themselves and others. The person who is simply incapable of self-care is not eligible for hospitalization, in most cases. Most of the mentally ill people who are homeless have never been hospitalized, or have been hospitalized only briefly. Psychiatric emergency room responses to a mentally ill homeless person may be to send the person back to the streets with a supply of medication, but no support.

Mental health outreach and treatment teams have been organized to provide services to sheltered and unsheltered homeless persons. These teams gently and nonthreateningly build relationships of trust with mentally ill homeless people, often by providing food or some other simple service in a nondemanding manner. Their clients often are so distrustful of other people that building such relationships takes a very long time. Once a relationship has been established, the team would provide a further service that the homeless client recognizes as something needed. Step is built upon step, until the person is willing

to go to get services, and eventually enter a day program or a residence.

The mental health team may go so far as to bring medication to the homeless person who is living outdoors, establishing a pattern of regular administration of the medication. Experience has shown that it is very difficult to maintain consistent medication patterns in unstructured living situations. The team would also be prepared to call in the appropriate authorities to commit the homeless person to a hospital if the person's condition were to become dangerous.

As with medical services, a challenge for workers in this area is to balance sympathy for the client's problems with a demand for cooperation and self-care in a ratio that helps the person move forward without being scared off.

Social Services. Social services help to bridge the gap between the homeless person and the network of services that exist to assist the person. Connecting the person with publicly-funded benefits, with family members, with shelters, with counseling, meals, medical care, mental health care, and many other resources is the job of the social services team.

Social service workers have historically had the freedom to move from behind a desk or outside a service organization's building to overcome the limitations of bureaucratic boundaries and limited perspectives.

Social service workers are required to develop expertise in a number of roles. These include intake, in which the client's needs are identified and plans are made for the work the agency will do with the client. A second role is that of finding resources, such as housing, income, medical care or other resources that are not available within the agency. The third role is the one of referral, in which an attempt is made to make a positive connection between the client and the outside organization that can supply the client's needs. If an obstacle arises to meeting the person's needs, the worker may become an advocate, who speaks for the client or a whole class of clients in order to get the needed resource.

The social service worker may also function as a counselor, helping clients to focus when they are confused, or helping them to sort out their preferred choices among various alternatives.

There is a special type of social service worker called a case manager. This worker coordinates the process of meeting all of the needs that a particular client has. This may involve making comprehensive plans with and for the client, contacting a number of different organizations, and arranging contacts between the client and the organizations so that they don't make conflicting recommendations or requirements as the client's needs are addressed.

Special challenges for workers in social services are related to the multiple problems that homeless people have. These problems may have become quite severe over time. In addition, organizations that provide the services that are needed may place obstacles in the way of serving the client. In some communities, the needed services—especially affordable housing, or housing with supportive services—do not exist.

Job-Related Services.   Helping a person end his or her homelessness involves connecting the person with an income. For some people, the income will be derived from disability payments or public assistance. But even those who are disabled may be capable of supporting themselves through work. This service is one that comes toward the end of the homeless process, after medical, mental health and at least temporary housing needs are met.

People who have been homeless for a period of time may need more than help in getting a job. They may need job readiness training, which provides job-like activities to help the homeless person accept the time structures that are so important to employers: regular attendance and on-time attendance. Job readiness may also address issues such as acceptable dress, grooming, résumé, speech patterns, and attitudes toward supervisors

and co-workers. In addition, work skills may need to be taught or polished. Practical problems, such as child care, money for transportation, an address for responses to applications and other, similar factors may need to be arranged.

Self-confidence may need to be built up through worklike activities in nonwork settings. Many shelters and other homeless programs involve clients in helping activities in order to build their self-confidence.

For clients who are disabled, some special rehabilitative measures may be appropriate. One of these may be the provision of a job coach, whose duties are to accompany the trainee to a regular work site, to teach the required skills on the job, and to help the person reach competitive levels of work. The job coach then gradually leaves the site to train another person elsewhere.

The most distressing special challenge for workers in this area is that even good training cannot overcome the problems of a poor economy. This factor is exacerbated by the fact that racial or ethnic discrimination may deny well-prepared candidates opportunities to learn or to demonstrate their skills. The stigma of homelessness may accompany the potential employee to the workplace, and limit her or his chances to relate professionally to employer, colleagues, and customers.

Education Services for Homeless Children. Just as adults need jobs, children need an education. Homelessness, by requiring families to move from one area to another, breaks up the relationship between children and their schools. Homeless parents are often completely occupied with carrying out the survival tasks of the family, or overwhelmed with a sense of failure, so that the educational needs of their children are neglected.

Shelters where children will be temporarily housed sometimes develop one-room schools to provide tutoring and informal classes. Such efforts cannot replace the resources of a regular school. However, homeless children admitted to regular schools are often subjected to the scorn of other children. They often try to keep the others from learning of their homeless status.

Challenges for workers in this area stem primarily from the interruptions in orderly schooling that children have experienced, leaving them behind others in their garde levels in many instances. In addition, a worker may form a strong educational relationship with a child, only to have the child disappear from the school or the community when the family either chooses or is forced to move on.

Legal Services.   In many communities, services for homeless people are difficult to access. Bureaucratic barriers may make it difficult to get benefits to which homeless persons may be entitled. Legal services provide information, instruction, and, when necessary, legal action to enable the homeless individuals to qualify for these benefits. Often nonlawyers are trained in the procedures that are necessary to prepare individuals to present their claims.

In addition, homeless people as a class may be treated badly or refused services they need in a particular community. In many cases, it has been through the efforts of advocates who have brought suits to compel communities to provide what homeless people need that any support or accommodation was offered to them at all. In some cases, the suits merely sought protection for homeless people to be free from harassment by police forces and other municipal employees.

One challenge facing workers in this area is frustration that the original plaintiff may not enjoy justice, even if the case is won. Lawsuits often take years to resolve. The original plaintiffs may not be around to benefit from the decision, if it is favorable. Lawsuits may also create a situation in which officials can claim that they can do nothing until the lawsuit is resolved.

Courts have been reluctant to compel states and cities to spend money to provide services. Results of court actions have often been minimal or only made after months and years of delay. (For a fuller discussion, see Hopper, 1990.)

Having said this, it must be recognized that it is often only through court action that any positive movement toward justice has occurred. Bringing a suit can sometimes create a climate in which officials take action to solve the problem, making the case moot.

Housing.   In the late 1970s and the 1980s, the price of housing in the United States reached a very high level. Inexpensive apartments in urban areas became attractive to middle-class city-dwellers. Many of these were turned into cooperative dwelling units that required substantial sums of money for purchase, as well as high maintenance costs. Many people with low incomes were priced out of the market, and became homeless. People—young adults, first-time parents, persons leaving a relationship—who in earlier decades would have had little trouble establishing a household were unable to do so.

Before this time, even persons with other severe problems—substance abuse, mental illness, family conflict, low income, etc.—could count on finding some sort of affordable housing. But after 1980, steep cutbacks in federal support for low-income housing coincided with factors like neighborhood resistance to the siting of low-income housing to sharply curtail the availability of affordable housing. A substantial increase in the supply of affordable housing would bring much of homelessness to an end.

Housing services for homeless people provide support for the transition from living outdoors or in shelters into regular housing. Where the service itself owns or controls the housing space, the service becomes the landlord as well as the service provider. These roles may conflict, especially when concern for the welfare or peace of mind of other residents leads the organization to make the difficult decision to evict a resident who is causing problems. On the other hand, the service provider as landlord has more control over the situation than if other landlords are providing the housing.

Among the factors that housing providers must take into account are helping newly housed people to take responsibility for cleaning and maintaining the living space, taking medication (where appropriate), and participating in on- and off-premises activities that help clients meet their assigned goals.

When the landlord is another person or organization, the service provider must locate the housing unit, prepare the client to survive the screening interview and other requirements, assure the landlord of the availability of problem-solving support, and refer and connect the newly housed client to local services.

The major challenge confronting the worker in this area is the lack of housing. Even when units can be found, the landlord or screening committee may be very particular about who is allowed to occupy the scarce housing unit. The landlord may not feel bound to put the housing unit into livable condition, so the client may be plagued by vermin, lack of heat, or safety and security problems. And the landlord may feel comfortable with evicting a difficult tenant, since there is plenty of demand for the housing unit.

A second type of challenge is based on the difficulty many clients have in adjusting to being good tenants. They may not have quite the same sense of urgency that the worker has about keeping their housing. Or they may be unable or unwilling to focus on paying rent on time, being quiet at late hours, and cleaning up after themselves—all important elements of successful tenancy. In any event, they may need time and consistent feedback to become accustomed to these practices.

Clothing Services.   Clothing services seldom stand alone. They are usually included as part of a day program or a shelter. The homeless person has great difficulty getting clothing washed, keeping it from being stolen, keeping it clean and undamaged (while having no secure or dry place to store it), and getting it mended when it is torn. The person's prospects of getting a job or even

being treated decently on the street depend in part on wearing clean, well-pressed clothes.

Nearly all homeless programs either have second-hand clothing to distribute or know where such clothing can be found. In some cases, manufacturers contribute out-of-style, faded, off-color, or otherwise unsellable clothing to programs for homeless people.

Some programs attempt to launder or clean the clothing of homeless people. This requires care because of the possibility that the clothes may be infested by lice or other body parasites. Washing and cleaning methods must be used that will kill these parasites.

Personal Sanitation Facilities.   One of the persistent problems faced by homeless people is the quest for opportunities for washing, bathing, washing hair, and cleaning teeth. While offensive body odor may be used as a defense against harassment, especially by women, being clean is a widely held value among residents of the United States, including homeless people. Public restrooms are often the only place that homeless people can use for this purpose. In an effort to keep them out, communities and businesses have locked or closed many of the public restrooms across the United States.

Personal sanitation facilities are usually included in other programs for homeless people, such as day programs and shelters. Where they are available to persons who live out of doors, they are very popular.

Personal Storage Facilities.   Homeless people have great difficulty keeping personal belongings, including identification papers, from being lost, damaged, or stolen. The personal possessions, family photographs, documents, clothing, and odds and ends that all of us collect are at great risk when a person becomes homeless. Such things are important reminders of our personal history and identity. "Sweeps" of squatters' camps by sanitation personnel or police in which all belongings are destroyed are particularly cruel.

Programs for homeless people are often reluctant to provide places to keep personal belongings, partly because these are sometimes left behind when the homeless person moves on, and partly because some homeless people collect large quantities of objects that appear to other people to be of little value. There is not enough spare space in many programs for all the things that guests would like to store. Nevertheless, some programs provide a small locker for each resident or client in order to facilitate personal storage.

Mail Drops and Addresses.   Homeless people, like everyone else, need to be able to receive mail. Some programs provide mail drops where a person can pick up mail. Having an address for job applications, benefit applications, voter registration and other important functions is essential. This is another service that is usually included within a more diverse program.

Travel Support.   In many communities, services for homeless people are conceived of as rest stops for homeless travelers who are traveling to one of the coasts or to a large city. Stays are limited to a few days, or even one day. Meals, personal sanitation, and some petty cash for travel assistance are available. Homeless persons are not encouraged to stay longer to find work or housing in the community, because the community does not wish to accommodate persons who are likely to become dependent on local taxpayers or charitable organizations. This type of service is usually located in small communities along major travel routes. Residents of these communities who become homeless usually move elsewhere in order to avoid having to face their former neighbors on the street or in the store.

Self-Help.   While much of the homeless service system is based on "doing for" homeless people, there are a number of types of projects that show that homeless people can often do things for them-

selves. These organizations range from standard agencies in which homeless people have been given a clear responsibility for a certain aspect of the work, e.g., managing a shelter or providing counseling services, to self-help organizations where nonhomeless people are considered unqualified to take on any responsible role. One of the principles of self-help is that only those who have been through a particular experience are qualified to help others go through it, because they understand the experience better than an outsider could.

Other principles of self-help (Long, 1988, p. 18ff.) include:

— that the person who has been through the situation and is now successful can be a powerful role model for a person who is now struggling with the same situation

— that a person with a problem who is placed in the role of helper becomes stronger and more self-disciplined through assuming the helping role

— that a person who becomes a helper enjoys enhanced status that helps the person to overcome the stigmatized condition that led to the need for help in the first place

— that belonging to a self-help group provides support and a social network

— that having an active, supporting role helps the person overcome the dependent, passive role that is so unacceptable in U.S. culture

— that the best way to challenge the stigma associated with an undesirable condition (such as homelessness) is for those who are going through it to demonstrate their strengths by becoming advocates for themselves.

Given these factors, it may be very helpful to hire a person who has been homeless to assist professional staff people in homeless service programs. This person may be useful in teaching the staff what the experience of homelessness is really like, as well as being effective in reaching out to homeless people.

One challenge related to working in this area is that homelessness, unlike other stigmatized conditions, is one that a person may recover from completely. Many people, once they have been housed, have no wish to identify with other people who are now homeless. Housed persons often do not regard themselves as being potentially homeless, requiring continuing support. Therefore, the potential leadership of a homeless self-help group may continually be lost to the mainstream. While this is often wonderful for the individual, it weakens the group's ability to maintain and renew itself.

A second challenge—for human services professionals—is that they will probably be excluded from, or given a limited role in, any true self-help group. It is often difficult for professionals to accept the idea that experience is the sole qualification for effective human services work. But unless they accept this principle, they will find themselves undermining the essential self-help dynamic.

Special Problems of Services for Homeless People

Many programs to meet the needs of homeless people began as the result of enormous efforts by deeply dedicated persons who worked for very low pay, or no pay at all, in order to help those who were seen as most helpless.

"Doing For." It is this "helpless" image that leads to one of the problems with homeless services: more than other types of assistance programs, homeless services have "done for" rather than "done with" their clients. The resurgence of homelessness occurred at the same time as, and in some cases was caused by, substantial cutbacks in various types of governmentally-sponsored aid programs. Many established social agencies were slow to provide services that met the needs of homeless people. Volunteers with little social welfare experience stepped into the breach to assist those who had lost their housing. Their style reflected the assumptions of an earlier era characterized by *noblesse oblige*, when it was assumed that well-to-do people knew what was best for poorer folks. Several decades of lessons of the value of client participation and self-help, learned in the 1960s and 1970s, were largely ignored in

the case of homelessness. The result was that homeless people were not encouraged to develop their own organizations and movements to address their problems. They ended up as dependent clients, rather than as advocates for themselves.

Built-in Deterrents. A second type of problem with homeless services is the fear that homeless people would become too comfortable as recipients of services, and not be motivated to rehabilitate themselves. Therefore, many services have built-in limitations or irritating features that are intended to block indefinite dependency. This echoes the ambivalence that is reflected in the restrictive nature of many human services in the United States. U.S. culture does not encourage providing unconditional assistance to people in need (Piven and Cloward, 1971). Among the features that are intended to be deterrents:

- Strict and burdensome eligibility procedures
- Lack of comfort and privacy
- Limits to services—such as length of stay in shelters—even when alternatives do not exist
- Unpleasant, demeaning or patronizing attitudes by staff members toward clients.

Fragmented Services. A third type of problem with homeless services is that they are seldom integrated into a set of services that address all the needs of a person. Often an organization may meet just one need, and that in a limited way. There may be a number of different soup kitchens in the community, each of which serves food on a different day. Different shelters may have different rules about eligibility, length of stay, required behavior, and other features. In addition, services for families and those for single individuals are often provided by different service organizations.

While services are fragmented and specialized, homeless people nearly always have a cluster of problems. An early mental health worker commented:

You can't separate the problems. They go hand in hand. We have a lot of hybrid people in our program—such as the woman we were working with earlier this week who abuses drugs, who may have hepatitis, who also has symptomatology that at times looks schizophrenic, who has a seizure disorder and is having seizures regularly at the shelter, and who also is five months pregnant (Alcohol, Drug Abuse and Mental Health Administration, 1983, p. 14).

Not Focused on Permanent Housing. A fourth type of problem with homeless services is that they often do not assist the homeless person to make a transition to permanent housing. This is most often due to a lack of affordable permanent housing in the community.

Another factor keeping homeless services from focusing on placing homeless people in permanent housing is that the funds that support homeless services are restricted to emergency aid, and may not be used to provide permanent housing. The Untied States government throughout the 1980s and early 1990s sharply limited the amount of money available to support the provision of permanent housing, while allowing the amounts used for emergency aid to balloon.

In addition, many homeless persons belong to racial or ethnic groups that are subjected to discrimination in housing. Thus the service would have to overcome not only prejudice against homeless people, but also prejudice against historic victims of housing discrimination in the services' communities. Such an approach could seriously weaken the service program's base of support, as well as requiring members of the agency's staff to come to terms with their own discriminatory attitudes.

Staff Resentment. Some workers in homeless programs are paid so little that they are only a step away from homelessness themselves. They may have strong feelings of jealousy toward their homeless clients, who may be eligible for valued services or housing opportunities that the staff members desperately need themselves.

Denial of Services. Many communities have taken the position that providing services of any kind to homeless people will attract them from other parts of the area or nation. These communities have done their best to remove any amenity that could be seen as making existence within the community possible for homeless people. In some cases, police forces have been allowed to harass homeless people, with the hope that those who were pressured would go elsewhere. In many of these communities, legal suits have been brought in behalf of the homeless people; these suits are usually successful, because courts have held that homelessness is not *per se* a violation of the law. Therefore, courts reason, homeless people are entitled to equal protection under the law. Localities that have been forced to provide services through this means may do so in a hostile manner that is meant to subvert the decision of the court.

EPILOGUE

For a lack of adequate amounts of affordable housing, full employment, and support services that would help people live more successfully in their communities, a visible incidence of homelessness has spread to every area of the United States. A new industry, with many different services, large numbers of employees, high costs (550 million dollars in 1994 in New York City alone) and hundreds of thousands of clients, has sprung up. Once thought to be temporary, the homelessness industry has become a well-established arm of the service-providing network.

Without actually saying so, the nation has apparently "decided" that homelessness, with its personal and public costs, is more desirable than its alternatives. And human services has, opportunistically, benefitted from this trend. It is important to remember that other choices could have been made, indeed, can still be made, to reverse this policy, and return the nation to a condition that existed before 1980, when homelessness was rare and shocking, as well it should be.

REFERENCES

Alcohol, Drug Abuse and Mental Health Administration, (1983). *Alcohol, Drug Abuse and Mental Health Problems of the Homeless: Proceedings of a Roundtable.* Rockville, MD: U.S. Department of Health and Human Services.

Bassuk, Ellen L., ed., (1990). *Community Care for Homeless Families: A Program Design Manual.* Newton Centre: The Better Homes Foundation. MA.

Bingham, Richard D., Roy E. Green, and Sammis B. White, eds., (1987). *The Homeless in Contemporary Society.* Newbury Park, CA: Sage Publications.

Caton, Carol L.M., ed., (1990). *Homeless in America.* New York: Oxford University Press.

Cohen, Neal L., ed., (1990). *Psychiatry Takes to the Streets: Outreach and Crisis Intervention for the Mentally Ill.* New York: The Guilford Press.

Haus, Amy, ed., (1988). *Working with Homeless People: A Guide for Staff and Volunteers.* New York: Columbia University Community Services.

Hopper, Kim, (1990). "Advocacy for the Homeless in the 1980s," in Caton, ed., (1990), pp. 160–173.

Jahiel, Rene, ed., (1992). *Homelessness: A Prevention-Oriented Approach.* Baltimore: Johns Hopkins Press.

Long, Lorence A., (1988). *Consumer-Run Self-Help Programs Serving Homeless People with a Mental Illness. Vol. 3.* Rockville, MD: National Institute of Mental Health.

Molnar, Janice, (1988). *Home Is Where the Heart Is: The Crisis of Homeless Children and Families in New York City.* New York: Bank Street College of Education.

National Housing Institute, (1993). *Preventing Homelessness: A Study of State and Local Homelessness Prevention Programs.* Orange, NJ: National Housing Institute.

Piven, Francis, and Cloward, Richard, (1971). *Regulating the Poor: The Functions of Public Welfare.* New York: Vintage Books.

Torrey, E. Fuller, (1988). *Nowhere to Go: The Tragic Odyssey of the Homeless Mentally Ill.* New York: Harper Roe.

Wright, James D., (1989). *Address Unknown: The Homeless in America.* Hawthorne, NY: Aldine de Gruyter.

CHAPTER 19

PEOPLE LIVING WITH HIV AND AIDS
THE PROBLEM AND HUMAN SERVICES

WM. LYNN MCKINNEY

As a human service worker, you will almost certainly work closely with people living with Human Immunodeficiency Virus (HIV) and persons living with AIDS (PWAs). This is true because AIDS affects people of all ages, sexual orientations, and ethnic and minority groups, and because the needs of PWAs and people living with HIV are numerous and span virtually all human service programs. Because AIDS is an illness, there are medical needs. Since most PWAs eventually must stop working, they have income needs. The number of children who have HIV is growing, and these young people may have educational needs. For several reasons, there are likely to be psychological and social needs. For one, since AIDS occurs primarily in people younger than fifty, early in their lives people must confront a fatal illness. For another, AIDS is found predominantly in marginalized people such as homosexual men, injection drug users, and racial and ethnic minorities. Still another reason that PWAs may have psychological needs is that many of them will have lost nearly all of their friends. For example, a friend of the author who is a PWA in the past four years has attended thirty-one memorial services for people he was close to. The effects of such losses are potentially enormous. Thus, the entire human service system is involved in working with people living with AIDS and HIV. As you enter the field, it is important that you know about HIV and AIDS and society's reactions to the disease.

Working with people with AIDS and HIV presents particular challenges. Many people with this illness will not have close ties with their families who may have turned their backs on what is perceived to be a social embarrassment. Most will be poor, some because they were poor when they became sick, and others because the disease is impoverishing. Death from AIDS-related causes can be horrible; the diseases and infections which affect a sufferer can leave people thin and weak and close to death for long periods of time. Unlike those with other illnesses, PWAs may be very sick and close to death for a while and then go through long periods of good health when they can lead happy, productive lives. As more cases of AIDS are diagnosed among drug users, more clients may be difficult to work with and prone to violence. Finally, with more women contracting the virus and dying, there are orphaned children who are not infected and also children who were born with the virus. Many of these children are not or cannot be cared for by their mothers or other relatives.

As you must know since you are planning to enter the human service field, working with all people is rewarding. If your interest is in research, you can become involved with learning more about the disease, thus increasing the probability of a cure, a vaccine, or better care for people who have the virus. If you work with individual clients, you will no doubt develop intense, deep relationships with many of them; some of these will be enormously enriching, revealing to you some of the best about humanity. AIDS work will probably stretch you professionally, broadening your knowledge and experience so that, should you decide to change jobs, you will present an attractive array of qualifications to prospective employers. Finally, you can gain satisfaction knowing that you are working with people, many of whom live on society's margins, doing what you can in response to a pandemic—a worldwide outbreak of a disease affecting an extraordinarily large percentage of the population.

You probably knew some things about AIDS by the time you entered college. But because it is a politically-charged issue, the quantity and quality of AIDS education varies greatly. While we may review in this chapter some material that you already know, there will also be material that is new to you. The objectives of this chapter are: (1) to solidify your basic understanding of AIDS as an illness, (2) to help you understand some of the social ramifications of AIDS, and (3) to acquaint you with current issues. This chapter is only an introduction to the topic. Reading about AIDS and HIV in books, newspapers, and professional journals should be a part of your professional growth. We urge you to become involved in AIDS service organizations, too. Practical experience is an excellent means to expand your knowledge.

AIDS AND HIV AS MEDICAL ISSUES

In 1985, the specific virus which is believed to cause AIDS was identified. It is Human Immunodeficiency Virus or HIV. Today we believe that there are actually two viruses which are active in the United States. They are referred to as HIV-1 and HIV-2. HIV-1 has been with us since the early 1980s and is much more common. At this time HIV-2 seems somewhat less vicious than HIV-1. We still know much less about HIV and AIDS than we wish we did. Fortunately, research is regularly revealing new information to us.

Acquired Immune Deficiency Syndrome or AIDS was first noted in the United States in very early 1981, but it was not until three or four years later that it was identified as a syndrome and given a name. Doctors in San Francisco and New York began to notice that they were treating a new group of patients, primarily gay and bisexual men in their twenties and thirties, for a series of diseases which were highly unusual in this country. For a few years there was no agreement on a name for what they were seeing, but eventually the medical profession developed the description Acquired Immune Deficiency Syndrome (AIDS). The words which make up the acronym AIDS provide specific meaning. (For an incisive account of the early years of the disease in the United States and for insight into the politics of this illness, read *And the Band Played On* by Randy Shilts.)

The *A* in AIDS stands for acquired which indicates how a person gets the disease. AIDS is a communicable disease; a person must get it from someone else. In this sense, it is like hepatitis, a cold, or gonorrhea. AIDS is not inherited like some diseases such as sickle cell anemia and Tay Sachs. Unlike some other diseases, cancer for example, it does not just begin inside an individual, in many cases for unknown reasons. People have to get AIDS from someone else. AIDS is not easy to get, and we emphasize this and explain what it means later in the chapter.

The *I* and the *D* stand for immune deficiency which refer to the characteristics of this disease which makes it unlike other diseases. Instead of making you sick directly, HIV attacks the helper T cells in our body. These helper T cells are important for us to be able to fight off infections. When they become weakened, our bodies become vulnerable to other diseases, virtually all of which we are ordinarily resistant to. This literally causes a deficiency of the body's immune system, leaving the infected individual susceptible to a wide variety of infections which would not ordinarily affect noninfected individuals.

Finally, the *S* stands for syndrome. A syndrome is a collection of symptoms and effects of other diseases. AIDS is considered to be a syndrome because a person with AIDS does not die of AIDS but rather of other diseases, most of which were rarely seen in the United States until the advent of AIDS. These diseases, commonly called "opportunistic infections," can occur because T cells are destroyed and can no longer ward off infections.

Because AIDS is a syndrome which affects different people differently, it is still somewhat difficult for medical people to state definitely that an individual does or does not have AIDS—to say with certainty when an infected individual progresses from having the virus to having what has been called "full-blown AIDS." For two reasons, it is important to make a clear diagnosis. First, there is a psychological impact on the infected individual of having AIDS versus having HIV. Different sorts of supportive services may be necessary as an individual progresses from knowing that s/he is infected with HIV to knowing that s/he has AIDS.

Second, once someone is determined to have AIDS, s/he may become eligible for a variety of state and federal programs. Initially a person was diagnosed as suffering from AIDS if s/he had any one of two or three diseases or opportunistic infections: pneumocystis carinii pneumonia (PCP) and Kaposi's sarcoma, a rare form of skin cancer, were the most common. In early 1993, the Centers for Disease Control (CDC) changed the way in which it defined whether or not a person had AIDS. Now a person is classified as having AIDS if his/her T helper lymphocyte count falls below 200 (ordinarily our helper T count ranges from 800 to 1,200) and if s/he also has at least two of the specific diseases associated with AIDS.

The definition has changed because it had been much more useful in diagnosing AIDS in men that it was in women. Since women experience the disease differently and since more and more women now have AIDS, it was important to change the definition.

The two opportunistic infections which are the greatest killers of men in 1993 are PCP (described above) and toxoplasmosis. Toxoplasmosis is a chronic, severe brain infection. Toxo is a common parasite which is found in most of us. As is true of all other opportunistic infections, most of us are immune to it. However, in individuals whose immune systems are compromised, toxo can

become activated, resulting in blindness, paralysis, and dementia. Fortunately, there are now prophylactic treatments for both of these diseases.

Women with HIV and AIDS are more likely to develop other diseases, particularly yeast infections, invasive cervical cancer, recurrent bacterial pneumonias, and blood stream infections. Recently, an increase in the number of cases of pulmonary tuberculosis has been noted.

Knowledge about AIDS and HIV continues to increase through research. Diseases associated with AIDS now can be classified into three groups: Primary HIV disease, cancers, and opportunistic infections. Primary HIV diseases are directly caused by the virus itself. Unlike other diseases of AIDS, they are not due solely to a weakened immune system. Two examples are encephalopathy (AIDS Dementia) and wasting syndrome. Often dementia is the earliest sign of the development of AIDS in an individual; mental difficulties may be experienced before there are other physical symptoms.

The two most common opportunistic cancers are Kaposi's sarcoma and lymphoma. Finally, opportunistic infections are classified in four groups: virus, bacteria, protozoa, and fungus. Common viruses are cytomegalovirus (CMV) and herpes. Bacteria are mycobacterium avium intracellulare (MAI) and tuberculosis. Protozoa are pneumocystis carinii pneumonia and toxoplasmosis. Finally, funguses are Candidiasis (thrush) Cryptococcal Meningitis, and Histoplasmosis.

Unless it is your intention to enter the medical field, this is probably enough for you to know about the medical aspects of AIDS and HIV. As you become involved with PWAs, you may need to increase your medical knowledge, but, as we repeat often in this chapter, knowledge about AIDS is increasing rapidly, and you should learn more as part of your continuing professional development and as the need confronts you.

The Transmission of HIV

HIV is spread through body fluids, specifically blood and semen. While the virus is present in other body fluids such as tears and sweat, it is in such slight concentration that these fluids are not considered dangerous. AIDS is difficult to get. There are very few ways in which AIDS can be transmitted from one person to another. Unprotected sex and sharing needles are the two most common. A third means is across the placenta from an infected woman to her unborn child. Until 1985 AIDS was occasionally spread by blood transfusions, but since that time the American blood supply has been considered safe because of donor screening, and because all blood to be used for transfusions is tested before it is given to someone.

HIV is not easy to catch because, for a person to be exposed to the virus, it must penetrate his or her skin. This can occur when individuals share an unsterilized needle to inject steroids or other drugs. It can also occur during unprotected sex, either vaginal, anal, or oral. But again, for infection to occur, the skin must be broken. This often occurs during anal intercourse, can occur during vaginal intercourse, and can occur during oral sex if the person performing oral sex has skin breaks such as canker sores or unhealthy gums. Tears in the skin need only to be microscopic in size for transmission to occur.

Sexual transmission of HIV from men to women is much more common than from women to men. This is true because the skin must be broken for the virus to cross from one individual to another and because the virus is present in dangerous concentrations in semen. It is more likely that the lining of the vagina or anus will experience a tear during sex than it is that the penis will suffer some sort of skin break. Infection from a man to a woman is more likely because sex commonly results in the ejaculation of semen. The most dangerous form of sex between men is unprotected (that is, without a condom) anal intercourse.

Infection is less likely during oral sex but can occur if semen is ejaculated. It is possible for the person performing oral sex to infect his or her partner only if infected blood somehow enters the sexual partner's penis such as if s/he has strep throat or

other infectious lesions in the throat. Sex between two women and oral sex by a man on a woman rarely result in transmission, but it is possible. Use of dental dams during such oral sex is urged.

It is estimated that one-third of babies born to infected mothers are born with the virus. This figure has decreased as more pregnant infected women began taking AZT. Why the virus crosses the placenta in some cases and not in others is not known at this time. As part of your continuing professional growth, you should regularly read newspaper and journal articles about AIDS and HIV to stay informed. Research is making great strides, and you, as a human service student and professional, are responsible for keeping your knowledge current.

Epidemiology

The epidemiology of a disease is the way in which it spreads. AIDS was first recognized among gay men in New York and San Francisco when doctors began treating patients who were suffering from pneumocystis carinii pneumonia (PCP) and from Kaposi's sarcoma, a skin and/or lymph node cancer. Ordinarily most people are immune to both of these diseases unless they are pregnant or elderly, but because HIV destroys the immune system, infected people can develop these and other opportunistic infections. It is believed that AIDS was introduced to the North American continent by an infected gay man who had sex with other men who then had sex with others. Because of this, for the first decade of its existence, AIDS has most heavily affected the gay male population in the United States. This is not true of the epidemiology of the disease in other countries where it is almost exclusively a heterosexual disease.

Because large numbers of gay men live in the largest American cities, nearly all early recognized AIDS cases were found in New York, San Francisco, Chicago, and Los Angeles. However, the epidemiology of the disease has changed in recent years. AIDS is still primarily an urban disease, but cases are now reported in virtually all cities and towns across the country and among all demographics.

Many gay males have modified their sexual behaviors, thus somewhat slowing the spread of AIDS in the homosexual population, although recent reports about the sexual behavior of young gay men in San Francisco indicate that the rate of infection is not declining despite determined efforts to educate young people about the disease. In San Francisco in 1993 there were two hundred new cases diagnosed and slightly more than one hundred deaths every month. There continues to be a very high rate of infection across the country. There has been slow spread of the disease into the general heterosexual population, and minority populations are now particularly vulnerable.

In part because of the spread of the illness and in part because people with HIV are living longer, there are now many more people who have the virus. While progress may seem maddeningly slow, researchers are regularly discovering new prophylactic and infection treatments. Many of these delay the onset of opportunistic infections and thus improve the quality of life of PWAs and people living with HIV.

Predictions for the Future

The Centers for Disease Control (CDC) in Atlanta is the reporting body which tracks AIDS and other diseases. Their predictions about the spread of AIDS have been reasonably accurate for the past several years. The CDC has reported that AIDS replaced murder as the tenth most common cause of death in the United States in 1990 and the ninth most common cause in 1991 and would probably continue to climb the statistical ladder. Among young people in 1990, AIDS was the third most common cause of death; only cancer and accidents killed more young Americans. In 1993, AIDS became the most common cause of death among men ages twenty-five to forty-five.

The CDC had documented roughly a quarter of a million cases of AIDS and 160,000 deaths

from AIDS by September 1992. In 1995 it is estimated that between one and one and a half million Americans are carrying the virus. It is expected that the number of cases reported annually will plateau at 60,000 to 70,000 by 1995. However, these are only estimates, and the politics of estimating the pervasiveness of the illness are heated. Some believe that there may already be nearly 2,000,000 infected Americans. These numbers are important as decisions about funding levels for AIDS research, treatment, and education are made.

The epidemiology of AIDS is different in different countries. In some African countries, AIDS is much more prevalent than in the United States and is exclusively a heterosexual disease. In Zimbabwe, for example, one of every seven persons is believed to be infected, or 1.5 million out of a population of only 10.5 million people. Roughly 80 percent of new infections are occurring in developing countries. It is expected that by the year 2000, 2 percent of the world's population will be infected with HIV. It is unlikely that there will be a vaccine before the twenty-first century begins.

These grim predictions underscore the importance of clear, early AIDS education for all people. But this education may not be enough. Many young Americans do not believe that they are vulnerable to the virus because they are not members of the groups most heavily infected; and because of the length of time it takes to show symptoms (perhaps ten or more years), most believe that they don't know anyone with HIV. Their "invincibility" results in their engaging in high risk sexual practices. As a human service worker, you must take responsibility for helping everyone with whom you work understand this disease and how it is spread.

AIDS AND HIV AS SOCIAL ISSUES

Throughout this chapter we use the terms AIDS and HIV in a variety of ways. It is important that you remember that HIV is the infectious agent and AIDS is the name for the resulting decline in the body's immune system.

As is true of many new diseases, AIDS raised an array of sociopolitical issues. These issues resulted from the unusual epidemiology which was discussed above and from the fact that AIDS was transmitted by practices which Americans would prefer not to talk about. We will discuss four major social issues in this chapter: (1) who has AIDS, (2) AIDS education, (3) immigration, and (4) infection as the result of personal behavior.

Who Is Most at Risk for AIDS?

Quite likely no disease which has affected and will affect virtually all Americans has been so poorly understood as AIDS. It is clearly the most political disease of the last half of this century. This is primarily because it initially was found only in gay and bisexual men and was thought of as a "gay disease." To have AIDS meant shame and embarrassment for many sufferers and their families, and people tried to hide it. Initially people tried to cover up the fact that both Rock Hudson and Liberace had AIDS. More recently, after Rudolph Nureyev died, his relatives brought suit against his doctor in France for revealing that AIDS-related diseases had killed the legendary dancer. Obituaries in large and small cities and towns across the country routinely veil the real cause of death with such phrases as, "after a lengthy illness." Surviving family members continue to deny that the deceased had AIDS and, in many cases, that s/he was gay, bisexual, or a needle drug user. The revelations by Arthur Ashe, Magic Johnson, and Greg Louganis have improved this situation enormously.

Most heterosexual Americans, unless they are touched through family members or friends or become particularly interested in the disease, assume that AIDS is something that they would never have to worry about. We now know that everyone must be concerned about AIDS. It is almost certain that everyone of us knows someone who has HIV or AIDS or who has died of the disease. If you do not know someone who has the virus, it may be because they have chosen not to reveal their status to you. From college classrooms to corporate boardrooms, HIV and AIDS are affecting all racial, religious, and socioeconomic groups.

HIV quickly spread beyond the gay male population, primarily into the population of injection drug users, and then into racial and ethnic minorities. In 1993, 46 percent of all AIDS cases in the U.S. were among African-Americans and Latinos. African-Americans are only 12 percent of our population yet account for 30 percent of AIDS cases, and Latinos, who comprise 9 percent of the population, account for 17 percent. The projected spread of HIV is much higher among these groups, too. In 1990 and 1991 while reported cases among whites dropped 0.5 percent, reported cases rose 11.5 percent among Latinos and 10 percent among African-Americans. The presence of AIDS largely within minority populations has become a social and political issue in our society, one which we will discuss at greater length below.

Because AIDS is spread almost exclusively by sex and drug use, the American population has been squeamish about discussing it. Because children are considered to be asexual and because society legislates as if it disapproved of sex between unmarried people and between members of the same sex, we have been unable to develop a consistent policy concerning AIDS education.

AIDS Education Issues

The spread of AIDS could be greatly reduced if everyone stopped having sex and using drugs. Equally true is that tuberculosis would soon be a disease of the past if we all stopped breathing. All of these have about the same probability. The spread would also be slowed if everyone who is not in a long-term, monogamous relationship in which both partners know they are HIV negative would always use a condom when having sex and if everyone who used injection drugs would either never share their needles or would "cleanse their works," that is, use bleach to clean needles before passing them on to the next person. Since we know this, it would seem to be a simple matter to teach people to use condoms and to clean their works. However, education about these two forms of AIDS prevention have encountered great resistance in our society.

Much of our society shuns gay people and drug users and is squeamish about discussing sex. In numerous communities, elementary and secondary schools are not allowed to discuss sex at all. The 1993 reigning Miss America was prohibited from using the words condom and AIDS in some high schools while on a speaking tour in Florida. In some schools in which sex education is allowed, gay sex may not be discussed. Many people make the erroneous assumption that young people are actually encouraged to try out behaviors they might learn about in sex education classes. Use of condoms conflicts with some religious teachings. And many people believe that they and no one they know could ever possibly become infected or even know someone with AIDS or HIV. So, some Americans are growing up not knowing they may be vulnerable to a fatal illness, and they are not being taught how to avoid contracting it.

Reluctance to be clear about AIDS has resulted in the following: a 1992 survey revealed that 25 percent responding believed that you could get AIDS from a mosquito, 33 percent thought that you could contract the disease by donating blood, and 25 percent believed that an AIDS vaccine exists. All of these are absolutely false.

There is continuing resistance in this country to advertising about condoms on radio and television, on billboards, and in the print media. Virtually everyone in our society probably knows about condoms, but without advertising, the use of condoms has not increased as much as needed. Instead of promoting condom use, we have continued to pretend that young people are not having sex, and we have continued to tell them not to. A 1993 survey of teenagers revealed that 56 percent of teens ages sixteen and seventeen had had intercourse at least once. It may be best for young people not to have sex, but until we can insure that, it is important for us to convince them to protect themselves from a disease that currently is absolutely fatal.

The resistance to helping people cleanse their needles with bleach has been even stronger. In only a very few places in the country are needle exchange programs operating. In such programs, injection drug users are encouraged to turn in their used needles for clean needles each time they use them. In most parts of our country it continues to be illegal to own drug paraphernalia such as needles, unless licensed for a legitimate use such as injecting insulin. While this continues to be true, needle exchange programs are also going to be viewed as illegal.

There are three very important AIDS education messages which every American, particularly young people, ought to know. First, don't have sex outside marriage, or, if you do, learn the HIV status of your partner and still always use a condom during sex. To be blunt, the message is, "If it is up, it is covered." And, always use a dental dam if performing oral sex on a woman. Second, don't use drugs or, if you do, either never share needles or rinse your needles carefully with a bleach solution after each injection. And third, women who are HIV positive should carefully consider the risks for becoming pregnant, both to themselves and their unborn children.

As the gay community learned early in the epidemic, sex without penetration is not only possible but quite erotic and, for many gay males, has become the method of choice. It certainly is preferable to contracting an almost certainly fatal illness.

Immigration

Once we began to learn about AIDS and a reliable test for the virus was developed, many countries decided that one form of slowing or stopping the spread of the illness was to require an AIDS test of everyone entering. As soon as we had a test, the Immigration and Naturalization Bureau of the U.S. government began to require an AIDS test for everyone requesting to immigrate into the United States. Anyone whose HIV status was positive was denied. The United States is the only western country with this policy. This has continued to be an issue into the middle of the 1990s, particularly in regard to Haitians, some of who have been caught in a hopeless situation. As HIV positive people, they were denied admission to the U.S., but they could not return to Haiti because they were likely to be imprisoned for political reasons. Public arguments about the matter were played out in the media during the early months of the Clinton administration in 1993.

The policy also affects short-term visitors. Perhaps the amazing decision concerning people entering the U.S. came in 1992 shortly before an international AIDS conference scheduled for Boston when immigration officials prevented people coming to the conference from entering if they were HIV positive. These people were coming for the purpose of either sharing or gaining new knowledge about the disease. Because the impasse could not be resolved, the conference moved abroad.

NEEDS OF PERSONS LIVING WITH AIDS AND HIV

A 1992 survey conducted by the National Association of PWAs identified the three most-frequently identified needs of PWAs as: (1) fighting discrimination and violence, (2) affordable health care, and (3) receiving assistance with everyday life. As you can see, these needs span all of the human service field, involving politics, economics, psychology, and human development. If you decide to work in the AIDS field, your clients will have many problems which most of us may never have to confront.

The first step that a PWA or you, if you are an advocate or case manager, should take is to contact your local AIDS service organization. Virtually every city now has one, and many smaller areas do, too. These organizations are usually non-profit, but there is an increasing number of for-profit agencies which will provide an array of services. These may be affordable if your client has insurance coverage. In the southeastern New England area there are several nonprofit agencies. One is Rhode Island Project AIDS in Providence, RI. It was formally incorporated in 1985 by a small group of volunteers in response to the growing numbers of AIDS cases in the area. With an annual budget of roughly $1.5 million, the Project offers education, outreach to the gay and minority communities, case management, and a national newsletter in Spanish entitled *Quipu.*

AIDS organizations vary. Some focus more on education and less on direct services. They may provide a strong referral service. Others are direct service organizations and assist clients with a broad range of needs. And now more non-AIDS organizations are providing AIDS-related services such as support groups, counseling, and testing. An AIDS organization may provide a case worker to your client, in which instance you may no longer need to be involved with regard to HIV issues, but you may need to follow your client for other reasons not related to AIDS. You should stay involved until you are certain that your client is being well-served.

Medical and Dental Needs

There is no vaccine for AIDS, and we do not expect one until after the beginning of the next century. Nor is there a cure for AIDS. The medical needs of persons with AIDS and HIV focus on prevention and treatment of the specific opportunistic infections to which an individual becomes vulnerable. Dental needs are greater than those of people who do not have the virus. HIV positive people should have their teeth cleaned four times yearly. More symptoms appear in the oral cavity than elsewhere, so regular examinations are very important. PWAs need high quality dental care. The problem that many confront is finding one of the small number of dentists who are willing to treat them.

Many people, once they learn they are HIV positive, begin to take one of a small number of medications which are believed both to prolong and to improve the quality of life of those living with HIV. The choice of which drug to take depends on a variety of factors including the preferences of one's doctor, the drug currently thought to be most effective, and the insurance plan of the patient. The three most commonly used now are

AZT, ddl, and ddC. All three improve the quality of life of PWAs, but it is not clear that they prolong life. Because these are highly toxic drugs, each has potential side effects which may affect people differently.

From the view of the medical profession, PWAs present risks to medical personnel. Many medical and dental procedures result in blood loss, and that blood must be viewed as lethal. Astute and ethical physicians and dentists insist that all of their staff take universal precautions such as wearing rubber gloves when working with all of their patients, not just PWAs. They may not know, and their patients may not know, who is and who is not carrying the virus. Universal precautions reduce enormously the risk of transmission, although there have been a small number of accidents which resulted in infected blood entering the blood stream of a medical worker. People with the virus should also insist that medical personnel use universal precautions since they are at much greater risk for other diseases than are noninfected people. In fact, all of us should insist that universal precautions be taken by all medical and dental personnel who treat us and our clients. This measure serves to protect all of us.

As a human service worker, you may have to advocate for or be a case manager for a PWA. This will require your negotiating with the medical establishment. For some PWAs, this presents no problems, but in many cases it is quite difficult. There are still only a few doctors, mostly in cities, who have chosen to specialize in treating PWAs and therefore know enough about the disease to be "patient friendly." In your role as advocate, you may need to be very tough in insisting that your client get the treatment that s/he needs. There may be times when your client has no one else to help him or her and may be too ill to manage his/her health care effectively.

Income Assistance

Because of prophylaxis and newly developed treatments, PWAs may live for many years after learning of their HIV status. People with HIV and AIDS almost always eventually have to quit work because their energy levels simply do not permit them to continue. This will likely result in a dramatic reduction in income. They may need assistance in getting access to the government programs to which they are entitled. Many PWAs have never had to rely on income assistance programs, and they may be completely ignorant of the process.

By federal law, having AIDS means that a person is disabled. This entitles PWAs to Supplemental Security Disability Income (SSDI). The process of applying is not terribly complicated, but it can be nearly impossible for someone who is very ill. If the disease requires hospitalization or relocation, your client may need your dedicated and skilled assistance. Beyond that, it takes five months to begin to collect SSDI benefits. The federal government wants to make sure that they are supporting people only if they are truly sick, so they have imposed a waiting period. Once begun, the benefits are paid retroactively, but the delay can be financially devastating. Many must apply for AFDC or General Public Assistance to support themselves while waiting for their SSDI benefits to begin.

We noted above that the change in the definition of who has AIDS has had an impact on the lives of PWAs. Because the disease is now defined by a combination of helper T cell count and at least two diseases commonly associated with AIDS, many more people qualify for SSDI. Previously it was necessary to have either Kaposi's or PCP. Since many women PWAs never develop either of these diseases, they were prevented from qualifying for disability income. This change in federal law has helped ease some of the money problems of many PWAs, particularly women. For all sufferers of AIDS, the changing medical picture also affects who becomes eligible for federal benefits.

Housing

Housing may be an issue for your clients living with HIV and AIDS. The Americans with Disabilities Act (ADA) of 1992 protects PWAs, but by late 1993, this had not yet been challenged in court. While some states have recently passed laws protecting PWAs from eviction, over forty have not. This may mean that an individual who suddenly becomes sick, loses his or her job, and may have to "come out" to family and friends, now also has no place to live. Subsidized housing is a possibility, but the waiting lists in virtually all cities are so long that this is not a feasible alternative.

Many PWAs own their own homes and are able to stay in them. Others move in with friends or family. Some, however, may have no place to go. Fortunately, there is a small but growing number of places which are dedicated to PWAs who otherwise might be homeless. One example is Sunrise House in Providence, RI. It currently provides beds for nine people. Each has his or her own room. Meals are communal and, like the housekeeping, are the responsibility of the residents. People live there, paying according to their income levels, until they are able to make other arrangements, or they die. Sunrise House is supported by a nonprofit corporation which, like many other AIDS organizations, is quite effective in raising money to support its operation. A second option in Providence is a Hospice facility in The Miriam Hospital, a ten-bed ward where seriously ill people may live.

Finally, also in Providence, is Family AIDS Center for Treatment and Support (FACTS), a home for up to seven children, born to HIV positive mothers, who may or may not have the virus and whose families cannot or will not care for them. These examples from Providence were chosen to illustrate the breadth of services available even in a small city (population slightly under 200,000).

Employment

Most PWAs eventually must quit their jobs. As noted above, the disease is unpredictable. After a serious bout of one of the infections, PCP for example, a PWA may enter a long phase in which s/he feels well, has good energy, and lives a normal life. Some people find part-time jobs; others

return to their previous jobs; and some volunteer their time, most of them to AIDS-serving organizations. Again, federal law protects these workers. They may not be discriminated against because they have AIDS. However, this law does not prevent some employers from firing their employees if they suspect they are ill. You may have to assist your clients in returning to or maintaining their jobs. If you plan to work in the AIDS field, you should begin to learn the process for filing discrimination complaints.

Social Services

PWAs may need a range of social services such as transportation, counseling, assistance with meals, legal aid, and companionship. These services may be available through a variety of sources, but you may need to help your clients access them. Again, the best first step is to contact your local AIDS organization and ask for assistance. They may provide a case worker, a buddy program, counseling, support groups, and the like. Or, you may need to find those services from a variety of sources. The nature and extent of needed services will depend on how capable and/or how ill your client is.

An excellent example of a social service program is the Food and Friends program which operates in Washington, DC. PWAs who are too ill to shop and cook for themselves, who cannot leave their apartments or houses, and who have no one to care for them can call Food and Friends which will deliver nutritious, abundant meals directly to the PWA. Many PWAs, once they are functioning well again, become volunteers in the program, helping to prepare and to deliver meals. In this way, the cost of the program is kept to a minimum and people invest in caring for one another.

WORKING WITH PWAs

Working with persons with HIV and AIDS will be both challenging and rewarding. Some are very angry that they are ill and vent their anger on anyone who comes close. Others may focus on being as healthy as possible, including maintaining strong mental health. Others, following the stages of dying outlined years ago by Elisabeth Kubler-Ross, will react differently at different times.

Working with PWAs is much different now than it was a few years ago because the stigma of the disease is less, there are many more organizations to which you may turn for help, we know more about the illness, people are living longer, and there are vastly more competent, knowledgeable people who can provide assistance.

AIDS Agencies

Starting with the Gay Men's Health Crisis in New York and the Shanti Project in San Francisco in the early 1980s, nonprofit AIDS organizations were created as the need arose. They are funded in part by federal, state, and local government dollars, but most rely for the majority of their income on grant funds, fundraisers, and other donations. Most have major fund-raising events annually. A common one is a walk of some sort, such as the Walk for Life in Providence. Usually held on the first Sunday of June, The Walk is the major annual fundraiser for Rhode Island Project AIDS. Individuals who plan to walk ask their friends and relatives to sponsor them, usually a specific amount for each of the ten kilometers of the walk. The proceeds, regularly around $200,000, are sometimes shared with other, smaller AIDS agencies in the area. Such walks are festive occasions with balloons, politicians, food, entertainment, and good cheer. Local media now provide good coverage of these events.

Self-Help Groups

Many cities and towns have self-help groups. These groups use peer-helper models to provide a broad array of services. These groups lower the cost of caring for people with HIV and AIDS since they are low- or no-cost organizations. Examples include PWAs themselves, people living with HIV, partners of PWAs who test negative, and the "wor-

ried well"—groups of individuals who attempt to deal with emotions of being HIV negative while so many of their friends are sick or dead.

Volunteers as Important Resources

All AIDS organizations rely heavily on volunteers. The best examples are probably the buddy programs. Most were started in the early 1980s with the (accurate) belief that the human services needs resulting from the AIDS crisis would far exceed the capability of the system to respond. They are also evidence that, for a long time, the system refused to respond and did not provide necessary services.

The Buddy Program at Rhode Island Project AIDS is a good example. Started in 1985 by a small group of volunteers, it now provides training and support for over 150 buddies. Buddies undergo a forty-hour training program which teaches them about AIDS and how to work effectively with HIV positive people. They then may be assigned a buddy, a person living with HIV or AIDS who has requested a buddy. Each pair negotiates its own terms, but commonly the relationship provides emotional support and companionship plus whatever tangible assistance is needed. The buddy may, for example, provide transportation, pick up prescriptions from a pharmacy, arrange for hospitalization or visits to the doctor, see that the PWA is eating properly, or negotiate with landlords. Buddy programs have provided emotional support and help for thousands of people who, without them, would have died sooner and much more isolated. Being a buddy can be emotionally wrenching, so Buddy Groups are common. Groups of buddies meet biweekly or monthly to provide one another with necessary emotional support and periodically with AIDS agency staff for support and direction.

Special Needs and Skills of Workers

Human service workers who work with people living with HIV and AIDS must have the customary set of skills, knowledge, and attitudes that all human service workers should have. They should go beyond these, however. To begin, we remind you that these people are living, not dying. This is very important for you to remember. However, courses about and experience with death and dying with people who are terminally ill are useful. Second, a solid understanding of the entire human service system and how to make it respond is essential since PWAs nearly always need a broad array of services. If not dealing directly with all involved governmental and nonprofit agencies and organizations, you will at least be making referrals, so you must know the entire system. Third, advocacy skills are critical. You may have to act on behalf of your client who, for whatever reasons, may be unable to do so for him or herself. Finally, and very important, you must be aware of cultural differences.

Your clients may be of racial and ethnic groups other than yours. AIDS educations issues vary among different populations and so do reactions to the disease. Part of the reason that the death rates from AIDS among minorities seem to be higher than that of whites is that members of minority groups have less access to appropriate medical care and because, even if they have access, may choose not to fully avail themselves of the care.

CURRENT ISSUES

Some issues have been with us nearly since the beginning of the epidemic. For example, questions and concerns about testing for the virus arose as soon as there was a test. Other issues, such as insurance coverage, arose later. Issues will change over time, and you must read widely so that you will know what the issues are at any given time. Unlike the early days of the 1980s when we were just beginning to notice AIDS, the media now cover the topic extensively and in a balanced way. It should not be difficult for you to be aware of how the illness and treatments are changing.

Mandatory Testing

Some Americans believe that one way to stop the spread of the disease is to test everyone or, if not all people, at least selected groups such as gay men, drug users, and people applying for marriage licenses. Setting aside civil rights questions for the moment, the issues around testing everyone concern the costs and benefits and the latent period between infection and positive test results. Is it more effective to spend scarce AIDS resources on AIDS education and research than on testing? Which has the most probability of slowing the spread of the disease? At the present time, mandatory testing affects very few people; people entering and serving in the military are a good example of a population which is regularly tested. While our testing technology is greatly improved and continues to get better, it seems that the virus can lie dormant and undetected in some individuals, thereby resulting in a negative test result. Until more is known about this, there are lingering questions about mandatory testing. The issue was more hotly debated in the 1980s than it is today, but it has not been decisively settled.

Partner Notification

It has been community health policy and practice for many years that individuals testing positive for gonorrhea or syphilis provide the names of their recent sex partners. This has not been true for people testing positive for HIV, due in large measure to the intense pressure from AIDS activist groups who feared that individual civil rights would be trammeled and from the concern of pubic policy officials that even fewer people would choose to be tested if they had to provide the names of partners. So, the issue continues to be debated. Should the state have the right to demand the names of sex partners of anyone testing positive for HIV and then to notify those people? If so, what happens to anonymous testing?

Whether or Not to Be Tested

People who have engaged in high-risk behaviors such as unprotected sex and sharing needles must decide whether they should be tested for the virus. This is not an easy decision to make. The strongest argument for being tested is that, if positive, an individual can choose to take medication such as ZAT, ddl, or ddC; since the long-term effectiveness of these medications continues to be in question, this may not be sufficient reason for some people to choose to be tested. The argument against being tested is that the news of a positive result can serve as a death sentence. Some individuals know that they could not cope with such information. The best source of counseling about the testing issue is probably an AIDS organization.

Health Insurance Coverage

As we are painfully aware in the 1990s, health insurance coverage in the United States is variable. Many people are insured through their places of employment while others are not. Even people who are insured may find that their insurance is not adequate after a diagnosis of AIDS. In court cases in 1992, it was determined that employers who self-insure have the right to revoke insurance coverage after learning that an insuree has been diagnosed with AIDS. This seems to be a reprehensible and impossible decision, and it seems clear that there will be further court cases. As we have said often in this chapter, you should pay attention to all issues about AIDS through print and other media.

People who are not insured must rely on governmental programs, particularly Medicaid, the program which provides health care coverage for indigent people. While Medicaid provides basic care, it does not cover many additional services that PWAs may want or need. Coverage varies from state to state.

Medications

Because AIDS is fatal, those who contract it have an enormous investment in which medications are available to them and, perhaps even more so, in AIDS research and the speed with which the Federal Drug Administration (FDA) approves new drugs for general use. There are always rumors, and sometimes facts, about experimental treatments that are available in other countries but not in the United States. Because of the protests of AIDS activist groups such as AIDS Coalition to Unleash Power (ACT UP), the speed with which drug trials are conducted and new drugs approved by the FDA has been increased.

Strain on the U.S. Health Care System

AIDS is an expensive disease because people who have it may need a variety of intensive interventions over many years, many of them requiring hospitalization. The common medications are very expensive with the average monthly cost of AZT and ddl alone about $1,000. Let's take a young man in Providence as an example; we'll call him Greg. He is working full-time. His T count dipped below 200 once but usually is between 220 and 300. He has none of the diseases associated with AIDS. Each month he spends $680 for AZT and $360 for ddC. He also takes a monthly aerosolized pentamadine treatment (prophylactic against PCP) at a cost of between $650 and $800. Monthly visits to the doctor and blood work add another $75 to $250, depending on what needs to be done. Plus, he uses a variety of shelf medications such as Advil and Ibuprophin. These costs do not include those associated with his quarterly visits to his dentist. As his disease progresses, it is possible that it could cost another $1,000 monthly. Greg's monthly expenses (fortunately, his insurance plan pays for virtually all of these costs) range from $1,765 to $2,090. And all of this is on an outpatient basis. The costs zoom when people are hospitalized.

People with HIV and AIDS can suddenly become very ill with life-threatening infections. After hospitalization and appropriate medication, they may return to their lives for months or years without further enormous expense. Or, they may suffer a series of costly hospitalizations, one right after another. The course of the disease is unpredictable. What is predictable is the expense. Current estimates are that each case of AIDS costs roughly $100,000.

Questions about health care always must revolve around how we value a human life. For some, no expense is too great. For others, particularly when the causal factor is AIDS, nearly any cost is too great. The issue of cost will only escalate in the future as more people become infected and ill.

Who Is Responsible for AIDS?

While the U.S. Constitution is thought to protect all Americans, those of us in human services know well that discrimination continues in our society. Recent examples include the Rodney King beating in Los Angeles in 1992, the passage of Amendment 2 by Colorado voters in November, 1992, and the enormous public reaction to President Clinton's 1993 efforts to allow openly gay men and lesbians into the military.

In the example of AIDS, this discrimination manifests itself as a form of "blaming the victim." According to this way of thinking, people who contract AIDS do so because they violate society's norms by either using needle drugs or engaging in illicit or socially unaccepted (gay, extramarital, or premarital) sex. Some groups in our society then find it easy to adopt the position that people bring AIDS upon themselves. Since individuals are responsible for their own behaviors, some of which result in contracting AIDS, these individuals are ultimately responsible themselves for becoming ill. Thus, society should have no responsibility toward them. The rule then would seem to be: either obey society's rules or we don't care if you sicken and die. Taken to its logical extreme, this should mean that we refuse to provide treatment for victims of skin cancer who had spent time trying to get a tan, for victims of lung cancer who had smoked, for victims of cirrhosis who were heavy drinkers, and so on. So, we essentially would have groups of disposable people.

When translated into policy, this could mean that people with AIDS should be openly discriminated against, in housing or employment or public accommodation. It could mean the reduction in access to health care benefits. It could mean the stripping of civil liberties such as the right to privacy. People with HIV and AIDS could find that their health status is public information.

Because the disease initially affected gay men almost exclusively, public attitudes toward homosexuality are closely tied to antipathy toward PWAs. Some segments of American society would immediately stop all AIDS education, relying instead on exhortations for there to be no sex except between legally married heterosexual couples. However noble or ideal that goal, it ignores the data on sexual activity in America.

As long as AIDS continues to spread, these issues will be debated. As a human service worker, you will find yourself in an important role. You could be asked to provide expert testimony in court. You may be interviewed by people from the media. At the very least you are a voter who should be well-informed about the issues.

CONCLUSION

We reiterate that you will almost certainly work with people living with HIV and AIDS if you become a human service worker. This work can be richly rewarding, as can any human service work. But, because it involves serious illness and death, it can be debilitating as well. Only you can decide if this would be a good choice for you.

We urge you to consider a career working in one of the many kinds of AIDS organizations. In order to make such a decision, you must carefully examine your attitudes toward homosexuality, toward members of racial and ethnic minority groups, and toward people who use needle drugs. If you are disapproving or squeamish, either work through your issues or select another area in which to specialize. Do not enter this line of work as a means for improving your attitudes toward gay people, members of minority groups, or drug users, or for proselytizing or preaching. People with AIDS are or will become ill. They need your help and support. It would be unethical for you to use them for your own purposes.

To help you decide if AIDS work would be a good choice for you, begin to volunteer in a setting which provides services to people living with HIV and AIDS. Answer the telephone, raise money through phonathons or a Walk for Life or other means, stuff envelopes, staff the hotline, or become a buddy. Interview people who work in such agencies. Get to know other volunteers. You can gain valuable additional experience by doing a field placement or internship working with peo-

ple living with HIV and AIDS. Even if working with AIDS is not your preference, you will undoubtedly work with people who are HIV positive, so you must learn as much as you can about the disease and the needs of people who have it.

RESOURCES

There is a vast array of books available on the subject of HIV and AIDS; the card catalog of your library will be useful. But remember that knowledge about AIDS and HIV changes quickly. Daily newspapers and current periodicals and medical journals provide the most up-to-date information. Reading a daily newspaper, including the editorial pages and letters to the editor will also provide you with glimpses of your community's thoughts and beliefs about the epidemic. As noted in the chapter, *And the Band Played On* by Randy Shilts is a highly readable history of the earlier years of the disease; it is certainly not the only one available. To become involved and active in your local community, look under AIDS in your local telephone book. Most communities now have a hot-

line which can offer you direction. AIDS organizations almost always need help and money. You could also call your state department of health, and some areas have city or county health departments. Finally, there are several national hotlines which you can call for information, referrals, and printed material:

U.S. Department of Health/Center for Disease Control Hotline: 1-800-342-AIDS (24 hours, every day)

AIDS Clearinghouse for ordering materials in bulk: 1-800-458-5231

Spanish hotline: 1-800-344-7432 (8:00 A.M. to 2:00 A.M.)

TDD hotline: 1-800-243-7889 (10:00 A.M. to 10:00 P.M., weekdays)

CHAPTER 20

HELPING FOR ALCOHOL AND DRUG ABUSE

MARCEL A. DUCLOS
MARIANNE GFROERER

The statistics describing the use and abuse of alcohol and other mind-altering drugs ring familiar on the nightly news, find bold print in the newspapers, and flavor everyday conversations. General hospitals treat medical/surgical patients suffering from medical complications due to abuse and dependency. Emergency mental health and medical services are often faced with management of the intoxicated person. Community mental health centers daily confront the detrimental poly-drug use of scores of deinstitutionalized patients, including the dually diagnosed. School personnel, counselors, teachers, and administrators alike, witness the ebb and flow of the season's most preferred or most accessible substance on the school grounds. They must additionally contend with the far-reaching effects of substance use on students, families, and neighborhoods. Along with community workers and social service agency staff, law enforcement officers also struggle to overcome a gnawing defeatism when children and youth sustain, as victims, the ravages of their own or others' use in a cycle of destruction and even death.

No age group, no socioeconomic status, no level of education, no geographic area, urban, suburban, or rural, mountain, plain, or coast, no occupation or profession, no religious affiliation whether church, temple, synagogue, or mosque, protects from the insidious and infectious spread of the problem. Our society's cultural heritage of ambivalence reveals itself by the earliest promotion of the use of alcohol in the colonies and the colonial militia, combined with a primitive "righteous" response to inebriation. No time period in U.S. history, not even the years of Prohibition, provided a drug abuse-free environment for the growth and development of citizens. Nor can such an environment be anticipated for the near future. It is a dream, an idealistic vision. Human services practitioners must face the disillusionment of the present reality and continue to attend hopefully in the expectation of manageable goals realistically attainable by troubled and afflicted clients.

At-risk behaviors due to disinhibition and impaired judgment caused by mind-altering substances obligate human services practitioners to consider strategies—educational, medical, economic, political, sociological, psychological, and spiritual—to address the problems on the contemporary scene. These include those the nation shuns the most: the growing AIDS epidemic, all forms of child abuse, and the persisting plague of violence in our society. The long multicultural history of the human services teaches that the "cure" of human ills, including substance abuse problems, does not come from logic alone, but also from authentic caring. For the human services practitioner, caring in its concrete, active form means consistent and care-filled attention to the details of a realistic treatment plan.

The human services worker stands, as a generalist, in the middle of the network of providers, ready to work cooperatively with the many specialists assessing, developing treatment/service plans, delivering care, evaluations, and outcomes. In the arena of alcohol and drug abuse, the key challenge to the worker remains the same: achieving the earliest detection for possible prevention. Yet in the reality of the service delivery systems, the challenge almost always involves the detection of intoxication, the history of abuse, the possibility of dependence, and/or risk as victim or victimizer. No accurate or appropriate care can be designed and provided in any context without knowledge of the effects of drugs on a client's life. Failure to identify the contributing and resulting connections between substance abuse and the client's presenting problems with health, the law, money, work, school, society, family, and self will spell a decisive failure in care, however well-packaged the plan and well-intentioned the delivery. The old psychiatric rule "diagnosis predicts prognosis and therefore directs treatment" applies here as well.

The first challenge, then, is one of accuracy. However, much client care may be a matter of heart; it must be guided by knowledge and experience. Accurate knowledge of the Psychoactive Substance Use Disorders and their associated intoxication and withdrawal syndromes arms the worker with necessary information to intervene at the earliest possible moment. This continuum of care reaches from direct immediate crisis intervention to consultation and referral as required.

The second challenge lies in the subjective domain, in the human services worker's own personal story. Few individuals can claim never to have been touched by the effects of substance-induced behaviors, though they might claim, for themselves, lifelong abstinence. Whether in personal, social, or professional experiences, the human services worker will have accumulated learned responses to this population. The challenge of empathic acceptance, of healthy emotional distance, or dis-identification, of a client-enhancing response to countertransference, calls for clear, helpful supervision. Whether the service being delivered to the client entails modest assistance with some agency paperwork, or involves the complex, long-term work of case manage-

ment, the energy at the meeting of client and practitioner will generate the atmosphere of change. It therefore becomes an inner challenge for the worker to know her/his own story and to use that level of awareness to promote the client's good and to attempt to cause no harm.

The third challenge pertains to the temptation of the human services practitioner to view his/herself as competent to function as a substance abuse counselor though lacking the specialized academic training and clinical experience. The treatment of substance abuse and dependence is a multidisciplinary enterprise. The work of a substance abuse counselor is defined by observable and measurable competencies. For the human services worker who serves an addicted population, it is an ethical imperative to know his/her limits of competence and role within the agency, and to consult and refer as necessary.

The worker who is unfamiliar with the neurological impairments caused by particular substances abused would be in danger of placing the client, self, and others in physical and/or psychological jeopardy. Depressants, stimulants, narcotics, and hallucinogens present their own sets of impairments and their own relative levels of danger. Confusion about the client's antecedent or resultant developmental and personality disorders would make the adoption of an individualized helping style difficult. Early trauma in combination with many years, even decades, of substance abuse exacts heroic transformational work on the part of the recovering person. Overestimation of the addicted person's ability to stop using and become sober without sufficient time for emotional healing and behavior change would lead to errors in the selection of strategy, expectation of outcomes, and in the fundamental process of defining the real problems. The nature of the disorder, and of rehabilitation, leads to paradox for the recovering addict as well as for the human services practitioner.

Again, the history of drug use gives us a clue about the paradoxical nature of psychoactive substances, of the disease of substance addiction, and of the recovery process. The ancients and the alchemists taught that nature cured disease with either similars or opposites, depending on the illness. Substance abuse and dependence is such a disease. The substances themselves produce their opposites: depressants can rebound into anxiety; stimulants can plunge into depression; narcotics produce their own pain; hallucinogens can lead to loss of self. That which the user originally sought through partaking of the drug eventually eludes the abuser. The drug exacts due payment for all experiences—soothing, exciting, painless, or expansive. All that was beyond the ego's humble ability to integrate into the psyche and beyond the body's physiological capacity to metabolize into vital energy returns with a vengeance.

The enslaving addiction to the drug releases the abuser to an opposite dependence, binding her/him to a committed pursuit of inner freedom hard won by selfless courage. In the tradition of recovery, the paradox of the twelve-step program of Alcoholics Anonymous (and Narcotics Anonymous) describe that which will nurse the recovering person back to sanity with an elixir of opposites—a bitter medicine that many will reject. No recovery program anywhere can sidestep the necessary laws of nature that direct bodies, minds, and souls from illness to health.

The client's life calls for a complete turnaround—nothing less will do. The cleverness and cunning that characterized the addiction must become slowness and carefulness, accepting the wisdom of another, allowing the unshakable inner self to put aside the false grandiose ego projected by the substance. A new life begins only with the death of the old one. It is ultimately the paradox of life and death, because substance dependency is a matter of life and death.

The human services respond to the problem of addiction in society in three ways: education, prevention, and treatment. The choice of response is determined by the level of addiction which is the target of the approach. Limiting considerations to the individual, the human services distinguish between the person who has never used drugs for recreation, the one who only rarely uses chemicals for recreation, the person who uses frequently and whose abuse leads to some personal and professional problems, the individual who is dependent

to the point of resulting medical complications, and the small percentage of individuals who, in their chemical dependency, are also socially isolated and face predictable death. Because chemical dependency is potentially life threatening, the human services respond according to the immediacy of the danger to self and others.

Successful drug education programs have incorporated in their materials and services the knowledge, attitudes, and behavior necessary to optimize the choice of a drug-abuse-free life. Some programs emphasize convincing the audience of the dangers of drugs, while other programs underline the objective facts about the substances, neither advocating abstinence nor reasonable use. Other programs utilize the power of identification with a noteworthy person in recovery to score a point with the listeners or viewers. Other programs, especially those geared toward the school and college-age population, are even more direct in their approach, providing training in assertively resisting encircling pressures.

Prevention does not only refer to those persuasive efforts aimed at stopping abuse before it starts. It also involves those interventions aimed at signaling to a user in the early stages of abuse that continued use could result in damaging consequences. Early diagnosis, with crisis monitoring, crisis intervention, and referral, are such interventions. For those individuals who are in the later stages of abuse that lead to dependency, the prevention efforts address the goal of halting the slide to that conclusion. In this instance, intervention efforts could take the form of early treatment, monitored maintenance, or social/medical detoxification. The motto "the best defense is a good offense" applies in this domain.

Because drug abuse and drug dependence are characterized as mental disorders in the Diagnostic and Statistical Manual of Mental Disorders (DSM-IV), medicine, nursing, and psychology are the disciplines that have traditionally taken responsibility for the treatment of these illnesses. Social work and mental health counseling have also sought to remedy the social and societal ills due to substance addiction. The profession of substance abuse counseling, newly emergent in the early

1970s, has now taken on a prominent role in the treatment of individuals suffering from substance related disorders. Human services providers who are certified by the International Certification Reciprocity Consortium as alcohol and drug abuse counselors have given evidence of specialized competence in their assigned roles and functions as they work along side of the other traditional professions. These particular individuals have passed an objective exam and have been successful in an oral defense of a case presentation before a member State Board. They also may choose to be a member of the National Association of Alcoholism and Drug Abuse Counselors (NAADAC).

All of these professionals, according to their own training and skills, cooperate to achieve the client's goals of physical and psychological health, social and financial stability, and behavioral and interpersonal satisfaction. In all of this, there still remains a key role for the generalist in the human services field: that of case manager, as the coordinator of all of those services that promote follow-through and the attainment of the treatment goals.

Whether the goals are abstinence after detoxification, management of disruptive behavior, stability of employment or housing, or improved overall self-care and health, the variety of treatment settings and assortment of approaches employed is as diverse as the developmental needs and problems of the clients. Depending on the severity of the addiction, the setting might be an in-hospital treatment program, a residential center, a day program, or outpatient individual, family, or group contact. The human services worker has a valuable role in all of these, as a team member with other providers.

It is important to note that treatment facilities vary depending on the population served and the substance treated. Though they have commonalities worth acknowledging, treatment facilities may, in order to focus on specific areas of need, specialize in the elderly, adolescents, womens' issues, cocaine or heroin abuse, homeless individuals, or the dually diagnosed. In each case, the facility will function along standard guidelines of substance abuse treatment but with its own particular focus. With this in mind, an outline of generally-found treatment facilities follows:

In-Hospital Treatment Program

Used for:

— detoxification from physical dependence
— individuals unable to remain substance-free without supervision

Provides:

— medical monitoring of withdrawal
— emphasis is on group psychoeducational counseling and introduction to support groups such as AA/NA
— may provide some social services/case management

Length of Stay:

— 12 to 28 days (some may be as brief as 3–7 days depending on insurance coverage)
— may transition into outpatient program

Residential Treatment Center

Used for:

— long-term maintenance of sobriety/drug abstinence after detoxification
— individuals without financial resources in need of halfway house/therapeutic community for recovery

Provides:

— necessities of daily living, i.e., shelter, nutrition, life-skills training, education
— emphasis is on role modeling, direct reality-based feedback in daily living situations and self-discipline

Length of Stay:

— three months to two years (usually funded by public or private nonprofit agencies)
— includes assistance for vocational, social, and emotional transition back into community/family living

Outpatient Services

Used for:

— transitional treatment after detoxification or residential treatment
— individuals with early stage or less severe problems, those not physically addicted, those able to maintain employment during treatment, or those living in a stable and supportive environment
— individuals unable to afford or not eligible for In-Hospital or Residential treatment programs

Provides:

- counseling, education, support system
- emphasis is on individual, couples, family, and group
- may also include case management, transportation, socialization
- assessment and referral to more intensive types of treatment if needed

Length of Stay:

- participation varies according to need and facility; may be once a day, all day, each evening, twice weekly, to once every two weeks. Some facilities provide open-ended "drop-in" type groups for occasional support of program "graduates"
- no set limit on length of service use; may be fee for service based on ability to pay, or public or private non-profit funded

In order to function as a valuable and valued team member in such settings, the human services student must be attentive to the skills needed in the field. Employers expect trained human services practitioners to understand how the health and human services work. Students must, therefore, gain skills in coordinating the services a client receives, while also being able to help the same client access the services of other agencies as the need arises. Given the multiplicity of needs and problems that the substance abuser presents, the student is obligated to at least know how to access the multiple services required to meet treatment goals developed by the program.

Knowing the resources is one thing; but helping the client to choose and use a service is another. Perhaps the most fundamental skill that the student has to offer this troubled client is the skill of professional helping. To be more specific, this is the art of attending: the quiet, focused, other-centered attention that develops an investment in the process of change on the part of the client. Consistent, focused attending can raise a client's self-esteem, foster, perhaps even repair, trust, and increase feelings of effectiveness. These basic building blocks of a successful life are the inevitable results of the authentic, professional, helping relationship. This is really the central gift at the heart of all the human services practitioner's efforts. To attend in a way

that invites the client into eventual self-direction stands out as the main contribution which can enliven the delivery of care.

Students in the field of human services who seek additional proficiency in the area of alcohol and drug abuse may seek specific training in the following skills:

1. Taking an alcohol and drug use history
2. Identifying abuse and dependency, including the withdrawal syndromes
3. Recognizing the complications of drug interactions
4. Using the pertinent resources in the community
5. Imparting accurate information about abusable substances
6. Adapting services to the needs of specific populations

A question remains to be addressed: What specific body of knowledge and array of skills would provide the proficiency required to work effectively in the service delivery field of alcohol and drug abuse as an independent professional? For the sake of brevity, this article will only identify and parenthetically discuss major categories of competency.

These categories have been grouped under the headings of the Twelve Core Functions of a Counselor, which define and describe a professional human services provider as a specialist in over forty states. Furthermore, training for these core functions is available at the associate, bachelor, and master's level of formal education. It is also available to individuals through approved professional workshops, staff development, and continuing education courses. Currently, the federally funded Project for Addictions Counselor Training (PACT) offers knowledge and skill-based instruction leading to eligibility for certification, registration, or licensure through the aforementioned Consortium under the laws of member state boards.

Under these guidelines, a specialist/counselor in this field must be able to screen potential clients to determine whether they are eligible and appropriate for admission into the available program. If the person in need meets the established criteria for admission, the counselor will conduct the intake process so as to insure the clarity of the emerging treatment contract and trusting rapport between the client and the program. At this point, the counselor will orient the client in the ways and means, rules, and structure of the recovery program, providing an inner and outer safe millieu for the start of the work of recovery. With the information gathered so far, by all of the professionals involved, the counselor will pursue the formulation of an assessment of the individual's strengths, weaknesses, problems, and needs relevant to the mutual work of change. The focus of both client and counselor becomes the partnership necessary to decide on an individualized treatment plan. Problem identification, rank ordering of changeable problems, time lines of change, and methodologies all become part of the client-approved plan or strategy for change.

This plan must be multidimensional. It must include all the domains of human growth and development and all of the health and human services as necessary. To this end, the specialist must be a fundamentally sound individual, group, and family counselor. Because of the problems and needs of clients beset by the ravages of chemical addiction, the specialist must be able to coordinate the many services prescribed in the treatment plan. In the course of treatment, there will almost always be at least one crisis. The certified counselor will be able to respond to crises in a way that maximizes safeguarding the client's rehabilitation and turns the threat to recovery into an opportunity for continuing growth.

Throughout the treatment efforts, imparting accurate and germaine information about addic-tions and the road to recovery remains a major function of the trained counselor. When the needs of the client cannot be met by a particular provider or by a particular program, the obligation to refer guides the accessing of other sources of help. This obligation may be exercised from the moment of screening to the time of discharge, aftercare, and follow-up.

Finally, in carrying out all of the above functions, including intra- and interagency consultations, the human services specialist, in this field of addictions as in all the other branches of this profession, must be able to accurately keep records and write reports. It is essential that all records and reports maintain overall privacy and confidentiality, while being clear, understandable, and complete. This allows for the effective continuum of care for the client's benefit.

Alcohol and drugs are perhaps the most constant variable in the synergistic forces that trouble the lives of human services clients. The arguments in favor of continued specialized training flow from the case management records of service delivery agencies. Whether a generalist, specialist/counselor, or student practitioner, the goal of the human services in helping for alcohol and drug abuse remains ultimately the same. It is to encourage, assist, and enhance the recovery process with specific skills, knowledge, humanity, and genuine caring. It is to promote a life that will empower the recovering person to be, as the poet (Anon.) wrote, "tender enough to cry, human enough to make mistakes, strong enough to absorb pain, and resilient enough to come back and try again."

SELECTED BIBLIOGRAPHY_____

Abadinsky, H., (1993). *Drug Abuse: An Introduction,* 2nd ed. Chicago: Nelson-Hall.

Ackerman, R.J., ed., (1986). *Growing in the Shadow: Children of* Alcoholics. Pompano Beach, FL: Health Communications.

Alcoholics Anonymous: *The Story of How Many Thousands of Men and Women Have Recovered from Alcoholism,* (1976). New York Alcoholics Anonymous World Services.

Bauer, J., (1982). *Alcoholism and Women: The Background and the Psychology.* Toronto: Inner City Books.

Boaz, D., (1993). *Embrace Your Child-Self: Change Your Life—A Workbook.* Seattle: Lane's End Publishing.

Chandler, M., (1987). *Whiskey's Song: An Explicit Story of Surviving in an Alcoholic Home.* Pompano Beach, FL: Health Communications.

Chappelle, F., T.G. Durham, D. Lauderman, D.J. Powell, L. Siembad, and N. Simonds, eds., (1992). Counselor development: A training manual for drug and alcohol abuse counselors.

Clayton, L., and R. Van Nostrand, (1993). *The Professional Alcohol and Drug Counselor Supervisor's Handbook.* Holmes Beach, FL: Learning Publications, Inc.

Cultural Competence for Evaluators: Guide for Alcohol and Other Drug Abuse Practitioners Working with Ethnic and Racial Communities (1992). DHHS—A&DA and MH Administration.

Doweiko, H.F., (1993). *Concepts of Chemical Dependence,* 2nd ed. Pacific Grove, CA: Brooks/Cole.

Dusek, D.E., and D.A. Girdano, (1993). *Drug: A Factual Account.* New York: McGraw-Hill.

Estes, N.J., and M. Heinemann, (1992). *Alcoholism: Development, Consequences, and Interventions.* St. Louis: Mosby.

Evans, K., and J.M. Sullivan, (1990). *Dual Diagnosis: Counseling the Mentally Ill Substance Abuser.* New York: Guilford.

Flores, P.J., (1988). *Group Psychotherapy with Addicted Populations.* New York: Haworth.

Freeman, E.M., (1992). *The Addiction Process: Effective Social Work Approaches.* New York: Longman.

Goode, E., (1993). *Drugs in American Society.* New York: McGraw-Hill.

Goodwin, D., (1975). *Is Alcoholism Hereditary?* New York: Oxford University Press.

Inaba, D.S. and W.H. Cohen, (1993). *Uppers, Downers, All Arounders: Physical and Mental Effects of Psychoactive Drugs.* Ashland, OR: CNS Productions, Inc.

Jacobs, M.R., (1981). *Problems Presented by Alcoholic Clients: A Handbook of Counseling Strategies.* Toronto: Addiction Research Foundation.

Journal of Counseling and Development, (1991). *Special Issue: Multiculturalism as a Fourth Force in Counseling.* Vol. 70.

Hanson, G., and P. Venturelli, (1995). *Drugs and Society.* Boston: Jones and Bartlett.

Khantzian, E.J., K.S. Halliday, and W.E. McAuliffe, (1990). *Addiction and the Vulnerable Self: Modified Dynamic Group Therapy for Substance Abusers.* New York: Guilford.

Kinney, J.K., (1992). *Clinical Manual of Substance Abuse.* St. Louis: Mosby.

Kinney, J.K., and G. Leaton, (1995). *Loosening the Grip.* St. Louis: Mosby.

Kleinman, M.A., (1992). *Against Excess: Drug Policy for Results.* New York: Basic Books.

Kulewicz, S.F., (1990). *The Twelve Core Functions of a Counselor.* Malborough: Counselor Publications.

Lawson, G., and A. Lawson, (1989). *Alcoholism and Substance Abuse in Special Populations.* Rockfield: Aspen.

Leonard, L.S., (1989). *Witness to the Fire: Creativity and the Veil of Addiction.* Boston: Shambala.

McNeece, C.A., and D.M. DiNitto, (1994). *Chemical Dependency: A Systems Approach.* Englewood Cliffs, NJ: Prentice-Hall.

Roebuck, J.B., and R.G. Kessler, (1972). *The Etiology of Alcoholism.* Springfield, IL: Charles C. Thomas.

Roy, O., and C. Ksir, (1993). *Drugs, Society, and Human Behavior.* St. Louis: Mosby.

Royce, J.E., (1989). *Alcohol Problems and Alcoholism: A Comprehensive Survey.* New York: Free Press.

Steinglass, P., (1987). *The Alcoholic Family.* New York: Basic Books.

Vaillant, G.E., (1983). *The Natural History of Alcoholism.* Boston: Harvard University Press.

Ward, D.A., (1983). *Alcoholism: Introduction to Theory and Treatment.* Dubuque, IA: Kendall/Hunt.

KEY TERMS FOR PART FIVE

In completing Chapters 15, 16, 17, 18, 19, and 20 you will have a command of the following key terms, major concepts, and principal topical references:

Cycle of Abuse	Gerontology	Self-Help
Societal Denial	American Association of	Substance-Related Disorders
Domestic Violence	Retired Persons (AARP)	Counter Transference
Battered Women	AIDS/PWAs	A.A. & N.(narcotics)A.
Honeymoon Phase	HIV-1, -2	DSMIV
Empowerment	Centers for Disease Control	Project for Addictions
"Graying of America"	Americans with Disabilities	Counselor Training (PACT)
Alzheimer's Disease	(ADA) Act (1992)	International Certification
Age Discrimination in	Eviction Prevention Services	Reciprocity Consortium
Employment Act	Shelters	NAADAC

PIVOTAL ISSUES FOR DISCUSSION OF PART FIVE

1. Make a series of lists of special consumer (clients) populations in human services. Organize the lists by major demographic variables (i.e., age, gender, ethnicity, race, level of intellectual functioning, mental status, employment, income, number in family, physical condition, amount of education, criminal backgrounds). How and where are these consumers served? By whom? What are their special issues in receiving and responding to help?

2. What are the major causes of child sexual abuse? What can be done to reduce and/or eliminate this social issue?

3. What is the relationship between drug and alcohol abuse and domestic violence? How does spousal abuse, in some cases, continue to be perpetuated in 2nd or 3rd primary relationships involving the same woman? What can be done to help such a person?

4. Visit an NA meeting. Visit an Al-anon meeting. What were your impressions, feelings, and reactions to what you observed? Are there similar resources on your campus? If not, what can you do to initiate the organization of a similar group for students on campus?

SUGGESTED READINGS FOR PART FIVE

1. Lamb, H.R., (1984). *The Homeless Mentally Ill*. Wash. DC: American Psychiatric Association.

2. Hope, M. and Young, J., (1986). *The Faces of Homelessness*. Lexington MA: Lexington Books.

3. Kozol, Jonathan, (1988). *Rachel and Her Children: Homeless Families in America*, New York: Crown Pub. Co.

4. Estes, C.L., (1979). *The Aging Enterprise. A Critical Examination of Social Policies and Services for the Aged*. San Francisco: Jossey-Bass Publications.

5. Hilts, P.J., (1991). *AIDS Panel Backs Efforts to Exchange Drug Users Needles*, NY Times, August 7, p. A1.

PART SIX

HUMAN SERVICES: POLITICS, PROMOTION, AND DELIVERY SYSTEMS

Part Six includes the topics of the political process, advocacy, empowerment, prevention, and community-based service delivery.

As a human services professional you will find yourself fully challenged with demands and seemingly insurmountable problems of our job tasks. However, it is also necessary to save some time and energy for a large overriding issue: the social context of human service problems and solutions. Frequently, securing public support through legislation and money for programs is the major first step needed to solve a problem. This chapter deals with various aspects of getting the public committed to help with solving a problem.

Harold McPheeters in Chapter 21 discusses the importance of public policy and policies to human services. The article is instructive on how to be involved in getting your concern into political focus. There are different avenues of involvement and influence. It may be necessary, for example, to lobby regulatory bodies or launch a media campaign. Additionally, there are different ways, from voter registration drives to coalition-building, to have an impact on who becomes the elected official, and/or what that elected official represents. At the conclusion of the chapter is a Special Focus Feature on empowerment by Audrey Cohen which illustrates a training model designed to produce change agents and how this curriculum, in turn, bears upon the empowerment of the student/consumer it serves. In the cycle of change and influence, it places the urban consumer at the hub of catalystic reform.

In Chapter 22, David Liederman, Madelyn DeWoody and Megan Sylvester describe the work of the Child Welfare Delivery System in the United States. When this chapter was written, the authors worked for the Child Welfare League of America, which is a private umbrella organization which is devoted to serving the needs and solving the problems of children. In addition to the wide variety of child welfare services, the league has another function which is to advocate for children. It is important to note that they maintain an extensive research effort so that, when campaigning for an issue, they can present the strongest case based on facts.

Iris Heckman in Chapter 23 discusses prevention as the too often neglected but basic approach to solving a problem. So many problems can be traced to social injustice, and the human services focus on prevention is part of the struggle for humane social change. The chapter argues that more emphasis, resources, and effort should be given to preventing a problem before it becomes a crisis.

Now that you have an understanding of advocating and promoting human services, you should also be aware of the direction of some human services programs. Chapter 24 by Joseph Mehr deals with an important direction for human service programs. The chapter discussion covers the historical changes in how mental health services are delivered. Analysis of the impact of these shifts from institutional care to community-based mental health supports is also examined. You will see how policymakers in the legislature and bureaucratic organizations influence the distribution of funding for delivery systems and how these processes impact on training and education of human service workers. In the chapter, you learn about a variety of new approaches to treatment programming and case management and thusly will appreciate the outcomes of these dynamic sociopolitical systems of influence.

In this part's second Special Focus Feature, Mary Di Giovanni presents a very comprehensive description of an innovative and unique training program. The Residence Manager Certificate Program at Northern Essex Community College serves as an exemplary nondegree education program for human service workers in mental health and mental retardation, and has enjoyed a history of recognition and respect. In your continued exposure to the ever-changing dimensions of the field of human services you will be increasingly aware of the need for creative development of new and more relevant delivery systems. What have been presented have been examples of both broadbased, system-change shifts in delivery services and a specific, focused nondegree training program for resident managers in mental health and mental retardation.

Part Six has provided some contemporary insights into the political process, the role of advocacy, empowerment and the origins of changing delivery systems, and the influences those shifts have on training and education in human services. What is also changing for human services is recognition of the increasing importance of taking into account both issues of technology and a global perspective. This is discussed in Part Seven.

LEARNING OBJECTIVES FOR PART SIX:
HUMAN SERVICES: POLITICS, PROMOTION, AND DELIVERY SYSTEMS

Upon reading and studying Chapters 21, 22, 23, and 24:

- You will understand the process of social change utilizing the political and legislative systems.
- You will know how to use local, state, and federal contacts in gathering information about social issues and to identify available resources in dealing with these issues.
- You will understand the concept of advocacy as it applies to the work of the human services professional.
- You will be able to describe the contemporary models of delivering services to those needing help and the implications of recent changes in the focus of these programs.
- You will appreciate the meaning and impact of the process of empowerment and how the human services professional uses this process to effect social change.
- You will become familiar with the concept and practice of prevention in human services.
- You will be aware of exemplary programs in human services training that credential students in management skills and orient students to creating and promoting the empowerment of clients.

CHAPTER 21

POLICY, POLITICS, AND HUMAN SERVICES

FOR THE NATIONAL ORGANIZATION FOR HUMAN SERVICE EDUCATION, 9 OCTOBER 1992

HAROLD L. McPHEETERS

I wish to begin with a few words of special appreciation for Dr. Ron Feinstein of your organization. Dr. Feinstein was one of the pioneers of the human services education movement. I have been privileged to have been with him in perhaps two dozen meetings as we forged some of the concepts and directions for the movement. I always found him to be knowledgeable, critical, analytic and positively involved. It was a pleasure to have known him and worked with him, but I especially want to mention his leadership here, because he was one of our most active human services educators in the area of public policy development and political action. A few months ago he died from a heart affliction while in the office of a Pennsylvania state senator on such a mission. We shall miss him.

In modern times the primary sanction and funding for both human services delivery programs and human services educational programs is government. The days when churches or private charitable organizations provided the major impetus for health and welfare services and funding have long receded despite some nostalgic urgings that somehow a "thousand points of light" might assume this responsibility. There are still many private and charitable groups involved in human services delivery, but most of them receive both their sanction and much of their funding from federal, state, or county governments. By sanction I mean their

charters and licenses for the programs and their staffs, required standards of operation, tax exemption, liability, and often public oversight. Funding may be through direct governmental grants or contracts or the fees from programs such as Medicaid and Medicare. Virtually all of the human services educational programs are located in either public institutions or in institutions that receive much of their funding from governmental sources.

Thus, for self interest alone, human services educators must be involved in public policy and politics related to human services. In addition, human services educators, with their depth of understanding of human service needs and programs, should be involved in helping key government officials make better policy decisions for the human services. It is sometimes sad to see educators from the human services education programs turn away from involvement in policy development and politics, or worse yet, to constantly criticize and express contempt for public officials and politicians. Such an attitude helps no one, least of all one's own program and its graduates. Many of the most effective human services educators are active in public policy developments and find that their programs and graduates are more frequently requested and better regarded as a consequence.

The two areas of public policy and politics are closely related.

Public policy development is the process of helping national, state, and local governments and professional and voluntary associations decide what laws, regulations, programs, philosophies, and values are to be implemented and how. It also involves deciding how to obtain the funds and other necessary resources for the programs.

Politics is the process of nominating and electing officials to legislative and top executive positions in local, state, and federal governments (and sometimes judges) and drafting and enacting legislation to implement major policy directions.

PUBLIC POLICY

It is generally in the area of public policy development that human services professionals can have their greatest impact, but it is also the area in which they are least involved—at least as organized groups. This is probably because public policy development is not as well defined or as well-publicized as politics. In fact, many times elected and appointed officials of government seem to have no particular interest in policy development—they have no vision of where they want their agency to be or how to get there. This is no different from private corporations or voluntary organizations that have no policy or planning mechanism for the future, but simply keep on doing what they have always done despite changing times and needs.

There seem to be cycles in our society when we expect our institutions to behave in progressive and purposeful ways, while at other times in the cycle there is a trend to be preoccupied with the immediate bottom line. Such conservative thinking discourages policy development and planning; planning staff and research and development personnel are let go as "unnecessary middle level managers." The disadvantages soon become evident, and then the cycle changes. As a nation we have been through a twelve-year cycle of conservatism, but now the tide appears to be turning. Unfortunately, the excesses of the recent past have left huge deficits and debts which will impede our nation and our institutions for some time to come.

But that is all the more reason for careful policy development, and it is likely that we shall see much more of it in the future. However, governments and all of our agencies and institutions, primarily as a result of litigation and court orders, have recently begun to establish mechanisms for more sharply defining their policies and procedures, and those mechanisms provide the route for our inputs into the policy-making process. Among them are:

1. *Regulation writing.* Legislation is generally very broad in scope and leaves to the operating agencies the responsibility for developing the necessary policies, procedures, regulations, etc. This is the process called "administrative law." Thirty years ago, this was likely to be a haphazard process that too frequently was never formally done or committed to writing. However, as a result of lawsuits from clients, families, staff, etc., governments have instituted a whole set of legally mandated procedures for "administrative rule making." The procedures almost always provide for public hearings and comments and suggestions from interested individuals and organizations. This is where the inputs of human services educators should be made through the following steps:

a. Learn the legal requirements and procedures of the administrative rule making process for the relevant units of government and get on their mailing lists to receive notices of the public hearings, dates, and names of responsible official persons to receive comments, etc., for the writing of specific regulations.

b. Participate in the public hearings. This may require making appointments to appear on the program and preparing written statements for the hearings. It is generally desirable to participate in hearings as an organization rather than as an individual, but either is generally acceptable. Presentations at hearings should be documented as much as possible and be cognizant of the realities of budgets, geographic realities, etc., facing the agency.

c. Send in written comments to preliminary drafts of regulations if one is unable to be present at the hearing. This is an entirely acceptable forum for letters from individuals. It is always best to make specific and well-documented suggestions, rather than simple statements that the drafts are unacceptable or one-sided statements with no documentation or with biased documentation.

2. *Advisory Bodies to Public and Voluntary Agencies.* At still another level, public and voluntary agencies increasingly make use of citizen boards, advisory groups, and private consultants. Human services educators should be represented on such citizen bodies. Their organizations should take the initiative to suggest names of their members who will serve on those bodies, especially at the national and state levels, but there is nothing wrong with the educators suggesting their own names and their willingness to serve, especially to local agencies. Here, too, the persons who serve in such capacities should expect to represent the best interests of the total agency, but also speak to the interests of the human services profession and its educational programs. This implies that the person becomes knowledgeable about the broadest issues affecting the agency and its operations.

3. *Special Task Groups and Studies.* Public and voluntary agencies and legislative research bodies frequently find themselves faced with the need for special studies of problems and the development of recommendations for addressing them. These special studies range from clinical issues such as how to best manage the problems of AIDS patients in the prisons or mental hospitals to organizational issues, such as how to best relate the state institutions organizationally and financially to local public and voluntary programs. Here again human services educators should be represented on at least some of these citizen study bodies or as consultants to them.

4. *Networking with Other Organizations.* Many professional and advocacy organizations are also interested in public policy and will be using some of these same strategies to influence it. Human services educators should join with them. Most educators come from one of the traditional professions of social work, psychology, counseling, etc. Join those professional organizations as well as advocacy organizations, such as mental health associations, associations for retarded citizens, and public welfare associations, and become active in their affairs so that you multiply your impact on the public policy process.

5. *Participation in Media Activities.* Another way of participating in the public policy debate, especially at the local level, is to take part in media activities, such as writing letters to editors, writing special articles for newspapers and magazines, and appearing on media panels and radio talk shows. These activities require some special talent at being brief and to-the-point with a special sensitivity to the perspective of the general public.

6. *Inviting Agency Officials and Policy Makers to Participate in your Programs.* Many human services educators have found it useful to invite key persons from human service agencies and local policy makers to participate in their educational programs as speakers, panelists or as advisory committee members. In that way they come to know you and your program, so that they are likely to call upon you when they face policy questions that they feel you may be able to answer. In any case, such persons should be invited to participate in such activities and kept on the mailing list to receive reports, newsletters, etc., from your program.

POLITICS

Participation in the political process is a more directed, promotional, and often adversarial process of working for the election of specific candidates or the enactment of specific pieces of legislation by the legislative body and then getting the responsible executive officer to sign the legislation. This process is better known, and it is the one that human services educators are more likely to use. However, because of the nature of the democratic process of our governments, it is also one in which there is a strong possibility of being on the losing side. This may be no problem unless it means that your candidate and all that he/she stands for is defeated and everyone in a responsible position is replaced.

The processes of working for the election of candidates and working for legislation are somewhat different although related. It should be clear to human services educators, as it is to members of Political Action Committees (PACs), that an elected official is much more likely to be responsive to someone who has worked actively in the election campaign than to a complete stranger.

Electing Candidates Supportive of Human Services

The general process of electing candidates to office is familiar to each of you, but there are a few specific pointers to keep in mind.

Register and Vote. This seems obvious, but it is astounding that so few eligible voters bother to get themselves registered or vote, and I am regularly surprised to discover that some of those nonvoters are persons who have very significant stakes in the election. In most jurisdictions it is better to register in a specific political party rather than as an independent. In many places "independents" are not allowed to vote in primary elections where some of the most critical decisions are made.

Learn the Candidates and Help Them Take Stands on Issues. Meet the candidates or learn about them and their positions on human services issues. At local and state levels it is not difficult to attend programs and events where the candidates are in attendance and discuss human services issues with them. At Congressional and Presidential levels this becomes more difficult and is best done through established organizations. If it is not possible to reach the candidates themselves, talk with their campaign staff persons, but the most effective personal contacts will be made early before the heat of campaigning consumes all the candidate's time. Send candidates letters and ask for their response and commitments. Most candidates are anxious to reply to such letters of concern.

Make Financial Contributions to Candidates and Parties. Political campaigns cost money, and many a campaign has been lost because money ran out too soon. This has been a special problem for women candidates. The political parties do not provide much financial support for candidates until the later stages of the campaign. At the early stages, especially at the level of the primaries, the candidates are on their own to finance their campaigns, and it is at this stage that individual contributions are especially welcomed. It is at this stage that candidates learn whether there is real *public* interest in their candidacies or whether it is just the special interests. Such early contributions are especially likely to be remembered.

EMILY's (Early Money Is Like Yeast) List is an organized effort to help with the early financing of the campaigns of Democratic women who support free choice, but the individual supporters from EMILY's List are sure to be remembered.

The two major sources of funds for political campaigns are (a) individual contributions and (b) contributions from PACS or private organizations with vested interests in the outcome of the election. Later contributions to political campaigns are important whether they come from individuals or organizations, but they are likely to be more substantial and memorable when they come from groups that can pool their contributions as the PACS do. Be careful not to violate the ethics rules for political contributions. Do not make large contributions in cash; use a check and note that it is a campaign contribution.

Join Political Parties and Work in Campaigns. Join the political parties and work in the campaigns to reach the candidates with your suggestions and influence. It will help the candidate's campaign to have your organizational work and moral support. Organizational work is frequently crucial to a campaign, especially for a lesser known candidate. When you work in their campaigns, the candidates get to know you as individuals and are likely to respect your opinions later on when and if they are elected. This can also be a useful way to get to know some of the other campaign workers who may later become the staff workers for the official if the campaign is successful.

Influencing Legislation

Influencing legislation is tricky business. It has been said that the public is better off not to see how sausage is made or how bills become laws. There are many considerations.

Learn the Legislative Procedures. Learn the legislative procedures for how bills may be introduced and by which house, how they are referred to committees, which kinds of bills go to which committees, how they are likely to be amended, how they pass from house to house, and how they go to the executive officer for signature or veto. The procedures vary from place to place and even from time to time. To a considerable extent they depend on unwritten customs and temporary political alliances. Learn about these!

Keep Informed of All Bills of Interest.   Keep on top of bills introduced in your legislative body and get copies of the ones relevant to your interests. There is almost always some kind of published daily record of the bills that have been introduced, to which committees they have been assigned, and their progress through the legislative session. Arrange to subscribe to this legislative journal or examine it regularly in a library that subscribes to it. It is not unusual to find bills that either conflict with ones that you are following or duplicate all or parts of them. Copies of bills are usually available the day following their introduction.

It is also important to keep aware of any amendments made in any of the bills that interest you. Opposition groups may have succeeded in totally reversing the intent of your bill or amending it with completely unacceptable changes. In the political process anything can happen! There is no widely published account of such amendments. It is vital to check with key committee members or staff persons (if there are staff persons).

Attend and Participate in Committee Hearings. Committee hearings are usually short of time to consider all persons and groups who desire to be heard, so appointments may be required. Also, be brief and to the point with documentation whenever possible. Have your statement written and duplicated for handout. Be aware of the broad implications of your testimony (e.g., its cost implications, its impact on rural areas or minority groups) and be prepared for any kind of question or criticism. It is well to anticipate organized opposition and acknowledge it and any efforts that have been made to work out conflicts. Legislators take a dim view of proposals that draw opposition where there has been no indication of efforts of the opposing parties to negotiate their difference. Such bills very likely will be tabled until the next session when they will have to be re-introduced.

If you cannot arrange to participate in the hearings, try to get a written statement to the committee for its consideration. If the statement comes from an organized group that has documented support from relevant organizations (e.g., public agency administrators, health insurers), so much the better. It is better to get these statements to members of the specific committees that are considering the bills rather than to your personal representative or senator, but send your own representative an information copy. And be timely with such statements! Be aware of the committee's schedule for when a vote is likely to be taken, and get statements to them ahead of that time.

Personal calls to committee members are also helpful, especially if they include the logic and reasoning for your position rather than just a message to vote for or against a specific bill. Formal petitions and messages that urge votes for one side or the other are tabulated, but play little role in the committee's decision.

Contact Your Personal Legislators.   Your personal legislator should know what you want done, either from personal contacts or letters or telephone calls. The more different legislators who are approached by different members of a group with a common interest, the better, especially when it comes to the vote, if and when the bill comes to the floor for a full vote. Your personal legislator may be willing and able to negotiate with committee members of the committee that is considering your bill while the bill is in committee. Be aware, however, that the issue should then probably have to be one with considerable political importance to justify your legislator's using his/her political capital.

Bills are introduced by individual legislators, but it is usually wise to carefully choose which legislator to make the introduction—usually one with some tenure and reputation for expertise in the area of the bill's concern. It is necessary to meet with that legislator and present your proposal and follow the legislator's advice. Keep in mind that bills introduced early in the session have a much better chance of passage than those introduced later.

Model bills will probably have to be rewritten to fit the state or local government's format. Most states have a bill-drafting unit to do that, but they require time to do this, so the initial contacts for a new bill should be made *well* ahead of the legislative session. It will definitely help to contact additional legislators who are willing to sign the bill as co-sponsors. This shows wider interest.

Build Coalitions with Other Groups. In the political process it is most important to build coalitions with other interest groups (e.g., other professional groups, public agencies, voluntary agencies), so that they support your bills while you support theirs. Remember, the political process is a democratic process that requires a majority vote. It is most difficult for an isolated group to generate that much clout. This also means that you must be willing and able to negotiate and compromise—sometimes on very short notice. But remain alert to the implications of your negotiations and compromises. Be especially careful of wording. A careless word or phrase can completely change the meaning of your bill!

Working with other groups in the political process will also give you a broader perspective on the community's or the state's problems and needs and the concerns of the legislators in addressing them. Legislators appreciate the advice of lobby groups with broad perspectives, because they see so many narrow interest groups who are oblivious to the broader concerns of the society. I recently heard a state legislator say that the most credible lobby group he sees is the medical society because it is prepared to discuss everything from public health and clinical treatment issues (e.g., AIDS, mental health commitment laws) to rehabilitation, licensure of various health professionals, organizational and financial issues such as Medicaid fees, health insurance for state employees, workers' compensation, and managed care organizations.

Be Prepared to Try Again Next Session. Be prepared for your bill to die in committee or fail to pass both houses or to be vetoed. Most state legislatures have between 3,500 and 4,000 bills introduced each session, but only a few hundred, at most, pass and become signed into law. Many of those bills that succeed have been around for several previous sessions. Their sponsors have persisted and compromised and honed their political skills by developing coalitions, strengthening public support and meeting with additional legislators. Representative democracy is a great concept, but it is frequently not a tidy or efficient process. However, it works in its own fashion, and it is important that you be there!

EMPOWERMENT
TOWARD A NEW DEFINITION OF SELF-HELP

AUDREY COHEN

The purpose of human service is to empower people.

What are human services®?[1] Stated most simply, they are the complex interactions that address and respond to human concerns. When successful, they make positive and lasting differences in peoples' lives, and they help improve the world. Now, in the final years of the twentieth century, a major portion of our work force is engaged in these very activities, and the phenomenon extends even to those areas not normally considered as human services. In manufacturing companies, for example, there are key human service components—i.e., customer service and human resource management—which may spell the difference between these companies' success and their failure.

The importance of human service cannot be overstated. While we can agree on the overall nature of human services, the question is whether there is an overarching purpose which gives continuity to this broad and varied field? I believe there is. Empowerment is the purpose of human service. Not only must human service professionals themselves be empowered, but in addition, their goal is to help others to become empowered;

to increase their ability to manage their lives more effectively and realize their potential as creative, responsible, and productive members of society.

This is not a small charge, but it is essential and is achievable. Empowerment is both the result of effective human service and the force that makes such results possible. It should be an integral part of human development and education, and the basis upon which professional effectiveness is assessed.

Unfortunately, educational institutions rarely address empowerment as their central concern. In addition, the rapidly changing nature of our economy transformed the types of knowledge and skills that people require in order to be empowered and to empower others. Most educational institutions are still based on a paradigm of learning developed for industrial societies, whereas today we live in a technologically sophisticated and service-centered post-industrial age.

In 1964, I founded an educational institution whose specific purpose was to develop a method

[1]Audrey Cohen College holds a trademark (1967) on the word combination "human services." That term was registered as part of its original name "The College for Human Services." However, the approved and official registration certificate from the U.S. Patent Office specifically exempts the words "The College" from trademark protection, leaving "human services" as the protected entity. This is an interesting note when one considers how generic the term "human services" has become.

of teaching and learning that was based on principles of empowerment and that prepared people for professional work in the new economy. During the more than thirty years of the institution's existence, it has expanded into both graduate and undergraduate education. Audrey Cohen College's unique educational approach—its Purpose-Centered System of Education®[2]—also is being applied in public elementary and secondary schools throughout the country, and has become a model for educational approaches for the twenty-first century. For three decades, the College has tested its ability to promote and achieve empowerment in the world outside the classroom. My hope is that in reaching out to you, the future generation of professionals preparing for careers in human service, I will help you achieve your own empowerment and that of the citizens you serve.[3]

Empowerment is reciprocal. You become empowered as you assist in the empowerment of others. To achieve this reciprocity, education and implementation must occur simultaneously. Theory and practice must prevail throughout the preparation for professional practice.

A FOCUS ON PURPOSE

How does one achieve this necessary synthesis of theory and practice? At our institution, we addressed this question by first defining what constituted an effective human service professional. Our goal was to use this definition to determine the outcomes on which to base professional education. It took four years of extensive research to identify the principal characteristics of effective service. That research focused on exemplary professionals throughout the country and determined, through the use of the "critical incident" and other social science methodology, the tasks and results, the knowledge and actions, which made them out-

---

[2]Audrey Cohen College currently has a patent pending on its Purpose-Centered System of Education. In addition, the college has trademarks on a number of key concepts describing its system of education, including the following terms and descriptive phrases that appear in this text: Purpose-Centered System of Education, Constructive Action, Dimension, and Purpose.

[3]From 1964–1970, the College was the vanguard of what became the national paraprofessional movement. In our initial efforts to address what constituted effective human service, I worked with people throughout New York City to design new, above entry level positions that could meet the need for improved human services and also address the lack of job opportunities, particularly for the poor. Based on my research and our work with community organizations, we defined about a dozen new job categories including Educational Assistant, Legal Services Assistant, Case Manager, Social Work Assistant and Counseling Assistant. The College then designed the first rudimentary model of the empowering human service curriculum. It then educated and trained low income community members to fill these new positions, integrated the positions into the New York City and State personnel structure, and generated widespread support for the new roles. The need for these positions was demonstrated, and we helped disseminate them for hundreds of thousands of people throughout the country. In 1970, the College moved on to its total redesign of professional education.

[4]The plan for development of a professional education required the involvement of those who were identified as excellent examples of the kind of professional the program was intended to prepare. For the purpose of gathering and analyzing this material, the College hired a research firm to interview sixty outstanding professionals in the area of human service. When the data produced a number of areas of performance that seemed generic to the work of outstanding professionals, a team of planners from the College, working with a group of consultants which included researchers, content specialists, curriculum experts, faculty, and agency officials, began to take the elements that emerged from the research—the skills, knowledge and values of the outstanding professionals—and tried to separate and make sense of them. The new ideas which emerged could not provide us with a new paradigm for educating a new human service professional, if we used the traditional model of higher education.

standing. We discovered that there were eight critical, complex areas of effective performance that creative professionals mastered. These professionals, whether they were corporation presidents, managers, social workers, educators, lawyers, physicians, etc., continually and effectively addressed the identified areas of performance. These were also the key areas of empowering human service work that, qualitatively and quantitatively made a positive difference in people's lives.[4]

At the College, we called these areas of performance Purposes®. Our first major educational breakthrough came when I decided to develop a curriculum focused around the Purposes, so that each semester students training to become human service professionals develop competency in one of the eight generic areas of performance. The eight Purposes which empowering and creative service professionals master are: self-assessment and preparation for practice; developing professional relationships; working in groups; teaching and communication; counseling; working as a community liaison; supervising; and managing change. Figure 21.1 illustrates these Purposes.

The College's curriculum moves human service professionals toward full self-empowerment by training them to address each of the eight Purposes we have identified. Equally important, students learn that their goal as human service professionals[5] includes consciously working to teach citizens to deal effectively with these Purposes themselves—to become less and less dependent. In other words, citizens would become empowered. As part of the human service process, our professional helps empower others. Our professional helps them recognize obstacles and call on resources, both internal and external, to overcome these barriers. Human service performance, under the College's paradigm, is successful on both societal and personal levels.

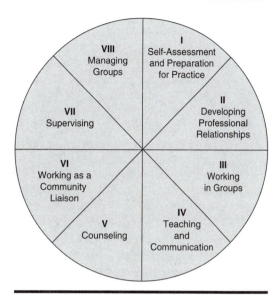

FIGURE 21.1   The Eight Performance Areas

Dimensions of Knowledge and Action

While defining the Purposes of human service education was the first step in implementing the concept of empowerment in the new curriculum, we also learned that our exemplary professionals worked holistically. This "holism" was clearly another critical factor in their success. Each time they addressed one of the Purposes in question, they considered a number of parameters, or Dimensions®, of their performance which they knew contributed to their success. Five essential Dimensions, key aspects of effective performance, were embedded in their empowering human service work. These Dimensions were concerned with selecting and achieving appropriate goals, acting ethically and resolving value conflicts, understanding oneself and others, understanding the systems within which people function, and developing the specific skills needed to achieve goals. These Dimensions, which

---

[5]In June, 1974, the Conference to Found a New Profession, sponsored by Audrey Cohen College (formerly The College for Human Services), New York City, marked the establishment of the Human Service Profession and the definition of a new professional role. A broad spectrum of national decision makers voiced their support for the profession and its practitioner: the human service professional.

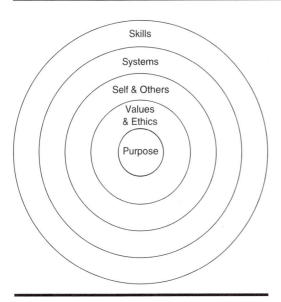

FIGURE 21.2   The Essential Dimensions® of Empowering Human Service

remain constant whatever the situation, are shown in Figure 21.2.

This led to the second breakthrough in our human service paradigm: the decision to use these Dimensions as the organizers of the knowledge for each of the Purposes. They became the names of the classes students attended throughout their eight undergraduate semesters of study.

The first Dimension pertains to establishing appropriate goals and developing strategies for achieving them. Each term students are required to set a service goal in relation to the semester's Purpose, work to achieve it, and apply both learning and practice in the context of this planned effort. They also are expected to teach those with whom they work the same purposive and self-directing skills. The second Dimension calls on the student to demonstrate a clear and consistent understanding of his/her values and those of others. It presupposes a belief in the unique value of each person and the capacity of each person for growth, increasing self-direction and creative and responsible participation in the world around

them. The third Dimension involves a commitment to understanding oneself and others through both study and experience, and is based on the understanding that everything we do is affected by our perception of ourselves and others. The fourth Dimension relates to understanding the role of systems in our daily life. As human service professionals, we are often incapacitated by lack of knowledge not only of the organizational systems that are closest to us—the particular office for which we work, for example. We also are often incapacitated by our lack of knowledge about how this system relates to other offices, the total organization, and outside systems. A vital ingredient in becoming an effective human service professional is the acquisition of a thorough understanding of relevant systems, and the ability to use them as resources. The final Dimension of performance relates to the acquisition of the written technical and interpersonal skills that are an essential part of professional behavior.

These Dimensions of effective performance become the lenses through which our students see the world of learning. They provide the framework by which we can teach and assess empowering practice.

At Audrey Cohen College, our students extrapolate from the theory drawn from the humanities, the social sciences, the sciences, and professional studies, and this theory is covered in the Dimension classes. Students learn how to work with people and organizations directly in order to identify their special needs. They master skills which include not only those involved in analysis and communications, but also less tangible ones such as effective interviewing and effective listening. They learn how to help others articulate their feelings, their strengths, their needs, and their goals. They learn how to encourage them to make realistic plans. Our students evaluate citizens' needs in relation to the resources that are available and the help the service provider can properly give in the situation. They learn that citizens are likely to have multiple needs which must be balanced and which may require

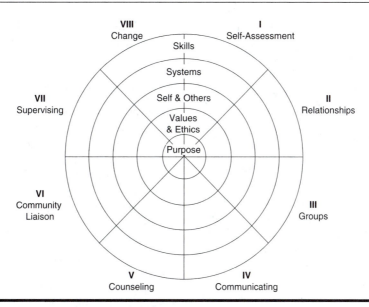

FIGURE 21.3   The Intersection of Dimensions® and Purposes

quite different kinds of special help. Our professionals in training learn to look for other sources to provide the help that they cannot provide themselves. They learn to do all this with the goal of empowering those they are helping, empowering these citizens to meet the needs they themselves have defined and make their own choices as to the best methods of achieving their goals.

A Purpose-Centered System of Education®

The intersection of the eight performance areas and the Dimensions in Figure 21.3 illustrate the general framework for human service practice. Wherever you are working, i.e., in a hospital, day care center, a school, mental retardation facility, etc., this framework facilitates integrated, rather than fragmented, service. It underscores, once again, a basic tenet of empowering human service practice: human service professionals must perceive their work as a totality, not only meeting the needs of the citizen, but also fostering a learning process which helps the same citizen to become empowered.

Constructive Action®

Assessment at Audrey Cohen College concentrates on students' abilities to effectively empower others. It cannot be concerned with minutiae. Our methodology for assessing the achievement of each semester's Purpose, and ultimately assessing empowerment, requires that a student take Constructive Action®. A Constructive Action is a major service, designed and carried out in an organization during the semester, and related to that semester's Purpose. The Constructive Action demonstrates how a student uses knowledge (what he/she is learning inside the classroom) as a basis for effective human services outside the classroom. It documents the knowledge used and the process followed during the period of the Constructive Action. A successful Constructive Action improves the lives of citizens. It is conceived with the help of the citizens it serves. It can be carried out almost anywhere—in nursing homes, hospitals, schools, halfway houses, public and private agencies, and in the organizations that define the for-profit sector as well. Above all, it is a complex process of empowerment. It is a living case study.

Over the years, thousands of Constructive Actions have been carried out by students at our institution. They have ranged from reclaiming abandoned land and transforming it into a small neighborhood park in an area where no such resource had been available, to subtly incorporating necessary literacy training into parent education components in a Head Start program (many of those parents have earned general equivalency diplomas and are now pursuing higher education), to designing a training program for substance abuse counselors which was subsequently mandated for state-wide use, to building bridges for young people at risk as they move from elementary to junior high school. In the latter instance, this meant that the human service practitioner in training, our student (who worked with these youngsters in elementary school), reached out to design support services with the prospective junior high school. Thus, the necessary special support and counseling was continued as the youngsters moved to the larger, far more impersonal arena of junior high school. In carrying out these and thousands of other Constructive Actions, students must address issues of values and ethics, relationships, skills and systems, and above all they must demonstrate they can integrate them from all of the Dimensions and use it to pursue their Purpose.

The Constructive Action begins with a proposal that addresses the goals and needs of a citizen or group of citizens. Upon approval, a plan of action is developed. This is done by our student (the human service professional in training), together with the citizen or citizens in question, a faculty member, and the student's supervisor in the organization in which the Constructive Action is to be performed.

The Constructive Action identifies academic success with professional accountability. This reflects the principle that classroom learning should be applicable to one's life, and it can only be considered successful if it helps both the student and the citizen to become empowered.

Empowerment from the Citizen's Viewpoint

In the process of carrying out the Constructive Action, both the human service professionals-in-training and the citizen whose needs are being addressed learn to ask the right questions. If the citizen is not directly involved in the Constructive Action process, then the Purpose of the human service activity is illusory at best. Its achievement is difficult to assess.

While a chapter does not present sufficient space to outline all the appropriate questions which a citizen should be able to answer, a sampling helps provide insight into their depth and appropriateness. Like learning and assessment under the empowerment model, questions are framed around the Dimensions of learning and action.

Purpose®.   When addressing the Purpose and assessment of the empowering Constructive Action, a citizen might be asked: Were you clear about your reason for seeking service? Did the professional listen carefully and help you to have a clearer idea about your problems? Do you feel that the questions asked by the professional were helpful, and could you answer them? Did you take part in planning what you ought to do to help solve your problem? Did you feel that the plan which was developed included **your** ideas of what you hoped would happen to **you**? As a result of the professional's services, did the things that were supposed to happen to you in the plan actually happen? In answering these, and other questions, considerable detail is expected from the citizen.

Values and Ethics.   In assessing whether the professional was effective in the area of Values, some questions include: Did the professional draw conclusions about you and your problems that you felt were not true? Did the professional respect your feelings and opinions? Did the professional see your problem in a different way than you see your problem? Did **you** question the professional's judgement of what is most important or did you just accept them? Here, as in all areas of questioning, yes or no answers are not acceptable. The citizen is expected to provide a rationale for his/her actions.

Self and Others.   In determining whether the citizen has made progress in self-understanding as well as in understanding others, appropriate questions might include: Did the professional try to cooperate with you? Did you learn anything from the professional about yourself that would help you to solve your problems? Did the professional really help you to solve your problem?

System.   In looking at whether the citizen has expanded his/her ability to identify and work the systems that provide service delivery, appropriate questions might include: Did the professional provide you with information about organizations that could help you? Were you able to meet your goals through accessing these organizations? Do you have a better understanding of the different organizations that can support you in your goals, and their relation to each other?

Skills.   The citizen is expected to have learned additional skills from empowering human service practice. That citizen might well be asked: Can you now be specific about how you can handle your own problems better? Did you acquire any of the following skills: to investigate resources for yourself; to plan ways and carry them out for dealing with this and similar problems? Can you write a record of what is happening to you each day, and

indicate how any of the events you describe might be part of your problem?

Assessment: The Empowerment Chart.   In 1978, we developed the first Empowerment Chart, a further tool to guide the student practitioner and the Purpose instructor through both the empowerment process and its assessment.[6] Two basic principles underlie the Chart's content: (1) providers of service can and should demonstrate the effectiveness of their services; and (2) recipients of services are empowered to the extent that they are involved in the planning and assessing of the services they receive.

The Empowerment Chart is designed for use by the citizen and practitioner as an integral part of the helping relationship. It is an instrument for planning and assessing service. Within the context of the citizen's needs, it helps the students see to what extent they receive. He/she is being effective in meeting three sets of goals simultaneously: the student's goals with regard to the citizen; the organizational/supervisor goals with regard to the same citizen; and, equally important, and too often overlooked, the citizen's goals with regard to the need he/she has defined.

Because these goals can be quite different, the Chart becomes a most effective educational tool. It will show the student to what extent he/she has been effective in meeting these three sets of goals. It will show whether the student has been able to bring the three points of view closer together. It will show whether there is true accomplishment.

It is not possible, within the confines of one chapter, to detail all the elements of the Empowerment Chart. However, let me begin the process with you by illustrating step one of the Empowerment Chart, setting the long term Purpose (Goal).

[6]Productivity in the human services was described in detail in a monograph I wrote in 1978. *The Citizen As The Integrating Agent: Productivity in the Human Services* was published by Project Share, a national clearinghouse for improving the management of human services under the U.S. Department of Health, Education and Welfare, and was distributed through the U.S. Government Printing Office. The Empowerment Chart was shown in that monograph, and a step by step description of the process was included.

Our citizen is an abusing parent. Abusing parents represent a category of citizen far from empowerment. They are beset by such frustrations and difficulties that continued direct care and help are essential. Our citizen hurts his wife and his children. He hurts them physically and psychologically. He says he wants to change. If this is to occur, a broad range of services and skills are necessary. To actively involve this parent in the decision making processes, to encourage him to take responsibilities in trying to change his life, to teach him how to do this, while respecting him as an individual, are challenges enough. However, our student must also simultaneously deal with the professional at the organization providing service who may have a very specific service approach which is not necessarily harmonious with empowering human service practice. Finally, our student has to confront his/her own perceptions about the citizen. Because of this totality, the Empowerment Chart helps define on an individual by individual, step by step basis, a new way to deliver human services. Figure 21.4 illustrates the start of this process.

Our student is immediately aware of the three points of view he/she must strive to bring closer together. Other portions of the chart are derived from the long term Purpose or goal. Throughout the empowering service process, the primary issue is what is it that the citizen wants to accomplish. The citizen's goals may change during the service period, and such a change is often a positive one. At its best, it will indicate a growing capacity to deal with reality. Because the Citizen Empowerment Chart is intended to evaluate progress and service effectiveness over a period of time, it facilitates a concentration on outcomes rather than processes.[7]

Audrey Cohen College has now spent over thirty years delineating empowerment and making it a reality for both citizens and human service professionals. In that period, so much has happened. It has been gratifying to see a change from the time we truly were small voices in a large wilderness, to the present, when the concepts of "empowerment" and "human services" are in common usage. What remains critical, however, is making these terms a reality. Here is where I believe the work of Audrey Cohen College has not only made a critical contribution, but continues to represent the vanguard in designing a new paradigm for the preparation of effective professionals and assessing empowering human services.

1. LONG TERM PURPOSE (GOAL)

as stated by:

CITIZEN(S): _Stop hurting children and live better with others_

AGENCY/SUPERVISOR: _Develop self-esteem and improve relations with children_

PRACTITIONER: _Develop self-esteem and improve relations with children_

After you have completed your needs analysis, write down the problem or issue you feel you should address in your Constructive Action. Then write down the problem or issue as your Purpose® Instructor sees it. You may or may not agree.

FIGURE 21.4   The Empowerment Chart, Section 1

[7]A full example illustrating the usefulness of the Empowerment Chart is found in the monograph previously referred to: *The Citizen as the Integrating Agent: Productivity in the Human Services,* U.S. Government Printing Office, 1978.

CHAPTER 22

THE CHILD WELFARE DELIVERY SYSTEM IN THE UNITED STATES

DAVID S. LIEDERMAN
MADELYN DEWOODY
MEGAN C. SYLVESTER

Child welfare is a field of human services that focuses on the general well-being of children. It incorporates services and efforts designed to promote children's physical, psychological, and social development. Child welfare and social service agencies offer a range of services to children and their families to ensure the health and well-being of children.

The general principle is that child welfare is the responsibility, first and foremost, of the child's family, and human services support and complement the role of the family. There are situations, however, when families encounter difficulties meeting the needs and fostering the development of their children. These difficulties may be so severe as to put the children at risk of physical, emotional, or developmental harm. Government has organized a system of child welfare services specifically designed to assist children and their families, supporting the strengths of families whenever possible, and intervening when necessary to ensure the safety and well-being of children. Child welfare services may be provided by public and private nonprofit agencies and usually are provided by social workers. They may take many forms, depending on the child's and family's situation and needs.

THE CORE CHILD WELFARE SERVICES

In general, child welfare services fall into four core categories:

1. services to support and strengthen families;
2. protective services;
3. out-of-home care services; and
4. adoption services.

Services to Support and Strengthen Families

For many children and their families, child welfare services involve supportive services that are provided to assist the family in remaining together. These services are designed to support, reinforce, and strengthen the ability of parents to meet the needs of their children. When a child welfare agency provides services to support and strengthen families, it does not assume the responsibilities of the parent. Instead, the agency supports parents in protecting and promoting the well-being of their children and strengthens parents' ability to solve problems that may result in the abuse or neglect of their children.

There are three major types of supportive services: family resource, support, and education services; family-centered services; and intensive family crisis services.

Family Resource, Support, and Education Services. These services, which are broad and often overlap, assist adults in their roles as parents. Resource services are varied and include, as examples, providing referrals for services needed by the family and helping with transportation. Support services are likewise diverse and include, as one example, parent support groups, often facilitated by the group members themselves. Educational services seek to develop parenting skills, and often involve parenting classes where parents learn, among other things, children's stages of development.

Family-Centered Services. These services help families with problems that threaten the well-being of children and the family as a whole. They are designed to remedy problems as early as possible. These services can include:

— Family counseling;
— Parent education programs designed to enhance parents' knowledge and skills;
— The identification and use of social support networks that include individuals, groups, and organizations;
— Advocacy to obtain services for families when services do not currently exist; and
— Case management services to facilitate access to needed services and coordinate multiple resources.

Intensive Family-Centered Crisis Services. These services are designed to assist a family when a crisis is so serious that it may result in the removal of the child from the home. Intensive family-centered crisis services attempt to ensure the safety and well-being of the child and strengthen and preserve the family in order to avoid the unnecessary placement of children outside the home. Services may include crisis intervention counseling, alcohol and drug treatment, and parenting education.

Three specific services that can support and strengthen families are child day care, housing, and adolescent pregnancy prevention and parenting services. *Child day-care* responds to the needs of children, families, and communities. Child day-care can be provided in family day-care homes, group child day-care homes, and child day-care centers, and may be offered part-day, full-day, or in the case of respite care, twenty-four hours a day. *Adolescent pregnancy prevention and parenting services* have become an important component of

child welfare services as the rate of teenagers giving birth to children has increased dramatically over the last decade. Child welfare services include education and referral services related to preventing pregnancy and services for parenting teenagers, such as assistance in locating child care and completing their education, and parenting education. *Housing services* have become increasingly important as the number of homeless children and families in America and the number of children who live in substandard conditions have risen. Child welfare agencies help meet the housing needs of children and their families by linking them to public housing resources and social services and by advocating for more and better affordable housing.

Protective Services

Protective services are designed to protect children from abuse or neglect (sometimes referred to as maltreatment) by their parents or caregivers and to improve the functioning of the family so that children are no longer at risk. The specific types of maltreatment to which child welfare services respond include:[1]

— Physical abuse: physical injury to a child;
— Sexual abuse: sexual maltreatment of a child;
— Emotional abuse and neglect: emotional injury to a child or failure to meet the child's emotional or affectional needs;
— Deprivation of necessities: failure to provide adequate food, shelter, or clothing;
— Inadequate supervision: leaving children for long periods of time without access to an adult who can meet their needs and protect them from harm;
— Medical neglect: failure to seek essential medical care for the child;
— Educational neglect: failure to enroll a child in school or indifference to the child's failure to attend school;
— Exploitation or overwork: forcing a child to work for unreasonably long periods of time or to perform unreasonable work; and

[1]Katz-Sanford, Ruth, Arlene W. Howe, and Melba McGrath, (1975). "Child Neglect Laws in America." *Family Law Quarterly* 9(1), entire issue.

— Exposure of a child to unhealthy circumstances: subjecting a child to adult behavior that is considered "morally injurious," such as a criminal activity, prostitution, alcoholism, or drug addiction.

Protective services are provided by the public agency—often referred to as Child Protective Services (CPS)—mandated by law to respond to reports of child abuse and neglect and to intervene to protect children.

Protective services are offered to accomplish several purposes: to strengthen families who are experiencing problems that can lead or have led to abuse or neglect; to enable children to remain safely with their parents; to temporarily separate a child at imminent risk of harm from his or her parent; to reunify children with their parents whenever possible; and to assure a child permanency with another family when the child cannot return to his or her parent without serious risk of harm.[2]

Protective services include:

Case Finding and Intake.
Receipt of reports of child abuse and neglect. Reports received by protective services agencies generally fall into two categories: problems in the parent-child relationship, such as physical abuse, neglect, abandonment, the absence of the parent, or conflict between a parent and an adolescent; and problems that a child is experiencing, such as emotional difficulties, runaway behavior, failure to attend school, or physical problems.

When a report of abuse or neglect is made, the child protective service agency is responsible for investigating the situation. Contact is made with the family, others with knowledge of the situation, and the child. The agency will determine whether abuse or neglect has occurred (often referred to as "substantiation" of the report) and whether there is a substantial and immediate risk to the child that would warrant taking steps to remove the child from the home to a setting of safety.

Case Planning.
Helping families after abuse or neglect is reported and substantiated. At the heart of protective services is work with the family to prevent further abuse or neglect and to correct the problems that led to maltreatment of the child. The needs of the parents and the child are addressed through a range of services such as extended day care centers and crisis nurseries to prevent further maltreatment; homemaker services; counseling services; and emergency caregiving services.

Court Involvement in Protective Services.
Decisions are made by the courts regarding where a child will live and the changes that a family must make. Protective service agencies seek court action when parents are not able or willing to make the changes needed for their child's well-being or the situation presents a danger to the child so that the child can be protected only by placing him or her outside the family. In these situations, the court will order the child to be removed from custody of his or her parents and placed in out-of-home care. Only about 20 percent of the cases reported to protective services agencies require court action.

Out-of-Home Care Services for Children

Out-of-home care services are utilized when the situation presents such a risk to the child that the child must be separated from his or her parents and placed with another family or in another setting. In these situations, the public agency responsible for protecting children will seek court action to authorize placement of the child outside of the home. There are three major types of out-of-home care services: family foster care, kinship care, and residential group care. These services, provided as twenty-four-hours-a-day care, are designed as temporary services for the child while the agency works with the family to correct the problems that led to placement of the child. Out-of-home care in

[2]Association of Public Child Welfare Administrators, (1988). *Guidelines for a Model System of Protective Services for Abused and Neglected Children and Their Families.* Washington, DC: American Public Welfare Association.

all settings also includes services to meet the social, emotional, educational, and developmental needs of the child.

- *Family foster care.* Family foster care is provided by adults who are not related to the child and who are licensed or approved as foster parents by a child welfare agency.
- *Kinship care.* Kinship care is the placement of children with relatives. Many agencies consider relatives as the first choice for out-of-home care because remaining with family members is often less disruptive for the child.
- *Group residential care.* Group residential care is comprised of a variety of services. One type is group care, that is, living facilities located within residential communities that care for a small group of unrelated children, usually four to eight in number. Residential care, another type of care, is usually provided to a larger number of children or adolescents and involves highly structured, intensive, and planned therapeutic interventions for children and adolescents who have significant emotional or behavioral disorders.

Adoption Services

Adoption is a child welfare service that provides a new permanent family for children whose birth parents are unable or unwilling to provide them with the love, support and nurturing they need. Adoption services meet the needs of three groups of children who need adoptive families: (1) healthy infants; (2) children with "special needs," such as children with disabilities, older children seeking permanent families, and sibling groups of children to be placed together with an adoptive family; and (3) children from other countries.

Agencies that provide adoption services identify prospective adoptive parents for children awaiting adoption; assess the ability of prospective parents to meet the needs of children waiting to be adopted; prepare the child and birth parent(s) for adoption; place the child with the adoptive family; assist the adoptive family in finalizing the adoption; and provide post-adoption support services, such as casework services, linkages to community resources, and parenting groups.

EMERGING CHILD WELFARE ISSUES

Pediatric AIDS and HIV Infection

Child welfare professionals are confronting a new reality in the form of acquired immunodeficiency syndrome (AIDS) and the human immunodeficiency virus (HIV) that causes AIDS. Growing numbers of children are acquiring HIV from mothers who are themselves infected with HIV and, as a result, their lives are medically, psychologically, and socially threatened. Some of these children are "boarder babies," in hospitals awaiting homes because they are ready for discharge, but their parents are unable to take responsibility for them or bring them home. Other children who have been infected with HIV live with their parents who cannot provide for them. In many instances, their parents are also involved with drugs, which compounds the problem. In addition to children with HIV infection, there are children who are not infected with HIV whose parents are dying, leaving them orphaned by AIDS. Child welfare agencies must be prepared to help through such services as placing the children with extended families or by finding adoptive families to care for them.

Child welfare agencies respond to the needs of children and families who are affected by HIV/AIDS with a range of services. Some programs are community-based and provide services to ensure that children who are infected with HIV receive the therapeutic, developmental, and educational services they need; help parents understand and manage the child's illness; and support the efforts of the child and the family to deal with the grief and bereavement issues that accompany the disease. Specific services may include information and referral for needed financial, medical, mental health, and social services; crisis intervention services when the immediate needs of the child place stress on the family; family therapy; and case management and coordination of medical and psychological treatment. For children whose families are not available or able to care for them, child welfare agencies provide specialized foster care—twenty-four-hour-a-day care by foster parents who are specially trained to meet the special needs of these children. Children who are healthy or who have been infected with HIV and have lost their parents to AIDS likewise need child welfare services. Child welfare agencies work with the extended family to prepare them to care for children who are attempting to cope with the loss of their parents from AIDS, and provide ongoing supportive services to both the child and family after placing the child. For other children, child welfare agencies recruit and train adoptive parents, offering a broad range of education and supportive services to ensure that adoptive families understand and can meet the significant psychosocial needs of these children.

Substance Abuse

As the abuse of alcohol and other drugs has continued to escalate and growing numbers of women have begun to use illegal drugs, child welfare agencies have observed a significant relationship between alcohol and other drug abuse and the well-being of children. Dramatic increases in the number of child abuse reports and in the number of children entering foster care have been specifically tied to parental alcohol and drug abuse. Child welfare agencies are responding to record numbers of child protective service referrals concerning drug-exposed infants, many of whom may also have been infected with the AIDS virus and who may be medically fragile, and older children who have experienced abuse or neglect because of their parents' substance abuse. In all age groups, growing numbers of children who have been affected by their parents' alcohol and drug problems are entering foster care.

Child welfare agencies are called on to respond to the needs of families who need immediate and intensive help in resolving their alcohol or drug dependency. Agencies must also help families correct the problems that alcohol and drugs create for their children. Child welfare agencies provide services to prevent and intervene early in situations where there exists child abuse and substance abuse, such as outreach to newborns and mothers; referrals for needed financial, housing, and social services; child day-care; and coordination with community alcohol and drug treatment services. Special services may be needed by pregnant women who are abusing alcohol or other drugs. Early detection, proper prenatal care and medical and substance abuse treatment services can be mobilized to reduce the damage that alcohol and drugs can cause for both the mother and fetus.

Child welfare agencies also meet the needs of infants and toddlers who were prenatally exposed to alcohol and other drugs and older children whose parents, because of substance abuse, have not provided the psychological, social, and developmental environment that children need for healthy growth. Child welfare agencies, through child protective services, assess the risk to children posed by parental substance abuse; determine whether the child may remain safely at home with the parent or should be placed away from the parent to assure the child's safety; and provide or coordinate the range of health, educational, and developmental services that children need. Substance abuse, which is often a complex and long-standing problem, presents the child welfare system with special challenges to protect children, provide effective services to parents and to children who may have significant health and developmental needs, and plan for permanent families for children whose parents are unable to care for them because of substance abuse.

INSTITUTIONAL SYSTEMS

Child welfare services are provided by agencies in both the public and private sectors. Services to support and strengthen families, out-of-home care services, and adoption services are provided by public child welfare agencies and private non-profit agencies in the voluntary sector. Public child welfare agencies often combine the way in which they provide these services, directly providing some services and contracting with private nonprofit agencies to provide other services.

Private nonprofit agencies may provide a range of child welfare services, or may specialize in certain services such as adoption or residential care for children with serious emotional disturbances.

Protective services traditionally have been undertaken only by governmental agencies charged by law with the protection of children—child protective services (CPS) agencies located within public welfare departments; law enforcement agencies; and the courts. Although CPS agencies and law enforcement agencies both investigate reports of child abuse and neglect, CPS and law enforcement investigations differ. CPS agencies are concerned only with child protection; their efforts focus on determining whether a child has been mistreated and whether the child can remain safely with his or her parents. Law enforcement agencies focus on whether criminal charges should be filed in response to child maltreatment. Family and juvenile courts consider cases arising from CPS and law enforcement investigations. The courts will, when appropriate, declare a child in need of protection; remove custody of the child from the parent(s) and place the child in the custody of the CPS agency; and approve the child's placement in out-of-home care. When the court has made such decisions, the court will periodically review the progress that is being made toward resolving the problems that led to the child's placement and the progress that is being made toward finding a permanent family for the child. When criminal charges are filed, the court with jurisdiction over criminal matters may also become involved in the case.

CHILD WELFARE LAW

Child welfare services are shaped largely by federal and state law.

Federal Law

The Child Abuse Prevention and Treatment Act (CAPTA) of 1974. This federal legislation, enacted in response to growing public concern about child abuse, provides financial assistance to states and communities to prevent, identify and treat child abuse and neglect. In order to receive funds, states must designate an agency with responsibility for investigating abuse and neglect; establish a reporting system for all known or suspected instances of child abuse and neglect; enact laws that protect all children under the age of eighteen from mental injury, physical injury, and sexual abuse; and develop a system that provides a *guardian ad litem* who represents the interests of abused and neglected children when their cases go to court.

The Indian Child Welfare Act of 1978. This legislation was designed to strengthen the services available to support and strengthen Native American families and to put safeguards in place regarding the custody and placement of Native American children. The law directs agencies to work closely with Native American children, families, and tribes when there has been a report of child abuse or neglect and requires the placement of Native American children who have been abused or neglected with Native American families whenever possible. Importantly, the law also recognizes the authority of tribal courts to handle Native American child welfare matters.

The Adoption Assistance and Child Welfare Act of 1980 (P. L. 96–272). This legislation, also known as Public Law 96–272, is considered the most important child welfare legislation enacted over the past several decades. Public Law 96–272 provides federal support for children in foster care; requires that states have in place a planning process designed to ensure that children who are placed out of their homes will have a permanent home in a reasonable period of time; and provides a subsidy program to meet the special needs of children who are adopted. The law sets forth certain standards for child welfare services that states must meet to receive federal funds. These standards have had a significant impact on the way that child welfare services are provided, and they include:

— "Reasonable efforts" to attempt to keep children with their families whenever possible. States are expected to have in place prevention, intervention, and crisis services such as day care, crisis counseling, and access to emergency financial assistance.

— Permanency planning services. These services are provided to children and their families when children have been removed from their parents' custody because of abuse and neglect. These services include "reasonable efforts" to reunite children and their families whenever possible. When reunification is not possible, alternative permanent plans are required, such as placement with extended family or adoption.

— Out-of-home placements in the "least restrictive setting." When children are placed in out of home care, the type of care selected for the child must be in the most "family-like" setting appropriate to the child's needs and in close proximity to parents. Generally, a child will be placed with extended family or in family foster care. If the child has special medical, mental health, or developmental needs, a group or residential care setting may be most appropriate.

— Detailed case plans and regular case reviews to help ensure that the child has a permanent home as soon as possible after being placed in out-of-home care.

The Independent Living Initiative Title IV-E of the Social Security Act.

This legislation funds services for adolescents in out-of-home care who will not be reunited with their families and who will leave care at age eighteen to live on their own. Services must be designed to teach basic living skills, provide educational and job training opportunities, and assist youth in locating housing.

State Law

Each state addresses child welfare services in its statutes. In most states, the law:

— Directs that services be available to help strengthen and support families;

— Defines the conduct that constitutes child abuse and neglect;

— Identifies the agency responsible for receiving, screening, and investigating reports of child abuse and neglect and protecting children;

— Identifies the court that has jurisdiction over child abuse and neglect cases and that has the authority to remove the custody of children from their parents;

— Specifies the duties of the agency in working with children and families toward preserving and reunifying families;

— Sets forth the conditions under which parental rights can be terminated and a child freed for adoption; and

— Describes the procedures for adoption.

PUBLIC POLICY

Child welfare services also include efforts to ensure that government decision-making is based on what children and their families need. It involves clearly defining child welfare issues and analyzing the merits of various approaches to enhancing the strengths of children and their families and meeting their needs. There are a number of child welfare policy issues that have been and will continue to be debated including: the proper role of the federal and state governments in protecting children; the balance between protecting children and preserving families; determinations about when in-home services are most appropriate and when out-of-home care should be used; and the extent to which resources should be allocated between prevention and treatment services.

THE CHILD WELFARE LEAGUE OF AMERICA, INC.

The Child Welfare League of America, Inc. (CWLA), the largest and oldest membership organization in North America, represents the public and voluntary child welfare sectors. CWLA supports its over 800 member organizations through policy, practice, and research initiatives within seven major program areas: adolescent pregnancy services, child protection, services to support and strengthen families, family foster care and kinship care, group care, adoption, and child day-care. In addition, CWLA has eleven special initiatives: cultural competence, HIV infection and AIDS, chemical dependency, youth services, child and youth care credentialing, housing and homelessness, recruiting and retaining competent staff, state commissioners roundtable, performance evaluation, child welfare and the law, and rural child welfare services.

The Child Welfare League of America is the world's largest publisher of child welfare materials. CWLA's Publications Division reaches over one-half million professionals annually through its production and distribution of books, monographs, research reports, newsletters, a quarterly magazine, and a scholarly professional journal.

A major component of CWLA's work is its advocacy on Capitol Hill on behalf of children. CWLA's Public Policy Division is committed to significantly improving the full array of federally-funded services and supports needed to address the escalating crisis facing at-risk children and families and the child welfare system itself.

REFERENCES

Association of Public Child Welfare Administrators, (1988). *Guidelines for a Model System of Protective Services for Abused and Neglected Children and Their Families.* Washington, DC.

Costin, L.B., C.J. Bell, and S.W. Downs, eds., (1991). *Child Welfare: Policies and Practice,* 4th ed. New York: Longman.

Kadushin, A., and J.A. Martin, (1988). *Child Welfare Services,* 4th ed. New York: Macmillan.

Katz-Sanford. R., A.W. Howe, and M. McGrath, eds. (1975, Spring). "Child Neglect Laws in America" [Special issue]. *Family Law Quarterly* 9 (1).

Laird, J., and A. Hartman, eds., (1985). *A Handbook of Child Welfare: Context, Knowledge, and Practice.* New York: The Free Press.

Pecora, P. J., J. K. Whittaker, and A. N. Maluccio, eds., (1992). *The Child Welfare Challenge: Policy, Practice, and Research.* New York: Aldine De Gruyter.

SUGGESTED FURTHER READING

Helfer, R.E., and R.S. Kempe, (1987). *The Battered Child,* 4th ed. Chicago: The University of Chicago.

Maidman, F., ed., (1984). *Child Welfare: A Sourcebook of Knowledge and Practice.* New York: The Child Welfare League of America, Inc.

CHAPTER 23

GOING UPSTREAM
PREVENTION IN HUMAN SERVICES

IRIS HECKMAN

An old folktale tells the story of the very first prevention program. There was a village along a river where every day a drowned body from upstream would wash up on the bank. Every day the town's people would go out and pull in the poor soul and arrange a decent burial. The leaders of the village held many councils and called upon the wisest in the land to solve the problem of the drownings. The tradespeople wanted to build big nets that would catch the bodies before they got to the town. This was a great idea because it would give people construction jobs and stop the problem. A safety net was built. Unfortunately, large tears in the net were common and still the drowned bodies would wash up on shore. Sometimes, even when no holes could be found in the net, bodies would still wash up on shore. Occasionally, a victim would wash up still clinging desperately to life. The healers of the village were brought in and would resuscitate the poor souls. These "saved" individuals were still a problem to the village. They were often fearful, demanding, and needy people and required a lot of attention. Sometimes the recovering drowning victims were even ostracized. The people in the village became even more upset about the problem. Finally, one day a curious villager said, "Why don't we go upstream and see what is making the people drown?" Prevention! What a concept!

Prevention is the heart and soul of human services. Yet, prevention is misunderstood and often given lip service but with meager investments of resources, attention, effort, and time. Few colleges and universities across the country provide a curriculum to prepare students to work in prevention. Few graduates are employed in prevention. How can this be? Isn't an ounce of prevention worth a pound of cure? In this chapter, a picture of prevention will be painted that will hopefully make the reader curious enough to go upstream.

When the Community Mental Health Centers Act (Public Law 88–164) became law in 1963, the intent of the legislation was to move people out of institutions into community-based services. The development of community mental health centers created a need for a new type of worker, the "forerunners of today's entry level human service professional" (McClam and Woodside, 1990). A major thrust of the community mental health movement was to focus on prevention. Although the intention was to develop prevention programs to reduce the number of people in the community experiencing mental health problems, the safety net of community mental health had a lot of snags.

Osher (1990) argues that human services developed in a "cauldron" of social upheaval. In addition to the community mental health movement, human services developed in response to the increasing needs identified through the civil rights movement of the 1960s. The lack of social justice and the failure of the established helping professions of social work, nursing, psychology, and psychiatry to effectively alleviate social problems lead to grass-roots advocacy efforts which ultimately became a part of the human services movement. Osher points out that, although there was great potential in the beginning for the human services to create revolutionary social change, in fact, human services has not been a transforming force in our society. The drownings are still a daily event. The safety net is full of holes, and the horror of the bodies washing up on shore is simply status quo. "This stunted growth can be traced to the contradictory functions of human services—social control (the safety net), assistance (resuscitation), empowerment (going upstream)" (Osher, 1990).

Human services missed the boat, so to speak. Instead of investing in prevention as a means of empowerment, prevention has been seen primarily as social control. The public health model became the basis for prevention. Bernard Bloom, a leader in the community mental health movement, noted in his book *Community Mental Health: An Introduction* (1984) that "it is an important public health axiom that most illnesses are controlled by prevention rather than by treatment." This idea that prevention is a form of control has created obstacles to reaching the best approach to prevention: empowerment" (p. 191).

Empowerment is defined as the restoration and creation of hope in an individual or a community. Empowerment means to enable, to give power to. Prevention through empowerment is nothing new. The wisdom of this approach attracted the thinking of the Spanish philosopher Maimonides in the twelfth century regarding charity:

The first and lowest degree is to give, but with reluctance or regret. This is the gift of the hand but not of the heart. The second is to give cheerfully but not proportionately to the distress of the sufferer. The third is to give cheerfully and proportionately, but not until solicited. The fourth is to give cheerfully, proportionately and even unsolicited, but to put it in the poor man's hand, thereby exciting in him the painful emotion of shame. The fifth is to give charity in such a way that the distressed may receive the bounty and know their benefactor. The sixth, which rises still higher, is to know the objects of our bounty, but remain unknown to them. The seventh is still more

meritorious, namely, to bestow charity in such a way that the benefactor may not know the relieved persons, nor they the names of their benefactors. The eighth and the most meritorious of all, is to anticipate charity by preventing poverty, namely, to assist the reduced fellow man, either by considerable fight, or a sum of money or by teaching him a trade, or by putting man in the way of business so that he may earn an honest livelihood, and not be forced to the dreadful alternative of holding out his hand for charity (Cohen, 1927).

Maimonides realized that the most meritorious form of human service was to prevent the need for assistance by empowering people. This ancient and wise Spanish philosopher saw that empowerment would occur through the redistribution of wealth to create greater social equity or through education to enable the individual to have a livelihood. Social control would be the least meritorious form of charity. Maimonides did not describe charity as creating rules and laws that would prohibit despair. Yet much of our current prevention strategies are simply public policy aimed at social control through prohibitions and laws that punish those already suffering.

In the 1700s the miasmatists singled out odors and filth as the cause of all disease, and proposed sanitation as the way to prevent the scourges of malaria, typhoid fever, typhus, cholera, and tuberculosis. Miasmas, or noxious odors, polluted the environment through filth in the soil, rising into the air and spreading through the shifting winds. Most of the sanitation efforts were focused on the crowded urban areas swelled by growing numbers of immigrants. The approach was to cleanse the cesspools of tenements and slums through the establishment of sanitary controls. Little attention was given to the cause of the slum conditions, unfair housing practices, greedy landlords, and horrible working conditions in the factories that brought swarms of desperate people looking for the hope of work. The tactic was once again to control, prohibit, and create rules and regulations directed at the individual to prevent the problems rather than empower the immigrants in this "cloacal inferno" (Rosen, 1958). It is probable that the filth associated with the urban slums was identified with the people living in these environs rather than the economic forces causing these conditions. Irish immigrants were "poor, white trash." Immigration laws were developed to control the flow of "dirt" into the country.

The public health model of prevention developed following the discovery of germs and their role in creating disease. The public health model considers three components—the host or vulnerable individual, the environment, and the agent, or that which contributes to the disease. So, for example, in the prevention of malaria, it has been determined that the agent is a specific type of mosquito. Malaria can be prevented by increasing the individual host's resistance to the disease, rendering the mosquito sterile, or altering the environment by eliminating the breeding grounds of the mosquito. In the case of malaria, the last strategy has been utilized.

Another example would be drug addiction. The public health model would consider all of the factors that would put the individual host at risk for drug addiction, such as genetics, personality, past history, etc. The factors in the environment contributing to drug abuse would be assessed, including family dynamics, housing conditions, availability of jobs, quality of educational opportunities, etc. Finally, the agent or the drug itself, such as alcohol, would be identified and controlled or eliminated. It is apparent that the recent "war on drugs" attempted to control the agent by investing resources in law enforcement and supply reduction. Once again, prevention has failed because little attention has been given to provide the means for people to avoid falling into the trap of drug use in the first place. Go upstream and find out why people are falling in the river and drowning.

Catalano and Dooley (1980) divide prevention into either proactive or reactive programs. Proactive strategies focus on preventing specific problems before they occur, and reactive strategies try to enhance coping abilities to deal with problems once they occur. To date, prevention has been primarily reactive. Reactive prevention efforts are described by Schmolling, Youkeles, and Berger (1993) with their questions, "What can one do to

help prevent the spread of AIDS? Isolate victims from the uninfected populations? Prohibit children infected with the AIDS virus from attending regular school of day-care centers? Mandate testing for the virus and specify who shall be tested? Make the names of those who test positive available to the public?" (p. 281). Proactive prevention would demand social activism leading to social change, not social control. Examples of proactive prevention could include suggestions made by Jeanne Gibbs in her unpublished manuscript, "A Timely Paradigm Shift from the Delivery of Services to the Empowerment of Community for Prevention and Care," where she recommends greater utilization of self-help groups, peer learning-teaching strategies, changing public policy, and increased use of media in prevention.

In the mid-1960s, when human services were first emerging in response to the failure of the established system, Bolman and Westman in their article, "Prevention of Mental Disorders: An Overview of Current Programs," categorized prevention as person-centered, family-centered and society-centered. The society-centered prevention approach called for social action to provide education, community organization, development, and mobilization. Now, thirty years later, we are recognizing the importance of community empowerment for prevention and the revitalization of human services.

Before human services can return to its original vision of prevention, much work must be done. Many practitioners in human services have been socialized into the established belief that treatment is a far more valued activity than prevention. Often, it is now hard to discern the difference between human service practitioners and the established helping professions that gave birth to the rise of human services, because they were not responsive to the true needs of the community, such as prevention! Human service practitioners are unprepared as a result of lack of training and an ideology that has sold out to the status quo to advocate for the needed social change necessary to effect real prevention efforts. Finally, human service practitioners are clamoring to become third-party reimbursable along with their traditional, established counterparts (social workers, psychologists, nurses, and psychiatrists) and become a part of a system that promotes the provision of treatment, not prevention!

George Albee, in his remarkable work *Mental Health Manpower Trends* (1959), gave impetus for the development of a new type of human service practitioner. Albee continues to argue that prevention must occur through political action and social change (1981).

Patchwork solutions will not do, and . . . the whole structure of our polluted, industrialized, overpopulated, overenergized, overcrowded, sexist, and racist society breeds such massive human injustice and distress that the only hope for prevention is for major social reorganization. To prevent mental and emotional disorders, it is argued, we must abolish such injustices as unemployment, bad housing, social discrimination, personal insecurity, and poverty. As a consequence of the threat all of this holds to the status quo, the Establishment does little to encourage or support efforts at primary prevention in the social sphere because it believes, with some justification, that it would be funding programs aimed at a major redistribution of its power (Kessler and Albee, 1975, p. 576).

Albee (1980) also articulates the failure of prevention due to an ethnocentric defect model that has essentially blamed the victim and persists because it insures professional status and advantage for traditional established helping professionals. Albee promotes a competence model that builds upon an egalitarian political and moral philosophy emphasizing the concept of adaptive potential—empowerment.

Over a decade ago, Kelly, Snowden, and Munoz (1977) argued for the importance of inclusion of members at the bottom of the economic ladder to actively participate in planning and implementing prevention services. Unfortunately, today we continue to see the dominant culture controlling the provision of prevention services in the community. Prevention must listen to all of the voices in the community in order to make a difference today. What we will hear is a call for social justice, not social control.

Clark (1981) described a community prevention program based in Harlem, NY. He concluded that the following must occur before prevention can be effective in the face of severe social problems:

1. There must be commitment to social justice on the part of public policymakers;
2. There must be social and economic support of these programs, not just rhetoric; and,
3. Indigenous human service practitioners must be trained and given an active role to play in decision making.

Gisela Konopka fled to the United States from Germany after imprisonment in a Nazi concentration camp. She worked in social services for fifty years and in 1981 wrote about the important lessons people working in prevention need to keep in mind. Social change requires hard work and cannot be taken for granted. Do not get involved in advocating for social action if you are not prepared to face the adverse responses you will get. Understand your own value system and how this drives your work. Be honest. The means do not always justify the ends.

The means, the activities, and the process of prevention through empowerment are a dynamic and integral aspect of a new ecological paradigm. In this approach, empowerment is seen as the restoration and creation of hope in a community—the sense that "we can do it together" (Roberts and Thorsheim, 1987). In the ecological approach to empowerment of a community, the community member is seen as the real expert, knowledgeable of the history, hopes, fears, and weavings of human relationships that can be converted into resources for prevention. Hess (1987) shared the lines of a Japanese haiku to give the sense of this new ecological paradigm of prevention through empowerment:

> *If the cuckoo doesn't sing, make it sing*
> *If the cuckoo doesn't sing, kill it*
> *If the cuckoo doesn't sing, wait until it sings*

The last line reflects empowerment; the first two lines the tactics of social control.

Kelly (1987) presents ten principles for the ecological paradigm of prevention through empowerment.

These principles serve as useful guidelines for human service practitioners attracted to the work of prevention through social activism.

Ten principles of the ecological paradigm

1. Attend to aspects of the total environment that are supportive of change.
2. Learn how people are interwoven.
3. Be aware of social norms and processes of the systems in the community.
4. Reflect on how you are interacting with the environment.
5. Assess people, places, and events over time. Be patient and give it time.
6. Conserve existing resources.
7. Activate potential resources.
8. Be flexible and open to improvisation.
9. Support the process of coping and adaptation.
10. Be alert for unexpected outcomes.

A tremendous opportunity for revitalizing the empowerment approach to prevention lies in recent legislation enacted by the 101st Congress: the National and Community Service Act of 1990. This act will provide funding for programs enabling (empowering) students from kindergarten through college and older Americans to volunteer in environmental and human service areas. Senator Edward Kennedy (1991) wrote that through service, people will learn that they can make a difference in the lives of others and discover the power of their own life.

This legislation has promise, but more is needed. "It simply won't work to go on living as we do, consuming as we please, profiting as much as we can and running the economy as we do, while using the money that is left over to 'help the poor.' There won't be enough left over, and the poor will lose the political debate. It is we who must change, and our patterns and institutions that must be transformed. There is much work to do and there are jobs to be found in creating the things we all need—education, health, energy efficiency, a safe and restored environment, healthy food, good roads, strong bridges, better transportation, affordable housing, stable families, and vital communities. Such things can only be achieved by a combination of solid moral values and sound social policy. This requires a number of fundamental shifts in perspective—from unlimited growth to a sustainable society; from endless consumer goods to the reprioritizing of social goods; from the habit of self-protection to an ethic of community; from viewing life as an acquisitive venture to restoring the sacred value of our relationship with our neighbor and our environment. These shifts will not be easy, nor will they come without cost. The only thing more costly is not to change" (Willis, 1992).

Human services must rededicate its commitment to this spirit of social change. If human services practitioners are not ready for this call, a new wave of activists will rise up from the miasma, a fresh breath of renewing, hopeful, and empowering voices. We must go upstream. Prevention is the vital force of human services. Prevention is our heart and soul. Working in the community, "we learn that survival does not belong to the 'fittest.' Survival is about learning how to fit into our community and how the community fits us" (Fox, 1991, p. 50).

REFERENCES

Albee, G. W., (1959). *Mental Health Manpower Trends*. New York: Basic Books.

Albee, G. W., (1980). "A Competency Model Must Replace the Defect Model." In L. A. Bond and J. C. Rosen, eds., *Primary Prevention of Psychopathology, vol. 4: Competency and Coping During Adulthood*. Hanover, NH: University Press of New England.

Albee, G. W., (1981). "Politics, Power, Prevention, and Social Change." In J. M. Joffe and G. W. Albee, eds., *Prevention Through Political Action and Social Change*. Hanover, NH: University Press of New England.

Bloom, B. L., (1984). *Community Mental Health: A General Introduction*. Monterey, CA: Brooks/Cole.

Clark, K. B., (1981). "Community Action Programs—An Appraisal." In J. M. Joffe and G. W. Albee, eds., *Primary Prevention of Psychopathology, Vol. 5: Prevention Through Political Action and Social Change*. Hanover, NH: University Press of New England.

Cohen, A., (1927). *Teaching of Maimonides*. London: Routledge.

Fox, M., (1991). *Creation Spirituality: Liberating Gifts for the Peoples of the Earth*. San Francisco: Harper Collins.

Gibbs, J., (no date). "*A Timely Shift from the Delivery of Services to the Empowerment of Community for Prevention and Care*." Unpublished manuscript. The Center for Human Development, Lafayette, CA.

Hess, R.E., (1987). *The Ecology of Prevention: Illustrating Mental Health Consultation*. New York: Haworth Press.

Kelly, J.G., L.R. Snowden, and R.P. Munoz, (1977). "Social and Community Interventions." *Annual Review of Psychology* 28:323–361.

Kelly, J.G., (1987). "An Ecological Paradigm: Defining Mental Health Consultation as a Preventative Service." In Kelly, J.G. and Hess, R.E., eds., *The Ecology of Prevention: Illustrating Mental Health Consultation*. New York: Haworth Press.

Kennedy, E.M., (1991). "National Service and Education for Citizenship." *Phi Delta Kappan* 72: 771–773.

Kessler, M. and Albee, G.W., (1975). "Primary Prevention." Annual Review of Psychology, 26:557–592.

Konopka, G., (1981). "Social Change, Social Action as Prevention: The Role of the Professional." In J.M. Joffe, and G.W. Albee, eds., *Primary Prevention of Psychopathology, Vol. 5: Prevention Through Political Action and Social Change*. Hanover, NH: University Press of New England.

McClam, T. and M. Woodside, (1990). *An Introduction to Human Services*. Pacific Grove, CA: Brooks/Cole Publishing.

Osher, D., (1990). "The Antecedent and Concurrent Social Conditions that Influenced the Human Services Movement." In Fullerton and Osher, eds., *History of the Human Services Movement*. Council for Standards in Human Service Education, Monograph Series, Issue Number 7.

Robert, B.B. and H.I. Thorsheim, (1987). "A Partnership Approach to Consultation: The Process and Results of a Major Primary Prevention Field Experiment." In J.G. Kelly and R.E. Hess, eds., *The Ecology of Prevention: Illustrating Mental Health Consultation*. New York: Haworth Press.

Schmolling, P., M. Youkeles, and W.R. Burger, (1993). *Human Services in Contemporary America*. Pacific Grove, CA: Brooks/Cole.

Willis, J., (1992). "No Justice, No Peace." *Sojourners* 21:11–14.

CHAPTER 24

HUMAN SERVICES IN THE MENTAL HEALTH ARENA
FROM INSTITUTION TO COMMUNITY

JOSEPH MEHR

As human services enters what is arguably its fourth decade, the field continues to be characterized by dramatic change. In the mental health arena, the past thirty years have seen a move from the provision of public services in monolithic residential institutions (state hospitals) through an emphasis on institutional closure and the promotion of an ideal of community-based services. Some state hospitals have, in fact, closed, almost all are significantly smaller than they were, and those that remain are likely to become smaller yet. Unfortunately, while there has been growth in community mental health services during this period, that growth has not paralleled the need for services for the chronically mentally ill in most parts of the country. The decades of the seventies and particularly the eighties were times of severe fiscal constraints for state and federal government. In many states the savings from closing institutions were not channeled into community services, but were used to cover governmental budget deficits from other programs, most notably the soaring medical health care costs of medicaid programs. It was an era with a lack of public and political will to pay the cost of needed human services in the mental health sector, if such services would require the politician's nightmare— a tax increase.

Times continue to change. In 1993, the sequential Republican administrations of Presidents Ron-ald Reagan and George Bush were replaced by the Democratic administration of President Bill Clinton. Although President Clinton recognizes the need to reduce the federal deficit and has made it a major initiative, he also appears to recognize the need for improved public services. His administration appears committed to national health care reform, and if such reform is successful, it is likely to include increased access for mental health services for all citizens, regardless of their ability to pay. Of particular importance for the field of human services is the possibility that this health care reform may include funding both for the provision of mental health services in hospitals and for services in the community for persons with serious and persistent mental illness (NASMHPD, 1993). That is, services may be funded for persons who in the past were either placed in mental hospitals, or due to lack of funding, received typically inadequate services in community programs, or received no services at all.

The Democratic administration faces a difficult balancing act. It will be no easy task to successfully reduce the federal deficit and stimulate the economy, while at the same time push through health care reform and otherwise improve human services. If President Clinton and the Democratic administration are successful, there could be sweeping changes in many human service systems, particularly in mental health. However, even if changes at the federal level are not successful or only partially successful, one can still anticipate continued change in the delivery of human services in the mental health arena. The changes that have occurred in the mental health arena over the past three decades have developed a momentum that will continue either more quickly or more slowly—but they will continue.

Understanding the immediate future (the next decade) of human services in public mental health systems is best achieved by viewing the impact over time of changes in mental health service delivery, and the roles of human services that developed along with those changes. A detailed history of mental health service systems in the United States is available from a variety of sources including Fisher, Mehr, and Truckenbrod (1974); Grob (1991); and Mehr (1983, 1995). For our purposes here, a brief overview will suffice.

THE EARLY YEARS: A GRAND PLAN

After World War II, public policy regarding mental health services began to change drastically, and that change accelerated over the following decade. Through the mid-1950s the public mental hospital was the primary provider of mental health services, with inpatient census reaching a peak in 1955 of 558,922 (Mechanic and Rochefort, 1992). Public mental hospitals had become huge warehouses of the mentally ill, isolating patients from community life. In 1958, Harry C. Solomon, the new president of the American Psychiatric Association, described them as "antiquated, outmoded and rapidly becoming obsolctc" (Grob, 1991).

Disenchantment with large public mental hospitals stemmed from a variety of sources. Intolerable conditions had been exposed through a variety of public media venues including books, movies, and newspapers. Advances in treatment approaches, particularly the discovery of psychopharmacological medications that reduced the symptoms of major mental illness and the growing popularity of psychotherapy, suggested that the mentally ill could be treated in less restrictive settings.

From the late 1950s on, it became more and more accepted that the mentally ill could be treated in community clinics on an outpatient basis, and that chronic hospitalization should be only a last resort. Community mental health centers had been opened all across the country, and as early as 1959 there were more than 1,400 such clinics in the United States.

Major legislative changes reflected the changing opinions of the times and added impetus to the growing community movement. In 1946 legislation was passed to establish the National Institute for Mental Health (NIMH). The Mental Health Study Act was passed in 1955, providing funding for a Joint Commission on Mental Illness and Health that was to analyze and evaluate the needs of and resources for the mentally ill, and make recommendations for a national mental health program. Of particular significance for human services were the manpower development recommendations of the commission (Albee, 1961). These recommendations suggested that, due to a lack of medical staff, nonmedical mental health workers (i.e., human service workers) would be a necessary part of providing mental health services, if such services were increased. The recommendations of the commission regarding dramatically increasing community mental health services were sympathetically received by the Kennedy Administration and Congress, and were codified in the Community Mental Health Centers Act of 1963, which proposed the development of 2,000 and funded the establishment of over 600 community mental health centers during the next decade.

From the mid-1960s to the mid-1970s the principles of the community mental health movement were broadly accepted, and the locus of mental health services shifted dramatically from the public mental hospital to the community clinic. The community movement was, in a sense, a "grand plan" that had at its foundation a belief by many that the public mental hospital could be abandoned and replaced by a comprehensive community service system. That belief was, in fact, even shared by many who worked in public mental hospitals. The growing emphasis on community treatment, improvement in treatment technology, the passage of Medicare and Medicaid legislation in 1965, and expansion of Supplemental Security Income, Social Security Disability Insurance, and housing subsidies to the mentally ill lead to a dramatic reduction in the number of public mental hospital patients to 193,436 by 1975. It appeared that the community mental health movement was well on its way to changing the mental health delivery system, and the phenomenon of declining public mental hospital populations was given the name of "deinstitutionalization."

At the dawn of the community mental health movement, the terms *human services* and *human service worker* had yet to be coined; there were, however, "human service workers" in fact, if not in name. Most were nonprofessionals who worked in public mental hospitals under titles such as Psychiatric Aide, Psychiatric Technicians, or Nurse's Aide. Their role was initially quite limited. However, of all the staff in such settings, it was they who provided the lion's share of staff contact with patients. The growing recognition that traditional professionals would always be in short supply led to a number or organized efforts to expand the role of such workers and increase their competence. Some early efforts in this direction occurred at a few state mental hospitals, funded by NIMH Hospital Improvement Program (HIP) grants (Mehr, 1966, 1971). Later at NIMH, a special division was created, the Paraprofessional Manpower Development Branch, whose purpose was to provide technical assistance and grant funds to organizations (such as State Departments of Mental Health and Community Mental Health Agencies) in order to develop training programs and career ladders for such individuals. On the academic side, in 1964 an associate-level degree program was started at Purdue University to train this type of mental health worker both for jobs in the community and in the mental hospital. In 1966, the Southern Regional Education Board (SREB) sponsored a national conference of mental health and community college professionals to explore the training of mental health workers at two-year colleges, and subsequently SREB received an NIMH grant to assist in the development of associate degree or certificate programs in fourteen southern states.

The Southern Regional Education Board's Mental Health Division became a leader in the early human services/mental health manpower development arena. In 1969 SREB published a document that defined a series of roles and functions for mental health workers (SREB, 1969). In the monograph SREB described thirteen proposed roles and four competence levels. The thirteen roles were:

> Outreach Worker
> Broker
> Advocate
> Evaluator
> Teacher Educator
> Behavior Changer
> Mobilizer
> Consultant
> Community Planner
> Caregiver
> Data Manager
> Administrator
> Assistant to Specialist

Nine of the thirteen roles can be appropriate for an inpatient setting, but the focus of the roles and their definition was clearly on services in a community setting. The rapid expansion of community services during the era saw a concomitant expansion of the employment and use of nontraditional staff, both in public mental hospitals and community mental health centers. The changes in the mental health system were viewed as so dramatic that they were often described as "revolutionary" (Rochefort, 1984), and great expectations were held for the success of the approach.

THE MIDDLE YEARS: DREAM VS. REALITY

Advocates of the community mental health movement had a dream—a vision of what the mental health system should look like. The nation would be fully covered by a network of 2,000 community mental health centers, each serving a population base of up to 250,000 people. The services offered would effectively replace the large public mental hospital. The chronically mentally ill would be served in less restrictive community programs and the public mental hospitals would be either entirely eliminated or be small and designed to serve only a very small segment of the mentally ill population. The services that would replace the public mental hospital were defined in a number of sources as: (1) to provide treatment by a basic mental health team for persons with acute mental illness, (2) to care for incompletely recovered mental patients either short of admission to a hospital or following discharge from the hospital, and (3) to provide a headquarters base for mental health consultants working with mental health counselors. In the early period, federally funded community mental health centers were required to have at least five essential services: (1) inpatient, (2) outpatient, (3) emergency services, (4) pre- and posthospital care, and (5) education and mental health consultation.

For a number of years it appeared that the dream was becoming a reality. Public mental hospitals were getting smaller; some were closed. The community mental health center network was growing, and statistical data were being generated that documented the growth of community services. By 1985 the number of public mental hospital patients had declined to about 100,000 from over 550,000. In spite of that decline, patient care episodes for all types of mental health services had increased from 1.7 million in 1955 to 6.9 million in 1983 (Mechanic and Rochefort, 1992). Well over 50 percent of the patient care episodes in 1985 occurred in nonhospital settings. There had been a profound shift in the location of services as well as in the rate of episodes (Grob, 1991). A superficial view of the data supported the notion that the community mental health movement was moving towards success.

In fact, in many of the community mental health centers the severely mentally ill person discharged from the public mental hospital did not receive adequate and comprehensive care. The increase in patient care episodes reflected a broadening of the clientele to new groups that in previous years had no access to the mental health system—persons with problems of crisis, problems of satisfaction, and milder psychological problems rather than severe mental illness (Grob, 1991). More typically, the chronically and severely mentally ill person discharged from the public mental hospital was placed in a nursing home, or entered a cycle of short-term stays in the public mental hospital, discharge, and readmission. To be sure, there were many community mental health centers that did provide adequate service that could maintain a severely mentally ill person in his or her community, but the reality did not approach the dream.

A compounding problem for the vision of a reformed mental health system was the impact of declining fiscal support from government entities. In 1981, federal support for comprehensive community mental health centers was eliminated after only slightly more than 600 of the proposed 2,000 were established (Kiesler, 1992). Medicaid did not keep pace with the growth of the number of poor, and Congress required states to review SSI and SSDI eligibility, resulting in 500,000 people losing benefits, which disproportionately affected the mentally ill. In general, the Reagan-Bush years saw significant cuts in funding for social programs even though the federal deficit continued to soar. In addition, a general antitax, antigovernment spending sentiment at the local level resulted in social service funding stagnation at the state level. By the mid to late 1980s, only a few state systems saw any increases in funding for mental health services.

The plight of the mentally ill in the community was further compromised by a general loss of housing availability. Federal housing programs suffered cutbacks, low cost housing units were converted to middle class housing through gentrification in most cities, and single-room-occupancy (SRO) hotels virtually disappeared. Homelessness has become a problem of much greater magnitude, highly visible on the nightly news, and present in every city in the country. It is estimated that on any night about 600,000 people are homeless (Burt and Cohen, 1989). The growth in numbers of homeless people is viewed by many to be a sign of the failure of the deinstitutionalization of public mental hospitals and the community mental health movement (Torrey, 1988). In fact, the two groups, the homeless and the mentally ill, are quite different populations, even though they do overlap. Only about one quarter of the homeless have ever experienced prior psychiatric hospitalization (Rossi, 1990).

A number of factors came together in the 1980s to result in a bifurcated system consisting of continued use and need for public mental hospitals, and a community mental health system substantially lacking in a full range of services for the most needy of the mentally ill. With a lack of new or expanded fiscal sources, the two sides of the system competed for the same funds. In most states the downsizing of public mental hospitals continued. The fiscal savings from the downsizing in some states was put into funding new community programs. In other states, unfortunately, the mental health system lost the savings; they were used to cover state deficits in other areas. The bifurcated system was characterized by weak institutional linkages or mechanisms to ensure continuity and coordination of services. Severely mentally ill people were often released from public mental hospitals, after relatively brief periods of time, into communities without adequate support mechanisms (Grob, 1991).

Through the 1980s the term human services became more and more commonly used in the mental health arena, as the general field of human services developed. By 1987 there were almost 400 certificate, associate, and bachelor's level academic programs around the country and a growing number of master's degree programs. (Cogan and Wood, 1987). The roles of human service workers in mental health have paralleled the changes in service from institutions to community. Although about as many human service workers continue to be employed in public mental hospitals, far more are working in community

agencies. There has been a significant expansion in the number of human service workers who engage in the activity of case management due to the expansion of community mental health services, although the fiscal constraints of the eighties did, for a time, slow the growth of positions for human service workers.

RECENT TIMES: RETURN OF THE PENDULUM

The late 1980s and early 1990s saw a reconsideration of the overly optimistic promises of the original community mental health movement. With few exceptions, most authorities no longer believe that public mental hospitals can be entirely eliminated. However, they will continue to be smaller, and the total available beds will be less than the 92,000 available in 1990 (Mahtesian, 1993). Although plagued by the negative stereotypes of decades past, which are reinforced by occasional scandals portrayed in the popular media, most public mental hospitals are consistently improving as they get smaller and become better staffed. The pendulum has swung to a somewhat more centrist position that has a goal of a system of mental health care that is not only balanced between public mental hospitals and a comprehensive community mental health system, but that integrates public mental hospitals into the community mental health system.

The challenge for mental health policy makers and planners has recently been to find ways to fund the expansion of a community mental health system that is responsible to the public health needs of the indigent chronically and severely mentally ill. Some states have made dramatic efforts in this direction by systematically redirecting funds from downsizing public mental hospitals and putting those funds in community programs specifically for the severely mentally ill. Notable examples include Massachusetts, Connecticut, Vermont, New Hampshire, Ohio, Kansas, and more recently, New York, which reduced the number of resident patients by 30 percent between 1987 and 1991

(Mechanic and Rochefort, 1992). The costs of aggressive comprehensive community care, while not cheap, are substantially less than care in a public mental hospital, and thus equivalent funds can purchase much more community care than hospital care. However, most states have discovered that additional revenues from the tax base will be needed if a fully comprehensive system is to be established to adequately address the mental health needs of the severely mentally ill.

A comprehensive system of mental health care has a number of characteristics:

— An organized, managed, coordinated system of care at the *local level* provides the best opportunity for individuals to access mental health services in, or close to, their home communities.

— Each community area should have sufficient core services to meet the needs of individuals who are most in need and most dependent on state-funded care. Core services will be immediately available and accessible to priority populations. Immediate priorities include: assertive case management, residential/housing options, crisis/emergency response services (including prescreening to assure appropriateness of admissions to restrictive levels of care, and coordination services to assure continuity of care regardless of the location of the client).

— Individuals who are most in need and least able to afford care must be the priority for state-funded services.

— Individuals with special needs must be able to access services tailored to fit their needs.

— Services must be culturally relevant.

— Continuity of care between hospital and community services must be a consistent feature of the service system.

— An appropriate balance between inpatient, outpatient, and residential services must be achieved and maintained with the utilization of the most costly, restrictive levels of care being justified on the basis of clinical necessity.

— All service settings must provide high-quality care and treatment consistent with professional, nationally recognized standards of care.

— The system of care must be accountable to its users and the taxpayers for its outcomes, quality, efficiency, and effectiveness.

— The responsibility for ongoing planning and service system development at the local level must be shared between primary and secondary consumers, providers, advocates, and other interested stakeholders and interested parties.

By 1995 comprehensive systems of mental health care have been well on their way to development in a number of states, with dramatic results. Illinois, in contrast, is just beginning a reform movement with the goal of developing a more comprehensive system, and can be used as a comparison with states that are already implementing such a system. In Illinois, the admission (and readmission) rate to public mental hospitals in fiscal year 1991 was 150 people per 100,000 population. Although some states have admission rates that are substantially higher, a number of states with more comprehensive community systems have been able to achieve significantly lower rates of admission. States that are similar to Illinois in population and urban-rural mix that have more comprehensive community systems and significantly lower admission rates include California (22/100,000), Florida (26/100,000), Michigan (89/100,000), Ohio (121/100,000), Pennsylvania (56/100,000), and Texas (82/100,000).

Several states have been singled out in the literature for special notice due to their success in decreasing admissions to state-operated facilities. One such state is Vermont, a small state that, although very different from Illinois, has become one of the models for what can be done in this approach. In Vermont, the admission and readmission rate per 100,000 population to their state hospital in 1991 was 92/100,000 (Pandiani and Girardi, 1991). Before implementation of the comprehensive community alternatives, the Vermont admission rate was approximately 275 per 100,000. Thus, admissions to the state hospital were reduced almost 200 percent. In Illinois, the admission and readmission rate to public mental hospitals in fiscal year 1991 was almost 40 percent higher than in Vermont.

A similar difference exists between Illinois and one part of Massachusetts (their Region I), which developed comprehensive community alternatives to hospitalization under a federal consent decree. In that section of Massachusetts, the hospitalization rate was reduced to 103 per 100,000 population. Prior to the complete implementation of comprehensive community programs, their admission rate was as high as 165 per 100,000 (Geller, 1991), or 38 percent higher. Of these two examples, Massachusetts is probably most comparable to Illinois, and the data suggest that implementation of effective comprehensive community alternatives in Illinois could decrease admissions and readmissions by almost forty percent, from over 16,000 per year in 1992 to around 10,000 per year. Thus, 6,000 episodes of care would occur in less restrictive environments at substantially less cost, and fewer public mental hospital beds would be utilized.

In planning for a comprehensive system of care in Illinois, it has become clear that fiscal savings in public mental hospitals can contribute to funding the system but are not sufficient. Additional revenues will have to be found to accomplish the task. Had the funds from downsizing during the past two decades all been moved into the community system, those new revenues might not be necessary today, and a comprehensive mental health system could already have been in place, as it is in a number of other states.

HUMAN SERVICES IN MENTAL HEALTH: WHERE DO WE GO FROM HERE?

What direction will mental health service systems take in the next ten years? Prediction is a risky process, particularly on the eve of a possible national health care reform. However, as pointed out earlier, whether or not community services for the severely and chronically mental ill are included in the national health care plan, the changes we have seen in the past several decades will continue. Public mental hospitals will be an integral part of the mental health service system, although they will be smaller, there will be fewer of them, and those that remain will provide a higher quality of care. They will be fully inte-

grated into the networks of community care offered in their geographic areas. The community services offered by local agencies for the severely mentally ill will expand significantly as public mental hospitals continue to downsize, and as priorities are set for the limited fiscal resources available for public mental health services.

As the community service system expands to provide adequate comprehensive services for the priority population of the severely and chronically mentally ill, existing programs will be expanded and new, more effective programs will be developed, opening opportunities for human service workers. Two types of service approaches in particular will be implemented that will require additional staffing of both traditionally credentialed professionals and human service professionals. These two approaches have been documented and recognized as highly effective in maintaining the chronically mentally ill in the community and in improving their daily functioning. One approach is usually called Assertive Community Treatment (ACT) or Intensive Case Management (ICM); the other is called Psychosocial Rehabilitation.

Assertive Community Treatment has existed for more than twenty years, but has not been uniformly implemented. It involves aggressive psychiatric care and medication supervision, intensive daily case management, assistance with housing and welfare entitlements, and the ability to respond to crisis twenty-four hours a day. It is usually offered on a team basis, with case loads of about ten clients per case manager. Sustained care over long periods of the client's lifetime is typically essential to maintain favorable results (Stein and Test, 1980, 1985; Olfson, 1990).

Experience in discharging clients to the community during the past several decades demonstrated that a move to the community alone and traditional services were not the answer. Many clients who returned to the community were unable to remain there for long. Resources were not coordinated to assist clients in securing or maintaining needed services. The use of a service by individuals depends on their being knowledgeable not only about the nature of a problem, but also about which of numerous agencies should be turned to for help. Persons who are chronically mentally ill have special needs and present special problems. The disruption to the client and family, and the interruption of productivity and cost to the taxpayer is staggering when the client cannot be maintained in the community.

The role of the ACT case manager is to meet the needs of clients wherever and whenever required. The case manager's responsibility is not restricted to predefined functions or limited in time and location. They must be available twenty-four hours a day, ready to go to the clients in their environment and perform assertively. What severely mentally ill clients need most is a person to help with their problems as they experience them, not as others might define them. They need a person whom they can count on for support. For case management to achieve its purpose, the case manager must have the authority required to assure client access to any of the programs or services provided by the agency. The case manager's effectiveness is defined in terms of client outcome. That means assisting clients with the appropriate services so that they have a life that is as productive, satisfying, and self-sufficient as possible.

The responsibilities of an Assertive Community Treatment Case Manager are:

1. To identify members of the target population: includes being able to assess whether or not prospective clients meet eligibility criteria (i.e., that they are truly in the greatest need of attention); also entails maintaining good relationships with major referral sources—state hospitals, community mental health centers, shelters, single-room occupancy hotels, bus terminals and airports, and the families of people with mental illness or the individuals themselves—so that clients will be referred for service.

2. To engage the new referrals in the program: initial engagement of a new client must be slow and careful, so that the client will not be overwhelmed by offers of assistance; ideally, initial engagement should begin by assisting a client with a concrete task in order to demonstrate the advantages of participation in a case management program from the outset.

3. To conduct assessments and, subsequently, to plan interventions based on these assessments: consists of taking stock of a client's strengths, difficulties, existing resources, and remaining needs, and then searching out novel ways to interrupt the chain of events that previously led to the person's distress in the community, subsequent rehospitalization, and/or homelessness; develop the intervention strategy in consultation with the client, and his or her family if the client consents.

4. To assume ultimate professional responsibility for clients: includes helping clients assemble individually tailored packages of community supports that are provided either directly by the ACT team or set up by the team in conjunction with other service providers; also means showing unusual tolerance for unresponsive or difficult behavior and refusing to "give up" on clients.

5. To assist clients through home visiting: consists of meeting with individuals on their own turf where their problems generally arise, and where the solutions to their problems must be found; must have the flexibility to meet with clients in very unconventional places, if necessary, such as low-rent hotels, welfare offices, public shelters, police lock-ups, street corners, and neighborhood coffee shops.

6. To be able to attend to the concrete details of clients' everyday lives: entails paying close attention to matters of everyday living that might otherwise be taken for granted such as food, clothing, shelter, medical care, entitlements, and money management; helping to make concrete matters seem less overwhelming, so that living in the community becomes a viable and desirable alternative to institutional care.

7. To provide clients with *in vivo* assistance and training: includes giving on-the-spot help and skills training to clients regarding a wide range of independent living tasks such as grocery shopping, laundry, leasing an apartment, managing a checking account, or cleaning a room; also involves encouraging clients to become involved in social, vocational, recreational, and self-help programs and even attending the first few meetings of these programs with clients to ease the transition.

8. To arrange for psychiatric and other medical services for clients: entails helping clients obtain the highest quality services available, while at the same time diffusing some of the confusing and stressful nature of making such arrangements; in some cases, in addition to assisting clients in arranging the visit, the ACT staff will have to physically accompany them to their doctor or psychiatrist appointments in order to help them negotiate the entire process.

9. To provide interagency resource brokering and advocacy.

10. To develop new community resources: could entail searching for and making available to clients hidden resources, or possibly developing currently nonexistent resources "from scratch"; includes creatively combining resources in order to come up with a new avenue for addressing a client's need when that need cannot be met by an existing resource.

11. To facilitate inpatient psychiatric hospital admissions, when absolutely necessary, and working with the inpatient staff while the client must be in the hospital: consists of being able to recognize signs that the client is truly in need of rehospitalization, initiating hospitalization if the client is unwilling to go voluntarily, and working with inpatient staff once the client is safely hospitalized in order to have a voice in the client's inpatient treatment and to take part in the subsequent discharge plans.

12. To establish a partnership with families of clients in cases where client and family are still in contact, and the relationship between client and family is one that has potential to be of some benefit to the client.

The defined roles of an Assertive Community Treatment Case Manager overlap with the roles previously identified by SREB, and embody many of the philosophies and attitudes characteristic of human service workers (Mehr, 1995).

Psychosocial rehabilitation includes a variety of approaches that have as their goal to improve the daily social functioning of the chronically mentally ill by helping them to develop or acquire social and instrumental skills, and by developing environments that will support the maintenance of those skills. While many mental health professionals have contributed to the development of the approach, two in particular stand out: William Anthony in Boston and Robert Paul Liberman in California (Anthony and Liberman, 1986).

In Liberman's approach, social skills training is delivered in group settings using structured modules for teaching social and independent living skills (Vaccaro et al., 1992). All patients receive competency-based instruction in four core skill areas: medication management, symptom management, basic conversation, and recreation and leisure. Classes are run four days per week, three

hours per day, for a period of six months. Each of the classes is sixty to seventy-five minutes in length. The total length of instruction varies slightly from group to group, since clients do not proceed to the next skill area until the material is learned. Ongoing progress is monitored through the use of "pop quizzes" administered during and after the social skills training classes. Patients are further assessed for knowledge and skills acquisition and maintenance at the end of the six-month intensive treatment phase and every six to twelve months thereafter. Therapists' competency and adherence to the model are regularly assessed as well, ensuring high degrees of fidelity to the model. Once patients complete the first six months of skills training, they enter into the generalization phase of the program. Case management efforts are directed toward helping patients generalize the skills learned in the classroom to other life areas. Case managers use behavioral learning interventions such as structured problem solving and role play in their practice. All patients periodically update their individualized written rehabilitation plans. These plans address goals in major life domains such as housing and household maintenance, symptomatic status, occupation, social and family life, and finances. Substantial evaluative research has accumulated to document the effectiveness of a psychosocial rehabilitative approach in relapse prevention and maintenance of clients in community settings, and in the improvement of quality of life.

The implications for the future of human services in mental health that arise out of the broad expansion of ACT and psychosocial rehabilitation are significant. During the next ten years, there will be the need for thousands, perhaps tens of thousands, of new community staff nationwide who have, or can develop, the necessary attitudes, knowledge, and skills to be employed as assertive community treatment case managers and psychosocial rehabilitation technicians. While some traditionally trained mental health professionals perform these roles, the human service professional who is a graduate of a two- or four-year human service program is more likely to enter the work force with an appropriate set of attitudes and skills already in place. The potential skills market that will develop over the near future suggests that human service programs should evaluate their curricula to assure that extensive training and education in these two content areas are included in order to provide a supply of professionals who can meet the growing demand.

REFERENCES

Albee, G.W., (1961). *Mental Health Manpower Trends.* New York: Basic Books.

Anthony, W.A., and R.P. Liberman, (1986). "The Practice of Psychiatric Rehabilitation: Historical, Conceptual, and Research Base." *Schizophrenia Bulletin* 12(4), pp. 571–591.

Burt, M.R., and B.E. Cohen, (1989). *America's Homeless: Numbers, Characteristics, and Programs that Serve Them.* Washington, DC: Urban Institute Press.

Cogan, D.B., and A.C. Wood, (1987). "A Survey of the Introductory Course in Mental Health and Human Services." *Human Services Education* 8(2), pp. 22–27.

Fisher, W., J. Mehr, and P. Truckenbrod, (1974). *Human Services: The Third Revolution in Mental Health.* Port Washington, NY: Alfred Publishing Co.

Geller, J.L., (1991). "Anyplace But the State Hospital: Examining Assumptions About the Benefits of Admission Diversion." *Hospital and Community Psychiatry* 42(2), pp. 145–152.

Grob, G.N., (1991). "The Severely and Chronically Mentally Ill in America: Retrospect and Prospect." *Transactions: Studies of the College of Physicians of Philadelphia* 13(4), pp. 337–362.

Kiesler, C.A., (1992). "U.S. Mental Health Policy: Doomed to Fail." *American Psychologist* 47(9), pp. 1077–1082.

Mahtesian, C., (1993). "The Last Days of the Asylum." *Governing* (March), pp. 32–37.

Mechanic, D. and D.A. Rochefort, (1992). "A Policy of Inclusion for the Mentally Ill." *Health Affairs* (Spring), pp. 128–150.

Mehr, J., (1983). *Abnormal Psychology.* New York: Holt, Rinehart and Winston.

Mehr, J., (1971). "Evaluating Non-Traditional Training for Psychiatric Aides." *Hospital and Community Psychiatry* 22(1), pp. 315–319.

Mehr, J., (1966). "Hospital Staff Development Grant Proposal." Unpublished Manuscript, Elgin State Hospital, Elgin, IL.

Mehr, J., (1995). *Human Services: Concepts and Intervention Strategies,* 6th ed. Boston: Allyn and Bacon.

NASMHPD, (1993). Report #103–18, "Tipper Gore Mental Health Issues Group Considers the Role of Public Psych Hospitals in Health Care Reform." Alexandria, VA: National Association of State Mental Health Program Directors.

Olfson, M., (1990). "Assertive Community Treatment: An Evaluation of the Experimental Evidence." *Hospital and Community Psychiatry* 41(6), pp. 634–641.

Pandiani, J.A., and L. Girardi, (1991). "The Depopulation of Vermont State Hospital: Adventures in Historical Analysis." Waterbury, VT: Vermont Department of Mental Health.

Rochefort, D.A., (1984). "Origins of the Third Psychiatric Revolution: The Community Mental Health Centers Act of 1963." *Journal of Health Politics, Policy and Law* 9(1), 17–25.

Rossi, P.H., (1990). "The Old Homeless and the New Homelessness in Historical Perspective." *American Psychologist* 24(3), pp. 232–239.

SREB, (1969). "Roles and Functions for Different Levels of Mental Health Workers." Atlanta: Southern Regional Education Board.

Stein, L.I., and M.A. Test, (1980). "Alternative Mental Hospital Treatment: I. Conceptual Model Treatment Program and Clinical Evaluation." *Archives of General Psychiatry* 37(2), 392–397.

Stein, L.I. and M.A. Test, eds., (1985). *The Training In Community Living Model: A Decade of Experience.* San Francisco: Jossey-Bass.

Torrey, E.F., (1988). *Nowhere to Go: The Tragic Odyssey of the Homeless Mentally Ill.* New York: Harper and Row.

Vaccaro, J.V., R.P. Liberman, C.J. Wallace, and G. Blackwell, (1992). "Combining Social Skills Training and Assertive Case Management: The Social and Independent Living Skills Program of the Brentwood Veterans Affairs Medical Center." In Liberman, R.P., ed., "Effective Psychiatric Rehabilitation." *New Directions for Mental Health Services 53(Spring), 33–42.*

COMMUNITY RESIDENCE MANAGER CERTIFICATE PROGRAM
NORTHERN ESSEX COMMUNITY COLLEGE

MARY DI GIOVANNI

The development of human service career programs happened as a result of two major events occurring at the same time in history. First, the development of community college systems across the nation allowed for the initiation of human services paraprofessional programs; second, federal legislation mandated changes in the delivery of mental health care.

Northern Essex Community College, located in Haverhill, Massachusetts, is a public two-year institution of higher education that provides programs of study leading to an associate of arts degree, associate of science degree, and/or a certificate program completion.

In the 1960s, community leaders in the Merrimac Valley area of Massachusetts felt the need for a state community college. As a consequence, programs of study were developed in liberal arts, engineering, and business. Health career programs were developed when hospitals in the area no longer wanted to operate schools of nursing and allied health training. It was a new era, and career programs were needed that could educate individuals to provide direct care services at the local level. Very little was known or understood about new careers in human services. One of the purposes of developing new careers in mental health was to create a new manpower source and hope that the new professional would be able to enter the delivery system and modify it to better meet consumer needs. It was felt that individuals employed in the old mental health system had less opportunity to be "change agents" in a community-based system of care.

The Mental Health Technology Program began in 1972 with the primary goal of awarding an associate in science degree. At that time, no one knew what to call the program, but it was essential to name the new program with an existing job description in the Commonwealth of Massachusetts. Career programs were linked to direct job placement upon completion of the program. Meetings were held with community agencies and administrators from the Massachusetts Department of Mental Health to obtain support and cooperation for the new career program. Needs assessments were sent to individuals in agencies in Merrimac Valley to identify the type of educational curriculum that would be needed for the student population and to obtain commitment for field placements. The response was immediate, and plans for the Mental Health Technology Program were set in motion.

Community college systems were new and not used to the type of curriculum needed to prepare human service generalists. In the second year of planning, a program coordinator was officially identified and met with college administration and the faculty curriculum committee over a period of several months before the final curriculum was put into place. A core curriculum that would contain general liberal arts, science, elective courses, clinical courses, and practicum field courses was approved by the faculty curriculum committee and the Massachusetts Board of Regents. Courses such as English composition, psychology, abnormal psychology, sociology, human biology, creative experience, mental health practicums, group dynamics, modalities of treatment, introduction to mental health, observation and recording, seminar in mental health, and electives went into the program. The program was a competency-based curriculum, whereby students would be evaluated on their success in meeting the competencies in field placement. The program initially began with fifteen students in 1972, and by the academic year 1976–77 there were fifty-one students enrolled in the program. In 1993, ninety-five students were enrolled in the Mental Health Technology and Certificate Programs at Northern Essex.

CERTIFICATE PROGRAMS

The issue of a certificate program to train group home managers in the mental health technology curriculum was not easy to resolve in the early 1970s. At that time, there was a job recession in Massachusetts and in all areas of human services. Mental health technology graduates were concerned that they would have to compete with lesser-trained people for a position in the mental health and mental retardation field. Initiating a certificate program for entry-level human service students or for employees of state institutions was seen by some as a conflict with the community college commitment to training beginning professionals at the associate degree level.

The program coordinator viewed the certificate as a first step in the career ladder, and the opportunity existed for a three-year grant to develop this type of certificate. The program could integrate with the associate degree in the second year of operation in a true career ladder direction. This decision was the right decision for the time and was borne out in the years to follow. Today, state employment agencies, rehabilitation agencies, job placement centers, welfare work programs, and re-entry unemployment programs all look for certificate programs that will prepare workers to enter the career field with one year of training or less.

COMMUNITY RESIDENCE MANAGER CERTIFICATE PROGRAM

The Massachusetts Department of Education, Division of Occupational Education, awarded a nineteen-thousand-dollar grant to the Northern Essex Community College Mental Health Technology Program in 1978 to initiate a House Manager Certificate Program. Under this grant, recruitment for the program emphasized admission of students who were disadvantaged, handicapped, or limited in the English language. Applicants to the program had to be twenty years old in order to meet the guidelines for entry into this field at the time of graduation from the program. This program was first called House Manager because the job description of the program had to relate to a current job description in the Department of Labor. It was a time when community residences for the mentally retarded were being opened in the region, and trained staff were needed for the programs. The title was changed in 1982 to Community Residence Manager Certificate Program to reflect the true nature of the program, and changes in the residential system of care, which had expanded to many different types of residences. This program continues to be somewhat balanced in student population, as students who enter fit the same general characteristics as students entering all human service programs on a national basis. In the Community Residence Manager Program, there has been an increase in minority applications, older students in career changes due to job losses in industry, males, and single mothers.

Recruitment of applicants to the Community Residence Manager Certificate Program is an ongoing essential role of the college program. In order to interest people in this career option, faculty must believe in the program and be able to communicate their support of residential services at the community level. If a faculty member does not recognize that these programs provide a career option for new recruits, that competencies learned in the environment will be transferable to any other area of human services, and that staff in these settings have a genuine commitment to quality care, the message will not be received by potential applicants. These applicants come from the community and are usually somewhat ignorant about this field. Applicants also have to be educated immediately about changes in terminology relative to the individuals that they seek to help in the new career. The mentally ill person has a disease of the brain: a neurobiological disorder. The mentally retarded individual has a developmental and learning disability.

The main advantages of working in community residential services are the opportunity to work independently with residents, wide choice of residential programs, participation as a team member at case conferences, opportunity to learn new treatment modalities with residents, and excellent possibility to move up in the agency as a result of work experience and continuing education.

The decision to initiate the Community Residence Manager Certificate Program was based on several factors indicating that it was the right time to begin a program of this nature. Federal legislation leading to closure of institutions, the philosophy of deinstitutionalization, documented studies on the need for a different type of mental health manpower, anticipated development of community services, recognition of human rights, and the philosophy of normalization were the vital elements at this time.

RESIDENTIAL PROGRAMS
FOR THE MENTALLY RETARDED

The National Mental Health Study Act in 1955 was directed by the Joint Commission on Mental Illness and Health to analyze and evaluate the needs and resources of the mentally ill and make recommendations for a national plan. This study demonstrated the need for change in state institutions due to inhumane conditions, overcrowding, and inadequate therapeutic treatment plans. In 1961, the Joint Commission on Mental Illness and Health issued a report called *Action for Mental Health* that identified the need for community-based services and trained staff in new types of programs. State institutions never again increased in size to such a point that care became custodial.

Professionals providing care in the institutions had obtained knowledge and skills based on medical understanding and psychological theories not relevant to the treatment approaches of the 1960s. The traditional mental health disciplines of psychiatry, nursing, social work, psychology, and rehabilitation emerged and developed between 1900 and 1950.

Mental health professionals questioned the placement of individuals in the community who were once residents of state hospitals or schools; they were concerned about who was going to provide the care and services needed in residential and other types of community programs. Often, state employees in the institutions were fearful of losing their jobs and having no place to go in the new systems that were yet to be developed. Most institutions had employee unions and state contracts in collective bargaining that could not address the issue of community-based programs. If the state had developed these programs, then the state employees could have followed the patients into community-based settings. This did not happen. Good wages and working conditions in state institutions could not be appropriately implemented in the community network. Professionals began to leave the institutions in the late 1960s and 1970s to begin their own private practices, serve as consultants to new systems, or take administrative positions in human services created by a private system of care called the vendor system.

In Massachusetts, "the philosophical decision to provide community-based alternatives to institutionalization was accompanied by the pragmatic decision to purchase new services rather than rely on direct state provision. At the heart of the issue was the rejection of the institutional method of rendering care, the rigidity of state bureaucracy and the desire to reduce the stigma associated with state assistance."[1] In other words, the state is purchasing a service for a specific amount of money and the vendor must perform the service. Vendors write a program based on a request for a proposal for a specific service (RFP), and submit it to the Department of Mental Health or Department of Mental Retardation. A selection is made as to which vendor has submitted the best program at the lowest cost. Presently, the governor of Massachusetts advocates the closure of state programs and the privatization of state services.

President John Kennedy recognized the conditions of the institutions and became concerned with the issues of mental health care. He set in motion a plan to change the system and recommended that Congress authorize grants to the states for construction of comprehensive community mental health centers. The legislation was called the Mental Retardation and Community Mental Health Centers Construction Act of 1963. Five essential services were identified: inpatient, outpatient, partial hospitalization, emergency services, and consultation and education.

The Civil Rights movement of the 1960s made the nation conscious that individuals were being deprived of constitutional and statutory rights. This movement also helped the cause of people who were being held in state institutions without due process of equal protection under the U.S. Constitution. The Fifth and Fourteenth Amendments state in part that "nor shall individuals be deprived

of life, liberty, or property without the process of law," and "nor shall any individual deprive any person of his life, liberty, or property without due process of the law, or deny any person within its jurisdiction, the equal protection of the laws."[2]

Natural rights of being treated with dignity and respect were also ignored. There was an overwhelming need to educate staff about human rights and to prepare workers to adapt to the services needed by the deinstitutionalized patient. In the first group homes for the mentally retarded used for student placements, residences had small house committees composed of staff, students, and people from the community to evaluate and monitor the management of the group home. Highly dedicated individuals wanted the movement to succeed and made every effort to have continuous review of the residential program.

The curriculum in the Community Residence Manager Certificate Program has developed a learning module to educate students about human rights and rights of residents in group homes. They participate on the Human Rights Committee of the practicum agency and have the opportunity to listen to the type of resident situations that may be a cause of abuse. Recently, Massachusetts General Laws, Chapter 19 C, approved a Disabled Person Protection Commission. The intent of this commission is to investigate all reports of abuse of disabled individuals not covered by other laws. The disabled had been excluded in the past because no laws covered the ages between eighteen and fifty-nine. All persons who work with the disabled are mandated reporters.

In 1966, the Community Mental Health Act acknowledged the deplorable conditions of state public facilities and mandated that people should receive care in the least restrictive environment. Court decisions later led the way for some basic

[1]"Purchase of Services: Can State Government Gain Control?" (1980). Boston: Massachusetts Taxpayers Foundation, Inc. MA (June), p. 3.

[2]Morris, Richards B., ed., (1953). *Encyclopedia of American History.* NY: Harper Brothers, Publisher, p. 458, 459.

rights to be guaranteed to people in the institutions as well as in community-based programs. These rights are the right to habilitation, to the least restrictive environment, to treatment, to refuse treatment, to privacy, and the right to confidentiality. Once a medical or psychiatric diagnosis has been made, that individual has a right to expect a treatment plan for the disability with the ultimate goal of helping the person to reach the highest levels of functioning as a human being. Implementation of a treatment plan was directly related to trained staff with new knowledge and skills needed for community models of care.

In 1950, parents of retarded children formed the National Association for Retarded Children, later renamed the National Association for Retarded Citizens (NARC). They began to organize and call together professionals from every specialty to demand changes in the system and research into the causes of mental retardation. These parents were advocates, and by their efforts changes began to occur in the delivery of mental retardation services.

The development of residential programs was a major undertaking of this organization. They defined a community residence as "some type of housing other than the individual's natural home. It is usually designed for not more than twelve persons, all of whom have similar needs in terms of age, independence, and abilities. The residential service should provide a home environment with supervision and guidance, offer living experiences appropriate in the functional level and learning needs of the individuals, be located within the mainstream of community life, and provide access to necessary supportive habilitation programs."[3]

The major concept behind the development of group homes for the mentally retarded was that of normalization. The term normalization was first articulated in 1967 by Bengt Nirje, the director of the Swedish Association for Retarded Citizens. He stated that "normalization is making available to the mentally retarded, patterns and conditions of everyday life which are as close as possible to the norms and patterns of mainstream society."[4] Normalization implies that the mentally retarded person would no longer be placed in an institution away from the community and out of sight of the community. Residences would be located in communities and blend in with the rest of the neighborhood. No longer would social contact be limited to the mentally retarded as it was in the state institution. Staff in residential programs would have to develop new skills to help residents integrate into communities. This was not a skill learned as a caretaker in the institution.

Staff teach independent living skills that promote self-esteem and help the resident to reach maximum potential. These skills are self-care and grooming, clothes matching, meal planning and food preparation, telephone use, housekeeping, leisure skills, and social interaction. Of special concern are the community living skills that teach residents how to handle an emergency situation, self-preservation, safe mobility in the community, use of public transportation, and use of community resources.

One of my students, a woman in her mid-forties, a mother and grandmother, had been assigned to supervise two retarded men in an independent living situation. We planned a site visit to observe the residents' ability to plan, prepare, and serve a meal. The two men in their fifties had lived together in a group home situation and were able to progress on their own. The unit had one bedroom with twin beds, a kitchen, and a living room. The residents had access to the local workshop where they worked and could do all of their own shopping in the area. We arrived around 5:00 P.M. because we intended to watch the residents prepare

---

[3]"The Right to Choose." (1973). Arlington, Texas: NARC. (October), p. 8.

[4]Browning, Phillip, (1977). *Normalization: A Service Delivery Perspective.* Eugene: University of Oregon Press, p. 4.

the evening meal. They expected our visit and greeted us at the door with a big smile and showed us their home. Both had excellent verbal skills and were eager to talk to us about their day. A picture of Farrah Fawcett hung on the kitchen wall with a calendar under it. The table was set for two, and the food for preparation was sitting on the counter. The men had planned to cook fish, french fries, and green beans. They had made jello for dessert. As one of the men went to pull out the frying pan and turn on the oven, we noted that the fish had just been taken from the freezer, and that it was frozen solid. The resident had forgotten to take it out of the freezer the night before and put it in the refrigerator. He apologized to us, and it was apparent that he felt badly about the situation. Since there was no microwave, he tried to pound it with the can, but the ice would not break. The other resident was trying to open the can of string beans with a manual can opener. He had difficulty in manipulating it, and it took him thirty minutes before he achieved the task. It was difficult to watch them prepare this meal; we did not want to take over the activity for them. We asked them how they were going to thaw the fish, and one man said to put it in a pan of boiling water. The meal then changed to fish chowder, and they were pleased to have resolved the dilemma.

Another area of normalization concerned looking at the chronological age of retarded people and treating them in a manner appropriate to their age rather than their intellectual ability. Grooming and dressing skills were not learned in the institution. Residents would have to be taught about makeup, the use of personal care items, and appropriate clothing that was in style with the rest of the community. The goal was to make them look as normal as possible and to help them to have joy and pleasure from the world around them. On a site supervision visit to a group home, this concept was evident. It was about 4:00 P.M. in the afternoon, and residents were returning from a day at the workshop. A student led me to the upstairs bedroom where she introduced me to a

severely retarded forty-year-old man. She was assigned to him and her primary goal was teaching activities of daily living skills and socialization. This room was a single room with appropriate male decor, and everything was neatly in order on the bureau. He was sitting in the middle of the bed, twirling a Superman doll around his head. Hung on the curtain was a Batman doll that was poised to strike at any moment. The student explained that these dolls were with the man in the state institution and that they played a major part in his socialization in the institution. Staff had limited this activity to the bedroom and only when he returned from the workshop. This was the only area that he could use them, with the ultimate goal of weaning him from the dolls in small steps. The behavior plan seemed to be working— he no longer needed to take them to the workshop or any other area of the house.

All students in the Community Residence Manager Certificate Program must complete a course in behavior management techniques and principles. This treatment module is used in all types of residential and community-based programs. Students are responsible for implementing and documenting behavior plans with residents and applying accepted positive methods of behavior intervention. Students also need to learn to recognize adverse therapies and, if used, communicate with the agency supervisor immediately.

Students bring with them their own values and attitudes about what is right and what is wrong and are encouraged by faculty to express their views in the practicum setting. In one situation, a group home staff member felt that retarded residents who had no medications had the right to have wine or beer with their evening meals since this was a normal activity in many homes. The residents involved had been in an institution and had never been exposed to alcohol. The student felt that it was wrong to introduce them to alcohol, because of the residents' judgment and ability to handle this beverage could pose a major problem in the future. She had an excellent understanding of addiction and did not want to run the risk of harming the residents in her care.

One area that staff and students have difficulty addressing is the area of sexual expression. The Department of Mental Retardation had issued guidelines relative to the residents' rights to sexual expression, privacy, interaction with persons of the opposite sex, and birth control. Sex education was a major need for residents in group homes. It was recognized that staff in these settings were not prepared to provide this education, and that some staff may not wish to participate in this type of education due to their own personal, moral, cultural, or religious values. The rights of staff also needed to be respected. Community residence students are always confronted with this issue, and they must be made aware of and resolve personal feelings about it before they enter the residential situation. One student ran into a situation where two retarded men who had lived together in a state institution were placed together in the residence, and slept together in the same bed. This student was uncomfortable in this situation and was placed in another setting. The men later moved to an independent living situation. Health educators are often hired by vendors to teach residents about sexuality. They are the experts in this area and this teaching responsibility does not fall on untrained, unwilling staff. Some vendors have also implemented sexuality training programs for direct care residential staff.

It was not until 1968 that NARC issued a policy statement regarding patient care in the institution. They recognized the need to change the institutional practices that led to patient overdependency. Institution residents lacked personal identity, privacy, meaningful relationships, and lacked appropriate programming. Courts began to mandate improved conditions with adequate patient-staff ration, treatment plans, and integration into community programs. As the state schools continued to close due to decreasing numbers, parents of the mentally retarded children with severe disabilities in need of continuous supervised care began to

fear that if all of these schools closed, there would be no place for the children to live in the community. Across the nation, parents began a movement to slow down and look at the overall effects of closing state facilities at such a rapid rate without programs in the community to meet the residents' needs. Institutional medical records have documented that many of the disabilities found were conditions that had been permitted to exist and develop even though they could have been prevented or reduced by early management. Section 504 of the Rehabilitation Act of 1973 mandated the rights of individuals with handicaps under federal law. Court decisions recognized that even the most handicapped had a right to reach to their highest potential in the least restrictive environment.

The closure of state schools for the mentally retarded means that children now live at home in the community. These children are being serviced in special education classrooms and are mainstreamed into the regular classroom whenever possible. Under a concept called inclusion, severely handicapped children are now being placed into regular classrooms with supportive services. A question that one needs to ask is: Will these children always live with their parents? or Will more group homes and supported living situations be made available in the future?

The first residents to be integrated into group homes for the mentally retarded were individuals who had higher levels of functioning, minimal or no physical disability, and without serious medical or behavioral problems. These residents were more easily accepted by neighbors and were able to participate in community-based programs for integration. As time passed, it became obvious that only the more medically involved persons with severe mental retardation and behavior problems remained institutionalized.

In the 1980s small residences, called intermediate care facilities, ICF's, were developed to provide services for the multiply handicapped retarded that were left in the institution. These programs were intended to service six to eight residents, thus improving the quality of care to patients. These facilities have nursing staff and provide more direct care services for patients who are in need of special adaptive equipment to meet their needs. Several intermediate care facilities funded under XIX of the Social Security Act of 1971 have been built in Massachusetts, and require staff to be more actively involved in direct personal care situations. Students in the Community Manager Certificate Program have also been integrated into this type of residence and have been able to learn the care skills needed on site in the setting under nursing staff supervision. By the 1990s these facilities were no longer being advocated or built due to the costs involved with this type of program and changing philosophy of care.

Community ignorance about the mentally retarded and mentally ill can be a source of many problems. The opening of group homes in the community was not an easy task. Many neighbors resisted the opening of residential programs in their neighborhoods. This is called the NIMBY syndrome and means "not in my back yard." In some communities, zoning laws made it difficult to find an appropriate location for a group home.

A landmark decision in the case of the Harbour Schools, Inc., in Newburyport, Massachusetts, in October, 1977, led the way in overcoming this problem. Harbour Schools is a facility for emotionally disturbed adolescents, and one of the first programs that accepted community residence manager certificate students into placement. When the school proposed opening a community residence in Haverhill, Massachusetts, the zoning board, which had the authority to draw up zoning laws, revoked its zoning permit. They questioned its use as an educational facility. The Harbour Schools then appealed to the Appeals Court of Massachusetts. They stated, "Evidence, in suit

claiming zoning exemption for facility devoted to education and improvement of emotionally disturbed children, supported finding that operation of facility were of public nature, that its undertakings and objectives were not commercial in character and not motivated for personal profit of any group, and that facility was entitled to zoning exemption."[6] In ruling that Harbour Schools was a facility for education that was public and therefore exempt from zoning, the court allowed a broad definition of education.[6] Community residences were regarded as educational facilities and were thus exempt from zoning laws in the community. Over the years, other Harbour Schools residences have opened without resistance.

RESIDENTIAL PROGRAMS FOR THE MENTALLY ILL

Residential programs for the mentally ill were more difficult to establish than residences for the mentally retarded. The Association for Retarded Citizens had been in operation since 1955, but there was no strong parent organization to advocate on behalf of the mentally ill until the National Alliance for the Mentally Ill was founded in 1979. The primary goal of reducing the census of the state hospitals was accomplished, but the discharge of patients was conducted in a manner that did not always meet the needs of the patient. Initially, many of the patients from state hospitals were transferred to nursing homes or to public health hospitals. Others were released to their own homes, placed in boarding houses, or single-dwelling occupancies. The mentally ill person needed group homes, day treatment programs, outpatient services, medication clinics, habilitation programs, and psychosocial programs. These services were

[5]Harbour Schools, Inc., et al. Board of Appeals of Haverhill et al. Appeals Court of Massachusetts, Essex. Argued Nov. 16, 1976. Decided Aug. 19, 1977.

[6]DeLeo, Dale, (1993). *Enhancing the Lives of Adults with Disabilities: An Orientation Manual,* 2nd ed. St. Augustine, FL: Training Resource Network, p. B–1.

essential for the residents in group homes because they needed to have day programs that would assist them in integrating into community living. Residential programs were not intended to provide all of the comprehensive services.

Historically, people who suffered from mental illness as well as mental retardation spent their whole lives behind the walls of the institution. The American public was introduced to this world by such films as the *Snake Pit, One Flew Over the Cukoo's Nest,* and *Frances.* They learned about treatment models used by professionals in hospitals such as lobotomy, electric shock therapy, and the use of psychotrophic drugs to control patient behavior. Nonprofessionals were also depicted as abusive and noncaring. The image of a person working in this field was negative, and it was clear that training programs were needed to change the philosophy of care and attitudes of the mental health disciplines. The stereotype and image of these patients was entrenched in the community. No major public education programs were developed by the states or federal government on a consistent basis to prepare the nation to accept the mentally ill and retarded as members of society. Educating the public became the role of staff and students in residential programs at town meetings and legislative forums.

Chronic mentally ill persons had difficulty in adjusting to the community. Students in residential settings had to learn to cope with residents who had years of hospitalization that led to institutionalized behaviors that interfered with adaptation to the program. Institutions were dehumanizing environments, and it was assumed that the professionals knew best how to care for the patient in the institution. Patients had little or no input into their treatment plans, nor did they have to participate in any decision-making process relative to their own personal care and wants. The patient was in a powerless position, locked into the status of patient. The use of long-term hospitalization as a therapeutic intervention was a failure.

Students in the community residence program learned that residents needed to have experiences in the decision-making process, and that they had to be included in all aspects of living. Providing support to residents making decisions, helping them to problem solve, and teaching them to deal with the reality of living in the community are challenging experiences for students.

In Massachusetts, community residential programs for the mentally ill first developed under the auspices of the Massachusetts Department of Mental Health. Patients from a regional state hospital were prepared to go into community living on a living unit at the hospital. One of the early students in the Community Residence Manager Certificate Program was a state employee working at this hospital who lacked a formal college education. The supervisor of the unit recognized her potential to work with patients at the community setting and referred her to the college program. It was a time when direct care staff were not sure as to what direction to take since they had invested years into the system and were threatened by these changes. This employee took a chance and recognized that this new career option would allow her to master new skills assisting residents in community living and she became part of a whole new way of providing services for the mentally ill.

Residential programs for the mentally ill have changed over the years. Students need to learn to adapt to the needs of a younger person with mental illness who has never been hospitalized as a chronic patient in a state institution. Initially, older patients were placed in group homes, and they behaved in a manner common to chronic patients: passive, apathetic, enjoyed sitting more, dependent, did what staff told them to do, lost contact with family or friends, uninterested in working, limited or no work skills, little or no dating experience, difficulty in community integration, and complied with taking their medications. The younger residents today in group homes have lived in the community with their families, often remain in contact with family and friends, have been active in community living, are more educated, have been exposed to alcohol and other drugs, have had more sexual experiences, and question the use of medications.

The National Association for Retarded Citizens has tried to dispel the confusion between mental illness and mental retardation. The public accepted the high functioning mentally retarded adult into the community because they did not have a diagnosis of mental illness. Recent research suggests that 20–35 percent of the deinstitutionalized mentally retarded suffer from some form of mental illness. Some professionals in the mental health field believe that the answer may be to develop special residential homes for people with a dual diagnosis. These homes would have specialized staff to meet the mental health needs of these residents. Students in community residence manager certificate programs are placed in this new type of setting, and it is clear that this type of resident needs individual supervision and continuous treatment with the goal toward acceptable behavior.

Reports from shelters have documented that more mentally ill persons are being seen in shelters, and that these individuals are in need of residential services. Psychiatric hospitals do not have to accept mentally ill persons who relapse, unless it can be proved that they are a danger to themselves or others. The question of who is responsible for psychiatric patients when they are discharged from mental hospitals is a matter of the courts in many states. As homeless mentally ill people continue to use shelters for refuge, staff and city officials have requested the courts to determine the issue of follow-up care. In March 1993, the Massachusetts Supreme Court (SJC) ruled in *Williams vs. Secretary of the Executive Office of Human Services, 414, Mass 551* that there is no affirmative obligation under the federal

or state constitutions to provide treatment for persons not in custody of the state.[7]

SHELTERS: AS RESIDENCES

Students in community residence manager programs also have practicum placements in shelter programs. The original intent of shelters was to provide temporary relief for homeless persons, but we have created a new industry of human services that has in some part replaced state facilities that have closed. Shelters have become institutions where the same people seek refuge day after day. The actual composition of shelters depends on the area of the country that one lives, and each state has its own statistics on the reasons for shelters. As the number of persons in shelters began to increase, the shelters learned that these individuals had medical, psychological, social, and economic concerns that needed to be addressed. The problem that emerged is that shelters do not have professionally trained staff to meet these needs, and they were not intended to be treatment programs.

Students in community residential manager programs had specific classes in the mental health area as well as courses that taught therapeutic skills. It was natural to begin to expand the community residence program and place students from this curriculum in shelters for work experience. The same issues and concerns of other living environments were also in the homeless shelters. Shelters provided relief to mentally ill homeless, substance abusers, immigrants, battered women and children, minority poor, and the unemployed. Students select the type of shelter that is of interest to them and have been of value in these settings. They have learned intake procedures, been active in running support groups for women, conducted twelve-step meetings, taught mothers how to manage child care needs, taught

[7]"S.J.C., No Right to Treatment from DMH Clients." (1993). *The Provider.* (The Newsletter of the Massachusetts Council of Human Services Providers, Inc.) 14(5)(May), p. 4.

home and life management skills, taught guests in shelters how to use the community referral systems for services, taught meal planning and food preparation, and learned to develop interpersonal relationships with people from all walks of life.

Two of the major areas of concern have been health and safety. Specific content has been added to the community residence manager curriculum that deals with understanding infectious diseases and how to manage individuals who have a potential for violence. Students have learned how to observe guests for potential violent, suicidal, or antisocial behavior and how to search guests as they enter the shelters. These skills are useful in any human service setting and should be in every human service curriculum.

By 1985, over seven hundred community mental health centers had been created in the United States. A study was conducted by the National Institute for Mental Health to identify exemplary practices in mental health centers and other public health agencies. This study revealed problems in funding, administration, and service delivery. Reduced federal and state funding led to fiscal constraints and a lack of resources. There was a need for more decentralized coordination of state mental health systems, interagency advisory boards, new clinical management systems, and improving rela-

tionships among human service agencies. The service delivery system had problems in loss of accreditation, lack of continuity in care, need for crisis intervention services, need for housing and support services for the chronically mentally ill, lack of community resources, need for case managers, and underutilization of services for minorities. This study again documents the need for trained human service workers in all areas of the mental health system.

Wolf Wolfensberger, a mental retardation scientist at the Nebraska Institute in Omaha, wrote a paper in 1969 on twenty predictions about the future of residential services. It is interesting to look at his predictions now and evaluate what has happened. He believed that the concept of the institution would disappear, and a broader concept of residential services would take its place. Also, he predicted that the image of the mentally retarded as sick people and menaces to society would be replaced by a belief in the capacity of each mentally retarded individual. Most importantly, the concept of managing the mentally retarded would be replaced by the idea of normalizing them. It is hard to believe that such vast changes have occurred in the system, and that a new working system of human service generalists has evolved out of the resistance to change.

BIBLIOGRAPHY

Action For Mental Health: Joint Commission on Mental Illness and Health. Final Report of the Joint Commission on Mental Science and Health, 1961.

Action for Mental Health, (1961). Science Editions, New York: Basic Books, Inc.

Bloom, Bernard, (1984). Community Mental Health: A General Introduction. Monterey, CA: Brooks-Cole Publishing Co.

Browning, Phillip, (1977). Normalization: A Service Delivery Perspective. Eugene: University of Oregon Press.

DeLeo, Dale, Enhancing the Lives of Adults with Disabilities: an Orientation Manual. Training Resource Network, St. Augustine

Department of Mental Health: Division of Mental Retardation, (1980). The Massachusetts Consent Decrees for Mentally Retarded Persons. Boston: State Purchasing Agency.

Golann, Stuart, (1976). The Right To Treatment for Mental Patients. New York: John Wiley and Sons.

Harbour Schools, Inc., et al. v. Board of Appeals of Haverhill et al. Appeals Court of Massachusetts, Essex, argued Nov. 16, 1976, decided August 19, 1977.

Kruzich, Jean, (1985). "Milieu Factors Influencing Patients' Integration into Community Facilities." *Hospitals and Community Psychiatry* 36(4).

Landsberg, Gerald, (1987). "Developing a Comprehensive Community Care System for the Mentally Retarded, Mentally Ill." *Community Mental Health Journal* 23(2): 131–34.

Lehman, Anthony, (1986). "Quality of Life of Chronic Patients in a State Hospital and Community Residences." *Hospital Community Psychiatry* 37(9): 901–909.

Morris, Richard B., ed., (1953). *Encyclopedia of American History.* New York: Harper and Brothers Publishing Co., pp. 458–459.

Maitin, Leonard, ed., (1991). *Movies and Video Guide.* New York: Signet.

NARC The Right To Choose: Achieving Residential Alternatives in the Community. Texas: National Association for Retarded Citizens, Oct., 1973.

Purchase of Service: Can State Government Gain Control? (1980). Boston: Massachusetts Taxpapers Foundation, Inc., (June).

The Right To Choose. (1973). Arlington, TX, NARC. (October).

Wolfensberger, Wolf, (1969). "Twenty Predictions About the Future of Residential Services in Mental Retardation." *Mental Retardation* (December) pp. 51–54.

KEY TERMS FOR PART SIX

Upon completing Chapters 21, 22, 23, and 24, you will have a command of the following key terms, major concepts, and principle references:

Sanction

Public Policy

Administrative Law

Administrative Rule-Making

Public Hearings

Networking

Political Action Committees (PACs)

Emily's List

Coalitions

Adoption Assistance and Treatment Act (CAPTA, 1974)

Indian Child Welfare Act (1973)

Child Protective Services (CPS)

Child Welfare Services (CWS)

Intake

Kinship Care

Pediatric AIDS

Least Restrictive Setting

Child Welfare League of America (CWLA)

Integrated Mental Health Services

Healthcare Reform

National Health Policy

National Institute of Mental Health (NIMH)

Deinstitutionalization

Assertive Community Treatment

Intensive Case Management

Psychosocial Rehabilitation

Normalization

Community Residence Manager

National Assoc. of Retarded Citizens (NARC)

Intermediate Care Facilities (ICFs)

PIVOTAL ISSUES FOR DISCUSSION FOR PART SIX

1. Make one visit to each of the following public legislative activities and record your observations on each occasion.

   Public Legislative Hearing

   Subcommittee Hearing

   General Session—House

   General Session—Senate

   Make a list of all elected officials serving you as a constituent. Write to each and request a list of pending bills having to do with human services that they, individually, support. Record their responses, collate the materials, and present your work in class.

2. Outline the process of child adoption in your state. How long does it take and are there restrictive rules which discriminate against certain groups of people (for example, homosexual, elderly, recovering substance abusers, etc.)

3. What are the advantages and disadvantages to deinstitutionalization? How does this trend impact on homelessness, drug and alcohol abuse, crime and violence?

4. What is the role of prevention/promotion in future human services?

5. As a community leader, you are committed to maximizing prevention techniques in the delivery of community human services. Describe how you would develop "prevention/promotion" programs throughout your city or town. How would these programs be used in schools, in agencies, in hospitals and clinics, in housing, in police and public safety, etc.?

6. Visit a community-based group residence program. Interview the manager of the program and record the description of the program, the clients served, funding, and the problems and barriers encountered in administering the program. Be sure to include how to become a staff member, and what is required in this work.

SUGGESTED READINGS FOR PART SIX

1. Biegel, D. and A. Napanstek, *Community Support Systems and Mental Health: Practice, Policy, and Research.*

2. Woods, R.H., (1984). *The Law and the Practice of Human Services.* San Francisco: Jossey-Bass Pub.

3. Neugeboren, B., (1985). *Organization, Policy, and Practice in Human Services.* New York: Long Man Pub.

4. Fairweather, G., K. Sanders, and L. Tornatzky, (1974). *Creating Change in Mental Health Organizations.* Elmsford, NY: Pengamon Press, Inc.

5. Hasenfeld, Y., (1983). *Human Services Organizations.* Englewood Cliffs, NJ: Prentice-Hall Co.

PART SEVEN

EMERGING ISSUES OF TECHNOLOGY AND GLOBAL TRENDS

In this final part, the chapters represent a beginning attempt to introduce you to technical issues of research and computer usage and the global trends in human services of recognizing diversity and the need for international education.

In Chapter 25, Rod Underwood and Michael Lee clarify how research is used in human services and why it is important in the repertoire of skills of the contemporary human service worker. Clear descriptions of the many different types of research are presented, and each is detailed as to its methodology, purpose, and use. From this display of research techniques you can grasp how different research approaches are used for different purposes. Different research questions require different methods of technical inquiry. While many human service programs do not include computer literacy and programming or research techniques and analysis as part of core competencies, there is now growing evidence that these areas of training and the relevancy of the skills inherent to these areas will become progressively more important and recognized as necessary prerequisites to the competent human service worker.

In a Special Focus Feature, Tom Wisbey describes the growing use and applications of computers in human services management and intervention. In this reading you will see how fast-growing technology in computer software and interactive programming will provide the basis for radical changes in client care and human services in the decades to follow. More than a trend, the place of technology in human services is already established and will continue to be an area of study which will grow in importance and relevance.

As an effective human services professional you will have to understand that people may have different points of view that may stem from such background differences as ethnicity, religion, race, or economics. Broadly, to take into account these differences is to appreciate the multicultural perspective.

In Chapter 26, Donna Petrie deals with differences "between and within" groups by discussing the role of cultural diversity, its trends and challenges for human services. The future trends as well as cultural value differences, support the increasing need for the human service professional to take into account the multicultural perspective. Frequently, human services, in order to be effective, has to provide a different kind of caring for people in different groups. It is clear that a human service professional, regardless of background, must be sensitive to the diversity issue in order to be successful. The technological advances in telecommunication and travel have brought the rest of the world closer.

In Chapter 27, Dennis Cogan discusses the implications for human services of easier access to other areas of our planet. By reading a case study, you will see the relevance of international study for human services in enhancing your understanding of diversity. If you are interested in studying abroad, the article will tell you how to go about it.

In Chapter 28, Rod Underwood and Michael Lee describe an overview of human services in Australia. You will recognize much in Australia that is similar to the United States in terms of human services. The article will present population trends and historical background as well as the different kinds of human services programs. Many of the issues and trends that face human services are the same in both countries.

LEARNING OBJECTIVES FOR PART SEVEN: EMERGING ISSUES OF TECHNOLOGY AND GLOBAL TRENDS

Upon completing Chapters 25, 26, 27, and 28:

— You will appreciate the special concerns that cultural diversity presents in the profession of human services.
— You will be aware of the problem of professional subjectivity in the role of the human services worker.
— You will be familiar with general concepts and issues in the international education of human services professionals.
— You will learn how human services operates in Australia and understand the cultural influences that explain how that delivery system differs from Western societies.
— You will become aware of the growing role and use of computer technology in the field of human services.
— You will know the basic components of research models used in human services.

CHAPTER 25

RESEARCH MODELS IN HUMAN SERVICES

ROD UNDERWOOD
MICHAEL LEE

WHAT IS RESEARCH?

Research yields a particular form or type of information. Its value lies in the information which is collected rigorously in a systematic way, and it should be free from bias; when it is applied, its limitations are known. Another way of conceptualizing research is to think if it as a type of investigation, or a process leading to a greater understanding of the world. There are many different ways of gathering information. The scientific method is one procedure. Because it is so widespread, we commonly think that the scientific method is the only way to gain new knowledge. However, this is not the case. New knowledge can come from a variety of other processes such as a religious or spiritual experience. Such an experience can give new insights and different understandings on human problems. However, an important limitation to knowledge acquired by religious means is that it is difficult to verify. Another related procedure is philosophical analysis, which examines important issues and dilemmas in our lives, and, while it might sometimes use information that comes from research, it does not necessarily set out to investigate using the scientific method.

If research is information gained using a particular method, and as a consequence has distinctive characteristics, what are these characteristics? Research is objective; consequently, it is independent of the observer. Two or more people observ-ing the same situation, using the same procedures, should anticipate the same conclusions. Research is also systematic, and the information must be collected according to a set of standards. These standards allow the user of information to determine how the results of the research can be used and interpreted. Finally, research data must be seen as public and verifiable.

GOALS OF RESEARCH

Research attempts to do two things. First, it seeks to describe a phenomenon. For example, it is believed that as people reach old age their powers of reasoning decline. This belief gets support from observations we have all made at some time or other of an elderly person being mentally confused or having difficulty understanding. However, when this is investigated using research techniques, we find this common perception is not justified. Some elderly people have powers of reasoning as good as they have been at any time of their lives. Some aspects of memory become more acute for elderly people; some elderly seem to lose confidence in their ability to reason. If confidence is not lost, then reasoning continues to be maintained (Salthouse, 1982).

A second thing that research attempts to do is explain cause and effect relationships. We commonly observe in everyday life an association of events such that a result is preceded by a particular prior event. When we ask "What happened?" we assume that the outcome was caused by the prior event. In the human services we can observe an increase in the number of people turning to welfare agencies for financial assistance, or clothing, or food. We know from government statistics that unemployment is increasing, so we connect the two observations and deduce that the increase in unemployment has caused more people to seek relief. If you think about this problem, you can see that there might be alternative explanations as the cause. It is by using research methods that we can see which of the alternatives is the correct one.

So what is research? It is a method of collecting information, commonly referred to as data, which allows us to both describe and then explain the information we have gathered. It is systematic and, because it must follow certain procedures, is able to be replicated and verified or rejected by others using the same procedures.

Every day we have things occurring around us that influence our perception of the world. The way we view our environment is colored by a variety of circumstances, including our culture, our state of mind, and even our capacity to use language. Notwithstanding these factors, this information is still important to us, and we carry it as part of our storehouse of knowledge. Many people might carry the same or similar perceptions of information. For example, consider how widespread are certain stereotypes. Nevertheless, the information has not been gained by scientific means, and until it is "tested" it might be biased and flawed. However, such observations are often the starting points for research, but until they are "proven" they remain personal viewpoints and are described as "anecdotal."

WHY DO RESEARCH?

It is not always easy to convince the human service student of the necessity for research. Naturally enough, many human service professionals believe their time is best spent by providing services to those people in need rather than answering another questionnaire from a federal agency or being interviewed by another researcher. Clearly, then, there have to be good reasons for diverting human service workers from their primary goal.

Perhaps one of the most compelling reasons for human service workers to engage in research is the ever-present threat of funding cutbacks. Increasingly, funding authorities—both government and nongovernment—are expecting human service agencies to be more accountable for the funds they receive. There are several aspects of accountability. For example, agencies may need to demonstrate to the funding authority that every dollar spent has been within the original guidelines given to the agency. Another aspect of accountability is for the agency to show that an appropriate number of clients are receiving the services at a predetermined level of quality. This type of accountability is referred to as program evaluation.

Program evaluation requires an agency to demonstrate the effectiveness of a particular program, or show the extent to which the program is achieving its stated goals. To be able to do this, the program director needs to be familiar with the different research designs used in the social sciences and their limitations when applied to program evaluation. Any agency that makes claims about the effectiveness of its program that cannot be substantiated is likely to be critically reviewed by the funding authority.

At the other end of the continuum, agencies are often required to undertake a needs analysis within their community to determine the extent to which a particular service might be required. As with evaluation studies, needs analysis surveys are dependent upon research design logic. If, for example, you want to know how many people over the age of fifty are suffering from diabetes in your county, then you may have to draw upon the sampling procedures used in social science research.

If you need to identify social trends such as the increased number of women in the work force, the increasing number of high school dropouts, or the growing number of people with literacy problems, then you need a sound understanding of the principles of research design. Planning of future human services is essentially based on statistical analyses of data gathered according to the principles of research methodology. Of course, any human service planning is always guided by the values of society.

It is possible for research to have a significant impact on the development of human service policies. Often, it is the researcher who brings to the attention of the policy maker the existence of particular problems in the community. For example, in a recent study of emergency accommodation services it was found that more than 70 percent of workers reported having to deal frequently with young people suffering from mental illness (Underwood, Lee, and Jackson, 1991). Further, the investigation revealed that the accommodation workers had very little training in coping with behaviorally disturbed adolescents. The workers stated that they experienced significant difficulties in eliciting assistance from appropriate agencies. The study clearly showed that the policies applicable to emergency accommodation services required an urgent review.

Apart from the very pragmatic reasons for becoming a skilled researcher, the human service worker is inherently interested in understanding the dynamics of the community in which he or she operates. Unfortunately, social theory has not yet developed to the stage where it can provide an indepth analysis of any community. For example, you may believe that the increased crime rate has been the outcome of increased unemployment. On the other hand, the rate of domestic violence may be directly related to increased violence being shown on television. These are the sorts of questions that influence human service workers and the programs they offer. The answers depend very much on well-conducted, sophisticated social research.

RESEARCH STRATEGIES

There is no one research strategy that is best for investigating all issues in the human services. The variety and diversity of research questions reflect several features of this area. Different disciplines

contribute to human services. Psychology, sociology, political science, and economics are all important contributors to research method, but they have different techniques as well as differing types of information regarded as important.

Some methods of research have a long history. When Francis Bacon first wrote on the scientific method some four hundred years ago, he emphasized "cause and effect." This put great emphasis on experimental procedures. In very recent times, feminist writers have questioned the mainstream methods and called for fresh approaches to research technique and writing (Squire, 1989). These methods would recognize the importance of individual perceptions, feelings, and judgments as basic research data.

The Experimental Approach

The experimental paradigm is the most powerful means of determining whether a causal relationship exists between a particular intervention strategy or treatment and the outcomes. In its most rigorous form, the experimental paradigm is characterized by the random allocation of participants to experimental and control groups. Providing that those other features of experimental investigation such as validity and reliability of the measurements are sustained, then the researcher is in the position of drawing sound conclusions regarding the relationship between the independent and dependent variables. The investigator is also able to determine the magnitude of the treatment effects upon the outcomes.

According to Elliot (1980, p. 509), the experimental approach to social research involves the following sequence:

1. The causal model or theoretical paradigm, which identifies a set of variables (attributes, relationships, or circumstances) connected by some logical process to social behavior.
2. The identification of a set of program activities or interventions that are designed to manipulate these causal variables.
3. The implementation of the program with these manipulations operationalized as program objectives.

4. Information feedback during operation to determine if the program activities are, in fact, occurring and the objectives are being met.

5. Feedback to determine if the realization of these program objectives is having the theoretically expected effect on the participants.

6. The modification of the theoretical paradigm and/or the program activities and objectives as suggested by the analysis, in order to increase the program's effectiveness.

The Sherman and Berk (1984) study of the efficacy of different treatment strategies of police management of domestic violence incidents exemplifies the application of the experimental approach. The investigators examined the likelihood of repeat offenses occurring as a function of arrest or nonarrest interventions by the police. In a subsequent review of their study, Berk and Sherman (1985, p. 46) conclude:

> We are increasingly convinced that until there is a compelling body of social science theory with which to properly specify causal models, true experimental or strong quasi-experimental designs are essential for sound impact assessments.

The utility of the experimental approach depends on the degree to which the results of a study can be generalized to other situations. The decision maker is interested to know whether the outcomes of a particular study carried out in another place at another time, with different participants are likely to be replicated if he/she implements a similar program. A number of factors militate against generalizing the results in many studies. There may be problems in defining the population from which the sample has been drawn for the study. This is particularly the case when the population is defined in terms of psychological or sociological characteristics such as psychopathy or delinquency. The methods used to select the participants for the study will influence the degree to which the findings can be generalized. Participants can be randomly selected from a population, they may be volunteers for the study, or they may be induced to participate in a program. Thus, the selection method used may determine the way

in which the characteristics of the sample generalize to other groups. The conceptualization and measurement of variables, such as drug dependency or recidivism, suffer from a lack of universal agreement. Hence, the human service administrator who is implementing programs on the basis of other studies, should be cautious and recognize the limitations of those studies.

Social research studies undertaken in the 1960s and 1970s typically sought to employ the experimental approach. Increasingly, this mode of research has been criticized by practitioners. Cook and Shadish (1986, p. 226) argue that "early experience suggested that they [that is, randomized experiments] were fundamentally flawed as models." The experimental approach came under attack from researchers because:

1. It is not applicable to those situations in which possible causal factors cannot be manipulated such as economic circumstances. Such situations tend to be the norm in the human services;

2. The random allocation of participants in a study to different treatment groups or to a control group is fraught with difficulties. Not the least of these difficulties are the ethical and moral concerns raised in those studies where efficacious treatment is withheld from participants in the interests of science. In the United States, laws have been passed which specifically prohibit the use of randomized experimentation in certain circumstances (Empey, 1980);

3. A critical assumption of the experimental paradigm is the equivalence of the treatment and non-treatment groups. However, the very fact that the treatment conditions are differentially effective will bear significantly on the rate of attrition. For example, the rate of attendance of alcoholics assigned to different therapeutic milieus will vary, among other reasons, according to the nature of the treatment. Hence the rigor of the paradigm is seriously weakened. The difficulties associated with establishing comparable treatment groups are well described by Davidson, Koch, Lewis, and Wresinski (1981) in their study of youth service programs in the United States;

4. Members of a cohort, particularly in an institutional environment, who are assigned to different treatment conditions may lack commitment to the

program if they sense they are being put in the role of "guinea pigs." This may lead to deliberate sabotage of the program, or to the demoralization of the participants (Cook and Campbell, 1979);

5. The experimental paradigm may well identify the impact of a particular program, but the processes associated with achieving the effect are not always revealed. There is a tendency to assume the "black box" situation exists; that is, that the conditions under which the program is conducted remain constant and relatively impervious to influences of the total system. Such an assumption is clearly fallacious.

QUASI-EXPERIMENTAL RESEARCH MODELS

A great deal of social research does not meet all the criteria necessary to be called a "true experimental design." These studies often involve the investigation of important matters in human services. Consider the question, "Are antismoking health campaigns effective in reducing the number of people who smoke?" It would be extremely difficult to investigate this question using a true experimental design where it would be necessary to randomly assign smokers to an experimental group and a control group. That is, the experimental group would be exposed to the information presented in the public health campaign, such as television advertisements. The control group of smokers would not receive the information. Immediately, we are confronted with an ethical dilemma. Do researchers have the right to withhold from people information that may be of potential benefit to them, even though we are attempting to establish the efficacy of such health campaigns? It may be that such campaigns have no effect on reducing the prevalence of smokers in the community and the money could be spent on much more effective approaches to the problem.

Campbell and Stanley (1963) use the term "quasi-experimental" to describe the broad category of research designs which, while attempting to be rigorous, are employed to seek answers to questions which cannot be addressed using an experimental design. The limitation of the quasi-experimental research design is that it does not permit the investigator to ascribe a causal relationship between the independent and dependent variables of a study. For example, a social scientist may be interested to learn whether people who attend church are less likely to get divorced than those who do not attend church. Obviously this is a question that cannot be investigated using an experimental design. We cannot ask some married couples to attend church and other couples not to attend in order to answer the question. However, we may gather information about married couples who do, or do not, attend church. We may find that one in five married couples who attend church eventually get divorced compared with one in three couples who do not attend. We may be tempted to conclude that the divorce rate, that is, the dependent variable, is determined by church attendance, that is, the independent variable. However, it may turn out that some factor other than church attendance accounts for the different rates of divorce. For example, it may be the case that married couples who attend church regularly have a higher level of income than nonattendees. Perhaps economic security leads to marital stability.

Correlation Studies

As human service professionals we are continually looking for relationships between different variables. Do daughters of alcoholic parents tend to select partners predisposed towards alcoholism? Is crime rate related to the level of unemployment in a community? Are males who have vasectomies more likely to get cancer of the prostate in later years? We are looking to see if there is a correlation between these variables.

Knowing that two variables are correlated does not permit us to assume that a causal relationship exists, as discussed in the preceding section. Let us examine another example. We have known for many years that young people who play sports regularly are less likely to engage in delinquent behavior than their nonsporting counterparts. In fact, national youth policies of a number of countries have been based on this premise. So what have social scientists learned about the relationship between sports and delinquency? In their recent review of the literature on this issue, Mason and Wilson (1988) found that:

1. Those boys who participate in sporting activities are delinquent in lesser numbers than those who do not participate in sports.
2. While sporting male youths commit less crime than their nonsporting counterparts, they are also involved to an even lesser degree in the more serious offenses.
3. Boys participating in major sports (for example, football and baseball) tend to be more delinquent than those engaged in minor sports (such as badminton and volleyball).
4. Some sports of an aggressive nature may even have adverse effects upon participants, and a highly aggressive sport, such as ice hockey, has been seen to have a greater number of male participants who are involved in delinquent acts than comparable nonathletes.

Unfortunately, no amount of research has been able to demonstrate a causal link between playing sports and not indulging in antisocial behavior. The fundamental question remains unanswered. That is, are young people well behaved because they play sports, or are well-behaved young people more likely to play sports? Only if the former statement is true does it make sense for governments to invest millions of dollars in recreational programs for the nation's youth.

Survey studies will often yield correlational information. We know that a relationship exists between years of education and level of income, between regular exercise and the probability of a heart attack, between the age of a mother and the likelihood of giving birth to a Down syndrome child. Although we may not be able to say that a causal relationship exists between these variables, nevertheless knowledge of the correlation is valuable for two reasons. First, the identification of a correlation between variables provides researchers with clues as to where they should direct their resources in seeking to understand the world in which we live. Second, the fact that variables are correlated permits us to make certain predictions. For example, we can predict that a high achiever in high school is likely to succeed at a university, or that people who are abused as children may become abusing parents. Again, this type of information assists us in the allocation of resources for intervention programs.

Time-Series Design

The quasi-experimental model that deserves greater attention in social science research is the time-series design. Where it is not possible to implement an experimental design to determine a cause-effect relationship between two variables, the time-series design may be the best alternative. For example, the time-series design might be used to determine the impact of legislation requiring people in automobiles to wear seat belts. The important feature of the time-series design is that it requires more than one pre- and postintervention measurement. Essentially, the researcher is looking at trends over a period of time, and changes in the direction of the trends that can be attributed to a particular intervention. In the seat belt example, the researcher will be interested in the number of automobile fatalities occurring at least three years prior, and subsequent to the introduction of the legislation. By taking a series of measurements over a period of time, the effects of random fluctuations are ameliorated.

The time-series design is an important option for program evaluation. It is particularly applicable where the program affects everyone and where, therefore, a proper control group cannot be constituted. Campbell (1979) believes that if comparison group data are available, the time-series approach ranks as the strongest of all quasi-experimental designs.

Janus (1982) used the time-series design to evaluate the impact of organizational changes in federal correctional institutions. Other applications of the time-series design include a study of the effect of removing restrictions on the sale of pornography on the incidence of sex crimes in

Denmark (Kutchinsky, 1973); measuring the impact of restrictive abortion laws on birth rates in Romania (David and Wright, 1971); and assessing the effects of the introduction of breathanalyzer testing in the U.K. on traffic casualties (Ross, 1973). McCleary and Riggs (1982) used time-series analysis to assess the impact of the 1975 Australian Family Law Act on divorce rates. The time-series analysis can be used to strengthen a traditional study or to evaluate human service programs in which it has not been possible to create a control or comparison group. In the latter case, the experimental group can serve as its own control under certain conditions. According to Grizzle and Witte (1980, p. 290):

> Time-series analysis produces strongest evaluations when good, consistent time series data are available, program implementation is relatively abrupt, and the nature of program effects are relatively well understood.

The greatest threat to the validity of time series is the possibility of "historical factors influencing the outcome" (Cook, Cook, and Mark, 1977). In the case of the McCleary and Rigg study, for example, the investigators would need to establish that the increased rate of divorce that occurred after the introduction of the Family Law Act was not influenced by events such as economic recession or the impact of the Vietnam War on marital stability.

Single Subject Design

In many human service settings the researcher is interested in the effect of an intervention strategy upon the behavior of an individual. For example, an aged person living alone at home may be encouraged to prepare a daily meal by being positively reinforced for doing so by the home care worker. Or, the disruptive behavior of a school-aged child may be reduced by using a time-out strategy. In these cases it is not possible for the researcher to establish experimental and control groups to determine the efficacy of the proposed intervention strategy. Indeed, in some situations

the withholding of a potentially useful treatment or intervention strategy—which applies to those people who form the control group in any formal experimental study—may be unethical behavior.

In the single-subject design, there are usually at least three phases. In phase one the researcher will observe the number of times the target behavior occurs prior to the introduction of the intervention strategy. This process is called establishing the baseline rate of behavior. Thus, the home care worker may observe that the aged person prepares a meal on only three days a week over a period of three weeks. The second phase of the single subject design refers to the period when the treatment or intervention strategy is introduced. For example, the home care worker might provide positive verbal reinforcement whenever meals are prepared by the aged person. If the reinforcement strategy is successful, then the worker may observe that the aged person is preparing up to five daily meals per weak over a period of three weeks. The third phase is a return to the baseline conditions for a short period of time. That is, the worker may withhold positive reinforcement for meal preparation for a period of one to two weeks. If the rate of meal preparation declines it is reasonable to infer that the rate is influenced by the intervention strategy. Reintroducing the reinforcement schedule, which hopefully provides confirming evidence, constitutes the fourth phase of the design. The sequence of Baseline-Treatment-Baseline-Treatment is normally referred to as an A-B-A-B design.

The above description of the A-B-A-B design is a very elementary type of single-subject study. The procedures for this type of research can become quite complex. However, regardless of the complexity of the study, the single-subject design is always limited by the extent to which the results of a study can be generalized to a particular population. No human service researcher would recommend, on the basis of a single study, that the dietary problems of aged persons can be solved by having home care workers provide positive reinforcement at appropriate times. If the study is replicated on several occasions then, of course, increasing confidence can be placed in the strategy.

FIELD RESEARCH

For the purposes of the present discussion, the term "field research" will be used to refer to that research which is conducted in a naturalistic setting, which must account for most of the human service research. The term "ethnographic research," which you will come across from time to time, can be taken as synonymous with field research.

In essence, the field research approach requires the researcher to gather information by observation and interview about naturally occurring social phenomena in a predetermined environment. The eminent anthropologist Malinowski is recognized as having developed the research strategy with his study of the Trobriand Islanders in the early part of this century (Holy, 1984). Since that time the approach has been used extensively by sociologists to study communities (Kornblum, 1974), religious groups (Festinger, Reiter, and Schacter, 1956), and occupational groups (Miller, 1986). Educational researchers have undertaken field research studies in the classroom (Schultz and Florio, 1979).

Clearly, the field research approach can make a significant contribution towards our understanding the needs of the community. Human service researchers have used field research strategies to study mental illness in homeless people (Herrman et al., 1988), people in asylums (Goffman, 1961) and people in poverty (Lewis, 1966). Through using this approach researchers are able to provide insights into the human condition not normally accessible to other research strategies.

The field research approach requires the researcher to collect information across a number of variables over an extended period of time. For example, if the researcher is conducting a study of a community facility for aged persons then he/she would be interested to learn about such matters as the perceived quality of care provided by staff, the degree of independence accorded to the aged persons, the opportunities for leisure and recreational activities, to name but a few variables. To gather sufficient data, the investigator is committed to conducting formal and informal interviews with the aged residents, as well as recording systematic observations about the activities occurring in the facilities which are relevant to the study.

In most field studies the researcher gathers information by becoming a participant-observer. That is, the researcher seeks to become a member of the community being studied. Researchers have carried out the role of participant-observer to varying degrees. In some cases, the community has been completely unaware of the fact that the researcher is anybody other than a bona fide member of the group (Pryce, 1979). Researchers who take on the role of the complete participant believe that by doing so they are able to come much closer to the perspective of the community on those issues pertinent to the study. Clearly, there are serious ethical problems associated with this approach. By becoming a complete participant, the researcher engages in an act of deception. For this reason most ethnographic researchers will declare the purpose of their presence in a community. It has been found that adopting a strategy of openness does not adversely impact upon the study (Coffield, Robinson, and Sarsby, 1981).

There are a number of methodological issues to be considered by the researcher when conducting field research. It is essential that the researcher has a clear understanding of the purpose of the study. This approach involves more than a person recording vast amounts of information about a group of people in the hope of being able to yield interesting insights about their behavior. The competent researcher will have at least tentative hypotheses to be tested by the study. Hence, the variables to be observed will be clearly defined. For example, in a study of the quality of life experienced by deinstitutionalized mental patients there are a number of variables requiring careful definition for the purposes of observation. In making these observations, the researcher will have established a predetermined method of recording the data to be sure that samples of the target behaviors are representative of the total occurrence of those behaviors. The researcher will also need to be able to demonstrate that steps have been taken to reduce possible bias in the observations. In a review of ethnographic research Gay (1990, p. 212) cautions us that "as more and more people have gotten into the ethnography act, some with little or no related training, there has been an increase in the number of poorly conducted, allegedly ethnographic studies." The same observation applies to field research.

THE CASE STUDY

In the human services, the case study may be used as a means of conducting an in-depth investigation of one or more individuals, an institution, or an exemplar community project. In order to ascertain the effectiveness of a drug rehabilitation program, for example, the researcher may conduct a case study of several participants. As well as undertaking to conduct extended in-depth interviews with each of the selected participants, the researcher may also seek information from family members, friends, workmates, and others. By this means of building a comprehensive picture, the investigator is seeking to understand how the processes of the rehabilitation program impact upon the individual.

Is there a difference between field research studies and case studies? Yes. The case study will tend to focus on only one individual, or a very limited number of individuals, while a field study will include data obtained from a sufficient number of individuals to allow the researcher to talk in terms of the behavior of a group of people. In the study of a human service agency, the field research approach will be focused on the individual clients; whereas the case study will not only deal with a number of individuals, but will have a much broader frame of reference including, for example, a cost analysis.

Case studies have been carried out on institutions for a variety of purposes. A recent study by Cocks (1989) has documented the process of an institution for mentally retarded persons moving its clients into community-based residential units in accordance with current policies of deinstitutionalization. The primary purpose of the study was to identify those issues of concern to management, staff, and clients as they progressively moved into the residential units. The outcomes of the study showed where management needed to allocate its resources for maximum effectiveness, the training needs of staff, and those events likely to cause distress to the clients.

Often the case study approach is used in state or federally funded programs. By undertaking an in-depth analysis of, for example, a youth employment project the researchers are able to gain insights into those factors likely to contribute to the success or failure of the program. Such an analysis may reveal which youth should be targeted by the program—long-term unemployed, high school drop-outs, homeless youth, etc.; the types of training programs which are most successful—relatively unskilled activities such as farm laboring, courses in automotive mechanics, computer programming, and so on.

The primary purpose of a case study is to identify the range of variables, and the relationships among the variables which account for the project outcomes. The experimental design is best used to determine the impact of an intervention strategy. For example, by using the experimental approach one may be able to show that the crime rate in a particular community has dropped by 20 percent since the introduction of Neighborhood Watch. However, it is by using the case study that we are able to understand why the crime rate has diminished. It may be simply that people are reporting suspicious incidents more frequently to the police who, in turn, are making more arrests. Hence, the crime rate has dropped because all the burglars are behind bars. On the other hand, it may turn out that the police have made no more arrests than is normally the case. However, the investigator learns that there has been a concomitant increase in crime rate in the adjacent community which has yet to introduce the Neighborhood Watch scheme. That is, the burglars are just as busy as ever, they have merely shifted to new ground.

A major problem with case studies is possible observer bias. That is, the observer sees what he or she wants to see. For example, the husband who has been attending marriage counseling sessions for an extended period of time now appears to be much more content in his relationship. It may be a case of the husband learning to behave in a socially acceptable manner in the public eye, while at night he is busy in the garage sharpening his chain saw. To reduce the possibility of observer bias it is always desirable to have more than one person collecting information in a case study.

The case study approach is limited by the fact that it is not possible to generalize the findings. That is, because one individual has been successfully weaned off heroin by participating in a particular methadone program does not mean that the program is going to be universally successful. The insights gained by the investigator in one case may not apply to any other case for a variety of reasons. Case studies can, however, suggest hypotheses which can be tested using another method of research.

PARTICIPATORY RESEARCH

The research endeavors of social scientists in the sixties and seventies were dominated by the application of the experimental paradigm. However, there has been a growing awareness, particularly in the field of community development, that social scientists are not the repository of all wisdom. Those issues deemed to have a high priority by social researchers are not always accorded the same status by members of the community. The solutions proposed by the "experts" are not always put forward with a full understanding of the social dynamics of the community. As a consequence, the outcomes of community development programs were sometimes less than satisfactory. At the same time, community development personnel recognized that any program had a far greater chance of success if the participants developed a sense of ownership through involvement in its planning and implementation. Leviton and Hughes (1981) cite a substantial number of studies which demonstrate the importance of stakeholder involvement in social research.

Deutscher (1976) foreshadowed the application of the participatory paradigm to research by advocating the concept of "negotiating a scenario." He argued that is was possible to identify realistic program goals through the process of negotiation which actively involved all stakeholders.

According to the International Council for Adult Education (1982) the participatory paradigm is characterized by three processes:

1. Collective investigation of problems and issues with the active participation of the constituency in the entire process.

The participatory approach to community development grew out of a reaction to bureaucratic domination of the social agenda and attendant problems. For example, it was found that the imposition of ideas and perceived needs from "outside" researchers can lead to a diminution of the status of community leaders which, in turn, is likely to militate against the success of the program.

The participatory approach should be distinguished from field research. In field research, or observational research, the investigator is essentially recording observations according to some predetermined criteria and seeking to explain the collected data in terms of relevant theories. In participatory research the agenda is determined by the participants with the investigator taking more of an advisory role in the process.

2. Collective analysis, in which the constituency develops a better understanding not only of the problem at hand but also of the underlying structural causes (socioeconomic, political, cultural) of the problem.

The researcher working in communities defined by such characteristics as ethnic composition or geographical isolation becomes as much a facilitator as an investigator. Healy (1985) provides some useful insights into the methodological difficulties arising from attempting to gather data from a socially powerless constituency such as women who are the victims of domestic violence. These difficulties not only include the very real problems of locating the women after they have left the refuge, and ensuring respondent confidentiality, but also dealing with the extremely negative attitudes that some women have developed towards society, including those endeavoring to provide support.

3. Collective action by the constituency is aimed at long-term as well as short-term solutions to identified problems.

It has been suggested that because the participants have a commitment to the well-being of their community and not constrained by the whims of voters, as are politicians, they will forego the "quick fix" in preference to the achievement of more substantive goals.

In addition, the process of participatory research does not concern itself with the issue of generalizing findings to other programs or projects (Cook and Shadish, 1986). Rather, the emphasis of this approach is to account for the success or failures of a program within a particular community setting.

The participatory approach has had only limited application in human service areas such as health, education, and the criminal justice system. However, the model is seen to have particular relevance to areas such as crime prevention and services to victims of crime. According to Maguire (1986), for example, there are more than 300 voluntary organizations in the U.K. which provide support services to victims. The creation of these organizations has been a community response to a perceived shortcoming in meeting the needs of victims by the statutory authorities. Programs such as Neighborhood Watch and the Safe Houses project clearly depend upon active community support for continued success. Healy (1985) advocates the application of the participatory model to evaluate women's shelters:

> . . . the women's movement, and the shelter movement generally, have always argued that the women users should be able to participate in running their own services, for example, be on the management committees of women's shelters. Therefore the push for more consumer planning and evaluation should strike a responsive chord (p. 231).

The participatory approach puts the researcher in a very different role. The issues of concern are determined by the participants in any program. Questions such as whether the program had an effect on the participants, or to what extent the program achieved the initial objectives, or how the program can be improved, are addressed from the point of view of the constituents. If the program has been implemented to the full extent, that is, the goals have been set by the participants, and the process has been guided by the participants, then the researcher takes on the role of an educator. The researcher shares with the participants his or her knowledge regarding social research. Essentially, the research is undertaken by the participants.

The participatory model is structured on the assumption that it will be necessary to collect different information to serve the needs of different audiences including community members, funding authorities, other researchers, and the general public. An inherent component of the research process is the imparting of knowledge and skills to the participants to enable them to take ultimate responsibility for the program. At the outset of the process, consideration is given to the clarification of goals, identification of the data required to measure progress towards those goals, the decision-making processes, and utilitarian skills such as record keeping and budgeting.

The initial stage of the research process is characterized by the active solicitation of feedback from members of the community, reviewing the relationship between the funding authorities and the program, as well as looking to any modifications. In addition to assessing the progress made towards achieving the objectives of the program during the summative stage of the process, attention is also given to the lessons learned by the participants and identifying future directions.

Cook and Shadish (1986, p. 228) make the point that the participatory paradigm is not without its critics:

> It is argued that social problem solving is dependent upon a stakeholder seeking a solution to a given problem under this approach. Thus, there are concerns that issues of significance may not be addressed. Also, the trade-offs between the accuracy, timeliness, and comprehensiveness of results are not yet well known, but adherents of the stakeholders service approach run the risk of providing timely information that is wrong in its claims or is misleading because of its incompleteness.

Other problems associated with the participatory model of research are highlighted by Brown and Ringma (1989). They make the point that the role of the participant may be seen as that of a commentator, a representative, a lobbyist, a partner, or a controller of services. The contribution that participants make towards program research will depend largely on their role in any program. In addition, Brown and Ringma claim that there is evidence to indicate that participants "have difficulty in finding a language with which to talk about and to evaluate services" (p. 37).

SECONDARY DATA ANALYSIS

So far, our discussion of different research paradigms has been based on the premise that the research data have been gathered directly by the investigator for the purposes of a particular study. That is, the investigator or his/her assistants have conducted interviews, and recorded observations and client responses in order to answer a specified research question. However, in the secondary data analysis approach the researcher undertakes an analysis of data previously collected for other purposes. For example, the Current Population Survey, a monthly survey conducted by the Census Bureau might be used by the human service researcher to identify the need for social programs for unemployed persons in a particular region.

There are significant advantages to using secondary data for research purposes. Clearly, the tasks of the researcher are reduced significantly if he/she has access to archival information which is relevant to the topic of investigation. In some cases, the information may be more extensive than the researcher would be able to gather as an individual. It may be, for example, that an organization has conducted a particular survey over a period of years and is able to provide the investigator with valuable longitudinal data for a project.

A variety of agencies hold large data banks of information which may be of interest to the social scientist. For example, the Census Bureau is a repository for vast amounts of social data. In addition to the ten yearly censuses of the population, the Bureau conducts other activities such as the American Housing Survey and the Consumer Expenditure Survey. The Interuniversity Consortium for Political and Social Research (ICPSR) at the University of Michigan will provide data to social scientists from its extensive archives. ICPSR is part of an international network of similar agencies in countries throughout the world. Other sources of secondary data which may be of interest to the human service researcher include the Roper Center at the University of Connecticut, the Federal Bureau of Investigation, State agencies, and hospital and school records.

Frankfort-Nachmias and Nachmias (1992) have identified three problems in secondary data analysis. First, the data may not fit precisely with what the researcher requires. For example, the sampling method used to collect the secondary data may not have been entirely appropriate for the particular investigation currently being undertaken. Definitions of the same social variables can differ from one study to the next. For example, in one study the "recidivism rate" might be measured by the number of released prisoners who are charged by the police within twelve months of being paroled, while a second study might define the same variable as the number of prisoners returned to prison within two years of release. Even more problematic is the notion of a universal definition for concepts such as "delinquency," "homelessness," "learning difficulty," or "promiscuity."

Second, it may not be easy for the researcher to access the various archives for relevant information. Agencies are always concerned about the confidentiality of the information they have about their clients. It may be expensive in terms of staff time for agencies which do not normally provide data for research purposes to provide the information which has been requested.

Third, it is not always possible for the researcher to determine the quality of the data stored in archival form. There may well be sampling problems which have biased the data, problems of reliability, and data of questionable validity. Some organizations such as ICPSR are attempting to address these issues by grading their data by different criteria. However, this is a long way from being the case with most sources of secondary data.

META-ANALYSIS

The traditional method of scientific research involves looking at a problem, attempting to control for extraneous factors, and showing links, either correlational or causal, between the variables. As research on a topic continues to receive attention, so more and more studies are conducted. Sometimes these studies will attempt to replicate the earlier studies, others will look to investigate variations which lead to improved understanding, while some will seek to disprove the theories or explanations which have been proposed.

However, this increasing body of literature is not always consistent in its findings. Rosenthal (1991) believes that the existence of many studies with differing conclusions leads to confusion and eventually pessimism on the part of those who use research to guide their decisions. Glass (1976, 1977) describes a procedure called "meta-analysis" which enables the disparate findings of different studies of the same topic to be integrated.

What then is a meta-analysis? The principle is relatively easy to describe but does not reflect the complexity of the procedure. First, the researcher

identifies as many studies as can be found on the topic of interest from a variety of sources including journals, technical reports, and unpublished dissertations. The primary criterion for selection is that the study has used an experimental and control group. By a complex statistical process, the researcher then is able to calculate an "effect size," which is a measure of the difference between the experimental and control groups in each study. It is then possible to calculate a mean (average) effect size for all studies as well as other statistical properties. The meta-analysis enables the researcher to determine when an overall effect size exists or whether the treatment has no significant effect on the dependent variable.

Let us consider a meta-analysis of studies on the efficacy of perceptual-motor training by Kavale and Mattson (1983). Perceptual-motor training is a procedure widely used in the treatment of children with a learning disability. In all, 180 studies on the topic were reviewed by the investigators, who report that the results of thirty-four studies support the use of perceptual-motor training while seventeen studies were found to be negative or neutral about the same procedures. Using meta-analytic procedures Kavale and Mattson are able to show that perceptual-motor training is not effective in ameliorating the condition of children with a learning disability.

Meta-analytic studies have been used to compare the effects of psychotherapy to the effects of placebo treatments (Rosenthal, 1983); to investigate sex differences in conformity research (Cooper, 1979); and the effects of teacher expectancies on academic achievement (Dusek and Joseph, 1983). There is no doubt that the human services will see many more meta-analytic studies being conducted in the future.

COST ANALYSIS

In essence, the information provided by much social research is used by decision makers to determine the extent to which a program is achieving its goals, or to determine ways in which the delivery of services may be improved. However, this is only part of the total picture. On the basis of information yielded, programs will be maintained, enhanced, expanded, cut back, or discontinued. Decisions regarding the future directions of a program generally cannot be taken without consideration being given to the costs associated with the derived benefits.

The allocation of resources to one program inevitably means less resources available to pursue other social objectives. Cost analysis, then, is a tool used by policy makers and administrators to arrive at decisions pertaining to the distribution of limited resources. A variety of cost-analysis models have been developed in response to the nature of the issues about which decisions are required, and the form of information available to the investigator. Two of the most widely used models in social research will be examined, namely cost-effectiveness and cost-benefit analysis.

Cost Effectiveness

The cost-effectiveness model was originally developed by the Pentagon to evaluate the effectiveness of different weapon systems in achieving certain defense objectives. The model is distinguished from the cost-benefit approach in that the outcomes of the program are not expressed in monetary terms. Rather, the model simply yields the cost of achieving a given objective per unit of outcome, and provides a basis for selecting between alternative means that might be used to reach that objective.

A study by Knapp and Robertson (1986) illustrates the application of the cost-effectiveness model to the justice system. The investigators compared the cost per sentence for youths committed to a detention center with youths given intermediate treatment such as a community service order. Not surprisingly, it was found that the intermediate treatment was found to be a cost-effective alternative to custody for juvenile offenders. However, as the researchers point out, this conclusion is based on the assumption that effects on the juvenile offenders are the same for both forms of sanctions.

A further application of the cost-effectiveness analysis is to compare the unit cost for the same service delivered in different circumstances. For example, Raine (1986) compared the costs of different judicial court services in different counties throughout the U.K. He found that the "amount devoted to staffing costs was calculated to vary from just over $25 per case in Liverpool to over $60 in Cornwall" (p. 54). Obviously, this information alone is not sufficient to justify either increasing the budget of the court's services in Liverpool, or reducing the funds allocated to their southern counterparts. It may be that differences in the quality of services provided account for the cost differential between the two counties.

The underlying assumption in the application of the cost-effective model to the comparison of services is that of equivalence. The uncritical acceptance of this assumption may lead to counterproductive decisions being taken by administrators. As suggested above, similar services or the same service delivered in different environments may differ on various dimensions. Not only may there be a difference in the quality of the service provided, but significant differences may also occur in the characteristics of the target populations, the experience of the staff delivering the service, the length of time the services have been operational, or the geographical locations of the service operations. Any comparison of services on a cost-effective basis must take these factors into consideration.

A major limitation to the cost-effectiveness model is the quality of the cost-accounting operations in many human service areas (Grizzle and Witte, 1980; Grabosky, 1988). In reviewing the application of the cost-effectiveness model to evaluating the impact of victimless crime legislation, Geis (1980, p. 411) cautions that:

In short, judiciousness would probably dictate that costs are best handled as longitudinal data indicating a real rise or decrease in the amounts involved in particular activities and the implications to be drawn from such information—rather than as very firm bases for policy-relevant conclusions.

Cost-Benefit Analysis

The cost-benefit analysis model used primarily by economists guides decision makers in choosing the public policy option which will derive the greatest benefits for the community. For example, the issue of crime prevention might be tackled by increasing the size of the police force, or by allocating funds to an urban renewal project, or by implementing an employment program for young people. In carrying out a cost-benefit analysis the evaluator is required to quantify all the costs and benefits associated with each option in monetary terms. The preferred option should be that which provides the greatest benefits-for-costs ratio.

The cost of increasing the size of the police force by 10 percent can be readily calculated. However, it must be assumed that there will be a concomitant increase in the number of arrests and convictions. Thus, the attendant increase in courts and prison costs must be taken into account. Of course, assuming that the level of productivity remains constant, more lawyers will need to be trained, more parole officers appointed, and so on. Economists have developed techniques for measuring these reverberations, such as the general equilibrium analysis (see, for example, Rothenberg, 1975). To complicate the cost side of the equation even more, it is necessary to introduce the concept of opportunity costs. The allocation of financial resources to the justice system will be at the expense of other social programs. Hence, the cost of less employment opportunities for young people, for example, would need to be considered.

Quantifying, in monetary terms, the benefits arising from the implementation of a particular social policy, such as increasing the size of the police force, is even more complex than estimating the costs. In the case of our example, the measurement of crime prevention is a fundamental issue. The notion that the increased number of arrests and convictions that have occurred as a result of recruiting more police can be taken as an indicator of the number of crimes prevented is problematic at best. Another strategy might be to calculate the economic cost of burglaries over a

given period of time, both before and after the policy has been implemented. But how does one determine the monetary value of corporate crimes not committed, or the number of incest incidents that have not occurred? Just as intangible is attempting to cost the reduced level of fear of crime within the community that, hopefully, is an outcome of the policy decision.

A strength of the cost-benefit analysis approach is that it provides the policy-maker with information which makes it possible to choose between very different options or solutions to problems in the field of human services. The major limitation of the model is the quality of the data available from the field. As Rothenberg (1975, p. 88) states:

> . . . regardless of its methodological claims, its practical usefulness will be most decisively at the mercy of the availability of data. Very serious inadequacy of relevant data exists in almost every area for which cost-benefit analyses have been undertaken.

A second limitation is the costs involved in undertaking such an analysis. However, as Grizzle and Witte (1980) point out, it is possible to apply effectively the methodology in a more limited form. A modest application of the model, for example, would be the calculation of the costs incurred and benefits derived from the introduction of the legislation requiring seat belts to be worn in motor vehicles. Any agency would find it useful to document all the costs and benefits associated with a particular policy or program.

Short (1980) makes the point that while cost-benefit evaluation studies are important to the development of public policy, such studies do not contribute significantly to our theoretical understanding of the issues involved. Cho (1980) has taken a different approach to analyzing public policy. Using a multiple regression model Cho has been able to measure the impact of different public policies on crime rates in major U.S. cities. Cho reports that service policies, such as expenditure for education and for parks and recreation, affect crime rates more often than control policies, such as employing more police or reducing prison crowdedness. While not directly addressing the criticisms of Short, the correlational model developed by Cho can point the way for undertaking future impact studies.

ROLE OF THE HUMAN SERVICE WORKER AND RESEARCH

As a human service worker you are likely to become involved in research in a variety of ways. Perhaps the most common involvement occurs when your agency is being evaluated by the funding authorities. It is important that you have a clear understanding of the purpose of such an evaluation study. If the funding authority is interested in the effectiveness of the program, for example, the evaluator will be seeking different information to an investigation concerned with determining the efficiency of the program. In the first case, the researcher is primarily interested in the extent to which people benefit from the services provided by the agency. If you are working in a drug rehabilitation center, the obvious question is how many people remain off drugs once they have been discharged? An efficiency study, on the other hand, is essentially concerned with the costs of the program. Here the investigator is dealing with questions like which is the better of two programs: Program A successfully rehabilitates twenty drug addicts per month at a cost of $5,000 per person while Program B only rehabilitates ten addicts per month but at a cost of $2,000 per person. In these types of studies your role as a human service worker may be focused on the provision of information. It may sound trite to say that it is essential that you provide accurate and reliable information. However, any social scientist is constantly concerned about the quality of information obtained from participants.

Another research scenario often includes the human service worker as a member of the investigation team. You may become involved in a study examining the effects of a recently released drug on the behavior of mentally disturbed adolescents. As a member of the investigation team

you will be concerned about the implementation and maintenance of the program. Again, it is critical that you understand the purpose of the study. If the investigation is looking at the effects of different schedules of reinforcement on the rate at which an autistic child engages in disruptive behavior, then you should have an understanding of the rationale for the research.

In other circumstances, as a human service worker you may be the sole researcher. You may have applied for and received a grant from the federal government to develop a program aimed at reducing the amount of domestic violence that occurs behind the closed doors of suburban middle America. You will want to demonstrate that your program is more effective than any other program currently operating. You will have to design and implement a research project which will convince the funding authorities that they should continue to support your program. In this situation, you will need to demonstrate that your cautious, but convincing, claims for success are soundly based on data that are both valid and reliable.

As a professional human service worker you will be a consumer of research findings. This means you will be required to keep abreast of relevant research developments occurring in your particular sphere of interest. You will need to be able to critically review published research findings and synthesize the results of those studies with the outcomes of earlier related investigations. For example, should current research into the applications of primal scream therapy indicate that this technique is particularly effective in dealing with the neuroses of anal-retentive bank managers you would want to reflect upon the potential usefulness of this therapeutic approach in dealing with the problems of people with whom you work. Here, of course, you need to think about the critical issue of generalizing the results of research studies. Only after you are convinced that the evidence suggests that you are likely to achieve more effective results with primal scream therapy than, say, your current neurolinguistic programming approach, would you implement the change. This is where you exercise your professional judgment. You may be concerned with developing social policy statements based upon empirical research findings. For example, the latest research may indicate that adolescents who play sports do not engage in delinquent behavior to the same extent as adolescents who do not play sports. Hence, your policy for reducing the rate of antisocial behavior is to introduce a comprehensive sports program for young people. Your social policy is based on the assumption that young people will not engage in undesirable behavior if they are busy playing football, baseball, and basketball. That is, you have inferred that a causal relationship exists between the two variables of sport and delinquent behavior. As discussed earlier, it is interesting to note that while national youth policies have been based on the assumption that such a relationship exists, social scientists have never been able to demonstrate that such is the case. The moral of the story, of course, is that you cannot accept uncritically the findings of contemporary social research.

REFERENCES

Campbell, D.T., (1979). "Assessing the Impact of Social Change." *Evaluation and Program Planning* 2, 67–90.

Cho, Y. H., (1980). "A Multiple Regression Model for the Measurement of the Public Policy Impact on Big City Crime." In D. Nachmias, ed., *The Practice of Policy Evaluation.* New York: St Martin's Press.

Cocks, E., (1989). "Working Together with Your Community." *National Council on Intellectual Disability: Interaction* 3, 39–48.

Coffield, F., P. Robinson, and J. Sarsby, (1981). *A Cycle of Deprivation? A Case Study of Four Families.* London: Heinemann.

Cook, T. D. and D. T. Campbell, (1979). *Quasi-Experimentation: Design and Analysis Issues for Field Settings.* Skokie, IL: Rand-McNally.

Cook, T.D., F.L. Cook, and M.M. Mark, (1977). "Randomized and Quasi-Experimental Designs in Evaluation Research: An Introduction." In L. Rutman, ed., *Evaluation Research Methods: A Basic Guide.* London: Sage Publications.

Cook, T.D. and W.R. Shadish, (1986). "Program Evaluation: The Worldly Science." *Annual Review of Psychology* 37, 193–232.

Cooper, H.M., (1979). "Statistically Combining Independent Studies: A Meta-Analysis of Sex Differences in Conformity Research." *Journal of Personality and Social Psychology* 37, 131–146.

David, H.P. and N.H. Wright, (1971). "Abortion Legislation: The Romanian Experience Studies." *Family Planning* 2, 205–210.

Davidson, W. S., J. R. Koch, R. G. Lewis, and M. D. Wresinski, (1981). *Evaluation Strategies in Criminal Justice.* New York: Pergamon Press.

Deutscher, I., (1976). "Toward Avoiding the Goal-Trap in Evaluation Research." In C. G. Abt, ed., *The Evaluation of Social Programs.* London: Sage Publications.

Dusek, J. B. and G. Joseph, (1983). "The Bases of Teacher Experiences: A Meta-Analysis." *Journal of Educational Psychology* 75, 327–346.

Empey, L. T., (1980). "Field Experimentation in Criminal Justice: Rationale and Design." In M. W. Klein and T. S. Teilman, eds., *Handbook of Criminal Justice Evaluation.* London: Sage Publications.

Festinger, L., H. Reicken, and S. Schacter, (1956). *When Prophecy Fails.* New York: Harper & Row.

Frankfort-Nachmias, C. and D. Nacmias, (1992). *Research Methods in the Social Sciences,* 4th ed. London: Hodder & Stoughton.

Gay, L. R., (1990). *Educational Research: Competencies for Analysis and Application,* 3rd ed. New York: Merrill Publishing Co.

Geis, G., (1980). "Evaluation Issues and Victimless Crimes." In M. W. Klein and T. S. Teilman, eds., *Handbook of Criminal Justice Evaluation.* London: Sage Publications.

Glass, G. V., (1976). "Primary, Secondary and Meta-Analysis of Research." *Educational Researcher* 5, 3–8.

Glass, G. V., (1977). "Integrating Findings: The Meta-Analysis of Research." *Review of Research in Education* 5, 351–379.

Goffman, E., (1961). *Asylums.* New York: Doubleday.

Grabosky, P., (1988). "Efficiency and Effectiveness in Australian Policing: A Citizen's Guide to Police Services." In J. Vernon and D. Bracey, eds., *Police Resources and Effectiveness.* Seminar Proceedings

No. 16, Australian Institute of Criminology, Canberra.

Grizzle, G.A. and A.D. Witte, (1980). "Criminal Justice Evaluation Techniques: Methods Other Than Random Assignment." In M. W. Klein and T. S. Teilman, eds., *Handbook of Criminal Justice Evaluation*. London: Sage Publications.

Healy, J., (1985). "After the Refuge: Methodological Issues in Follow-Up Surveys." In S. E. Hatty, ed., *National Conference on Domestic Violence*. Seminar Proceedings No 12, Australian Institute of Criminology, Canberra.

Herrman, H., P. McGorry, P. Bennett, R. Van Riel, P. Wellington, D. McKenzie, and B. Singh, (1988). *Homeless People with Severe Mental Disorders in Inner Melbourne*. Council to Homeless Persons Victoria, Melbourne.

Holy, L., (1984). "Theory, Methodology and the Research Process." In R. F. Ellen, ed., *Ethnographic Research: A Guide to General Conduct*. London: Academic Press.

Janus, M., (1982). "Functional Unit Management: Organizational Effectiveness in the Federal Prison System." In G. A. Forehand, ed., *Applications of Time-Series Analysis to Evaluation*. San Francisco: Jossey-Bass Inc.

International Council for Adult Education, (1982). *Participatory Research: An Introduction*. New Delhi: Society for Participatory Research in Asia.

Knapp, M. and E. Robertson, (1986). "Has Intermediate Treatment Proved Cost-Effective?" In A. Harrison and J. Gretton, eds., *Crime U.K. 1986: An Economic, Social and Policy Audit*. Newbury, Berkshire: Policy Journals.

Kornblum, W., (1974). *Blue-Collar Community*. Chicago: University of Chicago Press.

Leviton, L. C. and E. F. X. Hughes, (1981). "Research on the Utilization of Evaluations: A Review and Synthesis." *Evaluation Review* 5(4), 525–548.

Lewis, O., (1966). *La Vida: A Puerto Rican Family in the Culture of Poverty*. New York: Random House.

Maguire, M., (1986). "Victims' Rights: Slowly Redressing the Balance." In A. Harrison and J. Gretton, eds., *Crime U.K. 1986: An Economic, Social and Policy Audit*. Newbury, Berkshire: Policy Journals.

Mason, G. and P. Wilson, (1988). *Sport and Juvenile Crime*. Canberra: Australian Institute of Criminology.

McCleary, R. and J. E. Riggs, (1982). "The 1975 Australian Law Act: A Model for Assessing Legal Impacts." In G. A. Forehand, ed., *Applications of Time Series Analysis to Evaluation*. San Francisco: Jossey-Bass Inc.

Miller, E., (1986). *Street Woman*. Philadelphia: Temple University Press.

Pryce, K., (1979). *Endless Pressure*. Harmondsworth, England: Penguin.

Raine, J., (1986). "Do Magistrates' Courts Give Value for Money?" In A. Harrison and J. Gretton, eds., *Crime U.K.: An Economic, Social and Policy Audit*. Newbury, Berkshire: Policy Journals.

Rosenthal, R., (1983). "Improving Meta-Analytic Procedures for Assessing the Effects of Psychotherapy vs. Placebo." *The Behavioral and Brain Sciences* 6, 298–299.

Rosenthal, R., (1991). *Meta-Analytic Procedures for Social Research*. Newbury Park, CA: Sage Publications.

Ross, H.L., (1973). "Law, Science, and Accidents: The British Road Safety Act of 1967." *Journal of Legal Studies* 2, 1–75.

Rothenberg, J., (1975). "Cost-Benefit Analysis: A Methodological Exposition." In M. Guttentag and E. L. Streuning, eds., *Handbook of Evaluation Research* Vol. 2. London: Sage Publications.

Salthouse, T. A., (1982). *Adult Cognition: An Experimental Psychology of Human Aging*. New York: Springer-Verlag.

Schultz, J. and S. Florio, (1979). "Stop and Freeze: The Negotiation of Social and Physical Space in a Kindergarten/First Grade Classroom." *Anthropology & Education Quarterly* 10, 166–181.

Sherman, L.W. and R.A. Berk, (1984). "The Specific Deterrent Effects of Arrest for Domestic Assault." *American Sociological Review* 49, 261–272.

Short, J. F., (1980). "Evaluation as Knowledge Building—and Vice Versa." In M. W. Klein and T. S. Teilman, eds., *Handbook of Criminal Justice Evaluation*. London: Sage Publications.

Squire, C., (1989). *Significant Differences—Feminism in Psychology*. London: Routledge.

Underwood, R., M. Lee, and R. Jackson, (1991). "Community Support Services for Mentally Ill Young People." Paper presented at the Australian Sociological Association annual conference, Perth.

THE IMPORTANCE OF COMPUTER USAGE IN HUMAN SERVICES

TOM WISBEY

What do you know about computers and their application to your profession? You may have taken a computer course or used word processing for your school papers, but how does that experience relate to clients or a professional human service practitioner? The computer is an expandable tool for the human services with many yet unexplored uses.

The introduction of computers has changed the present orientation to human services in much the same way that introduction of the wide-body jet aircraft fundamentally changed our orientation to travel. The distances remain the same, and the human yearning to see far-away places continues, but now, the possibilities available to the average person are far beyond all but the most audacious and fertile imaginations of the even recent past (Guzetta, 1993, p. 248).

Presently computers are mostly used in the human service agencies for management purposes rather than for, and by, providers and clients.

The use of computer capabilities appears to be concentrated primarily at the managerial level, with direct service assistance and research applications much less prevalent (Mutschler, 1987). In this area, the human services disciplines and agencies have not kept pace with other fields, such as psychology and medicine. Reasons for this discrepancy seem to fall into four categories: (1) equipment and software limitations (lack of discipline-specific software), (2) expense, (3) ethical and practice concerns, and (4) practitioner resistance (Lamb, 1990, p. 32).

This limited computer use in direct service applications needs attention if the profession is to help people help themselves. The computer is one of many tools the practitioner has to master to be an effective helper.

The computer is a TOOL. Therefore, its use must be guided by the values, knowledge base, and practice activities of the profession in question (Nurius, Hudson, 1993, p. 1).

As we help people to help themselves, the question of what helping is will be redefined in both human and technological terms. As practitioners we are taught to use the senses of smell, touch, and feeling to help the client. Now we add to these senses the tools of the computer which can help to analyze data and client decision making. The computer can also allow the client the opportunity to see through simulation exercises the consequences of their actions for various forms of behavior and then become involved in decision making with the practitioner. However, the most important tool that the microcomputer has added to a practitioner's skills is in the area of communication. Communication has always been a major aspect of human service work. Now the computer is adding new forms of communication for both practitioner and client. These new forms of communication include professional and computer networks and new forms of client education and follow-up services. The way human service practitioners use computers for communication will affect the way helping will be defined in the future.

Information technology can impact the way information is communicated between service recipient and practitioner, between practitioner and management, between agency and funding source, and between a funding source and its constituents. The change in communication mechanisms also impacts what is communicated (Schoech, 1990, p. 84).

The year is 1998. You are working in a clinic. The psychiatrist has been given a new family case which involves some type of child abuse. The family has come into the clinic where the mother and father are seen by the psychologist. You have been given the task of working with the child in question. The child you will be working with for the next hour-and-a-half has no siblings and is not very verbal. She is four years old and her parents have been married for the past five years. How would you use the computer as a human service tool with this child?

You take the child into a room containing toys, blocks, puppets, and painting materials. She spots a computer in the corner of the room and goes over to push the keys. You help her by turning it on and bringing up a Muppet software program. When she pushes the keys, Kermit the Frog begins to jump, and she gets a smile on her face because she made him jump. After five minutes you and your client are laughing and talking. Within fifteen minutes you have begun to establish a relationship that allows her to share her fun and fears. The computer game was fun and allowed her to control the situation. When people are having fun, communication is inevitable.

Using computer games in therapy is relatively new, yet it begins to redefine what and how therapeutic helping can occur. When working with adults, some clinics are now using the computer for client training or as follow-up to therapeutic sessions.

More intensive forms of client education are emerging as an adjunct to treatment. For example, interactive software has been designed to educate clients on topics such as how to comply with medication instructions and medical care, what to expect upon leaving a residential treatment program, and how to alter attitudes toward alcohol and drinking (Ellis, 1987; Meier, 1988). This type of software obviously takes us into the realm of using computer tools in the direct provision of service to clients. This arena is developing unevenly with supports in some domains, such as intervention with the disabled (Ridgeway and McKears, 1985) and therapeutic games, far outpacing others (Nurius and Hudson, 1993, p. 389).

The year is now 1999. You have just received communication from one of your clients. He is sixty-two years of age, married with three children and six grandchildren. His family lives in California. He and his wife have been married for forty years, always living in Southern Maine. His wife died this past month and he was picked up by the police for drunken driving and fired from his job. He is calling you for help and needs several kinds of resources. Your task is to refer him to the appropriate services. What computer tools would you use in accomplishing this?

This is a difficult case that involves the family, court system, and alcohol services of two different states. Where do you turn? Who will be able to help this client with all his issues? In the past you would pick a resource, probably a person in one of the delivery systems that you trust. Now there is a better and more efficient way. You turn on your personal computer and put in your information and referral discs. With the aid of the modum you are able to search the available services in both states. Now you can assess the services and see what is available and their restrictions. With data in hand you and your client can sit down and make out a series of action steps. Do you call his family in California? Should he go there or stay in Maine? The two of you can now use a computer decision-making simulation to help plot several scenarios from which he can pick. Once you isolate the places he should go or people he should see he can be given a printout to take with him.

The year is 2000. You have been a case worker in a community agency for ten years. Your day is filled with people in crisis. The agency is able to only provide a two-hour staff meeting once per week which usually addresses administrative tasks that need to be completed. Your immediate supervisor is often unavailable and overworked. You begin to feel burned out and wonder if you belong in another profession. You question whether your skills are appropriate for the kinds of clients you are now seeing. Can you imagine using the computer as a personal tool for this situation?

That evening after work you turn on your personal computer with its modum in order to access your professional network. You type up several messages to other professionals throughout the world to check out your feelings and skills in crisis work. The next morning there are several ideas including resources for new jobs that a colleague has suggested. The feeling of isolation and burnout begins to diminish as you realize that practitioners throughout the world care for you and understand demands of human service work. You have also developed new friends that you can continue to correspond with regarding your work and future aspirations.

As a new human service practitioner how do you begin to explore the tools of computers and your new career field? If you were lucky, your educational experience taught you the uses of the computer, because each human service course you took used the computer for various types of course activities. In fact, the computer network you experienced between your field placement, the college, and your home was very beneficial.

If you didn't have this type of educational experience—and most of you probably didn't—start your experimentation with yourself. Get people together and begin to play with computer games. Have fun, learn, and enjoy the communication. Now join a local computer society and get into an interest group. When you explore your professional field on computer, you will find an excellent journal to read called *Computers in Human Services* published by the Haworth Press.

Also there are some excellent books now being written. Finally, there are worldwide networks such as BITNET where you can get the experiences of those practitioners who have been using or experimenting with this technology. Great Britain and the Netherlands have been using computers in human services for over ten years and can easily give you a picture of the plusses and minuses of various applications.

The importance of the microcomputer lies not just in its assistance for decision making but in its communication capabilities for yourself and your client. As in all communication, there is a possibility that you will not really engage in two-way communication but simply give or dictate a message. The field of human services and you will need to insure true two-way communication and empowerment. This is the cornerstone of the human service movement. As you communicate and teach yourself or your client, the issue of personal control becomes a critical element. It is the computer and its potential for facilitating personal control that can insure good communication, empowerment, and learning.

The perception of personal control is also a central issue for intrinsic motivation in learning (McCombs, 1984); higher efficacy has been shown to enhance motivation (Dickens and Perry, 1982; Reinoehl, 1990, p. 171).

This self-control that has enhanced learning and individual motivation can be harnessed for yourself and clients through computer applications that allow interaction and simulation.

The positive effect of self-efficacy on learners is well documented. Human bonding with computers can also promote learning, particularly when combined with realistic graphic images providing modeling, role playing and feedback. Beyond their potential in human services education, the impact of computers on our thinking will play an increasingly important role in our lives and in our very conception and understanding of self (Reinoehl, 1990, p. 173).

The computer, like any tool, can be used for good and bad purposes. That is why a professional network of human service practitioners will continuously need to look at ethical and practical issues of computers. As larger computer systems become developed into smart machines (expert systems) that increasingly think like humans, issues of data collection, privacy, and job displacement will transform the human service profession and redefine helping services. Your participation in this change process will insure that professional values of communication and empowerment continue and become a part of the system for our next generation of smart machines.

Privacy is threatened as databases store and exchange information about most members of society. Job displacement and privacy are concerns, but a more basic challenge may be the sanctity of our human nature. We humans have always set ourselves apart due to a greater ability to reason and communicate. As smart machines become more sophisticated, we have to reexamine this separateness. Especially critical are our beliefs about what makes us human and the roles of humans versus machines in society (Schoech, 1990, p. 3).

REFERENCES

Guzetta, C., (1993). "Introduction." *Computers in Human Services* 9, 247–248.

Lamb, J., (1990). "Teaching Computer Literacy to Human Service Students." *Computers in Human Services* 7, 31–43.

Nurius, P. and Hudson, W., (1993). *Human Services Practice, Evaluation, and Computers*. Pacific Grove, CA: Brooks-Cole Pub.

Reinoehl, R., (1990). "Partners in Thinking and Learning." *Computers in Human Services* 7, 167–175.

Schoech, D., (1990). *Human Service Computing*. New York: The Haworth Press.

CHAPTER 26

TRENDS AND CHALLENGES OF CULTURAL DIVERSITY

R. DONNA PETRIE

We are born in families, whether small or large, with one or more parenting figures. These families are embedded in a web of other families, all of which are part of a particular society or culture. In the United States families share a common culture because they all live in one country, but they also share a family culture which may or may not be like the culture of the nation. It is virtually impossible to overemphasize the influence an individual's family culture has on the day-to-day activities of any given person's life. In this country it is also nearly impossible to overestimate the points of difference within cultures and between cultures. Diversity is a major principle of American life (Kluckhorn, 1967), but many individuals think the way they grew up is the "only" way to live life.

The purpose of this chapter is to broadly introduce the challenges of multicultural human services work. The challenge is threefold. First, human services professionals need to have an understanding of specific value areas wherein misunderstanding between cultures is likely to occur; secondly, workers need to understand different cultural models of healing and caring; and finally, human services professionals, whether they think of themselves as bicultural or as "American," need to understand how they are seen as "agents" of mainstream American culture.

FUTURE POPULATION TRENDS

Recently the New York Times reported that the United States Census Bureau has had to recalcu-
late population growth (Peer, 1992, December 2). The population of the United States, it appears, will continue to grow through 2050 rather than decline after the year 2038. To summarize, for the years 1990 to 2025 there will be more babies, particularly of new immigrants, and the proportion of men to women is likely to even out, as the life expectancy of men appears to be rising faster than that of women.

Despite this overall increase in the number of people in the United States, Whites will account for a declining share in the population. The numbers of Black Americans, Asian Americans, and Hispanic Americans will grow appreciably. Using the 1990 census, the Bureau predicts a 412.5 percent population growth for Asian and Pacific Islanders, a 237.5 percent growth in numbers for Hispanic Americans, a 109.1 percent increase in the number of Native American Indians, Eskimos, and Aleuts, and a 93.8 percent increase for Black Americans. These figures contrast significantly with the 29.4 percent projected growth of White Americans from 1992 to the year 2050.

The Census Bureau makes the future trends somewhat more complex by noting that immigration by itself will account for the expected growth in the Asian American population and not the number of births. Birth rates are increasing among the Black and Hispanic populations. The birth rate of Whites, however, will not increase. In the United States the youngest population group is the Hispanic American group. In fact, whereas the median age of all Americans is

389

thirty-three, more than one-third of the Hispanic population in the United States is under the age of eighteen.

Interestingly, at the same time that the population is expanding with more babies, more new immigrants, more people of color, and more elderly—people who typically live in cities—more jobs are moving from the cities to the suburbs thus making access to employment much more difficult (Barringer, 1992, December 4). With this economic picture, human services workers on the two coasts (namely New York, North New Jersey, Long Island, Los Angeles, Anaheim, and Riverside, California) will likely experience more interpersonal racial and ethnic conflict because of the greater numbers of immigrants and the greater density mixes of black, white, yellow, and brown cultures. Other urban areas such as: Miami, and Fort Lauderdale in Florida; Houston, Galveston, and Brazoria in Texas; and San Francisco, Oakland, and San Jose in California may also experience the effects of polarized differences between Hispanics and Asians, and Asians and Blacks (Statistical Abstracts, 1991). Color consciousness and ethnic intolerance, although longstanding and typically a white-black issue in this country, is no less a problem between and within other racial and ethnic groupings.

Social characteristics of various cultural groups in this country add to the complexity of the challenge of working with culturally diverse client populations. While the percentage of persons twenty-five years of age and over who have not completed an elementary school education (zero to eight years) is lowest for Asian Americans (6.4 percent up to five years completed), and highest for Hispanic Americans (34 percent), the percentage of Whites is 11 percent and for Blacks is 17 percent. Level of education, unemployment, and poverty have a high degree of correspondence for all cultural groups in America except for those who are born White. The unemployment rate for Whites is the lowest of all groups, as are their numbers in families living below the poverty line, and this despite the fact that 11 percent of the White population only has an elementary school education (U.S. Department of Commerce, 1991).

Using these population trends, current and future clients seeking human services can be summarized rather easily. People of color will continue to dominate the social welfare client rolls and they will continue to have multiple problems. The clients will be very young or very old, their formal education will be limited, and they will have trouble finding work. If they are immigrants or children of immigrants, they will likely have problems navigating family and personal cultural issues as well.

While individuals from this client population profile are well known to any entry-level human services professional, the human services model of helping does not automatically attribute deficiency or mental illness to these individuals (Schmolling, Jr., Yonkeles and Burger, 1992; Papajohn and Spiegel, 1975). On the contrary many such clients, although wanting economic security, may not subscribe at all to the American values of materialism and of being "bigger and better" or more successful than one's forebears. Indeed, on many levels their needs and wants may be different not only from mainstream cultural stereotypes presented in the media, but individual clients may be very different from the culture or family in which they were raised (Pedersen, 1976).

BASIC AREAS OF DIFFERENCE IN CULTURAL VALUES

Assume that all people in the United States, regardless of cultural affiliation, want to have an *optimal life* (Speight, Myers, Cox, and Highlen, 1991). Given that definitions of an optimal life differ, and that individuals living in an increasingly multicultural and multilingual society will often have to interact or negotiate with others of another culture, on what subjects are they likely to have interpersonal misunderstandings?

Apart from differences in individual communication style and language usage (Sarbaugh, 1988; Baroth and Manning, 1991) cultural anthropologists have categorized differences between ethnic groups in the following ways: (1) their understanding of authority (2) their definitions of success, and finally (3) their beliefs about how people should conduct themselves and their relationships (Carter, 1991; Barlith and Manning, 1991; Spiegel, 1982). Understanding the values of each client group on the previously stated dimensions is helpful in understanding how an individual may be in conflict with their own culture or with the larger multiethnic culture. In the next several paragraphs we will look at a number of ethnic groups' general responses to these questions.

What motivates human beings? Are they basically good or well meaning or are they born with evil intentions? The answer to this question is a basic building block of an individual's belief structure. Research has shown that Blacks and Puerto Ricans often contrast sharply with Eurocentric Americans in their view of human nature (Carter, 1991). While several studies of white-middle-class Americans provide mixed views of human nature, none offer evidence that Euro-Americans think human beings are born malevolent in character; whereas Blacks and Puerto Ricans are more fatalistic, believing some people do evil because they are evil.

Similarly, Euro-Americans tend to differ from Blacks, Chinese, Africans, Italians, Cubans, and Native American Indians because they believe that individuals exert control over life events, and that each person should use willpower for one's own gain (Carter, 1991; Helms, 1992; Pinderhughes, 1989). While many Blacks, Cubans, and Native Americans believe people live in nature and are partners with all of nature, other Blacks, Italians, and Chinese believe that people have little control over natural forces or what happens to people, and also what they can do about what has happened. Clearly helping an individual who believes that personal effort is futile because "that's the way things are," that all anyone can do is to comply with what has happened is likely to "feel" frustrating and futile to Euro-American and Japanese-American intake workers who have put themselves through college. Euro-American culture

believes in action, in achievement, and in self-expression (Carter, 1991; Helms, 1992). Action is centered in the individual and the individual not only has the right, but he or she is expected to be autonomous from the group—to, in effect, place his or her goals ahead of those in the group (Carter, 1991). This "rugged individualism" or "do-for-self" value is so widespread in the United States, it has become almost synonymous with American culture. But not all cultures in America believe that it is better to become better. Puerto Ricans, Italians, and Greeks, to name a few, do not (Carter, 1991), and, interestingly, some studies of Euro-American college students indicate a movement away from mastery over nature and action value orientations (Carter, 1991).

What is success and what should be emphasized in social relations between people? Typically Euro-Americans believe success occurs somewhere in the future and that success is usually gained through individual effort and will be observable in material gain or achievements (Carter, 1991; Helms, 1991). Few other cultures put as much emphasis on the value of delayed gratification or material well-being that white middle-class Americans do. For other cultures, either traditional customs or the activities and events of the present are of central importance (Carter, 1991). So, again, the majority of human services college graduates who seek to help individuals, the majority whom are from a different culture, must be very careful to accept a different cultural response to success and achievement (Pinderhughes, 1989).

To summarize this section, a human services worker who has graduated from college has learned how to function successfully within the mainstream value culture of this country. Specifically, they have been encultured by others who believe in rugged individualism, delayed gratification, material success, personal effort and responsibility, and the basic goodness of human nature. Because a human services worker has negotiated the educational system, they can assist in educating clients about American culture and work habits so that clients may also become multicultural.

The helper's self-knowledge can also prevent possible misunderstandings in interpersonal communication.

Still and all, there is no way to simplify cross-cultural diversity. As Pinderhughes (1989) lists, there are at least fourteen different sources of cultural differences between people. When within-group differences are added, as in immigrant second and third generation groups, the problem of gaining knowledge of any single culture is impossible. The best students can do to meet the challenges inherent in cross-cultural helping is to know their own culture, to stay open and accepting of other cultures, and to keep an eye on what "works" in the dominant or mainstream culture. C. Gilbert Wrenn (1987), a longtime researcher in cross-culture counseling and therapy, suggests: (1) read positive long-range-thinking scholars who talk about the spiritual as well as the beautiful; (2) unlearn something everyday to make way for change; (3) trust that there is a light at the end of the tunnel; (4) risk acceptance and validation of another's experience. The latter point is important to the next section—kinds of caring.

KINDS OF CARING

Textbooks in human services usually emphasize one-on-one talking, or group talking as the most frequently used helping interventions. Sometimes the skills of brokering, advocacy, outreach, and community organizing are also added (Schmolling, Youkeles, and Burger, 1992; Okun, 1992; Shulman, 1982). There are other ways of intervening with clients. Madeleine M. Leininger (1987) persuasively argues for *transcultural caring* as an innovative and essential approach to helping people "live and survive in diverse and changing contexts" (p. 107). Leininger (1987) believes that helpers must learn what "cultural-care" behaviors are accepted by helpees before "real care" or service can be given. Other researchers have highlighted culturally specific interventions, too. What follows are summary findings from Leininger (1987); McGowan (1988); Vontress (1991); Prince (1980); Tseng and McDermott (1981) about kinds of caring in different cultures. The summaries are not meant to be exhaustive but rather to provide evidence of the diversity of helping methods.

Leininger (1987), from a study of thirty-five cultures, determined forty-two different ideas about caring for others. Those on the list which are usually taught in human services classes, are trust, understanding, empathy, listening, and respect. But there were others current education does not suggest as appropriate to American culture: touching, loving, succoring, protecting, and sharing (Leininger, 1987). Whether there are universal or elements basic to all cultures has not been determined because the problem of helping is complex, and there is often a very hazy boundary between psychological and physical problems (Prince, 1980). Methods are made more complicated, too, because some cultures believe psychological suffering is a fact of living to be accepted rather than an idiosyncratic personality outlook that can be changed (Prince, 1980).

Aside from these qualities and purposes of helping, each culture has a characteristic stance on who can effectively do the helping. In many cultures only an expert can be a "healer." This point of view is true of mainstream American culture—our experts being those who have managed to successfully complete a number of years of post-secondary education. In Africa, as Vontress (1991) writes, the healing specialists include the Herbalist, the Fetish Man, the Medium (usually women who are able to transmit messages from the dead to the living), the Sorcerer (usually one who can do evil), and the Healers, (perhaps an equivalent to our generalists). Although different from our experts, experts nonetheless.

In other cultures the community, using traditional rituals, acts in a collateral fashion with individuals to relieve their suffering. McGowan (1988) presents the effectiveness of a community center providing preventive service programs for Puerto Ricans in a Brooklyn, New York neighborhood. In effect, the program provided sociotherapy in that it maintained over a dozen programs for at-risk families—programs that included an after school drop-in, a thrift shop, a mother's group, an advocacy clinic, an employment service, and a foster grandparent program. Clearly for Puerto Ricans being with members of their community is important for healing. Another study (Leininger, 1987) found family sharing was a particularly important ingredient in helping for the Vietnamese, Philippine Americans, and Mexican Americans. Ethnotherapy is another within-group treatment used by various cultural groups to explore and understand personal identity (Klein, 1976).

A final method of helping or caring, one form of which is currently sweeping the United States through twelve-step programs, is the use of self-healing methods. Aron (1992) describes *testimonio* or testimony as a therapeutic tool in the treatment of people who have suffered psychological trauma. This method is not unlike the "qualification" at a twelve-step recovery meeting. There are other examples of self-healing techniques: prolonged sleep or social isolation found in Weir Mitchell's "rest cure," and the Japanese Morita treatment (Prince, 1980; Tseng and McDermott, 1981). Autogenic training, a form of self-hypnosis, is also practiced in Germany (Prince, 1980; Tseng and McDermott, 1981).

In summary, the challenges of cultural diversity in human services include not only the differences in beliefs, attitudes, and customs between and within cultures, but also about who can help and how that help can be carried out. Clearly the combinations are infinite so that any beginning professional might think working with other than one's own culture is impossible. It isn't if the helping professional is accepting and open to others and has the knowledge found in the next section.

TABLE 26.1   Value Emphases—Four Major Cultural Groups

	Value Authority	Value Extended Family Relationships	Value Personal Independence	Value Nature	Prefer Expert as Helper
Asian Americans (Includes individuals of island or mainland descent who understand Mandarin or Cantonese dialects)	H*	H	L	M	L
Black Americans (Includes individuals who identify with Caribbean or African origins)	H	H	H	M	H
Euro-Americans (Those individuals who would identify themselves as Caucasian or White or of European descent)	L	L	H	M	H
Hispanic Americans (Those individuals who speak or understand Spanish or a variant dialect)	M	H	M	M	M

*Legend: H = high value or emphasis; M = some emphasis; L= low value or little emphasis

AMERICAN HUMAN SERVICES PROFESSIONALS

Service professionals who are immigrants or first generation Americans, especially if they are fluent in a language other than English, clearly have an "edge" in working within the culture in which they have their origins. The edge is linguistic. This is not to suggest that anyone who speaks Spanish is going to be a "better" helper to the Hispanic client population. Indeed, if the helper is Mexican American, she or he may have no point of reference, other than a brand of Spanish, with an Argentinean or Cuban client.

The question remains—can an American-trained human services entry-level professional, regardless of cultural background, work with diverse cultural groups? Clinicians answer "yes" if that helper understands he or she is an agent of Euro-American culture and thus a helper, who by definition has power (Pinderhughes, 1989; Carter, 1991). While it is important not to be "culturally encapsulated" (Pedersen, 1976), it is imperative to have specific knowledge of dominant American values (Carter, 1991). For Helms (1992), Carter (1991), and Pinderhughes (1989) that knowledge involves knowing history affects how our institutions operate, and that American history is a history of racial-cultural inequalities. Racism, sexism, ageism, and heterosexism operate unconsciously so helpers must work to stay open, flexible, and empathic. Central to all "isms" is power and the underlying "better-than" or "less-than" dynamic between helper and helpee that is implicit or inherent to American values. Americans believe in power, in influence, and in the "better-than" ability of the expert. While mainstream American culture does not value authority, we paradoxically give power to our "experts."

Thus, power exists with powerlessness; dominance with subservience; control with helplessness; and capability with incompetence. Dangerous autonyms, but ones which those who seek help often carry within them. In effect, as Pinderhughes (1989) suggests, those who are without

status or power in American culture often identify with the aggressor and feel doubly victimized. In other words, the "have-nots" not only don't have, but they also hate themselves (thereby believing they deserve what they get) for not having. Thus helpers, by recognizing that power is built into a helping experience, can speak the unspeakable (Rubens and White, 1992) and clarify the needs and expectations of those interacting. That, by the way, includes the helper's needs and expectations of the client as well. In short, helpers must diminish their own defensiveness (Pedersen, 1988) and monitor and manage their own feelings, perceptions, and attitudes (Pinderhughes, 1989). As helpers we must realize we have power and be willing to acknowledge what we know and can do and what we don't know and can't do.

As Pinderhughes (1989) further suggests, helpers need to believe that all people need to feel positive about their cultural identity and that it is the responsibility of the helper to demonstrate mutuality, self-respect, and other respect in the helping relationship. Helpers need to allow clients the opportunity to exercise choice, to collaborate in treatment goals, and in treatment methods. And given that all people in America live in culturally diverse communities, it is important that the helper help all clients become multicultural. Learning to live harmoniously and with self-expression, both within a culture and with others of another culture, are the great rewards and challenges of living in a democratic republic.

SUMMARY

Human services workers face the challenges of cross-cultural social service work. Cultural diversity demands an understanding of possible value differences in world view, in who can be a helper, and how helping is experienced. The human services worker needs to be fully aware and culturally sensitive to self, other, and the helping relationship's interpersonal variables.

REFERENCES

Aron, A., (1991). "Testimonio, a Bridge between Psychotherapy and Sociotherapy." In E. Cole, E.D. Rothblum, and O.M. Espin, eds., *Refugee Women and Their Mental Health Vol. 2, Women and Therapy* 13, 173–189.

Baruth, L.G. and M.L. Manning, (1991). *Multicultural Counseling and Psychotherapy: A Life Span Perspective.* New York: Macmillan.

Carter, R.T., (1991). "Cultural Values: A Review of Empirical Research and Implications for Counseling." *Journal of Counseling and Development* 70, 164–173.

Helms, J.E., (1992). *A Race Is a Nice Thing to Have.* Topeka, KA: Content Communications.

Klein, J., (1976). "Ethnotherapy with Jews." *International Journal of Mental Health* 5(2), 26–38.

Leininger, M.M., (1987). "Transcultural Caring: A Different Way to Help People." In P. Pedersen, ed., *Handbook of Cross-Cultural Counseling and Therapy.* New York: Praeger, pp. 107–115.

McGowan, B.G., (1988). "Helping Puerto Rican Families at Risk: Responsive Use of Time, Space, and Relationships," In C. Jacobs and D.D. Bowles, eds., *Ethnicity and Race: Critical Concepts in Social Work.* Silver Springs, MD: National Association of Social Workers, Inc., pp. 48–66.

Okun, B.F., (1992). *Effective Helping: Interviewing and Counseling Techniques,* 4th ed. Pacific Gross, CA: Brooks/Cole.

Papajohn, J. and J. Spiegel, (1975). *Transactions in Families.* San Francisco, CA: Jossey-Bass.

Pear, J., (December 4, 1992). "Population Growth Outstrips Earlier U.S. Census Estimates." *The New York Times,* pp. A1, D18.

Pedersen, P., (1976). "The Field of Intercultural Counseling." In P. Pedersen, W.J. Lonner, and J.G. Draguns, eds., *Counseling Across Cultures.* Honolulu: The University Press of Hawaii, pp. 17–42.

Pedersen, P., (1988). *A Handbook for Developing Multicultural Awareness.* Alexandria, VA: AACD.

Pinderhughes, E., (1989). *Understanding Race, Ethnicity, and Power.* New York: Macmillan.

Prince, R., (1980). "Variations in Psychotherapeutic Procedures." In H. Triandis and J.G. Durgens, eds., *Psychopathology, Vol. 6: Handbook of Cross-Cultural Psychology.* Boston: Allyn and Bacon, pp. 291–349.

Ruebens, P. and J. White, (1992). "Speaking the Unspeakable: Race, Class, and Ethnicity: Differences within the Treatment Setting." Women's Therapy Centre Institute Workshop, October 24.

Sarbaugh, L.E., (1988). *Intercultural Communication.* New Brunswick: Transaction Books.

Schmolling, P. Jr., M. Yonkeles, and W.R. Burger, (1992). *Human Services in Contemporary America.* Monterey, CA: Brooks/Cole.

Shulman, E.D., (1982). *Intervention in the Human Services* 3rd ed. St. Louis: C.V. Mosby.

Speight, S.L., L.J. Myers, C.I. Cox, and P.S. Highlen, (1991). "A Redefinition of Multicultural Counseling." *Journal of Counseling and Development* 70, 29–36.

Tseng, W. and J.F. McDermott, Jr., (1981). *Culture, Mind, and Therapy.* New York: Brunner/Mazel.

U.S. Department of Commerce, (1991). *Statistical Abstract of United States, 1991.* Washington, DC: National Data Book.

Vontress, C.E., (1991). "Traditional Healing in Africa: Implications for Cross-Cultural Counseling." *Journal of Counseling and Development* 70, 242–249.

Wrenn, C.G., (1987). "Afterword: The Culturally Encapsulated Counselor Revisited." In P. Pedersen, ed., *Handbook of Cross-Cultural Counseling and Therapy.* New York: Praeger, pp. 323–329.

CHAPTER 27

INTERNATIONAL EDUCATION IN HUMAN SERVICES

DENNIS B. COGAN

INTRODUCTION

International studies are relevant to those who work in the field of human services for three fundamental reasons. The first is that the United States has become home to a people with a great deal of cultural diversity. The number of different ethnic groups in the United States with a significant population has grown tremendously in the last fifty years. Ethnic groups that Americans had never heard of twenty years ago have become next-door neighbors. International studies can help us appreciate more fully the richness of other cultures. And as a result, we can recognize the richness of our own culture.

The second reason for international studies is that we are now living in a global world. We have left the industrial society and have moved into a high-technological society. The ease of transportation and advances in all phases of communications technology are making the world more like one instead of many. It might be said that the age of technology and communications has shrunk our planet. We now compete in business with corporations from around the world, along with other countries we provide humanitarian assistance in feeding many parts of the world, we intervene in international political decision making, we assist any place in the world that a natural disaster occurs, and there is more evidence that international law will one day govern much more of our lives than is currently the case.

The third reason for the relevance of international studies is that the world has become a very complex place to live. We literally cannot get along without each other. Just as each of us has to rely on experts (accountants, builders, nutritionist, etc.) to keep up with all the changes that effect our daily life, countries are having to do the same. Countries are facing demands to remain competitive and to keep up with technology that improves the quality of life of its citizens but are finding it increasingly difficult to do this on their own. Even the United States, with all of its resources, is finding that it does not have the resources to be first in all areas. As resources dwindle, countries will have to work together and will have to share their discoveries with other countries (Griffin and Spence, p. 6).

RELEVANCE FOR HUMAN SERVICES

Because the United States has become home to people of tremendous cultural diversity (Baruth and Manning, p. 348), it is important that we understand the clients to whom we will be providing services. People from Asia, the Middle East, Africa, Latin America, and other parts of the world bring culturally-based life experiences that influence their ability to understand and effectively utilize the social, health, and educational systems that exist in the United States (Brislin, p. 18). For many, some of the services offered in the United States were not part of their experience or were unavailable in their country. For others, the services were available, but were designed differently (but culturally appropriate) because of the cultural context in which they were offered (Baruth and Manning, p. 350).

Most of those who graduate from a university/college program in the United States will end up working in the United States. Graduates who have been trained to work with people in a social, health, and/or educational setting will work with or provide services to a multicultural population. A few graduates will also work outside the United States, for agencies like the Peace Corps, Red Cross, or newly developed international agencies. For all of the above reasons, it is important that students have an appreciation and understanding of the diversity of the cultures they will encounter when they assume professional positions.

Segall (1979, p. 22) points out that due to the richness of resources available in this country in the area of psychology, most of the research and the publications are done in the United States. I suspect that this is true in many other areas of the human services. The fact that so much research is going on in the United States and so much information is available is the positive part. But, Segall goes on to caution that we not lose sight of the fact that there are differences in cultures. And if the majority of resources are U.S. based, and ethnically Western, the possibility of losing sight of the cultural differences that exist become greater. And because of the ease of access we are fortunate enough to have to all these resources, we can become lazy and miss out on all the discoveries taking place elsewhere in the world.

Professional organizations have become more aware of the need to provide students with training to work with people of differing backgrounds. At the Vail Conference in 1973, the American Psychological Association stated that it was unethical to those not competent in understanding people with culturally different backgrounds to provide services to such groups. Many human services professional organizations include in their ethical standards the recognition of the uniqueness of each individual, and instruct their members to respect the worth and dignity of the individuals with whom they work. Multicultural counseling also has the support of NCATE (National Council for the Accreditation of Teacher Education), and CACREP (Council for the Accreditation of Counseling and Related Education Programs) (Baruth and Manning, p. 330).

Now there is a body of knowledge available that supports cross-cultural efforts in the social, health, and education disciplines (Reid, p. vii). Developments in technology and new methods of interventions are easily accessible, transferable, and lend themselves to shared participation. The Israeli model of crisis intervention is currently used in many facilities throughout the United States. The Center for Disease Control monitors and compares current health concerns in many parts of the world, and then shares this information internationally. Education programs like the Montessori program from England have been adopted by many schools in the United States. Each country has unique problems and situations that require culturally relevant interventions for their remediation. By these countries sharing the results of their treatment approaches with professionals in other countries, students and professionals may gain insight into alternative methods for problem solving in their home country.

Through international studies, we can begin to understand all people better. For instance, we can see that in a country rich in resources, like the United States, academic achievement (wisdom/intelligence) is often equated with literacy. We sometimes assume a superior attitude when we negatively evaluate underdeveloped countries where the literacy rate is much lower. By developing a better understanding of other countries and other cultures, we might discover that, where access to schools is limited, wisdom is evaluated differently. In some countries it might be related to age and the ability to make wise choices for one's life circumstances (Griffin and Spence, p. v).

The United States has a long history of cooperative ventures with other countries. The major impetus for the development of international education came after World War II, when universities realized that international awareness was important (Backman, p. 1). In addition, the general public began to take an interest in foreign affairs, and the government entered into contracts with universities for developmental assistance.

There has also been a growing awareness that the transfer of knowledge and experience from one country to another can be successful. Knowledge can be shared that enhances the quality of services provided, and the sharing of this knowledge increases the competence of the professional staff. Past efforts have shown to be of general benefit to all countries involved.

CHAPTER OVERVIEW

In this chapter, I will discuss the contribution that can be made to human services education through international studies. I will look at what can be learned about human services from an international perspective and how the information gleaned can be applied and made relevant in the context of the work we perform here in the United States. In addition, I will briefly discuss the most traditional approaches to international studies. These will include: (1) international studies, (2) study-abroad programs, international research, (3) cooperative research programs and international exchange agreements, (4) faculty exchange programs, and (5) area studies and foreign languages programs.

In this first section I want to answer the question of how the study of human services in some faraway place can be of value to the practice of human services in the United States. With all that is going on in human services in the United States, it would hardly seem necessary to look at what is happening overseas. There is hardly enough time to understand all that is happening right here.

But, please consider the possibility that maybe, just maybe, by examining what is happening overseas we can better understand what it is we are dealing with here. Maybe by better understanding what is happening overseas, we can find new solutions to assist us in our efforts here. Maybe by understanding what is effective with people living in another culture outside the United States, we can learn what would be effective with people from that culture who live in the United States. Though it may sound strange, maybe by finding out what is not a problem overseas, we can learn something about what is happening in the United States. If we have a problem and it does not exist in another country, can that help us isolate the variable in our country that is responsible for the problem here?

On the other hand, maybe all that I mentioned in the previous paragraph is true in the reverse. Maybe we have something to contribute to other countries by sharing what we have discovered here. In 1991 (Jerusalem Post, p. 12) a group of thirty individuals from public housing projects in Chicago went to Israel to live on a Kibbutz to see if anything learned from rural communal living could be applied to urban projects full of crime and drugs.

Maybe by being involved with the international aspects of humans services, we can help another country cope with their problems through a transfer of information on what has worked in the United States under similar circumstances. A lot of "maybes," but a lot of possibilities for mutual assistance toward improving the world conditions.

INTERNATIONAL STUDIES: A CASE STUDY

So what is it that we can learn through our involvement in international studies? The following case study will help to answer this question. I worked with a student who was interested in family planning. I was interested in human service issues in the Middle East. We agreed on a joint research project of interest to both of us. By means of a literature review, we agreed to an in-depth study on family planning in the Middle East. By each of us getting something out of the project, we would both stay interested in the topic and would each encourage the other in our efforts to move forward on the task at hand.

We already had the basic information on family planning programs in the United States from earlier work that had been completed. We knew that family planning in the United States was initially established in the 1920s by Margaret Sanger with the goal of saving women's lives. We knew that current estimates from throughout the world show that 500,000 women die annually from pregnancy related causes. Ninety-nine percent of these deaths are in the developing countries.

The Middle East includes twenty countries, mostly third world developing nations whose names many people have never heard. We included in this geographic area of study (in alphabetical order) Algeria, Bahrain, Egypt, Iran, Iraq, Israel, Jordan, Kuwait, Lebanon, Libya, Oman, Qatar, Saudi Arabia, Sudan, Syria, Tunisia, Turkey, the United Arab Emirates, the Yemen Arab Republic, and the Yemen People's Democratic Republic.

Together we designed a plan of study which included a review of the literature, as well as contacting as many international agencies, centers, institutes, embassies, and foreign universities as we felt was reasonable within our working time frame. The end product would be a written report of our findings that could be presented at professional conferences and a possible article for publication. So in addition to enhancing our expertise in family planning (the student's primary goal) and for learning more about how Middle Eastern countries (my primary goal) deal with this issue of health/mental health, we would get some professional (résumé) mileage out of the project.

We found more than sixty articles that were published in English as a result of the literature review. The review of the literature included a review of Psychological Abstracts, Sociological Abstracts, Education Abstracts, and Medline. As a result of the literature review, we identified various worldwide agencies/organizations that dealt with various aspects of the topic in which we were interested. We wrote to these agencies/organizations and received additional information from International Planned Parenthood Association, and the World Health Organization. Materials received from consular offices were too general to be useful for a technical research project.

What did we discover by looking at family planning in the Middle East that might be useful for human service professionals studying, working, or teaching in the United States? We learned that:

1. There are efforts going on in Middle Eastern countries, to varying degrees, to encourage family planning.

2. As the level of education increases, the success of family planning increases.

3. Where there is a strong fundamental religious foundation, in this case it was primarily Islam and Judaism, family planning is viewed with a great deal of caution.

4. In Middle Eastern countries, as the level of male dominance/control increased, family planning was less successful.

5. In Middle Eastern countries where women have increased social status and higher education, family planning was more successful.

6. The family's financial situation and the national economy of the country have an impact on family planning. We learned that the reverse was also true. Better family planning had a positive impact on the financial resources of the family and the economy of the nation as a whole.

7. Family planning is a major issue in the overall health of the population of a country.

8. Birth spacing is important in maintaining the health of the mother.

9. When a mother breast fed each child for the maximum appropriate time, the health of both the mother and the new born was significantly affected in a positive sense.

10. When religious leaders support the concept of family planning, family planning is more successful.

11. Where there is poverty and a low level of general health care, family planning is emphasized less.

12. In Middle Eastern countries the circumstances under which an abortion, as a means for birth control, is approved is largely determined by religious laws.

13. Where there is a higher use of contraceptives as a means for birth control, there appears to be a higher number of abortions.

14. Religion plays a significant role in the choice of contraceptive devices or birth control methods used.

15. In Middle Eastern countries where there is a high infant mortality rate, there appears to be a desire to replace the lost child with another.

16. Government policies are a major determiner for or against family planning.

17. There is widespread cultural encouragement of early marriages in many Middle Eastern countries which works contrary to family planning.

18. There is a cultural prestige in many of these countries for women to have large numbers of male children.

19. In many Middle Eastern countries, children are seen as an important and necessary part of the labor force.

HOW CAN THIS BE OF USE TO HUMAN SERVICE PROFESSIONALS?

Keep in mind that this was one study, from one part of the world. But I believe much was gained that is of value to human service professionals teaching, studying, and working in the United States.

1. Because the United States is becoming home to people of tremendous cultural diversity, we are better able to understand what influences their acceptance or reluctance to utilize family planning methods.

2. We can see that there are common problems in communities where there is poor family planning. We see that poor family planning negatively affects the health of mother and child, and we can see that there is a relationship between the birth mortality rate and poor family planning.

3. We can see that economics, education, and poor health care are contributing factors to the problems that come from lack of family planning.

4. We can see that religion is a significant factor in acceptance of family planning in fundamentalist religious communities. This becomes even more significant in the United States where fundamental religious beliefs are increasing.

5. We found that in societies where there is a higher level of male dominance/control, family planning is less successful. We might want to develop programs that are designed to work with educating the males instead of the female.

6. If the finances of the family and the economy of the nation are negatively affected by poor family planning, political advocacy programs might be developed to increase support for family planning.

7. Because overall health of the mother and the infant is affected by birth spacing, and poor health of either is an additional financial burden on any country, programs to encourage mothers to nurse their infants might be increased.

8. If we know that family planning programs are more effective in fundamental religious communities when they are supported by religious leaders, programs that include religious leaders where appropriate might be developed.

9. We learned that poor health conditions and poverty are related. We know that under these conditions family planning is emphasized less. And where there is poor family planning, there is a greater drain on the economy. Governments have to be shown that programs have to be developed that will improve family planning and will, over the long run, save money.

10. If the circumstances under which family planning techniques are utilized are largely determined by religious laws, it is important for human service workers to see if religion determines access to other human services.

11. If religion plays a significant role in the choice of contraceptive devices or methods of birth control, government support for these programs should consider whether the methods being developed are going to be culturally acceptable before investing the money into these programs.

12. If some cultures encourage early marriages which lead to a high birth rate, then hospitals in this country and organizations like Planned Parenthood that work with people from these cultural groups must revise their education programs to incorporate this information if they are to be successful.

13. From what we learned from the program instituted in the Sudan, we might develop similar programs in the United States. To reduce the burgeoning population in the Sudan, midwives were trained and then worked in conjunction with an Islamic scholar. They went into the village to assure the local population that certain family planning techniques were consistent with the teachings of the Koran. A follow-up study twelve months later showed that the use of contraceptives increased from ten percent to twenty-six percent.

14. We can see that developing the role of advocate may become a significant role for human services workers. In some cases, human services workers will not be allowed to do what they are trained for without human service advocates paving the way.

15. From what was learned from the literature review of the Middle East, we might put more efforts into prevention (education), and less into treatment, as a means for effectively dealing with some human service concerns.

16. As a result of this study, we can see that under certain conditions, where there is a significant number of specific culture, it might be more effective to go into the local community than to develop general policies on a national level. We might want to reexamine the concept of community intervention that was used in the 1960s as a means for treating some of the problems that we face today.

APPROACHES TO INTERNATIONAL STUDIES

We need to recognize that the world is a much smaller place than it was thirty years ago, or even ten years ago. With the demise of the Soviet Union, the freeing of Eastern Europe, the peace talks in the Middle East, and the need for cooperative economic ties with countries all over the world, we would be doing a disservice to our students and to ourselves if we were not prepared to function in a world community.

In this section, I will briefly describe the most typical approaches to international studies. These include: (1) international studies, (2) study-abroad programs, international research, (3) cooperative research programs and international exchange agreements, (4) faculty exchange programs, and (5) area studies and foreign languages programs.

INTERNATIONAL STUDIES AND RESEARCH IN HUMAN SERVICES

International studies and research in human services can be done in your local community. Like any other research problem, whether you are dealing with a developmental issue, a mental health problem, or a specific group of people (age, handicapping condition, etc.), you utilize traditional approaches to your study as if you were not involved in an international question. You collect your information by going to the library, doing case studies, or conducting a field survey.

This approach can be built into any existing program of study or course structure. Faculty could include classroom assignments or projects, or guest lecturers and field visits. The approach could also be handled as special readings, independent study, or as an honors project.

What is different from the traditional assignment is that the student through his/her work is introduced and utilizes international literature as the basis for the study or research project. After the information is collected, it can be compared to traditional approaches taken in the United States. The information gathered can be written or presented in a format designed to increase the student's multicultural sensitivity.

With the continued growth of minority populations in the United States, the recognition of the importance of multicultural counseling has become more important. There are texts on multicultural counseling (Dillard, 1987; Pedersen, Lonner, and Draguns, 1976), multicultural counseling from a developmental perspective (Baruth and Manning, 1991), transcultural counseling (Walz and Benjamin, 1978), and issues of special concern to minorities (Smith et. al., 1978).

If we become familiar with alternative approaches to treatments, new methods of research, and the theoretical literature from other countries and cultures we may be able to identify innovations that apply to the work we are doing in the United States. By understanding the cultural influences that affect the delivery of services in other cultures, we might be able to gain valuable knowledge that applies to the treatment of multicultural populations in the United States. We may also gain insight into alternative methods for problem solutions at home.

STUDY-ABROAD PROGRAMS, INTERNATIONAL RESEARCH

Unlike international studies and research, study-abroad programs are not accomplished in the local community; and the study-abroad programs require overseas travel. But like any other interest the student may have for developing his/her level of professional expertise, study-abroad programs can be designed with a focus on a particular human service concern or on a particular cultural group. These programs can be designed to increase the students understanding of human service issues that are of local concern (alcoholism, crisis intervention, child development, or a growing minority population in the local community).

For years there have been study-abroad programs and exchange programs for students who majored in foreign languages, the arts, literature, and more recently business. More than a million international exchanges take place annually (Reid, p. vii). The number of U.S. students who are participating in study-abroad programs has been increasing for the past ten years (Carlson et. al., p. xi). More than 200,000 foreign students enrolled in U.S. colleges and universities in 1978 (Mehlinger et. al., p. 10), and it is estimated that 60,000 U.S. undergraduate students study abroad annually (Franz and Hernandez, p. 32). Studying overseas is no longer limited to the privileged few who can afford to travel to some exotic land (Arndt, p. 9).

Study-abroad programs are designed to provide students with a first-hand experience in the subject area studied. The student is able to travel and experience another culture while studying in the field of their choice. For the field of human services, the study-abroad program is a relatively new innovation. Because of the number of new immigrants coming to the United States and the important globally dependent relations that are developing, we can no longer maintain a parochial attitude toward the value of international education.

Human service programs could join other disciplines already involved in the movement toward a global approach to education (Brungardt, p. 88). Being sensitive to cultural issues increases the individual's ability to make effective decisions in a multicultural society (Pedersen, p. 3). A study abroad program in human services can provide the students with a comparative background in multicultural issues in the field. The study-abroad program is designed for students to be exposed to the types of problems experienced by individuals of different cultures, how these problems are dealt with in their native country, and how to understand how other countries deal with similar types of people issues found in the United States. The study-abroad program can be designed to expose students in a focused and systematic manner to the

unique aspects of how human services are defined, funded, and provided for in other countries.

The following definition might be used as the broad goals for any study-abroad program.

Because the United States is becoming home to people of tremendous cultural diversity, each of these cultures brings with them their own way of functioning within a socioeconomic-political system. The majority of the employers of graduates of university programs will work in a multicultural setting. This program will assist students in developing an appreciation and understanding of the diversity of cultures they will encounter when they assume professional positions in the field. This program will assist students in becoming aware of their own cultural biases. And by learning about the knowledge base developed by other cultures and methods of the application of that knowledge with professionals from other countries/cultures, students will gain insight into alternative methods for problem solution at home (Brungardt, p. 88).

More specific objectives can be developed to meet the needs of the individual student. The objectives can be designed to be comparative to the United States or another country, or they can focus on specializations that are already offered in your local program (substance abuse, mental retardation, severely emotionally disturbed, etc.).

The world is getting smaller, and we all have to learn to relate to people from other countries and other cultures. A program like this brings recognition to your college. This forum provides opportunities to develop international cooperative research or exchange programs. Opportunities become available for funded projects. And finally, if the goal of the academic institution is a place for the students to learn and develop their character, the study-abroad program serves to enhance all aspects of the individual.

The study-abroad program can enrich the students' personal development, and contribute significantly to their knowledge of other cultures. The experience of traveling and/or living abroad enhances the understanding for other people and cultures. The potential is there for students to increase their self-confidence by dealing with the challenges of travel abroad. On a practical level, students should be more competitive in seeking employment after graduation.

COOPERATIVE RESEARCH AND INTERNATIONAL EXCHANGE AGREEMENTS

Cooperative research can be done in the local community, or in a community in another country. Though it does not require travel, travel typically facilitates the cooperative efforts, especially in the initial phases of the project. Because these projects require official agreements between two or more institutions, and between two or more countries, they are typically more faculty directed. However, it is not uncommon for students to be involved in all phases of the research and/or studies.

Selecting an area for study is a little more involved because it needs to be of mutual interest and benefit to both parties involved, who typically live in two different geographic locations. Identifying the area of study requires agreements that are mutually beneficial to both parties who may live in different locations. Again, students typically do not have to be concerned with whether or not a problem they are interested in exploring exists in another country, because the likelihood is that most countries experience similar types of problems. Often the research will be comparative in nature and will focus on process and resources, government policies, or causative factors and treatments.

International exchanges almost always require some overseas travel. These exchanges may be initiated separately or developed as a result of the cooperative research program. There can be student exchanges or faculty exchanges. Both parties can travel at the same time exchanging positions for a specified time frame, or each can take turns traveling while the other hosts the traveler. In both cases, the person who is visiting the other country is typically there to share his/her special expertise with the professionals and students in the country being visited.

The final three programs, faculty exchanges, area studies, and foreign language programs, will only be briefly described in this chapter. While they are beneficial, they do not have as direct a focus on the human services as the programs already discussed. Though they do not contribute specifically to the human services, they do have the potential to add significantly to the multicultural awareness component. They can be adapted to the focus of culturally common human services needs, training, interventions, or delivery systems.

FACULTY EXCHANGE PROGRAMS

Faculty exchange programs are designed to bring faculty members from another institution who have special expertise in a culture, topic, or content area to contribute to the local academic program. This could be a faculty member from another U.S. institution (national exchange), or a faculty member from another country (international exchange).

For example, faculty members within the U.S. with expertise in working with a particular population in their local community might be invited to another community with a large similar population, but limited resources regarding this population. The faculty members could also be from an overseas country, of the culture being studied locally (U.S.), and are coming to the U.S. to study our methods of treatment. They could share their expertise as to how their country deals with similar concerns.

Having firsthand information from an outside expert has the potential to enrich the student's educational experience. Having an outside expert also contributes to the development of the student's level of expertise. If the exchange faculty is from the culture being studied, the students have an opportunity to interact directly with the exchange faculty member and receive feedback from that interaction.

AREA STUDIES AND FOREIGN LANGUAGE PROGRAMS

These are traditional programs that colleges and universities have offered for years. They are for the most part done locally, but may have an overseas component as an option (few make it mandatory).

The area studies programs usually involve several countries in a particular geographic region. It may be Latin American studies, African studies, Middle Eastern, or European studies. Area studies are typically interdisciplinary and, in the past, have traditionally involved the disciplines of economics, political science, history, geography, and literature. There is no reason why the human services disciplines, and other health related disciplines could not develop an area studies program based on the health and social sciences disciplines. This might include some of the courses offered by disciplines from the arts and sciences, or business college.

The educational rationale for area studies is that students can understand an area better if it is viewed as a whole. Because they study the whole, it is expected that they will have a broader and more thorough understanding. When the students are done with the program, they will have depth and competence in this area and be able to explain changes that are occurring or act as consults on how change might be fostered.

Foreign language programs are self-defined. Students enrolled in these programs develop skills in the language of the country of choice. In addition to learning how to speak another language, students typically are expected to study the history of the countries where language is spoken, and to study the literature of the language. Through this process, students will gain a sensitivity and appreciation for the culture and the people who speak the language.

Today, more than ever, in the U.S. the need for a second language is becoming more important. Some of the clients we serve will not speak English. And yet it is not reasonable to assume that human service workers will have the facility, especially if they work in major metropolitan areas, to speak the languages of all the clients with whom they will work. But, languages can contribute significantly to our sensitivity to other cultures.

THE FUTURE OF INTERNATIONAL EDUCATION

The world community has become a good deal smaller. At one time, long ago, people were rela-tively independent, providing for their own daily needs. Then farm communities developed that encouraged the growth of small communities in which people worked together, and shared in some of the burdens that no individual could handle alone. Eventually the industrial revolution brought people together in the cities. Laws developed to guarantee that so many people living in such close quarters would be able to relate to each other. In the industrialized society, a greater degree of specialization of activities developed, resulting in the need for more cooperation between people and between communities. With the recent developments in high technology, communications, and modes of travel, we have become a world community. Each nation is becoming more dependent on the advances made by all other nations to improve the quality of life locally.

The future of human service education, like the future of other aspects of society, are going to demand sharing on an international level. This is not going to be an easy task. There are many factors that have historically tended to inhibit a cooperative approach. One of the first is the difficulty of many languages. Language is affected by culture and history. Culturally the nonverbal language communicated through body posture, timing, and distance can determine whether the communications were positive or negative. Historically, conflicts that have existed for a thousand years or more are carried forward in language.

Another factor is the differences that exist in the level of technological sophistication. The gap in this area seems to be widening. Economic differences between countries form another barrier to cooperation. The people who have, and those who do not have, develop attitudes toward each other that inhibit cooperative relationships. Differences in availability of resources is another consideration. Where there are no resources available for sharing, there is less desire for cooperation. There are also the individual psychological factors or human factors like the need for control and power that present barriers to cooperation. None of these factors are insurmountable, but they need to be considered if we are to move forward in reducing the differences.

On a positive note colleges and universities, not only in the United States but all over the world, must prepare their citizens to have a greater appreciation and understanding of the diverse cultures they will encounter in their everyday interactions at home and abroad.

How can the college/university get beyond the old, and move to a new and more relevant era in education that meets the needs of a movement toward worldwide cooperation? This might include a worldwide interdisciplinary approach to human services.

We are experiencing an "explosion of information," and no one person, no one nation, has the ability to master what is known. By taking a worldwide interdisciplinary approach to this unprecedented proliferation of knowledge, it is possible to develop a usable repository that is available to all through the improved technology of communications. This would include developing a knowledge and skills base that would be relevant for all cultures.

CONCLUSIONS

Colleges and universities that offer human service programs must provide students with information about other cultures. If a student is to graduate and be considered an "educated person," then it is incumbent on the universities to provide the student with knowledge of what is occurring in other countries.

In this chapter, I have presented information in an attempt to demonstrate the relevance of international studies for human service professionals. I have shared various methods of international study programs that can be built into existing curriculum at home, or that can be accomplished through various programs offered abroad. I provided a case example of what could be learned from international research and how it might be applied to similar concerns in the United States.

Human services is the providing of services by a helper to assist a client who is experiencing problems in living. Much of what the helper is able to do is based on the relationship that the helper has with the client. Sensitivity to the client's culture will improve the relationship the helper has with the client. Understanding the client's previous life experiences will assist the helper in providing the client appropriate services.

I hope that this chapter has, in a positive manner, communicated the challenge that we face in the United States by recognizing that we are living in a multicultural community. Internationally and nationally, the United States is made up of, and is part of, a multicultural community. I hope that I have communicated that the United States cannot afford to isolate itself, because knowledge from other countries can help us better relate to the many cultures that reside in the United States, and can help us relate better to the world community.

International studies can be a challenge to all of us. Besides the challenge of becoming part of the world community, I believe that it is a challenge with limitless opportunities from which to learn and grow. If we work together, because none of us has a monopoly on all the answers, we can solve many of the problems we face as a planet. If we work together, and respect the richness of each other's cultures, we can find the keys to many of the existing problems. If we work together, we can learn to respect the richness of each other's cultures, and perhaps have fewer problems to resolve.

REFERENCES

Arndt, R., (1988). "Developing All Its People: The University's Next Challenge." In J. Reid, ed., *Building the Professional Dimension of Educational Exchange* (pp. 9–21). Yarmouth, ME: Intercultural Press.

Backman, E., (1984). *Approaches to International Education.* New York: Macmillan Publishing.

Baruth, L. and M. Manning, (1991). *Multicultural Counseling and Psychotherapy: A Lifespan Perspective.* New York: Macmillan Publishing.

Brislin, R., (1981). *Cross-Cultural Encounters.* New York: Pergamon.

Brungardt, M., (1991). "Global Education and the American Student Abroad." In D. Hill, ed., *Global Edu-*

cation and the Study Abroad Program (pp. 88–94). Worthington, OH: Renaissance Publications.

Carlson, J., B. Burn, J. Useem, and D. Yachimowicz, (1990). *Study Abroad: The Experience of American Undergraduates.* New York: Greenwood Press.

Dillard, J., (1987). *Multicultural Counseling.* Chicago, IL: Nelson-Hall.

Franz, D. and L. Hernandez, eds., *Work, Study, Travel Abroad: The Whole World Handbook* 11th ed., New York: St. Martin's Press.

Griffin, W. and R. Spence, (1970). *Cooperative International Education.* Washington, DC: Association for Supervision and Curriculum Development.

Keinon, H., (November 9, 1991). *The Jerusalem Post International Edition,* N.Y.

Mehlinger, H., H. Hutson, V. Smith and B. Wright, (1979). *Global Studies for American Schools.* Washington, DC: National Education Association.

Pederson, P., W. Lonner, and J. Draguns, (1978). *Counseling Across Cultures.* Honolulu, HI: The University Press of Hawaii.

Pederson, P., (1988). *A Handbook for Developing Multicultural Awareness.* Alexandria, VA: American Association for Counseling and Development.

Reid, J., ed., (1988). *Building the Professional Dimension of Educational Exchange.* Yarmouth, ME: Intercultural Press.

Segall, M., (1979). *Cross-Cultural Psychology: Human Behavior in a Global Perspective.* Monterey, CA: Brooks/Cole Publishing Co.

Smith, W., A. Burlew, M. Mosley, and W. Whitney, (1978). *Minority Issues in Mental Health.* Reading, MA: Addison-Wesley.

Virgulti, V., (1991). "Maintaining Academic Standards: Academic vs. Non-Academic Learning." In D. Hill, ed., *Global Education and the Study Abroad Program* (pp. 95–108). Worthington, OH: Renaissance Publications.

Walz, G. and L. Benjamin, (1978). *Transcultural Counseling: Needs, Programs, and Techniques.* New York: Human Sciences Press.

PARTIAL LIST OF RELEVANT JOURNALS

American Journal of Orthopsychiatry
Association of International Educators
  Newsletter
British Journal of Clinical Psychiatry
Community Mental Health Journal
Comparative Education Review
Contemporary Family Therapy: An International
  Journal
Culture Medicine and Psychiatry
Ethos
International Journal of Addictions
International Journal of Adolescent Medicine and
  Health
International Journal for the Advancement of
  Counselling
International Journal of Family Therapy

International Journal of Partial Hospitalization
International Journal of Psychology
International Journal of Rehabilitation Research
International Social Work
International Studies Newsletter
Israel Journal of Psychiatry and Related Sciences
Israel Social Science Research
Journal of Community Psychology
Journal of Comparative Family Studies
Journal of Cross-Cultural Psychology
Journal of Multicultural Counseling and
  Development
Journal of Psychology and Judaism
Political Psychology
Research in Race and Ethnic Relations
Schizophrenia Bulletin

CHAPTER 28

HUMAN SERVICES IN AUSTRALIA

ROD UNDERWOOD
MICHAEL LEE

BRIEF DESCRIPTION OF AUSTRALIA

History of European Settlement

European settlement of Australia began in earnest after the American War of Independence. Australia was claimed as a British colony by Captain James Cook in 1770 and when the first settlement occurred in 1788 with Captain Arthur Phillip as governor, the task was to establish a penal colony. Further, the British authorities had determined that the colony was to become self-sufficient. This first settlement at Sydney was characterized by hardship and deprivation. Many of the people sent to the colony were convicts given sentences of transportation for seven or fourteen years, and so were unwilling settlers. However, faced with the reality that they could not return to England, they had no option but to make the best of their new life. Thus, unlike the North American colonies, the Australian settlers were mostly reluctant immigrants and would have preferred not to have been in their new land.

At the time of the first settlement, the British government proclaimed the new state to be "Terra Nullius." Under this principle the continent of Australia was regarded as uninhabited, and therefore early settlers were not required, nor expected, to negotiate any treaty or land title with the local indigenous people. It was only in 1992 that the High Court of Australia found that, under common law, some Australian Aboriginal people were entitled to native title of ownership of their tribal land. But the process of European settlement is still regarded as an "invasion" by some of the Aboriginal population.

Much of the present social structure, and particularly social policy, derives from features of the early European colonization. While considerable power resided with the governors in the early settlements in each state, when parliamentary government came to each state it was modeled on the English "Westminster" system. And when the states federated into a commonwealth in 1901, the British system was incorporated into the new parliamentary system with the Prime Minister and members of each house swearing allegiance to the British Crown.

By the mid-nineteenth century, settlement through transportation of criminals had ceased in most parts of Australia. The last contingent of convicts to be sent to an Australian colony from Britain arrived in 1869. After that time, the European settlement of Australia depended upon periodic "waves" of migration that influenced the nature of the emerging society.

The first wave of migration occurred during the 1850s after the discovery of gold. Between 1850 and 1860 the population of Australia increased tenfold. Again, in the 1890s there were further major gold discoveries that attracted migrants from many parts of the world. Other periods of significant migration have followed the 1914–18 War, the Great Depression of the 1930s, and the 1939–45 War. Since the Vietnam War in the 1970s there has been a significant influx of migrants from Southeast Asia.

Features of Australian Population Growth

The National Population Inquiry of 1975 (Borrie, 1975) estimates that at the time of European settlement in 1788 there were approximately 300,000 indigenous people living in Australia. It was not until one hundred years after settlement that more than half of the population could be described as born in Australia. By 1973 when the population had grown to 13.1 million it was estimated that 35 percent of the growth was due to overseas-born people settling in Australia.

Today, the population of Australia is nearly twenty million. While a significant majority of the population is of British descent, it can be said that Australia is increasingly becoming a multi-cultural country. Most of the population lives in the six state capital cities located around the coast. For this reason Australia has been described as the most urbanized of all the continents. In a country that is geographically almost the same size as the U.S.A., there are no more than ten cities with a population of greater than 100,000 people. The interior of Australia remains very sparsely populated. The distribution of the population has a significant influence on the provision of human services at the community level.

THE PROVISION OF HUMAN SERVICES IN AUSTRALIA

In 1901 the separate Australian colonies were federated into the Commonwealth of Australia. The constitutional conferences that preceded the federation spent considerable time on which powers were to be vested in the new federal government and which were to be retained by the states. At that time, forms of local government existed but were not a significant force. Some functions such as national defense and foreign relations were easy to assign to the federal government, while others such as education and the police forces were state responsibilities. Other powers came to be shared. Health and welfare responsibilities are two such areas where there is power sharing. The general principle was that required services should be pro-vided by the states as far as possible. On the other hand, the federal government assumed responsibility where a national policy was required, such as health issues related to immigration.

The decision to vest most taxation powers in the federal government and to limit the types of taxes that can be raised by state and local governments has impacted upon the provision of human services. The federal government collects substantial revenue through income tax and excise taxes which is disbursed to the States for the delivery of services. A variety of consultative mechanisms are used to facilitate the disbursement process. Inevitably there are conflicts and standoffs regarding the nature of disbursement, particularly where there are ideological differences between the two levels of government.

Local government has an important role in providing public health and recreational services in the community. Unlike many other countries, such as the United States and Great Britain, educational services and hospitals are not the responsibility of local government. For a long time local government had only a limited involvement in the provision of human services. In the past twenty years there has been a shift to local government provision from state and federal governments. Increasingly, where the running of facilities and services is becoming locally based with the assistance of community groups, the role of local government is changing. The shift in responsibilities will enable the delivery of human services to be more responsive to community needs.

The history of human services all over the world shows that religious and charitable bodies have played an important part in providing facilities and services in the community for people in need. While these groups remain significant in Australia today, the Non-Government Organization (NGO's) include a third group that have developed since the Second World War, that is the support or special interest groups. Generally, these groups promote community concern about a particular issue such as mental illness, AIDS, or lung diseases contracted by miners. Depending on the focus of the group and the extent of the problem in the community then their activities will range from lobby group to service provider. While there are many positive features about such community groups, such as effective service delivery and responsiveness to community needs, there are also issues such as a lack of coordinated service provision and unreliable funding sources that sometimes limit the valuable contribution of these agencies.

HUMAN SERVICE EDUCATION

People working in the human services in Australia have a wide variety of educational backgrounds, particularly in the nongovernment sector of the field. For example, Learner and Smith (1989) examined the qualifications of those workers providing services for older people, families, and children within agencies. They found that volunteers and personal care workers were generally without formal educational qualifications; most family aides had no qualifications, although some held part of a nursing or welfare studies award; child-care workers generally held a certificate in child care, while nursing staff, youth workers and social workers held a diploma or a degree. Human service administrators had a variety of professional qualifications, including nursing and social work, however very few had formal qualifications in management.

White, Omelczuk, and Underwood (1990) found that out of a sample of 110 youth workers 45 percent had no formal university qualifications; 24 percent had completed a youth work qualification; 6 percent had a degree in social work. The remaining 25 percent of workers had obtained other qualifications in areas such as child-care studies, psychology, residential and community care, and general liberal arts and social science courses. Only those youth workers who were in full-time employment participated in the study. Thus, the many part-time and voluntary workers who contribute so much to the provision of services for young people were not included in the analysis.

A major provider of training and education for the human services sector in Australia are Technical and Further Education (TAFE) colleges.

These colleges would equate most closely with community colleges in the U.S.A. The TAFE colleges maintain contact closely with industry to offer vocationally oriented programs in fields such as working with people with disabilities, child care, and welfare studies. These awards are usually the equivalent of two years full-time study, but may be of shorter duration for some programs. In many cases, students have already found employment in the human service field prior to admission to a TAFE program.

Edith Cowan University in Western Australia offered the first Australian degree program in human services in 1985. The program provided the opportunity for students to focus their studies on areas such as children's studies, habilitation studies, human service management, working with the aged, and youth work. Since that time the number of universities offering a similar program has steadily increased. People entering the human service degree programs come from diverse backgrounds. Just as many people with substantial relevant work experience enter the courses as do young people straight from school. People who have acquired a TAFE human service qualification are encouraged to continue their studies at degree level.

Several years ago the federal government introduced the Training Guarantee Scheme that requires organizations to spend a minimum of 1.5 percent of the annual budget on staff training. While many agencies already were satisfying this requirement, others have had to develop training programs where none had existed in the past. It is too soon to tell whether the Training Guarantee Scheme has been effective in raising the skill level of human service workers.

SERVICES FOR CHILDREN AND YOUNG PEOPLE

Children in Care

Traditionally, day-care services for children in Australia have been provided by the private sector. However, the federal government has become involved in the funding of child care through the

Children's Services Program. This program aims to facilitate workforce participation by women; ensure access to appropriate child care for special-needs groups including Aboriginal, migrant, and disabled children, and the children of sole parents attempting to reenter the workforce; and ensure that child care is affordable for low and moderate income families (Tapper, 1990).

According to Ife (1989, p. 99) "Governments have tended to confine their responsibility in childcare to the more traditional role of child protection that comprises the bulk of government expenditure in childcare." In recent years there has been a good deal of public concern about the apparent increase in the incidence of child abuse. Goldman and Goldman (1988) surveyed a thousand university students about their childhood sexual experiences. They found that 28 percent of the females and 9 percent of the males reported they experienced some form of sexual abuse as children. While these figures are cause for concern, Mathias (1992) urges caution in accepting any estimates of the prevalence of child abuse in Australia for a number of reasons, including the lack of an accepted definition of abuse, the lack of epidemiological research and the different ways in which the data are collected. However, the Goldman and Goldman (1988) findings are consistent with the results of similar studies conducted in North America and Great Britain.

The health and well being of Aboriginal children are cause for national concern. The infant mortality rate is unacceptably high, the incidence of chronic ear disease is a major problem, trachoma continues to cause blindness, nutritional deficiencies and respiratory infections remain far too common among Aboriginal children. Brady (1992) believes that the most effective means of addressing the child health problems of Aborigines is through those programs designed to improve the education and status of women.

Human service workers are to be found providing day-care and out-of-school care services for children; they are employed in residential services and women's refuges; they work in child protection agencies and in facilities for children with disabilities. With the expansion of the federal government's role in the provision of services there is an increasing need for suitably qualified staff in some areas.

Youth in Transition

Human service professionals working with young people in Australia are mostly concerned with the needs of youth after they have left high school and who are working through the process of finding their place in the world. In most of the seven Australian states children are required to complete ten years of formal education, comprising seven years of primary and three years of secondary education. Young people have the option of completing an additional two years of secondary education if they wish to proceed to university or enter the workforce with a higher level of education. In the past decade there has been a significant increase in the number of young people choosing to complete twelve years of formal education—from 36 percent in 1983 to 58 percent in 1988.

Federal government youth policy is strongly focussed on reducing the number of unemployed young people. The current level of unemployment for the sixteen to twenty-five years of age is around the 30 percent mark with significant variations from one community to another. Clearly, this degree of unemployment raises a number of social issues. The response of the federal government has been to increase the educational and training opportunities available to school leavers. The national target is to have 95 percent of nineteen year olds in education or training by the year 2000. Strategies that have been designed to help achieve this target include providing financial incentives to employers willing to take on young workers; creating traineeships in the public sector for unemployed young people; meet the needs of early school leavers, that is, those who leave school after completing Year 10, through programs which link education and training with work; provision of support services to enable school students with disabilities to have the same opportunities as other students; ensuring a greater focus on the needs of young people "at risk" within the school system through the provision of specialized support services and coordinated multiagency responses.

Youth homelessness is becoming a significant social issue in Australia. The number of young homeless people is not easy to estimate. The results of recent studies have suggested as few as 15,000 at any one time (MacKenzie and Chamberlain, 1992) to as many as 70,000 (Fopp, 1989). As is the case in Western countries generally, young homeless people are in the high risk category with regard to sexually transmitted diseases, youth suicide, alcohol and substance abuse, petty criminal activities, and poverty. Even those young people fortunate enough to find employment do not always earn enough to remain above the poverty line. In response to the problem the federal government implemented the Supported Assistance Accommodation Program (SAAP) in 1987. The SAAP program funds places in refuges, hostels, youth housing programs, emergency accommodation in large hostels, and services for families throughout Australia.

The human service worker who chooses to work with young people may become involved in any one of a number of different programs. White, Omelczuk, and Underwood (1991) found that nearly half of all youth workers are engaged in the accommodation field. Other areas of service significantly represented in their survey include community-based juvenile offender programs, recreational drop-in centers, employment assistance, streetwork, health and counselling, the provision of services to special groups such as non-English speaking migrants, and legal aid to young people in trouble. Most workers will be employed in state or federal government funded programs. Grierson (1992) found that slightly more than 10 percent of all youth workers were in nongovernment funded organizations in a survey of youth services in Sydney.

SERVICES FOR PEOPLE WITH DISABILITIES AND THE AGED

People with Intellectual Disabilities

Over the past one hundred years the services provided to people with intellectual disabilities in Australia have reflected the trends current in North America and Europe at the time. Until recently, these people were generally regarded as suffering from some form of mental illness and, hence, were seen to be the responsibility of the state health department. Even today, the distinction between people with an intellectual disability and people who are mentally ill is not widely understood (Indermaur, Underwood and Cockram, 1991). For much of this time the policy of each state has been to provide large institutional facilities into which significant numbers of these people were incarcerated for life.

Cocks (1989) has identified a number of factors that he believes will lead to an enhanced quality of life for people with intellectual disabilities living in Australia. First, there has been a significant movement of parents willing to become actively involved in forming voluntary associations dedicated to the well-being of their children. Typically, these voluntary associations have endeavored to provide services where none previously existed, such as special schools or sheltered workshops, or attempted to improve the quality of available services, such as residential facilities. Second, the growth of the human rights movement in Australia, which has mirrored the U.S. experience, has focussed attention on the needs of disadvantaged people. Cocks believes that the activities of self-advocacy groups are having a positive impact upon the community. A third factor is the legislative and financial support provided by state and federal governments over the past ten years. Legislation, such as the 1986 Federal Disability Services Act, is generally regarded by human service professionals as positively supporting the interests of people with disabilities.

Today, the Australian society recognizes the fact that people with intellectual disabilities have the right to live their lives with all the dignity accorded to anyone else in the community. The concept of normalization, or social role valorization as espoused by Wolfensberger (1972, 1983) has impacted upon the services provided for these people largely through the work of Cocks and his colleagues. The principle of "least restrictive alternative" has been applied by those agencies delivering services to these people. However, Cocks (1989, p. 22) observes that:

The principle stresses the importance of individual choice and this depends very much on resources and options which are available. Many restrictive alternatives such as large institutions are retained because of the lack of resources or, more likely, lack of political and bureaucratic will to change them.

The Federal Department of Human Services and Health, the various state government agencies and the voluntary sector each play a significant role in the provision of services to people with an intellectual disability. Essentially, the role of the federal department is to disburse funds to support the activities of the voluntary sector. The different state agencies are responsible primarily for residential facilities and increasingly, educational opportunities. As mentioned above, the voluntary agencies have been actively involved in provision of alternative residential accommodation, schools, and vocational services.

Most people with an intellectual disability in Australia live at home with their parents or guardians. They have the opportunity to attend school as children and find employment in sheltered workshops or other supported employment programs. The more able people are being accommodated in small home units in the community. They lead full and independent lives through the support of minimal supervisory services. However, an issue that is currently attracting the attention of policy makers is the matter of aging people with intellectual disability. Jackson and Patterson (1993) report that the life span of these people has increased dramatically over the past fifty years and now approximates the general population. They have found that, in comparison to their younger

counterparts, older people are less likely to participate in programs provided by formal service systems and, hence, tend to become socially isolated and live in a more restrictive environment. Policy makers are required to adapt their services to meet the particular needs of these people.

Human service professionals are actively involved in working with people with intellectual disabilities. They may be employed in the large institutional facilities to provide direct care services to the clients, they may be administering services provided by voluntary agencies, or facilitating the activities of self-advocacy groups.

People with Mental Health Problems

For some years there has been an Australia-wide trend to close hospitals that have catered only to mentally disturbed patients and to provide services for these people in major general hospitals. The care of people with mental health problems in hospitals and government-funded community services is the responsibility of psychiatrists, mental health nurses, and other health professionals. Increasingly, however, human service workers are involved in the delivery of services provided by voluntary agencies in community settings.

A national policy on the delivery and management of mental health services was announced by the Federal Government in 1992. Key elements of the National Mental Health Plan (1992, p. 10) include:

— developing initiatives and service models which improve integration and continuity of care for people with mental disorders;

— developing integrated community based mental health services to provide alternatives to separate psychiatric facilities;

— the collection and publication of a national data set, service standards and performance indicators;

— upgrading specialized psychiatric facilities for those who are appropriately placed in such facilities; facilitating the mainstreaming of acute psychiatric services into general hospitals; and the development of community residential and support facilities;

— developing models which provide effective services for those people with mental disorders identified as having special needs for mental health services (for example, Vietnam War veterans);

■ continuous training for health professionals involved in the delivery of mental health services; and

■ implementing and evaluating pilot preventative projects, and conducting surveys to measure the prevalence of mental health problems and mental disorders.

The National Mental Health Plan actively encourages the involvement of consumers and carers in the development of mental health policy. The important contribution of domiciliary carers and advocates in supporting and caring for people with mental health problems is acknowledged in the Plan. Hence, strategies are to be developed for providing education and training programs for carers; ensuring that effective support services, such as respite services, are available; and that carers have access to a range of advocacy services.

Unfortunately, the rhetoric of public policy is not always reflected in reality. For example, Waters, Molony, and Vandenberg (1992) identified a number of serious deficiencies in the provision of services to mentally disturbed adolescents. They found that most disturbed adolescents do not have access to appropriately specialized services, rather they are likely to receive care in inpatient units designed for adults; the coordination and integration of services for impaired young people is generally poor; there are often frequent changes of carers and a lack of communication between different levels of service; disturbed adolescents are sometimes treated as if they have few rights and little autonomy; and finally, too few medical, psychiatric and allied health staff are trained to work with mentally disturbed adolescents. Human service professionals working the field of mental health will recognize the concerns of Waters et al. (1992), and can only hope that the National Mental Health Plan will effectively address these issues.

Services for the Aged

The delivery of human services to the aged in any community is primarily determined by their "living arrangements." That is, human service policy makers need to know the answers to questions such as how many older people are living alone compared with the numbers living in a household of two or more people; is the primary caregiver a spouse or a daughter; what proportions of the elderly live in retirement villages, hostels, or nursing homes? The structure of living arrangements for the older population will impact upon home services, such as domiciliary care; community services, such as public transport; and institutional services, such as recreational facilities.

According to Rowland (1991) living arrangements for the aged in Australia parallel those in the U.S.A. to some extent. For example, in the 1980s about 5 percent of the elderly in both countries lived in institutions. The commonalities are not surprising given the similarities in terms of the life expectancy of males and females, marriage patterns, number of children per family, and income distribution. One area of significant difference is the extent to which the elderly live alone in the community. In Australia, about half of all elderly single women live alone, while the other half live with relatives. In the U.S.A., on the other hand, two-thirds of elderly single women live alone and one-third live with relatives. Rowland (1991) argues that the difference can be largely attributed to better financial situation of older women in the U.S.A.

The most common solution to dealing with the problem of frail aged dependency in Australia was institutionalization until the mid-eighties. When the federal government passed the Home and Community Care Act in 1985, there was a major shift in the allocation of expenditure on institutional care to the provision of domiciliary services. The fundamental goal of the Home and Community Care Program (HACC) is to defer institutional placement of the elderly for as long as possible by the provision of a range of home-based services. The HACC Program provides services such as home help and personal care, home maintenance, transport and community nursing. The program has allocated substantial resources to the training of service providers and to the availability of respite services and support for caregivers.

The Nursing Homes and Hostels Review undertaken by the federal government in 1986 recommended the redistribution of expenditure from intensive residential care to community services for the frail aged. The Residential Care Program is based on the following principles according to Rowland (1991, p. 202):

— people who are aged or have a disability should as far as possible be supported in their own homes, in their own communities;

— these people should be supported by residential services only when other support systems are not appropriate to meet their needs;

— as far as possible, services should promote rehabilitation and restoration of function. The manner in which services are provided should develop and enhance personal freedom and independent functioning of all residents; and

— services should be based on a recognition that for many people discharge to a less supported residential service or to a community-based support service will be a possible and desirable outcome.

Today, there is widespread agreement that the provision of community services to support elderly people in residential accommodation is far preferable to institutional placement. Certainly, these people seek to retain their autonomy, independence and dignity for as long as possible. The shift in service provision has meant that the role of the human service worker has changed significantly in recent years. Today, he/she is more likely to be engaged in the recruitment and training of volunteers to deliver a range of services to the elderly in their homes rather than providing institutional services. However, much remains to be done in Australia to enable older people to remain active in the community and participate in a far richer lifestyle that is potentially theirs to enjoy.

SERVICES FOR OTHER GROUPS

Aborigines

The indigenous people of Australia are known as Aborigines. They arrived in Australia from Southeast Asia at least 40,000 years ago and until 200 years ago they lived as hunter-gatherers throughout Australia. Aborigines now constitute less than 2 percent of the total population of Australia, that is, about 250,000 people. Approximately half that population live in the major cities with the remainder living in rural communities throughout Australia. A small number of Aborigines in the central and northern parts of Australia has had relatively little contact with non-Aboriginal Australians. In these communities English may be spoken only as a second language.

Aboriginal people in Australia have experienced the same fate as many indigenous people who have experienced the settlement of their lands by Europeans. In almost every sphere of life, evidence of the significant disadvantage is apparent. Proportionately, far fewer Aborigines complete high school than do non-Aboriginal Australians; they experience significantly more ill-health; a far greater number is unemployed; and too many are caught up in the criminal justice system. Over the past twenty years the federal government has designed and implemented a series of interventions designed to affirm the dignity and well-being of these people.

The health of Aboriginal people is a matter of particular concern. A recent report of the Australian Institute of Health revealed that Aboriginal life expectancy is nearly twenty-two years shorter than that for other Australians. Infant mortality is twice the national rate. In recent years the continuing impact of a number of communicable diseases (especially respiratory diseases, sexually transmitted diseases, hepatitis B, and ear and eye diseases) has been accompanied by a worsening incidence of noninfectious and chronic diseases such as hypertension, coronary heart disease and diabetes mellitus. This is despite a general improvement in the health of Aboriginal children over the last twenty years. In 1991 the federal government introduced a series of health programs focussed on the needs of Aboriginal children against hepatitis B; a national education program targeting heart disease and diabetes; and a program to address substance abuse among Aboriginal people (Department of Employment, Education and Training, 1991).

The Aboriginal Employment Development Policy (AEDP) is a major commitment by the federal government to develop employment and economic opportunities for Aborigines, and is designed to take account of the differing aspirations and needs of Aboriginal people in their various geographical and social contexts across Australia. The policy's three main elements are:

- creating jobs in rural and remote communities where almost half the Aboriginal population live;
- ensuring that Aboriginal people have fair access to jobs throughout the conventional labor market; and
- improving educational and training opportunities (Department of Employment, Education and Training, 1991, p. 18).

The substantial expenditure by the federal government on intervention strategies designed to enhance the quality of life for Aborigines is no cause for complacency. Human service workers remain concerned that these people confront insurmountable difficulties on a daily basis. However, until the major political issues are resolved, such as land rights for Aborigines, it is unlikely that a great deal of progress will be made on the issues of education, employment, health, and social welfare.

Ethnic Minorities

Essentially, Australia is a nation of immigrants. However, the immigration policies of Australia have at times been regarded as highly discriminatory and have been the subject of international criticism. For the first half of this century, the overwhelming majority of immigrants came from Great Britain. During this time the White Australia policy actively discourage people settling in Australia from African and Asian countries. After World War II the federal government embarked upon a vigorous campaign to attract people to Australia from Europe. More recently, Australia has been accepting refugees from Vietnam, China, and Lebanon. Immigrants are arriving now in significant numbers from countries such as Hong Kong and Singapore. Thus, since the federation of Australian states in 1901,

there have been a number of significant policy changes ranging from exclusion of Asian and African people, to integration and assimilation, to acceptance of multiculturalism.

A range of human services is required to sustain an active immigration program. On arrival, migrants with limited economic resources are accommodated in hostels established in each of the states of Australia. These hostels are staffed by federal employment officers, accommodation, and welfare officers. All non-English speaking migrants are given the opportunity to attend English classes.

Cox (1987) discusses the tenuous relationship that has existed between the federal government immigration authorities and ethnic community agencies. It has been a policy of the federal government not to involve ethnic agencies in the provision of services to immigrants at the on-arrival stage of settlement. Since the 1970s, however, the federal government has supported those agencies providing services in ethnic communities through the Commonwealth Grants to Community Agencies scheme.

The policy of ethnic community agencies has always been contentious. It has been claimed that essentially these agencies are duplicating the services offered by the departments of the federal government. Such agencies are doing so with significantly fewer resources. On the other hand, according to Cox (1987, p. 248), the federal departments have "used the existence of the ethnic minorities' welfare structures as an excuse for maintaining their own services on a largely mono-cultural basis."

To ensure equity and facilitate access to services by all members of the community "Ethnic Liaison Officers" have been appointed to all federal government departments. One outcome of this policy is a more effective relationship between ethnic community agencies and the government departments.

It is well recognized by human service workers that there are significantly different requirements for immigrant settlers compared with those who have arrived in Australia as refugees. For example, the needs of a financially secure German family that has voluntarily migrated to Australia are different to those of an impecunious Vietnamese family who has arrived from a war-ravaged country via the refugee camps of Thailand or Hong Kong. Much research remains to be done on the settlement of refugees. Preliminary studies indicate that the social problems associated with adjustment to a new way of life are exacerbated for refugees (e.g., Klimidas, Minas and Ata, 1993).

Human service workers are employed by the ethnic welfare agencies to provide services to newly arrived community members. These agencies are typically staffed by a small number of paid employees and a number of volunteer workers, although some of the church organizations engaged in migrant welfare services are considerably larger. Other human service professionals will find employment with the large federal government departments. The state governments have limited involvement in the provision of services to immigrants.

The Family

The structure of the nuclear Australian family has been transformed since World War II. In line with similar trends that have been occurring in other Western industrialized countries more and more women are seeking to remain in the workforce after they are married, either because of economic necessity or for their personal development. The consequences of this social phenomenon are still emerging. Nevertheless, as Graycar and Jamrozik (1989, p. 192) have observed:

> . . . the vast majority of the Australian population (90 percent) lives in family settings and the majority of families, both two and one parent, are family units with dependent children.

Since Australian divorce laws were relaxed in the mid-70s the rate of divorce has tripled. According to Tapper (1990, p. 2) nearly forty percent of "all recent marriages will end in divorce, many within the first ten years, many involving children and many resulting in loss of contact between chil-

dren and their noncustodial parent." The increasing number of single parents, together with working mothers from two parent families, has raised the demand for government funded child care facilities throughout Australia over the past decade.

The increase in unemployment and the divorce rate over the past twenty years has had dire economic consequences for many Australian families. Ochiltree (1990) estimates that 55 percent of all single-parent families are living in poverty. The Sole Parents Benefit was introduced in the 70s by the federal government to provide urgently needed assistance to single parents and their children. At the time this benefit was introduced, it was subjected to a good deal of public criticism. Concern was expressed about whether such a pension would contribute to the disintegration of the family unit because it made it possible for the mother to survive without the financial support of her husband. The Sole Parents Benefit has become a major item in the Australian social services budget today.

Two social issues pertinent to the well-being of the Australian family have emerged over the past twenty years. The influence of feminist thought on social policy has highlighted the incidence of domestic violence that occurs behind the closed doors of the family home. More and more women, unable to accept the continual brutality to which they have been exposed, are coming forward to report their experiences in public forums. As the community has become aware of the prevalence of domestic violence there has been a significant increase in the number of hostels providing refuge for women and their children. Again, this development was seen as a threat to the unity of the family in the early years. It is doubtful that such an argument against the need for such shelters today would attract any significant community support.

Related to the issue of domestic violence is the growing awareness of the extent to which children suffer physical and sexual abuse in the family home. As the taboos against speaking out about such abuse are removed, the community has recognized the need to provide a range of services to cope with the problem. Some states have made it mandatory for people such as teachers, human service workers, nurses, and doctors to report suspected child abuse. However, many aspects of mandatory reporting remain somewhat contentious so that other states are monitoring the outcomes where it has been introduced.

While many family programs are funded by the federal government, these services are generally administered by the state community services departments. Nongovernment agencies play an important role in the delivery of family support services. Human service workers may find themselves involved in the provision of respite care for disabled children living at home, emergency family accommodation services, child abuse prevention education, family planning and pregnancy support programs, Aboriginal homemaker services, as well as the conventional child care services. As Wolcott (1989) points out, the underlying rationale for all these services is to maintain the family unit and to avoid having to place children in the care of other persons such as foster parents or in institutional residential facilities.

SERVICES FOR SPECIAL NEEDS

There is a comprehensive range of services developed to address the needs of communities in Australia. Human service workers are to be found providing alcohol and drug programs for those with dependency problems, managing emergency accommodation facilities for the homeless, administering agencies trying to ameliorate the circumstances of the poverty stricken, and so on. In this section we will briefly introduce three fields of service: programs that divert people from the justice system, programs that deal with the social impact of unemployment, and programs established to assist victims of violence.

Diversionary Programs

Australia does not compare favorably with other industrialized nations in terms of the rate of incarceration of offenders. Next to the USA, Australia

has the highest rate of incarceration per capita of all OECD countries. In addition, the extraordinarily high proportion of the total prison population who are Aborigines remains a significant social issue. It is only in recent years that people working in the criminal justice system have seriously addressed the issue of diversionary programs. That is, alternatives to prison are proposed on the assumption that the rehabilitation of offenders is least likely to succeed behind prison walls.

Increasingly, a range of diversionary options are being developed. The options are generally being targeted at young people and Aborigines. For example, in most Australian jurisdictions police now have the authority to issue informal and formal cautions to alleged young offenders, or offenders with an intellectual disability, rather than being required to lay formal charges for minor offences.

The courts have a range of sentencing options that can be implemented, particularly with young offenders. These options include dismissing a case even if the offender is convicted; requiring the offender to attend law education lectures; or giving the offender a community service order. Typically, these options mean that no conviction is recorded against the offender. Other options available to the courts include placing an offender on a good behavior bond, or on probation. In many cases dealt with by the courts, however, the offender will receive a fine. Increasingly, a prison sentence is seen as an option of last resort.

The pattern of Aboriginal involvement in diversionary programs reflects their involvement in the justice system as a whole. In short, Aborigines are less likely to be diverted than are non-Aborigines. For example, although about 64 percent of juveniles in detention are Aborigines, only 40 percent of juveniles on community service orders are Aboriginals (Wilkie, 1991).

Human service workers become involved in different programs related to the criminal justice system. For example, they may be responsible for the management of preventative programs such as recreational activities for young people; they may supervise intellectually disabled offenders placed on a diversionary program; or they may coordinate rehabilitation programs, such as an employment project for ex-prisoners.

Unemployment

For the past decade the level of unemployment in Australia has hovered around the 10 percent mark. The rate of unemployment varies significantly from one sector of the community to another, and from region to region throughout the country. Young people have been severely affected with rates of unemployment exceeding 30 percent in some areas. Older workers have had lower unemployment rates than other age groups, but once unemployed, they find it very difficult to get work again. Non-English speaking migrants are particularly badly affected (Department of Employment, Education and Training, 1992).

Unlike most areas of the human services in Australia, services for the unemployed are provided by the federal government. The Department of Social Security provides a Job Search Allowance for those people who have been unemployed for under twelve months. Those who have been unemployed for more than a year may apply for a Newstart Allowance. To get that allowance, they are required to negotiate an agreement with the department that outlines a personal plan to help them get a job. These allowances provide minimum subsistence to those seeking employment.

Many human service workers are employed in a range of community-based programs funded by the Department of Employment, Education and Training to increase the work skills and employment prospects of people out of work. The Skillshare Program, for example, funds community agencies to train long-term unemployed people and other most disadvantaged people. The Disadvantaged Young People Services Program aims to assist young people, currently not attracted to and uncompetitive in mainstream programs, to get and keep a job, by providing relevant assistance for their needs. A variety of programs have been developed to assist specifically Aboriginal people in obtaining employment.

Victims of Violence

In 1968 a criminal injuries compensation program was first introduced into an Australian jurisdiction. Since that time victims of violence have been receiving an increased amount of attention over the past decade from the media, the criminal justice system, and human service professionals.

Throughout the 1970s activists from the women's movement drew increasing attention to victims of sexual assault and domestic violence. The first Australian Rape Crisis Center was opened in Sydney in 1974. Unfortunately, domestic violence and abuse is pervasive throughout Australian society. Brady (1992, pp. 27-28) has found that "the issues of domestic violence, sexual assault and child abuse are now being openly discussed among Aboriginal people throughout the country." Other vulnerable groups in the community include victims of child abuse, the aged, and unemployed victims.

There has been growing public concern in recent years about the incidence of elder abuse that may be occurring in the community. To date, there has been relatively little research undertaken on this issue in Australia. The first reported prevalence study of elder abuse estimates that about 4.6 percent of the total elderly population may be suffering from some form of abuse (Kurrle, Sadler and Cameron, 1992). These results are consistent with the findings of similar studies conducted in the U.S.A. and Great Britain (McCreadie, 1991; Pilemer and Finkelhor, 1988). Perhaps the saddest aspect of the problem is that these older people are being abused by close family or friends within the home rather than from strangers outside. The federal government has recently announced that it intends to establish a working party to look at ways of protecting older people from physical and psychological abuse.

Services established to meet the needs of victims of violence draw upon the knowledge and expertise of human service workers. These services include telephone counselling, women's refuges, sexual assault referral centers, victim support groups, and so on. Human service workers provide direct care to victims as well as manage or coordinate community programs.

Grabosky (1989) has identified three basic principles for the future development of victim services in Australia. First, further research is required to help us understand the nature of criminal victimization. Questions such as who are likely to become victims and under what circumstances need to be addressed. Second, although significant changes have been introduced in a number of Australian jurisdictions in recent years, there is still much that remains to be done in terms of criminal law reform. For example, many female sexual assault victims are still reluctant to seek redress through the courts because they fear the experience. Third, the services available to support victims of crime need to be enhanced. Grabosky (1989) believes that in today's society Australians are no longer able to rely upon support from family or neighbors in times of distress. Hence, crime victims are becoming more reliant upon the services provided by government and voluntary agencies for social and moral support.

ISSUES AND TRENDS
IN THE HUMAN SERVICES

Given the variety of stakeholders, including policy makers at different levels of government, administrators of large federal departments to small voluntary agencies, human service workers delivering multimillion dollar programs to organizing volunteer transport for old people, and consumers as well, it is a somewhat daunting task to comment on trends or issues common to the field of human services in Australia. At the level of national politics it can be argued that the Reaganomics of the 1980s even impacted upon the socialist government in power in Australia for most of the decade. There is always conflict between the federal and state governments over the disbursement of expenditure to finance human service programs. However, certain concepts can be identified as underlying assumptions for a range of services, there are characteristics of Australian society that are going to impact upon service delivery, and there are structural characteristics of human services in Australia bearing on the way in which services are provided. We will consider briefly some of these issues.

Deinstitutionalization

As we have seen throughout this chapter, the concept of deinstitutionalization has widespread acceptance in such fields as mental health, and services for the disabled and aged. Different services have been implementing the policy of deinstitutionalization at different rates over the past thirty years. For example, Graycar and Jamrozik (1989, p. 205) have observed that:

> . . . the general trend in child welfare provided by the states has been towards fewer children under residential care; towards smaller size residential establishments, in an attempt to provide a home-like atmosphere; more residential care provided by nongovernment organizations and maintaining foster care as the prevalent type of placement. However, the large majority of children under guardianship are still placed in substitute care, that is, they are separated from their natural parents and families.

Wherever deinstitutionalization is practiced there is always a concern that the concomitant community services needed to support such a program will not be available (Hayes, 1984). Many human service professionals in Australia have become disenchanted with the policy of deinstitutionalization because of the manifest lack of appropriate community support services. In a study of emergency accommodation services for people with intellectual disabilities by Underwood, Jackson, and Lee (1993) it was found that accommodation workers are experiencing difficulty in coping with these people and believe that individuals are at risk. Studies conducted in the

U.S. report similar findings (Intagliata, Kraus and Willer, 1980; Mechanic and Rochefort, 1990).

Accountability

Increasingly, both government and nongovernment human service agencies in Australia are being held more accountable for the services they provide. Not only are these agencies required to demonstrate to the funding authorities that they are delivering effective and efficient services, but they are also being held accountable by consumers and other stakeholders, such as consumer advocates, professional associations, and the public through the media.

Over the past ten years there has been a growing trend for both federal and state governments to incorporate into the legislation relating to human service programs specific requirements for service evaluation. Unfortunately, the emphasis on service evaluation has generally focussed on the efficiency of the services. That is, the funding authorities have looked to see how many people are receiving services from the funds provided. Of course, the efficiency of the program is a critical aspect of service evaluation but it should not be at the expense of the effectiveness of the services. Human service program evaluators need to be able to determine, for example, the extent to which an AIDS education program has reduced the incidence of that disease in the community, or to what extent the recidivism rate has been reduced by a diversionary program for juvenile offenders. It is not always easy to determine program effectiveness, however human service professionals must seek this information if they are to act in the interests of their clients.

A further trend that bears on the agency accountability has been the growing number of consumer groups being formed out of a realization that, as stakeholders, they need to be informing service providers of their needs. This development has generally been supported at the government level. Thus, at the state and federal levels, consumers actively participate in relevant advisory committees. In addition, advocacy groups, acting on behalf of different interest groups within the community, are having a significant influence on the responsiveness of service providers to issues of accountability.

Accountability means that services are required to be evaluated. Such evaluations can be undertaken in different ways. As indicated above, at a simplistic level, the evaluation may merely consist of counting the number of people who use a particular service. A more complex issue is to determine whether or not the service is effectively achieving its goals. Essentially, the evaluator is asking if there is a causal relationship between an intervention strategy, such as providing home-care services to the aged, and certain outcomes, such as fewer aged people requiring institutional residential care. A range of strategies is available to the evaluator. The selection of any particular strategy will depend on several factors including the nature of the question to be addressed, the financial resources available to undertake the evaluation and so on. It has become apparent that many agencies do not have the resources necessary to undertake an evaluation study of any complexity.

An Aging Society

The implications for the human services in Australia of a rapidly aging population have to be seriously considered. Current estimates indicate that the proportion of the population aged sixty years and over is expected to increase from 14 to 22 percent between 1981 and 2021 (Kendig and McCallum, 1986). Even though more than 90 percent of older people are living independently in the community they do use a large proportion of hospital beds and medical services. The need for services will increase as the numbers of aged persons over the age of seventy-five years increases. That is, there will be a significant increase in the numbers of older people in institutions and the numbers with disabilities.

The prime source of support for older persons in Australia is the family. The most common caregiver is a daughter of older parents. However, as the number of women participating in the labor force continues to increase, it remains extremely problematic as to whether daughters will continue to be the main form of support.

Current expenditure by federal and state governments is on an average twice as much for every older person as for every younger person. Population aging will increase government outlays by 131 percent between 1981 and 2001, assuming a continuation of current funding arrangements.

The 1990s could well see a crisis in care for the disabled aged. Investment in improved residential care and expanded community services would minimize the problems. However, judging from past experience, policy development probably will be influenced more by economic conditions and political priorities than by demographic aging.

A Plethora of Services

As discussed earlier in the chapter, human services in Australia are provided by the federal government, the seven state governments, and to a lesser extent local government authorities. In addition, a multitude of nongovernment agencies—many based on spiritual or ethnic affiliations—provide a range of services to different sectors of the community.

The fact that there are so many different agencies involved in the delivery of services is not in itself necessarily a bad thing. However, Ife (1989, pp. 81–82) makes an important comment when he observed that:

> The organization of welfare state provision in Australia is very fragmented, with no overall attempt to plan or coordinate. Different aspects of the social services operate in isolation and sometimes in conflict with each other, to the bewilderment and confusion of the general public and there is no integrated administrative structure which could serve as a unifying function.

In other words, the multiplicity of service providers has not led to the efficient targeting of community needs. On the contrary, in some areas it has led to a significant duplication of services and unnecessary competition for limited resources, while in other areas a service void will exist. The lack of an "integrated administrative structure" arises basically from the fact that the state governments actively seek to retain their involvement and are extremely reluctant to relinquish their responsibilities to the federal government.

As Ife points out, the plethora of services has led to confusion in the mind of the public and, therefore, in the minds of potential service recipients. Further, many workers often are not aware of the services that exist in the community. Underwood, Lee, and Jackson (1991), for example, found that emergency accommodation workers had little knowledge of agencies providing support services for mentally disturbed clients.

The multiplicity of services is consistently addressed in government inquiries into human services (Senate Standing Committee on Social Welfare, 1979) and social policy analysts (Graycar, 1983; Jones, 1983). However, Commissioner Elliott Johnson, who was involved in a recent government inquiry into Aboriginal deaths in custody, emphasizes the fact that the consumer is virtually powerless in this situation. Johnson observes that:

> The multiplicity of funding agencies, the obvious overlap between many programs from one department to another, the apparent competition for programs to be adopted by Aboriginal communities all present a grossly complex and unwieldy environment that is hardly conducive to effective self-determination and self-management. So far as I can see, no Aboriginal individual or organization, anywhere, has asked for this complex multi-layered, bureaucratic and organizational picture to be the reality of Aboriginal self-determination and self-management. All of these arrangements are the product of non-Aboriginal bureaucratic and political notions of the organizational needs and program needs for Aboriginal communities (Report, 1991, Vol. 4, para 27.3.13).

CONCLUSION

Human service workers in Australia provide an extraordinarily diverse range of services to meet the needs of people living in various circumstances. For example, a community development officer may be facilitating the establishment of a craft industry for a group of isolated desert Aborigines; a youth worker in the King's Cross area of Sydney may be concerned about the health needs of child prostitutes; an activities officer in a home for the aged may be endeavoring to enrich the daily lives of people suffering from Alzheimer's disease.

Human service workers may find themselves employed in large federal government departments, such as the Department of Employment, Education and Training that employs more than 13,000 people across Australia. Others will work on their own in an agency with as many volunteers as they can find. Too many are employed on short-term contracts with little certainty about their future prospects for employment. This situation does little for the morale of workers who typically work long hours for little reward.

Staff turnover in the human services has been high. Two reasons are the uncertain nature of the associated career structure and the absence of properly accredited training. For many workers their only source of training has been that provided within the agency in which they are employed. Increasingly, however, more educational and training opportunities are becoming available through community colleges and universities. Australian universities are actively exploiting modern communications technology that makes it possible to deliver human service professional development programs via satellite to people working in the most isolated parts of the country.

The role of the human service worker will be determined to some extent by the issues discussed above. The aging population means that a greater number of workers will be required to provide services to the elderly. As more and more large institutions continue to decant their clients into smaller community-based facilities, more creative options become available to human service workers. It is difficult to predict whether the number of services will ever diminish significantly, however it is clear that workers will always be at the mercy of the short-term decisions of policy makers.

REFERENCES

Brady, M., (1992). *The Health of Young Aborigines.* Hobart: National Clearinghouse for Youth Studies.

Borrie, W.D., (1975). *Population and Australia: A Demographic Analysis and Projection.* Canberra: Australian Government Publishing Service.

Cocks, E., (1989). *An Introduction to Intellectual Disability in Australia.* Canberra: Australian Institute on Intellectual Disability.

Cox, D.R., (1987). *Migration and Welfare: An Australian Perspective.* Sydney: Prentice Hall.

Department of Community Services and Health, (1986). *Nursing Homes and Hostels Review.* Canberra: Australian Government Publishing Service.

Department of Health, Housing and Community Services, (1991). *Social Justice for People with Disabilities.* Tabling statement by the Minister for Health, Housing and Community Services. Canberra: Australian Government Publishing Service.

Final Report of the Royal Commission into Aboriginal Deaths in Custody, (1991). Canberra: Australian Government Publishing Service.

Fopp, R., (1989). "Homeless Young People in Australia: Estimating Numbers and Incidence." In Human Rights and Equal Opportunity Commission, *Our Homeless Children.* Canberra: Australian Government Publishing Service.

Goldman, R.J. and D.G. Goldman, (1988). "The Prevalence and Nature of Child Sexual Abuse in Australia." *Australian Journal of Sex, Marriage and Family* 9, 94–106.

Grabosky, P.N., (1989). *Victims of Violence.* Canberra: Australian Institute of Criminology.

Graycar, A., (1983). "Retreat from the Welfare State." In A. Graycar, ed., *Retreat from the Welfare State.* Sydney: George Allen and Unwin.

Graycar, A. and A. Jamrozik, (1989). *How Australians Live: Social Policy in Theory and Practice.* Melbourne: Macmillan Company of Australia.

Grierson, M., (1992). "Sydney Youth Services Survey." *Youth Studies Australia* 11(4), 46–48.

Hayes, S.C., (1984). "Out of the Frying Pan—Making De-Institutionalization Work." *Australian & New Zealand Journal of Developmental Disabilities* 10(4), 187–190.

Ife, J., (1989). "AUSTRALIA—A Limited Commitment to State Social Services?" In B. Munday, ed.,

The Crisis in Welfare: An International Perspective on Social Services and Social Work. New York: Harvester Wheatsheaf, St. Martin's Press.

Indermaur, D., R. Underwood, and J. Cockram, (1991). "Police and the Intellectually Disabled." Paper presented at the 7th Annual Conference of the Australian and New Zealand Society for Criminology, Melbourne.

Intagliata, J., S. Kraus, and B. Willer, (1980). "The Impact of Deinstitutionalization on a Community Based Service System." *Mental Retardation* (December), 305–307.

Jackson, R. and Y. Patterson, (1993). *Seniors Policy: Summary of Work Completed and Policy Recommendations.* Perth, Western Australia: Authority for Intellectually Handicapped Persons.

Jones, M.A., (1983). *The Australian Welfare State.* Sydney: George, Allen and Unwin.

Kendig, H.L. and J. McCallum, (1986). *Greying Australia: Future Impacts of Population Aging.* Canberra: Australian Government Publishing Service.

Klimidis, S., I.H. Minas, and A. Ata, (1993). *Vietnamese Refugee Adolescents: A Preliminary Descriptive Analysis.* Melbourne: Victorian Transcultural Psychiatry Unit.

Kurrle, S.E., P.M. Sadler, and I.D. Cameron, (1993). "Patterns of Elder Abuse." *The Medical Journal of Australia* 157, 673–676.

Learner, E. and F. Smith, (1989). *Training in Social and Community Services.* Melbourne: Brotherhood of St. Laurance.

Mathias, J., (1992). "Cycles of Violence and Abuse." In R. Koski, H.S. Eshkevari, and G. Kneebone, eds., *Breaking Out: Challenges in Adolescent Mental Health in Australia.* Canberra: Australian Government Publishing Service.

MacKenzie, D. and C. Chamberlain, (1992). "How Many Homeless Youth?" *Youth Studies Australia* 11(4), 14–22.

McCreadie, C., (1991). *Elder Abuse: An Exploratory Study.* London: Age Concern Institute of Gerontology.

Mechanic, D. and D.A Rochefort, (1990). "Deinstitutionalization: An Appraisal of Reform." *Annual Review of Sociology* 16, 301–327.

Mendelsohn, R., (1985). "Creating a Fairer Future." *Australian Society* 4(11), 8–13.

Ochiltree, G., (1990). *Children in Australian Families.* Melbourne: Longman Cheshire.

Pilemer, K.A. and D. Finkelhor, (1988). "The Prevalence of Elder Abuse: A Random Sample Survey." *Gerontologist* 28, 51–57.

Rowland, D.T., (1991). *Aging in Australia.* Melbourne: Longman Cheshire.

Senate Standing Committee on Social Welfare, (1979). *Through a Glass Darkly—Evaluation in Australian Health and Welfare Services* Vol. 1. Canberra: Australian Government Publishing Service.

Tapper, A., (1990). *The Family in the Welfare State.* Sydney: Allen & Unwin.

Underwood, R., R. Jackson, and M. Lee, (1993). "Shelter in Crisis: Providing Emergency Services for Young People with Intellectual Disabilities." *Youth Studies Australia* 12(1), 48–50.

Waters, B., H. Molony, and D. Vandenberg, (1992). "Impaired Adolescents: Can We Offer Them Something Better?" In R. Koski, H.S. Eshkevari, and G. Kneebone, eds., *Breaking Out: Challenges in Adolescent Mental Health in Australia.* Canberra: Australian Government Publishing Service.

White, R., S. Omelczuk, and R. Underwood, (1990). *Youth Work Today: A Profile.* Technical Report No. 25, Edith Cowan University, Center for the Development of Human Resources, Western Australia.

White, R., S. Omelczuk, and R. Underwood, (1991). "Defining the Nature of Youth Work." *Youth Studies* 10(2), 46–50.

Wolcott, I., (1989). *Family Support Services: A Review of the Literature and Selected Annotated Bibliography.* Melbourne: Australian Institute of Family Studies.

Wolfensberger, W., (1972). *The Principle of Normalization in Human Services.* Toronto, Canada: NIMR.

Wolfensberger, W., (1983). "Social Role Valorization: A Proposed New Term for the Principle of Normalization." *Mental Retardation* 21(6), 234–239.

KEY TERMS FOR PART SEVEN

Upon reading and studying Chapters 25, 26, 27, and 28 you will have a command of the following key terms, major concepts, and principle references.

Census Bureau Trends	Foreign Language Programs	Diversionary Program
Optimal Life	Technical and Further	Experimental Research
Cross-Cultural Diversity	Education Colleges (TAFE)	Quasi-Experimental Research
Transcultural Caring	Training Guaranteed Scheme	Cohort
Twelve-step Programs	Aboriginal People	Correlational Research
Testimonio	Supported Assist and	Time-series Research
Culturally Encapsulated	Accommodation Program	Single-subject Design
Multicultural Counseling	(SAAP)	Field Research
International Studies	Home and Community Care	Case Study Research
Study-Abroad Programs	Act (1985)	Participatory Research
International Research	Aboriginal Employment	Secondary Data Analysis
International Exchange	Development Policy	Meta-analysis
Program	(AEDP)	Cost Analysis
Area Studies	Ethnic Liaison Officers	

PIVOTAL ISSUES FOR DISCUSSION FOR PART SEVEN

1. Identify three agencies or programs in your community which specifically advocate for ethnic or cultural minorities. How are these agencies integrated with other traditional human services agencies? How do these agencies support their consumer population?

2. What are three ways human services workers can better relate and respond to diversity in their client populations?

3. Discuss ways in which international education can be used to promote better understanding of cultural diversity and multicultural issues in human services. What can you do on campus and in your community to support these goals?

4. Design a basic human service research project utilizing one of the various designs described in the Underwood and Lee article on human services research. Outline your results and conclusions and present them in class for discussion.

5. List three instances where Australian human services parallel efforts in the United States. Cite similarities in target populations, legislation, and contemporary issues as your basis of comparison. How do they differ? What can we learn from these similarities and differences?

SUGGESTED READINGS FOR PART SEVEN

1. Dillard, J. M., (1987). *Multicultural Counseling*. Chicago: Nelson-Hall.

2. Pedersen, P., (1990). "The Constructs of Complexity and Balance in Multicultural Counseling." *Journal of Counseling and Development,* 68(5), 550–554.

3. Mehr, J. *Human Services: Concepts and Interventional Strategies*. Boston, MA: Allyn and Bacon Co.

4. World Health Organization., (1975). *Organization of Mental Health Services in Developing Countries: Sixteenth Report of the Committee on Mental Health.* (WHO Technical Report Series No. 564) Geneva: World Health Organization.

5. Atkinson, D., Morten, and D. Sue, (1993). *Counseling American Minorities.* Madison, WI: Brown and Benchmark.

6. Banks, J., (1991). *Teaching Strategies for Ethnic Studies.* Boston, MA: Allyn and Bacon.

7. Banks, J. and C. McGee Banks, (1993). *Multicultural Education.* Boston, MA: Allyn and Bacon.

8. Baruth, L. and M. Manning, (1992). *Multicultural Education.* Boston, MA: Allyn and Bacon.

9. Dana, R., (1993). *Multicultural Assessment Perspectives for Professional Psychology.* Boston, MA: Allyn and Bacon.

10. Ivey, A., M. Ivey, and L. Simek-Morgan, (1993). *Counseling and Psychotherapy: A Multicultural Perspective.* Boston, MA: Allyn and Bacon.

11. LeVine, E. and A. Padilla, (1980). *Cross Cultures in Therapy: Pluralistic Counseling for the Hispanic.* Monterey, CA: Brooks/Cole Publishing Company.

12. Tiedt, P. and I. Tiedt, (1990). *Multicultural Teaching.* Boston, MA: Allyn and Bacon.

ABOUT THE EDITORS

Howard S. Harris has chaired the Social Science Department at Bronx Community College for the past 16 years and he has taught psychology for more than 25 years. He is Vice President of Publications for the Council for Standards in Human Services Education and is a founder and current president of the Metropolitan New York Association of Human Services Education. Professor Harris has also assumed a wide range of leadership positions in faculty organizations, education, community service, and environmental advocacy. He is Bronx Community College Chapter Chairperson and a member of the Executive Committee of the Professional Staff Congress/CUNY. He was a trustee and president of the Yonkers School Board during the initial phase of the court-ordered desegregation plan. Also, Howard plays four-wall handball, which is said to be the perfect game.

David C. Maloney, Ed.D., is presently Professor of Psychology and Human Services and coordinator of the Human Services Program at Fitchburg State College, Fitchburg, Massachusetts. He is immediate past President of the National Organization for Human Services Education and is a recipient of the Lenore McNear and the Miriam Clubok Awards for leadership and professional contributions to both regional and national professional organizations. Dr. Maloney has twenty-nine years in the Human Service Education field and has an active clinical practice as a licensed psychologist in Massachusetts. His professional interests are in grant writing and social action research and in developing interactive software for teaching human services courses. He is an avid and international sailor and enjoys playing piano.

ABOUT THE AUTHORS

Peggy Anderson is a graduate student at Western Washington University, specializing in Adult Education Administration. She is currently working with Rob Lawson to implement a new Human Services concentration (Human Services & Education Coordination). She is a graduate of the Everett Human Services Program and Project Coordinator for Communities in Schools of Snohomish County.

Naydean Blair, LPC, LDC, SW, NCAC II, department head for mental health programs at Houston Community College since 1986, has completed most graduate work in curriculum development. Specialty areas include Substance Abuse, Counselor Training, Multicultural Interviewing Techniques and Human Service Ethics. She is the Vice President for program approval for the Council for Standards in Human Services Education.

Paul F. Cimmino, Ph.D., is an Assistant Professor and Coordinator of the Human Services Program at Montana State University at Billings. Cimmino's doctor-

ate is in counseling psychology, and he is a licensed clinical social worker/psychotherapist. He is the founder of the PEAT concept (Parental Emotional Awareness Training), and former chief of psychiatric social services division at UCLA, Olive View Medical Center, and assistant clinical professor at the UCLA School of Medicine/San Fernando Valley Psychiatry Training Program.

Miriam Clubok, MSW, has provided significant leadership throughout the development of the human services movement. Clubok was a founding member of NOHSE, and served as its president from 1982 to 1985. She has worked on many task forces sponsored by NIMH and SREB to develop competencies, curriculum, certification, and other issues important to the field. She was Director of Ohio University's Mental Health Technology program for thirteen years.

Dennis B. Cogan, Ph.D., is currently teaching and studying in Israel. Previously, he was Chair and Professor of the Department of Mental Health and Human

Services at Georgia State University. Dr. Cogan had extensive involvement in the human services movement, in association leadership positions, and in contributing to the literature.

Audrey Cohen, founder and president of the College (1964) which bears her name, has devoted her career to reinventing education for the information and service-based global society. Her Purpose-Centered System of Education®, first developed at the college, has been adopted by public schools throughout the country. Ms. Cohen also led the creation in the 1960s of ten new human service professional positions, including the first teacher, social worker, and legal assistants. In 1974, she founded the first national organization for human service professionals, the American Council for Human Service, Inc.

Madelyn DeWoody is associate director for program development with the Massachusetts Society for the Prevention of Cruelty to Children. Formally, she was legal counsel and director of program development for the Child Welfare League of America in Washington, DC. Ms. DeWoody is an attorney with a LLM from Georgetown University Law Center; a social worker with an MSW from Louisiana State University; and a public health practitioner with a MPH from the University of North Carolina at Chapel Hill. She has worked as a front line child welfare worker and supervisor in CWLA agencies. Her work most recently has focused on child welfare issues, particularly the health, mental health, and developmental needs of children, the financing of health care and social services for children, and legal issues that impact on children. Her recent books, *Medicaid and SSI: Options and Strategies for Child Welfare Agencies, Confronting Homelessness Among American Families: Federal Strategies and Programs*, and *Making Sense of Federal Dollars*, published by CWLA, explore a range of financing strategies for child welfare and housing services.

Mary Di Giovanni, RN, BS, MS, is a professor and coordinator of the Human Service programs in Mental Health Technology, Community Residence Manager Certificate Program, and the Alcohol Drug Abuse Counseling Certificate Program at Northern Essex Community College. DiGiovanni is a founding member of the New England Organization for Human Service Education (NEOHSE), and served as a member of the Southern Regional Education Board (SREB) Credentialing National Task Force in the late 1970s. She is current president of the Council for Standards in Human Service Education (CSHSE).

Maureen E. Doyle, MSW, CSW, is Assistant Professor of Human Services at LaGuardia Community College in Long Island City, NY. She has been a volunteer in service projects in Roxbury, MA, Northern Ireland, and Belize, and is a member of the Mayor's Increase the Peace Corps in NYC. She is a graduate of the Columbia University School of Social Work, and has served as director of a family service center and a senior center, and has coordinated a city-wide wellness program. She and her husband, Gerry, live in Connecticut.

Marcel A. Duclos, M.Th., M.Ed., CCMC, NCC, CADAC, LCPC, has been an educator and counselor for the past thirty years. He received an award for his pioneer work in human services in New England, has served on the board of the Council for Standards in Human Services Education, and is a presenter at regional and national conferences. He currently specializes in substance abuse counselor education and supervision, maintains a private practice in Jungian Psychotherapy, and is a professor of psychology and alcohol and drug abuse counseling at the New Hampshire Technical Institute. He is an approved clinical supervisor by the Academy of Clinical Mental Health Councils.

Sally Fullerton, Professor and Head of the Department of Human Services at the University of Oregon, has been a pioneer in human service education. After working in a variety of human service agencies, she completed a Ph.D. in Counseling Psychology and joined the University of Oregon faculty in 1970 in a program called the School of Community Service and Public Affairs (CSPA). CSPA, established in 1967, was one of the first bachelor-level human services programs in the country. Fullerton played an instrumental role in the development of that program, which later became the Department of Human Services. Throughout the 1980s, she was also involved with human service education at a national level. She served on the Board of Directors of the National Organization for Human Service Education and edited the newsletter of that organization, *The Link*. She also was co-editor of a monograph on the *History of the Human Service Movement*, part of the monograph series of the Council for Standards in Human Service Education.

Marianne Gfroerer, MA, NCC, is a psychotherapist/consultant in private practice, and an Adjunct Professor at the New Hampshire Technical Institute. In addition, she directs service programs for homeless children and families, and at-risk youth.

Kenneth J. Grew, Ph.D., currently serves as an arbitrator and mediator for the American Arbitration Association. He also functions as an educational consultant. He formerly worked as a superintendent of schools for seventeen years. Dr. Grew was an instructor at Northeastern University and an adjunct professor at several colleges in the greater Boston area. He taught science and mathematics at the secondary level.

Iris Heckman, Ed.D., is currently Associate Professor and Chairperson of the Human Services Department at Washburn University in Topeka, Kansas. Heckman received both her doctoral degree in higher education administration and her master's degree in counseling from the University of Kansas. She served as Secretary for the Board of Directors of the Council on Standards in Human Service Education. She was a member of the Board of Directors for the National Organization for Human Service Education for eight years. In addition, Heckman is active in the area of prevention, alcohol and drug abuse, and youth services in the state of Kansas. She is also interested in the spiritual aspects of human service work and alternative approaches to healing.

Robert Lawson, M.Ed., is Director of the Human Service Program at Everett Community College, as well as Director of Western's Everett Education Center, a 300 student satellite campus. Lawson has been a member of the NOSHE Board of Directors since 1989, and a Co-Editor of Human Service Education since 1991. A former special education teacher, Lawson has worked in the human service field for four years. He has been on the faculty of Western Washington University for eight years, in addition to teaching at Lummi Community College, a regional Native American College.

Michael Lee has recently been appointed Associate Dean, Faculty of Health and Human Sciences. He was formerly the Head of School of Community Studies at Edith Cowan University in Perth, Australia. Dean Lee has been active in community organizations in the aged care and disability fields. This, combined with research into such areas as values in child care and employer attitudes, has provided him with a diversity of experience in human services.

Judith Leff, Ph.D., is a sociologist and project director in the Institute for Education and Employment, within the Education Development Center (EDC), a private, nonprofit education research and development organization. She currently directs a national project to develop industry-wide skill standards in the bioscience industry and also directs EDC's work in similar projects for the chemical processing and human services industries. Together with her colleagues at EDC, Dr. Leff has developed techniques for creating industry-based skill standards, and education systems to meet them, by working collaboratively with employees, workers, educators, labor unions, and government.

H. Stephen Leff, Ph.D., is a psychologist who has considerable experience in designing and evaluating mental health programs. Dr. Leff is currently Senior Vice President at Human Services Research Institute in Cambridge, MA, and Director of The Evaluation Center@ HSRI, a technical assistance center for the evaluation of adult mental health system change, funded by the federal Center for Mental Health Services. He is also a clinical and administrative supervisor in the Harvard Medical School Department of Psychiatry at Cambridge Hospital.

David S. Liederman, BS, MA, MSW, is the Executive Director of the Child Welfare League of America, Inc. Mr. Liederman is national co-chair of Generations United, a coalition of more than one hundred national organizations established to promote cooperation between the generations. He also chairs the National Collaboration for Youth, a coalition of sixteen national youth-serving organizations.

Nan Littleton is the Director of the Mental Health/Human Services Programs at Northern Kentucky University, Highland Heights, KY. In addition to holding an associate degree in human services, she has a masters in adult education and counseling and a Ph.D. in Psychology. Nan is also the Director for the South Region, Council for Standards in Human Service Education.

Lorence A. Long, MSW, ACSW, is Professor of Human Services at LaGuardia Community College in Long Island City, NY. He has written training manuals on working with homeless people for the National Institute of Mental Health, and is author of the interactive computer course Human Services Worker. He is a graduate of the Adelphi University School of Social Work. He has been a social worker in an emergency room and a crisis unit, and has directed a mental health clinic. He and his wife Marjorie live in Long Island City.

James Edell is a doctoral candidate in anthropology at Columbia University and an MSW student at Hunter College School of Social Work. Mr. Edell has worked as Coordinator of Adolescent Development at the New York Foundling Hospital. Mr. Edell has worked in child welfare for over thirteen years, specializing in issues of foster care, teen pregnancy, and child maltreatment.

Jean Macht has been one of the prime leaders in the human services movement. She was involved in the faculty development conferences in the early 1970s which led to the establishment of the National Organization of Human Service Educators (NOHSE) in 1975, and she served as a regional representative on the first NOHSE Board. She was instrumental in establishing the Council for Standards in Human Service Education (CSHSE) in 1979, and has recently served as CSHSE

President. Macht has coordinated two national conferences, has contributed to the literature in the field, and in many other ways has provided leadership and tireless work toward the development of human services. Her long-time involvement on the faculty of the Human Services Program of Montgomery County Community College, where she recently retired from the position of Social Science Division Chair, has given her a particular perspective regarding AA-level programs.

Harold L. McPheeters, MD, is a psychiatrist who graduated from the University of Louisville School of Medicine and took his psychiatric training there. Much of his career was spent in administrative mental health work. He served as Assistant Commissioner and then as Commissioner of the Kentucky Department of Mental Health from 1955–1964 and then as Deputy Commissioner of the New York Department of Mental Hygiene. He served as Director of Health and Human Services Programs at the Southern Regional Education Board (SREB), an interstate compact organization of the fifteen southern states, from 1965 to his retirement in 1987. During the period of his work at SREB he was project director for several projects, funded by grants from the National Institute of Mental Health, to develop and implement educational programs for human services workers in the South and across the nation. He lives in Atlanta, Georgia.

Wm. Lynn McKinney, Ph.D., is professor of Education and Director of the bachelor's degree program in human science and services at the University of Rhode Island. He served as Interim Director of Rhode Island Project AIDS in the mid-eighties and continues to volunteer both his time and his money to caring for people with HIV and AIDS and for AIDS research.

Joseph Mehr, Ph.D., is currently Chief of Inpatient Planning and Program Development for the Division of Mental Health, State of Illinois. He has been associated with the human services field since the mid 1960s, first as principal investigator on a NIMH Hospital Improvement Grant, a NIMH New Careers Grant, and a Fund for the Improvement of Post Secondary Education Grant. All three sequential grants were focused on developing and implementing curricula for human service workers and developing human service worker career ladders. He has taught human service courses at the associate, bachelor's, and master's level. Dr. Mehr has written a broadly accepted college text, *Human Services: Concepts and Intervention Strategies,* first published by Allyn and Bacon in 1980, which will be available in its sixth revised edition in 1995.

Judith S. Morse, BA, MA, has spent twenty-two years teaching emotionally disturbed children at the Mt. Pleasant Cottage School. She is President of the Board of Directors of the Northern Westchester Shelter for Victims of Domestic Violence.

Virginia Mulkern, Ph.D., is a sociologist with experience in mental health evaluation and program planning. She has taught courses in research methods and medical sociology. Dr. Mulkern is currently a Vice President at the Human Services Research Institute (HSRI) in Cambridge, MA, and is Associate Director of The Evaluation Center@ HSRI, a technical assistance center for the evaluation of adult mental health system changes, funded by the federal Center for Mental Health Services.

Maria Munoz-Kantha, MSW, also has a Ph.D. from the NYU Graduate School of Social Work. She is currently a part-time Assistant Professor at the Columbia University School of Social Work. She was a child abuse trainer and provider for the Westchester County Department of Community Mental Health and a training consultant for the Fordham University Center for Training and Research in Child Abuse and Family Violence.

Kathleen J. Niccum, BA, MS, Ed.D., Ph.D., is currently the Patient Services Coordinator for Tri-State Renal Network, Inc., and part-time instructor at the University of Indianapolis and Indiana University. Ms. Niccum has a master's level Gerontology Certificate from Florida State University. She developed the first social services in long-term care training course in the state of Indiana. Further, she developed a noncredit, continuing education course for Indiana University on Motivating the Nursing Home Resident. Ms. Niccum is a past board member for NOHSE, and the Midwest/North Central Organization for Human Services Education.

Arthur W. Parlin, CAGS, has been in education as a teacher, counselor, and currently as an administrator. He is responsible for Psychological and Speech Education at the University of Massachusetts. Parlin has been an advocate for the inclusion of special needs students and has advanced programs to support those positions.

R. Donna Petrie, Ph.D., NCC, is an associate professor and coordinator of the four-year undergraduate human services major at St. John's University, Jamaica, NY, and she works part-time as a psychotherapist in a Brooklyn, NY, community mental health center.

Anita Runyan is an associate professor in the department of human services at the University of Oregon. She has taught at the university since 1972 and has directed the University/Community Action Program since 1976. Prior to her work with the University, she spent fifteen years in various human service positions. Ms. Runyan's graduate degrees are in rehabilitation counseling and counseling psychology.

Michael Seliger, Ph.D., is Associate Director of the University of New York Educational Opportunity Center of the Bronx where he is responsible for program development, research, and systems development. His experience has been with Head Start, VISTA, the Peace Corps, Community Action Programs, health institutions, employment, and economic development projects.

David Silberstein, CSW, established *The Rite of Passage* for the purpose of enrolling responsible men to initiate and mentor adolescent foster care boys. He earned an MSW from Hunter College. Mr. Silberstein has served as a project coordinator for the Grand Street settlement and in a variety of positions in counseling and service including the Peace Corps. David Silberstein has also had a career in business and sales.

Edwin Simon is a professor of human services at New York City Technical College in Brooklyn, where he has served as chair of the Human Services Department from 1980–1990. His educational background, which includes master's degrees in social work and in education as well as a doctoral degree in social welfare, has given him a broad perspective of the field. Simon has served as a member of the Board of Directors for the Council for Standards in Human Service Education, where he was Mid-Atlantic Regional Director for two years and then was Vice President for Publications and Technical Assistance from 1985–1989. He has also served as President of the Metropolitan New York Association of Human Service Educators.

Barbara Somerville, CSW, MSW, is an Assistant Professor of Social Sciences, and is a Human Services Fieldwork Coordinator. She was formerly the coordinator of the Marymount College BSW program, then part of the Westchester Social Work Education Consortium. Ms. Somerville was a Social Worker for many years both in New York City and Sydney, Australia.

H. Frederick Sweitzer, Ed.D., is the director of the human services program in the College of Education, Nursing, and Health Professions at the University of Hartford, where he has taught for the past nine years. Before coming to the University of Hartford, Fred taught in the human services program at the University of Massachusetts and served as clinical director of the Maple Valley School, a residential treatment center for emotionally dis-turbed adolescents. Fred is also Chairperson of the Division of Education. He has served on the Board of Directors for both the National and New England Organizations for Human Services Education and is currently the editor of *The LINK*, the newsletter for NOHSE. Fred has published several articles on human service education and practice and is on the editorial board of the journal, *Human Service Education*. His professional and consulting interests include human relations, group dynamics, support groups and experiential education.

Megan C. Sylvester, BA, MA, MSW, is currently a social worker for Baltimore County Department of Social Services working in the Families NOW program. She formally coordinated special projects and field training at the Child Welfare League of America. She has been a case manager for persons with chronic and acute mental illness. Ms. Sylvester is a Nationally Certified Counselor.

Professor **Rod Underwood** was appointed to the first chair in human services in Australia in 1991. Currently, he is Dean of the Faculty of Health and Human Sciences at Edith Cowan University in Perth, Western Australia. Dean Underwood's recent research activities have included a study of the needs of people with an intellectual disability in the criminal justice system, the mental health problems of people in rural communities, and legal issues confronting young people. He has been responsible for the development of human service courses at baccalaureate, masters, and doctoral levels over the past ten years.

Douglas Whyte teaches and was past chair of the Department of Human Services (Mental Health and Social Service program) at the Community College of Philadelphia. Doug was involved with SREB conferences, and the beginning of the human services movement. The Community College of Philadelphia had one of the first ten human services programs in the country. Doug is currently membership chair of NOHSE.

Tom Wisbey, MA, is currently the Human Service Division Chair at North Shore Community College in Danvers, Massachusetts. He is a past president of the New England Organization for Human Service Education. Currently a doctoral student at the University of Massachusetts at Amherst, he received his masters in social psychology at the University of Missouri at Kansas City.

Frank Dituri, who contributed the image for the cover of this book, has taught photography for over twenty-five years and holds a Masters of Fine Arts degree from Lehman College/City University of New York. He has given photography seminars and workshops worldwide and has recently been appointed Visiting Professor at C.W. Post, Long Island University. His work has been exhibited internationally and he has had numerous catalogs and books on his images published.

INDEX